CW01666051

DATSUN 240Z & 260Z

Road Test Portfolio

Compiled by
R M Clarke

ISBN 9781855209190

Brooklands Books

BROOKLANDS BOOKS LTD.
P.O. BOX 146, COBHAM,
SURREY, KT11 1LG. UK
sales@brooklands-books.com

www.brooklands-books.com

DA24RP

09T11/2089

Contents

Contents Continued

Acknowledgements

Our first 'road test' book on the Datsun 240Z was published in the late '70s and ran to a hundred pages and finally went out-of-print after 3 editions. Our second attempt to satisfy the needs of Datsun 240Z enthusiasts appeared in the '90s and this time we incorporated its successor - the 260Z range of cars. It ran to some 172 pages. We expect this 260 page portfolio to be our final anthology on these two highly collectible classic models. I have had first-hand knowledge of an early 240Z bought new by my good friend Chris Milton-Hall and which can be seen sporting New Jersey plates on the top left hand side of the back cover. It was raced in its younger days. It is now over 40 and is still in his loving hands and living peacefully in Maine.

Regular readers of Brooklands books will know that our aim is to make available to enthusiasts material about their cars which has become hard to find. In putting such books together, we depend on the generosity and understanding of those who originally published the copyright material we reproduce. Our thanks in this instance go to managements of: *Asian Auto, Autocar, Automobile, Autosport, Car and Driver, Cars International, Car Life, Classic & Sports Car, Classic Cars, Competition Car, Driving, Modern Motor, Motor, Motor International, Motor Manual, Motor Sport, Motor Trend, NZ Classic Car, Popular Imported Cars, Practical Classics, Road & Track, Road & Track Specials, Road Test, Sports Car Graphic, Sports Car World, World Car Guide* and *What Car?*

R.M. Clarke

You can get some idea of the importance of the Datsun 240Z when you realise that Nissan, owners of the marque, in the '90s commissioned a specialist to restore batches of 25 year old 240Zs to 'as new' condition so that they could sell them through their own showrooms alongside modern Nissan products. The 240Z, for Nissan, is its heritage.

You might wonder why the 260Z is not subjected to the same treatment, and the answer is that in the USA at least, the original is still considered to be the greatest. It was the 240Z which conquered the sports car market from the British, and the broadly similar 260Z which followed it was more of a relaxed boulevardier and less of a sporting machine.

None of that, of course, makes the 260Z a less worthy car, it is, quite simply, different because it aimed to do different things. American customers wanted more creature comforts - which is why they were offered an automatic option on the 240Z when other countries had only a five speed manual - and Datsun developed the car to meet the demands of its largest market.

The 240Z wasn't Datsun's first attempt at a sports car, of course, but the roadsters built between 1962 and 1971 never had anything like the same sales success. A cynic might argue that the moribund state of British sports cars in the early '70s gave more that a helping hand to the Japanese contender, but there can still be no doubt that the Datsun was a class act.

The 240Z and 260Z scored in reliability (where British models were increasingly failing), they scored in performance, and they scored in their excellent handling balance, achieved by setting the big straight-six engine well back in the structure. There was plenty of room inside, even though the cabin was a little austere to look at, and there was also no doubt that the Datsun's hardtop coupe configuration gave it additional appeal at a time when the safety aspect of open cars was beginning to be questioned. Attractive styling played its part too, and it is interesting that the 240Z and 260Z came from the drawing board of Albercht Goertz, the same man who had penned some of the classic BMW models of the later 1950s and early 1960s.

Enthusiasts today look upon the 240Z as one of the first really great (as distinct from merely competent) cars to come out of Japan. The articles reproduced in this book do a fine job of showing why that should be so.

James Taylor

The all-new Datsun 240Z is a people-sized car for two that is claimed to top 124 mph. Selling for an amazingly low $3500, it will be available here soon.

DATSUN...STARRING THE 240Z SPORTS

240Z Sports

One of the best kept secrets in recent automotive history was Datsun's 240Z Sports, a car first unveiled simultaneously at the Tokyo Motor Show and to U.S. dealers on October 22nd and 23rd, depending upon how you reckon the calendar.

It is also, at a projected price of $3500, as great an aesthetic and mechanical bargain as was the XK 120 Jaguar two decades ago. The 240Z is not only supremely good looking by any standard but when scaled to two passengers, it approaches U.S. definitions of dimension. It is on an 89.9-inch wheelbase and measures 161.3-inches long, 63.6-inches wide and 49.1-inches high. Comparable Corvette dimensions are 98, 182.5, 69, and 47.8 inches, respectively. Unlike the Fiat Sport Racer, it is people proportioned as well as pretty.

Power comes from a new-to-the-U.S. sohc in-line six rated at 150 horsepower which drives through a standard, fully synchronized four-speed gearbox. One would wish it could have been a fiver to give an overdrive and of course a growing percentage of those who buy a car of this type, if Corvettes and AMX's are any indication, actually prefer an automatic. Other mechanical features include a 3.364 final drive, an over-square 3.24- x 2.87-inch bore and stroke, rack and pinion steering, front disc brakes and twin SU-type carburetion by the Japanese licensee, Hitachi. A radio and radial tires are standard equipment. Complete, the all-steel two-seater weighs 2238 lbs.

Re-Powered Pickup

The unexpected popularity of the Datsun pickup with campers is undoubtedly what forced adoption of the 1600-cc, 96-hp sohc four introduced with the 510 passenger series in 1968. This gives a 40% increase over previous truck power. Other than this, Datsun's pickup, No. 1 import of its type, is not changed for '70. It's the only Datsun other than the roadsters with frame-type construction and unlike most U.S. pickups, a fully synchronized four-speed transmission is standard along with whitewall tires, package shelf and tie-down hooks.

DATSUN 240Z: The newest GT

And a bargain too. Who else offers a GT coupe with 2.4-liter sohc 6-cyl engine and all-independent suspension for $3500?

BY RON WAKEFIELD, Engineering Editor

LOOK AT THE specifications listed below. In them you'll find quite a few nice, compact imported GT coupes. You'll also find among them high prices (when you shop), small engines, unsophisticated chassis or various combinations thereof. Going alphabetically we find such as the Alfa Romeo 1750 GTV (2+2, 1779 cc, 132 bhp, 5-speed, live axle rear suspension, $4500); Fiat 124 Sports Coupe (2+2, 1438 cc, 96 bhp, 4-speed, live axle, $3000); Jaguar E-type Coupe (2 seats, 4235 cc, 246 bhp, 4-speed, independent rear, $5800); Mercedes-Benz 280SL Coupe (2 seats, 2778 cc, 180 bhp, 4-speed, independent rear, $7000); MGB GT (2+2, 1798 cc, 92 bhp, 4-speed, live axle, $3300); Opel GT (2 seats, 1897 cc, 102 bhp, 4-speed, live axle, $3500); Porsche 911T (2+2, 2195 cc, 142 bhp, 4-speed, independent rear, $6000), Triumph GT6+ (2 seats, 1998 cc, 95 bhp, 4-speed, independent rear, $3000); the Volvo 1808E (2 seats, 1986 cc, 130 bhp, 4-speed + OD, live axle, $4500). All good cars. But do you see any bargains there? Maybe the Triumph —maybe—but all the rest seem high-priced for what you're getting, *by American standards*. Compare, for instance, America's one sports car, the Corvette: 2 seats, 5735 cc, 300 bhp, 4-speed, independent rear and a gob of gadgets, $5100. A bargain, if you like a big, flashy car. And it seems that a good many Americans do.

For years I've said that it is possible to build a small GT with a generous-size engine, fully independent suspension, disc brakes, 4- or 5-speed gearbox and decent trim and fittings for well under $4000. All it would take, I reasoned, was a manufacturer with some appropriate parts on his shelves and the vision to tool up for enough production to pare the unit cost. An American company could do it; using one of the 6-cyl engines or even a "small" V-8 from their smaller sedans and the front suspension from same, they could build an independent rear suspension and an exclusive body with simple equipment and meet that sort of price target if the car were produced in quantities of, say, 50,000 per year. It's more difficult to envision a European maker doing it: they always think in terms of small-displacement engines, which immediately puts a damper on U.S. sales, and their GT cars tend to be premium items even in their home markets. The British have larger-displacement engines but lack the vision to invest capital in such a project. It was left to the Japanese, and somehow we knew a long time ago that they would do it. They did.

The car is the Datsun 240Z. The parts on the shelves were the 510 sedan engine and the 1800 Laurel (a sedan not imported to the U.S.) front suspension. From there the 240Z is an entirely new car, unique from other Datsuns. It's going to sell for about $3500 in the U.S. in (Datsun U.S.A. hopes) quantities of 1600 per month once production is in full swing.

Before anyone jumps to the conclusion that the 240Z's engine is a 1595-cc 4-cyl, let us hasten to add that it's actually a 2393-cc, 6-cyl unit derived from the 510 engine's reciprocating parts.

Body and Chassis

THE 240Z's body and chassis platform is a conventional unitized, all-steel structure whose rigidity is derived almost totally from the welded-together unit from the firewall back. Seating is for two only: the area behind the seats is a flat floor covering for luggage and under that is the spare tire and the fuel tank.

The wheelbase is 90.7 in., just 0.3 in. shorter than the MGB and 1.4 greater than that of the Porsche 911, and with an overall length of 162.8 in., the 240Z is 9.4 in. longer than the MGB and 1.1 in. shorter than the 2+2 911. So it is not particularly efficient in terms of fore-aft seating room relative to its overall length. Considerable wasted space ahead of the radiator for the sake of styling, and the long engine, account for this. It is 4.1 in. wider than the MG and 0.7 wider than the Porsche, and at 50.6 in. high is 0.8 in. taller than the MG and 1.4 in. lower than the Porsche. The track dimensions, 53.3 in. front and 53.0 rear, are much closer to those of the Porsche than the MG but it appears that there is plenty of room in the wheel wells for wheels with greater offset, which would increase the track further and improve the car's appearance.

Body appointments are on a par with other GTs in the same price class but is more up-to-date in appearance than most of them. True to current fashion there are no door ventwings—we hope that Datsun has solved the potential draft problem in the coupe better than they did in the 510—and the rear quarter windows are fixed. Flow-through exits are located under the rear window in the lift-up tailgate, the fresh air entering through flush cowl intakes and outlets in the center and at both ends of the molded and padded vinyl dash panel. Ventilation, even through the end vents, can be assisted by a 3-speed blower and there are the usual horizontal-moving levers for directing air to feet or windshield and controlling temperature.

Some of the standard equipment items are impressive. For instance, an AM radio with electrically powered antenna is standard (stereo, with speakers in the rear quarters, is optional) and a real wood steering wheel sets off an otherwise stark (if modern) interior. Carpeting is standard, as is an electrically heated rear window. Round, white-on-black instruments are set into molded hoods in the dash and controls are distributed among the dash, central console and a steering-column stalk in such a way that they can be operated without looking at them. The standard seats, which have the head restraints built in as extensions of their backs, have backs adjustable about 10 degrees but a 59-degree range is optional.

The front suspension parts are taken from the Datsun 1800 sedan, a stretched and more luxurious car based on the 510. A lateral subframe, mounted to the main structure with rubber isolation, carries pivots for the stamped lower suspension arms which, with the long MacPherson struts that angle up to their towers atop the wheel wells, determine the front wheels' camber characteristics. Rubber-mounted struts go forward from the underbody to the outboard ends of the lower arms, thereby taking braking loads and allowing fore-aft compliance as the front wheels hit bumps or dips. The coil springs are located near the top of the MacPherson struts and the shock absorbers at the bottom; a link-type anti-roll bar connected to the lower arms is standard.

Rear suspension is unique to the 240Z and is a departure from any previous Datsun practice. It is reminiscent of the Lotus Elan's independent rear suspension, though made from less expensive and weight-saving pieces, so we have taken the liberty of labeling it Chapman strut. Location of the wheels is the same as at the front: a very wide-based lower A-arm does the job of the front's lateral arm and compliance strut, and vertical struts (again including the coil spring and telescopic shock) angle upward to towers that protrude into the luggage area. Two constant-velocity universal joints and a ball-bearing spline are necessary in each axle halfshaft to accommodate the wheel movement. Mounting of the components to the underbody is most interesting: at the front a conventional-looking stamped crossmember bridging the driveshaft tunnel provides the front pivot for the A-arms and supports the differential nose. At its rear the differential is hung from a rather fragile-looking piece of sheet steel that goes sideways to rubber isolation mounts which fix it to the structure. Then, to the bottom side of a frame crossmember behind the differential, bolts another flat sheet steel brace that hangs straight down to form the rear pivot points for the A-arms. The whole support arrangement has a flimsy look about it but I'm willing to be persuaded that it really does the job—it must be fabulously inexpensive to produce!

Girling-type disc brakes are used at the front: solid discs of 10.7-in. diameter with single calipers. These discs are of smaller diameter than those of the 2000 sports car (10.7

Tuneups and oil filter changes will be easy with all that space around the engine. Cutaway shows the innards of the new 2.4-liter six, which is based on the reciprocating parts of the sturdy 1.6-liter 4-cyl engine used in the 510 series.

DATSUN 240Z

in., still a good size for a car in this weight range) but have larger pads so that the swept area is the same. The 240Z's rear drum brakes of 9.0 in. inner diameter and with linings 1.58 in. wide, are taken directly from the 2000. Front and rear brakes are self adjusting and are assisted by a vacuum booster.

The standard wheels aren't high-styled, being simply 14-in. steel disc with 4½-in.-wide rims. But 5½-in. rims are optional for a small extra charge, and all the styled wheels currently available for the 2000—American Racing, Empi, Minilite, Appliance Plating—in 5- to 6-in. rim widths will fit, which leaves the buyer with an easy route to some individuality with his 240Z.

Engine

NISSAN, DATSUN's parent company, has an almost staggering variety of unrelated engines in production, partly because of a merger some time ago with the Prince company and partly because some of its own more out-of-date engines are still in production alongside the new ones. The 240Z's 150-bhp, 6-cyl engine bears no relation to an existing 2-liter six in their Gloria Six sedan, nor to the 2.3-liter six in the Datsun 2300 sedan, nor to the 2-liter four in the 2000 sports car—and these are all unrelated inline single-overhead-cam designs! What it does amount to is a 6-cyl version of the 1.6-liter 4-cyl unit in the familiar Datsun 510, a relatively new and modern design that's bound to replace some of the older ones at Nissan.

The new engine shares the 510's bore, stroke, pistons, rods,

Hatches at rear corners of hood, similar to those on Toyota 2000 GT, uncover windshield washer reservoir (here, the left one) and the battery on the right side.

A nice touch borrowed from Porsche (below) is this rubber flap that flops out when the gasoline filler door is opened.

Instrumentation is complete, well arranged and readable except for distance to the small instruments from driver's eye. Rear suspension intrudes into rear cargo area but capacity is still generous; spare tire lives in well beneath floor.

rod bearings, valves, valve gear and general design characteristics and is a conventional inline, sohc design with cast iron block, aluminum head, seven main bearings and a single-stage duplex chain cam drive.

The 510 as sold in the U.S. has only a single Hitachi carburetor, relatively mild valve timing and 1.50-in. intake valves; it produces an advertised 96 bhp at 5600 rpm. For the home market there is a twin-carburetor (SU carbs built by Hitachi under license) SSS version with more radical valve timing and larger (1.65 in.) intake valves, producing 109 bhp @ 6000 rpm. The 240Z engine is closer to the SSS version, sharing its valves (the exhausts are the same for both 4-cyl and the 240Z at 1.30 in.), valve timing (16-52-54-14, 248°) and 9.0:1 compression ratio. Carburetors for the 240Z, however, are Hitachi-SU model HJG 46W (46-mm throat diameter) whereas the 510 SSS has 38-mm versions of the same carburetor. Exhaust emission control is accomplished by exhaust manifold air injection, which makes us wonder if the 510 SSS might now meet the emission regulations and be eligible for Federal certification and sale in the U.S.

Canted about 5 degrees to the right, the 240Z's engine looks much like a Mercedes 6-cyl unit except for its SU carburetors. It is well silenced—a rapping exhaust note was not considered desirable by Nissan—by a single exhaust system with muffler and resonator. The rev limit is 7000 rpm with a yellow band beginning at 6500 rpm on the tachometer, and viscous-drive fan clutch is standard to keep fan noise down at high revs.

A final note on the engine: it's surrounded by lots of wide-open spaces, which may not be so great for space utilization but which make things easy for the mechanic. Do-it-themself owners will find it exceedingly easy to change the oil filter, spark plugs and points and the like. Who says a car can't be sophisticated and still be entertaining to work on?

Geometry of rear (left) and front suspension (right) is similar, being determined by lower transverse link and spring-shock strut. Wide-based lower A-arm serves as lower link at rear; at front simple lateral arms combine with compliance struts.

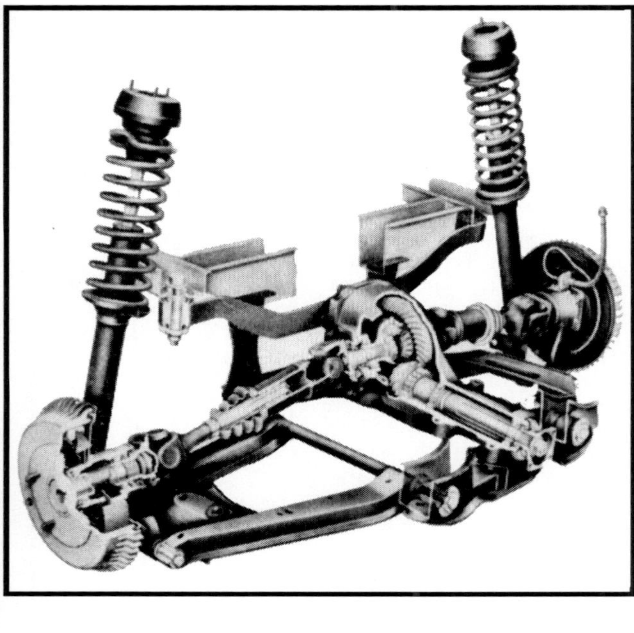

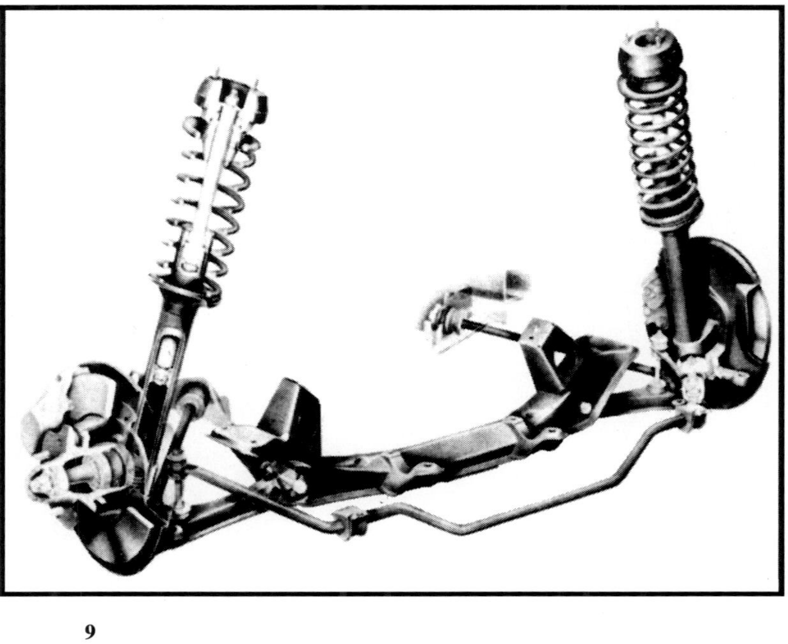

earlier. Both are familiar quantities; but more importantly the 240Z will sell for about the same price as the MG while offering performance—that is, acceleration and top speed—in the Porsche bracket. At the promised price the Datsun is neck-and-neck with a similarly equipped MGB GT and its combination of 150 bhp with 2238 lb sounds mighty like the 911T's 142 bhp and 2395 lb—allowing for the fact that Japanese horses seem to be somewhat smaller than German ones. Datsun's performance claims are for a top speed of 124 mph and a standing ¼-mile time of 16.3 sec; these line up almost exactly with what we recorded for last year's 125-bhp 911T, so projecting from that we might predict a 0-60 mph time of 8.9 sec. We'll have a road test before long.

As for handling, the standard tires and wheels should give moderately high ultimate cornering power; both front and rear suspension appear to have good camber characteristics and should therefore make for pleasant handling as well as respond well to larger wheels and tires for those who want still better results. Certainly the car is light enough to have no need for power steering even with relatively large amounts of rubber on the road. And what of braking? Our 2000 test car of a couple years ago did 0.9g in the panic stop and showed no fade in our brake fade test; the 240Z with the same brake area and about 130 lb more weight should be nearly as good. I haven't seen any evidence yet that a car this light really needs discs at all four wheels to give good braking performance, so the disc/drum setup seems appropriate.

DATSUN 240Z

Transmission

THE STANDARD 4-speed, all-synchromesh gearbox is combined with a conventional single-dry-plate diaphragm clutch and uses the Warner synchronizer design. The box is similar in design to that of the 510 but has a different set of ratios and stronger internals to handle the 6-cyl torque. The Dana Spicer differential, built by Nissan but of a design widely used in cars all over the world, comes in a 3.36:1 ratio with the 4-speed box, giving about 2800 engine revolutions per mile or 21.4 mph/1000 rpm.

Optional is the 5-speed manual gearbox as used in the 2000 sports car; its overdrive 5th gear (0.852:1) with the 3.70:1 final drive gives a slightly longer-legged 22.9 mph/1000 rpm. A 3-speed automatic transmission will be available later but at this point Nissan has not decided whether it will be the Borg-Warner 35, as used in the 510, or a unit produced by Nissan, Toyo Kogyo and Ford in Japan.

Performance

THERE WAS a definite reason for picking the MGB GT and the Porsche 911T for dimensional comparisons

WHAT, THEN is the 240Z and where does it fit in the scheme of things? From what we can tell—we haven't driven it yet—it's a bargain GT with most of the things Americans expect but don't always find in a GT. The relatively hefty engine is what really sets it apart from its competition, and it's certainly modern in concept and execution throughout. It doesn't have the handling potential of the mid-engine Porsche 914, another 2-seater, but at the same price it offers abundantly more straight-line performance and (probably) refinement of running. Our experience with other Datsuns to date tells us that it won't be assembled with the precision of a German car nor will it have the fine edge of "feel" found in the Italians—but the same package produced in either of those countries would undoubtedly cost $1000 to $2000 more. We think Datsun has a real winner.

DATSUN 240Z SPECIFICATIONS

Engine:
Type . . . 6 cyl inline, sohc
Bore x stroke, mm . . . 83.0 x 73.3
Equivalent in . . . 3.27 x 2.90
Displacement, cc/cu in . . . 2393/146
Compression ratio . . . 9.0:1
Bhp @ rpm . . . 150 @ 6000
Torque @ rpm, lb-ft . . . 148 @ 4400
Carburetion . . . two Hitachi-SU (1V)
Emission control . . . air injection

Drive Train:
Transmission . . . 4-speed manual (std) or 5-speed manual (opt); 3-speed automatic to be available later
Gear ratios: 4-speed
4th . . . 1.00 . . . 3.36:1
3rd . . . 1.42 . . . 4.77:1
2nd . . . 2.20 . . . 7.39:1
1st . . . 3.55 . . . 11.92:1
5-speed
5th . . . 0.85 . . . 3.14:1
4th . . . 1.00 . . . 3.70:1
3rd . . . 1.31 . . . 4.85:1
2nd . . . 1.86 . . . 6.88:1
1st . . . 2.96 . . . 10.95:1
Final drive ratios . . . 3.36:1 (4-speed), 3.70:1 (5-speed), 3.54:1 (automatic)

Chassis & Body:
Body/frame . . . unit steel
Brake type: 10.7-in. disc front, 9.0 x 1.58-in. drum rear; power assisted
Swept area, sq in . . . 310
Wheels . . . steel disc, 14 x 4½J
Tires . . . radial, 175-14
Steering type . . . rack & pinion
Gear ratio . . . 17.8:1
Turning circle, ft . . . 31.5
Front suspension: MacPherson struts, lower lateral arms, leading compliance struts, coil springs, tube shocks, anti-roll bar
Rear suspension: Chapman struts, lower A-arms, coil springs, tube shocks

General:
Curb weight, lb . . . 2238
Wheelbase, in . . . 90.7
Track, front/rear . . . 53.3/53.0
Overall length . . . 162.8
Width . . . 64.1
Height . . . 50.6
Ground clearance . . . 5.7
Fuel tank capacity, U.S. gal . . . 15.9

DATSUN 240Z

Datsun's new GT car has independent suspension all 'round, a 150-bhp six, and a sticker price of about $3500.

THE LIGHTS ARE GOING ON all over Europe, in engineering sections and boardrooms. Datsun has a GT car, with all the latest items and a lower-than-most price.

The specifications would put the 240Z into the competition no matter what the price: A two-seat fastback, with an 89.9 in. wheelbase, 161.3 in. long, and a claimed weight of 2238 lb. To move it, there's a 146-cid inline six, with a single overhead camshaft and two side-draft carburetors. Compression ratio is 9:1, low for such a car. Rated power is 150 bhp, with no peak rpm or torque figure given. With the low compression, high power-per-cubic inch, and an oversquare bore to stroke ratio (3.24 in. x 2.87 in.), the 240Z must wind high. Behind the engine is a four-speed transmission, perhaps the only component in the car that can't look the rivals in the eye. Where's the excellent five-speed optional on the 2000 sports car?

Suspension is independent front and rear. Discs in front, drums behind, a combination that works well, no matter what you hear from people who read the ads with fine print. The 240Z has a unit body, steel, naturally. Radial tires are standard equipment.

The interior is as attractive a cockpit as we've seen for some time. Real bucket seats, that adjust for rake, one feature the Europeans somehow include, and Detroit doesn't.

Plenty of instruments, with tachometer and speedometer set before the driver and the gauges sculpted into the dash above the gearshift. There's no trunk as such, but the rear window swings up and away, so you have a large door for a small closet.

Styling is a matter of taste, as we always say when the people here don't agree on how successful a body shape is. The 240Z is sleeker than, say, a Fiat 124, not as striking as an Opel GT, but it's up to date.

That (and the price) may be the key to success. We tested a fleet of Datsuns in 1968. The sedans were nice little boxes, and the sports cars were appreciated for their engines and transmissions. The suspensions were outmoded and the bodies looked like somebody copied the English and tried too hard. The 240Z appears to have taken care of both lacks. ■

PHOTOS / HENRY THOMAS, GERRY STILES

The world is not the same, especially when it comes to automobiles; the English MGB, German Opel GT and Japanese Datsun 240Z are as dissimilar as East and West

THREE WAYS TO APPROACH A GT

SCG ROAD TEST

MAYBE IT'S WRONG TO TELL YOU at this point in the story, but the Datsun "Z Car" won. Sorry to give away the punch line, but we're so enthused about this newest Japanese sports car we couldn't restrain ourselves. Yet, we found that even though the Datsun 240Z fits into the same category and price range with the MGB GT and Opel GT, it's a completely different automobile and greatly resembles the more sophisticated Jaguar XKE and Toyota 2000 GT, but for half the price.

There has been quite a change in the sports car concept during the past couple of years. The old familiar ragtops and their tweedy drivers are now mentioned in the same breath with the Jowett Jupiter and Cad-Allard. Manufacturers have been avoiding building roadsters, and started concentrating on the hardtop GTs. In fact, most English auto builders have eliminated the drophead from their model lines. What's happening? Doesn't anyone enjoy fresh air anymore? Or is it just that there's very little fresh air left to enjoy?

Our three test cars represent the most active GT sales market, and each approaches it with a different concept. The MGB GT is merely a roadster with a different roof. The Opel GT is based on the kit-car theory: put a new body on a nothing chassis. But the Datsun 240Z is totally new from chassis to ventilation system.

The MGB GT is the nostalgic piece in our trio. It was the MG that brought sports car interest to a crescendo in the United States with the TC and TD models. Even today it remains as the link trainer for anyone who wants to learn the hard way. "You'll appreciate it more," we remember our dad used to say. And be sure to get a radio with it, too, so you can practice listening between the static. It's all part of the learning process. Hell, it wouldn't be any fun to start off with a Ferrari, now would it?

Despite the hardships of poor ventilation, inadequate heating and pre-1950 engineering, you'd love it – if you have never driven a sports car before, that is. So, for those of you that are just starting out, we recommend you don't read beyond the MGB GT portion of this test and only look at the MG data panel. You've just gotta start with this car, so you'll know what the rest of us had to endure before we got to drive the Datsun 240Z.

Now don't let that jostle and bounce and rattle and clatter fool you, because the MGB still is the best handling car in its class, in both left- and right-hand turns, if you can overcome the large, truck-like steering wheel with only two hands. With six more pounds of air pressure in the rear tires, which is recommended by the factory, the little B was quite controllable on the Digitek skidpad. It was the only one of our three cars that we could consistently hold on the white stripe that outlined the 200-foot circle. Even with higher tire pressures in the rear, the car's

back-end still hung out slightly, belying inherent understeer so common to front-engined automobiles. Even while lifting the inside front wheel while cornering, the B never felt as if it were out of control.

The brakes were another standout feature, bred through what was once an extensive racing program run by MG. And gearshifting, always a fine feature of this little car, was easier and more direct than the other two.

Although the MGB GT was competent in the performance aspects, there was one major fault – disregard by the designers that it would be occupied by human beings – sensitive, impressionable, compare-it-to-the-other-car human beings. There has been little thought to comfort and use of modern techniques when building this car; the same car that was nice eight years ago, has not improved today. Everyone is building past MG.

Even people who love MGs get warm in the summer and cold in the winter. Thank England for the rear wing windows, or the little MGB GT would be unbearable in the summer. With the rear wings open, you can at least get some air circulating, even though your feet do get warm from the poorly insulated firewall and transmission tunnel. But that's part of the MG mystique, that's the learning process we were telling you about. And for winter, just bundle up real good, close all the windows and breathe hard, because that's about the best way we can think of to keep your body temperature out of the critical range. Anything below 40 degrees outside, takes perseverance inside. Thermal underwear is good for openers.

Then there's that matter about engine noise. In a race car you don't mind being deaf after several exhilarating laps. But after a 60-mile drive to Riverside Raceway, you'd like to be able to hear what the technical assistant has to say while he's hooking up the equipment, because he might say you're set up to do aerodynamics tests and you go out and do brake stops. We gave our secretary a ride in the car and she mumbled something. We turned to her and asked, "What?" She replied very loudly, "Noisy, isn't it?"

Then there's the matter of the seats. Oh, they're formed right, but hard . . . and hard to adjust. As a matter of fact, in order to operate the handbrake, the passenger seat must be reclined fully so you can pull back on the lever without getting your arm hung up between the lever's second click and the seatback.

Instrumentation is in front of you, where you can see it after about three or four different glances. An archaic method of arrangement. Most manufacturers today are grouping their instruments so the needles can be read at one glance. Remember those old cars with instruments strung across the length of the dashboard? You get the impression that, besides the tachometer and speedometer, the other gauges were placed wherever there was room.

Speaking of dashboards, when the government laid down its safety regulations, MG was caught with its knobs protruding.

THREE WAYS

Now, that in itself is amazing, and indicative of the forethought given to the production of MG automobiles. The regulations were available to everyone before they went into effect – apparently everyone except MG, because an entire shipload of new MGCs was impounded by U.S. Customs because the dashboards didn't meet the newly inaugurated safety regulations. Once the British firm did legalize its dashes, they were hideous, looking as though they were hastily and incompletely manufactured. That was two years ago, and they haven't changed since.

The small jumpseat in the back was made for a toy poodle and can easily be done away with, which would cut costs in producing this car. No one can sit in it anyway, so why is it there? When the seat folds down, however, it gives pretty good luggage space in the rear. And the door at the back of the car gives easy access for storing or removing items.

To give you a hint that maybe some TD parts are still being used on the B, the rear-view mirror retains the same jiggling action. It seldom gives a single image, except maybe after a New Year's Eve party.

Ah, nostalgia. It reminds us of many fond memories, just like riding in Ted West's 1948 Chrysler does.

Yes sir, all you would-be sports car nuts, everybody has to own an MG once in his life. Take it like a man. And if you don't like it, you're not one of us, because this is where it was at.

STOP! All you novices quit reading, because we're going to be talking about the new breed. You've gotta pass the MG grade school before you go on.

This next car is for the pseudo sports car nut. If we could only take the MG handling and add some of the Datsun quietness and reassurance to it, we might have a good car in the Opel GT. But when you hop into something as eye-catching as the Opel and become embarrassed by a damned Volkswagen Beetle while chasing him up an off-ramp, you somehow get the feeling you're not getting your money's worth out of the whole thing.

The Opel GT isn't a *real* sports car, but then Buick never claimed it was. It's like discovering a beautiful woman, and after she disrobes and removes the padding, you find out it's really a man.

Other than those funny small wheels and tires, the Opel GT is pretty as can be – sort of Corvette-like, isn't it? And once you flop behind that small Grand Prix steering wheel, you know you're in a different class from that MGB GT you just climbed out of. The well-detailed interior and easily read instruments, the softer seating, being able to stretch your legs, the quiet note of the idling engine and, what do you know, you can hear the radio without trying because the speakers are properly mounted behind you. Wow, what a car. This one should really go! You think.

Like gaping barndoors, the open trunklids of the Datsun (right) and MGB GT (far left) expose large luggage areas, previously considered a premium in sports cars. The Opel, however (foreground), clandestinely keeps its conservative luggage space behind the rear seat.

Interiors are important to the driver, since this is where he spends his motoring hours. The Datsun (top) and Opel (middle) furnish a modern, easy-to-use dash arrangement. The MGB GT, however (bottom), relies on the fact that the driver should be kept busy.

But there are awakenings ahead, not serious and uncorrectable, but unexpected.

The beauty doesn't overwhelm you after a couple of days, because you're caught up in overcoming the deficiencies. You learn from the local gas station attendant that the front pivot bushings go bad at 1000 miles. You still can't get the hang of driving it smoothly because of the sloppy rubber bushings in the U-joints. The clatter of the solid lifters you hadn't noticed when first hopping in, because you were still deaf from the MG. And that last turn on Laurel Canyon, you weren't quite sure you'd stop drifting – maybe it was limited by the tires, or the severe front-wheel camber change might be the reason. Yet, it's still an improvement over the MGB GT – a status improvement if nothing else. And you know that if you wanted to sell it right now, you could get within a few dollars of what you paid for it new, and put your order in for a Z Car; after all, the Datsun dealer said you'd only be 51st on the list!

The Opel GT is nothing more than a Kadett with a new body. It feels much the same and, if anything, a little less sure-footed. This we can't understand, because by bringing some of that heavy metal lower to the ground, the center of gravity has been dropped.

Well, let's go to the good points, because it does have a few, and its main advantages over the MGB GT are creature comfort and up-to-date engineering techniques. Only the storage area behind the driver is difficult to get at. There's no rear door on the Opel GT – the rear-mounted gas tank gets in the way.

The Opel has surprisingly good brakes. We expected slow stops and early fade, but didn't encounter either after 12 stops. The car was very stable during hard braking, and actually was the only facet of the automobile that gave us confidence during hard driving. The power boost did tend to hang on a little too long, however.

Acceleration, too, was decent. We did the quarter-mile in 2 seconds less than the MG, after we thought we were going slower. The Opel, in fact, will do just about 120 mph at top end, which isn't bad for a *very* stock 1.9-liter engine.

We'd recommend the Opel for status, a nuance of comfort, economy and a step toward the ultimate in $3500 GT cars – the Datsun 240Z.

We're now talking about the Ferrari of under $10,000 automobiles. The car that considers the human race and its deficiencies. The sports car that has to be the greatest buy on the marketplace today: the "Z Car."

If you think we're prejudiced, brother, you bet we are. With only very minor modifications, the Datsun 240Z could be the perfect street car. Those changes would include adjustable Koni shocks, rear disc brakes and an AM/FM stereo radio. That's it, sweetheart.

DATSUN 240Z

AERODYNAMIC FORCES AT 100 MPH

CORNERING CONDITIONS

PRICE
Base (estimated) .... $3500 (POE L.A.)
As tested (estimated) $3500
With options .... None

ENGINE
Type .... In-line 6, water-cooled, iron block, alloy head
Displacement .... 146 cu. in. (2393 cc)
Horsepower .... 150 hp @ 6000 rpm
Torque .... 148 lbs.-ft. @ 4400 rpm
Bore & stroke .... 3.27 in. x 2.90 in. (83 mm x 73.7 mm)
Compression ratio .... 9.0 to 1
Valve actuation .... Single ohc
Induction system .... Dual S.U.
Exhaust system .... Iron headers, 5 into 2
Electrical system .... 12-volt alternator, point distributor
Fuel .... Premium
Recommended redline 7000

DRIVE TRAIN
Clutch .... Single dry diaphragm

Transmission	Gear Ratio	Overall Ratio
1st Synchro	3.55	11.92
2nd Synchro	2.20	7.39
3rd Synchro	1.42	4.77
4th Synchro	1.00	3.36

Differential .... 3.36 ratio

BODY
Type .... Unit steel, 3-door, 2-passenger
Seats .... Front buckets
Windows .... 2 manual, no vents
Luggage space .... Rear trunk, 9 cu. ft.
Instruments .. 160 mph speedo, 8000 rpm tach
Gauges: .... temp., oil pressure, amp, fuel
Lights: .... handbrake

OPEL GT

AERODYNAMIC FORCES AT 100 MPH

CORNERING CONDITIONS

PRICE
Base .... $3470 (POE L.A.)
As tested $3569.26
With options .... 1.9 S engine package

ENGINE
Type .... 4-cylinder, water-cooled, iron block, iron head
Displacement .... 115.8 cu. in. (1898 cc)
Horsepower .... 102 hp @ 5400 rpm
Torque .... 115 lbs.-ft. @ 3400 rpm
Bore & stroke .... 3.66 in. x 2.75 in. (93 mm x 69.8 mm)
Compression ratio .... 9.0 to 1
Valve actuation .... Mechanical
Induction system .... Solex 2-bbl.
Exhaust system .... Iron headers, 3 into 1
Electrical system .... 12-volt alternator, point distributor
Fuel .... Premium
Recommended redline 6500

DRIVE TRAIN
Clutch .... Single dry plate

Transmission	Gear Ratio	Overall Ratio
1st Synchro	3.428	11.79
2nd Synchro	2.156	7.42
3rd Synchro	1.366	4.70
4th Synchro	1.000	3.44

Differential .... 3.44 ratio

BODY
Type .... Unit steel, 2-door, 2-passenger
Seats .... Front buckets
Windows .... 2 manual, no vents
Luggage space .... Boot trunk, 8 cu. ft.
Instruments .. 150 mph speedo, 7000 rpm tach
Gauges: ..... temp., fuel, amp, oil pressure
Lights: .... oil, ignition, brake, headlights

MGB GT

AERODYNAMIC FORCES AT 100 MPH

CORNERING CONDITIONS

PRICE
Base .... $3453 (POE L.A.)
As tested $3603
With options .... AM/FM Radio

ENGINE
Type .... In-line 4, water-cooled, iron block, iron head
Displacement .... 109.8 cu. in. (1798 cc)
Horsepower .... 92 hp @ 5400 rpm
Torque .... 110 lbs.-ft. @ 3000 rpm
Bore & stroke .... 3.16 in. x 3.5 in. (80 mm x 89 mm)
Compression ratio .... 8.8 to 1
Valve actuation .... Mechanical, ohv
Induction system .... Dual S.U.
Exhaust system .... Cast-iron headers, 4 into 2
Electrical system .... 12-volt alternator, point distributor
Fuel .... Premium
Recommended redline 6000

DRIVE TRAIN
Clutch ..... Diaphragm, hydraulically operated

Transmission	Gear Ratio	Overall Ratio
1st Synchro	3.44	13.45
2nd Synchro	2.17	8.47
3rd Synchro	1.38	5.40
4th Synchro	1.00	3.91

Differential .... 3.91 ratio

BODY
Type ... Unit construction, 3-door, 4-passenger
Seats .... Front buckets, rear bench
Windows .... 2 manual, 4 vents
Luggage space .... Rear trunk
Instruments .. 120 mph speedo, 7000 rpm tach
Gauges: .... fuel, oil, temp
Lights: .... amp.

CHASSIS

Frame .... Unit steel, Front engine, rear drive
Front suspension ...... McPherson strut-type, with following arms, tube shocks
Rear suspension .... Chapman strut-type, tube shocks
Steering .... Rack and pinion, 2.75 turns, overall ratio 17.8 to 1, turning circle 31.5 feet
Brakes .... Front discs; rear drums; dual independent systems, 10.7-in. dia. front, 9.1-in. dia. rear, swept area 310 sq. in.
Wheels .... 14-in. dia.
Tires .... Bridgestone 175SR14 pressures F/R: 28/28 (rec.), 32/30 (test)

WEIGHTS AND MEASURES

Weight ...... 2320 lbs. (curb), 2515 lbs. (test)
Weight distribution F/R 53%/47%
Wheelbase .... 90 in.
Track F/R .... 53.5 in./53.5 in.
Height .... 50 in.
Width .... 61 in.
Length .... 157 in.
Ground clearance .... 6 in.
Oil capacity .... 5.3 qt.
Fuel capacity .... 15.9 gal.
Coolant capacity .... 8.3 qt.

MISCELLANEOUS

Weight/power ratio (curb/advertised) .... 15.5 lbs. per hp
Advertised hp/cu. in. 1.03
Speed per 1000 rpm (top gear) ..... 21.8 mph
Warranty .... 12 months/12,000 miles

PERFORMANCE

Acceleration .... 0-30 (3.1 sec.), 0-60 (8.2 sec.), 0-100 (23.7 sec.) 0-quarter mile (15.5 sec., 86.5 mph)

Top speed .... 135 mph (est.) at 6000 rpm (hp limited)

Braking .... Distance from 60 mph: 151 ft. (0.79 *g* av.)
Number of stops to fade: 6
Stability: Excellent
Maximum pitch angle: 2.4°

Handling .... Maximum lateral: 0.72 *g* right, 0.77 *g* left
Skidpad understeer: 5.6° right, 4.2 ° left
Maximum roll angle: 5.1°
Reaction to throttle, full: Understeer; off: Oversteer

Speedometer	30.0	40.0	50.0	60.0	70.0	80.0	90.0	100.0
Actual	30.5	41.0	51.0	61.0	71.5	81.5	91.5	102.0

Mileage .... Average: 20.8 mpg
Miles on car: 1440 to 2650

Aerodynamic forces at 100 mph:
Drag .... 270 lbs. (includes tire drag)
Lift F/R .... −85 lbs./−95 lbs.

TEST EXPLANATIONS

Fade test is successive maximum *g* stops from 60 mph each minute until wheels cannot be locked. Understeer is front minus rear tire slip angle at maximum lateral on 200-ft. dia. Digitek skidpad. Autoscan chassis dynamometer supplied by Humble Oil.

CHASSIS

Frame .... Unit steel, front engine, rear drive
Front suspension .... Double A-frames, transverse leaf spring, tube shocks
Rear suspension .... Live axle, coil springs, Panhard rod, tube shocks
Steering .... Rack and pinion, 3.0 turns, overall ratio 17.4 to 1, turning circle 33 feet
Brakes .... Front discs; rear drums; dual hydraulic system 9.4-in. dia. front, 9.0-in. dia. rear, swept area 277 sq. in.
Wheels .... 13-in. dia.
Tires .... Goodyear 165 HR 13, pressures F/R: 24/24 (rec.), 24/24 (test)

WEIGHTS AND MEASURES

Weight ...... 2130 lbs. (curb), 2325 lbs. (test)
Weight distribution F/R 55%/45%
Wheelbase .... 95.7 in.
Track F/R .... 49.4 in./50.6 in.
Height .... 48.2 in.
Width .... 62.2 in.
Length .... 161.9 in.
Ground clearance .... 5 in.
Oil capacity .... 3.25 qt.
Fuel capacity .... 14.5 gal.
Coolant capacity .... 6 qt.

MISCELLANEOUS

Weight/power ratio (curb/advertised) .... 20.9 lbs. per hp
Advertised hp/cu. in. 0.88
Speed per 1000 rpm (top gear) ..... 19.6 mph
Warranty .... 12 months/12,000 miles

PERFORMANCE

Acceleration .... 0-30 (3.5 sec.), 0-60 (10.1 sec.), 0-100 (N.A.) 0-quarter mile (16.6 sec., 76.3 mph)

Top speed .... 119 mph (est.) at 5400 rpm (hp limited)

Braking .... Distance from 60 mph: 150 ft. (0.80 *g* av.)
Number of stops to fade: N.A.
Stability: Good
Maximum pitch angle: 1.9°

Handling .... Maximum lateral: 0.67 *g* right, 0.68 *g* left
Skidpad understeer: 4.6° right, 3.8° left
Maximum roll angle: 6.7°
Reaction to throttle, full: Understeer; off: Oversteer

Speedometer	30.0	40.0	50.0	60.0	70.0	80.0	90.0	100.0
Actual mph	27.0	38.0	47.5	58.0	68.0	78.0	88.5	98.0

Mileage .... Average: 24.0 mpg
Miles on car: 865 to 1400

Aerodynamic forces at 100 mph:
Drag .... 230 lbs. (includes tire drag)
Lift F/R .... 130 lbs./155 lbs.

TEST EXPLANATIONS

Fade test is successive maximum *g* stops from 60 mph each minute until wheels cannot be locked. Understeer is front minus rear tire slip angle at maximum lateral on 200-ft. dia. Digitek skidpad. Autoscan chassis dynamometer supplied by Humble Oil.

CHASSIS

Frame .... Unit steel, front engine, rear drive
Front suspension .... Unequal A-arms, coil springs, lever-arm shocks, anti-roll bar
Rear suspension ...... Live axle, leaf springs, lever shocks
Steering .... Rack and pinion, 2.9 turns, turning circle 32 feet
Brakes .... Front discs; rear drums; split hydraulic 10.6-in. dia. front, 10.0-in. dia. rear
Wheels .... 14-in. dia.
Tires .... Goodyear 5.60 S14 pressures F/R: 26/33 (rec.), 30/37 (test)

WEIGHTS AND MEASURES

Weight ...... 2305 lbs. (curb), 2525 lbs. (test)
Weight distribution F/R 49/51%
Wheelbase .... 91 in.
Track F/R .... 49.25 in./49.25 in.
Height .... 49.4 in.
Width .... 59.9 in.
Length .... 152.5 in.
Ground clearance .... 5 in.
Oil capacity .... 4.5 qt.
Fuel capacity .... 14.0 gal.
Coolant capacity .... 6 qt.

MISCELLANEOUS

Weight/power ratio (curb/advertised) .... 25 lbs. per hp
Advertised hp/cu. in. 0.84
Speed per 1000 rpm (top gear) ..... 17.5 mph
Warranty .... 12 months/12,000 miles

PERFORMANCE

Acceleration .... 0-30 (4.0 sec.), 0-60 (13.2 sec.), 0-100 (N.A.) 0-quarter mile (18.7 sec., 74.4 mph)

Top speed .... 105 mph (est.) at 6000 rpm (rpm limited)

Braking .... Distance from 60 mph: 152 ft. (0.79 *g* av.)
Number of stops to fade: Not attainable
Stability: Very good
Maximum pitch angle: 1.4°

Handling .... Maximum lateral: 0.76 *g* right, 0.77 *g* left
Reaction to throttle, full: Understeer; off: Oversteer

Speedometer	30.0	40.0	50.0	60.0	70.0	80.0
Actual mph	29.0	38.0	47.5	57.0	67.0	76.5

Mileage .... Average: 24.0 mpg
Miles on car: 2870 to 3200

Aerodynamic forces at 100 mph:
Drag .... 285 lbs. (includes tire drag)
Lift F/R .... 70 lbs./130 lbs.

TEST EXPLANATIONS

Fade test is successive maximum *g* stops from 60 mph each minute until wheels cannot be locked. Understeer is front minus rear tire slip angle at maximum lateral on 200-ft. dia. Digitek skidpad. Autoscan chassis dynamometer supplied by Humble Oil.

And in this corner, doors waving, is the winnah! The 240Z Datsun does everything so well that it makes us wonder whether the other manufacturers are trying to put us on.

THREE WAYS

There are only two cars we've had in the past couple of years that each of us has rated as tops. Those were the Mercedes-Benz 6.3 and the BMW 2800CS. Now there's a third, and for a helluva lot less money, we might add!

The Z Car is a little bulky looking, big, impressive. Big? My God, it's comfortably roomy. Oh, and that blissful silence. It's smooth. It bolsters your confidence. And everybody's looking – just look at them!

"A Datsun? That's not a Datsun," the man with the gas nozzle in his hand exclaimed. "It's one of those exotic European cars, right? You're putting me on."

It was difficult for people to think that the Japanese, who produced the Toyota and Datsun sedans and the kamikaze Subaru, would come out with something this interesting. Toyota never made enough GTs to fill one gas station, so few people saw them. But a Datsun? It was fun. We even held up one of our instruments and told the station attendant that it was a microphone and pointed across the street and told him he was on camera. You know, he believed us!

Nissan claims its Z Car will reach a top speed of 120 mph, but our tests disprove that. The Japanese are born pessimists. Why, we got almost 120 in third gear! Our estimates for the car are closer to a 135-mph top end.

Although acceleration shows 15.51 seconds in the quarter-mile, we believe the car will go another two or three tenths quicker, since we didn't make as many runs as we hoped. And that's going through the traps halfway wound out in third, so you know the gears are tall. At first we hoped the Datsun we received for test would have a five-speed transmission, but it's unnecessary in this car. The only time Datsun may revert to a five-speed is in competition.

You know, there are little details you always look for in an automobile and somehow never find. But the Z Car has some. That luggage area in the back, with its rear door, has tie-down straps for luggage. The ventilation system works with the effectiveness of air-conditioning. And the heater in this one will keep you warm. The seats mold to your body delicately, and are fully adjustable in just about any direction your curves happen to go. At 75 mph you feel like you're going 40. Everything is at your fingertips. You can talk in a whisper and your passenger will understand every word.

Before we get too carried away, let's move back to reality a minute. The rear brakes need fixing. Just like on the other two test cars, the rear brakes are drums, but fade quickly. This was a problem with a Datsun sedan we tested a year ago. The rear brakes became erratic after about the sixth stop. Stopping distances increased from 140 feet to over 200. We've never made 12 panic stops in succession on the road, so maybe it's not as significant as we think. Before we began testing, we did about a dozen hot laps around Riverside Raceway, just for fun, and never encountered any braking problems, despite some very hard stops from speeds in excess of 100 mph. Apparently, recovery is good.

There's never been a car in this price range that could compete in many ways with an elegant sports car in the over-$10,000 range. But this one can. It even reminds us a little of a Ferrari in its characteristics and appearance. Everything that comes for the Z Car is standard, including the radial tires, radio, power antenna, tinted glass and, eventually, rear-window defroster.

Datsun has done something with the 240Z that Triumph attempted with its TR 4A a few years ago – a successful independent suspension all around. Although there is a noticeable pitch during acceleration, it's not exaggerated as in the Triumph, nor is lateral sway a problem. Stiffer shocks could help here, but Nissan designed the car this way purposely, to bring it closer to the GT by offering an unusually smooth ride on high-speed Interstates.

Nissan thought of more than just the driver when it built this sports car. The mechanic was considered, too. There's so much room in the engine compartment that a repairman will find he won't need his $54 "ess"-shaped socket extension to do the simplest task. There's a light there for him, too, as well as easy accessibility to any component that makes the automobile run.

Let's look back at our results now. The MG has the edge on handling, with the Datsun a close second. The three are quite close on initial brake stops, but the Datsun has the acceleration race, tires down. It's nip-and-tuck between the Datsun and Opel for styling. As far as anything else goes, the Datsun is far and away the best of the lot.

Look out, world, or the Japanese are going to rule us . . . on the highway, at least.

DATSUN 240Z

New standards in performance and elegance for medium-priced 2-seat GT cars

DATSUN HAS HAD a sizable portion of the U.S. sports car market for a number of years now with the 1600 Sports and its 2-liter derivative. Both of these models are based on British design influences, which is logical since the British were dominating the sports car market when the Japanese first took a serious look at it. Although the 1600 and 2000 Sports have been greatly improved during the last few years, they still exemplify the old formula: stark 2-seat open bodywork, strong but noisy engine, good roadholding with few concessions to riding comfort, good performance for the money.

But Nissan Motors had been studying the latest German and Italian design practices (not to mention carefully examining the situation in this country) and two years ago we saw the first result: the totally modern Datsun 510 sedan, with its single-overhead-cam engine and all-independent suspension. It was to be expected that Nissan would not be long in producing a sports derivative of the 510. Perhaps we expected only a lower, lighter 2-seat version of the sedan, using the 4-cyl unit. But the resulting 240Z (fully described in the January issue) surprised everyone by having a structure all its own, entirely new independent rear suspension, a 6-cyl 2.4-liter stretch of the 510's 1.6-liter four, and a classy fastback body that owes nothing to any previous Nissan product.

Since the styling of the 240Z is the first thing you see (and probably the most important factor in what we think will be a tremendous penetration into the GT market), we'll begin

STROTHER MAC MINN PHOTOS

DATSUN 240Z

with the body lines. There are several obvious influences on the 240Z, among them the Jaguar E-Type coupe, the Toyota 2000 GT, the Porsche 911 series and even the Ferrari 275 GTB. In a Nissan-produced movie that we saw recently on the development of the 240Z, the exterior forms and seating packages of all the contemporary GT cars were carefully evaluated and compared to the forms that Nissan was considering (using R&T's own Road Test data panel drawings, we were pleased to note). The Jaguar was the one getting the most attention from the Nissan stylists and engineers; this is not surprising, because the E-Type opened up a market all its own nine years ago and the 240Z could do worse than be a $3500 equivalent with the proportionately higher sales potential. Regardless of its influences, the 240Z is a very good design: clean, crisp and contemporary if perhaps sitting a bit high on its wheels. Our capable artist Werner Bührer has again produced a thorough R&T Styling Analysis, which appears on pages 64-65. Driving around in the car, one thing that surprised us slightly was the lack of attention it received; while it was admired by those who had the occasion to see it up close, it didn't make anyone gawk as it went by. A handsome but not startling shape.

Inside the car, the driver and passenger are immediately impressed by a very modern layout which would seem almost Corvette-like if it weren't more tastefully done in

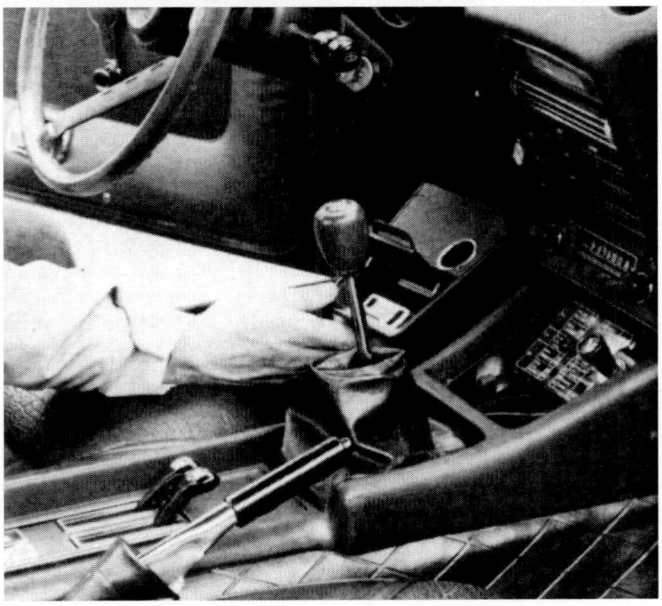

A clever touch, typical of the well-thought-out interior, is the lift-out ash tray which gives access to the fuses.

black vinyl. In fact, the lack of color is so severe that only the warm wood grains of the steering wheel rim (simulated) and gearshift knob (real) provide relief. For one interested in the business of driving, this simplicity is satisfyingly functional. The seats and the positions of all the controls are equally right: every member of our staff found the seating comfortable for him, a rare occurrence on even the most luxurious cars. The backrests are adjustable only through about 10 degrees, sufficient for seating variations but not permitting full reclining. Speedometer and tachometer are large dials right in front of the driver; both were steady and accurate, actually reading about 1 percent slow. The speedometer was a bit disconcerting, beginning at 20 mph; we realize that accuracy suffers below this speed, but we'd like to see the 10 and 0 at least marked on the instrument. The central console is topped by three dials containing the water temperature/oil pressure and alternator charge/fuel level gauges plus an accurate clock. These three faces are a bit far from the normal line of sight to suit us, but they are clearly readable. Below them are the heater/ventilation controls, which are comprehensive and should be very effective. We weren't able to evaluate them properly, however, because the Nissan people were still having trouble getting them connected up right (ours was an early preproduction 240Z). Beneath these controls, and the standard-equipment signal seeking radio with its delightfully fast electric antenna, is a lift-out ashtray which very conveniently exposes the fuse box. Between the shift lever and the handbrake are the choke and hand throttle.

Much appreciated little touches are the padded headliner and push-on-and-off flush interior light lenses. Not so well appreciated were the day/night mirror knob, which didn't provide the same field of view in both positions; the windshield wipers, which as often as not would stop in midstroke rather than park themselves when switched off; and the fact that the backrests don't swing forward to give access to the luggage platform from the side. Rear access from the lift-up window/tailgate is fine, however, and the 240Z accepts a really generous amount of luggage, as much as two people would want to take along. This is a good result of designing a car specifically for two passengers—no awkward compromises as are often forced by the 2+2 configuration. The luggage platform is well detailed, with handsome carpeting and useful straps for suitcases.

The 240Z six is quiet and smooth at low engine speeds, as you would expect, but has an almost unpleasant rumbly growl when wound out. We found the power peak to be at about 5500 rpm rather than the 6000 quoted; there is certainly no value in going up to the 7000-rpm redline! By

COMPARISON DATA	Datsun 240Z	Alfa Romeo 1750 GTV	Fiat 124 Coupe	Opel GT
List price	$3526	$4681	$3174	$3395
Curb weight, lb	2355	2288	2110	2105
0–60 mph, sec	8.7	9.9	11.3	10.8
Standing ¼-mi	17.1	17.3	18.6	17.7
Speed at end	84.5	80	74	77
Panic stop from 80 mph, % g	84	90	81	81
Fade in 6 stops from 60 mph, %	10	nil	54	nil
R&T wear index	39	60	74	42
R&T steering index	1.10	1.26	0.99	0.99
Fuel economy, mpg	21.0	22.0	24.0	27.5

DATSUN 240Z

European standards, the output is probably less than the 150 bhp claimed, but the 17.1-sec quarter-mile time was in the ballpark for the calculated lb/bhp figure. Acceleration is better than that of any other GT in its price class and along with the styling this will be a major selling point. Getting off the line is smooth with only moderate wheelspin. Gearing is intentionally tall to give the 240Z good cruising performance and a high top speed (we got 122 mph at 5800 rpm), but means that there is a definite lack of snap when trying to accelerate from a low engine speed in 4th, or even 3rd. The gearbox has a nice action with good short throws, but the synchromesh was all too easy to beat, especially in 2nd.

The steering was a bit of an enigma. When we first had the car it seemed light, precise and absolutly first-rate. On our second experience (to recheck the fuel economy which had been disappointingly low at about 17 mpg) the steering was unaccountably heavy, requiring real effort on tight turns. Since the tires were the same, we can only conclude that the steering is highly sensitive to front-end adjustments and that some incorrect setting was made. Except for this, handling is very good and roadholding really excellent. On the skid pad, we recorded 33.0 mph, equal to 0.728g. This is just a hair better than the speed achieved by the Porsche 914! The Datsun can really be driven hard; flung enthusiastically into corners, its near-neutral handling (helped by the near 50/50 weight distribution) makes it very stable, with just a hint of oversteer allowing the tail to hang out but not come around. Ride is far better than on previous Datsun sports cars but still quite abrupt on choppy surfaces; it would seem that Nissan engineers still have something to learn about shock absorbers. The noise level is low, except for the rear axle, which "comes in" at 40-50 mph; at 70 the car is a pleasure to cruise, with the engine turning only 3350 rpm and the wind noise slight. The hood panel tended to vibrate at highway speeds.

The spoked wheels shown in the photos are an extra-cost option. We weren't able to get them properly balanced in time for our performance runs, so we ran with the standard disc wheels and covers and Bridgestone 175-14 radials.

The brakes were very strong, recording 84%g with excellent control in the panic stop and only 10% increase in pedal pressure over the six half-g stops. Under wet driving conditions, however, they were badly affected by spray and had to be ridden to remain effective.

The basic list price of the 240Z is $3526 and at this price it is a super-bargain, with a combination of styling, performance and handling far ahead of anything else under $4000. None of the shortcomings mentioned are serious; they are certainly not obtrusive at the asking price and many of the minor ones will probably disappear as the car gets into full production. One thousand units per month are expected for the American market initially, with more later when the market is established. What will the 240Z compete with? The accompanying Comparison Data panel lists the Opel GT, Fiat 124 Coupe and the Alfa Romeo 1750 GTV; because of price, the 4-cyl Porsche 914 (tested in this issue) can also be included. The Fiat 124 Coupe is almost a full 4-seater, but with comparatively modest performance; the Alfa GTV is a 2+2 with performance very close to that of the Datsun but costing $1000 more. So the Opel GT, with a price near that of the 240Z but lacking some of its performance, style, comfort and sophistication, is perhaps the closest competitor (and the one which could suffer in sales as a result). But we expect to see the Datsun establish a market of its own, one which will force other makers to come up with entirely new models to gain a share in it. The Japanese industry is no longer borrowing anything from other nations. In fact, a great struggle may be ahead just to prevent a complete reversal of that cliché.

ROAD TEST
DATSUN 240Z

PRICE

List price, all POE $3526
Price includes radial tires, signal seeking radio with power antenna (standard equipment)

IMPORTER

Nissan Motor Corp. USA
137 E. Alondra, Gardena, Calif.

ENGINE

Type .... 6 cyl inline, sohc
Bore x stroke, mm ..... 83.0 x 73.3
Equivalent in .... 3.27 x 2.90
Displacement, cc/cu in .. 2393/146
Compression ratio 9.0:1
Bhp @ rpm .... 150 @ 6000
Equivalent mph 126
Torque @ rpm .... 148 @ 4400
Equivalent mph 92
Carburetion ... two Hitachi-SU (1V)
Type fuel required ...... premium
Emission control ...... air injection

DRIVE TRAIN

Transmission ..... 4-speed manual
Gear ratios: 4th (1.00) 3.36:1
3rd (1.42) 4.77:1
2nd (2.20) 7.39:1
1st (3.55) 11.92:1
Final drive ratio 3.36:1

CHASSIS & BODY

Layout .... front engine, rear drive
Body/frame .... unit steel
Brake type: 10.7-in. disc front, 9.0 x 1.6-in. drum rear, vacuum assisted
Swept area, sq in 310
Wheels .... steel disc, 14 x 4½J
Tires .... Bridgestone 175 SR-14 radials
Steering type .... rack & pinion
Overall ratio 17.8:1
Turns, lock-to-lock 3.5
Turning circle, ft 31.5
Front suspension: MacPherson struts, lower lateral arms, compliance struts, coil springs, tube shocks, anti-roll bar
Rear suspension: Chapman struts, lower A-arms, coil springs, tube shocks

ACCOMMODATION

Seating capacity, persons 2
Seat width .... 2 x 21.0
Head room 36.5
Seat back adjustment, degrees .. 10
Driver comfort rating (scale of 100):
Driver 69 in. tall 90
Driver 72 in. tall 70
Driver 75 in. tall 65

INSTRUMENTATION

Instruments: 160-mph speedo, main & trip odo, 8000-rpm tach, water temp, oil pressure, ammeter, fuel level, clock
Warning lights: directionals, high beam, handbrake, emergency flashers

MAINTENANCE

Service intervals, mi:
Oil change 3000
Filter change 6000
Chassis lube 30,000
Minor tuneup 6,000
Major tuneup 12,000
Warranty, mo/mi 12/12,000

GENERAL

Curb weight, lb 2355
Test weight 2769
Weight distribution (with driver), front/rear, % 51/49
Wheelbase, in 90.7
Track, front/rear 53.3/53.0
Overall length 162.8
Width 64.1
Height 50.6
Ground clearance 5.7
Overhang, front/rear 34.4/37.7
Usable trunk space, cu ft 8.5
Fuel tank capacity, U.S. gal ... 15.9

CALCULATED DATA

Lb/bhp (test weight) 18.4
Mph/1000 rpm (4th gear) 21.0
Engine revs/mi (60 mph) 2850
Engine speed @ 70 mph 3350
Piston travel, ft/mi 1378
Cu ft/ton mi 87.2
R&T wear index 39
R&T steering index 1.10
Brake swept area sq in/ton 263

ROAD TEST RESULTS

ACCELERATION

Time to distance, sec:
0–100 ft 4.3
0–250 ft 6.4
0–500 ft 9.5
0–750 ft 12.2
0–1000 ft 14.5
0–1320 ft (¼ mi) 17.1
Speed at end of ¼ mi, mph ... 84.5
Time to speed, sec:
0–30 mph 3.2
0–40 mph 4.9
0–50 mph 6.6
0–60 mph 8.7
0–70 mph 11.8
0–80 mph 15.2
0–100 mph 27.1
Passing exposure time, sec:
To pass car going 50 mph 6.3

FUEL CONSUMPTION

Normal driving, mpg 21.0
Cruising range, mi 335

SPEEDS IN GEARS

4th gear (5800 rpm) 122
3rd (6500) 97
2nd (6500) 63
1st (6500) 37

BRAKES

Panic stop from 80 mph:
Max. deceleration rate, % g .. 84
Stopping distance, ft 287
Control .... excellent
Fade test: percent increase in pedal effort to maintain 50%-g deceleration rate in 6 stops from 60 mph 10
Parking: Hold 30% grade? ..... yes
Overall brake rating ..... very good

SPEEDOMETER ERROR

30 mph indicated is actually .. 31.5
40 mph 41.5
60 mph 61.3
80 mph 81.0
100 mph 100.6
Odometer, 10.0 mi 10.1

ACCELERATION & COASTING

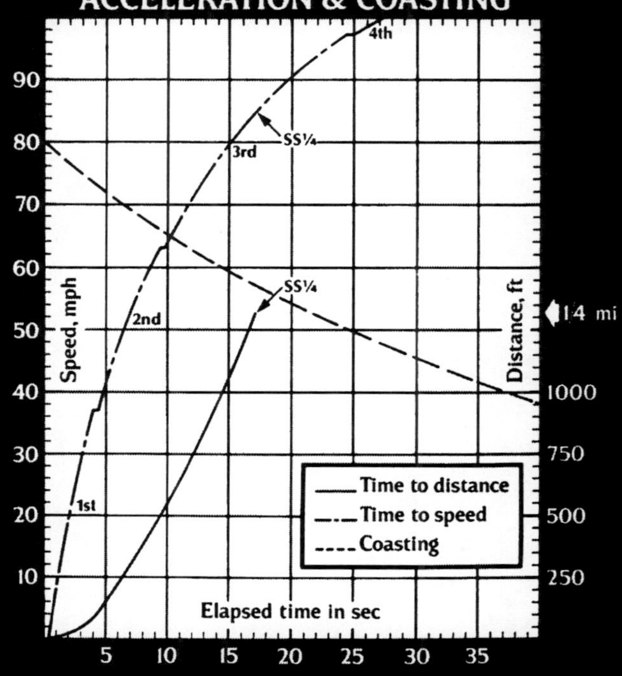

R&T STYLING ANALYSIS
DATSUN 240Z

DRAWINGS BY WERNER BÜHRER

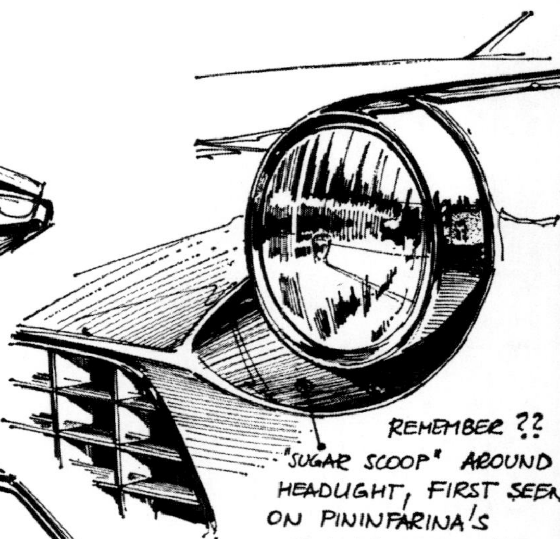

QUARTER WINDOW AND ROOF LINE MIGHT BE ONLY SERIOUS POINT OF DISCUSSION
ANY SPORTIER COCKPIT WANTED ?
BÜHRER '70
VERY NICE DETAIL, SPOILED ONLY BY SEAM – UNFORTUNATELY NECESSARY AT THE LOW PRICE.
BEST VIEW FOR THIS CAR : VERY NICE CHARACTER LINES, GOOD PROPORTIONS BETWEEN BODY AND GREENHOUSE.
WHEELCOVERS ONLY – CONSEQUENCE OF THE PRICE.

IMPRESSIONS DATSUN 240Z

New and sporting Grand Touring car from Nissan

The newest sports car from Japan arrived in the United States just before the new year to be displayed at various auto shows. The Datsun 240 Z has been promised to ROAD TEST for the full treatment in the very near future, for now we bring you a sampling of the Grand Touring car with impressions gathered by our Japanese correspondent.

A few years ago the planners at Nissan began work on the Z series of cars. The sportsters were developed with full independent suspension and a variety of engines, with both open and closed body styles considered. By 1967 the worldwide popularity of the GT body style prompted the decision to go ahead on the fastback closed coupe version for the Z series.

The single overhead cam engine that has done so well in the 510 sedan was chosen as the base for the export model of the Z. There is a hot two-liter dohc engine built for racing, but it is still in the development stage as far as export is concerned. The 240 Z engine has been modified to suit the demands of the U.S. Federal emission laws and has an exhaust manifold air injection system fitted. The engine is a six cylinder adaption of the 1600 unit, with the sohc, in-line configuration, cast iron block with a seven main bearing crank, alloy head and chain drive on the camshaft. The export model has two Hitachi-SU HJG 46W carburetors and 9.0 to 1 compression ratio. Displacement comes out to 2393 cubic centimeters. The new six produces 150 SAE horsepower at 6000 rpm.

The standard transmission is an all synchromesh four-speed and the five speed gearbox is an option. Later on a three speed automatic will become available. The front suspension parts are borrowed from the 1800 sedan that is not exported to America. It is the MacPherson strut type with coil springs, tubular shocks, and an anti-roll bar attached to the lower arms. The new rear suspension is completely different from any previous Datsun model. It utilizes 'Chapman' struts similar to the Lotus Elan with coil springs and tubular shocks. There are double constant velocity U-joints on the drive axles. Wheels are the steel disc type sized at 14 × 4½ J. There are, however, many different styles of wheels availabe in America that will fit the car. Girling type disc brakes are used at the front with drum brakes at the rear. There is a power assist for the brakes and the action is good.

The new car is styled in the contemporary fashion. The designers borrowed heavily from European coachbuilders tc produce the low nose, sloping rear deck profile on the 240 Z with its conventional configuration of front engine, rear drive. The big back window slopes down to a Kamm type tail treatment and the rear running lights are recessed into the vertical tail panel. The engine hood has a slight center bulge on top that comes down to the low mounted air intake for the radiator in a smooth line. Single headlights are recessed in the fenders forward of the wheel wells, and the U.S. version will be without the glass covers used for fairing in the lights. The front turn indicators are mounted under the bumper. Rubber faced bumper over riders protect the body from parking lot nicks. The doors open wide and are quite large to insure ease of entry into the low two seater.

The interior is done in vinyl with deep cushioned bucket seats. The seats adjust horizontally and vertically with a reclining back angle of up to ten degrees. The cockpit is spacious and there is a large carpeted cargo area behind the twin bucket seats. Instrumentation is complete with a large tachometer and speedometer in front of the driver and auxiliary gauges of smaller, but matching circular style on the center of the dash for fuel level, oil pressure/water temperature, and the third is a clock.

The rear view is pleasing and the styling all part of the whole. The rear window opens up for a cargo door ala' Jaguar XKE.

The 240 Z is docile on the road, runs quietly and without fuss. The ride is quite good with the independent rear suspension and handling is far more modern than the classic sportsters from Datsun.

Interior of the 240 Z is upholstered in richly padded vinyl. Seats are well cushioned and comfortable. The center mounted shift lever and steering wheel are standard with the wood trim and the Z has a full complement of instruments.

Three point safety harness is fitted and the optional radio can be placed under the heater controls above the center console. There is now a passenger foot rest.

The aerodynamic body on the 240 Z and the engineering advances on the car were designed for the American market. The idea was to blend race proven features with contemporary styling and luxury appointments for a high performance personal car — a segment of the American market that grows larger every year. Nissan feels that the new GT will suit the demanding tastes of the American buyer and meet all the requirements of the sports minded drivers with modern looks, good ride and handling, plenty of power, and many safety features. The 240 Z looks like an exotic and expensive car, but pricing will fall near the $3500 mark.

Our correspondent in Japan reports that road manners of the 240 Z are in the tradition of the excellent sports cars already produced by Nissan. He tells us, however, that we are in for a surprise in the *performance* of the car, "— it performs quite marvelously in a dash at more than about 3000 rpm." He goes on to say that on the high speed sections of the test track the 240 Z really comes into its own. The new independent rear suspension adds a new dimension in road holding to a vehicle already known for excellent cornering.

Our tester in Japan had a minor complaint and again we'll quote in his own words. "The seat, one of the equipments attached more importance on this kind of car, belonged to the bucket type, adopting the latest fashion in the construction integrating the head rest. The seat was quite magnificent, yet a little too large in size for the Japanese people."

Engine warm-up even in cold weather is reportedly quick and low end torque is good even though greatest pulling

The new 2.4 liter six is based on the 510 unit with two more cylinders. The sohc powerplant produces 150 horsepower.

power comes on at 3600 rpm.

The only real complaint our man in Tokyo has is over the inadequacy of the lighting at speed. He was unaware that such matters are legislated in the U.S.

Datsun feels it has covered all segments of the market now — from pickup trucks through sedans to the personal sports car. The 240 Z is a remarkable bargain too, and we predict a line of customers waiting for the first shipment to hit the showrooms. ROAD TEST will bring you a full report on the Z in the very near future. ♠

CAR AND DRIVER ROAD TEST

DATSUN 240Z

Datsun didn't invent the overhead cam engine, or disc brakes, or independent suspension but it has a habit of incorporating these sophisticated systems into brilliantly conceived and easily affordable cars

The difference between the Datsun 240Z and your everyday three-and-a-half thousand dollar sports car is that about twice as much thinking went into the Datsun. It shows. For the money the 240Z is an almost brilliant car.

The people at Datsun balk at calling the 240Z a sports car. To them it's a "personal" GT car. Even so, they know perfectly well who the customers will be—sports car buyers—adventuresome young Americans who were collecting their dollars for an Opel GT or MGB-GT or Porsche 914 until something better came along and changed their minds. Still, the "personal" GT car description somehow fits. It separates the Datsun from whimsical, superficial sports cars like the Opel GT and moves it off into a mature class of automobiles that has more to offer than just amusement. The Z-car, as it has come to be called, is a very real *transportation* automobile, meant as much for coast-to-coast journeys as it is for playing around on idyllic summer days. Datsun is probably right. The Z-car really isn't a sports car.

It is exactly the kind of car we have come to expect from Datsun, however. You can't really consider Datsun to be an innovator—it didn't invent the overhead cam engine or disc brakes or independent suspension—but it is one of the most ambitious car manufacturers alive these days and it has a habit of incorporating these sophisticated systems into easily affordable cars. The budget-priced PL510 sedan is the envy of all its competitors, and the vitality in the engine and gearbox of the 2000 sports car makes a Triumph feel like a first-round loser in the soapbox derby. With that kind of siblings, the Z-car would naturally be a gifted performer.

And it is. Curiously, a double standard has grown up through the years concerning sports cars and equivalently priced family sedans—the sedans are always more powerful. Not so with the Z-car. It will keep right up with your neighbor's Bonneville and leave all of the sports cars in its class scuttling along in the slow lane. At Orange County Raceway the test car ran through the quarter in 16.1 seconds at 86.5 mph—more than one second and 9 mph quicker than a Triumph TR6. It is also several mph faster than a 2-liter Porsche 911T, although the elapsed time is not quite as good because the Z-car continues Datsun's practice of using axle ratios suitable for the Bonneville salt flats.

Of course, it should also be obvious that the Z-car continues Datsun's practice of using exceptionally powerful engines—in this case a 2.4-liter single-overhead-cam Six. It's a new engine for Datsun—yet not really new because it is actually one-and-a-half of the Fours used in the PL510 sedan. With the help of two SUs and a 9.0-to-one compression ratio it generates 151 horsepower at 5600 rpm, and if you are so inclined you can turn it all the way to 7000 rpm before you hit the red line. We aren't inclined, however. Like all Datsuns, the torque curve is as flat as Nebraska and the engine noise is so unpleasant above 6500 that there is just no reason to ever go up there.

Datsun tackles the exhaust emission problem with three separate external devices: an air pump to inject air into the exhaust manifold, a valve that admits air into the intake manifold immediately after the throttle is closed to aid combustion of fuel that is already in the manifold; and a diaphragm which prevents the throttle from closing for several seconds after you lift your foot off the accelerator. Only one of these is noticeable to the driver—the last item. It keeps engine speed too high, making smooth upshifts impossible, and seriously detracts from the pleasure of driving. Throttle response, particularly at low speeds, also suffers, due to subtleties of the system.

In most other ways the Z-car is kind to its driver. The steering effort is moderate; the shifting motions are light and acceptably precise; and the driving position is excellent. The brakes—discs in front and leading/trailing shoes in finned aluminum drums at the rear—stop the car well enough, 259 feet (0.83G) from 80 mph, but very high pedal effort is required for a panic stop. In addition, the system is spongy and offers very little feel to help the driver control lock-up. In the rain things get even worse—at least in the test car. Water somehow splashes up onto the braking surfaces and sharply reduces stopping ability. In this respect the Z-car is not satisfactory.

The Datsun's suspension system—a fully independent MacPherson strut arrangement both front and rear—also has a few quirks. The test car would understeer more in right than in left turns. You would never notice it

PHOTOGRAPHY: HUMPHREY SUTTON

DATSUN 240Z

on the road but on the test track the car was very well balanced when cornering to the left but would plow heavily when turning right. There is no reason that this should be typical of all of the Z-cars. The test car had expanders between several coils in the left front spring to overcome a sag, and the asymmetric handling can probably be blamed on that spring. We don't know what to blame for the poor directional stability, however. When you'd like to be going straight down the road the Z-car would rather weave back and forth. The wiggles are small—and they seem to correct themselves—but they are annoying, nonetheless.

Neither Datsun nor we are entirely satisfied with the choice of tires. Bridgestone 175 SR 14 radials were selected as standard equipment because of their good handling characteristics, but they are also responsible for an abnormally high level of road noise, particularly over tar strips and small bumps. The ride quality of the Z-car is actually quite comfortable for a sporting car of its class but the noise tends to make you think otherwise. Knowing this, Datsun engineers were deeply involved in tire testing at the time of our road test and hoped to have a more compatible tire before very many Z-cars were imported.

While there are problems in the chassis that still must be worked out, it's an altogether different story in the cockpit. At times during the test we found ourselves being very critical of the Z-car—judging harshly where it fell short of perfection—and completely forgetting that it sells for $3601. It seems far more expensive than any competitive similarly-priced sports car We are back to the double standard for family cars and sports cars again. The Z-car has certain qualities that up to now were available only in sedans or very expensive GT cars. Silence is the best example. The engine noise level in the Datsun under normal operating conditions is roughly equal to that of an American intermediate sedan, which is to say that you hardly know it's there. That doesn't seem like a monumental achievement except that no one else in this price class has ever done it before.

And the 240Z is very comfortable which also makes it seem more expensive. The bucket seats are elaborately contoured and wrap around you slightly to keep you from sliding around. The backrest angle is adjustable in notches through a small range so you can find a position that suits. Head room, leg room and shoulder room are ample and the final little detail that makes it just right is the dead pedal.

The feeling of getting your money's worth is reinforced by the complete instrumentation and rather complex looking controls. The speedometer (which for some reason starts at 20 mph) and the 8000-rpm tach are directly in front of the driver, and all of the normal small gauges and a clock are angled toward him from three pods centrally located on top of the instrument panel. A curious rod projects out of the right side of the steering column which has turn-type switches for lights and windshield wipers and a button for the washers on its outer end. It works quite well when you get used to it but its biggest advantage is that it can be easily reached, even when you are strapped in with the shoulder belt. On the console are two levers that look like they should be for lowering the landing gear or adjusting the flaps—it turns out that one is a hand throttle and the other is the choke (the 240Z always has to be choked to start).

The 240Z is obviously well conceived by standards universal to good automobiles but there has been an East-West struggle in the interior trim. When you consider the tremendous cultural differences between the Japanese and the Americans it's surprising that any automotive styling could bridge the two. In some areas, like the 1953 Tijuana quilted vinyl on the console and on the sides of the luggage area and yellow wood rim on the steering wheel, the difference in taste is conspicuous. The instrument panel, too, has a characteristic flavor that is found in all Datsuns. It's a one-piece affair, molded of soft energy absorbing plastic foam, and deeply contoured in a way that suggests nothing but a Datsun instrument panel: Not GT car in the fashion originated by the Italians, not 2-ton nickelodeon in the style championed by Detroit, but just plain Datsun. Elsewhere, the Z-car seems international in its appearance. The exterior styling is smooth and appropriately GT-like, drawing remarks like, "That's not a Datsun, is it?" and "Man, how much did that thing cost ya?" It's obviously attractive enough to generate a little envy in everyone who sees it and that is at least half the value of any automobile other than a 4-door sedan.

But while they are envying you for having a sports car the Z-car doesn't shackle you with the normal sports car limitations. Not only is it comfortable and quiet but it also has a generous luggage area. From just behind the seats all the way back to the rear of the car is a flat area that will easily carry enough luggage for two people. Tie-down straps have been provided to secure small objects that like to roll around. And loading is easy because of the huge tailgate. It would be handier if the seat backs would fold forward so that small things could be unloaded from the front. As it is, the headrests are so high that there is little room left for passing bulky objects around them. Even so, the 240Z sets the new standard for utility in 2-passenger cars of this price.

And it is inevitable that we should come back to price because that ultimately decides the desirability of any car. At the time of the test the Z-car followed Datsun's typical pricing policy for its sporting cars—everything is standard equipment. Every car, as it comes from the factory, has radial ply tires and an excellent push-button AM radio with a power antenna. It's as simple as that. There will be options in the future, however. Tinted glass and a heated rear window will soon be available.

Price is the least of the Z-car's problems —and it does have a few problems. Although it is splendidly conceived, we have the feeling that it's not quite done yet. There is an annoying vibration somewhere in the drivetrain that you feel under full power, and as near as we can tell it is present in varying degrees in all cars. And as we mentioned before, the brakes are sensitive to splashed-up water which is a serious deficiency. Still, we are optimistic. After the test we sat down in a truth-telling session with the key men of Datsun USA, the importer, and they were intent on hearing any criticisms that we might put forth. It turned out that they were aware of every weakness that we had found and were working closely with the main engineering department in Japan to find solutions. We are confident that they will succeed. Since they were obviously bright enough technically to bring the Z-car this far along, the final rung on the ladder is within easy reach.

Even as it is, the 240Z is worth its price. Just between you and us, when Datsun gets it all straightened around, it might be worth a little more. ●

ACCELERATION standing ¼ mile, seconds

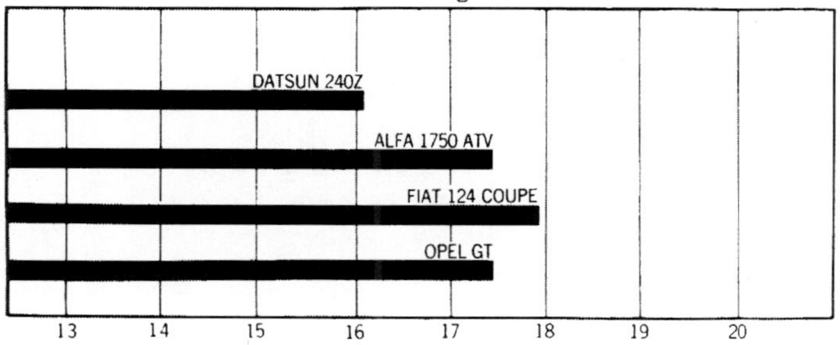

BRAKING 80-0 mph panic stop, feet

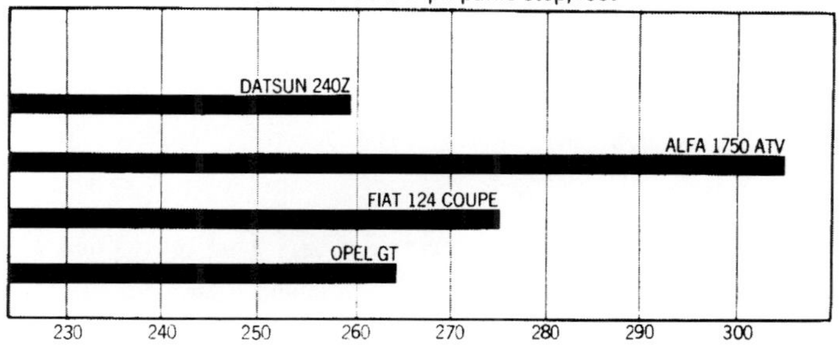

FUEL ECONOMY RANGE mpg

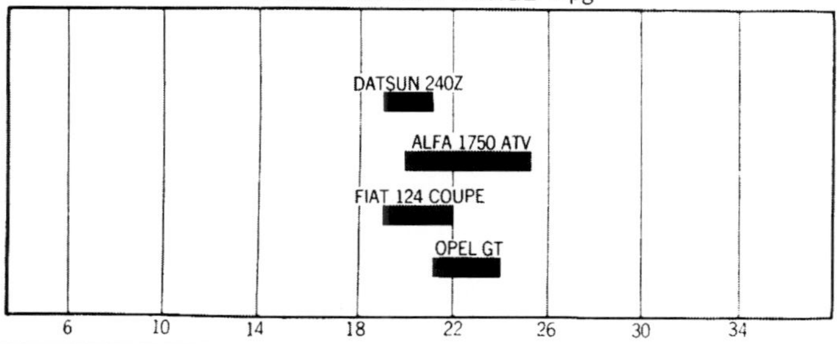

PRICE AS TESTED dollars x 1000

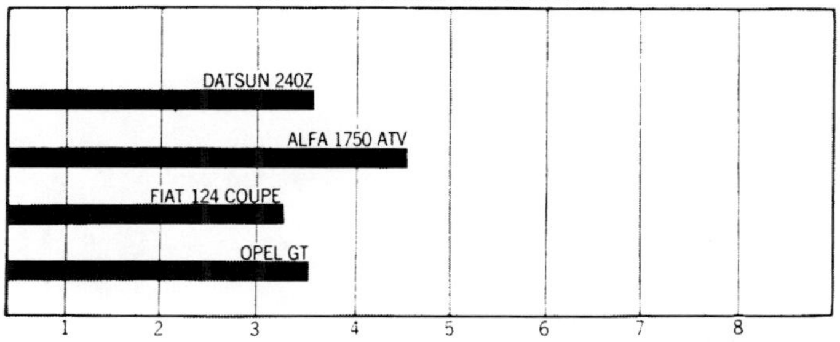

DATSUN 240Z

Importer: Datsun U.S.A.
137 E. Alondra Blvd.
Gardena, Calif. 90247

Vehicle type: Front engine, rear-wheel-drive, 2-passenger coupe

Price as tested: $3601.00
(Manufacturer's suggested retail price, including all options listed below, Federal excise tax, dealer preparation and delivery charges, does not include state and local taxes, license or freight charges)

Options on test car: Base car, $3526; dealer preparation, $75.00

ENGINE

Type: 6-in-line, water-cooled, cast iron block and aluminum head, 7 main bearings
Bore x stroke . . 3.27 x 2.90 in, 83.0 x 73.7 mm
Displacement . . . . 146.0 cu in, 2393 cc
Compression ratio . . . . 9.0 to one
Carburetion . . . . 2 x 1-bbl S.U.
Valve gear . . . . . . Chain-driven single overhead camshaft
Power (SAE) . . . . 151 bhp @ 5600 rpm
Torque (SAE) . . . . 146 lb-ft @ 4400 rpm
Specific power output . . . . 1.03 bhp/cu in, 63.2 bhp/liter
Max recommended engine speed . . . 7000 rpm

DRIVETRAIN

Transmission . . . . 4-speed, all-synchro
Final drive ratio . . . . 3.36 to one

Gear	Ratio	Mph/1000 rpm	Max. test speed
I	3.55	6.0	42 mph (7000 rpm)
II	2.20	9.7	68 mph (7000 rpm)
III	1.42	15.1	105 mph (7000 rpm)
IV	1.00	21.4	109 mph (5100 rpm)

DIMENSIONS AND CAPACITIES

Wheelbase . . . . 90.7 in
Track, F/R . . . . 53.3/53.0 in
Length . . . . 162.8 in
Width . . . . 64.1 in
Height . . . . 50.5 in
Ground clearance . . . . 6.3 in
Curb weight . . . . 2330 lbs
Weight distribution, F/R 50.5/49.5%
Battery capacity . . . . 12 volts, 55 amp/hr
Alternator capacity . . . . 540 watts
Fuel capacity . . . . 15.9 gal
Oil capacity . . . . 4.4 qts
Water capacity . . . . 8.4 qts

SUSPENSION

F: Ind., MacPherson strut, coil springs, anti-sway bar
R: Ind., MacPherson strut, coil springs

STEERING

Type . . . . Rack and pinion
Turns lock-to-lock 2.6
Turning circle curb-to-curb . . . . 33.0 ft

BRAKES

F: . . . . 10.7-in disc, power assist
R: . . . . . 9.0 x 1.58-in finned drum, power assist

WHEELS AND TIRES

Wheel size . . . . 14 x 4.5-in
Wheel type . . . . stamped steel, 4-bolt
Tire make and size . . . . Bridgestone 175 SR 14
Tire type . . . . Radial ply, tubeless
Test inflation pressures, F/R . . . . 28/28 psi
Tire load rating . . . . . 1230 lbs per tire @ 32 psi power assist

PERFORMANCE

Zero to	Seconds
30 mph	2.5
40 mph	3.8
50 mph	5.7
60 mph	7.8
70 mph	10.6
80 mph	13.8
90 mph	17.8
100 mph	22.8

Standing ¼-mile . . . . 16.1 sec @ 86.5 mph
Top speed (observed) . . . . 109 mph
80–0 mph . . . . 259 ft (0.83 G)
Fuel mileage . . . . . 19–21 mpg on premium fuel
Cruising range . . . . 302–334 mi

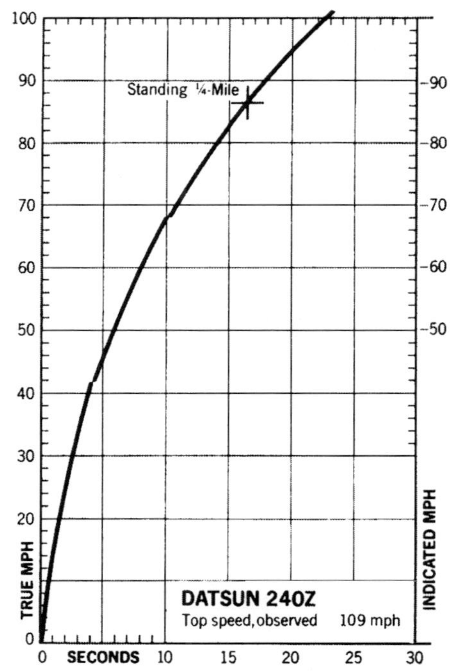

Front lights would look better with plexiglass covers, now illegal, but the 240-Z looks fast and expensive from every angle. Mag-type wheels are already available.

A SPORTSCAR'S SPORTSCAR

Considering the styling, the performance, and the price the only word for the new Datsun 240-Z is "sensational!"

Let's face it: the vast majority of automobiles on today's market are reliable, well-made, and completely uninspiring. The average road tester drives upwards of twenty new cars each year. Every once in awhile he'll get one with sparkling performance. Less often he'll get another with truly excellent body design. Rarer yet is a machine with both qualities. Even then, the price tag is almost invariably from $7000 to $12000. This is the realm of the Porsche 911S and the Ferrari.

The new Datsun 240-Z has these rare qualities, and the unbelievably low price of $3526! Your cheapest Porsche 911 is almost double this. The word "sensational" is overworked and usually incorrectly applied, but in this case it certainly fits. You can get some idea of the styling from the photographs with this road test. Just wait until you see a 240-Z on the street. If it's parked, you'll have to fight your way through the crowd to get near it. We did while we were testing it. The performance is in keeping with the body lines. We never had a chance to get the true top speed. The factory claims 125 mph. We see no reason to doubt it; top speed in third gear is 90 mph, and there's still another gear to go. This is only winding the engine to the orange line at 6500 rpm, not to the 7000-8000 rpm redline.

With the $3526 retail price, this means you can roll one off the showroom floor with tax, license, destination charge, financing, the whole bag, for under $4000. Go a little higher and they'll even throw in air conditioning. Try that on your imported GT cars, or even on a domestic pony car.

Drive Train

The engine in the 240-Z is a dual-carburetor inline-six with a single overhead cam. This makes it a high-winder, with the maximum horsepower at 5600 rpm. Both intake and exhaust ports are on the left side of the engine. A straight-through "tunnel port" head would be even better, and you can bet your driving gloves that someone will come out with one. This would be illegal for SCCA production car racing, at least until the factory begins to make them, but that doesn't have to take long. The first tests will be with the completely legal version that Pete Brock's "Brock Racing Enterprises" is preparing for SCCA road races. It should have had its first races by the time you read this. The Nissan Corp. which manufactures Datsuns will probably listen to Bre's advise on "factory options."

Power and Performance

The 240-Z weighs in at 2300 pounds, about half a ton less than most of the high-performance Detroit Iron, and around 500 pounds less than a stripped Trans-American pony car. This helps explain the impressive performance with "only" 150 horsepower. The factory claims 0-60 mph in under nine seconds. We were never able to make it quite this rapidly, but we didn't have a chance to time in on a dead level drag strip. Our best was one run holding first gear to 6000, then holding second up to near 7000, which came in right at 60 mph. This took 10.7 seconds, which still isn't bad. The car balked slightly at the start, which wouldn't have counted by the drag strip timing lights, but did by our hand-held stop-watch. Other testers, using a drag strip, have been able to do 0-60 in eight seconds.

Thinking of the top speeds in each gear as occurring at a conservative 6500 rpm, rather than the redlined 7000-8000, you get up to 35 mph in first, 55 mph in second, 90 mph in third, and 130 mph in fourth. The factory claims a top speed of 125 mph, which seems quite reasonable. If you could get the Datsun all the way up to 8000 rpm in top gear, you should be hitting the 160 mph top marking on the speedometer. Wind resistance, rolling friction, and other drags won't permit this with 150 horsepower, of course. That brings up that tunnel port head again. Working with the larger-displacement Pontiac single overhead cam inline-six, no longer in production, hot rodders were able to get 1.6 horsepower per cubic inch of displacement. That would mean 234 hp for the 146-cubic-inch Datsun engine. This is with three sets of dual-throat Webers, tuned intake and exhaust, tunnel port head, and full-race cam naturally. But gee, wouldn't that be a bear!

In checking 40-60 mph passing

From the rear the Datsun looks a little like a chopped Porsche 911, and looks better than most Detroit pony cars. Radio antenna is electrically controlled up and down.

Vigorous cornering can be accomplished with modest front end plow.

times, we worked it two ways. If you're cruising along at 40 mph in third gear, turning the engine at about 3000 rpm, you can make it to 60 mph in 6.5 seconds. If you're being sportier, and doing 40 mph in second gear, with the tach at 4500 rpm, a quick punch on the throttle will take you up to 60 mph (and 7000 rpm) in 4.2 seconds. It simply depends on which way you want to drive. With the new Datsun it's very apt to be the sportier way.

This brings up the gas mileage problem. With a sleek, two-seater

Rear section hinges up for loading baggage, engine hood opens forwards for better access to single overhead cam six engine. Note lowness of 240-Z with six-foot tester.

Instrumentation is fairly complete, with tach and speedometer in front of driver, secondary instruments in center nacel, but in easy and plain view.

Grand Touring car, gas consumption should be secondary. Still, it's not bad with the Z-Car. The factory claims 25 miles per gallon. Maybe. If one were to drive in the style of an old lady in a Volkswagen; it's simply not going to happen. We drove "sportingly" but not punishingly. The best we got was 19.0 miles per gallon, the worst 16.0. Say 17.7 as an overall average. Other testers claim 19.0-20.0. It's a small price to pay for constant fun, and compares quite favorably with a well-driven Porsche.

One interesting thing about the Z-Car engine, as it is set up for normal use: it doesn't lug at low rpm. Most engines with a horsepower curve peaking at 5800 rpm would be murder to drive if you ever let the revs drop below 3000 or 3500 rpm. This doesn't present the least problem with the Datsun. For example, 35 mph speeds on the streets in third gear will only get you 2500 rpm on the tach. If a low engine speed mentally disturbs you, drop back into second gear and pick the revs up to 4000. Freeway driving can be even more frustrating—if you're a tach watcher—as fourth gear almost amounts to an overdrive. Take the 240-Z up to 65 mph in third gear and you're right on 4700 rpm. Very nice and no complaints. Dump the box into fourth and the revs drop back to 3200 rpm.

This does allow you to roll along at a more economical engine speed, then easily and safely drop down a gear for a quick shot around a slower car or through a power-on bend. If you should forget you're in fourth gear and take the tach up to a respectable 4500 rpm, watch out: you're hitting 90 mph!

Roadability and Handling

The Datsun 240-Z has independent suspension all around, using single bottom "MacPherson" struts with an

Speedometer goes up to 160 mph, the theoretical top speed of the 240-Z, the tach to 8000 rpm, the end of the redline zone. Redline starts at 7000.

unusually long shock absorber and coil spring combination to allow for vertical strut travel. The coil spring surrounds only the top half of a tall telescopic shock. This necessitates having the "shock towers" stick up through the luggage platform in the rear, much as they do in the Lotus Elite. An anti-sway bar and compression link are used on the front. The weight distribution of the 2300-pound Z-Car is close to the theoretical ideal, with 52.4 percent on the front wheels and 47.6 percent on the rear.

Factory tires are 175 SR-14 Bridgestones, which are Japanese made and look very much like Perellis. They are radials, and work extremely well in every application we gave them. We went through some tight bends on the road racing circuit at the new Ontario Motor Speedway; we drove winding mountain roads. We never heard a squeal nor had that "there she goes" feeling in the stomach. There obviously is a point of no return with these tires and with the Z-Car's suspension. Few drivers will get anywhere near it except on a road racing circuit.

One great bit of sport with a car like this involves passing some cluck doing 60 mph or so. The ploy is to drop back to third gear just as you pull out to pass. Take it up to the redline in third as you go by. Then, just as he is looking up your exhaust pipe—and hearing it—casually shift into fourth and squirt ahead. He's been sure your funny little car was all wrung-out as you went by. If he has a chance to read the "Datsun" insignia on the rear, he'll really be shaken. Good grief! Blown off by a Datsun, and he wasn't even in top gear!

Brakes and Safety

Standard, no-extra-cost brakes with the Z-Car are 10.7-inch power-assisted discs on the front. These on a 2300-pound car, mind you. The 4800-pound Thunderbird only has discs one inch larger in diameter, and Ford thinks these are the hottest item on the safety market today. The rear brakes on the 240-Z are 9.0-inch power-assisted drums, but they're heavily finned to radiate braking heat rapidly. With this combination, the 240-Z stops dead true and with no

Panic stops are accomplished with little nose-dive, no loss of direction.

High speed cornering produces minimum body lean, it responds to road course conditions like a thoroughbred.

dramatics. With the big discs up front, you know it's going to keep doing it, too, come hail or high water.

The seat belts in the 240-Z are adequate without being particularly good. Average. Always getting lost down alongside the seats. That sort of mess. With this zippy two-seater we'd most certainly put in some well-anchored three-inch competition belts. They're safer and we have always found them more comfortable. It's possible to wear a wide belt tighter, as the loading is distributed over more body area.

Comfort and Convenience

The only complaint we heard in the ten days we had our test 240-Z was in a comparison with a Camaro—a $5000 optioned Camaro. The Chevy owner complained that the vinyl bucket seats in the Datsun weren't the vented or breathing type of material, so were overly warm. The complaint is a legitimate one, albeit minor. There are five little vents down low on the seat backs, but the rest of the backs are non-porous vinyl. This can make one's shirt a little damp on a warm day.

Other than this, the interior of the Z-Car is another of its very strong points of appeal. It is well-planned and luxurious looking. The steering wheel is a thin-rimmed racing type. Right dead center are a big 160-mph speedometer and an 8000 rpm tachometer. Over to the right, high up on the center console, are the temperature gauge/oil pressure, ammeter/fuel gauge, and an electric clock. As in the E-Jag, they're up where a flick of the eye checks them all. Down the center are the through-flow air vent, heater controls, three-speed fan, and below it the station-seeking AM radio. Next to the radio there's a little switch that retracts or extends the antenna on the left rear fender electrically. All this in the $3526 base price, mind you.

The gear shift lever is right at hand, with the throws of the all-synchro four-speed box being short and decisive. There's none of this "what gear am I in" nonsense, as occurs so frequently with American gearboxes. A quick glance at the lever answers the question. If it's up there, you're still in third. If it's down here you're in fourth. That sort of directness.

We would rate the little Z-Car as extremely good in general comfort. It is the type of GT or sporty car one wouldn't hesitate to take on a trip across the United States. There is room for all the luggage one would need, and the seats are extremely comfortable buckets. Engine and wind noise are low. Gas mileage is good. As local radio stations would

Body lines of Datsun 240-Z are smooth and modern, with fastback two-seater styling and chopped-off, Kamm-effect rear. Admirers estimated price at double the actual $3525.

Looking in through rear over the baggage platform, the shock absorber towers stick up alongside the wheel wells. Auxiliary instruments are in center.

fade out, you could tap the button and let the radio seek out another station.

Economy

The most important economy is the initial price, of course. As with the Datsun 510 sedan, one's first reaction is almost physical shock. ''You can't mean $3500! That's without the radio and the bucket seats and the carpeting and the radial plies.

The price alone is going to wipe out a lot of sales of Opel GTs, Fiat 124s, Alfa GTVs, Porsches . . . not to mention Camaros, Mustangs, Firebirds and Barracudas.

Although the Z-Car is not the sort of machine where gasoline economy is a critical factor, that of the Datsun is not bad. Our test got 17.7 miles per gallon average; other testers were

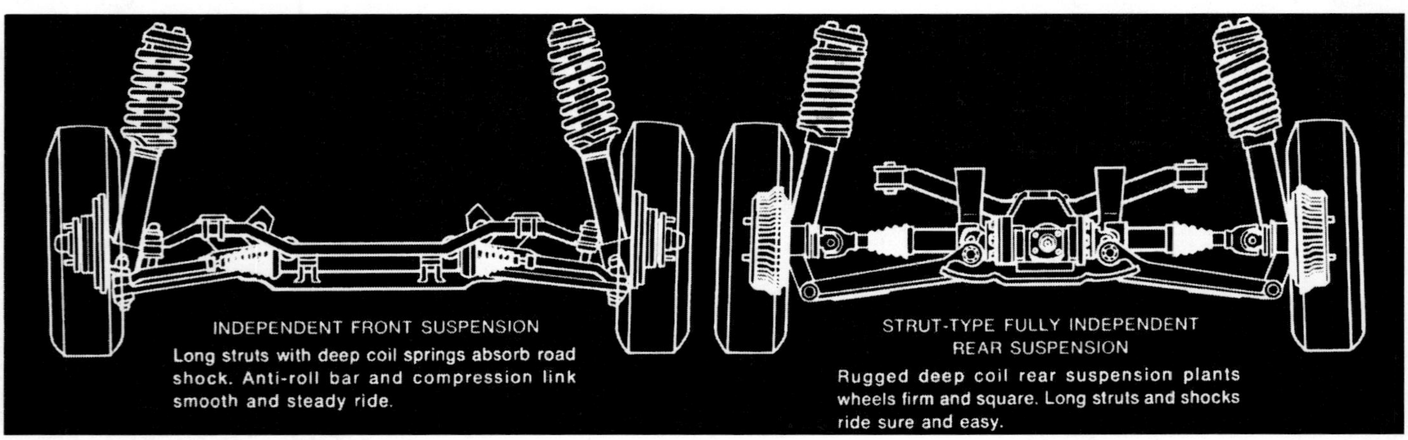

INDEPENDENT FRONT SUSPENSION
Long struts with deep coil springs absorb road shock. Anti-roll bar and compression link smooth and steady ride.

STRUT-TYPE FULLY INDEPENDENT REAR SUSPENSION
Rugged deep coil rear suspension plants wheels firm and square. Long struts and shocks ride sure and easy.

A. Dual S.U. type carburetors.

B. Oil Filler cap.

C. Easy access to dip stick, spark plugs, fuel pump, etc.

D. Spin on oil filter

E. Underhood service light.

F. Viscous drive fan.

With spark plugs on side away from intake and exhaust systems, plug changes are a cinch. Even with California smog devices, the 240-Z engine is uncluttered and accessible.

Big air cleaner partially hides two large, Japanese-made SU carburetors on side of single overhead cam inline-6 engine, which produces 150 leaping horses.

more in the 19-21 mpg range. Kept in proper tune, you can probably count on 20 mpg, which is quite acceptable for a 2.4 liter engine.

Summary

It is difficult to keep from seeming overly-enthusiastic when writing about the new Datsun 240-Z. At $500 or $1000 more it would be an attractive buy. With the going price of $3526, it is almost unbelievable.

Datsun plans to bring in 1000 a month initially, until they see how the Z-Car sells. We can tell the Nissan group right now that they could bring in 10,000 a month and have people standing in line with check books in their hands and drool running out of their mouths. We're willing to go so far as to bet that the 240-Z will be the biggest selling sports/GT car, import or domestic, of all times. Ten days of driving one makes that limb feel very solid. ●

Datsun 240-Z
Data in Brief

DIMENSIONS

Overall length (in.)	162.8
Wheelbase (in.)	90.7
Height (in.)	50.6
Width (in.)	64.1
Tread (front in.)	53.3
Tread (rear in.)	53.0
Fuel tank capacity (gal.)	15.9
Luggage capacity (cu. ft.)	8.5
Turning diameter (ft.)	31.5

ENGINE

Type	Overhead cam inline-6
Displacement (cu. in.)	145.7
Horsepower (at 5,600 rpm)	150
Torque (lb/ft. at 4400 rpm)	148

WEIGHT, TIRES, BRAKES

Weight	(2300 lb.)
Tires	175 SR-14 radial
Brakes, front	10.7-in. discs
Brakes, rear	9.0-in. finned drums

SUSPENSION

Front	Indep., MacPherson strut with coil springs and stabilizer bar
Rear	Indep., MacPherson strut with coil springs

PERFORMANCE

Zero-60 mph (sec.)	9.0
40-60 mph (sec.)	4.2

DATSUN 240Z

NIPPON'S MOST RAPID TRANSIT SYSTEM

ROAD TEST

CAR AT A GLANCE: As rapidly as we could legally travel all day long, 240Z produced from 21.3 to 23.4 miles per gallon including desert heat and mountain driving. City traffic and bumper-to-bumper fun during metro rush hours dropped mpg to 18.5 and during performance tests 240Z used exactly 16.0 mpg. An exhilarating car, difficult to fault seriously or to top at the price.

Taking stock of one's surroundings after first getting into the 240Z is as satisfying as was a somewhat similar experience when the writer found himself in the driver's seat of an XK-120 Jaguar back in 1952. In many respects the 240Z is as revelatory of a new age in sports cars as was that XK-120.

The first thing of which one is aware is that everything in the 240Z is where it should be except vent windows; they are absent. The steering wheel is at precisely the correct angle and the well-sized rim fits both hands on the ends of extended arms. The vinyl upholstery on the two individual seats is soft and looks and feels much like leather but, of course, does not smell like hide. The seats adjust through long courses and the backrests tilt by means of knurled knobs on the inside of each seat.

Let the right hand stray slightly downward to the right and the shift lever fills it. The "H" plus reverse pattern is sufficiently small for fast shifting but not so tight as to be fussy. The foot pedals are well proportioned and the accelerator pedal is spaced properly far enough to the right of the brake pedal to prevent stabbing for either and getting both. The unique choke control, a lever, is on the center console.

A no nonsense two-seater–there's not even a hint of an occasional seat aft of the office–the 240Z's space beneath the large, slanting back window has the capacity of the average sports car's luggage boot and then some. The makers have considerately installed nylon luggage belts to hold down whatever inanimate objects one might cart along.

The long, seat-level center console is padded on each side, a welcome leg rest for the driver's accelerator foot. The top of the console also contains the pull-up handbrake, an edged tray in two sections toward the rear, and the radio and heater/fresh air controls well forward beneath the dash. The flow-through system is excellent. The ash tray–if that item interests you–is large and sits on an angle just forward of the shift lever where it's out of the way of knuckles, blasts of fresh or warm air, and the like.

Full instrumentation includes everything necessary unless one desires oil operating and cylinder head temperature indicators. At night there is not the slightest reflection from any of the dials; they're well hooded and covered with convex glass set on an angle. Extending from the right side of the steering column on a horizontal arm are the headlight switch and windshield wiper controls. The 240Z is my first test car in years with properly adjusted lights. Everything is practical and well thought out even to the horn button which is on the wheel center which eliminates any accidental honking.

This efficient arranging of all components and controls extends beneath the engine bonnet which unlatches beneath the dash. Owners who prefer to do their own servicing and maintainance will find plenty of elbow room around the 2.4 litre 6-in-line engine which is rather quiet for an overhead camshaft job. Once the air cleaner is removed to reveal all of the twin SU carburetors, there is no impediment to tuning or other under-hood chores. As a matter of fact, one can remove the oil filter without beginning to stand on one's head. About the only routine reason for putting the 240Z on a hoist would be to drain the crankcase and to check the levels in the gearbox and the differential. This is about the cleanest, least cluttered engine compartment we have examined in recent years. What's more, there's ample space for air.

The 240Z in action is as pleasing as it is under close examination. We tried several variations in tire pressures and settled for 32 p.s.i. all around for the best handling; the ride remained uncannily good. True, road irregularities were felt, but not severely and control was quick and certain. When we finally got around to checking vital statistics in the Service Manual, we felt even better about our choice of tire pressure although our chosen 32 p.s.i. is listed for "over 100 mph."

Did we top that figure? Yes, on a course that has been used for competition. Datsun claims (rather modestly) 125 mph maximum for the 4-speed model tested and 129 mph for a 5-speed model (see specifications) which is not likely to be imported this year. On the road course we attained 111 mph (true) and would have done better had the straight stretches extended further. With the 3.36 to 1 rear axle ratio, each 1000 rpm in top (4th) gear gives 21 mph.

The 8000 rpm tachometer is yellow-lined for caution at 6500 rpm and red-lined at 7000 rpm. Theoretically a flat out run at 7000 rpm will produce 147 mph although top end performance usually falls a bit below the theoretical potential. WCG feels that extended in suitable surroundings and under the best conditions, one should have no trouble coaxing 135 mph or more out of a well tuned 240Z. The gear speeds in the bottom three ratios support this contention. Peaking to a maximum of approximately 7000 rpm in 1st gear produced a true corrected speed of 43 mph. Repeating this procedure in 2nd and 3rd gears resulted in 66 and 103 mph respectively.

Interior arrangement is difficult to fault; Datsun designers have put everything in the proper place for high speed comfort. RIB says: "This is a wonderful car; lots of fun and easy for a woman to drive for shopping or anywhere. I love it." Bettye Wherry.

Small lever this side of shift lever is choke. Three dials centered on dash contain water temperature, oil pressure, ammeter, fuel level and clock. Two large dials over steering column (other interior photo) contain 8,000 rpm tachometer and 160 mph speedometer; total and trip odometers are with speedometer. Console contains radio (standard) and lever controls for heating and fresh air system. The knurled knobs (bottom center) adjust the rakes of the backrests.

Acceleration was a bit disappointing; without doubt the test car could have used a new set of spark plugs, points and a bit of tuning for it had been vigorously used as a demonstration example prior to being turned over to WCG. Having heard reports of zero to 60 (the speedometer said 62) in around 8.0 seconds, we would like to report that we achieved this figure. With two aboard during acceleration runs as is our custom, the best we could do in a succession of two way runs to average out any wind was 9.8 seconds.

This figure is good but the 240Z will do better. I would say that zero to 60 should be 8.5 seconds. From zero to 45 mph took 6.6 seconds; obviously the 43 mph maximum in 1st gear required an up-shift to 2nd. Passing speeds, making use of the smooth and quiet gearbox, took 6.5 seconds from 40 to 60 mph, 5.9 seconds from 50 to 70 mph, and 11.6 seconds from 50 to 80 mph where the speedometer was only 5 mph off true. The latter is a passing check we rarely use but the snappy Datsun is the type of car that wants to go and to do so rapidly.

The brakes proved as nearly fade-free as one is likely to find on a production car. Rapid stops were made after each acceleration run and the brakes were still capable of stopping the car from 60 mph in 200 feet which is admirable. During our total test time we experienced several rain showers; the brakes were not adversely affected, the wipers did their chore without floating off the windshield at speed and the suspension (which has been criticized in some quarters) displayed no annoying tendencies. On rough roads, the ride is quiet.

Roadability of this fastest Datsun is excellent. In tight corners there is mild understeer, a virtue on mountain roads. The rack and pinion steering with just 2.7 turns lock-to-lock is sufficiently quick and the car is fun to drive and secure on the road. Straight line tracking on flat, uncrowned surfaces is good; it should be with a caster angle of 3 degrees.

One can force the 240Z to lift the inside rear wheel in a hard, full bore turn but it takes a bit of doing and accomplishes nothing. Our favorite tight corner for photographically recording lean is usually entered at approximately 30 mph in firmly suspended sports cars. The 240Z will enter this corner, a perfectly flat hairpin, at 35 mph and can be throttled through in 1st or 2nd gear without sliding, a tribute to the independent rear suspension. The lean is not excessive as the accompanying photo shows.

Our road test covered 1,575 miles from Datsun's national headquarters in Gardena, California to the San Francisco Bay area, throughout the North Bay counties and into the Coast Range. The North-bound first leg was via US-101 and the return to Southern California was through the hot and smoggy Central Valley and over the lower, desert end of the Tehachapi Mountains. The climate variations included sea level with spotty fog, dry heat and hot winds off the Mojave Desert to nearly 5,000 feet above sea level. No adjustments were made at any time.

Near the end of the test, one quart of oil was added; we learned later that the car had not been thoroughly serviced before we began our tests. The greatest fuel consumption was during the day of performance testing when premium fuel was consumed at the not surprising rate of 16.0 mpg. On the open road, consumption ranged from 21.3 to 23.4 mpg during which times liberal use was made of 3rd gear for

Minus styled wheel covers, 240Z was put through cornering tests. Generally neutral steering with very moderate understeer and resistance to leaning over indicate car is potential road racing mount.

Behind air cleaner are a pair of SU carburetors. Access panel (bottom right) covers dual brake master cylinders' reservoirs. Similar panel, opposite side, covers battery. Efficient layout provides generous work space for owner-mechanics.

overtaking other cars. City driving dropped as low as 18.5 mpg. The overall average was 20.52 miles per gallon. Conservative driving would have bettered this figure considerably but the 240Z is fun to drive, is the type of car that clears the head of an enthusiast once car and driver have gained to the relative freedom of the open road.

Quality of workmanship and assembly on the test car was excellent throughout. There were no unsightly lumps of dum-dum or filler visible in the engine compartment or elsewhere. The styling pleased us and must have pleased lots of people. Only the Amante GT garnered more onlookers demanding off-the-cuff press conferences. Most frequently asked questions were, "How fast will it go?" and "What's the horsepower?" as if this is all that matters.

When such curious types learned that the rated horsepower was 151, they invariably allowed as how such a weakling was unlikely to be a success and when we told them that the 240Z would exceed 125 mph we were not believed. Of course these horsepower types had learned from all the domestic advertising that 300 or more horses was necessary for status and to do much more than 100 in any case.

There were enthusiasts, on occasion, who knew the score. They asked to see the engine, expressed approval of the entire layout, and were surprised to learn that Datsun U.S.A., Inc. has suggested a delivered Port-of-Entry price of $3601 (see specs.). Several, including a waitress at a lunch stop, said they had tried to get their names on waiting lists and were told, by various dealers, that signing such a list means plunking down anywhere from $100 to $400 and that the delivered price is around $4400. Of course this included

Ancestor of the 240Z was this sporty two-seater of 1917. Loose brake cables can be seen beneath chassis. Note wheels' design is perpetuated in 240Z's wheel covers. First "Dat" cars were closed town car types in 1916. (Courtesy Jidosha Kogyo-Kia)

"mag wheels and a lot of other things I don't want." Don't blame Datsun; the dealers are independent merchants.

I must say that mag wheels would be nice but the stock wheels look great with the covers removed (see the cornering photo herewith). At test time, the only options listed were the tinted glass and the rear window defroster; the radio is standard. Air conditioning is in the works.

Datsun's 240Z is an excellent car, a value-packed sporting vehicle of excellent quality, and an economy car at that. It deserves success.

by Joseph H. Wherry

DATSUN

DATSUN 240Z SPECIFICATIONS

ENGINE: front, in-line 6 cyl, overhead camshaft; cast iron block, aluminum head; 7 main bearings. Bore and stroke 3.27 x 2.90 in. (83.0 x 73.7 mm.). Displacement 146 cu. in. (2393 cc.). Compression ratio 9.0 to 1. Carburetion dual 1-bbl SU; premium fuel. BHP (SAE) 151 @ 5600 rpm. Torque 146 lb. ft. @ 4400 rpm.

TRANSMISSION: Manual 4-speed fully synchronized, floor lever. Ratios overall: 1st - 11.93, 2nd - 7.38, 3rd - 4.77, 4th - 3.36. Rear axle ratio: 3.36 hypoid bevel; swing axle.

SUSPENSION: Front independent with transverse links, MacPherson coil spring struts around telescopic shocks, compression rods and anti-sway bar. Rear independent with transverse links and MacPherson coil spring/shock structs.

STEERING: Rack and pinion, ratio 17.8 to 1; 2.7 turns lock-to-lock, 31.5 feet diameter turning circle.

WHEELS AND TIRES: 14 inch steel disc, 4 lug bolts. 175 SR 14 Brigestone radial ply.

BRAKES: Front 10.7 in diam. discs. Rear 9 in. diam drums. Power assisted.

CAPACITIES: Fuel 15.9 US gal. Oil 4.5 US qts. incl. filter. Cooling system 8.4 US qts. Transmission 3.2 US pints.

BODY AND FRAME: All-steel integral.

DIMENSIONS: Wheelbase 90.7 in. Track front/rear 53.3/53.0 in. Length overall 162.8 in. Width 64.1 in. Height 50.5 in. Ground clearance 6.3 in. Curb weight 2340 lbs..

PRICE: Basic suggested list incl. radio and dealers' make-ready $3601. Optional equipment: tinted glass $30.00; back window defroster $40.00 (A 5-speed transmission with 3.90 rear axle is manufactured but Datsun U.S.A. states no plans at present for making this option available.)

DATSUN 240Z

New GT from Japan which may go on sale here

INTRODUCED at the Tokyo motor show last autumn, the Datsun 240Z is intended to run as a parallel model with the Fairlady open two-seater. It is what the MGC GT ought to have been like: a stylish coupé using a six-cylinder 2½-litre ohc engine taken from elsewhere in the Datsun range, and employing independent rear suspension.

To the sports-car minded Americans, the 240Z specification is exactly what they want, and, from the accounts we read in the USA press, the model is doing extremely well there. No decision has yet been made on whether it will be imported here, but it will be on the Datsun stand at Earls Court and a team of three 240Z rally cars will be going all out for an outright win, as well as for the team prize, in this year's RAC rally. Drivers will be Rauno Aaltonen, Tony Fall and probably Edgar Herman, who won this year's East African Safari in a Datsun.

In overall size the 240Z is about the same length as a Marcos, but 5in. higher. It is a two-seater with a lift-up tailgate like a Triumph GT6. The wheelbase is 7ft. 6.7in., which is the same as that of the MGB; the MGB is 9in. shorter, however, but the same height. The extra overhang compared with the MGB appears to be evenly split between front and rear.

The engine of the 240Z is an in-line six, with oversquare cylinder dimensions of 83 by 73.7mm. Exact capacity is 2,393 c.c. and the SAE power output 150 bhp at 5,600 rpm. (The equivalent SAE figure for the Triumph TR6 PI engine, which is about the same size, is 152 bhp at 5,500 rpm, so the two engines are comparable.) The Datsun engine, though, uses a single overhead camshaft and twin SU carburettors.

Quoted kerb weight for the 240Z is 2,300 lb (Triumph TR6: 2,473 lb) and the mph per 1,000 rpm in fourth gear (there is the option of a five-speed box with a direct fourth) is 19.2 (Triumph TR6: 21.2) so the top speed claimed of 125 mph seems well within the car's capabilities.

Front suspension is by MacPherson struts, with compression rods at their lower ends and an anti-roll bar. Rack and pinion steering is fitted and there are servo assisted front disc brakes. At the rear coil-spring struts are used again (as on the Fiat 130) with a lower wishbone for lateral location. Rear brakes are drums, with leading and trailing shoes.

High-backed seats have both vertical and horizontal adjustment, with the backrest adjustable also to any one of 10 angles of rake. Instruments are deeply recessed in a black padded facia, the rev counter reading to 8,000 rpm (amber warning from 6,500 to 7,000, red sector from 7,000 to 8,000) and the speedometer to 160 mph. On a central console the choke and hand throttle work in quadrant slides, with radio and heater controls on the vertical panel ahead of the gearlever. Lamps and wipers are operated by switches on a steering column arm.

A special luxury version known as the HLS30U is being sold now in the USA and Canada, and on this model items like the radio, tinted glass, clock and hazard warning flasher are standard. The UK specification (HS30U) has these items listed as optional extras, along with radial tyres, magnesium wide-base wheels, stereo tape player and fully reclining seats.

No possible price has been worked out, but it is not expected to be below £2,000. □

Anti-clockwise from top left: Recessed headlamps, wrap-round front bumper with rubber inserts, matt black grille and wing mirrors all give the 240Z a very modern sporty look. At the tail a spoiler has been added for 1971 and this car carries the domestic Japanese name of Fairlady Z. This side view shows the proportions of the car, which are mid-way between MGB and Marcos. The cockpit is well finished in padded pvc with full instrumentation

Datsun 240Z

Pete Brock gets the sleek new GT ready to do battle in SCCA competition

BY JAMES T. CROW

PETE BROCK knows what he's doing. Let's start with that. First, he's a designer/stylist. He went to Art Center School and later worked for two years in General Motors' Styling. After that he was with Shelby American and there his best known work was the very successful Cobra Daytona coupe. And since then he has been responsible for the exciting Ghia-DeTomaso racing car, the neat Hino Samurai experimental and the styled-up Triumph TR-250K. He's also done a lot of projects that have become familiar and accepted parts of the scene; things like the emblem at Riverside Raceway and the whole line of Shelby American accessories that ranged from T-shirts to valve covers. He's probably America's best-known stylist of high-performance parts and products. A tremendous talent.

Undoubtedly one of the reasons he has done so much good work during his 33 years is that he hasn't been secluded in a styling studio during his career. His designs have been consistently appropriate and vital because he has been involved with the objects he's worked on. He raced his own Cooper and Lotus sports cars, had a go or two in NASCAR stockers and spent two years as chief instructor for Shelby's School of High Performance Driving. Later he became involved with production car racing, first with Hino (which came to a disappointing end when Hino merged with Toyota and didn't enter the U.S. market) and now with Datsun. At the present time his firm, BRE (for Brock Racing Enterprises), is developing the Datsun 240Z for racing and it is typical of Pete that not only is the car fast and competitive but the machine itself is a pleasure to the eye all the way from the smart red and white paint to the beautiful engine detailing under the hood.

His association with Datsun began about two and a half years ago when BRE was asked to undertake a high-performance development program for the Datsun 2000. This

Goes Racing

GORDON CHITTENDEN PHOTOS

project led to a pair of Datsun 2000s being campaigned in SCCA club racing and the cars set lap records wherever they raced. During 1969 they won the Southern Pacific Division title in DP and only a freak circumstance of momentary fuel starvation on the bankings at Daytona which led to melted pistons kept them out of the winner's circle at the American Road Race of Champions. This year, driving one of the same cars, John McComb of Wichita has already clinched the 1970 Midwest Divisional title by winning eight races in a row and seems a sure thing for the ARRC.

Although BRE is an independent company working under contract to Nissan Motor Corporation's western office, Pete works in close liaison with Datsun national service manager Lee Wylie and under the benevolent eye of Datsun West's highly enthusiastic president, Yutaka Katayama. Contrary to outward appearances, such an operation as BRE does not operate with unlimited funds. In fact, Pete says that without the support they receive from other sponsors such as Champion, Goodyear, Valvoline and Fram, they could not exist. The high-performance parts they develop for sale to Datsun owners is also an important factor in their economic life (their contract specifies that all parts developed by BRE must be made available to any Datsun owner who wants to buy them) and Pete anticipates that the sale of such parts will enable his company to be completely self-sufficient within a couple years.

Pete saw a picture of the 240Z in late summer 1969 and finally got his hands on a car to start the development program in late January 1970. This was a pure production model straight from the first boat shipment of 20 cars and not anything specially prepared by the factory.

The coupe's first stop was the BRE shop in El Segundo, Calif. This facility, which covers about 10,000 sq ft, is a bit more complete than most pure racing shops and includes a dynamometer and engine assembly rooms as well as a machine shop and the usual welding and fabricating equipment. They aren't equipped to do forging, casting, gear cutting or cam grinding but just about everything else can be done in-house. In addition to their Datsun projects they specialize in dyno tuning of competition engines up to about five liters' displacement and will, on demand, design and fabricate special components for other competitors. Their whole capability is summed up by Pete as "Design, fabrication and development of high performance components."

In addition to Pete and the office girl there are seven other employees at BRE. As in most racing shops these men are not only specialists in one particular area but can also turn their hands to whatever needs doing. Mac Tilton, for

Datsun 240Z

instance, is not only the racing crew chief but is also an expert machinist. John Morton, driver of the Z car, is also an expert fabricator. John Caldwell, Floyd Link and Ray Gruss have engines as their main responsibility but also pitch in on other projects. George Boskoff, Pete's oldest employee, was formerly with Shelby and Bruce Meyers and can do anything. John Knepp is in charge of the electrics and transmissions but also handles the transporter. And Kirk Allegro specializes in versatility since he is mechanic, general helper and chief gopher.

When the 240Z arrived at BRE it was first of all stripped to the bare chassis. This was done not only to enable them to minutely examine every seam and weld but also as a part of the educational process for becoming intimately familiar with the new car. Some wires and some plumbing were relocated for more convenient access or for safety and as far as possible everything was made convenient for adjustment or replacement. The chassis did not require any trick beefing up to take the additional stresses that would be placed on it in competition and it was not necessary to reweld the chassis/body unit as is required on NASCAR or Trans-Am sedans to aid in stiffness.

As the car was reassembled, a number of special competition parts were installed; heavier springs, adjustable shocks, thicker swaybars, a limited slip rear end. A balance bar was added to the brake system so front and rear braking could be adjusted as needed; an aluminum radiator was installed, as were coolers for engine, gearbox and differential.

The shock absorbers that were used were a combination of Koni and Tokiko parts combined with special valving to achieve the bump and rebound control BRE wanted. They use Goodyear racing tires and the 7-in.-wide alloy wheels cast by American Mag to Pete's design weigh 12 lb each. Brake pads are Raybestos. They are now using a Detroit Locker in place of the clutch-type limited slip differential available from Datsun. With the locker the lubricants run at a lower temperature and this will allow them to run without the differential oil cooler in the future. The engine is equipped with Echlin ignition components. Oil coolers are Stewart Warner parts.

In the cockpit the stock instruments were replaced with those that would be needed on the development car—10,000-rpm tachometer plus gauges to monitor the engine oil temperature both in and out of the block, oil pressure,

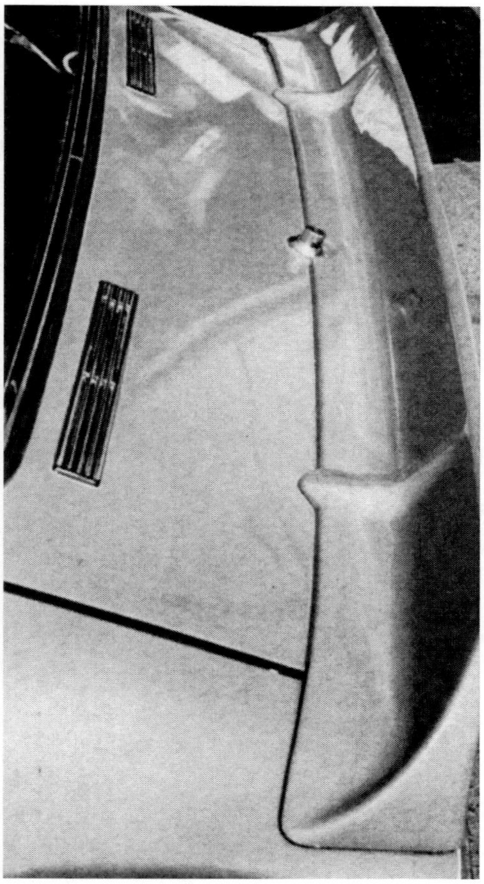

coolant temperature, gearbox lube temperature, differential lube temperature and alternator output. Once the development phase is complete they will be able to dispense with some of these. The driver's seat was replaced by a high-sided, completely adjustable competition bucket and all the electrical control switches were relocated to the driveshaft tunnel where the belted-in driver could reach them. The pedals were relocated to driver John Morton's dimensions and preferences, a rollbar was installed along with a Wink wide-angle mirror and the interior neatened up and painted with Zolatone for the sake of appearance. Pete likes his cars to look good too, remember?

Because the engine in the 240Z is basically that of the 4-cyl 510 with two more cylinders added, they were able to use the 510 engine for development and thus get started early. In this way everything they could learn about the combustion chamber shape, valve timing, breathing characteristics and so on would be directly applicable to the 6-cyl engine when it arrived.

The lower half of the engine is little altered. They use forged aluminum pistons that are machined by Venolia to BRE design but the rods are simply balanced, neither lightened nor polished. They have found that stronger rod bolts offer added reliability, however, and special 20-percent-stronger ones have been made for this purpose. A special oil pan has been fabricated to increase engine lubricant capacity and six "mouse traps" have been built in to direct (and keep) the oil in the area of the oil pickup.

The top end of the engine is considerably reworked. As Pete points out, "The added power comes from better breathing and better combustion; the other changes are made simply to let the engine live." They do a lot of flow bench work at BRE, studying engine breathing in order to understand how much is enough and, equally important, how much is too much.

The pistons, slightly domed and with light reliefs cut into the top for valve clearance, give a compression ratio of 12:1. The ports are opened up and smoothed, the valves lightened and polished; stock outer and special inner valve springs are used.

On the racing engine three Mikuni-Solex PPH-44 carburetors with 40-mm chokes replace the original Hitachi-SUs and these are altered only by such normal production category racing practices as tapering the butterflies, thinning the shafts and polishing the throats for better airflow. Feeding the carburetors are two Conelec pumps and a pressure regulator is used at each carburetor to assure even fuel delivery throughout the rev range. Also assisting in uninterrupted fuel delivery are molded soft rubber blocks between the carburetors and intake ports to isolate engine vibration and avoid frothing the fuel in the float bowls. The exhaust system, fabricated to BRE specs, consists of two sets of three headers collected into two tailpipes.

Pete prefers not to talk about cam timing and overlap but he will say they are using about 0.530 in. lift compared to 0.478 for the standard engine.

The only serious problem they have encountered with the engine thus far resulted from a high-frequency vibration from the 6-counterweight crankshaft with which the early engine was delivered. This curious harmonic (responsible for roughness at high speeds we noted in our 240Z road test) came in at just about

The BRE race crew. From left: John Knepp, Kirk Allegro, Pete Brock, Mac Tilton, John Caldwell and driver John Morton.

Bob Sharp's 240Z is already doing well in eastern SCCA racing.

Datsun 240Z

7000 rpm, right in the rev range they wanted to use, and did all sorts of strange things like breaking up the clutch after only brief periods of hard running. An 8-counterweight crank, ironically standard on all 240Zs since that first shipment, seems to have solved this problem.

The stock 240Z engine output is 150 horsepower at 6000 rpm and is safe to rev to 7000. The BRE racing engine develops more than 240 hp at 7600 and is now redlined at 8300. Pete declines to say how much more than 240 hp they are getting but as this represents a fairly mild 100 hp/liter, it is probably safe to assume there is more power to be had.

The completed BRE Datsun 240Z is aerodynamically very clean. A factory spoiler is used on the trunk lid and at the front there is a BRE "spook," Pete's contraction of its combined function as a spoiler and scoop. Pete says these devices are of little value except on the longest circuits where the speeds are such that aerodynamic aids are needed.

They have made no changes in the drive line and so far nothing has broken or fallen apart. They have three sets of ratios for the 5-speed gearbox from the 2000 roadster and they are as follows:

Gear	Standard	Optional	Optional
5th	0.85	0.85	0.85
4th	1.00	1.00	1.00
3rd	1.31	1.28	1.26
2nd	1.86	1.39	1.70
1st	2.96	1.86	2.68

These are combined with a 4.8 or 5.1:1 final drive ratio depending on the circuit and the size tires used.

HIGH PERFORMANCE PARTS

An important part of the BRE program—perhaps the most important part—is building high performance components to sell to Datsun owners who want something more from their cars. There's a large selection of performance equipment for the 510 sedans as well as for the two roadsters and now the equipment list for the 240Z is growing almost day by day. For the 240Z at the present time BRE has 7-in. mag wheels ($92 each), front spook ($32), oil filter remote block ($18), camshaft kit with springs, rockers, etc. ($280), forged 12:1 CR pistons ($210 per set), rollbar kit ($52), fuel cell ($375), fuel pumps ($37 each), pressure regulators ($8.50) and so on. The only item offered at present that is tailored to the street trade or for slalom and autocross competition is the "Mulholland" spring kit ($68) which lowers the car 1.625 in. All these BRE parts, as well as the special Datsun parts (such as the deck lid spoiler) can be ordered through Datsun dealers or through BRE. (Quicker through BRE, of course.) BRE has a parts and price list and you can get one by sending 25¢ to cover postage to BRE, 137 Oregon St., El Segundo, Calif. 90245.

The fuel is carried in a special tank that replaces the spare tire at the rear and this cell, which includes safety foam inside, has a capacity of 15 gal. Oil capacity is 10 qt and straight ethylene glycol is used in the engine for coolant.

The current car weighs just about 1960 lb in official racing trim (water and oil but no fuel) and it's likely that future 240Zs from BRE will be slightly lighter.

That the 240Z is going to be thoroughly competitive in its class in SCCA club racing has already been demonstrated in an SCCA national at Riverside when the five factory-supported team cars (two Porsche 914/6s from Richie Ginther, two TR-6s from Kas Kastner and the 240Z) all qualified within 0.6 second of each other. The showdown is yet to come, however, as the Z car dropped out of its first race with clutch failure from the crankshaft vibration and crippled home to a sixth place in the next outing with the same trouble since the new 8-counterweight crank still wasn't available.

In all-out top speed the Z car does about 130 mph on the long backstretch at Riverside and Pete expects it would be capable of about 155 on a longer circuit such as the high banking at Daytona.

Pete is very high on driver John Morton, not only for his ability as a competitive driver but also as a very sensitive and observant development driver. Morton says that he has found the 240Z to be a far different car to drive than the Datsun roadsters he has driven in the past: much more power, for one thing, but the handling is also considerably different because of the more sophisticated suspension, the wider track, the wider tires and greater bulk. It is very solid and smooth, it sticks better and because of its greater potential is that much more challenging to drive to its limit.

For other forms of competition, Pete is sanguine about the 240Z's chances. He expects it would do very well in the rugged European rally events, for example, because of its excellent suspension. In fact, he is so enthusiastic about the Z's suspension—a very simple but effective independent system at both ends—that he is building it into a single-seater mid-engine car to run in the Mexican 1000 race from Ensenada to La Paz this fall. With very few changes from stock, the 240Z should also be highly competitive in slalom or autocross competition, Pete says.

Though the final prices for all the competition components have not been settled yet because of the difficulty in separating development costs from production costs, Pete estimates that one of BRE's Datsun 240Zs, ready to race, would cost between $9500 and $11,000. Few competitors would desire, or even need, to buy a complete ready-to-race car and by buying the necessary components from BRE, including a race-prepared engine, most could probably field a potential winner for two or three thousand dollars less.

In the east there is a similar program being carried on by Bob Sharp in Darien, Conn. These are completely separate operations, you understand; Sharp working through Nissan Motor Corporation's eastern office and Pete through Datsun West. Sharp got his first 240Z somewhat earlier than BRE and was earlier into competition with it. The Sharp car has a better record in SCCA racing than the BRE 240Z and it is going to be extremely interesting to see the head-to-head results when the two cars meet at this year's national championships at Road Atlanta—providing John Morton can get enough CP points to qualify after BRE's late start.

A few other 240Zs are being raced around the country but these are privately entered cars and as such cannot be expected to have the muscle of the factory-supported teams. Next year, judging by the interest the BRE and the Sharp cars are generating this year among both competitors and dealers, there will undoubtedly be well prepared Z cars running in every division of SCCA.

So the Datsun 240Z, SCCA racing version, is well on its way and is going to do well. Watch for it. It will be worth seeing.

Datsun 240-Z

This 240-Z was built up by BRE Enterprises for John Parker of Palos Verdes Estates. The $1,000 worth of customizing includes spoilers fore and aft and a special paint job.

Considering the relative scarcity of true sports cars originating in Japan, it is all the more surprising that Datsun's Z-car should qualify so handily on its first appearance for *Road Test*'s Sports Car of the Year Award. In fact, with highway congestion and smog both more severe than the highly publicized conditions found in Los Angeles, it's rather amazing that the Japanese bother to design *any* sports cars. In their homeland they are viewed with suspicion through smarting eyes, their performance potential is somewhat short of useless when average speeds possible even in the country hover around 35 mph, and prices which seem moderate to us are beyond the reach of all but a small fraction of Japanese buyers. There isn't even very much in the way of organized sport to encourage the breed.

With the success of the Z-car here assured by four month's worth of orders currently on the books, Datsun wisely decided to stop importation of the 1600 and 2000 roadsters. It was not that these weren't popular but they are, or were, built on the same line as the Z-car and demand for the latter has reached phenomenal proportions. Datsun hasn't abandoned roadster enthusiasts as we understand one based on 1200 mechanical components is in the works but for the present, the company is understandably concentrating on easing embarrassing shortages.

One might fairly describe the 240-Z as combining all that is best in sophisticated but still orthodox engineering practice into a package of particularly pleasing appearance. On top of this, it is an unusually complete package at its $3,695 base price. Aside from dress-up and performance goodies supplied by such firms as AMCO and BRE Enterprises, there is very little in the way of options that you can buy or even need. They even set you up for the optional dealer-installed air conditioning (which is fully hidden behind the dash, by the way) by providing standard tinted glass. Full instrumentation including a tach, a clock, a signal-seeking radio with electric antenna and electric backlite de-misting, to name just a few items, all come at no extra cost.

We don't have to substantiate the fact that the 240-Z can be both raced successfully and driven comfortably on the street. Pete Brock's BRE-Datsun Team, as Southern Pacific Division C-Production champions, has already qualified to enter its 240-Z in the National event at Atlanta on November 29th, a month from this writing. As to the street, the 240-Z will survive lugging and any other abusive technique in the hands of the unskilled or respond in a manner that makes its price seem like a mistake with an empathetic and experienced driver behind the wheel.

In addition, the package is people-sized for two and lacks no luxury item found in cars at twice the price. No contortions are needed to get in or out and once in, there is ample head, leg and shoulder room. The pedals, too, are people-sized and well spaced, just one more bit of evidence that the car was designed with the world market in mind and not as a toy for stunted boulevardiers able to wear size 5 racing slippers. Proper proportions are the key to the pleasing lines as well. You don't look like you were driving your own cigar down the

240-Z dash is complete as shown here at the base $3,695 price except for the air conditioning controls for which are just to the right of the column.

BRE mag wheels weigh only 12 pounds each and the big Goodyears add and subtract to the handling, depending upon driving conditions.

Ashtray and housing easily remove to expose the complete fuse block. Control directly behind the shift lever is the choke.

road and there's no need to fit seats that support your sacrum and nothing else. The buckets allow a normal driving posture, give a measure of side support and the armrests are as well placed as in any Cadillac.

Readers of our August road test of the 240-Z, which drew a record number of mostly favorable letters in return, are aware that the ride served up by the fully independent MacPherson strut suspension front and rear is reasonably firm without being uncomfortable and that the car corners with mild understeer. If you opt for the Pete Brock treatment or its equivalent as did John Parker, owner of the 240-Z pictured on these pages, to the tune of about $1,100 for the body and chassis work and maybe $1,000 for tear-down, polish and dyno-tuning of the engine, you get a 240-Z that can cruise at 100 mph on Nevada roads at an easy 4,800 rpm. If you drop off to 80-90 mph, the economy is an amazing 23.3 miles to the gallon. This compares to the 17.7 mpg we got with our strictly stock test car.

Brock explains that it's a matter of both fine fitting and fine tuning, mostly the latter in the case of the Parker car. Apparently, it takes a finer touch than is applied at the end of the assembly line to properly balance the twin S.U.-type carburetors. A full blue-printing, Brock notes, would run closer to $3,000 whether you're setting up for street or racing.

A factor in the economy could well be switching from the standard 175SR14 Bridgestone radials to much larger F70 Goodyears mounted on 7-inch Brock magnesium wheels that weigh all of 12 pounds apiece. Obviously, the fatter the tire the further you'll roll per revolution of the engine but with the Goodyears, there is just too much bite for the clutch to handle and it was giving trouble by the 6,000-mile mark. We think Pete is wise in switching to RA-100 bias-ply racing Bridgestones on future conversions. Either type cures the slight wind-wandering found in the standard car.

Another part of the Brock package is what he calls "Mulholland" springs which you can buy and install yourself at just $68 a set. These are named after a winding mountain road in the Los Angeles area that in the past was the scene of many an impromptu and unofficial hill climb. The springs are noticeably stiffer and drop the car by 1½ inches, but they should not be used without suitable shock absorbers. If the standard shocks are kept, the car will bottom front and rear without much provocation.

Most of the visible money goes into the metallic paint job which isn't applied until all the glass is removed. Another chunk is for hiding the antenna (under the rocker panel on this car but in the trunk lid on future models) and adding spoilers to the front and rear. The front spoiler also functions as an effective scoop to cool the disc brakes. At the speeds of which this car is capable and where such speeds are legal, the spoilers are more necessary than decorative. The standard configuration tends to get a little light at the top end.

With the stiff Goodyear tires, feedback through the wheel was noticeable but never needed attention. Considering the fact that the car was designed or "tuned" for an entirely different type of tire, the fact that it will accept other types without much modification and still handle is somewhat of a compliment. You'll notice that we have yet to imply that it handles better for street use and we won't. Racing or extremely high-speed chicanes are something else. So, too, is the tasteful but hairy look of a Brock-treated car. Remembering how rare the 240-Z still is, four notes tucked under the wipers during a two-week period asking "where can

I get this done to *my* 240-Z?'' is also a compliment.

It was also interesting to live with a 240-Z that already had some mileage on it as our test cars otherwise have been nearly new. Aside from the clutch problem which was corrected (but not cured) by a simple adjustment, the Parker car suffered from side windows that weren't tight in their frames. Rather than rattling, they ''buzzed'' in the down position. Also, one of the little breathers in the seatback had disappeared, leaving a nasty hole in the upholstery of the driver's seat, and the oil pressure gauge was erratic to say the least, never showing what seemed like enough pressure and sometimes reading none at all. We gather that this is temporarily chronic to the 240-Z and of course, is of no matter unless real lubricating problems should develop and go undetected. To finalize what is really a very short list of nitpicks, we should note that front spoilers, however effective and pretty, preclude visits to automated washracks and develop scraping noises on sharply inclined driveways, particularly when the car is lowered beyond the designer's intent.

The 150-horsepower ohc six is willing and more than able, especially after Pete Brock performed approximately $1,000 worth of dyno tuning.

Standard 240-Z (left) sports power antenna which BRE buries in the trunk on current conversion. Note also relocated exhaust.

The 240-Z under discussion was air-conditioned but the only physical evidence of its presence was a small knob just to the right of the steering column. It uses the same outlets as the standard forced-flow ventilation system and the same three-speed fan. Actually, the latter is adequate for temperatures in the 80-90 range when combined with open windows. Here we should say that the 240-Z is one of those rare ventless birds that are relatively draftless with the windows down.

We hope Datsun never sees fit to tap Muncie, Indiana, for an automatic transmission for the 240-Z. A five-speed as an option, maybe, but anyone who needs or desires assistance in shifting this car has no business trading in his Buick. Come to think of it, Alfa Romeo has just as smooth a five-speed box that they might be willing to sell Datsun for a price. Anyway, such musings apart, we think you can now see why the 240-Z was chosen Sports Car of the Year. As we said in our road test, we're willing to bet that the 240-Z will be the biggest selling sports/GT car, import or domestic, of all times. That limb seems more solid after thirty days of driving one instead of just ten. Inquiries (not complaints about delivery delays) should be addressed to Nissan Motor Corp. in USA, 137 E. Alondra Blvd., Gardena, Calif. 90247. BRE Enterprise, Inc., lives at 137 Oregon St., El Segundo, Calif. 90245.

Data in Brief

240-Z

ENGINE: 6-cylinder sohc, 145.7 cu. ins., 2393cc, 150 hp at 5600 rpm, 148 lb.-ft. of torque at 4400 rpm, dual S.U.-type carburetion.

DRIVELINE: 4-speed manual transmission, rear drive.

SUSPENSION: MacPherson strut and coil, fully independent, front and rear, stabilizer front.

BRAKES: Disc front, finned drums rear, power assisted.

STEERING: Rack and pinion, manual.

DIMENSIONS: Wheelbase 89.9 ins., length 161.3 ins., width 63.6 ins., height 49.1 ins., weight 2238 lbs.

THIS ONE IS A WINNER! IT'S A TRUE GT IN THE MOST MODERN TRADITION. ITS LIST PRICE IS RIGHT, TOO

■ Dare we say it? Why not? The Datsun 240-Z is the best all-around sports-GT car we have ever driven that costs less than $6,000. Yes, we know that takes in a lot of territory. Yes, we know that includes most Corvettes, a lot of Porsches including the new 914, the Opel GT, a lot of British machinery and all kinds of other sports-GT cars. But that's the way we feel about it.

The 240-Z has got to be one of the most happening cars in the past ten years, maybe longer. It's got it all—handling, go-power, looks, comfort and convenience. And with all standard equipment—and that includes an AM signal seeking radio and power antenna—the list price is only $3526. Don't ask us how they can sell the car for $3526. We don't know. All we know is that they do and you're the benefactor.

Other standard equipment includes an overhead cam 6-cylinder engine, 4-speed manual transmission, power front disc brakes, radial tires, rear window de-icer, woodrim steering wheel, fully carpeted luggage area and all kinds of other little niceties that make driving the car a real pleasure. Everything you see in the photos is standard equipment and there are no options at this time. But some accessory companies like Amco and Frigiking have goodies in the

works right now.

Just sitting in the car is a complete gas. The real bucket seats—as opposed to those that claim to be buckets but really aren't—cradle you from the bottom of your shoulder blades to the backs of your thighs. The seats are infinitely and easily adjustable for rake and have yards of travel back and forth on their tracks. There's a dead pedal to the left of the clutch for bracing yourself in wild cornering maneuvers. The little touches are all there.

The steering wheel, gearshift lever and pedals are absolutely perfect. No improvement is possible in this area. Once you settle into your seat, you automatically take up the classic arms-out driving position. All controls are within easy reach including the headlights and wiper-washer control switches which are mounted on the ends of a steering column stalk ala European GT style.

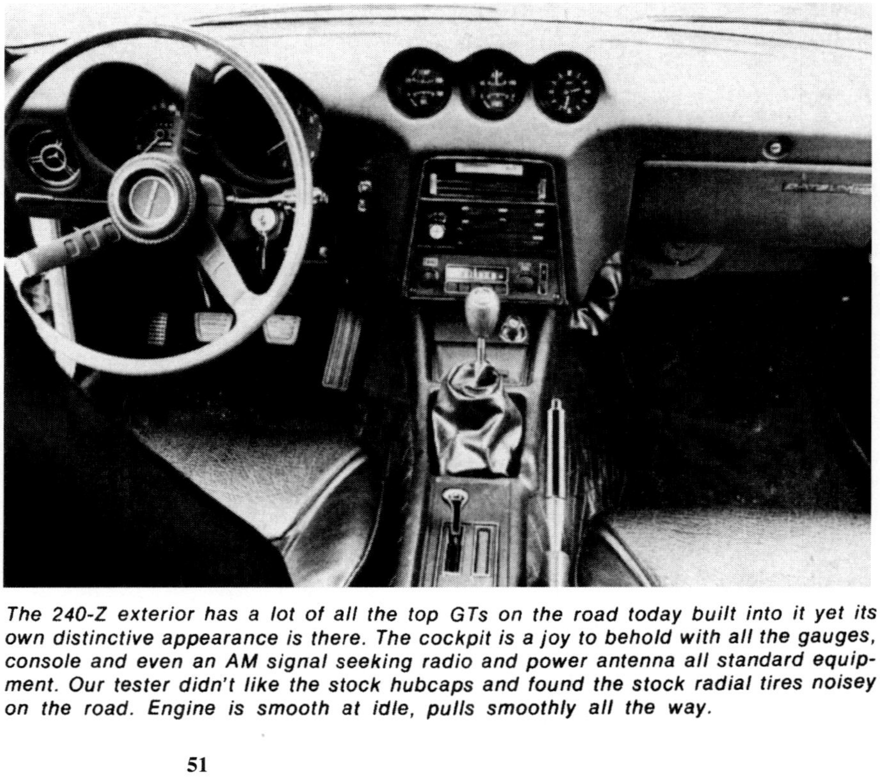

The 240-Z exterior has a lot of all the top GTs on the road today built into it yet its own distinctive appearance is there. The cockpit is a joy to behold with all the gauges, console and even an AM signal seeking radio and power antenna all standard equipment. Our tester didn't like the stock hubcaps and found the stock radial tires noisey on the road. Engine is smooth at idle, pulls smoothly all the way.

The 240-Z Sports is built on a 90 inch wheelbase. It is just about 49 inches high.

DATSUN 240-Z

Driving the car is something else. At first, the acceleration of the car was a disappointment. Considering the way it looks when it's standing still, we just expected it to be much much faster, acceleration-wise. Nissan engineers chose a 3.36 final drive ratio, which is too low numerically in our opinion. However, they wanted long legged cruising at low engine rpm rather than blast-you-in-the-back acceleration and they got it. With the 3.36 rear axle ratio, the engine is turning a lazy 3350 rpm at 70 mph. The engine is so quiet that they could easily have gone to a 3.70 or 3.90 ratio without running into an engine noise problem at crusing speeds.

As it was, our test 240-Z still performed admirably once you got used to the feeling that you weren't going to get that zap acceleration of a 454 cubic inch Corvette.

At Suffolk Country Raceway in Westhampton, New York, the car ran 0 to 60 in just under nine seconds on every run with a best of 8.8 seconds. The quarter mile times were always in the low 17-second bracket and always over 80 mph. Our best timeslip read 17.2 seconds and 83.68 mph. Our top speed was 118 mph but there was still revs left in fourth gear when we had to shut down for lack of room. Another magazine's road test reported a top end of 122 mph and we believe it. It's just that with the 3.36 gear ratio, you've got to have the Bonneville Salt Flats to wind the engine up high enough to reach it.

The engine is redlined at 7000 rpm and will rev easily to that point. However, we found that shifting at 6500 gave the best acceleration times.

The engine is a thoroughly modern design that is based on the Datsun 1600 sedan engine. What the Nissan engineers did is simply add two more cylinders onto their four and *Voila!* an overhead cam six of 2400cc (actually 2393). Compression ratio is 9 to 1 necessitating the use of premium grade fuel. Carburetion is by two one-barrel Hitachi-SU carburetors. The engine is rated 150 horsepower at 6000 rpm and 148 lbs./ft. of torque at 4400 rpm.

As we said before, the engine—and for that matter, the entire driveline—is dead quiet at anything below peak revs. The engine idles smoothly at 1000 rpm. Even the exhaust is quiet, which is really a shame. This car could use an exhaust more in keeping with the GT feel of the car. The engine is smooth at idle and pulls smoothly right up to the redline. There's no point in the rev range where the engine suddenly comes on the cam with a blast. It's just one smooth surge.

Handling is in a class by itself in this price range and right up to six grand. The suspension is independent all around. The front suspension is by MacPherson struts, lower lateral arms, compliance struts, coil springs, tube shocks and a fairly flimsy antiroll stabilizer bar. Rear suspension is by Chapman struts, lower A-arms, coil springs and tube shocks. The ride is pretty soft and very comfortable for a car that handles this well. In that, the car has a very Alfa-like feel to it with all kinds of wheel travel and lots of lean in the corners but good cornering power. The car could use a rear sway bar to cut lean. The steering is quick enough but has a somewhat ponderous feel to it. In tight corners, there's initial understeer until you apply more power. Then the rear starts to come around but in a completely controllable manner. Backing off the gas brings things right back in line. The more you toss it around, the more confidence you have that it will go right where you point it *if* you use just the right amount of steering lock and throttle. In a word, it's very forgiving.

The car would do even better on the handling course with wider wheels and more tire. Stock equipment consists of Bridgestone radials, size 175SR14 on 4½-inch wide steel rims. They're plenty noisy on the road. There's plenty of room in the wheelwells for bigger tires—even 205SR14s—on wider wheels. A big-

Styling is as fresh as anything offered today.

Through the traps the "Zee" did 0 to 60 in just under nine seconds which is hot!

ger offset to the rims would give the car a wider track and better looks too. The stock wheels are sunk into the wheelwells too far. Guess Datsun had to cut costs somewhere.

While we're on the bad points of the car—and they're few—the stock hubcaps have got to go. They look like a set of J.C. Whitney $3.95 specials and are just not in keeping with the rest of the car's quality feel. In addition, they kept throwing themselves off as we were snapping wild cornering shots so we just took them off once and for all and forgot them. A set of mags and fat tires would be completely out of sight on this car.

Styling is a matter of personal opinion and we're not about to tell you what to like and what no to like. But there are some stylists at Nissan Motors in Japan who have done a lot of homework and the 240-Z shows it The car's exterior design seems to take in the best points of the Carvette Sting Ray, the Jaguar XK-E, the Porshe 911 series, the Toyota 2000 GT and even some Ferraris. We like it—very much.

Here's a car that's going to give every Opel GT owner—and a few other marques to boot—the blue meenie fits. The car does everything the Opel GT pretends it can and for about the same price tag. You can't hardly go wrong by buying one. ●

Engine is a smooth 150 hp sohc in-line 6-cylinder plant capable of a good 125 mph.

Fastback rear has big top hinged tailgate but shock absorber towers cut into space.

Given the Works:

DATSUN 240Z

Driving Rauno Aaltonen's RAC Rally car; a first look at this exciting Japanese GT

By Ray Hutton

THE news, when published earlier this year, that Datsun were again to take part in the RAC Rally came as no surprise. In 1969 they had taken the team award with three 1600SSS saloons. Since then they had turned a 1969 team prize in the East African Safari into a win in the 1970 event and they clearly had hopes of a similar progression in the forests of Britain. What *did* surprise us was that the cars they entered were the new 240Z sports coupés, a model which, until this year's London Motor Show, had never been seen in England.

The Datsun 240Z was announced 12 months before at the Tokyo Motor Show and imports to the United States (at which market it is obviously primarily aimed) started early this year. Judging by the rave reviews it has received in the American enthusiast Press, it is a big success there and a few examples have already run in SCCA production car racing. The model has hardly been seen in Europe, and it has not yet been decided if it is to be marketed in Britain.

Datsun's RAC Rally effort should be an object lesson to some European manufacturers. Early in October, five rally-prepared 240Zs arrived in England for what was to be their first international event. Prepared to Group 3 (the RAC does not allow prototypes), they were equipped with modified engines, suitable gearing, lightweight panels and a whole string of special items. Engineer Takashi Wakabayashi and his team in Nissan's engineering laboratories had done a very thorough job to develop and get all these bits and pieces through the complex procedure of homologation (despite virtually no competition experience with the model) before the company's rally plans were made public.

To ensure that thorough preparation was carried through with the same professional approach, they enlisted top drivers Rauno Aaltonen (who had driven a 1600SSS in the 1969 RAC), Tony Fall and their Safari winner Edgar Hermann. A fourth, spare car was an additional last-minute entry for 1969 RAC Rally Champion John Bloxham. The fifth 240Z was used as a service car (taking a leaf out of Porsche's book, who use 0911s as high speed tenders) and joined the service vehicles

Performance Check

Maximum speeds

Gear	Top	4th	3rd	2nd	1st
mph	126*	112	84	60	36

Acceleration*

mph	30	40	50	60	70	80	90	100	110
sec	4.1	5.4	7.1	9.0	10.6	12.6	16.2	18.8	25.6

Standing ¼ mile: 16.0sec 89mph

Standing Kilometre: 27.5sec 117mph

*see text

operated by two mechanics from Japan and staff from Old Woking Service Station, the British base for the operation.

Aaltonen had carried out some testing with the model just after this year's Monte Carlo Rally and did a couple of days' rough road testing at Bagshot in the weeks preceding the RAC, while Tony Fall used his car in a British club event to acclimitize himself. Initial impressions of these big (by rally standards), brutish cars seemed to suggest that they were going to be quite a handful—one driver said that it was like an Austin Healey 3000 "before sorting".

Differentials spoil chances

The four-strong team of red and black 240Zs were together with the French Alpines (also making their first British appearance) the centre of attraction at the start of the Rally. Tony Fall, enjoying himself hugely, was well-placed in the early stages but became involved with Ove Andersson's already-spun Alpine on the Dalby South stage in Yorkshire on the first night and though he continued, retired on the next stage with a broken differential. Rauno Aaltonen had transmission trouble early on, when a drive-shaft broke on the first of the Clipstone stages. He thought at first that a tyre had punctured and drove to the end of the stage, where the broken drive-shaft and the brake pipes and cables it had damaged while flailing around were discovered. He and Easter removed the shaft and drove the next stage with one only (and no rear brakes) to reach their service crew, who fitted a shaft from their Datsun 1800. The brakes were progressively repaired by service crews throughout the night, but it was not until Bathgate control on the Sunday morning that the car's full braking was restored. On the return from the Scottish loop this car also suffered differential failure; fortunately they were able to get to the control and the unit was changed. Thereafter this car ran beautifully and steadily improved its position In the latter stages it proved as fast as the quickest of the opposition, particularly on the faster stages; Aaltonen set fastest time on three stages and finished a strong seventh; he would clearly have been much better placed had he not lost so much time early on. We had particular reason to be hopeful that this car would finish, for it was agreed that we could borrow it for the weekend after the rally had ended.

The two other team cars were victims of the same differential trouble; Datsun were by no means alone in this, for transmission failure was the universal cause of the mechanical retirements that affected the works teams.

The engine is a large lump for a 2.4 litre unit. The three carburettors are Japanese-made Solex. Access to the washer bottle and battery in the back corners of the bonnet is via small flaps on top of the wings.

A comfortable interior with well-planned controls but some lack of stowage space for odd essential items. The special seats are non-reclining; Willans full harnesses are fitted. Note the high windscreen washer post on the scuttle

Above: The 240Z is the first serious attempt to rally a big-rorty-front-engined sports car since the Austin Healey 3000. Aaltonen's car remained remarkably unblemished after 2,300 miles of RAC Rally

Far left: The doors and the bonnet are made of glass-fibre with plastic windows and the tailgate is so thin that it has a noticeable droop when supported open. Note the mud-flaps, mounted well back

First close look

Our weekend with number 18, the Aaltonen-Easter car, provided an opportunity not only to drive what is already a highly competitive rally car but also our first chance to examine the model in detail. Driving specially prepared competition cars is always an interesting exercise, and never more so than this, but it was curious to have no reference point by which to judge its performance and behaviour; none of us has driven a standard 240Z.

As it is so new to us, a run through the standard car's specification is perhaps appropriate. The 240Z is a front engine-rear drive coupé powered by a bulky in-line six-cylinder overhead camshaft engine of 2,393 c.c. which is, in effect, the familiar 1600 c.c. engine with two extra cylinders. It has bore and stroke measurements of 83mm x 73.3mm and produces 150 bhp (gross) at 5,600 rpm. It is available with either a four- or five-speed gearbox, has MacPherson strut and trailing link front suspension and an independent rear end, using struts again with lower wishbones. Rack and pinion steering and a mixed disc-drum brake set-up are employed. The two-seater steel coupé body has bits of several different cars in its styling (influences of the Jaguar E-type, Toyota 2000GT and several Ferraris are evident) but the overall effect is sporting, eye-catching and pleasing. A criticism might be its height off the ground—a feature which is of course of distinct advantage for rough-road rallying.

Exact details of all the internal modifications carried out in the preparation of the rally cars unfortunately are not available. The work was done in Japan and with characteristic inscrutability it was explained to us that the car was "fairly standard". The engine, which is normally equipped with two SU-type Hitachi carburettors, is fitted with three Mikuni-Solex twin-choke instruments and with a different camshaft; power has been increased to a quoted figure of 200 bhp (net). The gearbox, the five-speed version of course, has been re-ratioed and an ultra-low 4.87 final drive fitted (standard cars have a 3.9 axle; those sold in the US, 3.36). The limited-slip differentials, which proved the model's weakest link, had all suffered from loosening or breakage of the crown wheel bolts, not specifically from over-heating (as was suspected at the time). Aaltonen had been worried as to whether the renewed diff on his car would last, and we were worried too, since it made dreadful sounds like broken glass when the car was reversed. Incidentally, though the Datsun's US options list includes a clutch-type limited-slip differential, this one had the characteristics of the cam-and-plunger type.

A glance underneath the car, to examine the cause of a slight but audible movement at one of the mounting points of the sub-frame that carries the differential, suggested that very little underbody strengthening had been necessary. There is the usual front undershield (rather more than a sump guard) but otherwise it really did seem "fairly standard" and it is a credit to the car's strength that it survived 2,300 miles of RAC Rally without any apparent damage. The wheels fitted are Datsun magnesium alloy designs; 14in. diameter with 6in. wide rims.

GIVEN THE WORKS:

DATSUN 240Z . . .

Lightweight glass-fibre panels replace the doors, the bonnet and opening tailgate, and all side and rear windows are plastic. Outwardly the body changes are few—two strengthened jacking points at the sides, Safari-style mudflaps and a row of four modest-looking but highly effective Japanese supplementary lamps firmly outrigged in what seems a very damage-prone position. The standard bumpers remain. Oh, and there's two enormous megaphoned exhaust pipes.

No 18 on the road

Those exhausts give advance warning of the sort of noise the beast makes when it is fired up. The noise is "very considerable", absolutely glorious and of questionable legality when the engine is on song—the noise guessing game of "who comes next" on the stages of the RAC provided a lot of Datsuns mistaken for Porsches. Actual starting up (on the key) is no problem at all and is preceded by a subdued clatter from the electric fuel pump behind you (colleague Michael Scarlett insists that it be likened to a covey of ladies from a Japanese Womens' Institute all knitting furiously). Surprisingly, the engine will idle quite happily at 800 rpm. Moving off, gently, is no problem either; the clutch is not unduly heavy (though of the competition variety) and the engine remarkably tractable. The transition when the road clears and the throttles are opened is an experience of a very special kind—the harsh, raucous exhaust note is directly proportional to the rate at which the revs rise, almost as if the accelerator was a volume control. There is a leap forward after 3,500 rpm but the engine is not "cammy" in the racing sense, just beautifully responsive throughout. And it will pull in 5th gear from 1,100 rpm. Noise level towards maximum revs of 6,800 is too high for normal conversation—hence the inevitable intercom.

The gearbox, all-synchromesh and with its five speeds arranged Alfa Romeo-style (1st to 4th in the standard positions, 5th to the right of 3rd, above reverse) is one of the best five-speeders we have tried.

With the gearing arranged for short bursts between corners in the forests, we expected the acceleration to be impressive. Our figures show that it was (the 0-100 mph and standing quarter mile are closely comparable with those for a standard 4.2 Jaguar E-type) and they could certainly have been improved upon had we not felt inhibited by the sub-standard differential and tempered by our desire to return the car in running order. A gentle 3,000 rpm was used for our careful take-offs from rest (which gave just a touch of wheelspin) and 6,500 rpm used in the gears. Serious vibration from the rear (the same diff trouble) prevented an accurate maximum speed run, but with such a low axle ratio the theoretical maximum of 126 mph is obviously realistic. For the record, the speedometer (in mph) was dead accurate, before its cable broke. A run of some 400 miles allowed a check on fuel consumption, which came out at 20.3 mpg, only slightly less than figures obtained for the standard car by our American contemporaries.

How it handles

The car came to us exactly as it had finished the rally, numbers, mud and all. It was fitted with German-made Dunlop SP 215/70 SR14 radials which were used in the later stages, though the cars started the rally on some Japanese Dunlops not unlike the Dunlop "Hakka" snow tyre though with a harder compound, which were said to be excellent on dry, rough roads. Traction on tarmac on these big "chunkies" was excellent and directional stability good. Under smooth road conditions, understeer was moderate and power-induced rear-end breakaway easy to obtain and easy to catch, but on slippery corners the works drivers' reports of excessive understeer were confirmed, the front end "ploughing" out, even without a burst of power. But by "setting up" the car in the right gear with power to spare, cornering could be rapid indeed and the power was planted on the road to a surprisingly high degree. Under forestry conditions Aaltonen was using the handbrake to do this; hence his slower stage times when the rear brakes were not fully operative following the drive-shaft failure.

Not us—but the Little Finn himself, hurling the 240Z through the Grizedale stage on the RAC. Aaltonen finished seventh—one place better than he managed in 1969 with the Datsun 1600SSS saloon

The car's braking performance had remained good, if noisy and harsh at low speed and requiring a firm push. The steering is only moderately heavy, nicely geared (2.6 turns from lock to lock) and responsive. The dampers had also stood up well to the long pounding and the ride is very reasonable—if sharp over the bigger bumps. The works drivers expressed enthusiasm for the car's performance over "yumps" and the lack of drama on landing. Overall, we were most impressed by the 240Z's feeling of solidity but it seems a big and hairy lump of car to hurl through the forests (perhaps that is its only real similarity to the Healey) and we are once again filled with admiration for those who are able to do so at stage-winning speeds.

Both the driver and navigator are well catered for in the cockpit. Special cloth-covered seats are fitted; the passenger sits lower than the driver because Rauno is short and likes to sit high, but none the less the driving position proved comfortable even for our largest tester. The steering wheel is a comfortable, fat, leather-rimmed affair, while the pedals have been arranged for "proper" heel-and-toeing and a clutch footrest added. The handbrake, floor-mounted, is of the fly-off type. Visibility to the front is fine, though one is conscious of there being rather more of the long bonnet than is visible and of the heavy screen pillars. To the rear and at the rear three-quarters, the view is obstructed by the bodywork and also by the hefty four-strut roll-over bar and two spare wheels. This essential 'luggage' restricts interior storage space considerably.

Well-planned controls

The standard dashboard layout has an American flavour, with deeply recessed dials. The dominant instruments are the paired speedometer and rev-counter, the three smaller dials at the centre showing water temperature and oil pressure (a source of some concern to us as it was never much over 30 psi), amps and fuel level, and the time, respectively. All normal lighting and wiper-washer operations are contained on a multiple stalk to the left of the steering column and the indicator stalk to the right, while the auxiliary lamps are looked after by an extra panel of six switches above (and obstructing) the heater-ventilator controls. Two separate Halda Tripmasters are fitted instead of the more usual Twinmaster; a fail-safe operation since they are driven independently from the two front wheels.

As always, it is the details that are so fascinating—the separate flexible-stalk blue lights that illuminate the Haldas, the map light on the door, the intercom amplifier mounted on the roll-over bar, the passenger's floor button for the air-horns, the pockets, the Velcro-attached pads to prevent chafing knees on window winders, the multiplicity of straps to hold down wheels, tools and all manner of things in the back, and the sticky tape everywhere to hold spare fuses, keys and padding in place—and even to show the driver where dead centre on the steering wheel is.

It is things like this that make rally cars so different from the standard article. This Datsun 240Z, which impressed us tremendously, could be a very different kettle of fish from the standard car. But if the "cooking" version shows only a percentage of the flair of this car, we await its introduction to Britain (which must surely come) with eager anticipation. In the meantime, Datsun intend to follow up their promising rally debut with a full programme of events next year, starting off with the Monte, when their drivers will once again be Rauno Aaltonen and Tony Fall.

Z

One letter of the sports car alphabet which stands for comfort, style and $3,600

By Chuck Koch

Before getting into the narrative of this road test let me tell you that I was a bit prejudiced upon undertaking the whole Datsun 240Z assignment. You see, the first time I drove the car was almost a year ago and at the time I must admit to not being overly impressed. Sure, it was comfortable, stylish and fairly fast but I had this gut level feeling that maybe the 240Z was not a real sports car. Perhaps it was my tradition-bound thinking that the best sports cars come from Europe or maybe I had forgotten the shift of all automobiles from performance to comfort. Comfort is becoming more important in sports cars and the Datsun mirrors this change well. Reflecting on this fact and considering that intuition can be wrong, I am now willing to admit some of my thoughts concerning the car erred, especially doubts on its claim of being a sports car. That it is is indisputable.

There are still a few things about the car which draw negative comments, but on the whole these are outweighed by the positive features. One of the most positive is the price; $3,601 delivered out the showroom door and in your garage. In the sports car market for that paltry sum it is darn near impossible to go wrong. Consider what you get for the money: signal-seeking radio, power antenna, carpets, tilting seats, simulated wood-grain steering wheel, and a rear window defroster. What more do you want in a car? For a few extra bucks, about $200, you can get and, seemingly all California owners do, custom mag wheels (installed as dealer options) which add a great deal both in performance and appearance. We had our test 240Z outfitted with them to compare handling and steering between the stock and optional wheels.

Performance is definitely a part of the "Z" car's image, yet it must be outward appearance which accounts for the bulk of sales. Although just 11 months old, the car is apparently developing a styling mystique not unlike the '63-67 Corvette, the E-type Jaguar or even the Farina Ferrari GT coupe of 1959. Because of it this car will never grow old. And it's not surprising since in its way the 240Z is to Japanese cars what the 1963 'Vette was to American automobiles – a dramatic change from the norm. It follows in the footsteps of the Toyota 2000GT but goes a bit further because it's a real car anyone can have. The styling is dramatic yet subtle, with no wasted lines, and very smooth transitions. A long hood slopes gently upwards, accentuating the front, and a raked windshield serves to flow the lines to a peak height of 50.5 inches, while the fastback rear window slants quickly, gracefully, to its logical end.

The Japanese are known for exquisite detailing, particularly of interior appointments, and the 240Z does not fail this tradition. Once you enter and seat yourself, a very easy task due to the wide doors, you become part of the machine, as the bucket seats wrap snugly and comfortably about you. The seating position is low, almost too low since any attempt at resting an elbow on the window sill meets with the feeling that a public hanging is taking place, and the buckets tilt so that a comfortable driving posture can be easily assumed. Legroom is fantastic and even the driver's clutch foot has been taken care of, with a small foot rest provided when that pedal is not in use. The dashboard is stark but effective, with the tachometer and speedometer located directly in front of the driver. Above the center console are three dials containing the temperature, oil pressure, amperage and fuel gauges, along with a clock. They are all in easy view and at night light up with an eyepleasing green tint. Under the gauges are the heater/defroster/vent controls, pushbutton

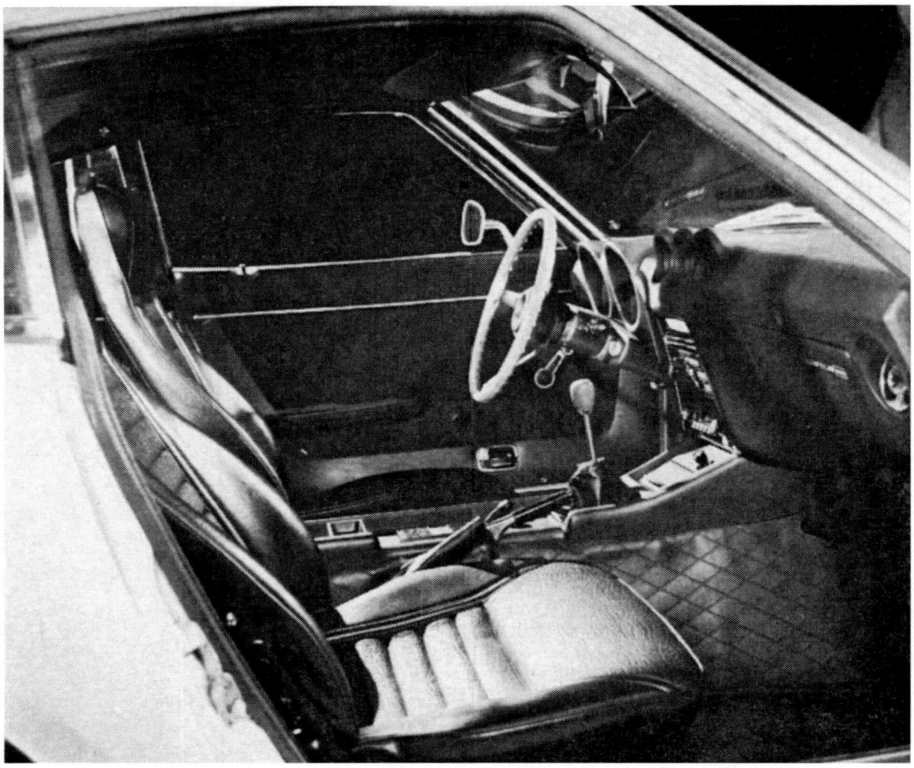

Detail appointments abound in the Datsun 240Z's interior which includes tilting bucket seats, simulated woodgrain steering wheel, a full complement of gauges and plush carpets. Only the cheap-looking vinyl quilting on the transmission tunnel detracts from the excellent design.

radio and ashtray. Of special note here is a heater which really heats and a ventillation system which does its job with the efficiency of air conditioning. The shift lever is mounted on the console and falls to reach easily, although when in second or third gear it does obstruct the way to the ashtray. On the steering column are the vaunted all-purpose levers made famous by foreign cars although Datsun reaches some kind of zenith of this art with a design bulk not seen since the electric-shift Hudson Terraplane. One controls the headlights and the windshield wiper/washer while the other takes care of turn signals and high beams. Behind the seats is a spacious luggage area, complete with straps for tying down cargo.

Interior noise is kept to a minimum, although some engine and wind howling does filter through and the rear window will rattle. Again, the only complaints are nit-picky and concern the carpeting which is nylon and tends to ball-up under repeated heel scruffings. Also, it would be a good idea to glue it down instead of snapping it in.

Next to comfort the 240Z's forte is straightline performance and it has plenty of that. Its power comes from an in-line 6-cylinder engine which has a displacement of 2393cc and produces 151 hp at 5,600 rpm. It is an overhead camshaft unit which uses numerous aluminum pieces to save weight and aid in cooling efficiency. The cylinder block is cast iron of a special monoblock construction with a seven main bearing support system for added quietness and high durability. Weight is saved through the OHC system which eliminates complicated tappet chambers. The block has a cylinder bore/stroke of 3.26 x 2.90 inches. For good cooling efficiency the cylinder head is made of aluminum alloy and uses cast aluminum seats on the intake valve, while a special cast seat is installed for the exhaust.

The overhead cam is cast iron and located inside the rocker cover. In the 240Z engine five aluminum alloy brackets support the cam and hold an oil pipe for proper lubrication of the cam pad surfaces. The valve system consists of two per cylinder with the intake having a diameter of 1.5 inches and the exhaust measuring 1.3 inches. The Mercedes-like system has a pivot type rocker arm activated directly by the camshaft mechanism making its moving parts much lighter and providing high-speed performance. Motive power for the cam and valve train is supplied by a double row of roller chains driven by the crankshaft. Constant chain tension is obtained through a spring and oil pressure arrangement. Fuel is fed to the engine through twin side-mounted SU carburetors attached to an aluminum intake manifold. The carbs work in synchronization and have primary/secondary venturi diameters of .98/1.10 inches. Despite recording excellent acceleration times for a sports car (quarter mile e.t. of 16.45 secs. at 83.72 mph), the 240Z still showed good fuel economy by registering an astounding average of 20.2 mpg. One thing I came away with after track testing the car was a healthy distrust of Japanese pessimism. The factory lists top speed at 120 mph but the engine feels extremely strong and it should be possible to reach at least 130 mph with ease.

As in most sports cars, the 240Z comes standard with a 4-speed transmission. Although the shifting action is good, I believe Datsun could improve

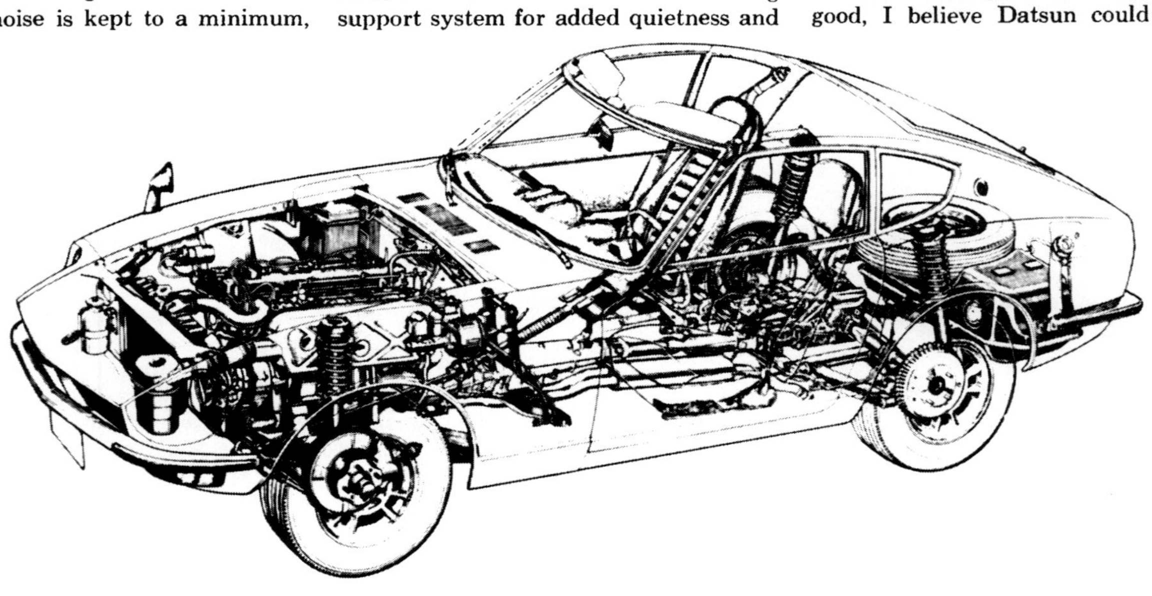

upon it. The throws, especially into third, are long and the movement is stiff (this problem does clear up to some extent after the car has been broken in). Datsun has an excellent 5-speed gearbox and one wonders why such a great combination is denied the 240Z. As it is, the car tops out too quickly in first and tends to die in the upper rev ranges of third. Most aggravating was the shift between second and third, where you have to literally think, "Now I go up into neutral, over, and then into third." It is most time consuming and robs the engine of at least 1,200 rpm. The clutch is a single dry disc diaphragm type.

Now we come to the nitty-gritty – handling. This is what makes or breaks a sports car and in the 240Z's case it makes it, but barely. Front suspension is of the independent strut type with the shock absorber and spindle combined in a single unit and supported by the coil spring at the upper end and a transverse link at the bottom. A ball joint is attached to the lower part of the spindle and connected with the lower link to the suspension member through a rubber bushing. The transverse link supports overall forward and backward motion by means of a compression rod fitted to the chassis, while the strut absorbs vertical inputs. In addition, a stabilizer bar is adapted in the suspension to maintain a connection between both struts. In the rear, suspension is comprised of independent struts with the wheels supported by the struts and transverse links. The differential is aligned separately from the wheels through a horizontal leaf spring at its rear and a mounting plate on the front. Incorporated in the strut is a coil spring which suspends the body. Driving power is supplied to the wheels through half shafts. This system makes it possible to separate the three major rear suspension components – the two wheels and differential – and provides the stiff, firm feeling a sports car should have.

However, stiff and firm feelings do not make for good cornering and this is one area where the 240Z could stand some improvement. The first time we took the car to the track it was equipped with the standard wheels, giving the car a front/rear tread of 53.3/53.0 inches. The automobile exhibited a goodly amount of understeer and often wanted to plow right off the corners when pushed too hard. Reaction to a full throttle was decided understeer, while the car lurched into a non-transitional oversteer attitude when the throttle was backed off. On the skid pad the car generated .77 lateral g's left and .72 right, merely acceptable.

We then had the custom wheels mounted. These are available from local Datsun dealers and are made by Ansen, Per Spec Industries, U.S. Mags, Minilite, and Empi. They have 6-inch rims, as opposed to the standard 4½ inches, and increase the car's front/rear tread dimensions to 55.5/54.5 inches. Due to the off-set cambers inherent in custom wheels, the automobile became a little harder to steer but you have to expect that from any sports car. Even with the wheels, the steering was quick, after exerting the necessary effort, and well it should be with a ratio of 17.8:1 from the rack and pinion gears.

As expected, the wider wheels did help out the cornering abilities of the car as it generated .80 lateral g's to the left and .73 to the right. However, there was still a very noticeable tendency towards understeer and body roll was poor, at times creating the sensation that the inside tires were leaving the pavement. The automobile was more agile, however, as it cornered quicker and for this reason alone I would recommend buying the custom wheels. What the 240Z really needs, though, is either an anti-roll bar in the back or stiffer coil springs, which are available from Nissan as well as outside supplies, such as Brock Racing Enterprises. The anti-roll bar increases the tendency towards oversteer and therefore brings the car into an almost neutral attitude during cornering.

DATSUN 240Z

Specifications

Engine	ohc in-line 6-cylinder
Bore & Stroke	3.62 x 2.90 in.
Displacement	2393 cc
Horsepower	151 @ 5,600 rpm
Torque	145.7 lb.-ft. @ 4,400 rpm
Compression ratio	9.0:1/premium fuel
Carburetion	2 SU sidedraught carbs
Transmission	4-speed all synchro
Final drive ratio	3.36:1
Steering type	rack & pinion
Ratio	17.8:1
Turning diameter	31.5 ft. curb-to-curb, 3.5 turns, lock-to-lock
Tires	175 SR 14
Brakes	Disc/Drum
Suspension: front	Independent strut, coil springs, stabilizer bar, transverse link
Suspension: rear	Independent strut, coil springs, transverse link
Body/frame construction	unitized
Dimensions, Weights, Capacities:	
Overall length	162.8 ins.
Overall width	64.1 ins.
Overall height	50.5 ins.
Wheelbase	90.7 ins.
Front track	53.3 ins.
Rear track	53.0 ins.
Curb weight	2325 lbs.
Fuel capacity	15.9 gals.
Oil capacity	8.7 gals.

Performance

Acceleration: (2 aboard)	
0-30 mph	3.45 secs.
0-45 mph	6.0 secs.
0-60 mph	9.4 secs.
0-75 mph	14.0 secs.
Standing Start ¼-mile	83.72 mph, 16.45 secs.
Passing Speeds: (2-3 gear)	
40-60 mph	4.9 secs.
50-70 mph	5.4 secs.
Speed in Gears:	
1st	34.0 mph @ 5,600 rpm
2nd	54.0 mph @ 5,600 rpm
3rd	83.0 mph @ 5,600 rpm
4th	105.5 mph @ 5,000 rpm
MPH per 1000 RPM: 21.1 mph	
Stopping Distances:	
from 30 mph	27.5 ft.
from 60 mph	134.7 ft.
Mileage:	
Range	18.9-24.6 mpg
Average	20.2 mpg

Braking is accomplished through a front disc/rear drum arrangement and provides good, safe stops as long as you don't overdo it. Up front there are 10.67-inch Girling-Sumitomo discs with two pistons operating the pad. The leading/trailing rear drums are equipped with an auto-adjuster for proper proportioning and the drums are finned aluminum to promote quicker cooling. Rear wheel skid during panic stops is controlled by a proportioning valve. From 60 mph the stops were straight and fairly short, 134.7 feet, although the right front wheel would lock up causing the car to lurch from side to side. If you do overdo the brake scene, rear fade sets in but recovery is quick with the aluminum drums.

So what does all this tell us? That Datsun has created a real sports GT which, with very few exceptions, combines good performance with the maximum of comfort. What is more important is that it has been done for a price of $3,601, an admirable job indeed. And with Datsun dealers selling all the 240Z's they can get their hands on, the automobile should be around for a long time. Unless, of course, my intuition is wrong. /MT

240Z

Some 10 months after its release in Japan, the Datsun 240 Z is now available in Australia and at a price around $4600 it should steal a few sales from some of the established prestige names.

WITH ALL this current chat about Supercars, XU-1s, four-barrel Hemis, and things like that, it might come as a shock to the system to find that manufacturers other than the Big Three, are still producing vehicles which exceed 125 mph.

Many manufacturers have been doing it for quite some time — like Jaguar, Aston Martin, Ferrari, Porsche and Maserati — to name a few. To that illustrious list you can now add the Datsun 240Z.

It is claimed that this device has a top speed of 130 mph and, even allowing for the traditional amount of Japanese over-enthusiasm for their own products, there is little doubt that the car will indeed better one-two-five.

That's quick!

But, as we read in all the dailies, "speed isn't everything." And in the case of the Datsun speed certainly isn't all it has to offer.

Styling is smooth and sleek and we'll back it in as one of the best looking sports coupes to be released for quite some time. To add further to our pleasant thoughts on the car is its price — as near as dammit to $4600 which is a long way short of that required for a similarly styled vehicle from the European scene.

Interior layout is strictly sports luxurious.

Directly ahead of the driver are the easily read tacho and speedo, while centrally located on the panel are a further three binnacle shrouded clusters containing auxiliary instrumentation.

The three-spoked, wood-rimmed steering wheel operates a 17.8:1 ratio rack and pinion assembly with light

switches, turn indicators, etc., sprouting from the steering column in standard Japanese fashion.

Ranking high on our list of desirable features for a car of this type is a five-speed gearbox — naturally enough the 240Z has one. A short lever is perfectly positioned on the centre console with the hand-brake sitting between the driver's seat and the console.

The seats themselves are deserving of special mention. Contoured for maximum support, they are vented for air circulation during the hot months, and have a well proportioned headrest. Certainly they look more like custom-made rally accommodation than normal GT seats.

One thing to bear in mind — whereas most coupes lay claim to 2 + 2 accommodation the 240Z makes no bones about it — two seats and that's that.

Mind you, where it may suffer slightly from this lack of accommodation, it more than gains from the fact that not only has it space to carry a tooth-brush, it can also carry a hefty amount of luggage with loading being easily accomplished via the wide rear opening door.

The car itself falls into something of a unique category. It costs considerably less than vehicles such as Porsche, Jaguar and, obviously, Ferrari. It has considerably greater engine capacity (2393 cc) than comparably priced cars like the Lotus Europa and Fiat 124 coupe and it has a greater top speed.

Finish, at least on the car we have seen, is excellent and compares more than favorably with some of the more expensive units. Appearance is a winner — it looks what it is — a luxurious, fast, GT type tourer.

Mechanically it features nothing that is revolutionary; disc brakes up front, drums at the rear — a single overhead camshaft engine with a sensible compression ratio of 9:1 and a horsepower output of 151 at 5600 rpm. Torque is 145 ft./lb. at 4400 rpm — as we said nothing revolutionary.

I think that it is probably in the price range that it comes close to being revolutionary.

When you speak of 130 mph performance, quality finish, sleek styling, and high-speed handling, you usually think of prices from $5000 upwards. There are exceptions to the rule, but not many. The Datsun is one of them. As readers will discover for themselves when they see one of these cars, the 240Z is indeed "something else."

Although it will sell in a limited demand market it is certain to capture sales which previously would have gone to the more expensive marques.

In short, it seems that Datsun has moved into yet another segment of the market long considered the strict domain of the European car. Such is life.

240Z

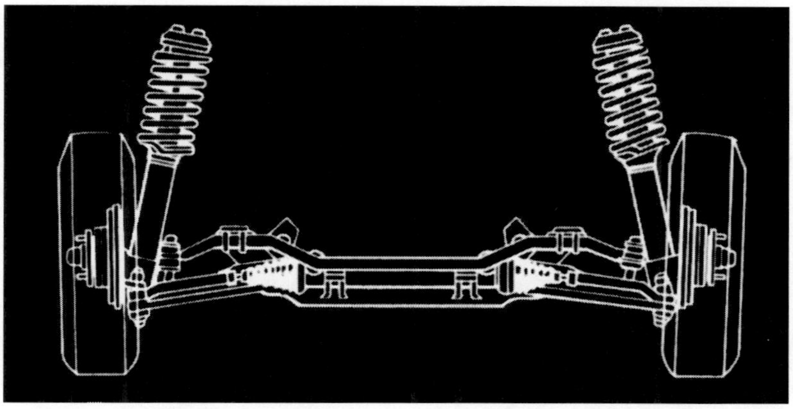

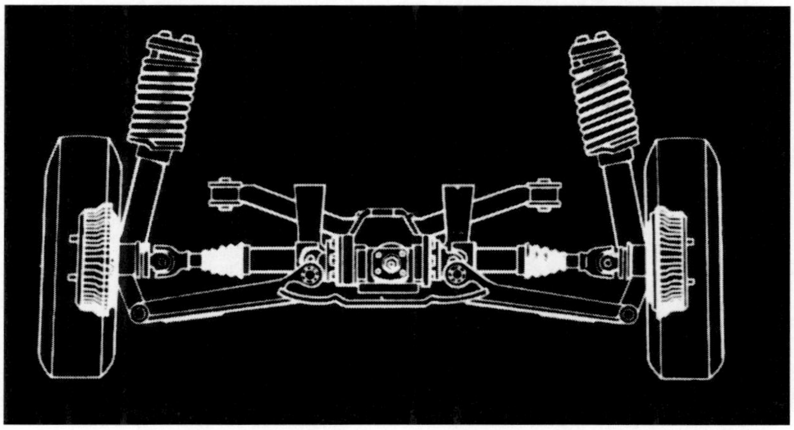

DATA

CAR FROM:
Nissan Motor Co. (Aust.) Pty. Ltd., 210 Victoria St., Melbourne.

PRICE AS TESTED:
$4567

OPTIONS FITTED: nil

ENGINE:

Type	s.o.h.c. six cyl
Bore and Stroke	83 x 73.7 mm
Capacity	2393 cc
Compression ratio	9:1
Power (gross)	151 bhp at 5600 rpm
Torque	145 ft lbs at 4400 rpm

TRANSMISSION:
Five speed manual, all synchro, floor mounted lever

Ratios

1st	2.957:1
2nd	1.858:1
3rd	1.311:1
4th	1:1
5th	0.852:1
Final drive	3.90:1

CHASSIS:

Wheelbase	90.7 inches
Length	162.8 inches
Track F	53.3 inches
Track R	53.0 inches
Width	64.1 inches
Clearance (Minimum)	6.5 inches
Test weight	2260 lbs
Fuel capacity	13.2 gallons
Overall height	50.6 inches

SUSPENSION:
Front: Independent by MacPherson struts, lower trailing links with compression rod, anti roll bar.
Rear: Independent, MacPherson struts, lower trailing links.

BRAKES:
Power assisted
Front: 10.7 inch discs
Rear: 9 inch drums

STEERING:
Type: Rack & Pinion
Ratio: 17.8:1

WHEELS/TYRES:
Steel disc wheels fitted 165HR x 14 radials.

PERFORMANCE:
Zero to

30 mph	3.8 seconds
40 mph	5.4 seconds
50 mph	7.0 seconds
60 mph	9.1 seconds
70 mph	11.6 seconds
80 mph	15.1 seconds
90 mph	22.4 seconds
100 mph	NA

Standing quarter mile 16.4 seconds.
Fuel consumption on test 22 mpg on S fuel.
Fuel consumption (expected) 25-30 mpg.
Cruising range 300 miles (approx.)

Speedometer error:

Indicated	30	40	50	60	70	80	90	100
Actual	30	38	47	56	65	74	81	NA

MAXIMUM SPEEDS IN GEARS:

1st.	36 mph at 6700 rpm
2nd.	63 mph at 6700 rpm
3rd.	87 mph at 6700 rpm
4th.	118 mph at 6700 rpm (estimate)
5th.	126 mph at 6000 rpm (estimate)

DATSUN'S NEW EXPORT WEAPON

Anthony Curtis drives the 240Z, an elegant new import but no E-type eater.

The first example of a new secret weapon in the Japanese invasion was slipped into Britain a few weeks ago by Datsun UK Ltd in the form of the 240Z, a sports coupe powered by a 2.4 litre six-cylinder sohc engine. The car has two comfortable seats, with behind them a large luggage space accessible through a lift-up tailgate. We were lucky enough to be able to borrow this car for a short time to record some initial road impressions pending a full test later on.

The 240Z is new only in this country, it was first announced in October 1969 at the Tokyo Show and has been selling well in the US for some time. And as sports enthusiasts will be aware, it has already begun to build itself a reputation through competition in a way that should help to increase its European sales. Although three of the four cars entered for the RAC rally dropped out in the early stages through final drive failure the survivor finished 7th. Another finished a creditable 6th in the Monte and others may appear in the Safari.

Whatever the rally circus may believe, it is unfair and inaccurate to categorize the 240Z by saying that "the big Healey is alive and well and living in Japan". Almost the only resemblance between the Datsun and the Healey is in having a front mounted six cylinder engine. It differs in its spaciousness, for example, and in the completeness of its equipment which make it a very practical long-distance, high-speed tourer for two. Moreover its rack-and-pinion steering and all-independent MacPherson strut suspension give it excellent handling and roadholding. In profile its styling is crisp and modern; full-face it is pleasant but a trifle tall, narrow and high off the ground for a sports car.

In Japan the 240Z is krcwn as the Nissan Fairlady Z where it is normally powered by a 2 litre sohc six developing 130 bhp (gross). It is also available with an entirely different 2 litre dohc 24-valve six which puts out 160 bhp. This engine was developed through Japanese saloon car racing by Prince Motors before they became absorbed into the Nissan group, and is also fitted to a GT-R variant of the Nissan Skyline hardtop. Export cars, however, have an enlarged 2.4 litre version of the "cooking" sohc unit which produces 151 bhp (gross) at 5600 rpm, using twin Japanese SUs.

As our test car had covered only 1000 miles we were restricted to a maximum of 5500 rpm, to which limit the engine revved sweetly and smoothly. It is at just this point, however, that the 2-litre home-market engine become particularly frenzied, according to Paul Frère who drove one in Japan and found the 7000 rpm red line ridiculously ambitious. As the increased capacity has been obtained by raising both the bore and stroke, the bigger engine remains comfortably oversquare, so there is no reason to believe that the 240Z will be any worse. We shall have to wait for a full road test to properly establish whether this genetic defect has been passed on to the 240Z.

High-back seats with enveloping squabs give good support, and the driving position and controls are good. Right: new shape for British roads—and an expensive one at about £2,300

In other respects this six cylinder unit is admirable. Though it is not as smooth as the Jaguar engine, it is very quiet and will pull without hesitation from 1000 rpm in fifth, strongly from 2500 rpm. The still-tight engine would comfortably pull an indicated 115 mph or so in top at our 5500 rpm limit, so the manufacturer's claimed 129 mph maximum speed shouldn't be too far off the mark. The car is said to weight around 1 ton, and we'd guess it to be rather quicker than a 3 litre Capri with a 0-60 mph acceleration time of around 9 sec.

The five-speed manual gearbox has a floor lever moving in the Alfa pattern with

fifth forwards and closest to the driver. Its ratios are well spaced and its action was reasonably light and precise except into first, perhaps because of newness. The throttle linkage, however, was very sticky and unprogressive, making smooth changes difficult. Like some other Datsun gearboxes, the transmission was very noisy in first, second and third, particularly third. Almost more irritating is the very marked rumble that builds up from 65 mph onwards and could be caused by bearing trouble rather than propshaft whirl as it is more apparent at lower speeds than high.

An unusual feature for a Japanese car is the rack-and-pinion steering, the use of which pays immediate dividends in precision and good feel: there is much less of the vagueness in the straight ahead position so often a characteristic of cars from Japan. At parking speeds the steering is perhaps a little heavy, though quite tolerable. But once on the road it becomes acceptably light; it is also fairly direct and responsive. Excellent adhesion in the dry with very little squeal is provided by the big 175-SR-14 Bridgestone radials which, unlike most Japanese tyres, did not seem unduly sensitive to the damp as far as we could tell from our limited experience of it. The lack of roll helps the MacPherson struts used at each end to keep the wheels at the right angles to the ground, though the car becomes rather lurchy when the tail loses grip on slow corners. The brakes (discs/drums) were progressive in action and did not fade.

The ride of the 240Z is not as good as its all-independent suspension should make it. It is knobbly at low speeds, fair on single wheel bumps, but badly caught out, especially at the rear, by waves or humps. Similarly a good deal of road noise is transmitted to the interior, road roar often being the predominant sound which drowns the engine at speed. Wind noise would be quite low were it not for a sealing hiss from the windows. We were not keen on the heating and ventilating which could be set to either one or the other but not both, and which leaked air to the footwells when set to defrost.

These defects are partially redeemed by the comfortable seats, which offer good lumbar and lateral support. The high backrests can be tilted through a small angle and the range of fore-and-aft adjustment is more than adequate for the tallest European driver. This roominess is matched by the size of the flat floor behind the seats on which a good deal of luggage can be stowed. The rear strut mountings intrude into the area but help to form little niches on either side in which objects can be retained, though there is a small tray on the transmission tunnel as well as a lockable glovebox and luggage straps are a standard fitting. This is just one of the many thoughtful features of the full set of equipment. Others are the inspection lamp under the bonnet, the clearly labelled fusebox on the transmission tunnel under the cigar lighter surround, the built-in towing hooks at each end, plus a full complement of armrests, coathooks and ashtrays.

We also liked the clear instruments, English in general style, but deeply recessed with angled glasses to prevent unwanted reflection. Better still was the combination stalk with a twist-round and press-in end that controls the lights, wipers and washers—just the sort of ergonomic arrangement we like. At the proposed price of around £2300 including the five-speed gearbox as a standard fitting, the 240Z should find a ready market. ■

AUTOTEST

DATSUN 240Z (2,393 c.c.)

AT-A-GLANCE: Excellent sports coupé from major Japanese manufacturer. High performance from lusty engine and excellent ratios in five-speed gearbox. Comfortable seating, but driving position more suitable for large men. Heavy but well-harmonised controls. Good handling; poor heating and ventilation system.

MANUFACTURER
Nissan Motor Co. Ltd., 2 Otemachi Building, Otemachi, Chiyoda-Ka, Tokyo, Japan.

UK CONCESSIONAIRES
Nissan-Datsun (UK) Ltd., 54-62 Regent St., London W.1.

PRICES

Basic	£1,751.00
Purchase Tax	£537.33
Total (in G.B.)	£2,288.33
PRICE AS TESTED	£2,288.33

PERFORMANCE SUMMARY

Mean maximum speed	125 mph
Standing ¼-mile	15.8 sec
0-60 mph	8.0 sec
30-70 mph through gears	8.4 sec
Typical fuel consumption	24 mpg
Miles per tankful	320

EVERYONE knows that nowadays it is hopelessly uneconomic to try to design a new sports car for mass production. Everyone, that is, except Datsun, whose 240Z appeared at the 1969 Tokyo motor show and is now in large-scale production, primarily for the American market. It is being supplied to some other markets as well, and is shortly to go on sale in Britain. It would have been eagerly awaited in any case, but its one-two success in the East African Safari Rally has really whetted British sporting appetites.

One main difference between the American-standard car and the one which will be sold by Datsun UK dealers is that over here, a five-speed gearbox will be standard. In return, some of the interior equipment in the American version has been deleted.

On paper, the 240Z looks quite tame. Its layout is thoroughly conventional, with a straight-six, 2.4-litre engine producing a claimed 151bhp (SAE) at a modest 5,600rpm. Datsun do not quote a DIN figure, but clearly this is going to give a specific output of less than 60bhp per litre, so the engine is not all that highly stressed.

Drive is taken through the five-speed gearbox (with overdrive top gear) to a 3.90 final drive. Suspension is by MacPherson struts at the front, and—less conventionally—at the rear as well. Disc brakes are used at the front, and radial-ply tyres are standard for the British market.

Although it is strictly a two-seater, the 240Z is quite big and heavy; getting on for 14ft long, it turns the scales at 20.4cwt with a half-full tank.

Excellent performance

As almost always the case in cars with SU-type carburettors, starting was easy. When the engine was cold, it was necessary to churn away for a second or two, but then it would come to life without fail. Once the engine was warm, starting took no more than a single twist of the key. Warming up was quick, but until a reading started to show on the gauge, engine response was a little hesitant.

If anything, performance is better than one would expect for the stated output of the engine. Two factors which help to make it so are the engine's splendid torque curve, and the excellently chosen ratios in the five-speed box. It proved possible to trickle the car along in fifth gear at 10mph or so, which was an enormous help in town driving. Full throttle could be applied in this gear from 20mph without any protest from the transmission, and the stepless nature of the torque curve can be seen from the way the 20mph increments in fifth are less than a second apart until 80mph is reached. Even then, there is no suggestion of a sudden limit to the car's powers of acceleration.

In the same way, there was no sign of the engine running into a rev limit once it was over its 5,600rpm power peak. The rev counter set the limit at 6,500rpm, and the engine would run to this and beyond if it was allowed to. It became noisier above 5,500rpm or so, but never started to feel rough. Allowing ourselves a momentary overspeed, we found that the car would comfortably exceed 40mph in first gear, with an indicated 70mph coming up in second and an indicated 100mph in third—with two gears still to come. Maximum speed in fourth, the direct-drive gear, gave us a mean of 117mph, equivalent to an engine speed well over the power peak, so it seems that the fall-off of power on the far side of the curve is only gradual. In the overdrive fifth gear we reached a mean maximum of 125mph, with the engine just over the power peak at 5,750rpm.

With massive torque, and gearing as intelligent as this, it was hardly surprising that the standing-start acceleration times were

The styling of the 240Z is attractive, and excited obvious admiration wherever it went; at least one onlooker thought it was a Ferrari. The good ground clearance and lack of projections on the underside show up here. With its relatively low build the car is not all that easy to get into, although the big doors help. The rear quarter panels do not interfere too much with the view, but the high-backed seats are rather obstructive

AUTOTEST DATSUN 240Z . . .

good. We found the actual start no problem at all; the clutch was let in smartly at 4,000rpm and the car leapt off the line, leaving a few yards of rubber on the road. Juggling with revs and clutch engagement produced no improvement on the 0-30mph time, which stayed obstinately at 3sec. From here on, progress was rapid indeed. We found it worth hanging on to each gear as long as possible with the result that 60 mph was reached in 8 sec exactly while still in second gear, and third gear, taken just before 70mph, whisked the car to 80mph in under 15sec, past the quarter-mile mark in under 16sec, and on to 100mph in less than 26sec. We reckon that any kilometre time under half a minute is the mark of a fast car; the Datsun managed to pass it in 27.7sec, doing 102mph.

To put things in perspective, the Datsun is quicker than any of the cars with which we have compared it, with the exception of the Jaguar E-type 4.2-litre. The Porsche 911T beats it on maximum speed but cannot match its acceleration times. Nor can the Triumph TR6.

Considering the weight of the Datsun and its performance potential, it is also surprisingly economical, although again, the remarkable E-type beats it by a short head. An overall consumption of 21.4mpg is quite an achievement; the best brim-to-brim figure we saw was 24.5. Our steady-speed consumption figures show why; unlike some high-performance engines, the Datsun unit has no disastrous hole at the low speed end of the fuel curve, achieving 40mpg at 40mph. Town driving therefore does not harm it the way it does the Porsche, for instance. At the other end of the scale, the fair aerodynamic shape shows up in the figure of 24mpg at a steady 80mph.

Handling and brakes

One would expect the 240Z to be a nose-heavy beast. In fact, the engine is not as heavy as it looks and is mounted quite a long way back, with the result that only 51.4 per cent of the dry weight rests on the front wheels. With two occupants, the balance is more likely to be the other way round, explaining why the same tyre pressures are recommended front and rear.

Datsun have actually achieved very consistent handling characteristics which remain just on the understeer side of neutral as long as the driver restrains his right foot. Aside from the even weight distribution, the very low roll angles must help to make this consistency possible. Driven smoothly, the car can be cornered very fast indeed. Our test car was fitted with Japanese Bridgestone radials, which held the road better than any Japanese tyres we have tried. On dry surfaces, the car would eventually slide sideways with all four wheels together, but this only happened when cornering faster than the average driver would ever dream of trying. When the roads were wet, the limit was lower, and the front wheels would lose their grip first.

There was, of course, quite enough torque available to provoke oversteer, especially in second or third gear (which were used far more than the others in fast driving along secondary roads). The tail could thus be pushed along way out of line without actually sliding in the full sense, and with the car still under full control. On a wet road the driver was even more tempted to take advantage of this behaviour, because it meant that the tendency of the front tyres to unstick was greatly reduced, making

The view through the back door, which lifts to provide access to the luggage space in the manner of the Triumph GT6, shows the high-backed front seats, the bulges in the carpeted platform caused by the tops of the rear MacPherson struts, and the luggage straps—a nice piece of detail thinking

The 240Z instrument panel is modern and comprehensive but rather plainly finished. The steering wheel is wood-rimmed, and there is a wooden gear lever knob. The controls on the centre console aft of the gear lever are the choke and hand throttle, the latter acting over the whole range of throttle travel

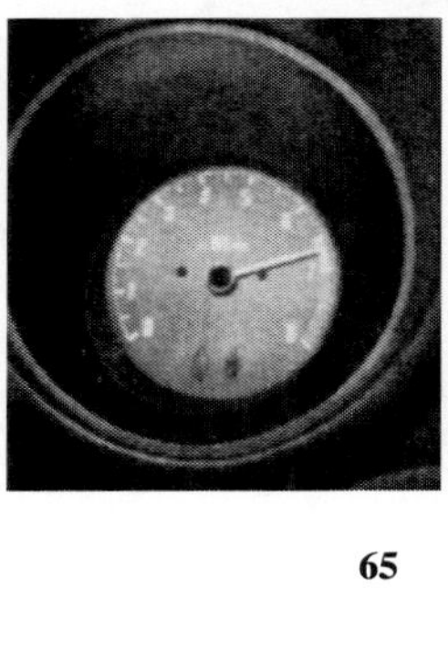

In established Japanese tradition, access to the big engine and all its surrounding parts is very simple. Maker's confidence in the engine is shown by the rev counter (left), yellow-lined at 6,500rpm and red-lined at 7,000

the handling more predictable.

The rack and pinion steering was most un-Japanese in its directness and instant response, helped by very high gearing (2.7 turns between extremes of a good 32ft lock). Inevitably, it was fairly heavy at low speeds and when parking.

As with the steering, so with the brakes, which were progressive but heavy, and stood up to our fade test very well. Gentle check braking could be achieved without a great deal of effort, but at the top end the brakes got much heavier and the ultimate stop of just over 1g indicated took a hefty 120lb shove on the pedal. The handbrake was poor, giving a feeble emergency stop when used on the level, and failing to hold the car on the 1-in-3 test hill. A restart on this hill was possible with the aid of some clutch slip, despite the high first gear.

Comfort and convenience

When one actually approaches the 240Z with the idea of getting into it, one realizes that it is not as big as first impressions suggest. The doors are wide, but the roofline is low and so are the seats, making it easier to get in than to get out, especially if one wishes to do it gracefully.

Once inside, the driver realizes, again with surprise, that the car is more suited to big people than small ones. The seats go back a very long way, and our tallest driver had no trouble at all making himself comfortable. Our shorter testers, on the other hand, found the seats set low enough to restrict their vision, and ended up able to see only two-thirds of the bonnet. In other directions, there are visibility problems for most occupants, principally caused by the intrusion of the high-backed seats. Wing mirrors would be almost essential for a driver who was going to use this car in town a good deal.

The seats are sculptured to provide excellent support, and have backrests which are adjustable through a small range of angles. All the driving controls are well placed. The pedals are a good size and well separated, and it is possible to heel-and-toe very nicely. The steering wheel is well placed and not too large, while the gear lever is short and mounted on the centre console with the handbrake just behind it. Lamps and wipers are controlled from a single column-mounted switch cluster; very nice ergonomic design. For the most part, the controls are well harmonized. As we have already said, the brakes and steering are both heavy but progressive. So is the clutch, which needs a 33lb push to free it, applied over 6in. of travel. The gearchange is precise but hardly fingerlight, although it feels substantial enough to put up with being pushed around. The whole impression is one of a man's car, which the average woman would find a bit of a handful in many respects. One thing which lets the car down is the accelerator linkage, which was sticky and non-progressive on our car, making it much more difficult to drive smoothly than it need have been.

The ride is poor at low speeds, with more of a feeling of over-damping than of over-springing. This pays off higher up the speed range, however, for as the car goes faster so the ride feels better, even over quite poor surfaces. The rear suspension does get caught out by undulating surfaces at some speeds, but the car feels immensely strong and able to put up with a good deal of abuse. For a sports car, it has very good ground clearance, and the underside is relatively smooth, clearly part of its rally inheritance.

The overall noise level is high, with mechanical, road and wind noise all playing their part. We suspected that the wind noise was due to sub-standard sealing on our car, but

ACCELERATION

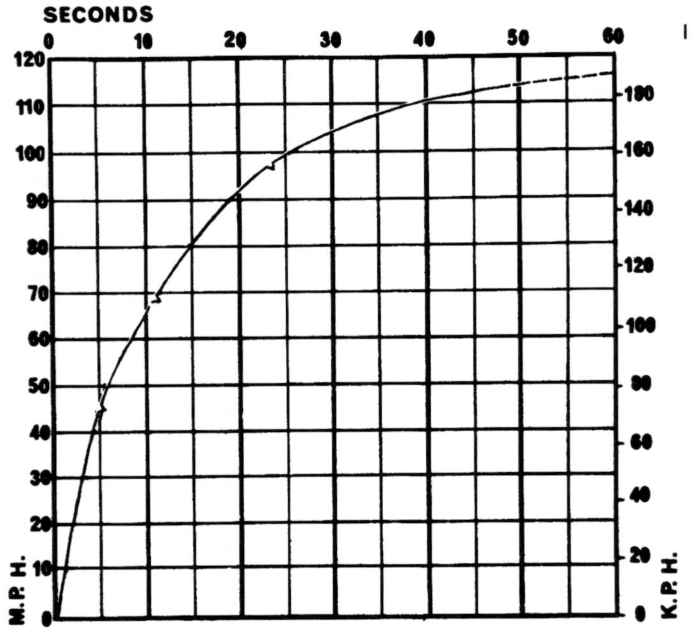

SPEED MPH TRUE	INDICATED	TIME IN SECS
30	30	3.0
40	41	4.6
50	51	6.0
60	62	8.0
70	73	11.4
80	84	14.8
90	95	19.2
100	106	25.6
110	117	

SPEED RANGE, GEAR RATIOS AND TIME IN SECONDS

mph	Top (3.32)	4th (3.90)	3rd (5.11)	2nd (7.24)	1st (11.52)
10–30	—	8.2	5.9	4.1	2.6
20–40	9.7	7.5	5.7	3.5	2.7
30–50	9.4	7.0	5.2	3.6	—
40–60	9.7	7.2	4.8	3.8	—
50–70	10.2	7.7	5.4	5.1	—
60–80	10.9	8.0	6.0	—	—
70–90	12.1	8.6	8.2	—	—
80–100	14.2	10.5	—	—	—

Standing ¼-mile
15.8 sec 82 mph

Standing kilometre
27.7 sec 102 mph

Test distance
1,170 miles

Mileage recorder
1 per cent
under-reading

PERFORMANCE

MAXIMUM SPEEDS

Gear	mph	kph	rpm
Top (mean)	125	201	5,750
(best)	126	203	5,850
4th (mean)	117	188	6,380
(best)	118	190	6,440
3rd	98	157	7,000
2nd	69	111	7,000
1st	44	71	7,000

BRAKES

(from 70 mph in neutral)
Pedal load for 0.5g stops in lb

1	40-45	6	50-55
2	45	7	55
3	45	8	55-60
4	45-50	9	55-60
5	50	10	55-60

RESPONSE (from 30 mph in neutral)

Load	g	Distance
20lb	0.24	125ft
40 lb	0.50	60ft
60 lb	0.69	44ft
80 lb	0.80	38ft
100 lb	0.96	31ft
120 lb	1.02	29.4ft
Handbrake	0.17	177ft

Max. Gradient 1 in 4

CLUTCH

Pedal 33 lb and 6in.

MOTORWAY CRUISING

Indicated speed at 70 mph . . . . 73 mph
Engine (rpm at 70 mph) . . . . 3,250 rpm
(mean piston speed) . . . . . 1,570 ft/min.
Fuel (mpg at 70 mph) . . . . 27.2 mpg
Passing (50-70 mph) . . . . 10.2 sec

COMPARISONS

MAXIMUM SPEED MPH

Jaguar E-type 4.2 coupé . . (£2,711) 140
Porsche 911T . . . . (£3,671 129

Datsun 240Z . . . . (£2,288) 125
Mercedes 280SL coupé . . . (£4,570) 121
Triumph TR6 coupé . . . . . (£1,498) 119

0-60 MPH, SEC

Jaguar E-type 4.2 . . . . 7.4
Datsun 240Z 8.0
Porsche 911T 8.1
Triumph TR6 . . . . 8.2
Mercedes 280SL 9.3

STANDING ¼-MILE, SEC

Jaguar E-type 4.2 . . . . 15.0
Datsun 240Z 15.8
Porsche 911T 16.0
Triumph TR6 . . . . 16.3
Mercedes 280SL 17.0

OVERALL MPG

Jaguar E-type 4.2 . . . . 21.8
Datsun 240Z 21.4
Triumph TR6 . . . . 19.8
Mercedes 280SL 19.0
Porsche 911T 17.9

GEARING (with 175-14in. tyres)

Top . . . . 21.55 mph per 1,000 rpm
4th . . . . 18.35 mph per 1,000 rpm
3rd . . . . 14.00 mph per 1,000 rpm
2nd . . . . 9.90 mph per 1,000 rpm
1st . . . . 6.20 mph per 1,000 rpm

TEST CONDITIONS:
Weather: Dull, snow flurries. Wind: 5 mph. Temperature: 0 deg. C. (32 deg. F). **Barometer** 29.5in. hg. Humidity: 60 per cent. Surfaces: dry concrete and asphalt.

WEIGHT:
Kerb weight 20.4 cwt (2,284lb—1,038kg) (with oil, water and half full fuel tank). Distribution, per cent F, 51.4; R, 48.6. Laden as tested: 24.9cwt (2,784lb—1,265kg).

TURNING CIRCLES:
Between kerbs L, 33ft 6in; R, 32ft 10in. Between Walls L, 35ft 2in.; R, 34ft 6in. steering wheel turns, lock to lock 2.7

Figures taken at 2,500 miles by our own staff at the Motor Industry Research Association proving ground at Nuneaton.

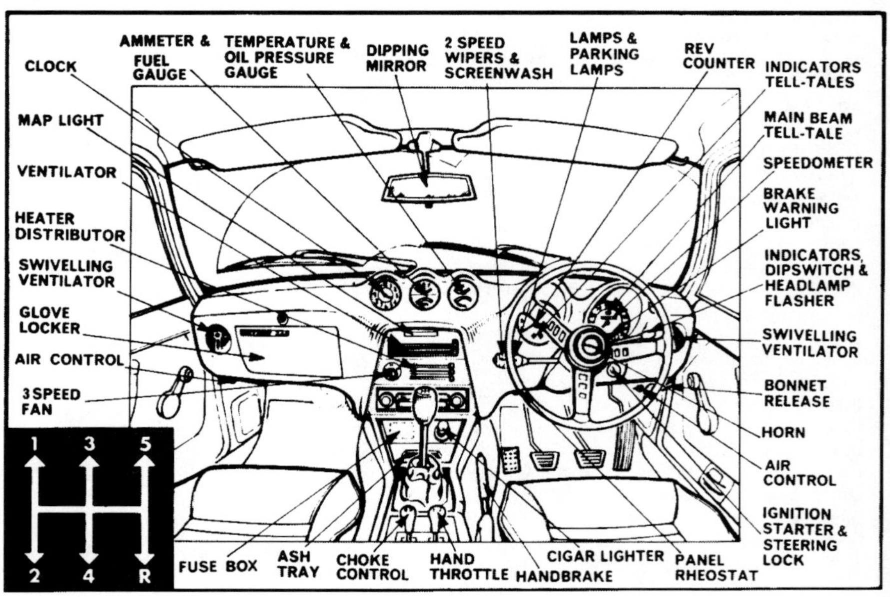

CONSUMPTION

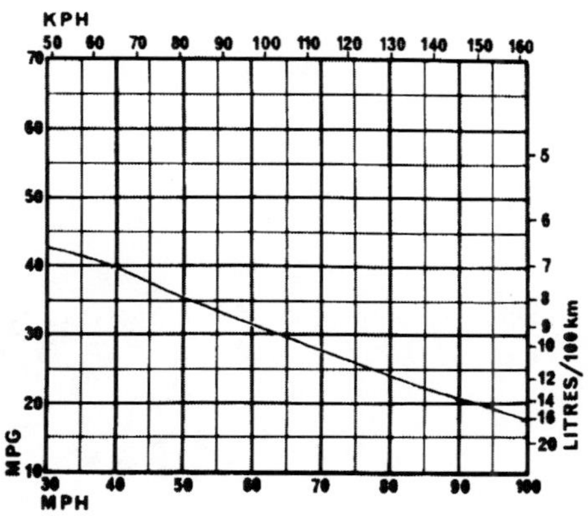

FUEL

(At constant speeds—mpg)

30 mph	42.6
40 mph	40.0
50 mph	35.4
60 mph	31.5
70 mph	27.2
80 mph	24.0
90 mph	20.4
100 mph	17.9

Typical mpg	24 (11.8 litres/100km)
Calculated (DIN) mpg	24.7 (11.4 litres/100km)
Overall mpg	21.4 (13.2 litres/100km)
Grade of fuel	Premium, 4-star (min. 98 RM)

OIL

Miles per pint (SAE 10W-40) . . . . negligible

SPECIFICATION FRONT ENGINE, REAR WHEEL DRIVE

ENGINE

Cylinders	6, in line
Main bearings	7
Cooling system	Water, pump, fan and thermostat
Bore	83.0mm (3.26in.)
Stroke	73.7mm (2.90 in.)
Displacement	2,393 c.c. (146 cu.in.)
Valve gear	Single overhead camshaft
Compression ratio	9.0-to-1 Min. octane rating: 98RM
Carburettors	2 Hitachi (SU type)
Fuel pump	Nikki mechanical
Oil filter	Full flow, replaceable
Max. power	151 bhp (SAE) at 5,600 rpm
Max. torque	146 lb.ft. (SAE) at 4,400 rpm

TRANSMISSION

Clutch	Single dry plate, diaphragm-spring
Gearbox	5-speed, all-synchromesh
Gear ratios	Top 0.85
	Fourth 1.0
	Third 1.31
	Second 1.86
	First 2.96
	Reverse 2.99
Final drive	Hypoid bevel, ratio 3.90-to-1

CHASSIS and BODY

Construction	Integral, with steel body

SUSPENSION

Front	Independent, MacPherson struts, lower links, coil springs, telescopic dampers, anti-roll bar
Rear	Independent, MacPherson struts, lower wishbones, coil springs, telescopic dampers

STEERING

Type	Rack and pinion
Wheel dia.	15.0 in.

BRAKES

Make and type	Girling, disc front, drum rear
Servo— make and type	Bendix vacuum

WHEELS

Type	Pressed steel disc, 4-stud fixing 4.5 in. wide rim.
Tyres—make	Bridgestone
type	Speed 20 radial ply/tubeless
size	175-14 in.

EQUIPMENT

Battery	12 Volt 50 Ah
Alternator	Hitachi 42 amp a.c.
Headlamps	Roito 150/100 watt (total)
Reversing lamp	Standard
Electric fuses	10
Screen wipers	2
Screen washer	Standard, electric
Interior heater	Standard
Heated backlight	Extra
Safety belts	Standard
Interior trim	pvc seats and headlining
Floor covering	Carpet
Jack	Screw scissor type
Jacking points	1 each side under sill
Windscreen	Laminated
Underbody protection	Phosphor treatment prior to painting

MAINTENANCE

Fuel tank	13.2 Imp. gallons (60 litres)
Cooling system	18 pints (including heater)
Engine sump	8.8 pints (5.0 litres) SAE 20W-50. Change oil every 3,000 miles. Change filter every 6,000 miles.
Gearbox	4.5 pints SAE 80 EP check level every 3,000 miles
Final drive	2 pints SAE 90 EP. Check level every 6,000 miles
Grease	2 points every 24,000 miles
Tyre pressures	F 28; R 28 psi (normal driving) F 32; R 32 psi (fast driving)
Max. payload	420 lb. (190 kg)

PERFORMANCE DATA

Top gear mph per 1,000 rpm	21.6
Mean piston speed at max. power	2,710 ft/min
Bhp per ton laden	121 (SAE)

STANDARD GARAGE 16ft x 8ft 6in.

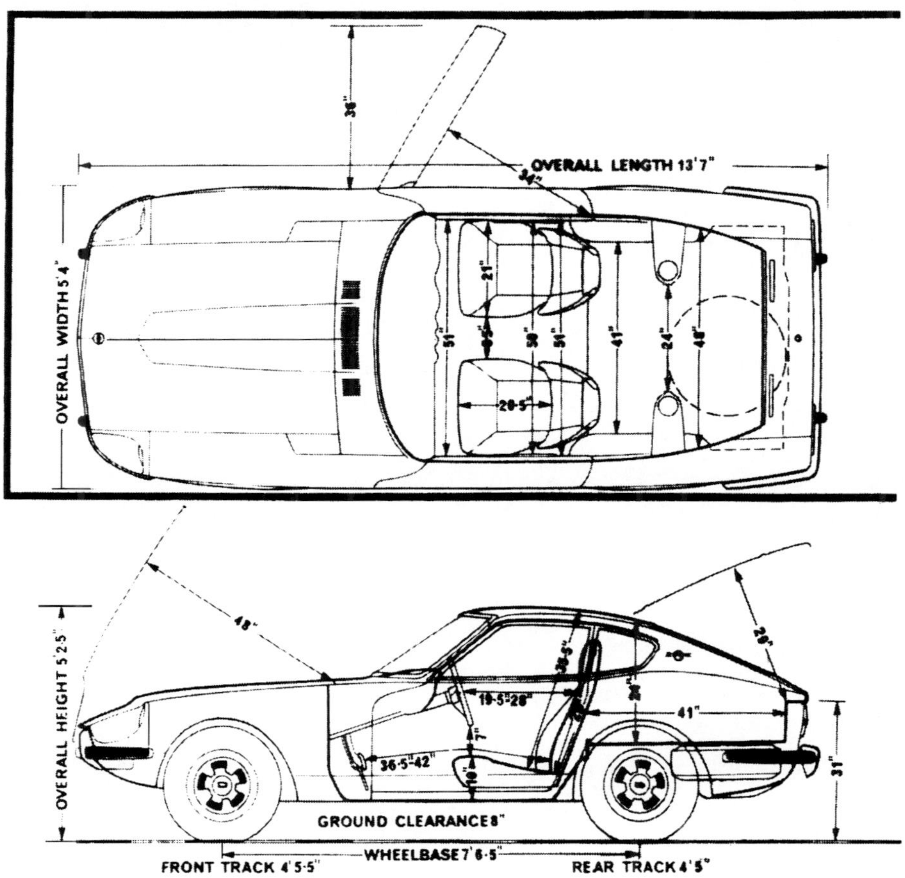

SCALE 0.3in. to 1ft
Cushions uncompressed

there was no denying the intensity of tyre roar on some surfaces. Most sporting drivers will be pleased by the purposeful roar of the engine, but the transmission whine, especially in the lower gears, will be less welcome. Our car also suffered from a driveline rumble which came in at around 3,300rpm: this unfortunately happens to be 70mph in fifth gear.

Although the control layout was liked and the instruments were rated satisfactory by all our drivers, the general design of the interior met with less approval. There was a feeling that it was too obviously plastic, and too simply put together, to be right for a car in this class—perhaps more in tune with American tastes than our own. One other thing which attracted adverse comment was the poor heating and ventilation system, which appeared to give a choice of one or the other, especially annoying when the water-valve heater gave such an all-or-nothing response.

Filling a need

There is a tendency to describe the Datsun as the natural successor to the big Healey. Perhaps it is; but it is so much more comfortable, so much roomier, and so much better-handling that comparisons are difficult. There is no denying, however, that the character is there. We would prefer to think of the 240Z as exemplifying what the MGC should (and might) have been. It is not a faultless car by any means, but in Britain, which has always had an appreciation for genuine sports cars, it is bound to find a market even at its relatively high price. □

DATSUN 240Z

Lively performance, a sophisticated all-independent suspension AND stunning good looks make Datsun's 240Z a $4600 bargain

WE find the handsome Datsun 240Z a little hard to place on the fragmented Australian market and feel it falls between two stools. Maybe it is unfair of us to categorise this car — which could be fore-runner of a new class of low-cost GT machinery.

But on current analysis the 240Z would not be sufficiently exotic for the jet-setters, (requiring a car for little more than decoration of their Toorak Road/Darling Point carport), nor the die-hard club racer who will find the ultimate handling clumsy and the engine's specific output for weight not quite up to the mark.

What then, is this wide-application compromise called 240Z?

It's an all-new car from Datsun released in Japan at the Tokyo show, October 1969 as the 1600 Silvia. It has since evolved as a 2.4 litre — not the Datsun 2400 Super Six engine nor a rejuvenated Skyline GTB two-litre (Datsun and Prince amalgamated some years ago) but an all new sohc six based on the 1600 cc four. The cylinder sizes, single overhead cam valve gear and cast-iron block with alloy head are all identical to the 1600 specification but two extra pots take the capacity out to 2393 cc for a 151 bhp rating at 5600 rpm and 145.7 lb.ft. of torque at 4400 rpm.

There is a five-speed gearbox, again based on the 1600 with strengthening and different ratios, while the suspension is independent all round, the brakes disc front, drum rear and the front engine rear drive layout quite conventional with 52.4/47.6 weight distribution.

Pandering to American taste, the cockpit is a working exercise in Naderism and pressure moulded plastics. The dash is disarmingly plain, with two deeply-recessed dials for speedo and tacho and three dash-top recesses. Such is the angling and sunken dials that the passenger is kept in oblivious innocence of the Zee's stirrings.

One dial is a clock, the other two combination gauges show oil, fuel, water, amps.

The whole approach is almost aeronautic, right down to the centre console with pull-back slides for choke and hand throttle, reminiscent of aircraft throttle controls.

By neatly stowing map light, centre ventilator, heater controls, radio, cigarette lighter and ashtray in a console ahead of the gearshift, there are vast expanses of uncluttered dash area. Lights, washers and wipers are all grouped at the end of a left side column stalk and are easy to use if not offering fingertip control.

There's no headlight flasher but the indicators are on the right and the strangled-sounding horn comes with a push of the awkward centre, Mustang-like, boss.

Drop into this cockpit and you have a classic driving position. The seats have a headrest extension built-in, the accelerator pedal has a long pad, the gearlever is where it should be and there's fresh air "eyeball" ventilation (from the 1600,) just to keep you cool.

Initial driving impressions show the twin (Hitachi) SU carburetted 2.4 six is quite cammy but smooth, the gearbox/clutch integration annoyingly jerky, but the ride superb.

Even when we had mastered smoothing the gearshift (and that took constant concentration for smooth,

MODERN MOTOR road TEST

DATSUN 240Z

slow-running), the Datsun became no easier to drive, in fact by the end of our test admittedly mostly traffic conditions, the Zee's charm had long disappeared for us.

The best part of the whole car is the excellent rear suspension which gives a soft ride with safe and controlled handling.

It was easy to squirt along with great bursts of acceleration but considerably harder to dribble along smoothly. Despite its capacity, the overhead cam six only gets "with-it" after 4000 rpm and then rushes through to the redline at 7000 rpm. There's little low speed torque and the Datsun only achieves its dramatic acceleration times with some hard driving — upon which it thrives. The heavy-handed driver should like the strong response to quite brutal treatment.

The test car had convex rear vision wing mirrors which, with a wide inside mirror to match the back window, a panoramic windscreen and no quarter vents gave clear all-round vision. It is unnecessary for the driver to swing around (except for backing) to position his car accurately in traffic or parking. The tall seats are no worry.

Although the gear shift is anything but brilliant, the ratios are well spaced and the overdrive fifth good for expressways. The shift is slow and the synchros obstructive rather than protective. The engine is quiet but will protest when revs run low on the higher ratios.

Using the gears liberally, the fuel figure was reasonable at 23.8 mpg and at worse will drop little under 20.

Revved through the ratios, we thought the 240Z sounded not unlike the Torana XU-1 with its crisp, hard six cylinder note.

In the Japanese industry, Datsun leads the way in independent rear suspension design — and the all new 240Z is no exception. Both front and back, the Datsun uses coil-strut towers — the front a typical MacPherson arrangement of lower A-arm supporting the coil/shocker unit and a link-type anti-roll bar. The exception is a trailing strut to brace the A-arm's lateral movement.

The rear is also a MacPherson set-up, or more correctly a Chapman rear end as it follows in essence the Lotus Elan configuration. The hub carrier is located on a very wide-base A-arm with the strut attached to the rear, and, at the top, inside the luggage area. The front A-arm pivot point is a strong cross-member but at the rear a frail-looking steel hanger holds the pivot point. A further pressed steel bracket supports the diff. housing at the rear, while the front is supported on the same crossmember as the front A-arm pivot. Drive is taken from a 3.7 to 1 Dana Spicer free differential via double universalled drive-shafts to the drum-braked rear wheels.

Overall the suspension gives a superb ride with road feel in the E-Type class — though a little too rubbery to give the precision of a Porsche. The front A-arms are rubber bushed and bolted to a separate rubber-insulated sub-assembly which in turn is attached to the chassis rails.

However the heavily canted spring towers control front camber and compliance to reduce any understeer. The rear suspension is ideally suited to Australian roads as it runs stiffer-rate shocks, is set higher and in direct comparison to the Jaguar's similar set-up, bottoms less.

Traction is so good we thought the car had a limited slip diff. The engine's torque curve also helps as there's no low speed brute torque to initiate wheelspin where the Powr-Lock diff is essential to get instant spread of torque from the Jaguar's flexible muscles.

However it is a feather in Datsun's cap that the Zee can be compared to the E, nearly twice the price!

When you do get the Datsun on cam and force power through the back wheels there is the tremendous sensation of controlled traction like the E-Type. Both cars will just sit their backsides into a corner and GO.

Like radial tyres, the breakaway point is less progressive. Because the back tyres dig-in under lateral forces (rather than sliding predictably like a well located live axle), a high-speed slide or spin could be a heart-stopping experience.

In the wet a power tail-slide is easy to control and fun but there are high lateral G-forces at the breakaway point in the dry.

Generally the Zee's handling is very secure, safe and inspiring. The test car was shod with Australian Dunlop SP radials. There was little squeal even when taking maximum advantage of the handling. Ride is very smooth with a feeling of solidarity. The 14-inch wheels will absorb major trauma without flinching — or unseating the passenger. That standard of compliance is hard to achieve while compromising for sports car handling and Nissan deserve full marks in the suspension and ride departments.

The only regression is a trifle too much "walk" at high speed, which suggests favouring low speed bump traction and ride rather than high speed stability. The same is true of an E-Type compared to the Porsche 911E.

The Datsun develops an unnerving "walk" at around 95 mph, the Jaguar at around 120 mph whereas you just don't find the limit in a Porsche.

This "walk" is closely associated with steering which in the Zee is fast-acting rack and pinion gear. For a 31¾ ft. circle there is three turns of lock on a 17.8 to ratio. There is tremendous steering "feel", and the car will "walk" its way through fast undulations very accurately. However this precision means the "walk" at ultra high speed becomes twitchiness.

As you can tell, although there may be some shortcomings in its high speed road manners, the Datsun is a real GT despite its modest price.

Once past the cam point, the six really turns on and will fly through to 6800 rpm — the limit which gave 41

mph in first, 65 in second and 91 in third. Fourth gives the 240Z its top speed of 119 as the lazy, touring fifth gear becomes a little breathless — which is surprising as it is useful around town.

The quarter mile from standstill will rush up in 16.7 seconds which puts the Datsun in the same performance-for-capacity-class as the Torana XU-1.

It is an easy car to tour although the restricted mileage in the Capitol Motor's test car kept us mostly in the city limits.

Although such high speed capacity may warrant four wheel disc brakes, the Datsun's disc front/drum rear brake system with tandem master cylinder and power assistance contains the car well. The pedal is quite heavy and not very sensitive, but there is tremendous stopping power due to good traction. In the wet with the Aquajet tread pattern (which suited the Datsun admirably) the brakes were most reassuring. We found ourselves committing the car to dry road braking distances with few qualms. And on the expressway the plume of spray behind the stubby tail showed just how well the SP radials squeegee away water.

We were disappointed with the quality of trim and fittings. Carpets around the seat runners, and head-lining trim was loose and ill-fitting. And this is where we feel the Datsun will fail in the eyes of many discerning buyers. The luggage compartment is neatly carpeted and has baggage securing straps. The luggage hatch (with a wide glass area and through-flow vents) is supported on a compressed nitrogen counterbalance stay but there is no interior courtesy light working from the hatch door. A roof light is set above the suspension towers and there's a glovebox courtesy light — neither operative on the test car, which left us the meagre glow of a neat dash ,map light. The headlights too were dismally poor for a car of this nature.

The wide arc two speed wipers (slow and slower) would be all at sea on an expressway too (as we found out) and the washers weren't up to the usual Japanese standard.

Ventilation on the other hand is very good with dash-end eyeballs, and a centre swivel grille. Boosted fresh air is fed through all three. The heater is most effective but the control slides jammed on the test car.

We can see the 240Z maintaining its pose value until availability becomes too wide — or the GTR-X Torana is released. Then it will have to look to its real abilities as a sports/GT car. There has been some careful thought behind the minor details — like the fuel filler spillage flap borrowed from Porsche, and the hinged bonnet hatches to make checking the washer water and battery easy, borrowed from the Toyota 2000 GT. But other points like tinny horn, no headlight flashers and no heated rear glass don't fit the GT image.

But what is there makes an overall bonus package — from the waste space in the nose for styling's sake to the magnificent rear suspension for handling and ride's sake. ■

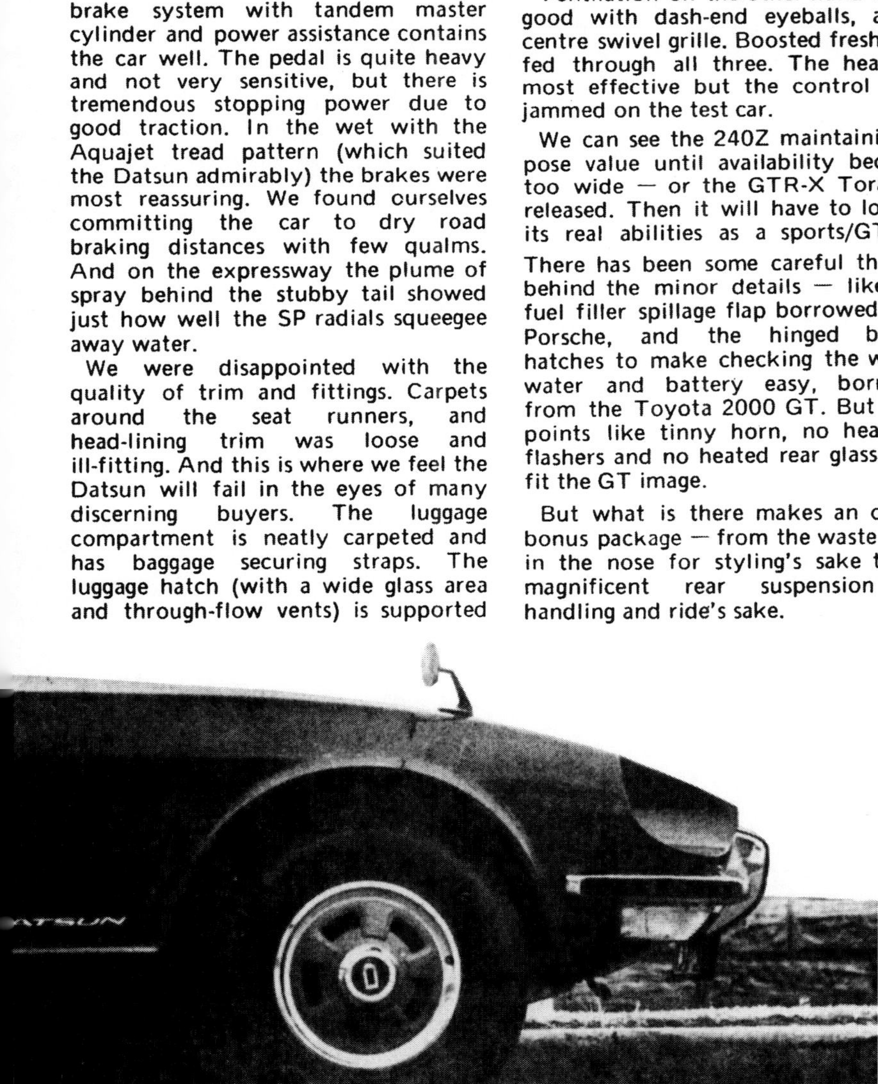

Manufacturer: Nissan Motor Co., Japan.
Test car supplied by: Capitol Motors Ltd., Sydney.
Price as tested: $4567

ENGINE

Water cooled, 6 cylinders in line. Cast iron block, 7 main bearings.

Bore x stroke .... 83.0 x 73.3 mm
Capacity 2393cc
Compression .... 9.0 to 1
Carburettor .... two Hitachi-SU
Fuel pump .... mechanical
Fuel tank .... 13.2 gallons
Fuel recommended .... super
Valve gear .... single ohc
Max. power (gross) .. 151 bhp at 5600 rpm
Max. torque ..... 145.7 lb. ft. at 4400 rpm
Specific power output ...... 63.2 bhp/litre
Electrical system ... 12v 40 amp hr battery
500 watt alternator

TRANSMISSION

Five speed manual all synchro gearbox. Single dry plate clutch.

Gear	Ratio	Mph/1000 Rpm	Max. mph
Rev.	2.922	6.05	—
1st	2.957	6.0	41
2nd	1.858	9.5	65
3rd	1.311	13.4	91
4th	1.00	17.6	119
5th	0.852	20.7	Not tested

Final drive ratio .... 3.90 to 1

CHASSIS

Wheelbase .... 7ft. 6¾in.
Track front .... 4ft. 5¼in.
Track rear .... 4ft. 5in.
Length .... 13ft. 6in.
Width .... 5ft. 4in.
Height .... 4ft. 2¾in.
Clearance .... 6½in.
Kerb weight .... 21 cwt.
Weight distribution front/rear 52/48 percent
lb/bhp .... 15lb.

SUSPENSION

Front: Independent by MacPherson coil spring, telescopic damper struts located on lower wishbones and trailing arm with link-type anti-roll bar.
Rear: Independent Chapman layout coil spring, telescopic damper struts located by wide base A-arms.
Brakes: Front disc rear drum, 10.7 in. dia. disc, 9in. dia. drum, servo-assisted: 67 sq. in. of lining area.
Steering .... rack and pinion
Turns lock to lock 3
Turning circle .... 31½ft.
Wheels: Steel disc with 175 by 14 tubeless radial ply Dunlop SP Aquajet tyres.

PERFORMANCE

Top speed .... 119 mph
Average (both ways) .... 119 mph
Standing quarter mile .... 16.7 sec.

Acceleration Zero to	seconds
30 mph	4.2
40 mph	5.0
50 mph	7.2
60 mph	10.0
70 mph	12.0
80 mph	16.5
90 mph	21.2

	3rd	4th	5th
20-40 mph	5.6	7.5	9.2
30-50	5.6	7.0	8.3
40-60	5.6	7.7	9.0
50-70	5.5	7.8	9.1

BRAKING: Five crash stops from 60 mph

Stop	percent G	pedal
1	.90	65lb
2	.89	65
3	.89	65
4	.92	70
5	.90	70

Consumption: 21.3 mpg over 170 miles including all tests: 22-24 mpg in normal country and suburban use.

Speedo error					
Indicated mph	30	40	50	60	70
Actual mph	29	39	48	58	69

DATSUN 240Z AUTOMATIC

The 3-speed automatic blends in nicely

THERE WAS NEVER any question in our minds that the 240Z would take nicely to an automatic transmission. Very simply, it has enough "cubes" to handle one. A torque converter may multiply torque, but in accelerating hard from rest it only multiplies for the first 200 feet or so,

and after that it's left to whatever gears there are in the transmission. Since there are usually fewer gears in an automatic than in the manual transmission for a given car, maximum performance usually suffers.

Thus many cars that work very well with their manual 4-speed gearboxes just don't make it with an automatic. Take away a gear, subtract a few horsepower for slippage loss and the hydraulic system of an automatic gearbox and what was a fairly spunky little car can become a slug. But the 240Z doesn't have that problem. With about a liter of engine displacement per 1000 lb of curb weight, its 6-cylinder, overhead-cam engine has enough torque and power to give the car sparkling performance with the 4-speed and more than adequate performance with the automatic.

The automatic is a perfectly conventional 3-speed, torque-converter unit produced by the new transmission plant of Nissan, Toyo Kogyo and Ford in Japan. Blending with the super-smooth 240Z engine, the transmission is also smooth, with silky upshifts and responsive "torque-demand" downshifts that don't necessarily require a floored throttle. But there are whirring noises on accelerating from rest and occasional slippage and whirring on upshifts from 2nd to 3rd. The final drive ratio is changed from 3.36:1 to 3.55:1 for the automatic version, and apparently the speedometer gearing had not been correspondingly changed on our test car; it was the first 240Z we'd driven with an optimistic speedometer and odometer.

The upshifts under wide-open throttle acceleration also occur too soon: at 5000-5100 rpm, well below the engine's power peak and not nearly high enough to extract maximum performance. Letting the unit do its own thing we measured 11.9 sec to get to 60 mph and 18.2 sec to cover the standing-start ¼-mile. But holding the gearbox manually in 1st and 2nd to 6500 rpm (where the yellow sector of the tach begins) gets figures substantially better. Here's how the automatic affects acceleration and economy.

	0-30 mph, sec	0-60 mph, sec	¼ mile sec @ mph	Fuel Economy, mpg
Automatic Transmission	4.3	10.4	17.6 @ 82.0	19.0
Manual Transmission	3.2	8.7	17.1 @ 84.5	21.0

It's difficult to drive the 240Z Automatic any way but briskly; its throttle linkage is just too eager. When moving off from rest the first bit of accelerator-pedal movement gets too much response from the engine and the car leaps ahead. One doesn't always want to drive this way, so we learned to carefully modulate the pedal to get a smooth start. The linkage isn't any "quicker" in the automatic car than in the manual, but one doesn't have a clutch to help smooth out things in the automatic so smooth starts become difficult. This problem, the slippage and whirring, and the too-low upshift points need correcting. A problem in the first Z automatics to come off the line—some driveline vibration—was solved by the addition of a vibration damper. In other words, the 240Z Automatic basically works very well, but little problems remain to be worked out. Nothing serious and presumably nothing that will cause the owner mechanical problems, but little imperfections in behavior that the Nissan engineers will want to eliminate as soon as possible.

Otherwise the 240Z's character is unaffected. The gearing lowers maximum speed a bit and there's no noticeable increase in engine noise at cruising speeds. There is still a manual choke, which these days seems to be a better way of getting going on a cold morning than an automatic one. The automatic transmission costs only $190 extra—a price as reasonable as the Z's basic price—and for those who like the unique combination of sportiness, style, compactness and performance the Z offers but don't like to shift, we can only say Go Ahead.

ROAD TEST RESULTS

PRICE

List price	$3596
Price as tested	$3861

ENGINE & DRIVE TRAIN

Engine	sohc inline 6
Bore x stroke, mm	83.0 x 73.3
Displacement, cc/cu in	2393/146
Compression ratio	9.0:1
Bhp @ rpm	150 @ 6000
Equivalent mph	115
Torque @ rpm, lb-ft	148 @ 4400
Equivalent mph	83
Transmission	3-sp automatic
Gear ratios: 3rd (1.00)	3.54:1
2nd (1.46)	5.16:1
1st (2.46)	8.70:1
1st (2.46 x 2.0)	17.4:1
Final drive ratio	3.54:1

GENERAL

Curb weight, lb	2405
Weight distribution (with driver), front/rear, %	50/50
Wheelbase, in	90.7
Track, front/rear	53.3/53.0
Overall length	162.8
Width	64.1
Height	50.6
Steering	rack & pinion
Turns, lock to lock	3.5

Brakes: 10.7-in. disc front, 9.0 x 1.6-in. drum rear, vacuum assisted.

ACCOMMODATION

Seating capacity, persons	2
Seat width	2 x 21.0
Head room	36.5
Seat back adjustment, degrees	10

PERFORMANCE

Top speed, high gear, mph	120
Acceleration, time to distance, sec:	
0–100 ft	4.3
0–250 ft	6.7
0–500 ft	9.6
0–750 ft	12.4
0–1000 ft	15.0
0–1320 ft (¼ mile)	17.6
Speed at end, mph	82
Time to speed, sec:	
0–30 mph	4.3
0–40 mph	5.9
0–50 mph	7.9
0–60 mph	10.4
0–80 mph	16.5
0–100 mph	32.5

BRAKE TESTS

Panic stop from 80 mph:	
Max deceleration rate, % g	84
Stopping distance, ft	287
Control	excellent
Fade test: percent increase in pedal effort to maintain 50% g deceleration rate in six stops from 60 mph	10
Overall brake rating	very good

HANDLING

Speed on 100-ft radius, mph	32.9
Lateral acceleration, g	0.723

SPEEDOMETER ERROR

30 mph indicated is actually	27.0
40 mph	36.0
60 mph	57.0

CALCULATED DATA

Lb/hp (test weight)	18.3
Mph/1000 rpm (high gear)	18.8
Engine revs/mi	3200
Piston travel, ft/mi	1540
R&T steering index	1.10
Brake swept area, sq in/ton	236

FUEL

Type fuel required	premium
Fuel tank capacity, U.S. gal	15.9
Normal consumption, mpg	19.0

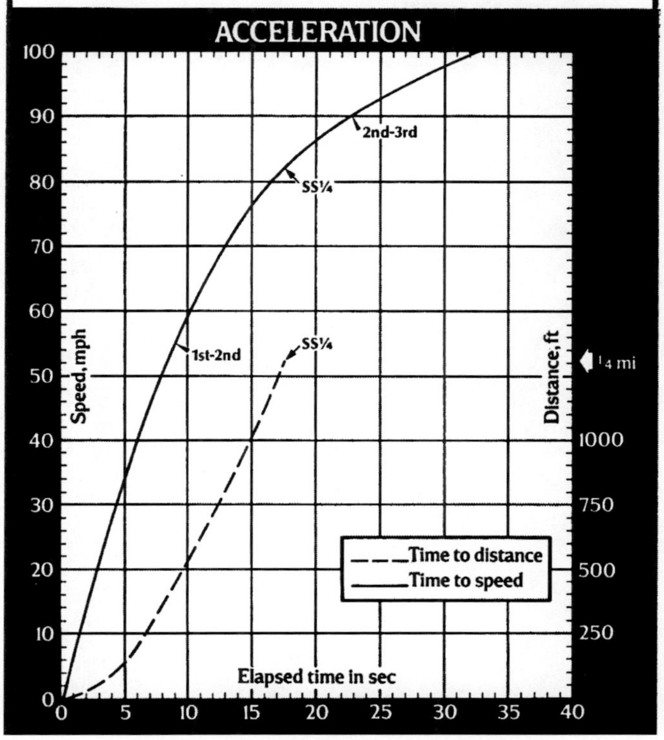

BEHIND the WHEEL of the DATSUN 240Z

A DELIGHTFULLY SMOOTH AUTOMATIC MEANS NO CHARACTER LOSS FOR THE "Z"

The Datsun 240Z is unequivocally the finest sports car for under $4000 that can be bought anywhere in the world. Consequently, the demand for the Z has been so great that in some cases it takes nearly six months to get the standard 4-speed version. But Datsun still hasn't been satisfied that they are luring in every potential customer. They felt that they were missing a sizeable portion of the newly created market because they just couldn't seem to draw those people who admired the 240Z's lines and low price but simply didn't want to be bothered with hassle of driving a sports car with a manual transmission. Needless to say, it didn't take long for

Nissan to realize that to get these people on their waiting lists they were going to have to stick in an automatic transmission of some sort.

At first it seemed like a fairly easy proposition. After all, they had a fully automatic transmission in the 510 sedan that could be beefed up to handle the additional torque of the 240Z's 150 hp. But the Borg-Warner unit used in the 510 sedan was no where near as smooth as it should be for a semi-luxurious sports car. It also had considerable lag between manual shifts, a problem you don't care about in an economy sedan, but something you want to avoid in a high-performance sports car. So Nissan decided to build their own automatic and, as you would expect, the result is a 3-speed automatic transmission that is every bit as smooth as those used on our large domestic cars.

The automatic is produced in a new

transmission plant owned by Nissan, Toyo Kogyo and Ford in Japan. This new transmission uses three speeds and a torque converter unit in the conventional manner. The final drive ratio has been upped slightly from 3.36-to-1 to 3.55-to-1, to achieve nearly the same torque curve as the 4-speed manual. As you can see in the data panel, this has been a wise decision. Our 240Z with automatic achieved nearly the same quarter-mile times as a 4-speed model we drove not too long ago. In fact, there was less than two-tenths of a second separating the two cars, and they both recorded identical trap speeds of just over 84 mph. These figures were, of course, obtained by manually shifting the automatic at 6500 rpm, but even with the transmission shifting itself, ETs were certainly respectable.

Driving the 240Z with automatic gives you virtually the same feeling as the 4-speed – there is plenty of power, excellent handling and good brakes. The only difference is that it's a little trickier to modulate the throttle for low speed acceleration from rest. This is primarily due to an overly sensitive throttle linkage setup. Dropping the transmission down into a lower "passing" gear, however, doesn't require the gas pedal to be floored, and works rapidly and smoothly. Other than the nice-looking quadrant with its T-handle lever and wide brake pedal, there have been no other alterations to the interior. Even the manual choke on the console has been retained, a feature we like in these days of lean-running, hard-to-start engines.

It seems that every time we drive a 240Z we find new little things to rave about. On the automatic we discovered a great little trouble light under the hood that we formerly had thought was only stationary. As it turns out, it has nearly five feet of cord to play with. Also, we found that although this car is somewhat more difficult to extract sheer cornering speeds out of, because the amount of power to the ground cannot be regulated as easily as with the 4-speed where you could ride the clutch and select a gear at will, it still corners as well as sports cars costing twice as much.

In our opinion, the automatic Z car is one of the finest driving cars to come our way. For an additional $190, the automatic transmission is certainly an inexpensive option for those who have lazy left feet, and one that doesn't detract from the overall character of the car.

TEST CAR: DATSUN 240Z AUTOMATIC

PRICE: *Basic list* – **$3596**
As tested – **$3865**
Options included:
Automatic transmission

ENGINE

Type – *6-cylinder inline sohc*
Bore x stroke, in. – *83.0 x 73.3*
Displacement, cu. in. – *146.0*
Compression ratio – *9.0:1*
Rated bhp @ rpm – *150 @ 6000*
Rated torque @ rpm – *148 @ 4400*
Induction system – *2 Hitachi-SU 1-bbl.*
Electrical system – *12V*
Type fuel required – *Premium*

DRIVE TRAIN

Transmission type – *3-speed automatic*
Clutch diameter – *N.A.*
Gear ratios: *1st* – *2.46*
2nd – *1.46*
3rd – *1.00*
Shift lever location – *Console*
Differential type – *Hypoid bevel*
Axle ratio – *3.54:1*

CHASSIS AND SUSPENSION

Frame type – *Unitary*
Brake type – *Disc/drum vacuum assisted*
Brake swept area, sq. in. – *310*
Steering type – *Rack and pinion*
Turns, lock-to-lock – *3.5*
Turning circle, ft. – *31.5*
Front suspension – *Independent with MacPherson struts, lower lateral arms, coil springs, tube shocks and anti-roll bar*
Rear suspension – *Independent with Chapman struts, lower A-arms, coil springs and tube shocks*

WHEELS AND TIRES

Wheel size and type – *4.5 x 14 pressed steel*
Optional size – *5.0*
Tire size and type – *175SR-14 Bridgestone radial*
Normal inflation, F/R, psi – *28/28*

DIMENSIONS AND CAPACITIES

Wheelbase, in. – *90.7*
Track, F/R, in. – *53.3/53.0*
Overall length, in. – *162.8*
Overall height, in. – *50.6*
Overall width, in. – *50.6*
Curb weight, lb. – *2320*
Weight distribution, F/R – *50/50*
Ground clearance, in. – *5.7*
Front seat hip room, in. – *2 x 21.0*
Shoulder room, in. – *45.6*
Head room, in. – *36.5*
No. of passengers – *2*
Luggage space, cu. ft. – *11.5*
Crankcase, qt. – *4.4*
Cooling system, qt. – *9.6*
Fuel capacity, gal. – *15.9*

MAINTENANCE

Engine oil change interval, mi./mo. – *3000/3*
Oil filter change interval, mi./mo. – *6000/6*
Chassis lube interval, mi. – *30,000*

PERFORMANCE

Zero to	Sec.
30 mph	4.3
40 mph	5.8
50 mph	7.9
60 mph	10.2
70 mph	13.1

Standing ¼-mile, sec. – *17.6, 17.1 (manual shifting @ 6500 rpm)*
Speed at end, mph – *79.5, 84.3 (manual shifting @ 6500 rpm)*
Top speed, mph – *121*
Braking performance – *Excellent*
Directional control – *Very good*

Speed ranges in gears	mph	rpm
1st	*45*	*6500*
2nd	*82*	*6500*
3rd	*121*	*6000*

Rpm redline – *7000*

The Z-car, Automatically

You can have all the glories of a Z-Car even if you don't like to shift for yourself!

When we first tested the Datsun 240-Z a year ago (see August 1970 *Road Test*) we unblushingly stated that, "Considering the styling, the performance, and the price, the only word for the new Datsun 240-Z is 'sensational!' " Since then we have driven several variations on that original test car, and have found no reason to even slightly retract what we said. The fact that there is a long waiting list and that many dealers are jacking up the amazingly low price for a quicker delivery speaks well for the overall acceptance of the Z-Car, if not for the factory's advance planning nor its control over its authorized dealers.

One of the joys of the 240-Z is that it is so complete as it is delivered, with its fine interior, its self-seeking radio and the likes. The only "option" as such is air conditioning, and now a three-speed automatic transmission. For the rallyist-slalomist-racer there are a long list of special high-performance parts, but these are not options in the normal sense: the part that is replaced is not taken back by the factory; you're stuck with it. The special parts list is available through the Competition Department, Nissan Motor Corp., 137 E. Alondra, Gardena, California 90249. It includes alternate gear ratios, special suspension, headers, exhausts—the type of equipment developed for racing by Pete Brock and Bob Sharp. It will be remembered that they set up the Z-Car teams which took the then-new Datsuns to the American Road Race of Champions last year and wiped out the factory Porsches and Triumphs by crossing the finish line 1-2-3.

But an *automatic* transmission in such a sleek sports and GT machine? It makes many enthusiasts shudder, but it is well to remember that the great Stirling Moss always drove an automatic Jaguar between races, and that Jim Hall's sensa-

Handling characteristics of the Z-Car, with its fully-independent suspension, is very good. The factory offers a line of specialized parts for serious racing competition.

Datsun 240-Z is strictly a two-seater, with a flat luggage shelf behind seats. Several suitcases can be easily carried. Shock tower, for extra long shocks and springs, is visible far left.

Standard equipment on the Z-Car includes a self-seeking radio. Vertical switch to right of radio knob electrically raises and lowers antenna on left rear fender, to prevent damage.

When the ashtray is lifted out of the center console, the neat and bi-lingual fuse box is uncovered, with the proper fuse amperage clearly marked alongside the fuses' functions.

The Datsun 240-Z comes with either a four-speed manual or a three-speed automatic transmission, but otherwise identical. The automatic adds $190 to the low base price of about $3600.

tional Chaparrals were (sob!) automatic. It boils down to a question of tradition and deciding your particular driving needs. Moss gave as his reason for favoring an automatic that he shifted enough every weekend whilst driving a race car, and wasn't about to be bothered with it on his own. Hall claimed that the driver had enough to do with steering and braking, without having to flip one foot on and off the clutch, and let go of the steering wheel at a critical moment to change gears.

Once the esthetics of whether or not you want an automatic in such a sporty machine as the Z-Car is settled, the next most important question should be "How does it affect performance?" After testing both versions of the Z-Car, we would say "Little, if any." The best zero-to-60 mph times we got with the stick shift version was 9.0 seconds. This was by popping the clutch in first at 6000 rpm and shifting up at the 7,000 red line. With the automatic we didn't get this violent, simply floorboarding it with the selector in Drive range. We consistently got 11.2 or 11.3 seconds. The two seconds difference could easily have been made up by manually snapping the selector handle up through 1-2-D or even 2-D.

The engine in the automatic Z-Car is identical to that in the stick shift model. It's an overhead cam, inline-six with dual SU-type carburetors, and is rated at 150 bhp at 5600 rpm in stock form. Set up for full-racing, with all the factory and BRE parts, you can expect more like 250 bhp.

Even though Nissan is selling factory racing parts, many other speed part manufacturers have quickly latched onto the Z-Car's obvious potential, and one can buy a wide variety of smooth-flow exhaust headers, stick-on racing stripes and alloy wheels.

We mentioned that the automatic transmission didn't, in our opinion, harm the performance of the Z-Car. Tests on drag strips have shown that the automatic is even slightly quicker than the stick shift, if you hold the selector in each range right up to the red line as you would with the manual. The automatic is a little slower off the line but, once the engine gets into a decent power range, the gearing of the automatic give it a slight but definite edge.

In these waning days of the big-engined Detroit "muscle cars," a 145.7-cubic-inch engine that delivers 150 horsepower doesn't seem like much, but don't forget that it's pushing an aerodynamically slippery car that weighs only slightly over 2300 pounds, easily half a ton less than the average Detroit sled. The factory claims a top speed of 125 miles an hour in street tune, and we have no reason to doubt it. When we tested the stick shift version, we calculated that with the tach at the 8000 rpm top limit of the redline zone, in fourth gear, the car would be hitting the 160-mile-an-hour top marking on the speedometer. Such factors as wind resistance, rolling friction and the like would never allow this speed with only 150 horsepower, but the factory-stated 125 shouldn't be all that difficult on the long and legal high-speed roads of Nevada. Don't try it in any other State, however.

Gasoline mileage is such a variable in car testing or in everyday driving, that we usually hesitate to report it. We always have to hedge and make all sorts of "We didn't drive for economy" statements. We never get anywhere near the factory claims, but then we never *do* test with

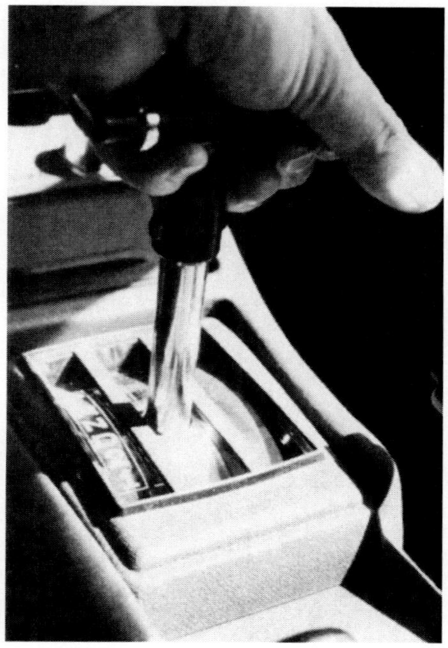

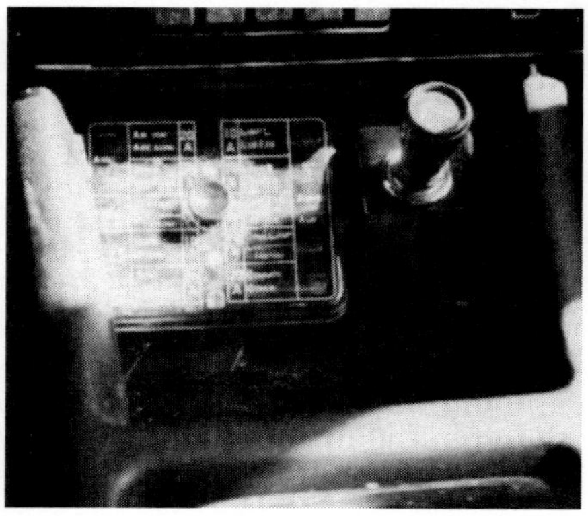

this in mind. The Datsun Z is a driver's car in the best sense of the phrase. Its performance almost necessitates full-power starts from every stop light, and this is not going to make for Volkswagen-level gas mileage. The factory claims 25 miles per gallon for the Z: we got about 18 but had more fun. With a light "Economy Run" foot on the throttle, and a more moderate pace, there is no reason one couldn't get 25 per gallon, but that's horsepower of a different color.

The Datsun 240-Z automatic has the same suspension as the stickshift model, independent on all four corners. The single bottom MacPherson strut needs a long vertical travel, so the shock absorbers and coil springs are unusually long. In the rear this necessitates the two shock towers which stick up through the parcel shelf, as seen in the Lotus Elite.

The factory tires are Japanese-made Bridgestone 175 SR-14 radials, with a very Pirelli-like tread pattern. We found no fault with them in any of our testing, and see no reason to replace them for anything short of the specialized needs of serious slaloming or road racing. If you want to go to larger-width alloy wheels, be careful that you don't overdo it. The factory recommends not going over 1½ inches wider than stock, making sure that the added width is reasonably lined-up with the centerline of the stock wheels. Going to super-widies which hang far out can play hell with the suspension of the car. If you simply *must* have fat weinies on your Z-Car, check with the Competition Department and switch to the heavy-duty "rally suspension."

The brakes on the Z-Car can be rated as excellent, with 10.7-inch discs on the front and finned 9.0-inch drums on the rear. By way of comparison, the Ford Thunderbird weighs well over twice as much as the Z-Car, and only uses front discs one inch larger in diameter. A recent test of the 240-Z along with the Opel GT, the MGB GT, the Fiat 124 Sports Coupe and the Triumph GT6 Mk. 3 showed only the Opel to stop shorter—by ten feet—from 80 miles an hour.

The lap and shoulder belt combination in the automatic Z-Car is the same as in the stickshift, and is still a pain. The two-inch straps get lost alongside the seat, and invariably ends up twisted into pathological designs. As we recommend in the earlier test, we will recommend again: buy a set of three-inch-wide "competition" belts. They are heavier webbing and don't get twisted about as easily; they are stronger, so give more real protection; they look real cool; they are more comfortable, having more area to distribute the loading.

Remember that driving safety is both a question of the situations you get yourself into and your ability to get yourself out of them—often long before they occur. With the excellent handling and performance of the Z-Car, automatic or stickshift, it should give you one of the safest rides on the road today. It is quite possible that the automatic Z would rate a little higher in this aspect, following Jim Hall's reasoning: at a critical time you can concentrate all your thoughts and actions on steering and on throttle control, with-

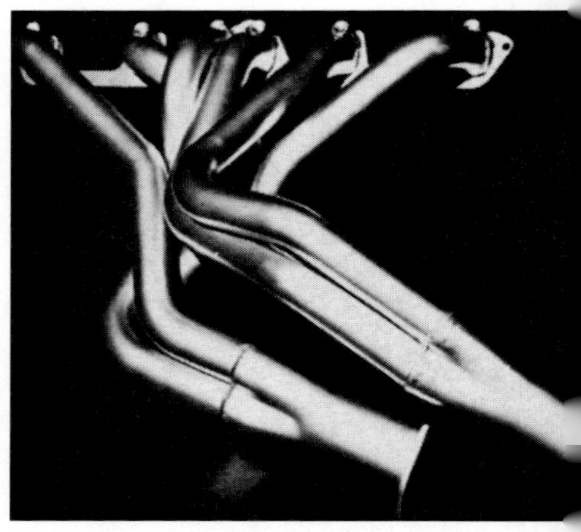

The body lines of the Datsun 240-Z are amongst the most pleasing in today's passenger car field, import or domestic. Access to the luggage space is over the seats or through rear panel. Many speed part manufacturers are already selling special parts for Z-Cars. This tuned, smooth-flow exhaust header is by Hooker. The biggest sales item is a set of alloy wheels, which have an identical pattern to the 510 sedan.

out having to worry about the clutch and gear lever.

The Z-Car is strictly a two-seater, period. None of this "two-plus-two" nonsense where there is room for two midgets behind the front seats. There is nothing back there but a flat luggage shelf, with two tie-down straps.

One of our best sources for comments on the Z-Car's interior has been parking lot attendants. They never get to drive a car far enough to make an intelligent report on its performance, but they sure get in and out of a lot of machinery each of their working days, or nights. Their comments have been universally favorable, to a point that when the Z-Car was relatively unknown, say a year ago, could almost get embarrassing. Names such as Porsche and Ferrari were mentioned, and price estimates usually bottomed in the $7000 stratum. This for a car retailing for well under $4000.

Since testing the first Z-Car over a year ago, we have driven several stick and automatic versions, plus one with most of the "rally" options on it. We have clocked several thousand miles, over desert and mountains, through a Mojave Desert dust storm, with adults and children as passengers (one at a time, of course) and have found the vinyl bucket seats extremely comfortable. One nice feature in both the stick and automatic versions is a small rubber-padded footrest on the left side of the pedals. It saves having your left foot grotesquely hunting around for something to do, and provides a solid platform when really arcing around bends in a mountain road.

The instrumentation in the Z-Car is as complete as one could want, with everything coming as standard; no extra-cost equipment. Directly in front of the thin-rimmed, simulated-wood steering wheel is a big 8000-rpm tachometer and the 160-mph speedometer, with a total odometer and a trip odometer. High on the center fascia are the water temperature/oil pressure gauge and the ammeter/fuel gauge, with an electric clock far right. Below this is the self-seeking radio, the air controls, and the ashtray with lighter. Lift out the ashtray and the fuse box is exposed, right where you can see everything. This feature sure beats squirming around on the floor trying to get a look at the fuse box mounted up under the dashboard, as is the common practice.

Down the center tunnel is the shift handle, then the manual choke. The Z-Car engine is cold-blooded, and needs heavy choking when started cold. It doesn't need it for long, but brother does it need it. One of our test cars had a broken choke linkage, and was that ever a bummer. The only solution seemed to be to pump the gas pedal a couple of times, trying to get some fuel rattling around the carburetors, hit the starter switch, and try to keep the revs at 3000 rpm. After half a dozen attempts, the fire would stay lit and it was possible to engage the gears, with only a couple of stalls before the engine warmed up enough to run without the nonworkable choke. If the engine could be kept running for a block or two, everything was fine.

With a car like the 240-Z you don't really ask about economy, not in its most niggardly sense. You have an exceptionally well-built, high-performance sports or Grand Touring car, that cries out to be driven rapidly and precisely. While you may well get somewhere just short of 20 miles per gallon, the actual per mile consumption should be of relatively minor interest to anyone who buys a Z-Car.

The one place where "economy" most

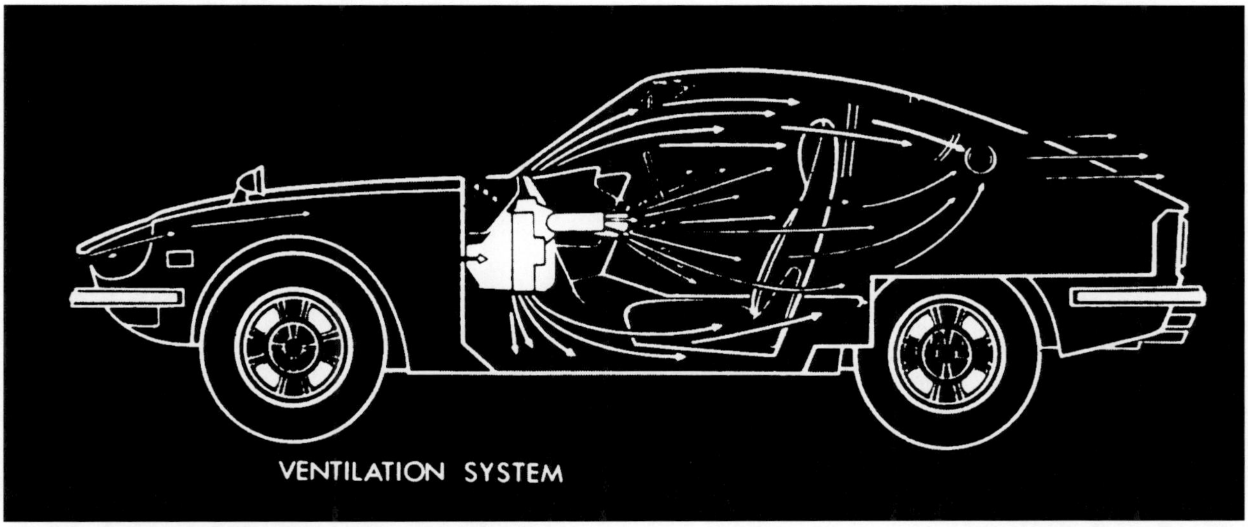

The Z-Car's engine is an inline-six with a single overhead camshaft, rated at 150 horsepower in stock configuration. Access to plugs and oil filter (left) is excellent, but the other side of the block gets a little busy with both exhaust and intake (right photo) coming off the same side.

definitely comes into the picture is with the initial price of the car. If you can find a dealer who doesn't insist on loading the few 240-Zs he is allotted with extra-cost options, you can, at least theoretically, walk out with a Z for about four big bills, tax and license included.

Try *that* on your neighborhood Porsche or Corvette dealer!

Better than a year and half later, and a dozen test Z-Cars after our initial road test, we still cannot speak too highly of the Datsun 240-Z, with either stickshift or automatic transmissions. If you dig the fastback, Kamm-effect bobbed-tail, two-seater configuration, as we do, you get it at its best in the Z-Car, the Opel GT and the Corvette. We'd rate the 240-Z superior to the Opel in many ways, particularly acceleration and cornering, and superior to the Corvette by over $2000 in showroom price.

The level of workmanship and quality control seemed to be quite high on the various Z-Cars we have driven—excepting the broken choke linkage we mentioned—which we cannot say for some of the other Datsun models. We trust that even with the great demand for more Z-Cars the factory in Japan will keep production down to a point where this quality control can be maintained.

We had trouble restraining our enthusiasm for the Datsun 240-Z stickshift a year ago, and have seen no reason to change our attitude with the automatic version. Road testers drive two or three dozen new cars each year, most of them quite adequate but really deathly dull. Once in a long, long time a new car comes along that combines the very best of body design, performance, handling and initial cost, so that all the tester can say is, "Now *that's* what I've been talking about all along!"

The Datsun 240-Z, automatic or stickshift, is such a vehicle.

Datsun 240-Z Automatic
Data in Brief

DIMENSIONS	
Length overall (in.)	162.8
Wheelbase (in.)	90.7
Width (in.)	64.1
Height (in.)	50.6
Tread, front (in.)	53.3
Tread, rear (in.)	53.0
Gas tank capacity (gal.)	15.9
Luggage capacity (cu. ft.)	8.5
Turning circle (ft.)	31.5
ENGINE	
Type	Inline-6, overhead cam
Displacement (cu. in.)	145.7
Horsepower @ rpm (SAE)	150 @ 5,600
Troque (lb.-ft.) @ rpm	148 @ 4,400
WEIGHT, TIRES, BRAKES	
Curb weight (lb.)	2300
Tires (as tested)	175 SR-14 radial
Brakes, front (in.)	10.7-in. discs
Brakes, rear (in.)	9.0-in. finned drums
SUSPENSION	
Front	Indep. MacPherson strut, coil springs, stabilizer bal.
Rear	Indep. MacPherson strut, coil springs
PERFORMANCE	
Acceleration, 0-60 mph (sec.)	11.2
Passing, 40-65 mph (sec.)	7.4
Passing, 50-65 mph (sec.)	4.8

ROAD TEST DATSUN 240Z

On paper there is nothing particularly impressive about the specification of the Datsun 240Z. True, it has independent suspension (by MacPherson struts) to all four wheels and, yes, its power unit does sport a single overhead camshaft. This engine is of the relatively outdated straight-six configuration, however, and even more unfashionably, is located in front of the driver under a long bonnet vaguely reminiscent of the E-type Jaguar. As a design, therefore, it is square rather than trendy, but this apparent handicap in the view of some does not prevent it front being an extremely competent sports car. It will accelerate smoothly up to 60 mph in 8.3sec. from standstill, for example, and then go on to achieve a maximum speed of just over 125 mph; its handling is exceptionally good and its adhesion in the dry is excellent, if not so good in the wet on the Japanese-made tyres fitted.

But its most important virtue by far is its clever packaging. It is fixed-roof packaging, but we believe that sportscar enthusiasts rightly don't set so much store by open-air motoring as they used. But they do like space with comfort, and without losing any sporting character — or becoming heavy — the 240Z is unusually roomy. There is enough legroom, and fore-and-aft adjustment, in its two seats for European-scale

giants, let alone Japanese ones, while behind them is a huge luggage platform easily accessible through a lift-up tail-gate. Thus with its sensibly sized fuel tank it provides two people with everything necessary for comfortable long-distance touring. In addition its instruments and controls are very well planned and it abounds with thoughtful details from the flaps which expose the washer bottle and battery, to the tool and oddments boxes behind the seats.

But the 24OZ is not perfect, of course. Our test car suffered badly from an assortment of transmission noises, loud tyre thump and roar as well as a distinctly knobbly low-speed ride. That most people find these defects outweighed by its virtues is shown by its current 6500 monthly sales in the States. In Britain at £2389 complete with five-speed gearbox it is much more expensive than it would be if made by an indigenous manufacturer — the TR6 costs only £1471, for example — but nearly £500 cheaper than the cheapest E-type. It is closely rivalled by the slightly cheaper, more refined and roomier Reliant Scimitar, but nevertheless represents excellent value for money and should sell well in this country.

PERFORMANCE AND ECONOMY

Although not bristling with technical innovations the 2393 cc Datsun engine is reasonably up to date for large volume production, with strongly oversquare (83 x 73.7mm) dimensions, a seven-bearing crankshaft, an aluminium cylinder head and a single overhead camshaft. It gives this large but fairly light sports car very respectable acceleration and top speed despite the rather modest claims made for it: 145.7 (gross) lb. ft. of torque at 4400 rpm, and 151 (gross) bhp at 5600 rpm — about the same as the *net* output of the Triumph 2.5-litre engine in TR6 form.

As with most SU-fed units — it is equipped with two Japanese-made instruments of this sort — starting was always rapid and warm-up from cold good, excellent

control of the idling speed being possible with the long-travel choke lever mounted between the seats. The exhaust note is almost too well subdued, while commendable smoothness is retained up to maximum rpm, though there are some smoother straight sixes around. On the overrun, however, a powerful vibration could be felt around 5000 rpm, accompanied by a loud buzz similar to an exhaust rasp, probably due to an out-of-true clutch. Datsun claim that this fault was peculiar to our test car and not common to 240Zs.

The engine will pull quite vigorously from 1000 rpm in top and feels flexible enough when driving at moderate speeds, but needs to be revved above 4000 rpm if good performance is to be obtained. Maximum torque is not developed until 4400 rpm is reached — 3000 rpm is a more usual maximum torque speed for an engine of this capacity — and the weakness is laid bare by our comparison chart since the smaller-engined Alfa 1750, for example, also has a five-speed gearbox but a better 30-50 acceleration time. On the other hand, the rev-counter has a 6500-7000 rpm yellow zone yet is fitted with an ignition cut-out to restrict revs to the lower of these two limits. Moreover, experiments with different change-up points during our acceleration tests showed that there was no point in exceeding 6000 rpm, above which the power falls off most noticeably. Within this relatively narrow power band, however, the engine sets to with a will, accelerating the car from a standstill to 60 mph in 8.3sec. and to 100 mph in 23.9sec.

It copes well, too, with a fairly large frontal area and spoilers at front and rear. The mean of four flying kilometre times on a Continental motorway gave a maximum speed of 125.1 mph and a best one-way speed of 129 mph. This doesn't do justice to the high-speed cruising capability revealed during our trip abroad it was quite unfussed when running for long periods at an indicated 115 mph (112 mph true).

This performance was accompanied by excellent fuel economy, the 31.2 mpg touring fuel consumption being outstanding for a car of this capacity. Over 17 mpg was obtained even when cruising at around 110 mph, while despite their lead-footed driving our testers managed to average 25.7 mpg during more representative motoring in Britain. The average owner should therefore

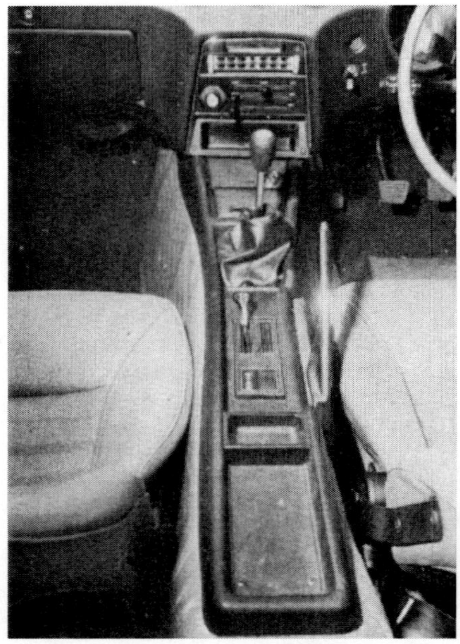

The seats provided good lateral and lumbar support but their cushions are rather too flat, creating a tendency to slide downwards. A small tray behind the gear and choke levers augments the oddments space provided by the lockable glove compartment. The small spaces behind the seats can be used to stow small parcels, and there is a toolbox and further oddments box in the forward edge of the luggage platform

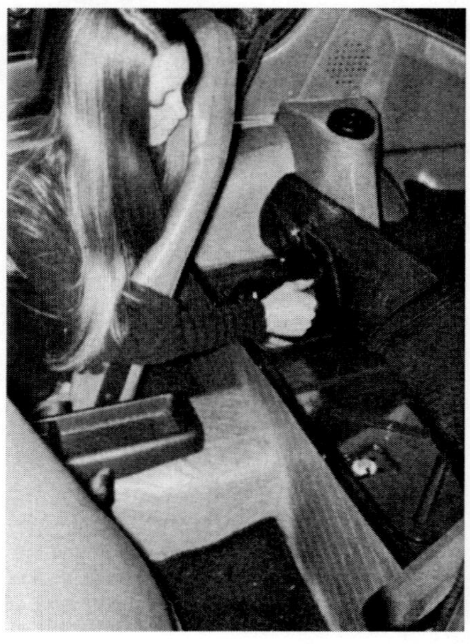

obtain nearly 30 mpg which will give him a range of well over 400 miles from the 15.5 gallon tank.

TRANSMISSION

Datsun's light and easy-to-use five-speed gearbox is one of the best in the business. Its well-placed lever moves between positions laid out in the classic Alfa Romeo pattern, first to fourth being in the normal "H" while fifth is towards the driver and forward. Spring biasing loads the lever towards the 3-4 plane so that very quick fifth to fourth changes can be accomplished with little more than a pull straight backwards even though the synchromesh on both these gears is a little strong. On all the others it is unobtrusive as well as unbeatable. The 32lb. clutch release pressure is not particularly low, but good positioning and angling of the pedal makes it feel considerably lighter. The clutch is additionally progressive in action and pleasant to use even in the heaviest traffic.

A careful and intelligent choice of ratios — intermediate speeds at 6000 rpm are approximately 37, 60, 84 and just over 110 mph — enables the engine to be kept in its power band without frantic revving; changing up at 5500 rpm in third, for instance, produces a drop of only 1300 rpm into fourth. Fifth and fourth gears are particularly convenient for high-speed motorway running, the extra power in fourth for overtaking and the relaxed cruising in fifth being most noticeable.

The gearbox was rather noisy, as it was on the other 240Z we tried earlier in the year. There is also a propshaft vibration which discourages the use of fifth gear below 35 mph and which builds up into a noticeable rumble at high speeds.

HANDLING AND BRAKES

We have become used to the sight of 240Zs in rallies cornering with truly amazing amounts of opposite lock, but such tail-out attitudes are a tribute to the feel and balance of the car rather than to its behaviour on proper surfaced roads. For the 240Z is a car which gives confidence to a driver at once because it always clearly telegraphs its intentions, partly through the seat of the pants and partly through the excellent feel provided by the light and direct rack and pinion steering. Indeed some drivers might consider that there is too much feel, since kickback is considerable on bumpy roads. Some front-end bump-steer is also apparent, though acceptable: keeping a chosen line around a bend is easy with a light grip giving the wheel freedom to execute small deviations from its mean position.

On dry roads cornering is extremely good, with initial understeer at first, eventually giving way to final oversteer. The behaviour through esses and tight, winding roads is particularly satisfying, partly because there is little roll even at the limit. At high speeds straight-line stability is excellent, and the car is little affected by side winds helped, no doubt, by spoilers at front and rear. In the wet cornering and handling are not so good, the car breaking away less predictably at either end, perhaps because the tread mix of the Japanese-made Dunlop SP68s may not be up to current European standards.

Motor Road Test No. 57/71 Datsun 240Z

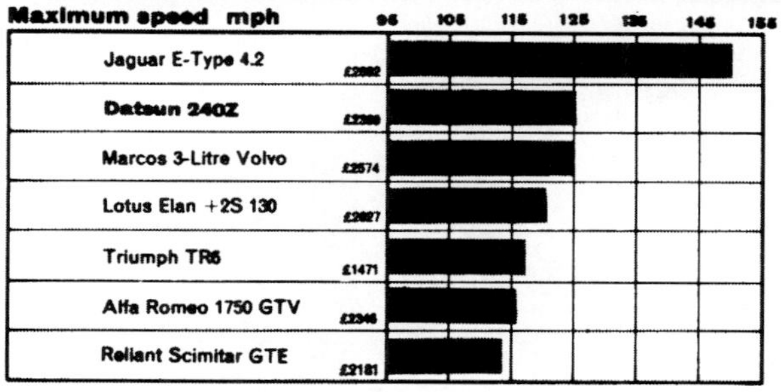

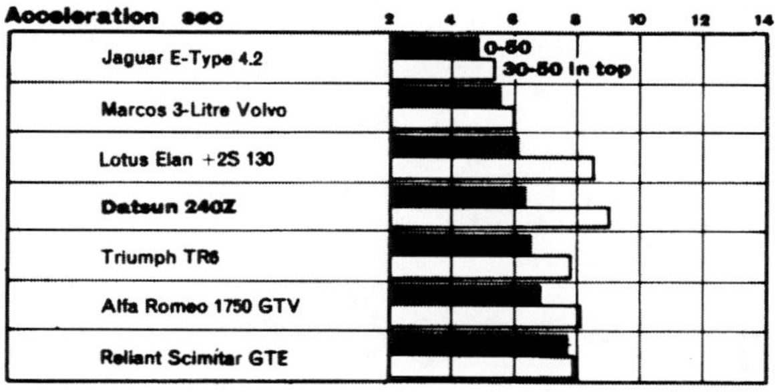

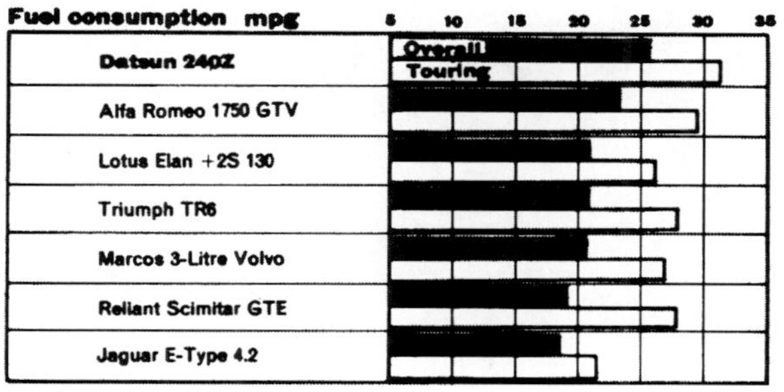

Make: Datsun.
Model: 240Z.
Makers: Nissan Motor Co. Ltd, Tokyo, Japan.
Concessionaires: Datsun UK Ltd, Datsun House, Brighton Rd., Worthing, Sussex.
Price: £1910 plus £479.37 purchase tax equals £2389.37.

Performance tests carried out by *Motor's* staff at the Motor Industry Research Association proving ground, Lindley.
Test Data: World copyright reserved: no unauthorized reproduction in whole or in part.

Conditions

Weather: Sunny becoming overcast.

Temperature: 40-43°F
Barometer: 29.25
Surface: Dry
Fuel: 98 octane (RM) 4 star rating

Maximum Speeds

		mph	kph
Flying Kilometre			
Mean		125.1	201.5
Best one way		129.0	207.5
4th gear	at 6500rpm	120	193
3rd gear	at 6500rpm	91	146
2nd gear	at 6500rpm	64	103
1st gear	at 6500rpm	40	64

"Maximile" speed: (Timed quarter mile after 1 mile accelerating from rest)

Mean	115.5
Best	116.1

Acceleration Times

mph	sec.
0- 30	2.8
0- 40	4.4
0- 50	6.3
0- 60	8.3
0- 70	11.3
0- 80	14.3
0- 90	19.1
0-100	23.9
Standing quarter mile	16.2
Standing Kilometre	29.9

mph	5th sec.	4th sec.	3rd sec.
10- 30			5.4
20- 40	8.9	6.9	5.4
30- 50	9.0	6.9	5.3
40- 60	9.2	7.2	5.0
50- 70	9.7	7.4	5.3
60- 80	10.8	7.6	5.8
70- 90	11.8	8.1	7.2
80-100	13.4	10.0	

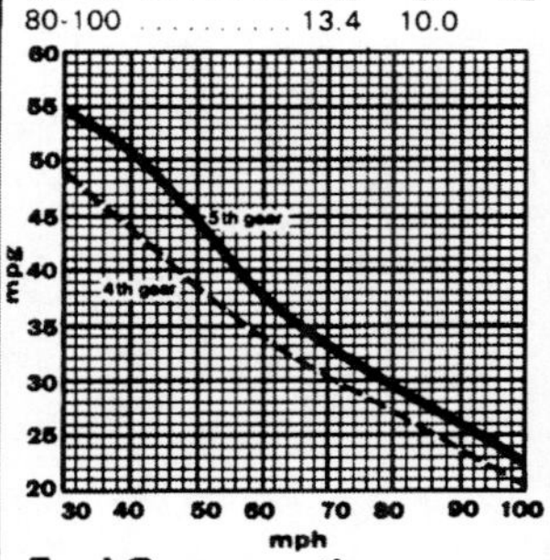

Fuel Consumption

Touring (consumption midway between 30 mph and maximum less 5% allowance for acceleration) . . 31.2 mpg
Overall . . . 25.7 mpg
(= 11.0 litres/100km)
Total test distance . . . 1992 miles

Brakes

Pedal pressure, deceleration and equivalent stopping distance from 30 mph

lb.	g.	ft.
25	0.30	100
50	0.55	55
75	0.74	41
100	0.90	33
125	0.99	30
Handbrake	0.44	68

Fade Test

20 stops at ½g deceleration at 1 min. intervals from a speed midway between 40 mph and maximum speed (=82 mph)

	lb
Pedal force at beginning	46
Pedal force at 10th stop	46
Pedal force at 20th stop	46

Steering

Turning circle between kerbs:
Left: . . . 32ft
Right . . . 31ft
Turns of steering wheel from lock to lock . . . 2.7
Steering wheel deflection for 50ft diameter circle . . . 0.7 turns

Clutch

Free pedal movement . . . = ¼in
Additional movement to disengage clutch completely . . . = 3in
Maximum pedal load . . . = 32lb

Speedometer

Indicated	30	40	50	60	70
True	30	39	50	61	71
Indicated	80	90	100		
True	81.5	93	104		

Distance Recorder 2.5% slow

Weight

Kerb weight (unladen with fuel for approximately 50 miles) . . . 20.3 cwt
Front/rear distribution . . . 52.9/47.1
Weight laden as tested . . . 24.0 cwt

Motor Road Test No. 57/71 Datsun 240Z

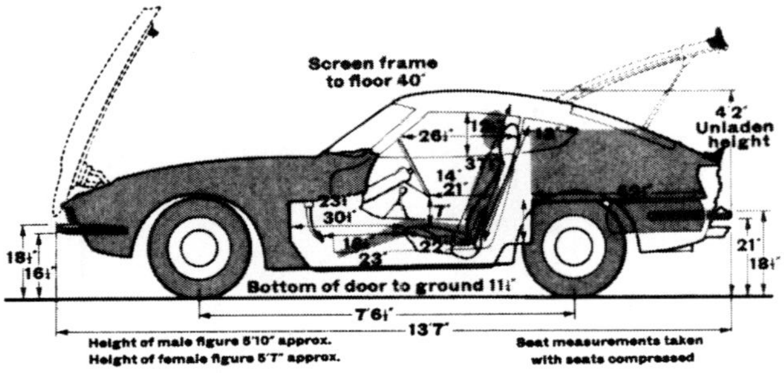

Engine

Block material . . . . . Cast iron
Head material . . Aluminium alloy
Cylinder . . . . 6 in line
Cooling system . . . . . . Water
Bore and stroke . 83mm. (3.268in.) 73.7mm. (2.902in.)
Cubic capacity 2393cc. (146 cu.in.)
Main bearings 7
Valves . . . . Single ohc
Compression ratio 9:1
Carburettor(s) . . . 2 S.U. constant depression/variable choke
Fuel pump . Mechanical diaphragm
Oil filter . . . . Full flow
Max. power (gross) . . 151 bhp at 5600 rpm
Max. torque (gross) . 145.7 lb.ft. at 4400 rpm

Transmission

Clutch . . Single dry plate—hydraulic 8.87in. diameter
Internal gear box ratios
5th gear 0.852
4th gear 1.000
3rd gear 1.311
2nd gear 1.858
1st gear 2.957
Reverse 2.922
Synchromesh . . All forward gears
Final drive . . . . . 3.90:1 hypoid
Mph at 1000 rpm:
Top gear 21.6
Fourth gear 18.4
Third gear 14.0
Second gear 9.9
First gear 6.2

Chassis and body

Construction Unit construction with energy absorbing front and rear section assemblies

Brakes

Type . Girling-Sumitomo servo assisted tandem system

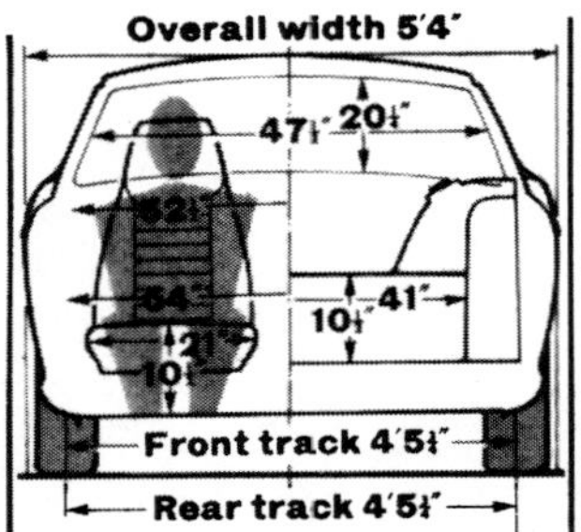

Ground clearance
Lowest point:
(under exhaust system) 5¼"
under front suspension 6"
under engine 6¼"

Dimensions . . 10.67in. disc front, 9.0in. drum rear

Suspension and steering

Front . Independent by Macpherson struts and coil springs
Rear . Independent by Macpherson struts and coil springs
Shock absorbers:
Front . . . . Telescopic
Rear . . . . Telescopic
Steering type . . . Rack and pinion
Tyres . . 175HR-14 radial Dunlop SP Sport
Wheels . . . . Steel
Rim size 4½J-14

Coachwork & equipment

Starting handle . . . Not provided
Tool kit contents Jack, jack handle, wheel brace, wheel chocks
Jack . . . . Screw scissors
Jacking points 4
Battery . . . . 12V/negative earth 50 amp hrs capacity
Number of electrical fuses . . . 10
Headlamps . . . . . . Two—7in.
Indicators . . . . Flashing
Reversing lamp . . . . Yes
Screen wipers . Electric two-speed
Screen washers . . . . . Electric
Sun visors . . . . Two
Locks:
With ignition key . . Ignition and steering lock
With other keys Doors, boot, glove box and fuel filler cap
Interior heater . . . . Yes
Upholstery . . . . Vinyl
Floor covering . . . . . . Carpet
Alternative body styles . . . None

Maintenance

Fuel tank capacity . . . 15½ galls
Sump . . . . 9 pints SAE 20W/50
Gearbox . . . . . 3 pints SAE 90
Rear axle . . . . 2 pints SAE 90
Steering gear . Multipurpose grease
Coolant 1 drain tap and 1 block plug
Chassis lubrication Every 24,000 miles to 6 points
Maximum service interval 3000 miles
Ignition timing 17°btdc at 650 rpm
Contact breaker gap 0.020±0.002in.
Sparking plug gap 0.033±0.002in.
Sparking plug type . . NGK BP6ES
Tappet clearance (hot)
Inlet . . . . 0.010in.
Exhaust . . . . 0.012in.
(between cam and rocker—not between rocker and valve)
Valve timing:
inlet opens . . . . . . 16°btdc
inlet closes . . . . . . 52°abdc
exhaust opens . . . . 54°bbdc
exhaust closes . . . . 18°atdc
Rear wheel toe-in . . . . . . 0°
Front wheel toe-in 2-5mm. unladen
Camber angle . . . . . 50'±30'
Castor angle . . . . . 2°55'±30'
King pin inclination . . . . 12°10'
Tyres pressures:
Front . . . . 28 psi
Rear . . . . 28 psi
(32 psi all round at over 100 mph)

1 Clock. **2** Map light. **3** Fuel gauge. **4** Ammeter. **5** Oil pressure gauge. **6** Water temperature gauge. **7** Hazard warning light switch. **8** Rev counter. **9** Horn push. **10** Trip distance recorder. **11** Speedometer. **12** Distance recorder. **13** Driver-side fresh air vent. **14** Centre fresh air vent. **15** Three speed fan control. **16** Air control. **17** Heater temperature control. **18** Heater distribution control. **19** Choke lever. **20** Cigarette lighter. **21** Combined washer/wipe/light stalk. **22** Foot rest. **23** Ignition and steering lock. **24** Driver-side foot well ventilator knob. **25** Indicator/dipswitch/flasher stalk. **26** Bonnet release.

With 10.67in. discs at the front and 9in. drums at the rear the 240Z is well equipped for a car weighing just over a ton, albeit one capable of nearly 130 mph. They lived up to their specification by their performance, although with a fairly low level of servo assistance they required a heavy 125lb. push to give 0.99g deceleration. But we liked their progressive feel and the way they retained their reassuring behaviour no matter how hard the car was driven — and we experienced no fade at all. The handbrake gave an exceptional 0.44g retardation.

COMFORT AND CONTROLS

The ride of the 240Z is not as good as its all-independent suspension should make it. On surfaces with small-amplitude bumps a very knobbly ride is evident and small high-frequency accelerations are transferred to the occupants, perhaps due to a high damping factor rather than stiff springs. This knobbliness is especially noticeable on town or suburban roads. At higher speeds, however, the ride is much better and undulations produce very little pitch or float.

We have often criticized Japanese cars for lack of seat adjustment but in this respect the export-biased design is very evident. There was sufficient adjustment for the tallest (6ft. 5in.) of our test drivers, while other staff members who often complain bitterly of being too close to the pedals found that with the seat fully back they couldn't even touch them. This tremendous range of adjustment, together with adequate lateral support and good lumbar support, gave a driving position that nearly everyone found comfortable even at the end of a long journey. But there were several complaints of excessive flatness in the cushions, creating a tendency to slide down the seat; a backrest rake adjuster with more notches to give finer adjustment would also be welcome. Provision has been made for 0.8in. spacers under the seat to raise it — for short drivers a must, we believe, since forward visibility is poor for them when the seat is in its lowest position.

For drivers of average height or above visibility from this rather high-waisted car is generally good except that most found it difficult at first to judge the position of the nearside front wing. The high-back seats obstruct rear visibility as, in the three-quarter areas, do the thickish back pillars. All the 240Zs arriving in this country do so without headlamps and it is up to the dealer to fit British units; Datsun recommend quartz-halogen lamps, and the blaze of light given by these on our test car was sufficient for full use of the performance at night.

One of the car's outstanding virtues is the excellent design of both major and minor controls — and their almost ideal placing. Worthy of special mention are the pedals laid out for easy heel and toe changes, a rest for the clutch foot (which is a considerable help in bracing oneself against lateral forces) and the combination control stalk on the left of the steering column. This puts the washer, wipers and lights under fingertip control. All these features make the car extremely safe and easy to drive under adverse conditions.

Few of our testers managed to master the complex heating and ventilation system. The admission of cold air by ram effect to the footwells is independently regulated by controls on each side of the car; while air passing through the separate heating system — heated or cold — can be directed to the centre and side vents, footwell or screen by using the central control slides. The temperature slide would not give fine control, but by setting the top slide to give a mixture of cool and heated air, an acceptable condition was found. Heating and ventilation capacity was adequate and both can be boosted by a three-speed fan.

Suppression of road noise is not one of the car's strong points, for at low speeds some radial thump intrudes and over concrete-washboard type surfaces (as on many of our motorways) a very loud roar and body drumming makes progress uncomfortable. Wind noise is well subdued up to about 105 mph when the driver's window lifts off its seal and begins to flutter; this effect is probably caused by pressurization of the interior for its onset could be delayed to around 115 mph by closing the various air inlet vents.

FITTINGS AND FURNITURE

A large, one-piece plastic facia moulding supports the attractively marked instruments — a clock with two small gauges above the central console and angled towards the driver, and the big speedometer and matching rev-counter right in front of him. Angled glasses ensure that reflections are never a problem with these two hooded and deeply recessed instruments. Beneath the three central dials is a maplight augmenting the interior light, beneath the heater controls is a space for a radio, and beneath that in turn is a cigarette lighter and ashtray. Reversing lamps and a heated rear window are also standard fittings.

For odds and ends there is a locker and a small tray behind the gearlever plus spaces between the seats and the luggage compartment as well as the toolbox and further oddments box set into its forward edge. An additional little pocket is set into the driver's sun visor, but there is no mirror on the passenger's. The luggage platform itself is huge: big enough to take an adult sitting crossways for short journeys or no less than 11.4 cu. ft. of our suitcases, safely held in position by the retaining straps provided and without in any way obscuring rear vision.

SERVICING AND ACCESSIBILITY

The bonnet lid is not self-supporting and was rather difficult to open after being released from inside the car. Once open, it reveals a large uncluttered engine compartment illuminated by a lamp that can be unclipped and moved around on a long lead. On either side are two special recesses, accessible through lift-up flaps in the front wings, containing the battery and the washer bottle. A similarly thoughtful detail is the chain holding the fuel filler cap and the associated flap which protects the bodywork. The spare wheel lives in a tray under the luggage compartment.

Servicing is required every 3000 miles at which the main job is a change of engine oil; some chassis greasing is required at 24,000 miles. There are 150 dealers and distributors in the UK. ■

No less than 11.4 cu. ft. of our suitcases could be stowed on the large luggage platform without obscuring rear vision. Retaining straps for the cases are provided. The roomy engine compartment is flanked by a pair of recesses with separate covers — the one for the battery can be seen on the far side

Road test/John Bolster

Datsun 240Z: A sports car for enjoyment

Most sports cars are treated as poor relations and have to use components which are well enough for family saloons but were not tailored for the job. The Datsun 240 Z makes a refreshing change for it has a really close-ratio five-speed gearbox, high-geared steering, independent rear suspension, and a body which shares no panels with bread-and-butter models.

The car is a two-seater coupé of sporting appearance, having a lot of interior space for the two occupants and a vast luggage compartment, with straps attached to secure suitcases. The suspension is by MacPherson struts all round, with disc front and drum rear brakes, the servo furnishing only moderate assistance to avoid blurring the responsiveness of the pedal. The rack and pinion steering gives an outstandingly compact turning circle and answers instantly to small movements of the wheel.

The engine is a very sturdy seven-bearing six-cylinder with a single chain-driven overhead camshaft. For balance, evenly-spaced firing impulses, and a pure exhaust note, the straight-six has no peer unless you can go to 12 cylinders. If it is mounted fairly well back, to obtain an advantageous weight distribution, it does require a rather long bonnet, which gives the Datsun an E-type look on a smaller scale. The gearbox is in unit with the engine and has the now generally accepted arrangement with fifth speed out on the right and forward.

Though the car is low, the large doors give quite easy entry and there is ample seat adjustment for the tallest driver. Similarly, the width at shoulder level is generous indeed. The controls are very well placed but the scuttle is on the high side which, coupled with the length of the bonnet, makes the driver feel that he is sitting rather low. Distance pieces are provided to bolt between the seat and its mountings, which would be almost essential for the smaller mortals and probably advantageous for others. The seats have the high backs which are not universally popular but are presumably intended for the US market. The interior is attractively trimmed and the instrument panel, with its impressive show of proper round dials, tells the enthusiast everything he wants to know.

Like most Japanese cars, the 240 Z has a very potent starter motor that brings instant results. The engine is outstandingly flexible, as a good six should be, allowing the car to wander along in traffic at 10 mph on the direct fourth gear. It gives a lot of power between 4000 and 6000 rpm, the curve starting to droop at 6500 rpm, but it remains smooth and unhurried anywhere within its range.

The Datsun reaches and holds 120 mph very easily and I covered some quite long distances at this speed. If everything is just right, an honest 125 or 126 mph can eventu-

The 240Z, a two-seater coupé of sporting appearance, makes a refreshing change from many sports cars.

ally be reached but the engine cannot over-rev on fifth gear. I normally selected that ratio at about 100 mph and there seems no point in retaining the direct drive up to its ultimate 120 mph, except to enjoy the *panache* of changing up after vanquishing a pugnacious opponent. On the *Autoroute du Nord*, I found nobody who could quite match my speed, but two Citroëns *à injection* and a V8 Mercedes caused me to travel for many kilometres with my foot hard on the floor, which the 240 Z seemed to enjoy as much as I did.

The ride is hard at low speeds but remarkably comfortable at high speeds on bad French roads. On some surfaces, such as the *autoroutes*, there is a complete absence of road noise, but on others, notably some British motorways with a sandpaper non-skid finish, the sound level is high. The engine is quiet though the exhaust occasionally blares at high speeds on the overrun. In contrast, the gearbox whines on the indirects and there is an occasional clonk from the driveshafts. There is a notable absence of wind noise below 100 mph but at 120 mph it is quite prominent. To summarise, the Datsun is not as refined as an expensive luxury saloon but it is by no means noisy compared with other sports cars.

With quick, responsive steering and excellent independent rear suspension, the car is a delight to handle. The degree of understeer is very moderate and there is enough power to alter all that. In this connection, the 5-speed box always provides the right gear

Thanks to some notable rally successes the 240Z is already regarded as quite a formidable car.

The seven-bearing six-cylinder engine is very flexible with a lot of power between 4000 *and* 6500 *rpm.*

ratio and the change is easy and certain. The car corners very fast with extremely little roll, the sensitive steering giving a wonderful feeling of control on wet roads. For ideal handling, the steering should be sufficiently light and high-geared to give a suspicion of kickback over the worst bumps, which is exactly how the Datsun is arranged; it is this steering which lifts it head and shoulders above its competitors. The brakes are powerful and fade-free, the independent suspension allowing them to be used to full advantage.

The heating is powerful and the fresh air vents are well arranged at the sides and centre of the instrument panel. The blower works both on the heated air and the cold breathing air, running sufficiently quietly to be inaudible at its lowest speed. It takes some juggling, however, to obtain warm feet, a demisted screen, and cool air to breathe, all at one time. The quartz-halogen lamps are very effective and when they were dipped nobody flashed at me in France, though I had naughtily forgotten to change them over. The engine is completely untemperamental and idled happily to itself in the worst traffic blocks that Paris could impose.

Thanks to some notable rally successes, the 240 Z is already regarded as quite a formidable car. I have driven one of the works rally cars which, though certainly having rather more power, was remarkably standard in most respects. The appearance attracts attention and the spoilers, front and rear, are more than a styling gimmick if one can judge by the steadiness of the car at speed.

For sheer driving enjoyment, I place this sports car very high indeed. Though it is a thoroughly practical fast tourer, nothing has been done to blunt its sporting character, and therein lies its charm. To the fat tycoon, who drives as he works out his next big deal, the 240 Z has nothing to offer, but to the man who still regards driving as a pleasure and an art, it promises unending enjoyment.

The interior is impressive and the array of well appointed dials tells the enthusiast everything he wants to know.

SPECIFICATION AND PERFORMANCE DATA

Car tested: Datsun 240 Z 2-seater sports coupé; price £2,389.37, including tax.

Engine: Six cylinders, 83 mm x 73.7 mm (2393 cc); single chain-driven overhead camshaft; twin Hitachi constant-vacuum carburetters; compression ratio 9 to 1; 151 bhp (gross) at 5600 rpm.

Transmission: Single dry plate clutch; 5-speed all-synchromesh gearbox, ratios 0.85, 1.0, 1.31, 1.86 and 2.96 to 1; hypoid final drive, ratio 3.90 to 1.

Chassis: Combired steel body and chassis; independent suspension of all four wheels by MacPherson struts, lower wishbores, and coil springs with telescopic dampers; rack and pinion steering; Girling disc front and drum rear brakes with vacuum Servo; bolt-on disc wheels fitted 175-14 radial ply tyres.

Equipment: 12-volt lighting and starting; speedometer; rev-counter; clock; ammeter; oil pressure, water temperature and fuel gauges; heating, demisting and ventilation system with electrically-heated rear window; 2-speed windscreen wipers and washers; flashing direction indicators with hazard warning; reversing lights.

Dimensions: Wheelbase, 7 ft 6½ in; track, 4 ft 5¾ in; overall length, 13 ft 7 in; width, 5 ft 4 in; weight, 1 ton.

Performance: Maximum speed, 125 mph; speeds in gears, fourth 120 mph, third 90 mph, second 65 mph, first 40 mph; standing quarter-mile, 15.8 s; acceleration, 0-30 mph 2.9 s, 0-50 mph 5.9 s, 0-60 mph 8.0 s, 0-80 mph 14.5 s, 0-100 mph 24.0 s.

Fuel consumption: 18 to 26 mpg.

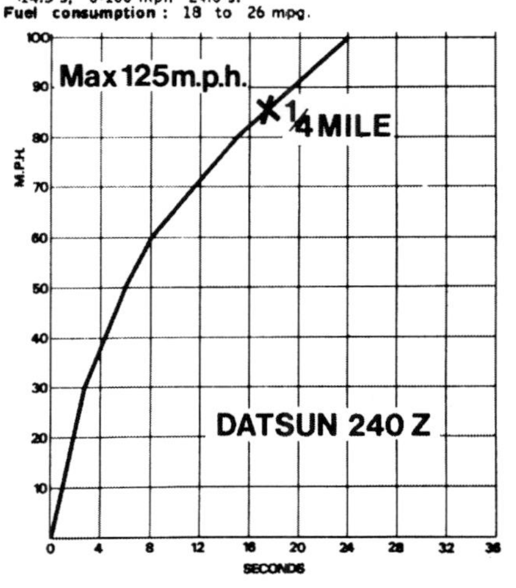

ROAD TEST

DATSUN 240Z

A Japanese Invader

THE PROUD LINES of the 240Z remind us of Ferrari GTOs. Note the front spoiler.

THE WORLD'S major Western motor manufacturers, for a number of reasons we will not go into here, have swung away from sports cars almost entirely over the past few years and their future plans do not, apparently, include any new models for the sports car enthusiasts. Therefore it seems we must look to the East for such vehicles as the Japanese manufacturers still feel there is a market and, judging by the results they are obtaining in the United States, they seem to be right. The Nissan Motor Company, with their Datsun cars, are making a tremendous impact at the moment with the 240Z model which competes directly in America with British cars like the MG-B GT.

The Datsun 240Z model was only introduced on to the British market at the October Motor Show but since then a good number have arrived in this country and we were recently able to try Datsun's demonstrator over a considerable mileage, which proved to be a most interesting experience. Before we drove the car we had the distinct impression that a 240Z was a fairly rorty sports car and the rally people kept telling us that it had many of the characteristics of the old Healey 3000. Perhaps the rallying versions do, but the standard machine is a civilised GT carriage which shows qualities of sturdiness and longevity. In fact it is far from a roaring monster and lacks the flair or handling of a Lotus. A drawback in Britain is the price, £2,389, within a few pounds of the Reliant Scimitar GTE which has two extra seats and very similar performance, but otherwise the 240Z has very few competitors. However, we feel that there is a very big market for exactly this kind of car which would appeal to an MG-B GT owner who possibly wishes to spend a little more money for added performance and prestige. It is a gap in the market that the new Healey-Jensen may well fill but unfortunately we cannot tell you more of that as the embargo date has us beaten by just seven days. The Healey-Jensen, however, is an open sports car while the Datsun falls into the GT category with its excellent lines which remind us of the Ferrari GTOs of the early 1960s. It is still a very proud shape from all angles and this is possibly one of the best selling points of the car.

The actual specification is not one to get excited about for the 240Z has a conventional front-engined steel unitary chassis with all-independent suspension, albeit by the rather unusual arrangement of McPherson struts both front and rear. The engine is a straight six with a single overhead camshaft mounted in the aluminium head and drives to the rear wheels through a five-speed gearbox. The Datsun is a two-seater only, although one can perch on the front of the parcels shelf for very short journeys. With the Datsun you get quite a lot of motor car for it tips the scales at just around a ton, unladen.

The 240Z was actually introduced in Japan at the 1969 Tokyo Motor Show as the top of the Datsun range and the same engine was used for a luxury saloon, the 240C, which is also available in the UK but has yet to be imported in any numbers. The Japanese firm now export a complete range of cars to Britain through Datsun UK Ltd., who operate from a rather anonymous building known as Datsun House, Brighton Road, Worthing, Sussex, to which we returned the car. Unfortunately we were not able to look around as the firm's Publicity Manager was apparently far too busy to see us!

It is interesting to note that during 1971 Datsun produced 1,730,000 passenger cars which puts them into fifth place in the World league overtaking Chrysler and Fiat in the process. For 1972 the firm expects to increase production to about 1.9 million of which 409,000 will be destined for North America and 100,000 for Europe. Datsun were only introduced into Britain in a small way at the end of 1968 through Nissan-Datsun Concessionaires of Shoreham and, over the next two years, sales hardly increased and the firm went into liquidation. This is when Datsun UK Ltd., which is a British owned and controlled company, took over with a factory site at Lancing and the offices already mentioned and became fully operational in March of last year. Since then 140 dealers have been appointed bringing up the strength to 170 and a further 25 are soon to be added. During 1971 a total of 8,000 vehicles were sold while, for the first full trading year, the figure should be up to 13,000 and a 12-15% increase is anticipated for the following 12 months. From all these figures one can see what a major company Datsun is by world terms, and also the aspirations of its new British off-shoot.

Back to the car itself and our test machine which was a very well used example in dark green which had been through a good few testers hands before ours. The two doors are amply large but the car is rather more difficult to climb into than one expects on the driver's side due to the largish wooden steering wheel and the high-built-up sides of the seats. The interior was finished in a particularly nasty shade of light "cardboard" brown and generally exuded a plastic look which was far from in keeping with the high standard of manufacture of the rest of the car. Japanese cars have, in the past, come in for considerable criticism for their seating usually failing to provide for the needs of the over six-footers. The 240Z has plenty of adjustment and a great number of sizes of driver cold make themselves comfortable. Provision is also made to raise the seat by almost an inch and this would definitely be necessary for smaller drivers. The high-backed seats do tend to obstruct rearward vision rather badly, making reversing rather tiresome.

We were immediately impressed by the design of the controls, both those operated by feet and hands. The pedals made heeling and toeing easy and there was a good footrest for the left shoe. A novel feature was the left-hand stalk on the steering column which was rigid and non-movable but put the windscreen washer/wiper controls and the lights right at the fingertips. In fact this is the best arrangement of such controls we have ever used for they were easy to operate with a minimum of fumbling. Likewise, the right-hand indicator stalk had a button on its end from which the lights could be flashed. This could be operated with one's little finger without taking the rest of the hand from the steering wheel. The horn was in the centre of the steering wheel. Directly in front of the wheel were two matching dials for speedometer (with an optimistic 160 m.p.h. maximum) and a rev-counter, red-lined at 7,000 r.p.m. Ranged to the left, above a central console containing the heater controls, were three smaller dials, one a clock and the other two informing on fuel level, electricity charge, oil pressure and water temperature. The heating and ventilating system seemed to lack fine adjustment and we never did master the difficu't combination of controls and the three-speed booster fan. Datsun had not seen fit to provide us with a handbook so that didn't help. One would think that making sure there was a handbook was one of the first lessons in preparing road test cars but it is amazing how often one fails to find such information. The gear lever, with its five-speed gate, and the handbrake came easily to the left hand.

As we mentioned in the introduction paragraphs, the Datsun 240Z is definitely only a two-seater for if a third travels for short distances perched on the parcels shelf it is only with discomfort. However, there is plenty of space in the sloping rear compartment for a great deal of luggage. The back lifts up, station-wagon style, although during winter one is bound to get one's hands dirty in the process as the rear fibreglass spoiler seems to attract road dirt.

Lifting the bonnet reveals the conventional-looking straight six engine with plenty of room around it. Housed either side with their own separate covers are the battery (on the offside) and the washer bottle (on the nearside). The engine compartment has a light which can be unclipped and moved around on a lead. The overhead camshaft engine is fed by two SU carburetters and the bore and stroke is 83 mm. x 73.7 mm. giving a cubic capacity of 2,393 c.c. on a 9-to-1 compression ratio.

For our first run in the car we had the misfortune to choose one of the nastiest snowy nights of the year for we had an evening appointment in Birmingham. Fortunately the Datsun is one of those cars one can climb into and immediately feel completely at home. The ease of operation of the essential controls for such a night, windscreen wipers and lights, obviously helped but the overall road manners of the 240Z were the major factor. The steering is by rack and pinion, is light in operation and gives excellent feel. The high speed stability is also first class and a marked contrast from the Europa we had been driving the week before while the brakes also give tremendous confidence. All this enables one to settle down with the Datsun so very quickly.

The five-speed gear-change is laid out with fifth gear away and across from fourth and in line with reverse. However, reverse is well protected by spring loading and the change down from fifth to fourth is very pleasant. The box is not finger-light and a little baulky and while getting used to it we were constantly changing from first to fourth instead of second and had to remember to hold the lever against the springing to the centre to perfect the change. For that matter the Datsun's transmission did not seem to be very strong and if we were changing up at high revs a horrible noise came from the gearbox as we depressed the clutch. This so worried us that we phoned Datsun to ask if it was serious but the aforementioned Publicity Manager had no explanation, and could not understand it. We later learned that the two previous road testers had encompassed the same trouble and also complained about it and when our weekly contemporary had the car for test, some weeks later, it was still doing it, only worse. However, presumably this is a fault in this particular car, probably a damaged thrust race in the gearbox, which Datsun UK cannot be bothered to remedy.

Braking is provided by 10.67-in. discs at the front and 9-in. drums at the rear and they have quite a job to do with a ton of motor car needing to be stopped from speeds in excess of 100 m.p.h. They are servo-assisted, but fairly lightly, so feel is still retained and they live up to the job extremely well pulling the car up square and with reassurance.

The Datsun's only chance of staying with something like an Elan +2S would be along the motorway where it will cruise happily at up to 120 m.p.h. and the top speed is generally considered to be 125 m.p.h. although our test model was panting hard to go very much faster than 115 m.p.h. and was vibrating fairly badly by then. On smooth surfaces the Datsun holds the road well, displaying fairly neutral characteristics, but on a run through Gloucestershire and in the Prescott hill-climb area we found it rather a handful on the bumpy back roads and the all-McPherson strut system was having to work very hard for its living. The test car was fitted up with Dunlop SP Sport tyres on 4½J rims which, on inspection, revealed that the rubber had been "made in Japan". Wider wheels and British made tyres may help the handling although the Japanese Dunlops did not seem nearly so bad in the wet as we had been led to believe.

Engine and wind noise is well silenced in the cockpit but the Datsun does seem to suffer very badly from road noise particularly at slowish speeds where driving over cats eyes or along a badly surfaced road makes far more din than any other car we can remember.

The engine is a willing worker, as would be expected from a unit of this type and delivers 151 b.h.p. (gross) at 5,600 r.p.m.

240Z MOTOR.—*Power comes from this straight-six engine.*

which is a little less than the fuel-injected Triumph 2.5 engine. Starting, with use of the choke which is mounted alongside the handbrake, was never a problem and the engine had a pleasant subdued rasp which definitely marked it as a six. The engine performance was perhaps a little disappointing for it really needs to be revved above 4,000 r.p.m. to start giving you a kick in the back while over 6,000 r.p.m. the power drops off. It starts to pant then and at 6,500 r.p.m. there is an ignition cut-out to stop you over-revving. However, once one has got the hang of utilising this fairly narrow torque band one can accelerate from standstill to 60 m.p.h. in under 8.5 sec. and see 100 m.p.h. in under 25.0 sec. The fuel consumption varies dramatically on how hard the car is driven but over a varied selection of roads we averaged a shade over 23 m.p.g. and that was with some hard driving. The tank incidentally held 15½ gallons but the fuel gauge showed empty with 5 gallons still to go.

Picking 6,000 r.p.m. as a change-up point, and with the previously described unpleasant noise as we made the changes, we found that 1st would take us to 37 m.p.h., 2nd to 60 m.p.h., 3rd to 84 m.p.h. and one could run right up to 110 m.p.h. in 4th before taking 5th. For this reason one tended to stay in 4th along the more twisty roads while normally one would change gear at around 4,000 r.p.m. or less for the engine has considerable torque and will actually pull in top from 40 m.p.h.

One has the feeling that the Datsun is strong and well built rather in the same way that Volvos are and the rally successes in Africa and elsewhere would certainly bear this out. Despite the rather restrictive price in Britain we are quite sure that the 240Z will find a ready sale in Britain somewhere upmarket of the MG-B GT set. March Engineering designer Robin Herd was one of the very first customers, having bought the actual Earls Court Show car and is delighted with it. The Datsun 240Z is what the MG-C GT should have been and wasn't and it seems a great shame that the British industry cannot offer a similar type of vehicle. Meanwhile the Japanese are on to a good thing and the best of luck to them.—A. R. M.

Z/28 vs 240-Z

Great Expectations --Unconfirmed

In the market research that produced the Z/28 and 240-Z, who did their homework best, them or us?/By John Christy

Ever wanted to feel like a statistic in a market researcher's report to Management? Drive a Z-car.

Competent market researchers are apparently cut from the same cloth whether they come from these United States or from 6,000 miles across the Pacific and the conclusions about the customers they are trying to reach are as remarkably similar. It is only in the manufacturing philosophy and execution of the parameters that the end result of the research differs. And in the starting point from which the realization of that product was launched.

Our two cases in point for this session are the two Z-cars, the '72 Camaro Z/28 and the Datsun 240-Z. The former had its beginnings in Chevrolet's answer to Ford's spin-off of the Shelby GT-350 Mustang for the Trans-American Challenge, the first of the Z/28 series. In street form it was a hairy, fierce, no-nonsense device that was the equal in almost every way of the Corvette of the same period but with more practicality. And about as irrelevant to the demands of the dawning '70s as it was suitable to the late '60s. The 240-Z was much longer in the cooking pot, being the end result of a long-term development of a tinny little offering of the mid-'50s called the Datsun Fairlady which was about as fierce as the name implied and homely enough to make one wonder about its makers' taste in ladies. In the early '60s a complete redesign transformed the Fairlady into a series of 1300, 1600 pushrod and finally 2000cc single OHC powered roadsters that strongly resembled the MGB in styling.

As the last decade drew to a close and the present one dawned it became obvious that those twin doom-words "safety" and "ecology" spelled the eventual end of such things as high power/displacement ratios and ragtop roadsters. Skyrocketing insurance rates on such machinery only reinforced the issue.

Enter the researchers. What could be done to satisfy customers with a sporting bent and still keep the forces of opposition at bay? Obviously horsepower as such had to go down and displacement had to go up to hold off the safety shouters and insurance underwriters. Cubic inches had to take the place of high compression ratios and rich mixtures to comply with the clean air laws. The hardtop had to replace the ragtop. Torque had to replace horsepower. The burning question was what combination or compromise of these parameters would people buy?

It is hard to say whether the market researchers started from some common ground-zero and by divergent trajectories arrived on the same target or whether they started from different sets of parameters to reach a common goal. However they got there, they did their work well and obviously touched the proper chord. The Z/28 is the last of those cars with any pretensions to the title of muscle car that is still selling, the others having gone all fatty, been emasculated or just plain discontinued. The 240-Z was a runaway sales success from the outset and, though dealers are no longer able to force the full load of extras on the customer that once brought the out-the-door price up to more than $5,000, it is still a brisk mover in the marketplace.

There are marked similarities between the two. Both are pleasing to the eye. The Camaro, reskinned as a sort of ultimate (short of the Sting Ray) expression of GM styling's "organic look," shows an Italo-American (out of NASCAR) influence with its natural flowing lines and flush side glass. The 240-Z is more along the Anglo-American line so beloved of Japanese stylists in recent years, but in this case they have eschewed the juvenile drive-in mini MoPar influence that has graced so many of the latter-day Japanese styling efforts. Both are strong on straight-line go-ahead performance, the Camaro especially so in high gear thanks to the hairier torque of its LT-1 V8, but strangely enough the 240-Z isn't all that far behind, particularly when it comes to a through-the-gears run. And both will hang onto the road surprisingly well if with a vagueness that takes the place of the handling precision of both their forebears. Perhaps this last,

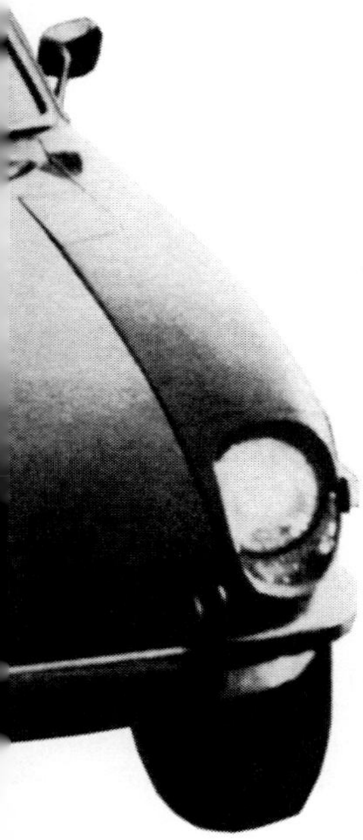

It would be hard to find two more attractive cars in the popular American genre than the 240-Z (far left). The crisp Anglo-Germanic lines of the Datsun and "organic" Italo-American appearance of the Camaro complement each other in an oddly similar way. Grace on the one hand and brutality on the other, efficiency on both. And it is this attractiveness that magnifies the shortcomings of each; expectations belied.

As attractive on the outside as the Datsun and, at first glance on the inside, the Z/28 lets you down when you start to drive. Pedals are all at different levels, the gearbox is harsh, the steering too soft and the instruments unreadable.

too, is a result of the computer read-outs from market research. Precision in handling is not a high priority want-item in mass surveys of the American car market — possibly through lack of exposure or experience in the higher planes of this particular commodity on the part of the buying public. If it stays on the road it's good; *where* it stays is of little moment. However, as far as precision goes, the 240-Z is a Group 5 racer by comparison to the Z/28.

Differences such as these are as intriguing as the similarities. As we have indicated, the Z/28 is in essence a downgraded racing car, or at least that's what the marketers would have one believe. The 240-Z, on the other hand is the end product of the upgrading and redesign of a production sports car. Actually it is the result of starting with a clean sheet of paper with the experience gained from the predecessors and the market research factors cranked in. However, if the current Z/28 were, in truth, a downgraded or civilized racing car (as was the original), it could have been a thing of beauty and joy forever in the manner of such delights as the various forms of Lotus, the Porsche and the Ferrari. Such devices are almost always infinitely superior to those which have come through the ranks, so to speak, of the plain-jane or cooking version of the passenger car. Is the current Z/28 one such? The answer, unfortunately, must be an unequivocal negative. The racy Camaro is just that; a cooking version of the Camaro that has been equipped with racy hardware. An upgraded sports-personal street machine of the genre of the latter part of the '60s rather than a re-trained racer. Thanks to its LT-1 engine option it moves; it produces responsive, go-ahead performance and does it in compliance with the Clean Air Act. It's probably as quick a small-block street machine as you can buy these days short of a five-figure price (except for the LT-1 Corvette). Thanks to a heavy-duty suspension and fat tires it stays on the road at speed. And, thanks to an excellent styling job and an instrumented, if somewhat gaudy interior aspect, it looks racy. But it is about as sophisticated as any other Camaro rebuilt by that knowledgeable kid down the street. A short run in an area where it can be exercised a little leaves one with the feeling that the people responsible for hammering it together should have gone down the hall and sought the advice of the guys who put together the '70 and '71 Nova SS 350. *That* one was a device with which you could lead Corvettes down the garden path, a machine that could shock the man with

Z/28

SPECIFICATIONS

Engine	90° OHV V8
Bore & Stroke — ins.	4.00 x 3.48
Displacement — cu. in.	350
HP @ RPM	255@5600
Torque: lbs.-ft. @ rpm	280@4000
Compression Ratio/Fuel	9.0:1/91 Octane
Carburetion	4v
Transmission	4-Speed, all snychro
Final Drive Ratio	3.73:1
Steering Type	Variable ratio power assist, recirculating ball
Steering Ratio	15.5-11.8:1
Turning Diameter (curb-to-curb-ft.)	41.1
Wheel Turns (lock-to-lock)	2.3
Tire Size	F60 x 15
Brakes	Power disc/drum
Front Suspension	Unequal length A-arms, coil springs, anti-roll bar
Rear Suspension	Live axle, leaf springs, anti-roll bar
Body/Frame Construction	Unitized w/ separate front subframe
Wheelbase — ins.	108 0
Overall Length — ins.	188.0
Width — ins.	74.4
Height — ins.	61.3
Front Track — ins.	61.3
Rear Track — ins.	60.0
Curb Weight — lbs.	
Fuel Capacity — gals.	18.0
Oil Capacity — qts.	4 (1)

PERFORMANCE

Acceleration	
0-30 mph	3.1
0-45 mph	5.0
0-60 mph	7.7
0-75 mph	11.8
Standing Start ¼-mile	
Mph	86.6
Elapsed time	15.2
Passing speeds	
40-60 mph	4.2
50-70 mph	4.0
Speeds in gears*	
1st ... mph @ rpm	52@6500
2nd ... mph @ rpm	71@6500
3rd ... mph @ rpm	89@6500
4th ... mph @ rpm	108@6000
Mph per 1000 rpm (in top gear)	18
Stopping distances	
From 30 mph	31.0 ft.
From 60 mph	139.2 ft.
Gas mileage range	10-14

Speedometer error

Car Speed	30	45	50	60	70	80
True Speed	28	44	49	59	68	78

Base Price	$3,919.00
Price as Tested	4,304.00
MT Road Test Score	64.54

*Speeds in gears are at shift points (limited by the length of track) and do not represent maximum speeds.

the five-figure import that has to be kept running by the little man with the pointy shoes and the stolen sunglasses.

By its very being and its past history anything bearing a Z/28 badge should be the equal, if not the superior, of the Nova SS. It isn't and disappointment in the general lack of expected precision causes one to look at the rest of the car with a somewhat jaundiced eye, causing one to carp at things that might otherwise be forgiven and one or two that couldn't.

Among the former is that group of equipment that faces the driver. The steering wheel is that same small rubbery item that is used in the Vega GT, the one with the groove around the inside that pinches the inside of your fingers. In this case it is connected to a power steering with an almost total lack of road-feel, a seeming anomaly since this particular Camaro is hardly geared to appeal to little old ladies. The wheel effectively hides most of the instrumentation. The tachometer and speedometer are visible but the others (fuel gauge, ammeter, clock and water temperature) are invisible unless one makes a conscious effort. The fact that they are about the size of the average wristwatch doesn't help matters. The lack of an oil-pressure gauge is also an annoyance in this sort of car. All except the dead-feeling power steering could be forgiven were it not for the two items that cannot be forgiven or ignored. The clutch pedal requires a strong left leg to deal with, which in itself is not uncommon among performance cars, but the throw is inordinately long and vague as to engagement and disengagement. A stiff clutch is supportable if the action is crisp and an abomination, especially in this age of hydraulics, if it is not. Coupled with a shifter that feels as though one were stirring at a keg of nails with a crowbar, the business of controlling the car becomes a chore where it could be a sensuous pleasure. The real annoyance comes with knowing that Chevrolet can do better; they've proven the fact abundantly in the Corvette and the Nova. Mix in the bumps, squeaks, jolts and rattles with which our test car came factory-equipped and what could and should be one of the better offerings *chez* Chevrolet, (or even Detroit), in this age, becomes one of their greater disappointments. Like leading a kid into a familiar candy store only to find that the wares are rubber and wax. Perhaps the thing that bugs us most is that this sort of thing is what lends unwarranted credence to those anti-bigness freaks who are continually wailing that all Detroit's Big Three are interested in is turning a profit and to hell with the customer. In this case it's just damnfool carelessness, not greed. An

The Datsun interior is well laid out in an ergonomic sense with all operations made easy and all instruments visible and readable. The effect is psychologically spoiled by the use of shiny, cheap-looking plastic for upholstery.

240-Z

SPECIFICATIONS

Engine	OHC in-line six
Bore & stroke — ins.	3.27 x 2.90
Displacement — cu. in.	146.0
HP @ RPM	150@6000
Torque: lbs.-ft @ rpm	148@4400
Compression Ratio/Fuel	8.8:1/Regular
Carburetion	2-2v
Transmission	4-Speed, all synchro
Final Drive Ratio	3.36:1
Steering Type	Rack & pinion
Steering Ratio	17.8:1
Turning Diameter (curb-to-curb-ft.)	31.4
Wheel Turns (lock-to-lock)	N.A.
Tire Size	175HR-14 radials
Brakes	Power disc/drum
Front Suspension	Independent strut, coil springs, anti-roll bar with compression link
Rear Suspension	Independent strut, coil springs
Body/Frame Construction	Unitized
Wheelbase — ins.	90.7
Overall Length — ins.	162.8
Width — ins.	64.1
Height — ins.	50.5
Front Track — ins.	N.A.
Rear Track — ins.	N.A.
Curb Weight — lbs.	2,230
Fuel Capacity — gals.	15.0
Oil Capacity — qts.	4 (1)

PERFORMANCE

Acceleration						
0-30 mph	3.0					
0-45 mph	5.7					
0-60 mph	9.0					
0-75 mph	14.0					
Standing Start ¼-mile						
Mph	81.7					
Elapsed time	16.3					
Passing speeds						
40-60 mph	3.6					
50-70 mph	6.0					
Speeds in gears*						
1st ... mph @ rpm	40@6500					
2nd ... mph @ rpm	64@6500					
3rd ... mph @ rpm	105@6500					
4th ... mph @ rpm	110@5000					
Mph per 1000 rpm (in top gear)	22					
Stopping distance						
From 30 mph	35.3 ft.					
From 60 mph	125.1 ft.					
Gas mileage range	15-21					
Speedometer error						
Car speed	30	45	50	60	70	80
True speed	30	45	49	58	68	77
Base Price	$4106.00					
Price as Tested	4552.30					
MT Road Test Score	68.4					

*Speeds in gears are at shift points (limited by the length of track) and do not represent maximum speeds.

Z/28 vs 240-Z

intracompany communications problem.

When we first met the 240-Z a couple of years ago, we, along with untold thousands of others, were caught up in the general enthusiasm and mystique the car generated. Here, we thought, was a modern successor to the Austin-Healey 100-6, a medium-priced, strong six-cylinder sports coupe on a modern chassis with more performance than its size and price implied — a tremendous value in terms of the amount of car per dollar. We obviously were not alone and demand, at least in those parts of the country where people are prone to that sort of thing, far exceeded the supply. Dealers, being dealers, were quick to take advantage of the situation and proceeded to load the things with everything but the kitchen sink and the price went sky-high. Some dealers in high-demand areas even scoured the hinterlands, offering retail for base, unloaded cars that they could cart home, load up and deliver to their panting customers, making their profit on the gingerbread. Since the add-ons were the usual run of dealer-option gimmicks rather than handling, convenience and performance equipment, the value per dollar ratio dropped. Now the rush is off and, if one looks, one can find a reasonably basic 240-Z without all the luxury or non-functional gingerbread. Until now that was a significant difference between the Z/28 and the 240-Z. If you wanted stereo tape decks, air, tinted glass, trick wheels and other gew-gaws on your Z/28 you could have them. If you didn't, all you had to take was the basic option group that turned the Camaro into a Z-car. In the case of the 240-Z you had to take what the man wanted to hang on the car, period. And if you wanted the other real handling bits all you got was a blank look.

Like the Z/28, Datsun's offering excels in go-ahead performance. It has that pure feeling of smooth torque that is the hallmark of a performing six that starts down *here* and seems to go on forever without let-up rather than that whang in the back that you get from a quick V8 or a hot four-banger. Each time you change up in gears it begins all over again. You can let the man next to you pull a minor hole-shot on take off and then, without a lot of rubber-burning, law-calling nonsense just drive on by while he's scratching second-gear rubber. Naturally we're not talking about economy sixes that run out of breath just as they're getting to run but rather the kind that are equipped to breathe deeply and run up to the 6000 rpm-and-up range.

Also, as mentioned, the 240-Z will stay on curving roads at immoderate rates of speed and will stop very well when so bidden — all points of similarity to the Z/28. It's how it does these things that shows the difference between the two in the engineering philosophy and interpretation of the original research. When the Z/28 does its act with a strong but harshly brutal manner reminiscent of backyard or early NASCAR practice, the 240-Z comes off all suave and, by comparison, butter-smooth. It's sensuous where the domestic rival is violent. It is also tireless in what it does. A bit of past experience coupled with a distinct gut-feeling indicates that were one to take showroom versions of both cars to some such area as Nevada or Montana and attempt a really high-speed cruise, the Z/28 would give the 240-Z fits for the first few minutes but after an hour or so it would be running a temperature and vomiting valve keepers trying to maintain the pace.

Another vast difference is apparent when you climb into the 240-Z. It's actually a rather small car but the first impression on settling in is that somehow it has expanded — it *feels* big and it indicates that the researchers did their work on the American market very well indeed. You know instantly where the target was — and it most definitely was not Japan. The next thing that catches the eye is the instrumentation. It's all there and it's all visible at a glance. The steering effort with the large wheel is on the high side and somewhat rubbery in feel, much like an unassisted domestic unit but faster. In contradistinction from its Yankee rival the shifting is effortless and it doesn't take a period of deep knee-bends to tone up for the clutch, which, though somewhat soft, is predictable. All this would lead one to expect that once underway the handling would match the appearance. Unfortunately, it just misses — another point of similarity to the Z/28 but in a different way. Where the domestic machine is harsh and somewhat inaccurate in aiming, the 240-Z is softly vague. If you painted a small spot on the apex of a corner and tried to hit it repeatedly with the appropriate front tire your average score would be something like three direct hits out of 10 tries and a couple of near-misses. According to Pete Brock of BRE it is largely due to the amount and softness of the rubber insulators. It feels like it. For the price of the stereo or air conditioner you didn't let the dealer install BRE can supply a total cure.

After a bit, if you're into sports cars at all, something else begins to irritate. There is an annoying feeling of fakery about the car — as though it were masquerading as something it isn't. It's hard to pinpoint, to lay a finger on any one item and say "that's it." At first it is a bit of *this* and an elusive impression of *that*, which forms the overall feeling. Part is a distinct feeling that the car was built to a strict schedule of price that was applied sometime after the build was started. One of the MT advertising staff who owns a 240-Z (and loves it) made the point that the fake plastic quilting on the tunnel was what put him off. ". . . like those Red Chinese quilted army jackets done by a plastics peddler." That certainly is part of it, along with the sleazy, shiny plastic in the seats and side panels that more resembles old fashioned oilcloth than modern vinyl-based leatherette. Not only does it look cheap, blatantly fake, but it feels odd, too, and is conducive to perspiration on even a mildly warm day, air conditioning notwithstanding.

At any rate, there they sit, two cars aimed at essentially the same market, meant for much the same purpose, and priced within the same range. Not-quite-sports-cars for people who aren't quite ready for sports cars and both excellent starting points for the real thing. Chauvinism aside, whether the Japanese market researchers did their homework just that touch better or the Japanese engineers assigned to interpret the research in metal did it better than our own is open to question. We prefer to think it's the latter since the point at which the Chevy falls down is in the second-string hardware. In the case of the Datsun the hardware is first rate, as is the application. Now if they can only find out where the Germans get their leatherette . . . /MT

Road & Track
Owner Survey

DATSUN

DATSUN 240Z

Is it worth seven months on the waiting list?

THE PROMISE OF value is the staple of automotive selling. Whatever the car, economy sedan or prestige sports model, nothing works nearly so well as telling the customer that he's getting the most for his money. In that sense, the Datsun 240Z was following a familiar trail. What made the difference was the way Datsun did it.

The extra values were exciting values. The styling was as close to faultless as a mass-produced car gets and the announced price put the "Z car" into a category occupied by cars that were merely attractive. And powered by fours, in the main, while the 240Z had an overhead-cam six with the performance of a domestic V-8. Plus independent suspension all around, generous front disc brakes . . . more than one buyer merely read the details and rushed down to his nearest Datsun dealer, deposit in hand.

Two years later they are still doing it. Some dealers still have a waiting list and many of those that don't are packing their allotted number of 240Zs with all possible options, secure in the knowledge that if one buyer doesn't want the alloy wheels, big tires, air conditioning and AM-FM radio, the man behind him does.

The 240Z, then, was an instant success. We said at its introduction in early 1970 that it was "the most exciting GT car in a decade," and it certainly was that, but even R&T has been amazed at the number of people who agreed and spent their money in agreeing. There are also indications that not even Datsun expected that many buyers to be that eager to have the car. And there are signs that the factory and the buyers have suffered for the under-supply of Zs.

The Owners

THIS SURVEY comes quite early in the Z car's history. Our rules require a car to have covered at least 5000 miles, so the owner will know if he has any problems, will have an opinion of his dealer, and will have formed his likes and dislikes before participating in the survey. A pleasantly large number of 240Z owners are R&T subscribers. And they do a lot of driving. In consequence, 106 owners qualified their cars for a survey despite the short time—less than two years—that the car has been available.

One indication of their reaction to the car's value was that they bought lots of equipment with the car. This may have been influenced by the aforementioned tendency of dealers to load the cars with extra stuff, but even so there were only one or two complaints from buyers who had to take the wheels, etc. to get the car. And we have no way of knowing whether the buyer took the car as it sat, ordered the options, or bought them later. In any case the installation rates were extremely high: 38% of the cars had air conditioning, 24% had alloy wheels and larger-than-standard tires, and 8% had BRE spoilers. There were also mentions of add-ons like driving lights, exhaust systems, Koni shock absorbers and leather-rimmed steering wheels, all proof that the 240Z buyer doesn't mind spending money to have his car the way he wants it. Especially if it's easy to do. One owner commented that the shop manual's wiring diagram comes complete with instructions for connecting driving lights and that the spoilers attach to holes already drilled.

The usage confirms this blend of price and enjoyment. While 53% of the owners have more than one car, only two of the 106 surveyed do not use their Z car for daily transportation, so utility is important. A predictable 78% take trips (it's a GT car, after all). There was only one racer, but 28% take part in rallies and 19% run in autocrosses or SCCA solo events, so the owners are competition-minded provided they can use their cars as driven daily.

For a final sporting note, in the welter of add-ons mentioned earlier we forgot to say that only two of the cars in the survey had an automatic transmission. Our owners bought their 240Zs to drive them.

Reasons for Buying

THE POWER factor is very strong here. The most popular reason for choosing the 240Z was what you'd expect, with 52% mentioning performance, i.e. acceleration, high cruising speed.

Next came value. Owner after owner noted, in essence, that he looked at the specifications, compared them with the other cars in the mid-price GT class and decided that the Z car had more of what he wanted. This is not just price, as another 20% mentioned the price as a factor.

Many of the cars were, so to speak, pre-sold. A surprising 20% said they placed their order because of what they read in R&T and/or other sources. More than one was bought on pure faith. "My father read your road test and went down and ordered one," a reader wrote. "He didn't know anything about cars—and still doesn't." Most flattering, especially as this owner went on to say that he likes the car very much, hasn't had any major troubles, hasn't been one bit disappointed and would happily buy another. We may decide that R&T road tests are all one needs to know about cars.

Most predictable was the 55% influenced by the styling. The Z looks exciting, certainly. And 14% liked the interior with its large stowage area and plenty of room for even the larger enthusiasts. (Two men in the 6 ft 6 in. range said they were delighted to find a sports car into which they could fit.) Handling wasn't as strong a sales point as one might expect, probably because there was no way for prospects to judge for themselves. Many dealers couldn't even keep demos on hand.

Just to illustrate the perils of moving up in the market, not one buyer said anything about Datsun's reputation. It's a good reputation, of course, but until the Z car it was based on fine little economy sedans and trucks and on the homely 1600 and 2000 convertibles. Though Ferrari and Mercedes can expect to sell cars to people who've yearned for an example of the marque and Porsche can even advertise the 914 as the car for people who've wanted a Porsche but couldn't afford a 911, Datsun had to sell to people who might even be diffident about buying the top of an economy-maker's line. That ain't easy.

Best Features

THE BUYERS got what they ordered, in that 36% said the performance of the car was its best feature. Perhaps the figure should be even higher, as another 4% like the car's ability to cruise at high speeds, which surely is affected by engine power and strength. Next was handling, with 33%. There may be some odd factors in that one, though, as we'll see in the next section. A welcome surprise must be comfort, as 21% said that being able to drive all day without cramps and aches was the best feature. For 9%, the model's high resale value was a best. This will surely become more important to owners as time passes. The survey included a large share of first owners, after all, and few of them said much about selling or trading, so maybe they don't know that in some sections of the country a low-mileage Z car brings close to the price of a new one.

Worst Features

A CONTRADICTION, or so it appears at first. Remember that 33% of the owners said the car's handling was a best feature? Well, 25% said that poor handling at high speed was a worst feature, and another 15% listed instability in cross winds in the same category. Sounds like a clear conflict, eh?

It isn't. A car can have good handling at speeds involved in normal daily driving and still lack high-speed stability. In our first test of the Z car, we were most impressed; the cornering figure on the skid pad was high, the car was nicely balanced and could be driven with great brio and control, the steering provided plenty of feel, etc. And our testing involved jaunts through the mountains, nipping through city traffic, commuting at 70 mph on the freeway, most conditions, in short, that are faced by a daily-driven enthusiast car. We also ran a top-speed test on a straight and level road with no side wind.

But when we got into a comparison test, with a convoy of sports/GT cars crossing the wide open spaces at close to wide open throttles, we found what some owners know. At speeds of more than 70 mph, the Z car *does* react badly to side winds and it does hunt about on ripply surfaces. As we said then, Datsun could stand to do some research into shock absorbers.

However, recall also that a number of owners have installed the BRE spoilers. Six of these owners, or 75%, said that the front dam, or "spook" in the BRE lexicon, and the rear blade cure the instability at speed. And one man said it helped, leaving only one owner who tried the equipment and wasn't pleased. Other owners reported great improvement from the installation of Koni shocks. It gives us great pleasure to pass along the results of these experiments, to predict maybe a cure and at least an improvement of a worst feature. Seldom is a flaw so readily taken care of. Sure, the factory ought to be doing something too, but meanwhile, better to bolt on spoilers and shocks than curse the manufacturer.

Besides, the factory gets its lumps in the next worst feature. It's quality control, involving a long list of minor bothers. Some show up as trouble areas but many don't, being complaints involving things that fell out, paint that rippled or flaked, components incorrectly assembled and the like. The consensus would seem to be summed up by the owner who said "They must really be cranking them out over there."

Then there's the parts shortage, which drew adverse comment from 22% of the owners. Like quality control, it didn't seem to be so much major as an accumulation of little things; a 10-month wait for a new hood release cable. The demand for the 240Z may have simply overpowered the supply of both cars and parts, but we're reminded that parts shortage was a problem also in our survey of Datsun 1600 and 2000 roadsters two years ago.

A fragile body was listed by 17% of the owners, meaning parking damage for the most part, as the front body panels get creased and dented in parallel parking. Several owners also reported dimpled fenders from just being leaned on by hand.

Service and Maintenance

THE DEALERS look very good. We included a section for "excellent" ratings because there were more of them (7%) than in most surveys. Several owners were appreciative enough to list the excellent dealers by name and location. The Datsun Dealer Honor Roll is: Bob Sharp, Wilton, Conn.; Palmer Datsun, Roseville, Calif.; Fayette Auto, Lexington, Ky.; Girard Motors, Groton, Conn., and Elmwood Auto Sales, West Hartford, Conn.

And 46% of the dealers were rated as good. Only 28% come into the "fair" rating, and 18% were poor ("They don't seem to have as much quality as the car," read one nicely ironic comment.)

The owners who considered their dealers to be poor no longer deal with them and have divided almost equally into taking their cars to independent shops or doing the work themselves. Only 4% of the owners fall into this last category, which is something of a surprise considering that the car is a sports car and the owners are interested in competition.

The owners take good care of their cars, 80% following

the factory recommendations and many of them going beyond that with more frequent oil and filter changes. Component life varies with driving style, or in the case of tires, maybe brand. Three owners said the original Toyo tires were replaced at 6000 miles but one man got 36,000 miles from his Bridgestones. The median would be somewhere between 16,000 and 20,000. Other lives reported were brakes, 20,000 mi; spark plugs, 6000-12,000, and shock absorbers, 20,000.

Trouble Spots

Good news first. This survey was close to being a record for non-disasters. Two owners said their cars locked in reverse gear, and one man had an engine failure caused, he thought, by paint flaking off the inside of the cam cover and clogging oil lines. (Fixed by the dealer, under warranty.) Those were the only incidents of genuine breakdown of troubles that called for a tow truck. Most impressive, especially as the 240Z is a new model and uses a new engine.

But there certainly were some trouble spots. A full 45% of the owners have had trouble with the instruments; the fuel gauge, oil gauge, tachometer, etc. And there's the parts problem, with waits of several months, and there's quality control, with as many as three replacements failing as rapidly as the original unit.

The brakes were more serious. The actual difficulties were sticky brakes and leaking master cylinders. No tow-ins or crashes reported, and evidently all cases were repaired with no hardship; but it does give one pause. In this area, but listed in the survey as a worst feature, was wet-weather braking. Poor, said 7% of the owners. This seems to be a design problem, as spray from the road splashes onto the rotors. The dealers say it's aggravated by those popular wide wheels, which is scant comfort.

The transmission shortcomings, those two locked-in-reverse instances aside, have to do with the synchromesh. Fifteen percent said the synchros were worn enough to warrant replacement, and many of them said the car still makes noises in 3rd and 4th gear, which the dealers say is normal.

The clutch doesn't break. It gets weaker and weaker, or the hydraulic linkage loses its seal and requires pumping.

We were expecting the reports of vibrations and balance problems, because we had already heard about this from owners and the factory. The early Z cars suffered from a high-speed vibration, which was frequently taken to be unbalanced tires, alignment, or unbalanced driveshafts and/or axles. Drove the mechanics batty. One owner said he visited three dealers before having his car fixed with a damper on the driveshaft, and that the line of other Z owners waiting for the fix stretched around the block.

The cause turned out to be too much driveshaft angularity. The differential is mounted with rubber to reduce shock and noise transmission, and it moves under braking and acceleration forces. On a '70 or early '71 model, this motion put the driveshaft into an angle that threw it out of line. Result, vibrations. Once this was learned the factory cured it by moving the differential back a bit. Simple but infuriating.

For the other trouble areas we turn back to quality control. This bends the meaning of this section, perhaps. We had mechanical difficulties in mind, and for the 240Z we got upholstery that ripped, choke cables that broke or fell off, hood releases that jammed. These are not big things. When a choke cable snaps, the driver can enlist a neighbor or wife to turn the key while he opens the hood and yanks on the stub. Still, when it becomes a habit, as it did on the car that needed three cables replaced, the owner regards it as a trouble spot; so that's where it's listed.

Would They Buy Another?

A vote of confidence, and not surprising. Beginning with the negatives, a majority of the nay-sayers based their "wouldn't" on combinations of bad service, poor quality control and handling.

As we've seen, the service is rated better than average. The parts are in short supply and sometimes faulty, and it remains to be seen if those shortcomings will cure themselves as supply catches demand. We are left with the 91% who would buy another Datsun—whose spokesman, so to speak, told us the Datsun 240Z is "A great car, especially considering the $5000 I have in it."

SUMMARY: DATSUN 240Z OWNER SURVEY

New or Used?

Bought New........95%
Bought Used.........5%

Annual Mileage

Less than 5000/yr...1%
5000-1000........17%
10,000-15,000.....38%
More than 15,000..44%

How owners feel about Datsun service

Rated "excellent"...7%
Rated "good"......46%
Rated "fair"........26%
Rated "poor"........17%
Don't use dealer.....4%

Driving Habits

Drivers who said they drove "moderately"..33%
Drivers who said they drove "Hard".........59%
Drivers who said they drove "Very hard".....8%

Problem Areas
Reported by more than 10% of owners:

Brakes	Transmission
Switches	Clutch
Instruments	Drivetrain
Choke Cable	Upholstery

Reported by 5-10% of owners:

Differential	Hood release
Alternator	Heater controls
Cooling system	

Owners reporting no problem areas...........6%

Would they buy another?

Yes..................91%
No...................9%

Five Best Features

Performance
Handling
Comfort
Value
Interior

Five Worst Features

High speed handling
Poor quality
Fragile body
Reaction to sidewinds
Scarcity of parts

Datsun 240Z

Although it is undeniably Datsun's best-known car, it comes as something of a shock to find the 240Z is actually the oldest of the Datsun models offered in Britain. When it was introduced in Japan in 1969 it was extremely advanced—to such an extent that many, perhaps, expected it to remain an exotic, small-production car like its rival the Toyota 2000GT. Instead, it was put into large-scale production, aimed primarily at the American market, and is now the world's most successful sports model.

While the 240Z is advanced in many ways, it is still essentially a practical car. There is plenty of room inside it, with no need for the occupants to contort themselves. All the controls are well laid out. Most important of all, the 240Z borrows heavily from Datsun's engineering tradition in that it is reliable rather than temperamental, and no trouble to run.

The engine, a 2·4-litre straight-six with a single overhead camshaft, offers reasonable power and excellent torque, and is cleared to rev much higher than many engines in its class, thanks in part to excellent balance and oversquare dimensions. Many people have asked the obvious question—when will it become the 260Z—but the bigger engine gains its extra capacity by having a longer stroke, which means it cannot rev as high and would spoil the sporting character of the car. It therefore remains the 240Z.

A notable feature of the car is its all-independent suspension, using MacPherson struts all round to ensure good handling even on rough roads, along with a better-than-average ride in the sports car class. As offered in Britain, the 240Z also offers a close-ratio five-speed gearbox, with a high enough top gear to allow restful (and relatively economical) 100mph cruising.

The competition record of the 240Z is too well known to require an exhaustive record. It is perhaps sufficient to refer to its recent success in the East African Safari Rally—its second in three years. It is in some ways the wrong sort of car to do well in the classic European winter events, being too much of a road car to compete strongly against the semi-racing cars which are now coming to the fore, but it has acquitted itself well none the less, with a constant chance of success in one of the rougher events.

By its very nature, the 240Z is destined for a longer production life than any Datsun saloon model. None of the cars introduced since its first appearance has yet been replaced, but presumably some of them will be before too long, simply because of competitive pressures. But there is still nothing which directly competes with the 240Z, and it is more likely to go from strength to strength than give way to a new model.

Car	Price £	Engine cc	Length ft	in	Width ft	in	Wheelbase ft	in	Weight lb.
Datsun 240Z	**2535**	**2393**	**13**	**7**	**5**	**4**	**7**	**6½**	**2285**
Alfa Romeo 2000GTV	2687	1962	13	5	5	2	7	8½	2290
Reliant Scimitar GTE	2314	2994	14	3	5	4½	8	4	2655
Triumph Stag	2533	2997	14	6	5	3½	8	4	2805
Porsche 911T 2·4	4562	2341	13	8	5	3½	7	5½	2250
Jaguar E-type	3319	5343	15	4½	5	6	8	9	3360

DATSUN

The Bright Green Pleasure Machine

By Ray Hutton

10,000 miles with a Fairlady —known as the Datsun 240Z

You can hardly fail to have realised that the Datsun 240Z has been a tremendous success in America. That was the market for which it was tailored and it was crying out for a new, fast, modern-looking traditional sports car at a reasonable price. Let's be honest—this Japanese coupé has taken a large number of customers, actual and potential, from British manufacturers in a corner of the US market which they have looked upon as their own. Now that its annual sales have surpassed the Chevrolet Corvette, Datsun can claim, that the 240Z is the world's best selling sports car.

The significance of the 240Z is that it illustrates the ability of Japanese industry to design and build a product for an existing export market, even if it has little relevance to their home conditions. Britain's largest manufacturer regularly reminds us that the idea of producing a new two-seater from scratch for mass production is not economic; that the world demand is changing to high-performance cars of a more conventional, more practical nature. Yet Nissan of Japan—where, I am told, taxation is prohibitive for all but the smallest cars, and speed limits and road congestion such that sports cars are impractical—have come up with an exciting-looking car which handles well and out-performs all its price competitors (at least in the United States).

The 240Z made its debut at the Tokyo Show in 1969 and first supplies were sent into America soon after. Only recently has the model been made available in Japan though a 2-litre version using the same body and known as the Fairlady Z has been sold there. The British Datsun importers hedged at first on whether or not the 240Z would be sold in this country—partly because of the supply problem (US demand far exceeded production) and also because it was clear that they would not be able to match the low American price. In the US it sells for less than 4,000 dollars (approx. £1,700). The final British price came out at £2,309, moving it away from the TR6/GT6 class and in amongst the Alfa Romeos and Lotuses.

So we had heard about the car a long time before we saw one—and when we finally did get our hands on a 240Z it was a rather special version. Datsun surprised the rally world by turning up at the 1970 RAC Rally with a team of 240Zs when the model had never previously appeared in a European event. After it was over we borrowed Rauno Aaltonen's rally car, complete with grumbling differential, for an article in our "Given the works" series. We were very impressed, but unsure of how great an improvement had been made over the standard product.

In due course a few production 240Zs were brought into this country and one of them came to us for road test (*Autocar,* 6 May 1971). We liked that one too, and were pleased to find that it had the five-speed gearbox of the rally car instead of the American spec. four-speed —part of the standard specification for the higher British price. It was during the preparation of this test that someone mistook the nought for a letter "o"; the car has been known in our office as the "24-ounce" ever since.

Late last year we were offered a 1972 model 240Z for 10,000 miles evaluation—something which pleased me particularly, since I was to run it.

The Datsun at rest on the fastest racing circuit in Europe—Spa-Francorchamps in Belgium. All but this short uphill section beyond the pits and L'Eau Rouge is comprised of public roads

The Bright Green Pleasure Machine

First impressions
So one cold morning in late January I set off gently back to London with a shiny new Datsun—metallic olive green with tan seats and trim and 528 miles on the clock. I see from my notes at the time that I thought that road and transmission noise were high and that some of the creaks we had noticed in the rally car were there (we think they emanate from the sub-frame which carries the independent rear suspension). The throttle linkage was jerky and, although the heater was powerful, I could not find a way of combining heat with fresh air ventilation. Six months and 10,000 miles later those criticisms are still valid. The differential, which at first growled loudly enough to suggest that it would be an early casualty, has quietened a little, but gearbox whine has increased. The road noise, a combination of tyres and insufficient sound insulation in the rear luggage area, is something one gets used to (and characteristic of cars without a separate luggage boot). The throttle linkage is still jerky, despite lubrication, and it takes both care and practice to move off smoothly from rest and prevent the joints in the drive-line clunking.

For the first 1,000 miles or so the car was used for commuting and a few trips to race meetings up and down the country, and we took care not to exceed 4,000 rpm. This was no real hardship, for it still allowed 90 mph in fifth gear and served to illustrate how very good the torque characteristics of this 150 bhp 2.4 litre ohc six-cylinder engine are. Coupled with a high first gear, giving over 40 mph when full (7,000) revs are used and well-spaced intermediate ratios, this means that the 240Z is a restful car to drive and has a set of gears which are just as useful in towns as on trans-continental journeys.

Our car was really given its head for the first time at the 2,000 mile mark when it was called upon to take part in our Sports Car Test Day at Silverstone. As luck would have it, commentary on the medium-range two-seater group fell to me. The car performed much better at Silverstone than I had expected; though it understeered it did so only moderately. It was almost as fast as the little Lotus Elan coupé, reaching 110 mph on the Hangar Straight yet still leaving comfortable space for stable braking for Stowe. The brakes—servo assisted, disc front, finned drums at the rear—proved powerful and fade free. At the end of the day I found myself torn between the relatively hefty, lazy Datsun and the lithe little Lotus and was rather surprised that when I considered all factors very carefully I decided that the 240Z just had the edge.

Tough and strong
It is an overall feeling of solidity which many passengers remark on when they first ride in the car. That is not an easy thing to analyse, but comes in part from the strong unstressed sound of the engine when running at normal revs (it becomes harsher above 4,500 rpm), the almost total lack of body roll and the secure feeling of sitting low within what seems, for a two-seater, to be a big car.

In fact, the 240Z seems a lot larger from the inside that it really is—at 13ft 7in. long it is 5in. shorter than a Ford Capri—but the low seating position means that neither the front or rear extremities can be seen from the cockpit. This caused one of our testers to report that he felt "boxed in". In fact, the view over the humped bonnet is good but the side windows are quite shallow and high for all but the largest drivers, and rearward vision, particularly through the rear quarters, is severely limited by the body itself and the high-backed "tombstone" seats.

The average Japanese may be small but when he's building a car for export, he makes sure that even the biggest American will be comfortable. I am just 6 foot but in most cars use the driving seat back as far as it will go. In the 240Z it can be adjusted so far that I can't even reach the pedals. The result is a car in which almost everyone can find a near-ideal driving position, aided by the seat rake adjusters which allow the backs to be reclined through about 30 degrees. The seats themselves are well shaped, if rather thinly padded, and proved comfortable even over the longest journey.

Someone has obviously put a great deal of thought into the layout of the 240Z's controls. The pedals are conveniently placed for heel-and-toe operation even for my small Size 7 feet and there is a footrest for the clutch foot. The one-piece moulded facia is rather stylised and its deeply cowled white-on-black instruments give it a superficial similarity to the Corvette; so that the Americans can feel at home, presumably.

All the important switchgear is incorporated in two column stalks—which is the way it should be done. That on the right is a conventional indicator switch with the headlamp flasher operated by a button in its end and the dipper by a single pull towards the wheel. The thicker stalk to the left incorporates a three-position light switch, that for the two-speed wipers and a button in its end which operates the electric screen washers. The wipers are only self-parking on the down-stroke from their centre position.

The centre of the facia has an excellent little map light (operated by pressing in the lens) and the heater and ventilator controls below the centre swivelling ventilator. The three-speed fan is operated by a knob to the left and is commendably quiet. Below that is a space for a radio into which, at the 3,000 mile mark we had fitted a Radiomobile 301 CS cassette tape player. At first we were disappointed with its performance and inclined to blame the machine but then I realized that the layout of the car was not well suited to stereo listening. Grilles are provided in the extreme rear of the luggage area for speakers (the similar ones nearer the door pillars are extractors for the ventilation system) and the combination of the narrowing tail plus the high seats means that the speaker balance is only right for someone in the centre of the car—where there isn't a seat.

There is a useful open compartment on top of the transmission tunnel for cassettes and other oddments (as well as a lockable and illuminated glove locker). This console also includes the convenient pull-up choke lever; cold starting was never a problem.

Left: Like most Japanese cars, the underbonnet layout is well planned for access to all major components. Air cleaner intake has "summer" and "winter" settings. The provision of a roving inspection light is a thoughtful touch

Below: Interior is stylised but well-equipped. All instruments are deeply recessed which eliminates reflections. Lights and wiper/washer switches are neatly assembled on left hand column stalk. The facia is a matt-black one-piece moulding

Below: The rear luggage platform is of generous size though the suspension strut housings obstruct it slightly. Small items can be housed in the centre tunnel trays or in the space behind the high-backed seats

Right: Jack and tools are housed in two rather irregularly shaped lockers underneath the rear carpet. The spare wheel is similarly concealed—and the carpet is held in place with Velcro pads

Below: The 240Z's body is a synthesis of ideas from other successful designs—like the Jaguar E-type, Toyota 2000GT and Fiat 850 coupé. It is a practical shape, though rear quarter visibility is poor; side mirrors would be a help. The rear quarter windows do not open

The Bright Green Pleasure Machine

The required servicing interval is 3,000 miles, when the handbook recommends that the engine oil should be changed. The oil filter should be replaced every 6,000 miles. There are no chassis greasing points.

At this stage the only fault which had occured was an occasional tendency to jump out of fifth gear on the motorway; this was not specifically attended to but did not reccur during the last 5,000 miles of the test. One of the vulnerable front indicator glasses had been smashed.

The Grand Tour

I made plans for a combined trip to the Spa 1000 Kms sports car race and the Monaco Grand Prix so that a lot of mileage could be concentrated into a short period and we could assess the car's touring capabilities. Since I feared that there would be few Datsun dealers in France (I was wrong) I asked the British importers to gather together a few essential spares to take with me. The box which arrived a few days later was big enough to house a spare Datsun—and as it turned out all I needed was one rear light bulb. But the spares kit could not cover the misfortune which occured the evening before I was to leave. The car was parked in a Knightsbridge side street and when I returned to it I discovered the rear offside had been hit, apparently hard, by something big enough to have missed the stout rubber-faced bumper completely and tear the bodywork above it. I was most grateful to a passer-by for reporting the accident to the police and identifying the offending Land Rover (which did not stop). Chelsea police are still looking for the driver. . . .

Fortunately the damage, though extensive, was no more than cosmetic and so I was able to set out on my journey as planned. The rear luggage platform accommodated all my gear with lots of room to spare; the rear window is at such a shallow angle that large pieces of luggage rarely obstruct the rearward view. Nylon straps are thoughtfully provided and are useful to stop isolated suitcases from moving around. The flat floor covers two small tool boxes and the spare wheel; other oddments can be conveniently stowed in the wells behind the seats. The lift-up rear door provides a generous opening and is supported by a hydraulic strut.

Less than an hour after leaving Calais I was cruising along the motorway towards Lille at over 100 mph at a relaxed and relatively quiet 4500 rpm in top. I soon found that 110 mph was a pleasant cruising speed for fast roads in

Left: Spoilers front and rear are part of the UK specification—and appear to perform a more useful function than their appearance suggests. The front "air dam" is made of hard rubber; the rear spoiler is glass fibre.

Below: Radiomobile stereo cassette player fitted neatly into the radio slot: high-backed seats plus the shape of the rear compartment reduced acoustic effect. The fuses are conveniently housed under a panel on the centre console.

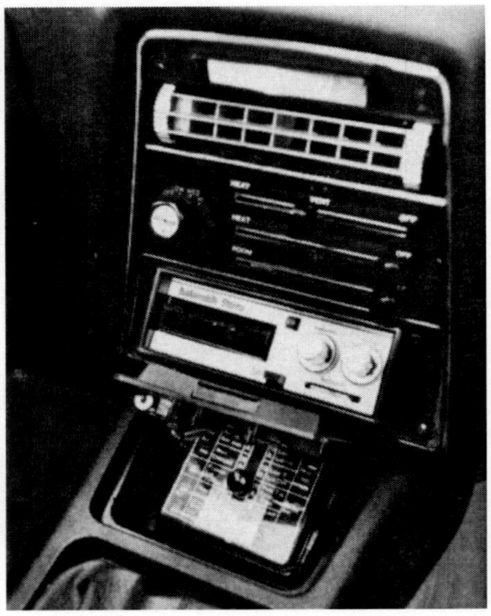

Access to the battery and washer reservoir, housed within the front wings is by opening flaps each side of the trailing edge of the bonnet.

Below right: Hub caps are unusual in that they have serrations locating them round the whole circumference on the wheel rim. But they tend to move round in use, threatening to cut the valve stems. This latest type of hub cap is much more elegant than the original fussy fittings

PERFORMANCE CHECK

Maximum speeds	mph		kph		rpm	
Gear	**R/T**	**Staff**	**R/T**	**Staff**	**R/T**	**Staff**
Top (mean)	125	121	201	195	5,750	5,600
(best)	126	123	203	198	5,850	5,800
4th	118	120	190	193	6,440	6,500
3rd	98	99	157	159	7,000	7,000
2nd	69	68	111	109	7,000	7,000
1st	44	44	71	71	7,000	7,000

Standing ¼-mile	**R/T:**	15.8 sec	82 mph
	Staff:	16.9 sec	82 mph
Standing kilometre	**R/T:**	27.7 sec	102 mph
	Staff:	30.2 sec	104 mph

Acceleration									
	R/T:	3.0	4.6	6.0	8.0	11.4	14.8	19.2	25.6
	Staff:	3.2	4.6	6.9	9.0	12.3	15.7	20.3	26.6
Time in seconds	0								

True speed mph		30	40	50	60	70	80	90	100	110
Indicated speed mph	**R/T**	30	41	51	62	73	84	95	106	117
Indicated speed mph	**Staff:**	32	42	51	62	72	83	93	104	115

Speed range, Gear Ratios and Time in seconds

Mph	Top		4th		3rd	
	R/T	**Staff**	**R/T**	**Staff**	**R/T**	**Staff**
10-30	—	—	8.2	8.1	5.9	6.0
20-40	9.7	9.6	7.5	7.1	5.7	5.4
30-50	9.4	9.3	7.0	7.0	5.2	5.2
40-60	9.7	10.0	7.2	7.5	4.8	5.5
50-70	10.2	10.9	7.7	7.9	5.4	5.6
60-80	10.9	11.9	8.0	8.2	6.0	6.1
70-90	12.1	12.6	8.6	9.1	8.2	8.1
80-100	14.2	15.5	10.5	10.8	—	12.6

Fuel Consumption

Overall mpg	**R/T:**	21.4 mpg (13.2 litres/100 km)
	Staff:	21.1 mph (13.4 litres/100 km)

NOTE: "R/T" denotes performance figures for Datsun 240Z tested in *Autocar* of 6 May 1971

those countries enlightened enough to allow it. At about 115 mph wind noise, which until that point is low, becomes excessive as the door frames start to pull away from the rubber seals. Later that day I checked the maximum speed, recording a best one-way figure of 123 mph (over 130 mph indicated) in fifth; 3 mph slower than our original test car, though the maximum in fourth (at the 6,500 rpm yellow line) was marginally greater, at 120 mph.

Straight line stability was good in even strong cross-winds, and better than I remember of the test car, which suggests that the new and gimmicky-looking add-on spoilers do perform a useful function.

The journey south from Spa took me through neat, pastoral Luxemburg, then on give-and-take roads skirting Annecy and Geneva to Grenoble—and the alps. Driving a fast, responsive car through the mountains on a hot, sunny day in May has to be one of life's most pleasurable experiences. I had plenty of time to get to Monte Carlo so I chose some of the less familiar *Cols*; they were virtually deserted and still back-clothed by snow-covered peaks.

Again the "24-ounce" impressed. The engine rushed responsively up to its high 7,000 rpm limit in second and third, the brakes responded perfectly to an admittedly hard push as the engine note barked on the overrun entering the next corner. The steering, which has a lively feel as it feeds back information about the road surface, is sufficiently high-geared to attack all but the sharpest hairpin without resorting to hand-over-hand techniques. On smooth roads the car holds the chosen line beautifully, but over rougher surfaces there is a certain amount of bump-steer which is disturbing at first but easily compensated for by allowing the wheel to make these small movements without correction. The quality of the ride improves as the car goes faster; at low speeds it is poor and jolty but the stiff dampers come into their own as the speed increases and several drivers have expressed surprise at the fast and sure-footed way it can be taken along poorly surfaced "B" roads. Those who have had experience of the 240Z in rallying also remark on this and it is worth noting that, even in standard form, the car has very generous ground clearance.

One tends to use a "point and squirt" approach to driving the car on a winding road: braking hard, cornering relatively slowly and accelerating hard again. In fact, the power can be applied quite early and this has the effect of neutralising the tendency to understeer. It can be made to oversteer quite spectacularly, but we didn't find this out until we tested at Silverstone. It is not scientific, sophisticated handling in the racing sense but it is predictable and quite satisfying. We have often had reason to criticise Japanese-made tyres, but the Dunlop SP Sports fitted to this car seemed every bit as good in the wet and dry as the British equivalents. This was puzzling, for Robin Herd of March Engineering, whose opinions of car handling and roadholding I trust, owns a 240Z and thought his, apparently identical, tyres were below standard. The answer came from Dunlop—their Japanese company has recently been persuaded to use the British tread compound for their SP Sport, so that the latest tyres are identical in composition to those supplied here.

COST of OWNERSHIP

Running Costs	**Life in Miles**	**Cost per 10,000 Miles**
		£ p
One gallon of 4-star fuel average cost today 35p	21.1	166.00
One pint of top-up oil, average cost today 21p	1,500	1.42
Front disc brake pads (set of 4)	10,000	12.64
Rear brake linings (set of 4)	10,000	5.40
Dunlop SP Sport tyres (front pair)	25,000	9.12
Dunlop SP Sport tyres (rear pair)	15,000	15.20
Service (main interval and actual costs incurred)	3,000	18.74
		Total 228.52
	Running cost per mile: 2.3p	

Approx. standing charges per year		
	*Insurance	63.70
	Tax	25.00

Depreciation		
	Trade in Cash Value (approx.)	1,700
	Typical Advertised Price (current)	2,000
	Price when new	2,309

**Insurance cost is quotation for 33-years-old driver, car garaged Surrey, 65 per cent no claims bonus deducted; named drivers over 30 only with clean driving record; compulsory £25 excess.*

I returned from Monaco by the quickest route—by *autoroute*, a journey of 12½ hours to Calais—and it was raining heavily for much of the distance. The limiting factor in these conditions turned out to be the wipers, which despite having anti-lift type arms were operating in mid-air at anything above 90 mph. This again emphasised the shortcomings of the quite complex heating and ventilation systems. The demisters make short work of clearing the screen (though they are ineffective on the mist-prone side windows) but in the summer particularly it would be nice to be able to enjoy a fresh air inlet at the same time. A heated rear window is fitted as standard and works well, though its switch failed after 7,500 miles.

From GP to rally

The 2,000 mile round trip brought the total mileage to 7,000; overall fuel consumption had been 21.3 mpg and the car had used just two pints of oil. A few weeks later Martin Lewis and Peter Cramer took the 240Z to cover the Scottish Rally and thus bring the mileage to our 10,000 target. Martin reported that it had coped with the undulating side roads of the highlands admirably and confirmed my views about the headlamps. They are Lucas Halogen, fitted by the importers here, and are so good that they make auxiliary lamps unnecessary for normal road conditions.

During the course of the test it had become more difficult to engage first gear from rest. The gearchange, arranged in Alfa Romeo style, with first to fourth in conventional positions and fifth forward opposite reverse, is spring-loaded towards the centre plane. Like the other controls the gear change is quite heavy (the 240Z could be a tiring car for a woman to drive) but changes through the first four gears are quick and precise. Changing into or out of fifth is a slower, more deliberate movement and the clumsy can easily touch the reverse cog.

Finishing it off

Though the metallic green paint always looks smart, it has shown a tendency to flake slightly around the inevitable stone chips. Some other details of the finish are a little below standard, though in general the car is stoutly built and the fit of the doors, for example, is good. The same applies to the interior which is nicely conceived but uses some cheap materials—notably the plastic mock quilting on the transmission tunnel and the wood grain plastic steering wheel rim.

Under the forward-opening bonnet, all the essential items are easy to get at—something which has become a Japanese tradition. Access to the sensibly large washer reservoir and the battery is via two small flaps either side of the bonnet opening; the battery never needed topping up but we found it impossible to disconnect the positive terminal without taking the battery out. The oil filler cap is screw-threaded into the cast-alloy cam cover and care must be taken not to cross-thread it; when this happened to ours a piece of the thread dropped into the bowels of the engine. Datsun deserve a minus mark for the jacking arrangements which look simple enough until one finds that the jack does not engage properly with the lifting points—and placing it elsewhere along the sides is asking for trouble.

But trouble was not a feature of our tenure of the 240Z. It provided us with fast, reliable transport, has a seemingly unburstable engine, and was always great fun to drive. Though it is a year since the model first appeared in this country its appearance is exciting enough to still draw interested and admiring glances. It has proved its worth in competition—winning the East African Safari and innumerable races in the USA—and is so highly thought of on the other side of the Atlantic that *Road & Track* voted it one of their "Ten best cars in the World" for 1971. It is encouraging, I think, that a car like this should be doing so well in a country where safety and pollution fears are taking the fun out of motoring. In Britain it is less of a bargain, but the other reasons for its popularity are just as valid. It is truly a Pleasure Machine. □

DATSUN 240Z

ALFA ROMEO 2000 GTV

This was not the most obvious of Two Car Tests; not at first. We began by wondering whether there was anything closely comparable with the Datsun 240Z, or whether the Japanese car had a slice of the market all to itself. Then, to our surprise, the Alfa Romeo 2000GTV emerged as a close contender.

The initial reaction was inevitable; what were we doing comparing a little Italian thoroughbred with such a hulking Japanese newcomer? But the figures speak for themselves. Whatever impression they give, the two cars are actually very similar in size and weight. As far as engines are concerned, would one rather have a twin-cam four or a single-cam six? And it is the Datsun not the Alfa, that has the independent rear suspension. Both cars, of course, boast a distinguished competitions record.

The Alfa coupé was never a cheap car and its price has risen along with its successive increases in engine size, until now this 2000 is listed at £2,587. It seems that a heated rear window and limited-slip differential, although listed as extras, are part of the British market specification, bringing the total price of the Alfa 2000 tested to £2,650.

This means that the Datsun is rather the cheaper car of the two, with a list price of £2,309. There are no major options for the 240Z.

Description — Alfa Romeo

THE 2000 GTV is the latest and most powerful of a range of Alfas to use the same 2-plus-2 Bertone coupé body. Increasing the bore of the previous 1,750cc twin-cam four-cylinder engine has raised the capacity to 1,962cc and the power output to 131 bhp at 5,500 rpm. The new model incorporated some revisions to the interior but few changes to the outward appearance, save for a new grille and wheel trims which dispense with hub caps.

Like all Alfas, the GTV has a five-speed gearbox with an overdrive top gear. The shift arranges first to fourth in the conventional four-speed pattern with fifth to the right and forward, opposite reverse.

The front suspension is conventional, using double wishbones and coil springs, but the Alfa is rare among today's cars of this type in continuing to have a live rear axle, albeit a well-located one with trailing arms, an A-bracket and anti-roll bar. The brakes are ATE discs all round with the handbrake operating through small drums machined into the rear disc centres. The wheels are 14-inch diameter and the tyres fitted to the test car were 165-14 Michelin XAS radials.

The GTV feels a compact car, having relatively little overhang front and rear and generous unobstructed glass areas. It has a wheelbase of 7 ft 8.5 in. and an overall length of 13 ft 5 in. It weighs just over a ton.

Description — Datsun

The stylish 240Z coupe was all-new at the time of its introduction late in 1969 but like the Alfa Romeo shares many of its components with saloons in the range. Thus the large 240C saloon also uses the bulky six-cylinder single overhead camshaft 2,393cc engine, which in the more developed form of the 240Z is rated at a conservative 150 bhp at 5,600 rpm.

The Datsun also has a five-speed gearbox as standard, with the shift pattern the same as the Alfas. Unlike the GTV the specification does not include a limited-slip differential.

The 240Z is unusual for a sports car of high performance in using the well-tried MacPherson strut medium for both front and rear suspension. At the rear, wide-based lower wishbones are used with the differential and suspension all mounted on a stout sub-frame bolted to the integral body/chassis. The brakes are Girling, made under licence by Sumitomo: disc at the front and with finned drums at the rear. The Datsun also uses 14-inch wheels, with narrower rims (4.5 to 5.5J) but wider section tyres than the Alfa: the test car had Dunlop SP Sport 175-14s.

Unlike the Alfa, the 240Z has only two seats and no provision for even the occasional carriage of an extra person. It has no separate boot but a generous flat loading area behind the cockpit and an opening rear window/door. It looks and feels bigger than the GTV but in fact is only two inches longer and two inches wider while the wheelbase is shorter by the same amount. It is marginally lighter.

Performance

There is bound to be some doubt about the relative power outputs of the two cars because while Alfa Romeo give figures according to the European DIN system, Datsun stick to the optimistic SAE ratings. This being so, the figures suggest very similar power outputs for the two cars, which is reasonable since the Alfa has a higher compression ratio and better breathing with its four carburettor chokes and opposed valves.

The torque figure is more puzzling: the Datsun should have a considerable advantage here, with its six cylinders and greater swept volume. Even more surprising is the high speed at which the Datsun's peak torque is developed: 4,400 rpm. Without actually seeing the torque curves, one can only guess that the Datsun's is very flat, with a minor peak at this speed.

This assumption is borne out by the acceleration figures. The fourth and top gear times show how strongly the Datsun pulls throughout the speed range, whereas the Alfa needs coaxing at the bottom end. The top gear figures are actually closely comparable, because the Datsun has the lower top gear but a higher final drive, and the two factors virtually cancel out to give the same mph per 1,000 rpm figure as the Alfa (21.6 against 21.9).

It has been pointed out often enough that where power and weight are more or less equal, the car with more torque will do better away from a standing start, and the Datsun is certainly faster than the Alfa — without ever scoring a runaway victory. The Japanese car is helped by the very high rev limit placed on its engine; the yellow line comes at 6,500rpm, the red at 7,000; corresponding figures for the Alfa are 5,700 and 6,000. The Datsun engine actually has a considerably shorter stroke, so one should not be too surprised — if anything, it is more a case of 6,000rpm being a low limit for a race-bred twin-cam like the Alfa power unit.

Thus it is that the Datsun can be powered away beyond 40mph in first (one change in the Alfa); to all but 70mph in second (the change to third comes at 50mph in the Alfa); and all but 100mph in third. The Datsun's gains, in fact, are partly due to its low-speed punch and partly to the time saved through not having to change gear so often. Once the cars are travelling at higher speeds in fourth gear, the Datsun maintains the gap but can no longer pull away — although it has marginally the higher maximum speed.

From a driver's point of view, therefore, the Datsun has the advantage for the lazy that it will pull strongly from much lower speeds. It also pleases the enthusiast with its much higher intermediate maxima. The gearchanges themselves are both on the heavy side, although totally different in character; the Alfa has long movements in a smooth, well-defined gate, compared with the Datsun's shorter, vaguer shift.

Fuel consumption

There was precious little to choose between the two cars overall, the Datsun showing a very small advantage — the equivalent of seven gallons difference in 10,000 miles. Driven gently, the Datsun showed more of an advantage (not entirely unexpected in a car with SU-type carburettors), giving 24.5 against 23.3mpg. This tendency was confirmed by the steady-speed fuel consumption figures, which showed the Datsun to be more economical up to 70mph, with the Alfa showing an advantage from 80mph onwards.

Ride, handling and brakes

There is one fundamental difference between the two cars, and that is the weight distribution. The Datsun *looks* a nose-heavy beast, but that is because it has gained a long nose through having its engine set well back. The weighbridge says it is excellently balanced, with 51.4 per cent of its weight on the front wheels. The Alfa, on the other hand, has over 56 per cent of its weight at the front.

Among other things, this means that the Datsun can get away with higher-geared steering; it has 2.7 turns of the wheel for a 33ft lock, compared with the Alfa's 3.6 turns for a 37ft lock. The Alfa's answer is to maintain its handling close to neutral, so that the driver does not have to indulge in too much

Above left: Datsun 240Z six-cylinder engine, which has a single chain-driven overhead camshaft and twin SU-type carburettors, made by Hitachi

Above right: The 2-litre Alfa engine is a four with twin overhead camshafts (chain driven) and two twin-choke Weber carburettors

Below: Despite appearances, the two cars are much the same size overall and not very different from each other on price

wheel-twirling except at low speeds. Considering the weight distribution, the fact that it *does* neutral-steer is a tribute to the cunning with which Alfa have tuned the chassis, using anti-roll bars at both ends. Especially with the extra power of the 2000, the limited-slip differential is needed to maintain traction in situations where the inside rear wheel would otherwise lift and spin.

The overall result is that the Alfa is a very agile car on the open road and maintains its line very closely right up to the point where it runs out of roadholding and slithers sideways. An earlier limit is set on uneven surfaces which can catch out the live back axle and cause it to skip sideways. On a wet surface, the Alfa's front wheels let go first unless the tail is provoked into a slide with the accelerator. Because of the limited slip differential, the whole tail slides at once, sometimes without much warning.

The Datsun's handling is also close to neutral, but naturally so because of its weight distribution and suspension geometry. The use of MacPherson struts at each end mean that the roll axis is virtually level, and quite high; the roll angle is therefore very small even when the car is cornered fast. Otherwise, the Datsun's

TWO CAR TEST...

behaviour mirrors that of the Alfa except that it is better behaved over poor surfaces because of its independent rear suspension. On a bumpy British "B" road, the Alfa cannot stay with the Datsun if the latter is driven with determination, for this reason.

While the Alfa has disc brakes all round, the Datsun makes do with the more conventional disc/drum combination. Both cars — despite their use of servo assistance — need a good deal of pedal pressure to stop quickly, though both will achieve a 1*g* stop in emergency. One reason for the heaviness is the use of fade-resistant brake linings. Neither car suffers detectable fade even in hard driving, and the Alfa's brakes in particular actually feel crisper when they are hot. Stability under braking is good in both cars, with little tendency to nose-dive. The Datsun handbrake is on the weak side, while the Alfa's works well but over too short a travel.

The Datsun feels more softly sprung but more stiffly damped than the Alfa, with the result that the latter has the better low-speed ride. Indeed, the Alfa's suspension is a good compromise over most surfaces, as long as the car is not overladen and the springs do not reach the end of their slightly limited travel. The Datsun on the other hand improves at high speed and gives a very comfortable motorway ride. It copes a great deal better with poor surfaces when travelling fast; its good ground clearance (especially for a sports car) helps it a good deal.

Noise

Since both are sporting cars, potential owners are unlikely to complain about their exhaust notes. The Alfa has a rich, lively and distinctive 'bark', while the Datsun has a much flatter, mechanical sound. Neither is obtrusive or unpleasant at motorway cruising speeds.

The Datsun's engine begins to sound rough and vibratory beyond about 4,700 (which is beyond the normal change-up points even in quite fast motoring) and can set up a slight but irritating vibration when running at steady speed around 4,000 rpm.

The wind noise in both cars is low — almost negligible up to 80 mph. Beyond that the Datsun is, if anything, a little quieter until 115 mph when the internal air pressure pushes the door frames away from the sealing rubbers.

The Alfa is remarkably free of creaks and rattles but the Datsun gives the occasional groan from the rear subframe and there is a noticeable clonk from the drive line on all but the smoothest take off. In addition the

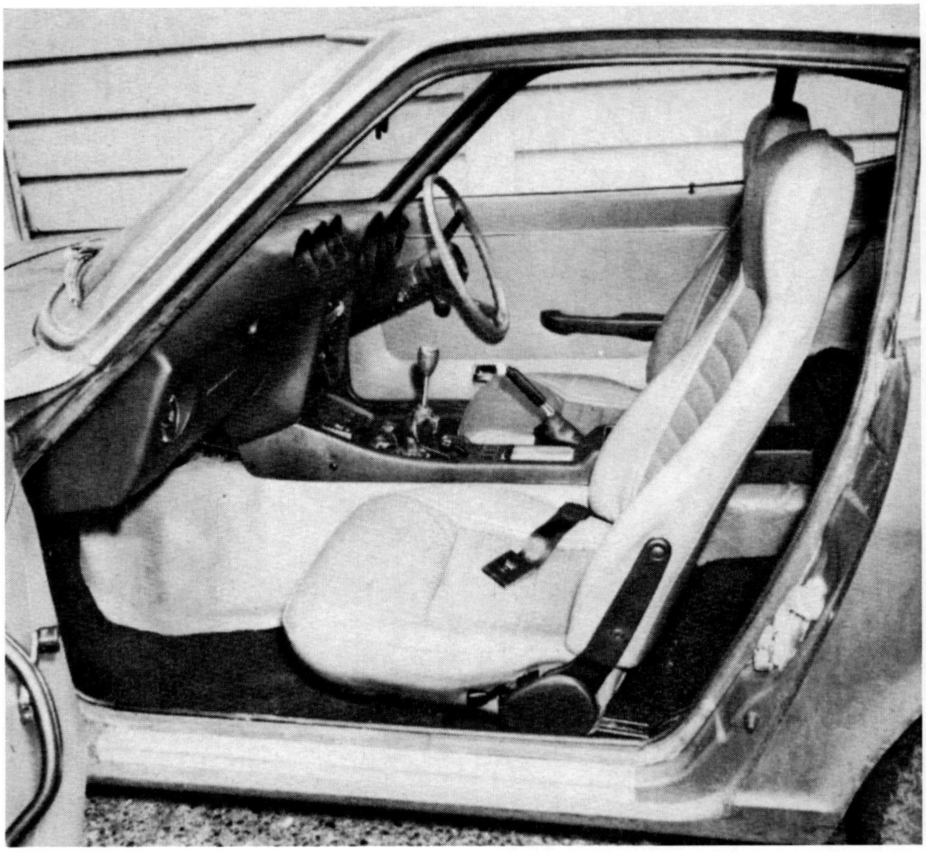

Top: Built-in head restraint is part of the seat structure on the Datsun, creating quite awkward blind spots. Steering wheel rim and gearlever knob are finished in mock wood

Bottom: The Alfa has cloth material on the wearing faces of the seats and the headrests can be adjusted for height or removed altogether. There is a real wood-rimmed steering wheel

transmission tends to whine and a lot of road noise (from the tyres) finds its way into the driving compartment; a function of inadequate insulation which would probably not be so if the 240Z had a separate luggage compartment.

Fittings and furniture — Alfa Romeo

Whether the facia revisions which came with Alfa's 2-litre engine represent an improvement over the 1750GTV layout is questionable. Repositioning the fuel and temperature gauges between the hooded speedometer and tachometer is a more sensible arrangement, but the gauges themselves are less clear than before and the instrument cluster has a cheap look about it, unworthy of the rest of the fittings. The binnacle includes eight warning lights arranged within two dial-shaped spaces. The switchgear is scattered. All lighting operations are looked after by a stout stalk on the left of the steering column; the indicators by a smaller and less precise one in front of it. The two-speed wipers (which are clap-hands type — and two short to clear the screen fully) and the heater fan have toggle switches on the console below the gearlever. The electric screen washer is operated by a foot pedal which also brings the wipers into operation for a few strokes. The heated rear window and hazard warning lights have large illuminated press buttons below the instrument panel, while lying flush with it on the right-hand side are the choke and hand throttle.

The heating and ventilation system has been improved by the fitting of proper flow-through ventilation with eye-ball sockets, but the heater is of the all-or-nothing type. Front and rear quarter-lights can be opened.

Alfa Romeo pedals are notoriously awkward until you get used to them — the clutch and brake being floor pivoted. The position of the steering wheel has been changed slightly in the latest model so that the gearlever knob when in fifth is no longer so close to its wooden rim. Thanks to good and widely adjustable seats it is not too difficult for most people to find a driving position that they like, though someone who is tall and bulky may find that they have to drive bow-legged to prevent contact of their knees with the wheel rim.

The seats themselves are among the best fitted to any production car, with support provided exactly where its needed — under the thighs and in the small of the back. They recline through about 30 degrees and have built-in headrests, adjusted for height by rather stiff thumb screws. The faces of the seats in the test car were covered with a high quality worsted-like cloth. The small rear seats are well shaped and comfortable and the headlining is thoughtfully cut away to give their occupants headroom — even if they are unlikely to have anywhere to put their legs.

Under normal circumstances the rear compartment would be used for light luggage. Access to the separate boot is via a lockable handle in the passenger's door pillar. It is smallish and has a high sill and its sides are single skinned, indicating that care should be taken when carrying heavy but sharp objects. The spare wheel is housed beneath the floor. Oddments can be stowed in a lockable glove compartment and a flimsy open tray between the front seats.

Right: The Alfa has a four-headlamp system with a large-diameter outer pair and smaller inner units for additional power on main beam

Below: The big difference between the two body styles is the occasional rear seat provided in the Alfa. It provides useful, but cramped accommodation

Right: The Datsun has only a two lamp system and all cars are supposed to have this front spoiler when imported to the UK. We have seen several without it

Fittings and furniture — Datsun

The Datsun's facia and controls are very well planned even if the rounded instrument panel seems a little garish at first glance. The dials are deeply hooded, with the centre-mounted ancillary gauges angled towards the driver. Two of those are split, indicating temperature/oil pressure and ammeter/fuel, while the farthest left is a clock. Only the handbrake, high beam and indicators have warning lights. An excellent left-hand column switch cluster controls all lights, the two-speed wipers and electric washers; the indicator stalk on the right includes the dipswitch and headlamp flasher. A separate toggle switch operates the hazard warning, while the illuminated switch for the rear window is incorporated on a little panel in front of the gearlever which encloses the neatly-labelled fuse panel. The choke is operated by a lever on the centre console.

The heating/ventilation system looks to be comprehensive, with air ducts at the centre and both ends of the facia, three slide controls and a quiet three-speed fan. But in practice it has the shortcoming of being unable to provide floor heating and fresh air at face level at the same time and the eyeball side ventilators do not adjust easily; the hearing and ventilating systems work well enough independently. The rear quarter windows do not open. Surprising as it may seem for a Japanese car, the 240Z is better suited to large people than small ones. The seats — comfortable and well-shaped but with rather thin cushions — have an enormous range of to-and-fro adjustment and also recline over a limited range. They have fixed head restraints as narrow extensions of the seat squabs. The pedals are well-placed and a long organ-type throttle makes heel-and-toe operation easy. The small steering wheel is set quite high; its rim is wood-grained plastic, though the gear lever knob is real wood.

The Datsun's interior trim is in various styles of plastic, from neat simulated pigskin used on the head lining to cheap-looking criss-cross patterned material on the side walls of the luggage compartment. The floor is fully carpeted.

The rear floor has two fitted straps to retain luggage which can be stowed through the lift-up rear door (supported by a hydraulic strut). The luggage bay has a false floor concealing the spare wheel and two small tool lockers. Other oddments can be stowed in the space behind the seats, in the shallow trays of the centre console or in the glove locker. The facia incorporates a neat map light.

Fittings and furniture — differences

Both cars are comprehensively equipped — as cars of this type should be. The Datsun has an ammeter and a clock which the Alfa does not, but the Italian car has a hand throttle and that item seems to have been deleted from the 240Z's current specification. Datsun's ergononic planning of the controls is much the better, but the quality of all the interior fitments and trim is higher in the Alfa. The latter has the better seats — though the Datsun's are by no means bad — and of course has the small rear seats that the Datsun lacks. In neither car are the seats fully reclining.

A person of average size should be able to find a comfortable driving position in either car. All-round visibility is better in the Alfa and short drivers find that their view from the low seating position of the Datsun is restricted. On the other hand, the 240Z is one of the few cars which has sufficient space and adjustment to accommodate the largest and tallest of customers.

If, for the purposes of comparison, one treats the rear seats of the Alfa as luggage space, the total carrying capacity of the two cars becomes about the same. There are undoubtedly some advantages in having a separate boot, but the Alfa's is a small one and the Datsun is the more versatile load carrier of the pair.

It is worth noting that the controls — steering, pedals and gearchange — are on the

TWO CAR TEST...

heavy side, so that neither is ideal as a woman's car.

Personal Opinion

A paper study tells me that these are two very similar cars. A lengthy drive, on the other hand, confirms my instinct, which is that they are two very different characters. The trouble is that they are both very attractive characters in their own way, making a choice between them an agonizing business.

The Alfa is the thoroughbred; the way it responds to the accelerator, the brakes and the steering almost put it in a class by itself. And it is comfortable, surprisingly comfortable even for my seventy-four inches, with excellent seats and a reasonable driving position (an improvement on the Alfa saloons in this respect). It is a car that repays driving skill and subtlety; there must be people driving Alfas who simply do not know how to get the best out of them.

By contrast, there must be those driving Datsun 240Zs who dare not get the best out of them. I imply no disrespect; it is just that the Datsun is a savage bootful of power rather than the Alfa's rapier thrust, a twitch of heavy steering rather than the Alfa's gentle persuasion. You have to be braver to drive the Datsun fast (except on poor roads, where the Alfa's behaviour deteriorates first), but not as skilled.

On the whole, the Datsun suits me better. I am not always in the mood for finesse and the Datsun's other character — that of the gentle, high-geared cruiser — is nice to fall back upon. Also, it fits me very well — though the Alfa is better in that respect than I thought — and I value its superior behaviour over inferior surfaces. Yes, it only has two seats while the Alfa in theory offers four (three, if one is realistic about it), but this is a personal choice and most of the time I only need two seats.

There would certainly be times when I would miss that feeling of being at one with the car, something the Alfa does so well. And in many other ways, the choice is difficult. But I shall stay with the Datsun (and be happy, in so doing, to save over £240).

Jeffrey Daniels

Personal opinion

I have been fortunate enough to use both of these models (the Alfa in its earlier but similar

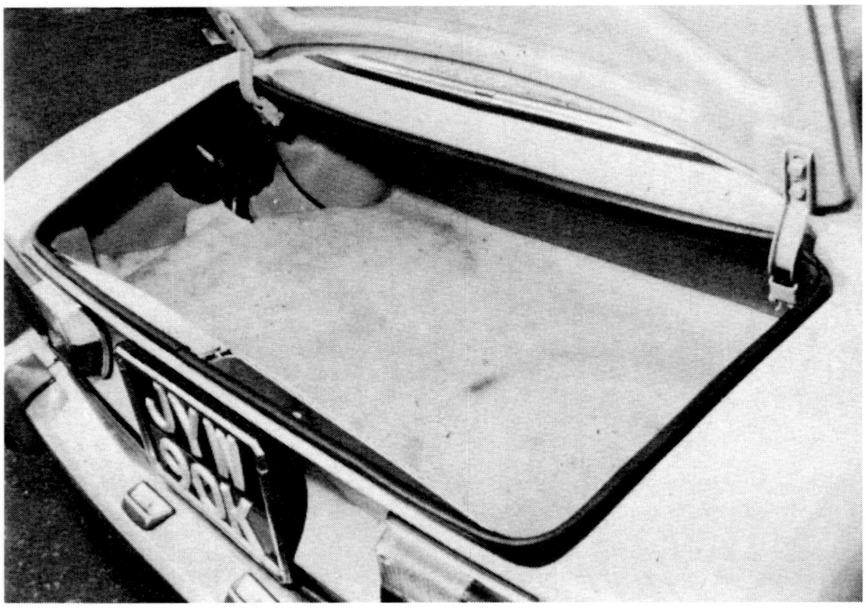

The Alfa boot is self-contained but restricted in the space it provides. On the Datsun there is a large rear tailgate giving access to a large rear platform, but one's luggage is then exposed to view

1750 GTV form) over extensive mileages as part of our long-term test programme. I enjoyed both very much — though in different ways.

However close their specifications are there are few similarities between them on the road. The Alfa is what Continental racing drivers would call "nervous'; highly responsive and very rewarding to drive quickly. By comparison the Dasun is more of a "point and squirt" car, though in fact its standards of adhesion are slightly better than the Italian car and it rides better at speed over rough surfaces. There is little to choose between them for long distance touring — both have the ability to cruise at high-speed without undue noise or drama. Both have excellent brakes, but I prefer the solid precision of the Alfa's gearchange.

Though it may not look so dramatic as the 240Z, the Alfa is in many ways a better package: it has better seats and two properly upholstered little seats in the back for the (very) occasional adult, children, dogs or other impedimenta. It feels a more manoeuvrable car thanks to an unfashionably large window area which allows the driver to very accurately gauge its size. On the other hand the Datsun has more scope for seat adjustment and usefully large luggage area; the Alfa's boot is rather small.

There are certain days and certain trips when I would want one of these cars much more than the other. The Datsun is in some ways the better all-rounder — it is easier to drive with its torque six-cylinder engine and would be, for most drivers, the faster of the two cars on a cross-country route. But it does not have quite the same air of mechanical precision, nor the quality of finish and trim of the Alfa. And as my colleague says, there is that feeling of car-and-driver togetherness which puts the Alfa apart from most other cars. Unlike him, I *just* come down in favour of the GTV for this reason. Isn't it odd that cars so different can be so difficult to choose between?

Ray Hutton

Performance Comparison

	Alfa Romeo 2000GTV £2,587		Datsun 240Z £2,309	
Maximum speeds	**MPH**	**RPM**	**MPH**	**RPM**
Top (mean)	120	5,480	125	5,750
(best)	122	5,570	126	5,850
4th	104	6,000	117	6,380
3rd	77	6,000	98	7,000
2nd	52	6,000	69	7,000
1st	31	6,000	44	7,000
Acceleration				
MPH	**sec**	**Ind. mph**	**sec**	**Ind. mph**
0–30	3.1	32	3.0	30
0–40	4.7	41	4.6	41
0–50	6.7	51	6.0	51
0–60	9.2	60	8.0	62
0–70	12.1	70	11.4	73
0–80	16.2	80	14.8	84
0–90	20.9	90	19.2	95
0–100	27.7	100	25.6	106
0–110	42.1	110	—	117
MPH	**4th gear**	**Top**	**4th gear**	**Top**
10–30	—	—	8.2	—
20–40	8.6	—	7.5	9.7
30–50	6.6	12.1	7.0	9.4
40–60	6.3	9.6	7.2	9.7
50–70	7.2	9.8	7.7	10.2
60–80	7.8	11.6	8.0	10.9
70–90	9.2	14.3	8.6	12.1
80–100	12.7	17.9	10.5	14.2
Fuel consumption				
Overall mpg	21.1		21.4	
Typical mpg	23		24	

Brief Specification

	(Alfa 2000GTV)	(Datsun 240Z)
Engine	4-cyl, in-line	6-cyl, in-line
Valve gear	Twin overhead camshafts	Single overhead camshaft
Capacity, c.c. (cu. in.)	1,962 (120.0)	2,393 (146.1)
Bore x stroke, mm (in.)	84.0 x 88.5 (3.31 x 3.48)	83.0 x 73.7 (3.26 x 2.90)
Compression ratio	9.5 to 1	9.0 to 1
Max. power, bhp/rpm	131 (DIN)/5,500	150 (SAE)/5,600
Max. torque, lb ft/rpm	134 (DIN)/3,000	146 (SAE)/4,400
Gearbox	5-speed, all-synchro	5-speed, all-synchro
Ratios, top/4/3/2/1	0.79/1.0/1.35/1.99/3.31	0.85/1.0/1.31/1.86/2.96
Final drive ratio	4.10 to 1	3.90 to 1
Mph/1,000rpm in top	21.9	21.6
Front suspension	Double wishbones Coil springs Telescopic dampers Anti-roll bar	MacPherson struts Lower links Coil springs Telescopic dampers Anti-roll bar
Rear suspension	Live axle Trailing arms A-bracket Coil springs Telescopic dampers Anti-roll bar	MacPherson struts Lower wishbones Coil springs Telescopic dampers
Steering	Worm and roller	Rack and pinion
Brakes	Disc front and rear, servo	Disc front, drum rear, servo
Tyres	165-14in.	175-14in.
Weight, kerb, cwt	20.6	20.4
Length overall	13ft 5in.	13ft 7in.
Width overall	5ft 2in.	5ft 4in.
Wheelbase	92.5in.	90.5in.

Triumph TR6 versus Datsun 240Z

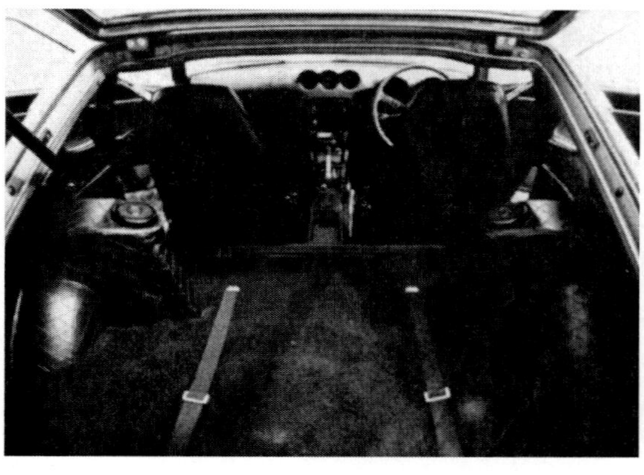

APART FROM the striking similarities in specification, performance and price between the TR and the Z, the comparison between the two is perhaps the most valid that could take place in the series for the simple reason that heavy sales on the US market have kept the TR marque alive for so long, and those sales are now being gobbled hand-over-fist by the 240Z.

As a soft-top "traditional" sports car in the 70s, the TR has excellent visual appeal, thanks to some slick sheet metal work by the Italian designer Ghia. And it has a truly marvellous engine.

But underneath that handsome skin and fine power plant hides an old, old motor car with a chassis and construction that's not far removed from the TRs of the fifties. That might have been fine then. It's certainly not now.

The TR6 is one of the few volume-produced cars still made with a separate chassis. It is a complicated and strong-looking structure of steel channelling, but it suffers nastily from lack of rigidity to become the basic failing point of the entire car.

Off this ailing chassis hangs independent suspension, true enough. But that, too, has its problems, merely compounding those created by the chassis. At the front, the TR runs upper and lower wishbones, with coil springs and telescopic shockers running inside them. There's an anti-roll bar.

At the back, the irs is worked by big semi-trailing arms with coil springs running from them straight onto the chassis. The shockers are lever arm jobs, rare these days. The steering is rack and pinion, but rather low geared.

Wheelbase is a short 88 inches, and track is narrow at 50.25 inches in front, 49.75 at the rear.

The engine — ah, the engine — is easily the nicest part of the car. Like the V12 of the E-type, it stands head and shoulders above its mount.

An in-line six of 2498 cc, oversquare and with quite a long stroke it is rather old-fashioned in design — there are only four main bearings. Fuel injection gives the engine strong power and a wonderful silky smoothness.

ABOVE:
Essential difference between the two cars' handling is shown immediately by this pic. With instantaneous response to throttle back-off, Datsun is nudging into oversteer to set up perfectly for the bend.

TOP LEFT:
Coming into the same bend, but at a slower speed, the TR6 maintains its understeer. Left front wheel is just beginning to tuck under as the weight goes onto it. Car does not respond to back-off until into the apex of the bend.

It pulls 150 bhp at 5500 rpm and 158 lb/ft of torque at 3000 rpm.

Taking this to the rear wheels is a four-speed box — on our car with the excellent, and highly-desirable overdrive on second, third and top — running to a quite tall 3.45 to one diff.

Though the specifications are similar, the 240Z is very much a new car by comparison with the TR. It was conceived and created during the late sixties to become a car for the 70s. Very much a "marketing" car, created in a similar way to Ford's Capri, the Z makes use of parts from mundane production sedans. This type of construction was essential for Nissan, of course. It realised, as many other companies before it have that building sports cars is a dubious game in terms of profitability and trouble.

So the MacPherson strut front end came straight from the Datsun Laurel sedan, and the floor pan is almost identical to the Laurel's. The rear end was all new though, and the engine was created simply by adding two pots onto the familiar 1600 cc four.

Typical of the way in which the Japanese are overhauling so many western manufacturers, the Z may be a sales-oriented "parts bin" car, but it is thoughtfully and very well executed.

Besides the MacPherson struts at the front, the Z has them at the rear too, with A-arms looking after the lower location.

Steering is rack-and-pinion, quite quickly geared at 2.8 turns lock-to-lock.

The in-line six is a very nice, modern engine with

an overhead cam but without a cross-flow head. At the bottom end it has seven main bearings. Decidedly oversquare, it's a revver with its 151 bhp (close to the TR, isn't it?) coming at 5600 rpm and the 146 lb/ft of torque at 4400 rpm.

The gearbox has five well-spaced ratios and runs to 3.9 to one diff.

Wheelbase on the Z is 90.7 inches, and the track is 53.3 inches.

Like the TR, the Datsun has disc brakes at the front and drums at the back. The Datsun's drums are finned for very efficient cooling, and the car has servo assistance (as does the Triumph).

ON THE ROAD: The TR starts out with tremendous appeal — top-down, brawny handsome lines, a lusty engine under the bonnet, roomy cockpit with attractive seats and smick genuine wood dashboard.

Unless you're taller than six foot one or so, the TR is very comfortable, with plenty of legroom and a long-arm reach to the leather-bound wheel.

Turning the ignition key brings a shrill whine as the injection equipment gets cracking. The engine settles down to a nice, smooth idle. You can't help but be impressed by this mill. It is strong — lusty is probably the most appropriate word — hauling the TR off the line with jet-like thrust and smoothness. Right through the rev range it's just as smooth and willing. But the age is revealed by a low 5500 rpm redline, although you can pull six without complaint.

The clutch is rather "soft", taking up progressively but rather mushily. This tends to take some of the sporty sharpness out of the car's drive-train. By contrast, the stubby little gearstick (which is well-placed) moves with snick-snick precision and very smartly too.

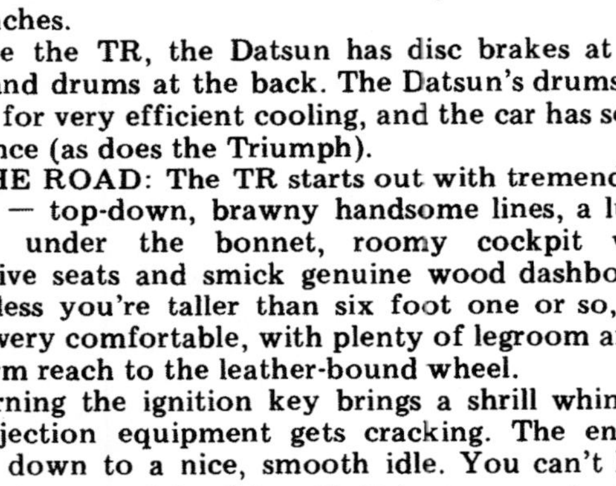

In its straight line performance, the TR is very good. It feels like a sports car should. With more torque, developed lower down, than the Datsun it gets off the line quicker and storms away very strongly. The gear ratios are good, and with the three overdrive ratios thrown in (by instant electric switch, and the nicest cut-in we've ever come across; it's so quick and smooth) you have gearing to play with.

Sidling around town, top-down on a sunny day the TR is marvellous. And for moderate pace touring on good roads with no sharp corners it's pleasant too, being comfortable up to 95 mph with the top down. Turbulence is low.

The steering isn't heavy, though a little low geared, and the ride is good.

But get onto twisting or bumpy roads and you may as well forget the TR6. Easily the worst handling sports or performance car we have ever driven, the car bump steers nastily, with the front skipping well and truly off line in any corner with a trace of irregularity. It is also a dogged understeerer, with blanc-mange response to throttle control so that trying to counteract the understeer coming into the bend is usually a battle of Napoleonic magnitude.

If you decide not to worry about getting rid of it and go into the bend in understeer — or just come in too damned fast anyway — the front wheels let go entirely and you're in a full front-end slide. Only in the wet have I ever had this happen in any other car.

In certain bends, particularly long, fast, slightly downhill curves, backing off the throttle suddenly produces very drastic results — the tail whips out into oversteer, and you'll need to be quick to catch it. This can be anticipated and used to advantage though. But I can't see that you'd ever learn to live with the bump steer or understeer slides — you'd just have to give up any pretensions of having a sporty car in the bends.

Brakes are good, with a progressive pedal. We had no fade nor lock-up.

The car is fairly well equipped. The instrumentation is good-looking with the tacho, speedo, oil and temperature gauges well located. Fuel and amps are obscured by the left hand though.

Minor controls are okay, except for the washers

and wipers which are placed quite stupidly and dangerously on the dashboard behind the stalks for the overdrive and indicators. Your hand fouls these two stalks, making reaching for the screen implement switches like going through on obstacle course.

Seats in the car recline a little, and are comfortable over long distances.

The TR's boot is the best of the soft-tops we've seen, taking a really good pile of luggage. The hood, which folds down behind the seats, takes a little fiddling to get up, but once in place is watertight and resists draughts and noise well.

The Datsun has an engine just as likeable as the TR's, but in a slightly different sort of way. It doesn't have the bottom end pull of the Triumph, nor quite the smoothness. It gets most of its charm up high, running to 6500 before the orange line starts and then onto 7000 for the red. It'll do it, too, though there's not much point since power drops off once much past six.

Because it's more of a revver, the Z's engine needs to be stirred much more than the TR to get full performance. You'll be using all those gears if you're trying hard. Yet its fuel consumption stays incredibly good, rarely dropping under 23 mpg and frequently giving 25 or more even under thrash conditions. The TR returns figures closer to 20 mpg when flat out.

Where the 240Z does score heavily is in its driver set-up. With a driving position that's one of the best integrated in any car — wheel and pedals distances, and seat travel, are tremendous — it immediately imparts a friendly, safe feeling to the driver.

Actually, "safe" is the best way to describe the way I've felt every time I've hopped into a Z. It comes from that rear end, which sits down on the road fabulously under power and allows you to get the tail so sideways it's almost unbelievable, and all the while feeling as safe as houses. The impression is helped by your backside being so close to the rear axle line.

However, the Z is sadly lacking in the front end. The steering and front-end feels really crappy. The steering is vague and rubbery (you'd never know it was a rack), but you do find yourself getting used to it after a while.

It's steering you have to be tough with — crank the lock you want on and hold it there. Very necessary, because the steering is quite heavy and will make your wrists ache when trying hard in tight bends.

Because of poor front end damping and spring rates, the Z's nose wavers around a lot in long fast bends and on bumpy roads. However, the wheels do not lose traction and it never feels dangerous like the TR — just messy.

The front gets very light at high speed; air seems to build up under that long nose, lifting it skyward. It needs a spoiler.

In tight bends, however, the Z can be driven exceptionally fast and with great fun and safety. You're working all on power here, and the rear end can come into its own.

The car can be brought into bends tremendously quickly because it has excellent response to the throttle when screwed up tightly. You come in with mild understeer, but a quick back off tucks the nose right in as the tail goes out. Then just plant your boot again and the thing stays glued on line to fly through. (Our cornering pic shows this perfectly.)

The Datsun will also outbrake the TR. It has one of the best balanced disc-drum set-ups of any car, hence there's no lockup. Fade is out, too.

To sum up: In tight bends, there's just no comparison between the two cars. The Z driver can just sit back and play games with the cloth-cap TR man. So, if handling is the essence of your definition of a sports car, then the Z will qualify but the TR won't — despite its soft-top.

For lazy touring on good roads it's much of a muchness, though the Z is roomier and quieter at high speed. Move out of those limited conditions and the Z's got it all over the TR as a point-to-point car.

Really, the TR6 is just a poor tired old thing with a ruggedly handsome body and a beautiful engine. With time and trouble and Koni shockers in the front you might be able to sort out the handling to at least make it reasonable. But what can you do about scuttle shake that's so bad I realised I didn't know what the word meant until I drove a TR?

The Z is basically an infinitely better motor car, although it has its problems with that poorly-developed front end, tasteless, plasticky trim and a noisy rear suspension that's harder than it should be.

At $5000, it doesn't have the quality detailing and finish it should. But the basics for a very fine motor car indeed are there rightly enough. Spend the $500 you save on a TR6 O/D price and you could get it set up to meet most of your desires — except taking the top down. *

HOW THEY COMPARE

	TR6	240Z
Cylinders	6	6
Capacity	2498	2396
Power	150 bhp at 5500 rpm	151 at 5600
Torque	158 lb/ft at 3000 rpm	146 at 4400
Weight	2410 lb	2284 lb
Lbs per bhp	16.1	15.1
Gear maximums		
First	37 mph at 5500 rpm	40 mph at 6500 rpm
Second	58	64
Second O/D	71	—
Third	88	91
Third O/D	107	—
Fourth	116	117
Fourth O/D	120	—
Fifth		121
Acceleration		
0-30 mph	3.2	3.0
0-40 mph	4.7	4.5
0-50 mph	6.5	6.5
0-60 mph	8.5	8.5
0-70 mph	10.9	10.8
0-80 mph	14.5	14.4
0-90 mph	18.6	18.4
0-100 mph	24.7	23.9
Standing Quarter Mile:	16.6	16.4

Insurance:

	Over 25, pay cash, full no-claim bonus		Under 25, HP, no no-claim bonus	
	TR6	240Z	TR6	240Z
GIO	$86.96	$90.42	not accepted	
NRMA	$87.50	$125.60	$332.20	$455
Tariff	$176	$176	$471.40	$471.40

Total basic service costs 0 to 24,000 miles (including oil, grease, oil filters, air filters, plugs and labor):

TR6 . . . .$203.05

240Z $182.70

Spare parts cost:	TR6	240Z
Exhaust system	$54	$60.50
Clutch assembly	$65	$53
Headlight unit	$2.90	$13350
Tail-light assembly	$28.73	$28
Disc pads (set)	$33.68	$33
Front mudguard	$58	$75
Windscreen	$60 (laminated)	$126
Battery	$30.52	$26
Warranty	6/6	6/6

The Z is typical of the long hood short deck GT, a design pioneered by the E Type Jaguar. New for '73 are some heavier bumper overriders, and radial tires are standard.

DATSUN

A sensation in sales, the 240Z is unchanged for the new year!

Few cars in memory have ever made such a sales impact, such an instant impact, as the 240Z from Datsun. Just three years ago Nissan announced the GT, and it was back ordered at every dealer before the first unit came off the boat. The Z was called the poor man's Porsche, and far more complimentary things. People bought them with any and all extras, any color, virtually sight unseen, and waiting lists grew to proportions that rivaled the 1946 Cadillac. One good reason for the popularity was the initial selling price in the 3500 dollar range. Dealers soon loaded their Zs with fancy wheels, fat tires, air conditioning, body stripes, and anything else that would boost the price and the profit, but the cars remained in short supply. With the extra government taxes on imports, the 240Z now lists for over four grand, and the average unit is still loaded with extras and sells for around five thousand, and Zs are still in short supply.

What makes the car so popular is the car itself. It looks like a sleek, high dollar GT, and it is far more of a sports car for the '70s than a good many models that cost much more. Nissan discovered the U.S. market in sports cars with their Fairlady roadster line, and when they put the Z car together, they borrowed a

The Datsun 240Z is an all weather Grand Touring machine in every sense of the word. Body style is unchanged since the car was introduced three years ago.

Z power comes from the big overhead cam six cylinder; emission control is extensive and fuel is fed by twin S.U. carburetors in the U.S. version of the engine.

bit from Europe, but actually eliminated the failings in creature comfort and suspension that made the open sportster a bit vintage in concept. The Z has all the good things a GT should — full reclining bucket seats, a dash full of instruments, sporty wood grained steering wheel, center console gadgetry and stowage, and plenty of cargo space. Access to the carpeted cargo deck is through the rear window/door that comes with a builtin defroster. The Z has all independent suspension, via MacPherson type struts front and rear, front disc brakes, radial tires, the lot. The powerplant is a husky 146 cubic inch, overhead cam, in-line six cylinder, fed by two S.U. type carburetors. The standard transmission is a smooth, four speed manual, all synchromesh unit, and a three speed automatic (Ford type) became available as an option in 1972.

As we go to press, the 1973 Datsun 240Z has yet to be unveiled. No changes in the successful car are anticipated, except for the mandatory impact absorbing bumpers. Our spies tell us that the new standards have been met by using hefty rubber bumper overriders both front and rear, and these bumpers add about four inches to the overall length of the Z car. There would be no reason to change anything else on the Z, but there might be the odd knick knack bit, lighting or some minor running change as the '73s evolve. The Datsun sports car is just that as it stands, and it has all the on road performance needed to match its zoomy appearance. There is more than sufficient power, and the handling and braking capabilities make it ideal on the back, winding roads that are fun to drive in a responsive car.

Another reason for the Z's popularity is the extensive racing program initiated by Datsun on the road courses in the U.S. The 240Z has been National Champion in Class C of Sports Car Club of America racing for the last two years, and it probably will have won the 1972 title by the time you read these words. A good bit of the racing hardware is available over the counter from Datsun dealers and companies like BRE's Interpart. Most popular items are the front and rear spoilers that really add to the looks of the Z car. There are full suspension mods too, and engine kits up to the full house number with three, dual throat Solex carbs. The latter, however, is not suitable for street use and doesn't meet emission control requirements. Available from the dealers is the smooth, five speeds forward manual transmission, but the car cannot be ordered with this unit. It is only sold on an exchange deal. The five speed is a good bet for owners who do a lot of highway driving, for the tall fifth gear is as effective as overdrive in bringing the rpms down on long interstate runs.

There is little to say about the new Z, since it is the same, wildly successful Z we have tested in the past. The horsepower figures may drop a few notches due to de-tuning for lower grade gasoline, but we'll bet the usable power stays pretty much the same. When the Z was introduced, the enthusiast magazines called it "the most exciting new Grand Touring car in a decade." It remains a sensation on the market, and Datsun has good reason to be proud of their sports car. It meets all the difficult federal standards in crashability and emission control, and it still looks like a proper Grand Touring machine. What is even more important to the buff, it still drives like a proper sports car too, and the after market goodies for the Z continue to proliferate. The sophisticated 240Z, dollar for pound of performance, is one of the best buys in the sports car world today.

240Z
Data in Brief

DIMENSIONS

Wheelbase	90.7 in.
Overall length	166.8 in.
Height	50.5 in.
Width	64.1 in.
Tread — front/rear	53.3/53.0 in.
Steering type & ratio	rack & pinion, 17.8 to 1
Fuel capacity	15.9 gal
Luggage capacity	8.5 cu ft
Design passenger load	2
Turning diameter	31.4 ft
Curb weight	2350 lbs

ENGINE — Standard

Type	in-line, six cylinder, SOHC
Displacement	2393cc/146 cu in.
Horsepower	151 at 5600 rpm
Torque	148 at 4400 rpm

DRIVELINE

Transmission	4-speed manual, all synchro
Drive axle ratio	3.36:1

BRAKES

Front	disc
Rear	drum

SUSPENSION

Front	independent, MacPherson strut, coil springs, tubular shocks, anti sway bar
Rear	independent, MacPherson strut, coil springs, tubular shocks

WHEELS & TIRES

Wheels, type & size	14 x 5 J, steel
Tires, type & size	175 HR x 14, radial

NA — Data not available
DNA — Data not applicable

Datsun 240Z

Engine is an in-line SOHC 6 delivering 150bhp at 6000rpm with a 4-speed box.

ZERO TO 60 MPH IN 8.8 SECONDS HELPS MAKE IT TOPS IN THE LOW-PRICED SPORTS CARS.

By BARRY LOPEZ

■ It's pretty tough to get up an argument over the performance characteristics of Datsun's 240Z. The car does have its drawbacks, being a little light on its feet at high speed and running a pretty hot engine, but there's no getting around the fact that it's the finest low-priced sports car in the world. Bar none. It's not only quick (0-60 mph/8.8 sec.), but accurate. It steers like a racing car with its four wheel independent suspension, and power assisted disc brakes (drums/ rear) haul it down from 80 to 0 mph in just 291 feet.

The 240Z's in-line, sohc 6 (150 bhp @6000 rpm) has plenty of oomph nicely spread through four synchroed gears and a 3.36 rear end. Third gear is a beauty with an effective range from 30-90 mph, very nice for passing. In fact, it's easy to forget fourth gear until you are out on the road, where you're turning only 3350 rpm at 70 mph. The engine is yellow-lined at 6500 rpm.

The 240Z has won accolades for its fine performance and been touted by a hundred odd automotive as the best thing they've driven in years. It's everybody's car-of-the-year, etc., so there's no point in my adding my two cents to it all. I agree with them. Of all the cars I've driven, this is one of the very few I really hated to give up.

What intrigued me about the Z car, however, was not so much its speed and performance. That's a matter of record. I wanted to know if you could live with the 240Z with no regrets. Had 240Z drivers formed the strong, informal bond that joins Corvette drivers? Would you end up hating yourself if you took it on a long trip? It was to answer these questions that we took the 240Z out for ten days. We wented to find a few answers for the guy who had read all the performance data but wanted to know more about what he was getting into.

One of the first questions we answered was one about space. Space for passengers and cargo is the most serious drawback to owning one of the foreign medium-priced GTs (Fiat 124, Opel GT, MGB GT, Triumph 6) if it's going to be the one car in the family. There's no way in the world the 240Z is going to be anything but a two-seater unless the additional passenger likes to ride curled up like a dog in the trunk or bent over like a croquet wicket in your lap. It's a good thing to keep in mind because some people have been led to believe "two-seater" means you can squeeze three into already limited confines. No way in this car. It's a sports car not a sedan.

Another thing you should know is that even if you're a family of two with no children planned for a few years, the 240Z is not the perfect family car. Sooner or later you're going to feel that pinch for space, especially if you like to hobby around with lumber or shop for antiques. If you're single and rarely carry anything around in the car but groceries and what you pick up shopping you may be very happy with it.

Cargo space is limited and anything stowed remains visible through the hatchback.

The economics of the Z car are interesting. List price ($3600) is excellent considering the quality of the product. On the other hand, insurance companies are sitting down pretty hard on 240Z owners, especially if they opt for the standard 4-speed over the optional 3-speed automatic.

Upkeep poses no special problems. Gas mileage was about 21 mpg on premium fuel, which is a must. Tune-ups might be a problem if you get some eager beaver with no brains, all hot to balance the dual side-draft carburetors. On the other hand, access to the engine is good so there's no reason why you can't do some of the work yourself.

Although it's not strictly an economic question, theft is something to consider, especially if you live in a big city. I have no figures to hand, but the 240Z is extremely popular and in short supply. This makes it a top priority item for thieves.

For typical around town driving, the 240Z is fine. It's good in traffic, easy to park, easy to load through the rear deck and it doesn't bottom out on driveways. The only drawbacks I felt were its lack of size which makes it difficult to see sometimes, and its see-through interior. The size is an occupational hazard. Protective bumper guards front and rear are a good idea to keep people from backing into you. The see-through interior is a problem with any hatchback. It forces you to leave everything out in the open because there's no closed trunk. In the city you have to lock the car up even in the hottest weather if you have anything in it.

As far as touring is concerned, the 240Z is a mighty fine piece of machinery. Before they built all those freeways with their 30 mile straightaways, their mile long turns and their dulling familiarity, cross country driving in a fast car on good roads was a gas. You were really driving. Prepare to recapture the experience in the 240Z. We packed our bags and went to Nevada and almost didn't come back.

Perhaps the greatest thing about touring in the 240Z is the tremendous feeling of being unencumbered. A full trunk load doesn't take much off the car's performance and it beats the

Good in traffic, 240Z is easy to park and easy to load through the rear deck but protective bumper guards in front and in back are a vital necessity with this sport car.

Datsun 240Z

pants off any style of travel but motorcycling, which it's a lot like. Coupled with this sense of being free and fast is a sense of safeness, of tightness, that there are no loose ends. When you shut those doors, they close with a crisp whumph and you're safe inside a high performance car with everything you need for your vacation. It's a good feeling.

The first hit you get when you climb into the 240Z is that this is really an automobile you are sitting in. It has real instruments and someone's put a lot of thought into designing a most functional and roomy interior. Set in deep wells behind the steering wheel are tachometer and speedometer with odometer and trip odometer. In the middle of the dash, canted toward the driver are temperature, oil, amps and fuel gauges and a clock that works.

With your hands on the steering wheel at 3 and 9 o'clock, your left finger tips brush the combination turn signal and headlight dimmer. Your right brushes controls for the lights and wiper/ washer, all mounted on a stalk on the steering column.

Drop your right hand to the console and you hit gear shift, hand brake (awkwardly), and manual choke lever. In the console extension that runs up to the dash are AM/FM radio with power antenna control, interior lights and interior weather control. Air conditioning controls are awkwardly mounted under the dash by the steering column. The stereo tape deck is hidden away in the glovebox.

There's something of the Jaguar XKE about the interior and you find yourself looking for that familiar bank of toggle switches. There's only one and that's for the four-way flasher. (Oddly, you get a similar feeling of XKE from the 240Z's front hinged

Full complement of instruments are fitted in the 240Z with big tachometer and speedometer immediately behind the dished, three-spoked steering wheel.

Visibility is good but not spectacular. When trunk is full of suitcases side mirrors alone offer vision to the rear. Cockpit is roomy but just for two people—no more.

hood and its in-line 6 with side draft carburetion.)

Vision from the driver's seat is good but not spectacular. With a trunk full of suitcases you have to depend on the side mirrors and the racing type is difficult to adjust. Forward vision over the sloping hood is fine. We had plenty of room in the cockpit, but 8.5 cubic feet of trunk space isn't huge. It's impossible to hang clothes up but we did fit two large suitcases and a small one in without any trouble. If you're a traveling salesman without a lot of sample cases, you can lay dress clothing flat and make out like a bandit.

As I indicated above, the real pleasure of the 240Z on a cross country drive is the sheer delight of the drive itself. In appropriate areas we were very comfortable cruising at 90. It was like cruising at 70 in any American car. Wind noise was slight, the ride was smooth and the car is tight enough to you feel very much in control of the situation. Conditions permitting we effortlessly moved over 100 mph. It was here that we encountered our only problems with the car. It was quite sensitive to side winds at speed and, with the air conditioner off, water temperature was well over 200. With the air conditioner on it moved over the boiling point. By the time you purchase a 240Z, Datsun may have both these problems worked out. If not, get a front end air spoiler and switch to forced air ventilation at speed.

In the upper Great Basin of Oregon and Nevada we drove long, 600-mile days without fatigue. The seating is comfortable and the car's suspension is excellent, but I think the real secret to the Datsun's comfortable ride over a 600-mile day is that you can really drive this car, you don't point it and then ooze down the road, the experience most of us are used to. It's a novel feeling for some and for the first few hours behind the wheel you are apt to be indulging your racing fantasies.

There are other factors that make a long drive pleasant—lack of heavy traffic, smooth road surfaces, a variety of road angle and topology—but for me, and many others I suspect, the real key to a pleasant long drive is having a car that's exhilarating to drive, something you can not only trust but work with, a car that is not an insult to the art of driving. The Datsun 240Z is such an automobile. Cruising at 90, over the rolling sagebrush hills of Nevada, dropping down to 60 to pass someone, back up to 90 in third and leveling out, going through turn after turn flat and tight, the sound of the pipes muttering in a downshift—all this hour after hour. It was a rare and very good experience. It made you feel alive. You felt like you could drive a thousand miles and at the end of the day be steady enough to balance a wine glass motionless on the tip of your finger.

You'll note a few nice small touches about the car: the rubber flap that keeps the attached gas cap from scratching the fender, a warning light for the choke, a work lamp under the hood. You'll note, too, that the radial ply tires, the AM/FM radio, the electric clock, the four speed, etc., are all standard. But in the end I don't think it's these things that sell you on the 240Z. The package is nice, but nice packages can mask a lemon. That's not true here. The 240Z is a truly fine automobile, done up, to be sure, in a fine package. What sells you is the idea that this is really an automobile, that for $3600 a man can buy a car that's better than its advertising.

About that fraternity of Corvette drivers. If you've never owned a Corvette you'd never understand it. The 240Z hasn't been around long enough to develop that sort of following and chances are it never will. It's built along very different lines. It's more subtle, more refined, much more the road machine than the dragster. •

DATSUN 240Z

America's best-selling sports car

WHEN DATSUN INTRODUCED the 240Z early in 1970 it changed our whole scale of values overnight. Suddenly the American sports-car buyer could get for $3500 the sort of premium sports car that had previously cost at least $5000. Well, theoretically he could get a 240Z for $3500; in reality the law of supply and demand prevailed, Datsun couldn't keep up with the demand, and very few people actually got 240Zs at anything like basic list price the first couple of years.

In the intervening three years the 240Z has become America's best-selling sports car, no surprise at all. Here it was, a slick-looking fastback 2-seater with an overhead-cam 6-cylinder engine, independent suspension all around, rack-and-pinion steering and most of the other features one expects in a high-class sports car, at a price that seemed almost incredible. It couldn't fail, even with dealers using its short supply to hawk all manner of add-on equipment (like alloy wheels) and hike its price up to around $5000.

The bargain days are gone, however. Two international money crises have devalued the dollar substantially and up-valued the yen just as substantially, and now a basic 240Z costs virtually as much as a loaded one did in 1970 and 1971. On the overall scale of things the Z is still good value for the money but its price is no longer remarkable and now we have to give it a more critical look.

Three years and the sight of swarms of 240Zs everywhere haven't diminished its styling appeal, however. Its smooth fast-back body wasn't startling when introduced but it was a very good design, relatively free of corny styling gimmicks—and that's important if a design is going to look good for a long time. Owners of 240Zs explore the limits of dressup items—fancy (and wider) wheels, Pete Brock's clever clear headlight fairings, spoilers, lowered suspension, rear-window shades—and many of these do enhance the car's looks, making a good thing better.

Inside the car, driver and passenger are impressed by a modern layout of instruments and controls. The materials aren't fancy; in fact the lack of contrast in color and materials is so severe that only the warm wood grain of the steering wheel (simulated) provides relief. Other than some very cheap-looking quilted vinyl, however, the simplicity is satisfyingly functional. The seats and positions of all the controls are equally right: every member of the staff found the seating comfortable, a rare occurrence on even the most luxurious cars. The seatbelt arrangement wasn't entirely satisfactory; its shoulder section rubbed the neck of our shortest driver when he had the seat

adjusted to suit him. Seat backrests are adjustable only through about 10 degrees, just sufficient for seating variations but not permitting reclining for the passenger. Speedometer and tachometer are large dials right in front of the driver, and the central console is topped by three dials containing the four minor gauges plus a clock. These three faces are a bit far from the normal line of sight to suit us, but they are clearly readable. Below them are the heater-ventilation controls, which are logically set up and command a highly effective system. The steering-column control on the right is a real do-all, for headlights, wipers and washer; a recent addition is an intermittent action setting for the wipers. Our test car's wiper mechanism had a curious trait in that it clicked loudly at about the 5-second interval used by the intermittent feature—even when the wipers were on one of their steady speeds. Another unusual control is the large-scale, long-travel choke in the console: it's particularly useful for a reason we'll get to later.

The backrests don't swing forward to give access to the

luggage platform from the side, but rear access through the lift-up window/tailgate is fine and the 240Z accepts a really generous amount of luggage for two traveling people. The luggage platform is well detailed, with handsome carpeting and useful straps for suitcases. The car is laid out specifically and well for two passengers—no awkward compromises as are often forced by 2 + 2 configurations.

The Z's 6-cylinder, 2.4-liter engine (related, naturally, to the 240 name) was derived from the 1.6-liter four of the 510 sedan and appears to be a sturdy, durable unit. It's quiet and smooth throughout its rev range though not so silky at high speeds as some more expensive sixes. An impressive exhaust note was not something the Datsun engineers strove for, but one can get that by fitting one of the accessory systems like that made by Interpart. Very strong performance used to be a 240Z strong suit, but Datsun has not been able to maintain it and meet 1973 emission regulations: our 1973 test car took 1.4 sec longer to reach 60 mph and 0.6 sec longer to cover the quarter-mile from a standing start. Fuel economy has suffered too, and the drivability of our test car (which already had modifications supposed to cure early 1973 drivability faults) was wholly unacceptable. That nice choke was handy because the Z needed it nearly all the time!

On to more pleasant things: the Z has an excellent 4-speed gearbox, with linkage that starts off a bit stiff when the car is new but becomes delightfully smooth and precise when broken in. And we cannot say that the Z is exactly a slug, even with the reduced 1973 performance.

Steering is light and precise—absolutely first-rate for cornering and not too heavy for parking—and there's a feeling of lots of cornering power, what with tires that are generously large for the car's weight. The car is nearly evenly balanced front-to-rear and has near-neutral handling that can be provoked into oversteer by the driver who likes to do that sort of thing. Skidpad testing shows that there is indeed a lot of cornering power, even without a rear anti-roll bar. But there are problems. In previous road tests we've reported high-speed stability problems and had been assured since that they'd been mostly solved, but in this test car they were there in abundance. In fact it tended to wander a bit even at speeds as low as 50 mph. The Bridgestone radials do well on dry pavement but aren't very convincing in the rain.

Brakes rate about average on the Z; they stop the car in average distances from highway speeds with no serious loss of control, and fade slightly in our 6-stop test. There have been recurring reports of sticking calipers in severe winter climates, a problem that is hopefully solved by now.

Now that the Z has to compete at a much higher price level, its deficiencies—which are few, to be sure—do become more serious, and we'd suggest that it's time for a "facelift" that would give it better stability at speed and acceptable drivability as well as perhaps restore its old performance. Its engine has an air-injection pump, something that usually allows good running, but somebody's not doing something right here and what would otherwise be a pleasant car has become almost unmanageable in everyday, moderate-speed driving. After all the accolades we've given the Z in the past, such a lukewarm conclusion may come as a shock—but times do change.

R&T

ROAD TEST

DATSUN 240Z

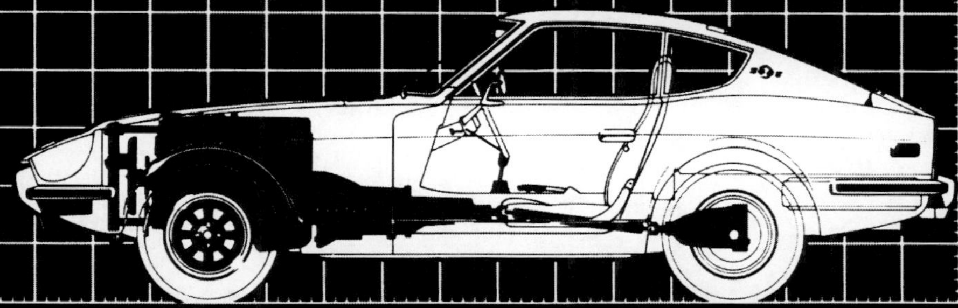

PRICE

List price, west coast	est $4600
Price as tested, west coast	est $4600

Price as tested includes radial tires, AM radio w/elec antenna, heated rear window (standard equip)

IMPORTER

Nissan Motor Corp in USA
18501 S Figueroa Ave
Carson, Calif. 90247

GENERAL

Curb weight, lb	2450
Test weight	2760
Weight distribution (with driver), front/rear, %	52/48
Wheelbase, in.	90.7
Track, front/rear	53.0/53.0
Length	162.8
Width	64.1
Height	50.6
Ground clearance	5.7
Overhang, front/rear	34.4/37.7
Usable trunk space, cu ft	8.5
Fuel capacity, U.S. gal.	15.1

ENGINE

Type	sohc inline 6
Bore x stroke, mm	83.0 x 73.3
Equivalent in.	3.27 x 2.90
Displacement, cc/cu in.	2393/146
Compression ratio	8.8:1
Bhp @ rpm, net	129 @ 6000
Equivalent mph	126
Torque @ rpm, lb-ft	127 @ 4400
Equivalent mph	92
Carburetion	two Hitachi-SU (IV)
Fuel requirement	regular
Emissions, gram/mile:	
Hydrocarbons	2.9
Carbon Monoxide	20
Nitrogen Oxides	1.8

DRIVE TRAIN

Transmission	4-sp manual
Gear ratios: 4th (1.00)	3.36:1
3rd (1.42)	4.77:1
2nd (2.20)	7.39:1
1st (3.55)	11.92:1
Final drive ratio	3.36:1

CHASSIS & BODY

Layout	front engine/rear drive
Body/frame	unit steel
Brake system	10.7-in. disc front, 9.0 x 1.6-in. drum rear, vacuum assisted
Swept area, sq in.	310
Wheels	steel disc, 14 x 5
Tires	Bridgestone radial, 175SR-14
Steering type	rack & pinion
Overall ratio	17.8:1
Turns, lock-to-lock	3.5
Turning circle, ft	31.5

Front suspension: MacPherson struts, lower lateral arms, compliance struts, coil springs, tube shocks, anti-roll bar

Rear suspension: Chapman struts, lower A-arms, coil springs, tube shocks

INSTRUMENTATION

Instruments: 160-mph speedo, 8000-rpm tach, 99,999 odo, 999.9 trip odo, oil press, coolant temp, ammeter, fuel level, clock

Warning lights: brake system, hazard, high beam, directionals, rear window heat, choke on, seatbelt

ACCOMMODATION

Seating capacity, persons	2
Seat width	2 x 21.0
Head room	36.5
Seat back adjustment, deg	10

MAINTENANCE

Service intervals, mi:	
Oil change	3000
Filter change	6000
Chassis lube	30,000
Minor tuneup	6000
Major tuneup	12,000
Warranty, mo/mi	12/12,000

CALCULATED DATA

Lb/bhp (test weight)	21.4
Mph/1000 rpm (4th gear)	21.0
Engine revs/mi (60 mph)	2850
Piston travel, ft/mi	1380
R&T steering index	1.10
Brake swept area, sq in./ton	225

RELIABILITY

From R&T Owner Surveys the average number of trouble areas for all models surveyed is 12. As owners of earlier-model Datsun 240Zs reported 13 trouble areas, we expect the reliability of the 240Z to be average.

ROAD TEST RESULTS

ACCELERATION

Time to distance, sec:	
0-100 ft	4.2
0-500 ft	9.8
0-1320 ft (¼ mi)	17.7
Speed at end of ¼-mi, mph	79.5
Time to speed, sec:	
0-30 mph	4.1
0-40 mph	5.6
0-50 mph	7.9
0-60 mph	10.1
0-70 mph	13.8
0-80 mph	18.1
0-100 mph	33.2

FUEL ECONOMY

Normal driving, mpg	19.0
Cruising range, mi (1-gal res.)	268

HANDLING

Speed on 100-ft radius, mph	33.0
Lateral acceleration, g	0.728

SPEEDS IN GEARS

4th gear (5500)	115
3rd (6800)	103
2nd (6800)	65
1st (6800)	40

BRAKES

Minimum stopping distances, ft:	
From 60 mph	169
From 80 mph	308
Control in panic stop	good
Pedal effort for 0.5g stop, lb	30
Fade: percent increase in pedal effort to maintain 0.5g deceleration in 6 stops from 60 mph	10
Parking: hold 30% grade?	yes
Overall brake rating	very good

INTERIOR NOISE

All noise readings in dBA:	
Idle in neutral	48
Constant 30 mph	67
50 mph	70
70 mph	75
90 mph	79

SPEEDOMETER ERROR

30 mph indicated is actually	27.5
50 mph	48.5
60 mph	58.0
70 mph	68.0
80 mph	77.0
Odometer, 10.0 mi	9.9

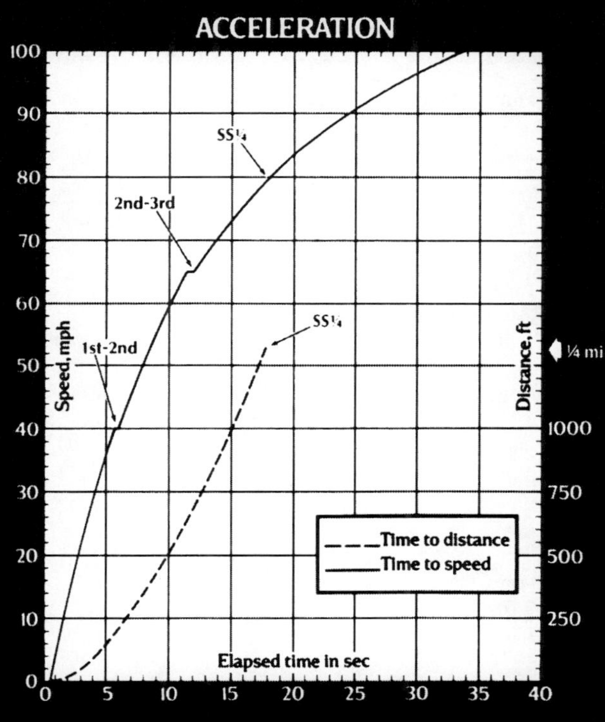

MOTORING PLUS

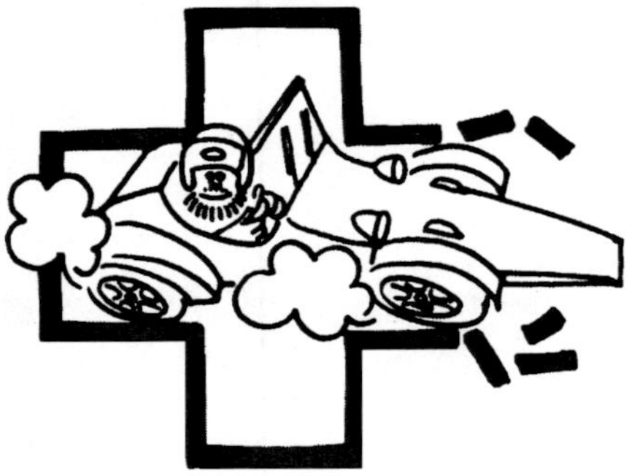

ORIENTAL MIND-BLOWER

A Samurai is a fierce Japanese warrior; a super Samurai must be an extra fierce one. So much for Japanese tradition. And now Mr Spike Anderson, a true British gentleman dwelling in rural England, has devised a suitable steed for said warrior—and turned Japanese tradition on its head.

For the aforementioned Mr Anderson is the sole perpetrator of the Super Samuri ('e's not fick, 'e can spel, it's deliberate), an honest and open (with that colour scheme you could disguise it?) road-going racing car. Unfortunately I ran out of superlatives last week, so what do I say about the performance? Amazing, astonishing—perhaps mind-blowing is best. Definitely mind-blowing. Welcome to the Motor League Leaders, 2000 to 3000 cc class.

A 0-60 time of 6.4 secs, a 0-100 time of 17.0 secs and a standing quarter of 14.8 puts it just behind the Porsche 911S, and pushing hard—for a lot less money. And 140 mph top speed should be possible although we had no chance to try to achieve it.

A study of the conversion shows it to be quite straightforward, with no exotic or peculiar tricks, and helps to explain some of the comments made here. If you want more power generally you put more fuel in and more air to burn it. Spike has taken the conventional route and replaced the twin SUs with triple 40 DCOE Webers without the hindrance of air cleaners, ports are matched, the valve seats are properly radiused (a trick of Spike's which he feels does as much as anything for tractability) and the compression ratio is raised by nearly half a ratio to 9.5:1. A competition type six branch manifold and exhaust system let the noxious fumes out with narry an obstacle. The conversion is thus primarily aimed at the top end of the rpm range, the bottom end being effectively left to look after itself. In fact the car exhibits all the symptoms of being overcarburetted—if the performance is used in full.

This may sound rather disparaging. Surprisingly, then, one of the outstanding features of the car is the tractability. The accelerator pedal is heavy, which in this instance is a

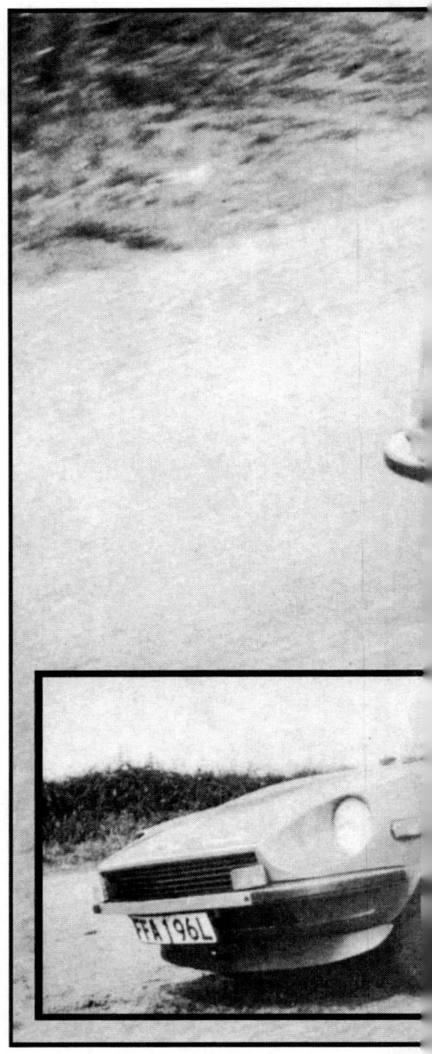

boon. Gentle pressure will just crack open those butterflies in the drainpipe sized carb throats, and (with a little clutch slip—first appears to be high with this set-up) the car will trickle in traffic as happily as any family saloon. That is not to say it likes it: too much pedal and it gives a warning cough and spit. But at no time did it display any temperament, idling lumpily if regularly at 600 rpm without stalling or getting overheated and with no sign of plug fouling. Starting was also instant after one or two jabs on the accelerator.

In spite of the lack of silencing devices the engine is surprisingly unobtrusive in normal driving. When used in anger, though, the note rises to become the glorious sound of a well tuned six with hiss and whistle overtones from the Webers. Superb if you like that sort of thing—and we do, we do! Even at high speeds, though, wind and mechanical noise allow normal conversation.

As has been indicated, below 2500 to 3000 rpm a gentle right foot is required if smoothness is the aim; between these speeds and 4000 rpm firm pressure is the order of the day; and it is really only above this figure that the full benefit of the conversion shows itself with a smooth flow of power. Flow is perhaps the wrong word—the power is instant and enormous. Overtaking is no longer a fraught experience, just a quick jab and a twitch. One has the feeling that the tachometer needle is attached to the red section of the dial by a particularly strong elastic band, so rapidly does it move.

To cater for this upsurge in performance Spike has tweeked the suspension via uprated and shortened springs though dampers remain standard—" for comfort," explains Spike. This

Car: Datsun 240Z.
Conversion by: Race Head Services, Dovehouse Lane, Harbury, Leamington Spa, Warwicks.
Conversion: Engine fitted with triple Weber 40 DCOEs, cylinder head gas-flowed, matched, and cr raised to 9.5:1. Six-branch exhaust manifold and competition silencer system. Suspension lowered and coils uprated. DS11 pads fitted to front brakes, harder linings to rear. 5½J wheels can take original tyres. Car repainted on top, around window and on sill in contrasting colour with white highlighting. " Super Samuri " signwritten front and back.

	£
Engine components	396.00
Suspension	52.00
Brakes	32.50
Wheels	82.50
Paintwork	82.50
Total (fitting charges included in cost of components)	645.50
Total as tested:	3180.50

MAXIMUM SPEED

	Super Samuri	Standard 240Z	Porsche 911S
	mph	mph	mph
	140*	125.1	145.3

ACCELERATION

mph	sec	sec	sec
0-30	2.4	2.8	2.5
0-40	3.6	4.4	3.5
0-50	4.9	6.3	4.8
0-60	6.4	8.3	6.2
0-70	8.5	11.3	8.7
0-80	10.7	14.3	10.9
0-90	13.4	19.1	13.2
0-100	17.0	23.9	17.1
Standing ¼ mile	14.8	16.2	14.7
Standing km	27.3	29.9	27.1

IN TOP

mph	sec	sec	sec
20-40	**	8.9	13.6
30-50		9.0	11.6
40-60	8.5	9.2	11.2
50-70	8.7	9.7	11.2
60-80	8.9	10.8	10.6
70-90	8.8	11.8	11.2
80-100	9.1	13.4	12.3

IN 4TH

mph	sec	sec	sec
20-40	**	6.9	8.8
30-50		6.9	7.6
40-60	5.7	7.2	6.4
50-70	6.5	7.4	6.4
60-80	6.9	7.6	6.8
70-90	6.1	8.1	6.7
80-100	7.0	10.0	7.0

IN 3RD

mph	sec	sec	sec
10-30	**	5.4	6.2
20-40		5.4	5.3
30-50	4.6	5.3	4.9
40-60	4.8	5.0	4.5
50-70	4.2	5.3	4.2
60-80	4.3	5.8	4.0
70-90	4.8	7.3	4.4

FUEL CONSUMPTION

Steady mph	mpg	mpg	mpg
30	32.6	54.8	***
40	35.1	50.8	
50	31.9	43.0	
60	28.8	37.5	
70	27.5	33.0	
80	25.8	29.8	
90	22.7	26.0	
100	20.6	22.6	
Overall	20.4	25.7	13.3

*See text
**Would not pull cleanly with full throttle
***Fuel injected—unable to measure with Petrometer

Top: handling is surprisingly neutral, and the car is at its best on fast winding roads. Midland Metallic alloy wheels with 5½J rims enhance the appearance—and the signwriting makes people's heads turn. Below: triple Webers and the six-branch exhaust system are the only outward hints of the power available

has the effect of accentuating the handling characteristics of the cooking 240Z as reported by your worthy scribes in December 1971. Basically an understeerer, tail-out cornering could be provoked by putting the boot in. There is some bump and steer which, when one is used to it, one can allow for by holding on to the steering wheel with a light grip and letting the wheel twitch; deviation from the chosen line is minimal. The road-holding and handling are at their best on fast twisty roads, when the car can be swooped through bends in what is to all intents and purposes a neutral condition. Superb.

A word here about tyres. Spike fits 5½J Midland Metallic alloy wheels which can take the standard Bridgestone tyres—and anyone contemplating this conversion is recommended to fit British made steel braced radials with decent rubber and tread. The Bridgestones are reasonable in the dry (no dramatic moments) but have the grip of greased banana skins in the wet—aquaplaning at 40 mph indeed!

And another word about brakes. With some 6000-plus miles on the clock a member of the staff experienced almost calamitous fade, followed by total failure. When checked the pads were worn completely away—right down to bare metal! Admittedly this is a fairly well used demonstrator, but such mileage (and these pads were "specials") is just not on. Spike is aware of the problem (so is anyone who drives the car) and now has on order sets of DS11s from the reliable Mr Ferodo. In addition he is working on sets of ventilated discs with four pot calipers. *That* should cure the problem.

This car does suffer from another problem—instant attention. The very attractive colour scheme of the example we tried was Datsun orange on the sides, a standard colour, and a deep metallic bronze on the bonnet, around the windows and on the door sills, picked out with white pinstriping. And in this instance, signwriting. Arresting, very. If you live on the proverbial envious glances, rush out now and purchase a Samuri. Without the colour scheme you can't call it a Samuri. Mr Anderson knows all about advertising.

Funny, really. I approached this car expecting it to be one of those "slowly round the corner, then squirt" types that objected to traffic, that was as hard as my office chair, that steered like a truck unless you were doing over the ton and were as cacaphonous as a modern hard rock group on full decibels. Funny how wrong you can be.

Mike McCarthy

Rally Car or

Since it first appeared back whenever it was the 240Z has acquired a rather enviable reputation, attracting the sort of oohs, aahs, and 'wouldn't half like one of thems' usually reserved for Porsches, Lotus and Vivien Neves. Why? Well that's the four-million yen question. In the States the Datz is a really huge seller, snaring a wide mouthful of the import pudding by virtue of a price tag similar to the MGB — and if you had the choice between a Z and a B, which would you go for? (That was a rhetorical question). So a certain amount of Stateside repute has filtered across the water, and sales have bumped up accordingly.

But that's by no means the whole story, which is my cue to introduce 'charisma'. Charisma is what John F. Kennedy had, but Enoch Powell will never have. Or, if you like, what Tudor cottages have over Centre Point, ie. charm and public appeal. Take a look at the standard Z. Step back a pace or two, tilt the head, narrow the eyes and observe the Datz in perspective. Without doubt it's a good looker, and sexy, with its long phallic bonnet and big butch wheels. The seats are practically over the axle, providing lean and hungry lines of which Yon Cassius would have been proud. These sort of characteristics make the birds go for a car, and if the birds go for a car then the blokes go for that same car, because most blokes are into the pulling game and a long sexy bonnet makes up for a fair bit of acne.

Now that little lot's all rather superficial and I'm sure the most real motoring fans aren't likely to be conned by the ego-extension syndrome, which brings me nicely to the sporting image. Unlike a certain British motor manufacturer whose name shall go unmentioned, the guys at Nissan Co of Japan are fully aware of the value of competition involvement related to showroom sales, hence the presence of the Zed in racing, rallying and, in the case of our old friend Shakey Matey, rolling. All great for the image of a hairy, snorting road-scorcher with red corpuscles in its 3-star and a daily diet of lesser forms of transport.

But is that the real story? Is the image fact or myth? I would be the last person to claim that the full-house works tanks are anything but the white-hot rally tools they're made out to be, and likewise I reckon the standard road car is a decently wild piece of machinery. The point is, is it worth a tag of £2535 or are you paying out a lot of loot for that sexy/rally/American image? The only way to decide is to look at what you get for the two-and-a-half grand. We did this by borrowing a standard 240Z from Datsun main dealers Ancaster Garage, 61 Croydon Road, London S.E.20, and chugging around in it for a week, and likewise with a rally prepared version.

The engine of the standard car is a six-in-line water cooled chunk with an aluminium alloy head and a capacity of 2393cc. There are seven main bearings, bore/stroke is 83mm/73.7mm, the camshaft is single overhead and the compression ratio 9:1. Breathing is by a pair of SU carburetters, and maximum power 151 bhp (gross) at 5600rpm; this works out at somewhere around 95-100 bhp at the wheels.

Sleek lines and rear spoiler make the 240Z a hungry looking beast. The nasty wood-effect plastic wheel spoils an otherwise excellent interior, with comfy seating and superb pedal layout. Six fat pots-worth of OHC engine fills the compartment, with alloy head and a pair of SU carbs.

The gearbox is 5-speed all-synchro with a 4th gear ratio of 1:1 and fifth of 0.852:1 making it effectively an overdrive gear. The clutch has a single dry plate and is 8.87in in diameter, and the final drive ratio is 3.9:1.

Suspension is independent all round by virtue of MacPherson struts and coil springs, steering is rack-and-pinion and brakes are tandem system, servo assisted discs and drums. The front discs are 10.67in diameter and the rear drums 9in diameter. The standard spec wheels are $4\frac{1}{2}$J × 14 steels, shod, in the case of our car, with those evil foreign Bridgestones.

The interior features a pair of vinyl reclining seats with in-built head restraints, behind which is a flat deck providing a large space for luggage or whatever, with access via a hinged tailgate. As this luggage area is not separated from the passenger compartment Datsun provide a pair of webbing straps for securing anything that might get thrown around under heavy braking or cornering (at which point I collapse with laughter at the thought of poor old Fido strapped down like a heretic during the Inquisition).

Instruments are excellent, and mounted snugly in a black vinyl-covered energy absorbing dash panel. The speedo and rev-counter are instantly visible through the top arc of the steering wheel, this latter item being the only bum-steer in the layout, with its rim of horrendous wood-effect plastic. At the centre of the dash we find three dials, one a clock and the other two dual gauges monitoring fuel/amps and water temp/oil pressure. The centre console houses the heater controls and vent, radio, cigar lighter, ashtray, rear screen heater switch and choke control. The driver is particularly well catered for, with eyeball ventilator (also provided for the passenger), foot-well ventilator, and a sturdy rest for the clutch foot. Pedal layout in general is ideal with the brake pedal set near enough to the accelerator to enable easy heel-toeing with no danger of the foot finding the wrong pedal at the

Street Machine?

Woolferace wheels really set off the looks of Richard Jackson's rally 240Z. Furry seat covers eliminate the soggy back problem of the standard car, while Britax full harness belts and beefy roll cage protect the occupants. Twin SU's pale into insignificance when compared to triple 40DCOEs.

wrong time.

The washer/wiper controls and the light controls are twist knobs on the end of the left hand column stalk — easily operated but prone to confusion; I often found that I had turned the lights on at the same time as the wipers. Or instead of the wipers. The stick on the other side operates indicators, dipped lights and flasher.

I drove the car during that amazing spell of hot weather in early July, and immediately discovered why so many manufacturers are making their seats with brushed nylon inserts. Unfortunately the Nissan Co isn't one of these manufacturers, and soggy shirt backs are mighty uncomfortable on a long run. However, the seats held one in well despite being rather uncomfortable around the lumbar regions after an hour or so's driving.

The ride is rather curious, in that the indy suspension manages to iron out largish bumps rather effectively but isn't as effective on smaller lumps and potholes, causing a certain degree of driver-judder. Visibility ain't too hot, rear-three quarter vision being particularly poor, and the sharply sloping nose can have the same effect on clean parking as that on the E-type, ie. if you aren't careful you can end up with a sharply dented nose.

The steering is rather heavy at low speed, but I find that eminently preferable to woolly power steering. Anyhow, it all lightens up when pressing on, and the car feels very stable at speed — in fact I felt more happy with it when galloping than when cruising. On bends everything is nicely predictable, with slight understeer fading nicely into progressive and controllable oversteer as the power is applied. However, on occasion the Z would give a little sideways hop if a bump was discovered on a bend — surprising in an all-independent setup.

As would be expected with six pots the power is smooth and useable, with a turbine-like effect in the middle rev ranges, most of the power raising its head at around 3500rpm.

Bridgestone seem to have been playing around with their compounds, for the tyres on the Z were far superior to those fitted to the Mazda RX3 tested a few months back. Mind you, that isn't to say they're particularly good — just that they're less bad. Perhaps happily, I didn't have the chance to try them in the wet.

But, in the final analysis, a most enjoyable car to drive, whether you prefer a good looker, a Kings Road-cruiser or a high-speed flyer; for the two-seat fan it is a veritable 'car for all reasons'.

And so to our variation on the theme.

The Rally Z tested is owned by Richard Jackson, marketing director of his family's clothing company in Leeds. Richard, a Triple C Championship contender, has been rallying for about two years, starting off with a 998cc Imp which developed the rather irritating habit of breaking down. This was chopped in for a secondhand Escort Twin Cam, the engine of which also proved unreliable. In an attempt to achieve some sort of finishing record Richard disposed of the TC lump and invested in a 2-litre SOHC chunk of machinery (thinks: could this have been the first RS2000?) and gave it a new lease of life by introducing it to a Piper turbocharger. Great. It went like the very clappers until the Jackson Gremlin struck once more and the car was consumed by fire on the Moss Tyres Rally.

The 240Z was purchased late last year, fitted with a sumpguard and rollcage, and rallied as a Group 3 car — which, in case you didn't know, is the sporty car equivalent of Group 1. In this form it gained a 2nd in class on the Mintex Dales, the Mini Miglia and, for a bit of variety, in one of the first Prod-Sport races. In fact, one of Richard's policies is to use the car for as great a variety of motor sport as possible — like sprints, production car trials, etc.

The Z's last event in Gp3 trim was the International Welsh, with a 62nd overall and four points in the CCC tables. And this despite starting at No. 206 and then getting baulked by a brace of back markers.

When viewed alongside the standard car, the Jackson Z looks even meaner, even more angry. The Cibiés protruding from the lamp bar on the nose give a peering, searching effect, and the low-profile Avons on Woolferace wheels create a squat, predatory effect. A real evil carnivore this one; the sort of thing that frightens nervy old ladies at dead of night.

Actually, speaking in purely relative terms, the tweaks are fairly conservative, being limited to general rally prep plus engine and suspension modifications of a conventional manner. No injection, rear wheel disc brakes or wild goodies like that. Most of the bits were developed by Jan Odor's Janspeed establishment and are now available for public consumption from Fletcher Motors, the car's sponsors, or, of course, Jan himself.

Let's look first at the power plant. Opening the bonnet the first thing that wallops the eye is the carburation: not one Weber, not two Webers, but three 40DCOE's perched on cast alloy manifolding. The cylinder head has been thoroughly cleaned up and made to work like all good heads should. Jan reckons that although the Zed-head is pretty good as standard there's a helluva lot can be done with it, and lots of removeable metal laying around. The compression ratio has been upped to 10:1, the chambers gas-flowed and polished, the ports opened up a bit and the valve seats worked on for greater efficiency. Let's face it, with all that extra fuel going through the Webers there's no point letting it linger aimlessly in unmodofided chambers. The valves have been left standard size, the camshaft is original, but a specially designed exhaust manifold is fitted, together with a plated two-silencer exhaust system of the straight through type. And that's about it. Nothing ultimately hairy but enough to produce a cool, useable 120-122 bhp at the wheels. Before moving on to the suspension I'll give you some prices for the engine mods. Work on the head comes out at about £80 — a high figure at first sight but one that has to be related to the amount of work required — for instance, Jan reckons that he can do at least three 1275GT heads in the time it takes to complete just one 240Z head. In kit form the carbs and inlet manifolding can be bought ready jetted, etc, at £128.00; this includes everything but the manifold gasket which comes as part of the £10 gasket set. Air cleaners can be bought for £5.25. The exhaust manifold costs £30, and the plated system a further £18.

Moving on to the suspension we find that modifications are limited to straight spring and shock absorber swaps. The rather choppy standard setup has been firmed by the fitting of Bilstein struts all round, and works specification coil springs at the front. Oh, and the rear wishbones have been strengthened by welded-on plates. And that's the sole extent of the suspension tweaking, costs working out at £16 for the springs and £66 for the full set of four shockers.

A sodding-great roll cage fills the interior, and laying around are all the usual bells and whistles required for rallying. Like a brace of fire extinguishers, one on each inner wheel bulge, a fat leather rimmed steering wheel, Halda, extra oil pressure gauge mounted next to the Halda, and furry sheepskin seat covers. Switches for the Cibiès are fitted, and a pair of full-harness belts. The driver has his clutch footrest of course, so to stop the co-driver (Dennis Dickinson) getting sulky a sturdy tubular footrest has been put in on the passenger-side floor.

The underside of the rally car is protected by a solid looking sumpshield made up from Dural by Richard and available from him at around £50, and a petrol tank guard in thin-guage steel with a rubber shock absorbing layer. Fuel and brake lines run inside the car of course.

Richard is lucky enough to have acquired a low ratio limited slip diff, essential on any good rally machine, and has enough good taste to have opted for a set of delicious 6½ x 14 Woolferace wheels. When I drove the car the wheels were coated in Avon radials, but for stages Richard fits the very popular Kleber M plus S tyres on steel wheels. All the bits that have gone into this car, plus a full rally preparation service, are available from Fletcher Motors (Leeds) Ltd, who are joint entrants of the car with the Trackrod Motor Club — see elsewhere in this issue — in which Richard is something of a big wheel. Fletchers are at Meadow Road, Leeds 11 (0532 29344) and the man to speak to is Alan Ford, the Sales Director.

All round visibility in the standard Z isn't the best, and what viewing area there is is further limited by the roll cage which runs along the top of the windscreen and down the centre of either rear side window. However, the feeling of security is adequate compensation, and the conspicuous spotlights perched up front make parking much easier.

Std 240Z Secs	mph	Rally 240Z secs
3.5	**0-30**	2.4
5.0	**0-40**	4.0
7.5	**0-50**	5.8
9.5	**0-60**	8.3
13.1	**0-70**	10.8
16.6	**0-80**	14.1
21.4	**0-90**	17.5
	In the gears:	
	3rd Gear	
5.7	**40-60**	5.2
5.9	**50-70**	5.5
	4th Gear	
7.5	**40-60**	6.2
8.3	**50-70**	5.5
8.5	**60-80**	7.4

MPH per 1000 rpm in 4th
Std, 17.5; Rally, 14.0
MPH per 1000 rpm in 5th
Std, 19.5; Rally, 16.5

On driving the rally car two things become immediately apparent — one, that the throttle pedal is incredibly heavy; the other that the steering is as well, the fat wheels adding to the already rather stiff steering-wheel action. But on loose surfaces neither of these factors is too much of a headache as much of the steering is done by stabbing the throttle, which one tends to have either fully open or fully closed. So responsive is the car that on stages fine degrees of throttle control become unnecessary. It's all a matter of turning that long nose into a bend — and then booting it. At which point the tail swings right out, the corrective lock goes on, and one negotiates the corner in a super power slide which is simply reduced by lifting off the hot pedal. Should one require to reduce it that is — it all depends what one finds on the exit from the corner. On a series of bends it's really easy to just lift on and off the power and whisk round all the twiddly bits in fine swooping style.

Mind you, the car's pretty heavy and a few laps of our handling course in blazing sunshine became bloody knackering.

Now, if you squint at the comparative figures on this page you'd be excused for thinking that the rally Z isn't quite as hot as one might expect. However, statistics can be misleading and the ordinary nought-to-umpty-ump figgies don't tell much of a story. But look at the in-gear mid-range times and you'll see where all the work has paid dividends. Like 1.3 secs off the 40-60 in 4th time, and nearly three secs off the 50-70 time. At the top range the rally car whittled practically 4 secs off the zero-ninety thrash. Which all goes to make this Datsun a responsive, pleasant and useable competition machine.

So where does that leave us on the Z price and value stakes. Well, as a standard sports car a 0 to 60 time of 9.5 secs isn't going to set the world afire; then again, it's by no means slow. Driveability is a real plus point, as is cockpit layout, and looks have already been praised extensively enough. In the same price range you could have a Lotus Europa or Elan Sprint, Lancia Fulvia 1.6 HF, BMW 2002, — shall I go on? OK — TVR 3000M, Alfa Romeo 2000GT Veloce, Scimitar GTE, Audi 100 Coupe or 1½ Capri 3000 GT's; and for much less you could have a Jensen-Healey, a Morgan Plus 8, or a Ginetta G21 1800.

And that all adds up to a lot of competition, without even considering various specs of Escort, with change left over for modification. On a strictly personal basis I would go for the Alfa if I wanted a Grand Tourer, the Lancia for rallying, or Morgan Plus 8 for sheer guts-and-thunder sports driving. Could it be the 240Z is the ideal compromise?

It certainly has a lot of charm and many plus points, and Jan Odor reckons he's sold more performance kits for the Z in the last six months than he has for the Marina since it was released . . . which must prove something. ■

DATSUN'S SAFARI WARRIOR

IN THE IDIOM of the traditional big Healey the Datsun 240Z is a big, brutish sports car. True, it's quicker, nicer-looking and more refined, but nevertheless that's the sort of market the 240Z takes so well. Originally marketed with the American dollar in mind and sold over there considerably cheaper than its current British price tag of £2535 all-paid, the 240Z with its strong combination of looks, performance and handling is a good seller over here. Like most Japanese cars, from the mini models right through to this level, the 240Z is very well equipped. It also performs very impressively with a 0-60mph time in the region of 8secs and a maximum of 125mph. In some respects it's very like a latter-day E-type in concept, and its recent East African Safari victory in the hands of Shekhar Mehta (preceded two years ago by a win by Edgar Herrmann) has shown up its superlative strength and durability.

Making no pretence of being anything other than a pure two-seater, the 240Z's lines are very much on E-type principles, although the Datsun is angular rather than curvaceous. The overall effect is aggressively stylish with the long bonnet with its carburettor bulge in the middle. Spoilers front and rear set off this powerful look, and indeed they do help towards the car's excellent high-speed stability.

Power for the 240Z comes from a single-overhead-camshaft straight six unit of 2.4 litres. Employing an aluminium head on a cast iron block, the engine is smooth and extremely sturdy. Twin Hitachi carburettors are used and peak gross power comes as 151bhp at 5600rpm, which may not sound a lot, but in practice provides great performance. The secret is the excellent torque curve and the five-speed gearbox with its well-chosen ratios. For one thing, the torque curve of the engine allows a driver to select virtually any gear in traffic: even in fifth the Datsun will pull away steadily from 15mph or so. The engine feels very strong indeed and heavy use of the right foot allows speeds of 35mph, 60, 85, 110 and 125 through the gears, and, of course, the fifth ratio provides ideal relaxed motorway cruising.

Mounted on the quilted (ugh!) covered transmission console the gear-shift proved heavy, notably the spring-loading, but otherwise the gearbox is excellent, save for some transmission vibration and general gear-train noise. The other impressive advantage of the ratios is the fuel consumption. Overall we got around 24mpg on average, and thrifty use of the throttle can produce even better economy on long, relaxed runs. For a big sports car, this is very economical indeed. A 15½ gallon fuel tank is fitted and so this gives a range of over 350 miles in most circumstances, and even a flat-out section of *autoroute* driving will give well over two hours running.

The steering, by rack and pinion, is on the heavy side, but precise and accurate, and braking by servo-assisted discs front and drums rear is well up to the job. As borne out by its rally performances, the 240Z is very much a driver's car. High-speed stability, no doubt greatly contributed to by the spoilers, is first-rate. On cornering, there is hardly any body roll, and unless the throttle is hard used, the Datsun is a mild understeerer. On power it transforms to easily controllable oversteer, and at its limits, as one sees from the Tony Falls, Rauno Aaltonens and Shekhar Mehtas of this world, the 240Z is a real opposite-lock machine. Suspension is independent all round by MacPherson struts and coilsprings, and the ride is pleasantly firm.

Tall high-backed seats are provided for the occupants and, while not being sumptuous, they are very comfortable. What really counts, though, is the availability of leg room for even the tallest of drivers, and the ability to get any sort of driving position. All this, plus easy to find and operate stalks for wipers, lights and washers, adds up to convenience and makes the 240Z and enjoyable long distance car. The heating and ventilation systems are superb, so much so that you really can get warm feet and a cool face simultaneously.

All in all the Datsun 240Z is a driver's car and a very desirable one at that. It ably fills the void in the big sports car market between the Triumph TR6 at one end of the scale to the V12 E-type Jaguar at the other. From our own experience, and from general impressions of others who have lived with the 240Z, the reliability factor is reported as excellent. Combine that with the looks, the full quota of equipment and the superlative performance and a 240Z at £2500 makes a lot of sense.

A PAIR OF Z CARS

We compare Bob Sharp's race-prepared 240Z with the new fuel-injected 280Z at Lime Rock

IN THE AUTOMOBILE business nothing in recent years, at least not in the sports/GT market, has enjoyed the success of the Datsun 240Z. Its instant stardom in the marketplace is the stuff automotive legends are made of. And the 260Z and 280Z that came later have done nothing to tarnish that five-year-old legend. The Datsun Z has been a favorite of *Road & Track* readers right along, and this year the R&T staff selected the 280Z the best car in its class in our "Ten Best Cars for a Changing World" in the June issue.

On race tracks around the country the Z has been almost equally successful thanks in large part to the efforts of Bob Sharp Racing in Wilton, Connecticut. Sharp has won two SCCA national championships in a Z car, has won 30 national races with a Z and as this was written was handily leading the IMSA Grand Touring Under 2.5-liter class and was tied for 4th in the SCCA's new Trans-Am series. So the choice of Datsun's fuel-injected 280Z and Sharp's current 240Z IMSA race car for this latest in our series of track comparison tests was really a natural.

For this test we went to Lime Rock Park, Connecticut. Sharp and crew were there with the 240Z that had won the IMSA GTU race the day before, setting qualifying and race-lap records in the process. The race car was matched with a new, but broken in, 1975 280Z conveniently provided by Bob Sharp Datsun. Although Sharp had been around Lime Rock scores of times in street Z cars they had always been slightly modified: heavier anti-roll bars, competition shock absorbers and the like. This would be his first time at pushing an absolutely street stock Z car around Lime Rock as quickly as he possibly could. He was as curious about the outcome as we were.

Sharp's race car is beautiful in the way a race car should be beautiful. Not necessarily sleek or svelte or graceful or any of the other adjectives that spew from the pens of ad copy writers. Rather, its beauty lies in the way it hunkers down menacingly nose-low on its suspension, the purposeful bulge of its fenders that can only be called sensuous, and up close, the meticulous attention to detail.

But any race car is only as good as it goes and going depends on what's under the skin. Sharp's 240Z is just about as much race car underneath as it can be. Datsun's knee-deep involvement in racing in this country has meant an on-going program of research and development by the factory, Sharp and other teams who derive no little support from Nissan, U.S.A.

The engine in the IMSA car is the 2.4-liter Z unit slightly stretched to 2450 cc which keeps it just under the 2.5-liter classification limit. It is fed by three 50-mm Mikuni-Solex carburetors and the compression ratio has been raised to 11.8:1, well up from the stock 280Z's 8.3:1. Horsepower is 258 at 8250 rpm, and torque peaks at 184 lb-ft at 6500 rpm. Although the redline is 8300 rpm, Sharp usually makes his shifts at an even 8000.

The car's 2200-lb curb weight is distributed 52% front, 48% rear. The stock 280Z's 2875-lb curb weight is split 50/50. There is a 22-gal. fuel cell and in normal race tune the car delivers approximately 6 mpg on the track. Unlike any production-line Z car sold in this country, the race car has a special, but legal, 5-speed transmission. The transmission is new from Datsun and only recently homologated for racing use. The 5th gear employs a direct-drive ratio rather than an overdrive as with most 5-speed boxes.

The disc brakes are a special Datsun Competition Department design manufactured by Hearst/Airheart. The front calipers are actuated by four pistons each; the rears, two. On the front Sharp has mounted 15 x 10-in. Minilite wheels. The rears are BBS 15 x 15 in. The racing tires are Goodyear, 24.5 x 10/15 in the front and 25.0 x 13/15 rear.

is three-fold: to show what goes into making a race car out of a production car, what it does when the job is finished and to find out just what a production version will do in the hands of a professional.

One figure you will find missing from the performance data of the race car is lateral acceleration. Much to our surprise Sharp has never had the car on a skidpad, which meant there were no existing figures we could pass on to you. And there just isn't a skidpad in the Lime Rock area where we could get our own numbers. However, we can do a little educated guessing based on experience with other race cars. In that June test the stock 280Z generated a lateral acceleration figure of 0.720g. Racing suspension and tires make a big difference, and we can safely assume (guess?) the race car would tour the skidpad at something like 1.100-1.200g. (In the September 1974 issue of R&T in a similar comparison test of a stock Jensen-Healey with Lee Mueller's race-prepared version, the street version recorded 0.758g on the skidpad. The race version did 1.112g.)

No problem, however, determining the race car's acceleration

The interior of the racing car bears little or no resemblance to the street car. There is a full complement of instruments; the bottle for the fire extinguishing system is in the right-side foot well. Roll-cage bars provide both protection and chassis stiffening.

Sharp in the Lime Rock winner's circle the day before our comparison test.

The suspension is "basically stock," according to Sharp. The struts and control arms are stock, or at least start life as stock components. The front and rear anti-roll bars are adjustable, as are the special competition shock absorbers. The coil springs have been made easily removable to allow quick spring-rate changes, and ride height is adjustable. Pick-up points have been relocated to improve the overall geometry.

The gutted interior now contains a single bucket seat. There is a complete roll cage, a fire extinguishing system and of course the stock instrument panel has been replaced with a simple flat metal affair containing a plethora of gauges which keep track of everything from engine rpm to differential temperature.

The street 280Z was box stock: no special equipment of any kind. The tires were Toyo 195/70-14 on the standard 14 x 5J steel disc wheels. The 2.8-liter engine (actually 2754 cc, 168 cu in.) produces 149 bhp net at 5600 rpm. In our test of the new 280 for the June issue the car's 0–60 mph time was 9.4 sec, with a 17.3-sec run through the quarter mile. It would, in power alone, be no match for the 250-bhp race car, but that isn't the purpose of these comparison tests. Our purpose

PERFORMANCE COMPARISON
Production & Racing Datsun Z Cars

	Production	Racing
Acceleration:		
Time to distance, sec:		
0-1320 ft (¼ mi)	17.3	15.8
Speed at end of ¼ mi, mph	81.0	103.0
Time to speed, sec:		
0-30 mph	3.2	4.4
0-60 mph	9.4	7.0
0-100 mph	30.2	14.8
Fuel economy:		
Mpg	19.5 (normal)	6.0 (race)
Brakes:		
Minimum stopping distances, ft:		
From 60 mph	130	106
From 80 mph	221	197
Pedal effort for 0.5g stop, lb	45	90
Fade, % increase in pedal effort, 6 stops from 60 mph @ 0.5 g	excessive	nil

R&T ROAD TEST

BOB SHARP 240Z

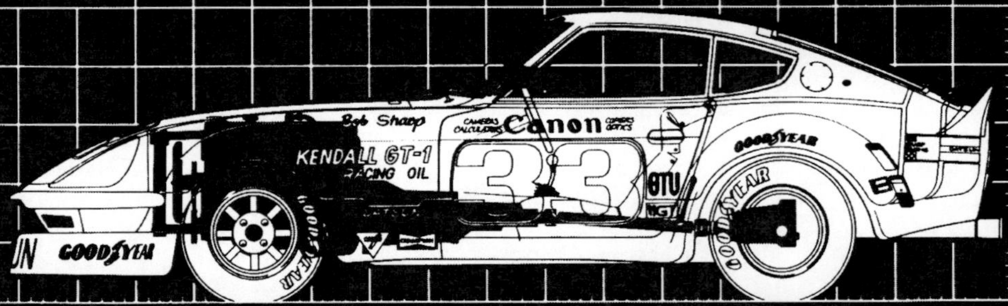

PRICE
List price $25,000

MANUFACTURER
Bob Sharp Racing
Danbury Rd
PO Box 278
Wilton, Conn. 06897

GENERAL
Race weight, lb 2200
Test weight 2540
Weight distribution (with driver), front/rear, % 52/48
Wheelbase, in. 90.7
Track, front/rear 58.0/63.5
Length 171.0
Width 82.0
Height 49.0
Ground clearance 3.6
Overhang, front/rear 42.2/38.1
Usable trunk space, cu ft .... nil
Fuel capacity, U.S. gal. 22.0

ENGINE
Type .... sohc inline 6
Bore x stroke, mm ...... 84.0 x 73.7
Equivalent in. .... 3.31 x 2.90
Displacement, cc/cu in. 2450/149
Compression ratio 11.8:1
Bhp @ rpm, net .... 258 @ 8250
Equivalent mph 146
Torque @ rpm, lb-ft .... 184 @ 6500
Equivalent mph 115
Carburetion .... three Mikuni-Solex (2V)
Fuel requirement .. premium, 102-oct

DRIVETRAIN
Transmission .... 5-sp manual
Gear ratios: 5th (1.00) 4.11:1
4th (1.14) 4.69:1
3rd (1.29) 5.30:1
2nd (1.60) 6.58:1
1st (2.35) 9.66:1
Final drive ratio 4.11:1

CHASSIS & BODY
Layout .... front engine/rear drive
Body/frame .... unit steel
Brake system .... 10.7-in. discs front and rear
Swept area, sq in. 394
Wheels .... Minilite 15 x 10 front, BBS 15 x 15 rear
Tires .... Goodyear Blue Streak; 24.5 x 10-15 front, 25.0 x 13-15 rear
Steering type .... rack & pinion
Overall ratio 18.0:1
Turns, lock-to-lock 3.1
Turning circle, ft 34.8
Front suspension: MacPherson struts, lower lateral arms, compliance struts, coil springs, adjustable tube shocks, adjustable anti-roll bar
Rear suspension: Chapman struts, A-arms, coil springs, adjustable tube shocks, adjustable anti-roll bar

INSTRUMENTATION
Instruments: 10,000-rpm tach, oil press., oil temp, coolant temp, ammeter, differential temp, transmission temp
Warning lights: oil pressure

ACCOMMODATION
Seating capacity, persons 1
Seat width 14.0
Head room 38.0
Seat back adjustment, deg 0

CALCULATED DATA
Lb/bhp (test weight) 9.8
Mph/1000 rpm (5th gear) 17.6
Engine revs/mi (60 mph) 3400
Piston travel, ft/mi 1645
R&T steering index 1.08
Brake swept area, sq in./ton .. 310

ROAD TEST RESULTS

ACCELERATION
Time to distance, sec:
0–100 ft 4.8
0–500 ft 9.5
0–1320 ft (¼ mi) 15.8
Speed at end of ¼ mi, mph 103.0
Time to speed, sec:
0–30 mph 4.4
0–40 mph 5.2
0–50 mph 6.0
0–60 mph 7.0
0–70 mph 8.6
0–80 mph 10.2
0–100 mph 14.8

SPEEDS IN GEARS
5th gear (8300 rpm) 147
4th (8000) 124
3rd (8000) 110
2nd (8000) 88
1st (8000) 60

FUEL ECONOMY
Race driving, mpg 6.0
Race range, mi (1-gal. res) 126

BRAKES
Minimum stopping distances, ft:
From 60 mph 106
From 80 mph 197
Control in panic stop ...... excellent
Pedal effort for 0.5g stop, lb 90
Fade: percent increase in pedal effort to maintain 0.5g deceleration in 6 stops from 60 mph .... nil
Overall brake rating .... excellent

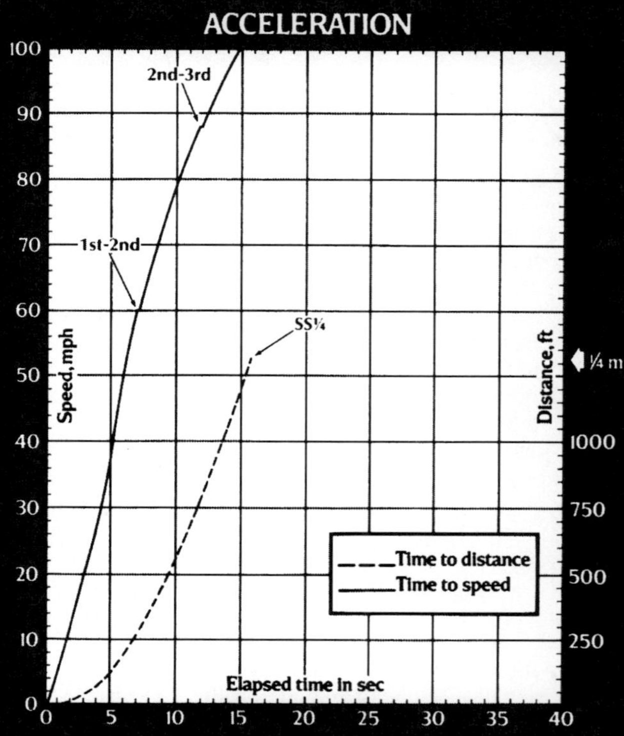

SPECIFICATIONS COMPARISON
Production & Racing Datsun Z Cars

	Production	Racing
Price	$6284	$25,000
General:		
Weight, lb	2875 (curb)	2200 (racing)
Weight distribution (with driver), front/rear, %	50/50	52/48
Track, front/rear, in.	53.3/53.0	58.0/63.5
Length, in.	173.2	171.0
Width, in.	64.2	82.0
Height, in.	51.0	49.0
Ground clearance, in.	5.7	3.6
Usable trunk space, cu ft	8.5	nil
Fuel capacity, U.S. gal	17.2	22.0
Engine:		
Bore x stroke, mm	86.1 x 79.0	84.0 x 73.7
Displacement, cc/cu in.	2754/168	2450/149
Compression ratio	8.3:1	11.8:1
Bhp @ rpm, net	149 @ 5600	258 @ 8250
Torque @ rpm, lb-ft	163 @ 4400	184 @ 6500
Carburetion/fuel injection	L-Jetronic injection	three Mikuni-Solex (2V)
Fuel requirement	regular, 91-oct	premium, 102-oct
Drive train:		
Transmission	4-sp manual	5-sp manual
Gear ratios:		
5th	—	1.00
4th	1.00	1.14
3rd	1.31	1.29
2nd	2.08	1.60
1st	3.32	2.35
Final drive ratio	3.55:1	4.11:1
Chassis:		
Brake system	10.7-in. discs front, 9.0 x 1.6-in. drums rear; vacuum assisted	10.7-in. discs front and rear
Swept area, sq in.	310	394
Wheels	steel disc, 14 x 5J	Minilite 10 x 15 front, BBS 15 x 15 rear
Tires	Bridgestone, Wide 70 195/70-14	Goodyear Blue Streak 24.5 x 10-15 front, 25.0 x 13-15 rear
Front suspension	MacPherson struts, lower lateral arms, compliance struts, coil springs, tube shocks, anti-roll bar	MacPherson struts, lower lateral arms, compliance struts, coil springs, adj tube shocks, adj anti-roll bar
Rear suspension	Chapman struts, A-arms, coil springs, tube shocks, anti-roll bar	Chapman struts, A-arms, coil springs, adj tube shocks, adj anti-roll bar
Instrumentation:		
Instruments	160-mph speedo, 8000-rpm tach, 99,999 odo, 999.9 trip odo, oil press., coolant temp, ammeter, fuel level, clock	10,000-rpm tach, oil press., oil temp, coolant temp, ammeter, differential temp, transmission temp
Warning lights	brake system, rear-window heat, seatbelts, egr, hazard, high beam, directionals	oil pressure
Accommodation:		
Seating capacity, persons	2	1
Seat width, in.	2 x 21.0	14.0
Head room, in.	36.5	38.0
Seat back adjustment, deg	40	0
Calculated data:		
Lb/bhp (test weight)	21.2	9.8
Mph/1000 rpm	20.3 (4th gear)	17.6 (5th gear)
Engine revs/mi (60 mph)	2960	3400
Piston travel, ft/mi	1535	1645
Brake swept area, sq in./ton	196	310

Three Mikuni carburetors feed the racing engine. The car gets approximately 6 mpg on the track.

With the rear hatch open, the racing car's dry-break fuel inlet and fuel filter are easily seen.

and braking capabilities. For that we moved to Lime Rock's front straight. Well, there was a slight problem. In today's era of rolling starts, race cars aren't set up for standing starts. The 240Z was no exception.

"It won't come off the line very quickly," team manager Gene Crowe warned as we set up the testing equipment. "The way the clutch is adjusted Bob has to do a lot of feathering to get underway from a complete stop. If he brought the revs way up and dumped the clutch the driveshaft and/or differential would probably twist right out trying to break the rear tires loose."

The figures reveal the problem. The watch was started when Sharp first engaged the clutch. There was bucking and snorting and a general reluctance to get underway which is reflected in the 0–30 mph time: 4.4 sec. The stock 280Z took only 3.2 sec. Continuing the comparison, the street version reached 50 mph in 6.9 sec. The race car, although still suffering from the slow start, began to come on and was almost a second quicker at 6.0 sec. But after that, when the race car could start operating in its accustomed range, things started happening in a hurry. The race car's 0-60 mph time was 7.0 sec, compared to 9.4. The race car got to 80 mph in only 10.2 sec vs 16.8. For the race car 100 mph came up in 14.8 sec. The street car took a half-minute—actually 30.2 sec—to reach the century mark. In the June test of the 280Z the car's top speed was 119 mph. According to the race car's gear chart at the 8200-rpm redline in 5th gear the 240Z would be clipping along at 150 mph, and that with a 4.11:1 final drive ratio. In the quarter-mile runs, the street car registered 17.3 sec at 81 mph. The race car, really storming at the end, did 15.8 sec, 103 mph.

The race car stops as well as it goes. Again, a race car is seldom, other than in emergency situations, asked to brake to a complete stop as quickly as it can, so Sharp's experience with such a maneuver was rather limited. The first time he tried it from 60 mph he locked up the rear wheels and amid much smoke and noise brought the car to a halt in 126 ft, a very good effort despite the "sloppy" technique. That first stop showed him what it was all about, so on the next attempt the job was done in a mere 106 ft. In two panic stops from 80 mph the figures were indeed extraordinary: 205 ft on the first attempt followed by 197 ft!

In the panic braking mode the race car stopped straight and without a hint of control loss. The street version exhibited much the same control. Its numbers for the 0-60 mph and 80-0 mph stops were 130 ft and 221 ft respectively. We experienced quite a bit of brake fade with the street car, however; something non-existent in the race car.

In the first panic braking test, Sharp locked up the Z car's rear brakes.

With the straight-line stuff completed, we could get on with the timed-laps portion of the comparison.

Lime Rock Park is a tough track. It is only 1.53-mi long, it has seven turns, is narrow and in some spots quite bumpy. A race at Lime Rock takes a lot out of both car and driver. The day before, when Sharp was dominating his class in the IMSA Camel GT race, we kept our fingers crossed the car would emerge unscathed and healthy. It did both. However, as healthy as it may have been Sharp explained that with the Mid-Ohio race just four days away there would be no time to correct any damage the engine might incur in our test. While he was more than willing to put the car through our standard battery of acceleration and braking tests we agreed there was no reason to subject the race car to more hot laps around the track. The figures from the previous day's racing would easily suffice.

Sharp, who is thoroughly familiar with the car and the track, very quickly got down to a 0:58.47 during qualifying, a record for the class. In the first heat of the race he set the fastest race lap record for the GTU class at 0:58.40 on his way to 1st in class and 10th overall. In the second heat he broke the class race lap record with a 0:57.70 (95.46 mph) on the way to another 1st in class and 9th overall. By comparison, Peter Gregg had set a qualifying record in his Porsche Carrera of 0:54.93 (100.27 mph) and Al Holbert, also in a Carrera, had the fastest race lap in both heats with identical 0:55.20 (99.78 mph) clockings.

For the laps in the street car we began by putting the Toyo tires at 36 lb front and rear. Sharp went out for a couple of laps in the 1:18 area. We then adjusted the pressures, putting 40 lb in the front and leaving the rears at 36 lb. The improvement was reasonable, dropping the laps down to a 1:17.8 and a 1:17.6. Bob felt the back end was still not quite to his liking so we also increased the pressure in the rear tires to 40 lb.

He had reported the tires were overheating rather quickly in those first trial laps, so he decided to make a five-lap charge at the clock: a lap to get up to speed, three hot laps and a cool-off.

As he came around to start his first hot lap we got the thumbs up sign and knew he was happy with the tire pressures. Obviously. The first lap dropped down to a 1:16.27. The second lap was a 1:15.79 and he finished the run with a final lap at 1:14.94. The best street car time was 17.24 seconds off the record-setting time of the race car.

Before describing the street car's handling characteristics Sharp promised he wouldn't let his strong Datsun prejudices cloud his objectivity, then he went on to say, "The street car is surprisingly neutral. It is easy to maneuver and is very controllable. There is slight oversteer coming out of a turn under power and a little trailing-throttle oversteer if you back off a little. The car, I think, is capable of more than the tires we are using would allow. They heated up pretty quickly.

"Any road car tends to feel soft and mushy when compared to a race car, but then I wouldn't want the race car suspension set-up on a road car. Balance is very important in a car and in that department the 280Z does a remarkable job for a street machine. In the esses it transitions nicely, although there is a lot of body roll with the stock suspension."

Bob went on to reiterate this was his first experience on a race track with a *completely* stock Z car. Although he lauds the car's handling as-is, he readily admits heavier anti-roll bars and competition-type shock absorbers make a big difference.

"Slow corners are a problem with the car," he went on. "It just isn't a throw-around car like the old Datsun 2000 roadster was. Now there was a pitch-it and point-it car. The Z is really more at home in the 60 to 80-mph bends.

"The brakes got hot, really hot, but didn't seem to lose their efficiency."

Although we were pleased with Datsun's decision to go to larger tires and wider wheels with the fuel-injected 280Z, we were less enamored with the rather sizable increase in steering effort the wider tires produced. However, Sharp found nothing there to criticize. The heaviness disappears at speed and the advantage of more rubber on the road takes precedence.

We were getting ready to record some more timed laps with the street car when a spring rainstorm blew up. Within minutes the track was awash, so our testing session was cut short. But further laps may not have resulted in much improvement in times.

"If we worked all afternoon I might have been able to knock off perhaps as much as a full second," Sharp explained. "But maybe not. The tires were being used about as hard as they would tolerate. I might have been able to improve as I worked more on the technique of driving the car. Regardless, I think we've shown the 280Z, as it comes from the factory, is a very good sports car."

The 280Z is a good sports car, and could be made even better, according to Sharp, with some very simple suspension modifications. The 240Z race car is also very good; state of the art, even. It's hard to imagine what could be done to make it any better.

DATSUN Z CARS

THE DATSUN 240Z has just been revitalised with the release of a two-plus-two version in Japan. To mark the occasion, we re-sample the four-year-old formula and also taste a high-spirited road-racer derivative available only in Japan . . .

IN THE PUBLIC mind, the Datsun 240Z has the reputation of a competition-bred sports car that's way ahead of its everyday competition. The sales figures confirm it — and as a projectile aimed at a slot in the market, the 240Z is right on target.

Its success and its popularity are well-reflected by our Readers' Poll. In the 1970 Poll (the first year the 240Z was released), the car recorded 10percent of the vote and ran third in its class. A year later, it doubled that percentage to 22.5percent and ran first. And in the latest Poll, the 240Z trebled the first Poll result by recording a massive 30.9percent, bringing it into first spot for the second consecutive year.

If you consider those figures represent only an absract indication of popularity, you might care to compare them with both the sales figures for that period and the value of the second-hand vehicles.

In 1970, the year of introduction, the car sold 110units. The next year, the total read 751! Stock shortages in 1972 due to a variety of factors cut sales to 534, although demand was calculated at several hundred in excess of that. This year, figures to date reveal 607units have been sold with more than two months of figures yet to be tallied-in. In any case, it seems that despite severe shortages again, more than 700 vehicles will be sold.

Now consider the resale value. The initial new price of a Datsun 240Z was $4567. Today that model in good condition still brings $3400. A 1972 model cost $4666 and today it still fetches around $4200. In sports car terminology, that represents good resale value.

Interestingly, the price of the Datsun 240Z has gone *down* since the beginning of 1973. The price drop is only $70 (from $5000), but in a climate of rapidly escalating new car prices (particularly from Japan) it's welcome.

Apart from its domestic popularity, the 240Z has done well in international motor sport, notably major world rally events. Its major success story must be a double in the East African Safari — perhaps the toughest enduro event in the world and one totally dominated by massive factory investment. It has proved only mildly successful in road racing — where ultimate power and handling are the criteria required for success — although it does dominate one US road racing category where the categories seem engineered for makes rather than competition.

With a background of motor sporting success that has been well-promoted in every country, the Datsun has reached a receptive market with the bare minimum of direct advertising. In view of that, it's a little surprising to find so little evidence of pure competition breeding in the road vehicle.

It's essentially a boulevarde car, with a soft, controlled ride, and certainly an absence of suspension harshness. It

THE two-seater cockpit — a place for a driver to work in comfort, accompanied by a passenger who is well provided for. In an amply-specified surrounding, the only missing element is good ventilation, and our test experience indicates an air-conditioning unit would be essential for Australian summer motoring.

handles well in road situations — but as a sports car its handling is only average. It rolls heavily into corners, and it negotiates them at limits considerably below the standards you'd require to be a successful weekend club racer.

At any speed above 60mph it starts to lift its nose and the phenomenon continues right up to 90mph-plus where a definite front-end "float" is experienced. Whether for aesthetic or practical reasons, it's interesting to note that over 90percent of NSW Datsun 240Zs are sold with the optional front-end spoiler — an item which has a considerable influence on front-end stability.

The high-speed stability can be further improved with steering box and front suspension adjustments, plus a set of high-performance shock absorbers such as Konis, and many owners are having these modifications carried out.

But it's equally significant that the car's original specifications (excluding the front-end float at high speed) suit the majority of owners. For example, the steering in its original factory condition has a noticeable amount of "lost motion" to either side of top dead centre (or the straight-ahead position). This can be cured with the afore-mentioned steering box and suspension adjustments, but these modifications increase the steering loads at parking speeds — obviously not a popular feature with either weak-wristed boulevarde heroes, or "the little lady". It seems the alternative of a vague, sloppy feel for open road cruising is immensely more acceptable to the majority of owners.

The car also has a tendency to shift off-line on harsh bumps, and the "dead-feel" steering isn't conducive to accurate control or correction. However, the alternative is there for the enthusiast, and at reasonable cost.

The suspension principle hasn't altered since day one — McPherson strut at the front and Chapman/Lotus/McPherson independent at the rear. There's no doubt it's this system which gives the good ride and the ability to handle rough surfaces as comfortably as it does — also allowing easy modification for competition.

Performance-wise, the 240Z acquits itself well. The acceleration-to-weight ratio was always a point for complaint by 240Z owners and despite the relative smoothness of the SOHC six the car is hard to drive at low, traffic speeds. This is highlighted by the notchy gearchange. From rest the car moves off well, but it's not until around 3800rpm that the engine gets down to business. After that it pulls strongly, if not a little noisily around maximum revs (6000).

In traffic, the transfer of power to the road is certainly not smooth. The clutch, though light in pressure, is jerky in operation and the stiffness of the syncros makes smooth movement in traffic difficult. Once in the wide open spaces it's a whole new bag. At

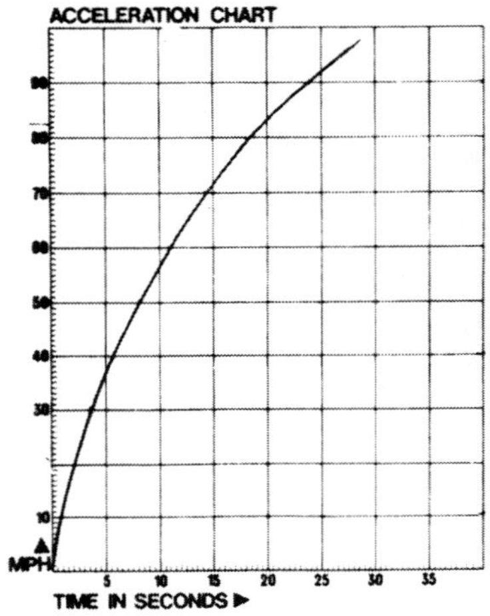

FLIP-UP panels on the hood provide access to windscreen washers (left) and battery (right). And the fuel filler (centre) is a masterpeice of logical design. It includes lockable trap-door, big easily-removed cap, plastic drip protector, and retaining chain. Eleven points out of ten.

ROAD TEST DATA – SPECIFICATIONS

Manufacturer: .... Nissan Motor Company Ltd, Tokyo, Japan
Make/Model: .... Datsun 240Z
Body type: .... 2-door, 2-seater coupe
Pricing: as tested: $5170
basic: $4940
options/prices: .... $75 — front spoiler; $50 — rear foil
Test car supplied by: .... Capitol Motors, 100 Parramatta Road, Auburn, NSW

ENGINE

Cylinders: .... Six-cylinder, in-line
Bore x stroke: .... 83 x 73.7mm (3.26 x 2.90in)
Capacity: 2393cc (146cu.in.)
Compression: .... 9.0 to 1
Aspiration: .... 2 x Hitachi (SU-type) 46mm (1¾in. sidedraft)
Fuel pump: .... Mechanical
Fuel recommended: .... Super
Valve gear: ..... SOHC inclined in-line valves — finger type rockers
Max. power (gross): .... 151(SAE)bhp @ 5600rpm
Max. torque: .... 145lb.ft @ 4400rpm

TRANSMISSION

Type/locations: .... Manual, syncromesh, five-speed
Clutch type: .... sdp diaphragm. 8.85in (225mm) diam.

Gear	Direct Ratio	Overall Ratio
1st	2.957	11.53
2nd	1.858	7.25
3rd	1.311	5.11
4th	1.0	3.9
5th	0.852	3.32

Final drive: 3.9

CHASSIS AND BODY

Type: .... Unit construction 2-door, 2-seater with tailgate-type .... rear window
Kerb weight: .... 2260lbs (1025 kilos)

SUSPENSION

Front: .... Independent McPherson coil springs with telescopic ..... damper struts and lower trailing links with compression rod, ... anti-roll bar
Rear: .... McPherson-coil springs, telescopic damper struts, ... lower trailing links
Shock absorbers: .... telescopic double acting in struts front .... and rear
Wheels: .... pressed steel 4½J x 14
Tyres: .... 175SR x 14 Bridgestone

STEERING

Type: .... Rack and pinion
Ratio: .... 17.8 to 1
Turns lock to lock: 2.7
Wheel diameter: .... 15in.
Turning circle, between kerbs: .... 4.8 mm (15.7ft)

BRAKES

Type: .... Discs front, drum rear
Dimensions: ...... 271mm (10.7ins (front, 228.6mm (9.0ins) rear.

DIMENSIONS

Wheelbase: 90.7in (230.38cm)
Track, front: 53.3in (135.38cm)
rear: 53.0in (134.62cm)
Overall length: 13ft 4.8in (413.51cm)
width: 5ft 4.1in (162.81cm)
height: 4ft 2.6in (128.52cm)
Ground clearance: 6.5in (16.51cm)
Overhang, front: 34in (86.3cm)
rear: 38.1in (96.8cm)

higher engine speeds the gearbox/clutch action becomes easier and the 240Z takes on its GT car image very convincingly.

Point-to-point, it is a delight to drive. It is quiet and the seats give great support, visibility and sense of control. The relationship of seats to steering wheel is suitable for most driver sizes. Our test crew ranged from short through tall and all commented on the comfortable driving position.

The range and layout of instruments is good. The centre console contains all the extra bits and pieces and the switchgear leaves nothing to be desired. Ergonomically the cabin is very close to perfect. That is with the exception of the seat belts which are diabolically *bad*.

The sash is badly located and feels uncomfortable, the buckle and its locating strap are hopelessly outdated (if you can find the buckle, after grovelling around at the side of the seat). Invariably the belt gets dirty, and adjustment is very difficult.

A car which, overall, is as acceptable as the 240Z should have an updated belt system — either a centre stalk and slide adjustment or a good inertia-reel system. It should be the next most important thing the makers pay attention to.

After that a close look at the ventilation. On the surface it looks fine, but in practice the Z is pretty hard to take on a hot summer day. The rear quarter windows don't open, it's unsafe and impractical to open the rear hatch and the heater/vent controls suffer from inscrutable Japanese labelling. Why can't we arrive at a standard marking system for ventilation controls?

With the two windows fully down, there is still insufficient draught for cooling and the capacity of the through-flow vents under these circumstances is almost laughable. The all-black interior doesn't help the situation.

The controls, as stated, are superb. Wipers are excellent, with good coverage and an intermittent facility. The light switch is right next door to the wipers (on the same multi-purpose stalk on the left side of the the tiller) and is very easy to use, especially at night. The choke is a lever (aircraft-style) situated at the side of the gear stick and is very positive.

The pedal location is good -- fine for heel-toe downshifts — but the brake and accelerator pedals might be just a bit too close together. The steering wheel is a good size, the wood rim is comfy to hold and generally contributes to the good driving feel of the car.

One very bad feature — the horn. Located in the centre boss it is very out-of-step with today's design layouts. Let's have it on the end of the trafficator stalk or on tabs set into the wheel spokes, but not where it is at the moment.

From a safety angle, there is not much you can say about the 240Z. Datsun were one of the first Japanese makers to get involved in

***FUSE-BOX** hides under panel in centre console, but is awkward to reach when panel is equipped with optional gear like rear-window screen-heater switch. Pedal arrangement (right) is good, with left-foot rest, clutch-pedal chock and heel-toe brake/throttle.*

***CENTRE CONSOLE** is based on aircraft design principles and generally works well. But heater controls are confusing and ventilation inadequate.*

EQUIPMENT

Battery:	Hitachi 12V — 50AH
Alternator:	Hitachi 12V — 45amps
Headlamps:	2 x 50/40 watts 12V
Jacking points:	In the rocker panel front and rear of door on both sides

CAPACITIES

Fuel tank:	13.2 gallons (59.4litres)
Engine sump:	10 pints (4.6litres)
Final drive:	1.8 pints (1 litre)
Gearbox:	3 pints (1.5litres)
Water system:	14.2 pints (8 litres)

PERFORMANCE

Test conditions for performance figures:

Weather:	Fine, clear
Wind:	2-4 knots
Humidity:	45percent
Max. Temp:	21degrees

Top Speed:

Average	118mph (190km/h)
Best Run:	122mph (195km/h)

Standing Quarter Mile

Average:	18.1 secs
Best run:	17.7 secs
Speed at end of Standing Quarter:	78mph (126km/h)

Acceleration, standing start:

0-30 mph:	3.8secs
0-40mph:	5.6secs
0-50mph:	8.1secs
0-60mph:	10.7secs
0-70mph:	14.5secs
0-80mph:	18.3secs
0-90mph:	24.4secs

Speeds in gears:

Gear	Max. mph	(km/h)	rpm
1st	35	(56)	6000
2nd	57	(91.1)	6000
3rd	88	(140.4)	6000
4th	124	(198.2)	6000
5th	129	(206.2)	6000

Acceleration holding gears:

	2nd	3rd	4th	5th
20-40	3.9	5.6	8.0	9.7
30-50	4.0	5.7	7.9	9.9
40-60	4.5	5.8	8.1	10.5
50-70	—	6.1	8.2	11.2
60-80	—	7.2	9.0	13.1

Fuel consumption

Average for test:	18.6mpg (6.56kpl)
Best recorded:	24.5mpg (8.71kpl)
City average:	19.2mpg (6.79kpl)
Country cruising:	18-24mpg (6.40-8.53kpl)

Braking: Five maximum stops from 60 mph

Stop	Time	Pedal
1	3.8secs	40psi
2	3.6secs	45psi
3	3.5secs	40psi
4	3.3secs	45psi
5	3.2secs	50psi

DATSUN 240Z

energy-absorbing panels. They have a crash-test program and the 240Z has benefitted from it.

Being a totally enclosed capsule-type cabin it is structurally rigid. The car feels rigid and despite the lack of side impact barriers in the doors, it doesn't seem to get much of a mention amongst the panel beating brigade.

The cabin itself is quite roomy and the (windows) are quite large. Vision is generally good apart from a blind-spot in the rear three-quarter panel.

At the optional extras level there is little, apart from dress-up items, a 240Z owner could add. Front and rear spoilers are a popular option — fitted to about 95percent of NSW registrations according to Capitol Motors. Heated rear screen, mag-type wheels, tape-player and air-conditioning are the top "extras". The suspension modifications listed earlier can be effected by Heasman or Selby in Sydney.

The finish on the test cars (three in total) was fair to good. Carpets don't fit well, but door trims, headlining and pillar coverings all fitted snugly. Outside, the body and paintwork was good. Welding was smooth, the paint job on all three cars looked even and without blemish and underbody finish was very good.

We like the detail things like brake-line retainers, under-bonnet light, twist-cable retainers for plug leads and the easy access to mechanicals. We thought Nissan might have progressed to sealed engine-cooling systems by now, but the car ran cool enough over several hot days and didn't seem to need undue topping up.

The clock kept good time, but on two test cars we had radio problems. On one, the radio simply didn't work, and on the other the auto-tuning device went absolutely berserk. The only way to stop the self-seeker from seeking and not locking was to switch off the ignition. Ah, such is the age of the machine.

These fiddly things aside, the latest 240Z confirms what we have all known for some time — that the car is well designed, well-equipped, a good overall performer and very good value-for-money.

CHARACTERISTIC nose-up accelerative pose of the Datsun is emphasised in this uphill shot. Condition is encouraged by relatively soft suspension settings which allow heavy front/rear weight transfer, but front-end spoiler helps greatly in reducing high-speed lift and resultant front-end float. The spoiler is now attached to 95percent of new Z-cars sold in NSW.

DATSUN was one of the first sports cars with opening tailgate layout — a remarkably popular fitment for its limited practicality. Floor straps sensibly assist in positive luggage location.

Z-CAR cuts a clean line through a tight uphill right-hander as it kicks the dust up in the apex. Oversteer is the end result of fast corner approaches and control is good with steering and throttle.

STRAIGHT-SIX is healthy performer, providing good acceleration and excellent terminal. However, it likes to be worked in the upper rev range and the five-speed gearbox is necessary to extract the best performance/economy compromise.

Z

DATSUN 240Z

THE DATSUN 240Z the car that won the 21st. East African Rally, one of the toughest rallies in teh world, is about the only two seater sport car that is available in Malaysia without having to place a special order. Tan Chong Motors, who import the 240Z in small quantities, but have a regular supply of this model, invited us to put a 240Z through its paces.

STYLING, ENGINEERING AND PRICE

At about $ 23,000/– it represents very good value for money, considering the fact that you get a unique shape (in this country) and a robust 2.4 litre engine that has a great potential for tuning and propels the car at around 120 mph. with brisk acceleration.

Its conventional sporty body with longish bonnet merging into a steeply raked screen and terminating in a camm tail by a fastback roof outlines the Datsun 240Z to true "Gran Tourismo" design. The smooth bonnet line is broken up by a central power bulge that serves the driver as a sight to point the car in the desired direction.

Deeply recessed headlights marr the sleek lines of the 240Z in our opinion. This however, can be remedied by a set of plastic headlight cowls, that are available as optional extras, which puts the car in the Maserati/Ferrari/Aston Martin league in looks.

Wrap round bumpers are thoughtfully placed as high as possible, just below the radiator grill in front and at about the same level at the rear thus making them effective in the event of a shunt. Under the bonnet lies the single overhead camshaft six cylinder (in line) power unit. Nissan Motors have sensibly standardised their production by maintaining a bore and stroke of 83 x 73.7 mm., similar to the four cylinder Datsun 1600SSS engine, obtaining the extra capacity of 2393cc. by the addition of two more cylinders. The cast iron engine has an aluminium cylinder head fed by two Japanese S.U. type carburettors, putting out a healthy 151 gross brake horsepower at 5600rpm If not watched carefully engine revolutions can be taken well above the tachometer's red lined 7000 rpm., thanks to a seven bearing crankshaft that spins with very little vibration.

A five speed gearbox transmits the power to the rear wheels. Ratios for the gearbox are well spaced with the first four in an 'H' pattern and fifth gear placed towards the driver and forward. The lever is spring loaded with a bias on the third and fourth plane enabling the driver to change from fifth to fourth in one movement without having to locate gear stick into the fourth gear position.

PERFORMANCE AND ECONOMY

Acceleration of the Datsun 240Z was unbelievably punchy. Each time a higher gear was selected at maximum permissible revs the occupants in the car would feel the seat dig into their backs as the 240Z surged forward with more velocity. With 150 odd bhp. pushing a car that is only around two hundred pounds heavier than its little 1600cc. saloon sister, there is more than enough power under the driver's right foot to nip by most vehicles on a highway.

Acceleration times were taken up to sixty miles an hour in a very sedate manner, owing to the newness of the car. The 240Z speedometer needle managed to reach the 60 mph. mark at just over 9 seconds without any spinning of the rear wheels.

We obtained 43,70 and 100 miles an hour in the first three gears (speedometer readings). The speedometer needle almost reached 120 mph. in fourth but we had to ease off and were unable to find out how much higher we could go before changing up to fifth because the straight came to an end. The car is capable of doing around 130 mph.

A mileage of around 25 mpg. can be returned in most cases of driving (unless we have a driver who always stays in the lower gears to be able to outdrag the first vehicle that makes an attempt to overtake), while with careful control of the throttle foot 30 mpg. can be achieved. With a 15½ gallon fuel tank the 240Z can be driven around for about 400 miles on a full tank without having to visit a petrol station.

HANDLING STEERING AND BRAKES

With its all independent suspension (struts all round) we had expected formidable handling. Somehow the car did not have any feel when travelling at 100 mph. The light weight of the car and the forward surge because of the power made it seem as if all the weight is transferred to the rear and the front wheels are hardly touching the tarmac.

When negotiating bends on the other hand the light rack and pinion steering provides excellent feel. The back of the car seems to be wanting to break away but when it does so it is gradual and can be brought well under control by a small amount of opposite lock, making the 240Z a car with oversteering tendencies. The steering wheel is 14 inches in diameter, one of the most sensibly sized wheels we have come across in a sport car. The front wheels can be brought from lock to lock in less than 3 turns giving the car a turning circle of just over 30 feet.

Servo assisted front discs (10.6 inches) and rear drums (9 inches) brought the Datsun 240Z to a stop very reassuringly every time. We experienced no fade whatsoever no matter how hard we drove the car. Suspension was rather soft as the car would nose-dive when the brakes were applied.

RIDE COMFORT AND NOISE

Suppression of noise is not one the Datsun 240Z's strong points. On heavy acceleration induction roar penetrated the passenger cabin and in some instances the occupants had to raise their voices to carry out any conversation. This induction roar is accompanied by axle or propeller shaft hum that was also transmitted to the cabin. The lack of a sealed off boot also contributed to poor sound damping.

The ride of the 240Z is not as good as its independent suspension should make it. At low speed bumps pass through the suspension and are felt in the passenger compartment. However at high speeds it improves and makes long distance trips quite bearable.

There is considerable steering kickback on bumpy roads because of the direct and light rack and pinion steering.

DRIVING POSITION AND ACCOMODATION

The seats although they look thinly padded are very comfortable and far from hard. There is enough adjustments both forward and backwards and for rake on the seat back to accomodate big sized people. Unfortunately for the average Malaysian they are set rather low, but there is provision for spacers to be placed underneath them in order to raise them almost an inch. Excessive flatness of the seats tends to make the passenger slide down forward. The driver has the steering wheel to help him stay in position.

Visibility up front is good once the driver has the right seat height, but judgement of the left side front wing takes some getting used to initially.

Built-in headrests on the seats make rear vision difficult. A centrally mounted rear view mirror gives good visibility directly behind through a generous though steeply raked rear screen. The rear three-quarter areas are blind because of the fastback roofline. A pair of

Z
DATSUN 240Z

wing mirrors, which are not fitted as standard to the car would be the ideal solution to enable the driver to see the rear right tip and have an idea of the rear left tip of the car.

Pedals in the 240Z are well spaced. Heel and toe gear changes are easily carried out thanks to the distance between the pedals. A rest for the left foot when it is not depressing the clutch complements the setup.

CONTROLS, INSTRUMENTS, EQUIPMENT AND FITTINGS

Five dials are recessed into the matt black fascia. The largest two, a 160mph speedometer matched by an 8000 rpm tachometer yellow lined at 6500 rpm and red lined between 7000 and 8000 rpm face the driver. Three smaller dials comprising of a clock, an ammeter and fuel gauge, and a water temperature and oil pressure gauge are situated above the centre console, and angled towards the driver. The Datsun 240Z driver has full knowledge of performance and the condition of the engine through these five dials.

On the central console is a space for a radio. Above this are the controls of the heater demister unit. Below the radio space is a cigarette lighter. A cover in front of the gear lever hides the car's fuses very neatly. The choke lever is conveniently placed just after the gear lever, both falling naturally under the driver's left hand. An ash tray with a sliding lid and two trays of different sizes complete the central console in between the seats.

The hand brake lies just on the left of the driver's seat, while a lookable glovebox occupies the left side of the fascia in front of the passenger.

A single stalk on the left of the steering column controls the lights, the wiper and the washer, well within easy reach of the finger tips. The indicator, dipswitch and flasher stalk lies on the right of the steering column also well within easy reach of the driver's finger tips.

Ventilation is taken care of by air passing through fish eye vents, one on each side of the fascia and a central vent, above the heater controls, that looked more decorative than functional. Air can also be admitted to the footwells by separate controls on each side of the car. There did not seem to be any extractor louvres apart from two little ones, one behind each rear quarter window.

It was disappointing to see the poor quality of carpets that come with the 240Z. Equally disappointing was the material used (thin PVC.) for the gear lever and hand brake boots.

LIGHTING

The headlights were ample for travelling at reasonably high speeds. Found under the front bumper and well protected by it are the side lights. These lights are badly placed by the manufacturers as they are difficult to see from high vehicles, thus the 240Z may not be noticed in the rear view mirrors of lorries at night. Lights at the rear are neatly placed in the back of the car in oblong clusters, consisting of the tail lights, brake lights, indicators and reversing lamps. Two small lights on the rear bumper provide illumination to the rear number plate.

BOOT

The boot consists of a platform that runs from the back of the seats to the rear of the car. A large number of suitcases can be carried and are tied down by straps to stop them from bouncing around in the cabin. Loading and un-

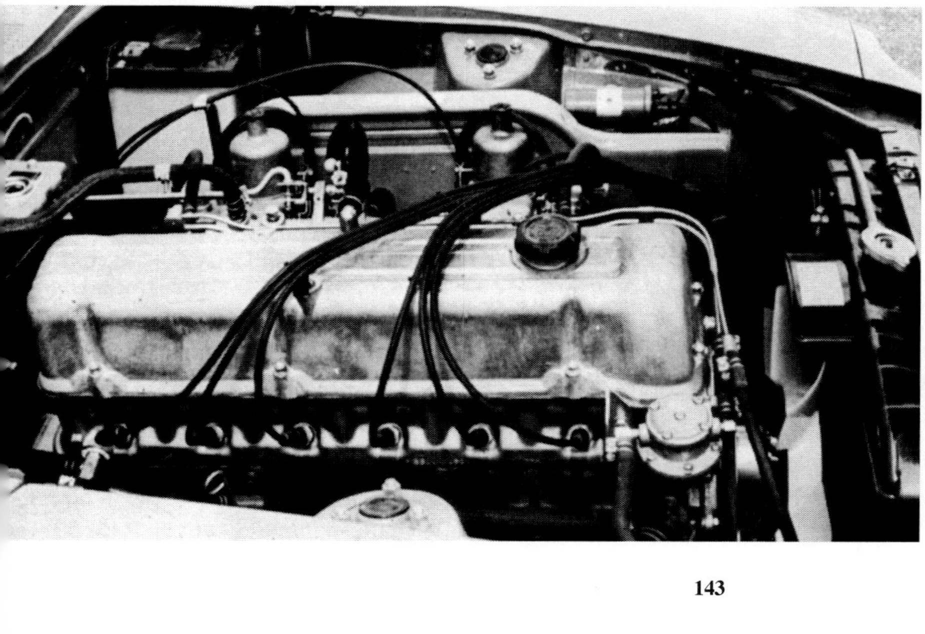

DATSUN 240Z

loading is facilitated by a large door that encompasses the rear screen and stays up hydraulically. The spare wheel is on a tray under the luggage compartment.

MAINTENANCE

The bonnet lid tilts forward after being released from inside the car. Once open it reveals the large uncluttered engine compartment. The necessary items that need to be checked such as water, oil level and battery are within easy reach enabling the owner to do so in no time at all. A lamp that can be unclipped and placed anywhere in the engine compartment is also supplied for night work.

An oil change is required every 3000 miles while greasing of the chassis need only be done after each 24000 miles.

CONCLUSION.

The Datsun 240Z is not a gimmicky car or an ultra modern one with mid-engine and space age styling. It is a sleek two seater GT vehicle built in a sound traditional and conventional manner. It is a car for the connoisseur who enjoys driving by himself or perhaps with another enthusiast. It is a car that has looks while at the same time offers simplicity in maintenance and repair.

DATSUN 260Z

They've done all the right things to the legendary bargain GT

PHOTOS BY JOE RUSZ

RARELY DO WE mark the passing of a car that we have in the recent past rated one of the world's most important sports-GT cars with a more blasé attitude than the Datsun 240Z. When the "Z car" was introduced four years ago it revolutionized the sports/GT market in America: it cost just over $3500 and was such an incredible buy at that price we tended to dismiss some of its failings, which were few anyway. But in the ensuing three years the plunge of the dollar, the upward-valued yen and the resulting near-$5000 price tag dictated a more critical look. On close inspection the 1973 Z was found wanting in two important areas: drivability and high-speed stability. So the 240Z is gone and R&T will not mourn its passing.

But hold on, Z-car lovers. Don't pick up that lynching rope and start heading for our offices just yet. The 240Z is dead—but in its place is the 260Z, a car that goes a long way toward eliminating all the criticism we leveled at the car last year.

On the surface it might appear that the 260Z is nothing more than a 240Z with slightly bigger engine and price tag. True, and not true. The shape—looking as crisp, clean and contemporary today as it did four years ago—is indeed the same. And mechanically it still has the same basic overhead-cam 6-cylinder engine, 4-wheel independent suspension, radial tires and rack-and-pinion steering. Inside, also, everything is much as it was. The keyword here is "subtle"; little changes in the 260Z make all the difference between last year's Z and the 1974 car.

Nissan obviously knows a good shape (selling as well as looking) and thankfully hasn't messed with the Z car's basic Albrecht Goertz styling. The biggest difference externally is the addition of shock-absorber bumpers front and rear, which increase overall length by 6.3 in. They are good-looking and well integrated, however, and should reduce the nose "dinging" the 240Z so often gets. At the rear the backup lights are now separate from the tail-stop lights and all body emblems say "260Z," but that's it for styling changes. There is an apparent improvement in paint quality too, and all 1974 colors except white and red are metallics. Our test car was a rich-looking silver and the best factory finish we've ever seen on a Z.

Last year's 240Z slipped very badly not only in drivability but in performance, and mid-year 1973 changes to improve drivability degraded its performance still further. We tested two Z cars last year: an early one with severe drivability problems and the same car after installation of a factory drivability "fix" kit. Here is a comparison of those cars, the original 1970 high-output Z and the current 260Z:

	Original Z	Early '73	Late '73	260 Z
0–60 mph, sec	8.7	10.1	11.9	10.0
0–1320 ft (¼ mi), sec	17.1	17.7	18.6	17.9
Speed in ¼ mi, mph	84.5	79.5	76.0	78.5
Drivability rating	excellent	poor	good	good

What we have, then, is a car that is still slower than the original—but one that performs as well as early 1973 cars and with drivability problems reduced to a level of the late 1973s. Confusing, maybe, but not a bad trade considering what one usually gets these days. The car is still quick and the reduction in drivability complaints makes the 260Z easily manageable on the road, something the early 1973s were not. Drivability isn't perfect—there's lean surge at light throttle openings between 40 and 55 mph—but we rarely find perfection these days, especially with a stickshift car that lacks a torque converter to absorb some of the engine's power pulsations.

Our car also suffered from two other problems which should be peculiar to this one car: difficult starting after a hot soak (cranking for 15-20 sec was not uncommon) and vapor lock during the second of back-to-back acceleration runs. The reason was that our 260Z was a prototype and did not have the asbestos-covered fuel lines (part of the fix for these problems last year) that will be standard on all production cars. It did, however, have the new transistorized breakerless ignition, which helped cold starting and should also reduce maintenance. There was some tendency to "diesel" after shutoff, now a common problem. We can't quarrel with the fuel economy: 20 mpg, only 1 mpg lower than the original Z.

The negative aspects of the longer-stroke engine occur at high rotational speed. A 6500-6800 rpm redline used to be usable; now 6000 is sufficient and the engine, which never was particularly smooth at high speed anyway, starts to sound labored above 5500.

High-speed stability—wandering in crosswinds and front-end lift—has never been a 240Z strong suit, but we had been assured that Datsun engineers had the problems well in hand last year. Our 1973 test cars told us differently; they tended to wander a bit even at speeds as low as 50 mph. Happily the 260Z behaves the way the 240Z should have all along, and though changes are few in number and subtle in nature they make a huge difference in the feel of the car.

The improvement results from two factors, we are told: the additional mass of the front bumper keeps the nose down at speed and the length of the rear springs has been increased more than the fronts to give the car a slight "wedge" attitude as it drives down the road. Whatever the factors, they work: we drove the 260Z at speeds of 90-100 mph over smooth, bumpy and undulating surfaces and never felt insecure.

Curb weight of the 260Z is up 200 lb over the car we tested last year: 130 lb from the heftier bumpers and the rest mainly from the air conditioning fitted to this car. Increased weight alone should dictate more cumbersome handling. Not so, however; the steering is a bit stiffer but the 260Z is as neutral as before and can be provoked into gentle oversteer as easily as previous models. To compensate for the increased weight, spring rates have been increased 20 lb/in. (front) and 3 lb/in. (rear). Stiffening the front spring rates proportionally more than the rears would normally result in additional understeer, so a rear anti-roll bar is now standard. The ride is improved: there is now less abrupt jerking of the car over bumps, though we are told the shock absorbers are the same. Perhaps the extra end masses decrease the car's pitch tendencies significantly.

Stopping distances are also improved, but again Datsun says there are no changes. We are inclined to credit the tires. Bridgestone seems to have learned a lot about tread design and traction in the past few years; all the cars we've tested recently with Bridgestones have been exceptionally good stoppers.

Except for the new steering wheel, subtle changes also characterize the interior of the 260Z. This year the wheel is thick and padded—a welcome change from the cheap-looking and slippery plastic fake-wood wheel used previously. The instrument panel is newly contoured and the door panels have also been upgraded with European-style armrests and integral door pulls (like on BMWs) added. We still criticize the cheap-looking vinyl used to cover the seats and the quilted material on the transmission tunnel but at least the pattern is now less gross.

The Japanese have the good sense to pick up on the good features of other cars, and the new integrated factory air conditioning-ventilation-heater system is a perfect example. The simple control panel with red and blue coloring for hot and cold temperatures and bi-level cool-heat mode is right out of General Motors. And it works just as well (a supreme compliment, as anyone who has driven a GM car with factory air conditioning is aware). There are separate center vents (only one last year) for the driver and passenger that now adjust side-to-side as well as up-and-down, plus adjustable eyeball vents at either end of the dash. Outside air is obtained only with the fan switched on but it's quiet at low speeds and really blows up a storm on the highest of its four settings. The air-conditioning compressor is also greatly improved: a rotary type, made in Japan and much quieter than the typical reciprocating design.

Several other detail changes make this the most livable Z: increased seat-adjustment travel, trip odometer and instrument-lighting controls relocated for easier access, larger warning lights for choke and rear-window heater, and column control stalk for lighting and wipe-wash functions tilted up for a clearer path to the ignition switch and a better view of the control itself. Our only complaint aside from the quality of some of the interior materials concerns the shoulder belt: it still rubs across the neck of some drivers.

Overall, Datsun has given the 260Z exactly the facelifting it needed, leaving the best things untouched and changing only those things that needed changing. As a result, at $5000 the 260Z is almost as impressive a value in terms of 1974 dollars as the 240Z was at $3500 in 1970. With its fine blend of performance, comfort and sportiness the 260Z again ranks as one of the world's best sports-GT values.

Datsun 260-Z

DATSUN

What the significance is for upping the Z car designation 20 points from 240 to 260 is not quite clear except that it might have some connection with increasing the displacement of the overhead cam in-line six cylinder engine 200 cc's. While the exterior styling remains pretty much the same with the exception of the energy absorbing bumpers. Under the hood however, extensive redesign of the emission controls and a few more cubic inches have upped the performance while still meeting pollution standards for 1974. While Datsun has not released any horsepower or torque figures for the enlarged power plant, they will be higher than the 151 horsepower and 148 lbs/ft of torque for the previous model.

With unitized construction and independent suspension on all 4 wheels, the 260-Z offers a smooth ride with true sports car handling. Rack and pinion steering and power assisted front disc brakes, and a slick shifting 4-speed manual gearbox are standard along with a host of other items that cost extra on many similar cars. About the only accessories that are listed as options are air conditioning, 3-speed automatic transmission, stereo radio, and some dress up items.

The Z-car suspension system is interesting, with strut type shocks inside a coil spring used on each wheel. There are some special shock/spring units developed for the Datsun by BRE that are used for racing and other motor sports that require a firmer suspension system. There are also some special engine goodies for modifying for racing or higher performance street use and include such things as dual 4-throat carburetion, cams, and pistons. Front and rear spoilers, extra wide alloy wheels, and a split exhaust system are among the extra cost items that can be ordered from Nissan's competition department. Radial ply tires are standard along with tinted glass, electric rear window defogger, reclining bucket seats, tachometer, electric clock, reset odometer, oil pressure and water temperature gauges, and an AM/FM radio with electric antenna.

Meeting the 1974 passenger restraint standards, the 260-Z has a 3-point self-adjusting belt/shoulder strap system that is interlocked to the ignition to prevent starting unless hooked up. Fire retardant interior material, a collapsible steering column, and padded dash complete the new interior equipment.

The four-seater version of the 260-Z, which Datsun calls a 2 by 2, will be available later in the year. The 2 by 2 wheelbase is about eight inches longer than the 2-seater model; this was accomplished by extending the rear section.

Datsun 260-Z

Datsun 260-Z 2 by 2

DATSUN 260-Z

Data in Brief

DIMENSIONS

Wheelbase	90.7 in.
Overall length	169.1 in.
Height	50.6 in.
Width	64.1 in.
Tread-front/rear	53.3/53 in.
Fuel capacity	15.9 gal
Steering type & ratio	rack & pinion, 18:1
Turning diameter	31.4 ft
Luggage capacity	NA
Design passenger load	2 passenger
Curb weight	2580 lbs

ENGINE—Standard

Type	single overhead cam in-line six
Displacement	157 cu in.
Horsepower	NA
Torque	NA

DRIVELINE

Transmission	4-speed all synchro manual
Drive axle ratio	3.36:1

BRAKES

Front	disc
Rear	drum

SUSPENSION

Front	independent strut type, coils over shocks
Rear	independent strut type, coils over shocks

WHEELS & TIRES

Wheels	14-inch steel disc, 5J rims
Tires	Radial ply 175HR-14

ROAD TEST

DATSUN 260 Z

The Z car for 1974 is still the same; possibly the best sports car value in the world/By John Fuchs

When Datsun's new and exciting sports / GT car, the 240Z, was introduced to the American market in early 1970, it was almost a guaranteed success. Its styling was dramatic, performance was very good, handling was far better than average, price was reasonable, and the interior was both comfortable and complete. But above all that was one important factor that figured significantly in the Z-car's favor: Datsun's marketing men had positioned the car so carefully in the automotive price and size spectrum that it literally had no head-to-head competition. They had zeroed in on that one empty niche, the two-seater sports coupe selling for $3600, that had gone begging since the Corvette became expensive.

Though only a few thousand Zs were imported in the beginning, nearly every one of them was sold at list price, and an enthused public clamored for more. Almost 25,000 were imported in each of the next two years and again sold at or above sticker prices. Enterprising dealers found that the 240Z's initial profit margin could be further enhanced by adding numerous extras like AM/FM stereo, air conditioning, and mag wheels, thus boosting the list price to almost $5500. No matter, prospective Z owners descended on Datsun showrooms in droves, all seemingly willing to pay these premium prices just for the privilege of owning one of these beauties.

Like most of the world's best-selling cars the 240Z, with its OHC engine, four-wheel independent suspension, radial tires, full instrumentation, and cavernous interior, was an excellent value for the money, and it soon developed a certain mystique about it, an aura normally associated with Porsches, BMWs, Ferraris, and the ever-popular Corvette. Owners forcefully denied its heritage by insisting that it was not a Datsun but simply a 240Z. It was as if there was a sense of shame and embarrassment at being associated with a family of economy cars.

But the heritage showed through nonetheless. The rugged 2393 cc six cylinder engine produced 150 horsepower, yet still delivered upwards of 20 miles on every gallon of gas. Even under hard flogging the miserly Z would seldom get less than 17 mpg, or almost twice the mileage of a Vette. Prophetically, exactly on target for the gasoline crisis.

Cognizant of their success, Datsun's product planners wisely let well enough alone. From '70 to '73 the changes in the car were mostly detail items, small

DATSUN 260Z

21.1 mpg

Fuel consumption calculated on a 73 mile loop of city, suburban, freeway and hilly roads. Speeds did not exceed 60 mph.

things corrected or improved as deemed necessary. But the U.S. smog regulations and the five mph bumpers loomed heavily on the horizon, and again they have taken their toll on one of the world's fine cars. The 240Z that we knew and loved is history, but its replacement, the 260Z, is an equally impressive machine.

Happily, the differences between the two cars are minor, with the most important ones being the extra 172 ccs of displacement and the addition of a rear anti-roll bar. The exciting sports/GT styling that by itself captured so many prospective buyers is virtually untouched. The five mph bumpers add nearly four inches of length to the Z, but Datsun's designers and engineers deserve special recognition for the excellent job they've done in integrating the safety bumpers with the sleek body design. The biggest visual change is in the rear panel, where the taillights have been enlarged and the backup lights are now separate from the brake and running lights. Inside, the wood-rim steering wheel, a favorite of the crocheted-back driving-glove set, has been replaced by a more comfortable padded-vinyl one, and the center console has been slightly redesigned.

Sadly, the ponderosity of the safety bumpers and other safety equipment has markedly increased the 260Z's curb weight. It's 2580 pound mass is almost 100 pounds heavier than the '73 240Z and over 250 pounds heavier than the original Z-car. Despite the bigger engine, performance suffers measurably, but not nearly as much as you might think. Quarter-mile times recorded at Irwindale Raceway in Irwindale, Calif., were in the high 16s, with the best run being a 16.72 at 81.66 mph. That's about .5-seconds and 2 mph slower than the previous model, but considering the performance deterioration of some domestic models, the 260Z is an engineering milestone. But where the extra pounds really show up is in the lower range and in the passing speeds. The 9.0-second 0-60 time of the 240 is now almost 10 seconds, and the 3.6-second 40-60 time is now 4.60. The 260Z is noticably slower, but you'd be hard pressed to name a car that isn't these days.

The fully independent McPherson strut/coil spring suspension is virtually the same as before, so the handling differences are due to the addition of an anti-roll bar at the rear and the extra weight. The pronounced understeer of the 240 has been replaced by a combination of slight understeer and throttle-induced oversteer. And since the radial tires are the same size as before, 175HR-14, the extra weight makes it easier to exceed the limit of adhesion. Consequently, the 260Z's handling is more nearly neutral and judicious use of the throttle allows you to select just the cornering attitude you desire. The 260Z also drifts quite nicely and is surprisingly predictable while drifting. The slightly vague feeling caused by the rubber-insulated suspension components is still present, but purists who object can easily cure it by installing BRE's racing suspension pieces. We also suspect that larger radials would be beneficial in the handling department. Since this is indeed a sports car for the masses, the improved handling characteristics, while not exactly Lotus or Dino-like, are far better than most Z owners will ever require.

The interior, with its slight revisions and factory air, continues to be comfortable, roomy, quiet, and relatively posh (if you can ignore the small amounts of cheap-looking quilted vinyl). Legroom is the best we've ever encountered in a sports car and the nice touches, like the "dead pedal" next to the clutch, reclining backrests, power antenna, inside hood release, and large easy-to-read white-on-black instruments, continue. Our only complaint is that some of the gauges, notably the oil pressure and water temperature, are so heavily damped that the response is too slow to be worth anything in an emergency. We're nitpicking, but a sports car should be more precise than that.

Most of the 260Z's other mechanical features like steering, transmission, power assisted disc/drum brakes, are the same as before and are similarly excellent. Even the fuel economy, despite the larger engine, is virtually the same. You may expect any figure from 17 to 24 mpg from the 260Z, depending only upon the enthusiasm with which you drive it. And when you consider that the under 17-second quarter-mile performance goes hand-in-hand with the 20 mpg fuel economy, part of the Z-car's mystique is all of a sudden very apparent.

And that's really the crux of the 260Z. It's an updated version of the 240 that includes the required safety equipment, yet continues the virtues of its forebear. Change for the sake of change was avoided, and change for the sake of improvement was not really necessary. The overwhelming success of the 240Z was not because it's the best sports car in the world, which it's not, but because it's possibly the best sports car value in the world. It was an extremely fine car for the amount it cost. The 260Z continues that tradition.

TEST DATA

Specifications	**Datsun 260Z**
Engine:	OHC in-line six
Bore & Stroke - ins.	3.27 x 3.11
Displacement - cu. in.	156.8 (2565 cc)
HP @ RPM	N/A
Torque: lbs.-ft. @ rpm	N/A
Compression Ratio	8.8:1
Carburetion	2 Hitachi (SU-type)
Transmission	4-speed manual
Final Drive Ratio	3.36:1
Steering Type	rack and pinion
Steering Ratio	18.0:1
Turning Diameter (curb-to-curb-ft.)	31.4
Wheel Turns (lock-to-lock)	2.7
Tire Size	175HR-14 radials
Brakes	power disc/drum
Front Suspension	Independent McPherson strut with coil springs, anti-roll bar with compression link
Rear Suspension	Independent McPherson strut with coil springs, anti-roll bar
Body/Frame Construction	Unitized
Wheelbase - ins.	90.7
Overall Length - ins.	169.1
Width - ins.	64.1
Height - ins.	50.6
Front Track - ins.	53.3
Rear Track - ins.	53.0
Curb Weight - lbs.	2580
Fuel Capacity - gals.	15.0
Oil Capacity - qts.	4.5
Base Price	$4995
Price as tested (includes A/C, freight, and handling)	$5526
Performance	
Acceleration	
0-30 mph	3.7
0-50 mph	7.4
0-60 mph	9.9
Standing Start ¼-mile	
Mph	81.66
Elapsed time	16.72
Passing speeds	
40-60 mph	4.6
50-70 mph	6.9
Speeds in gears*	
1st...mph @ rpm	41 @ 6500
2nd...mph @ rpm	66 @ 6500
3rd...mph @ rpm	97 @ 6500
4th...mph @ rpm	125 @ 6000 (est.)
Mph per 1000 rpm (in top gear)	22
Stopping distances	
From 30 mph	29' 0"
From 60 mph	133' 0"
Gas mileage range	17-24
Speedometer error	
Car speedometer	30 40 50 60 70
True speedometer	29 38 48 58 67

*Speeds in gears are at shift points (limited by the length of track) and do not represent maximum speeds.

THE DATSUN 260Z

A worthwhile improvement of the World's best-selling sports car. More flexibility and performance from 2.6 litres, excellent roadholding and handling — an exciting and practical 2-seater

The 260Z retains the same classic body style of its predecessor. Like the old Healey 3000 it exudes a unique character.

AT THE 1969 Tokyo Motor Show Nissan-Datsun revealed the hatchback, fixed-head 240Z and brought to an end BMC/British Leyland's halcyon days as supremos in the world of mass-production sports car manufacture. Aggressive, attractive looks, 125 m.p.h. from a single overhead camshaft, straight-six engine, five-speed gearbox and all independent suspension, excellent handling and what has since proved to be superb reliability contrived to make this newcomer into the World's best-selling sports car, which is distressing but not surprising when all its opposition from Britain had been designed in the 1950s. Now, five years later, the 240Z has been replaced by the 260Z, an even more exciting package in the same shell. And its competition from British Leyland? Still the same 1950s designs, with only the option of soft tops as an advantage. No wonder the 240Z sold 130,000 examples in the United States, the sports car market's barometer.

This latest sporting Datsun is an immensely satisfying car to drive; at £2,895 it represents to me the most covetable sporting car produced by a major manufacturer below the Porsche or Ferrari Dino class and it should be an object lesson to British Leyland, who could surely do even better if they so wished. It is fairly sophisticated and is not even mid-engined which many people tell us is the only way to build sports cars these days. Maybe so for ultimate cornering, but the 260Z reminds one just how much fun and, equally important, practical a conventional layout sports car can be. Unlike the MG-B V8 it makes no pretence at being anything more than a two-seater and as a result has a comparatively large luggage area accessible through the top-hinged, hydraulic-strut supported, rear door. Unfortunately the rear wheel arches and McPherson struts intrude to restrict what might otherwise have been an even more commodious area. The rear door window is heated, naturally, though in the period of my ownership all the windows remained permanently free of condensation, and suitcases can be prevented from sliding around loose by straps attached to the luggage bay floor. A handle moulded into the tail spoiler affixed to the boot lid would make it easier to open the lid against the force of the hydraulic struts.

Externally the 260Z is identifiable from the 240Z only by the badges attached to the front wings and a rearrangement of the rear light clusters, now flanked by separate reversing lights in the matt-black rear panel. Those familiar with the 240Z will spot that the 5½J x 14 in. wheels on this new model carry wider, low-profile Bridgestone tyres—195/70 instead of the old 175—a great help with the road behaviour and presenting a squatter appearance. Internally the facia and other details have been revised.

Mechanical modifications are the most important improvements made to the 240Z to create the 260Z and of these the most obvious is the increase in engine capacity from 2,393 c.c. to 2,565 c.c. by lengthening the stroke of the seven-bearing crankshaft from 73.7 mm. to 79 mm. The straight six thus remains slightly oversquare, the bore continuing at 83 mm.

I find it hard to believe that less than 200 extra c.c. can be the sole reason for the engine's improved performance. Claimed figures show an increase of 11 b.h.p. SAE to 162 b.h.p. at 5,600 r.p.m. and 152 lb. ft. torque instead of 146 lb. ft. torque at the same 4,400 r.p.m. and that while running on a lower compression ratio of 8.3 to 1 instead of 9.0 to 1 to suit low-lead three-star fuel. No emission equipment as such is fitted, but the two SU-type Hitachi carburetters and ignition have been recalibrated to meet more stringent anti-pollution requirements. Yet the 260Z feels much more flexible and much quicker than the old 240, suggesting that beneficial modifications to the cylinder head and/or camshaft may have been made also. Additional weight to that belief comes from the fact that the engine seems more willing to pull the higher final drive ratio (3.70 to 1) than the 240 engine did its 3.90 to 1 ratio. Overall gearing in 5th gives 22.3 m.p.h. per 1,000 r.p.m. as against 21.6 m.p.h. for the 240Z.

The whole of the drive train is said to have been beefed up and at the same time the gearbox ratios have been revised to make more efficient use of the torque and eliminate the 240s gap between 1st and 2nd gears. Or so the Press release tells us. It also says that 1st gear ratio is now 2.91 to 1 instead of 3.32 and 2nd gear is 1.90 to 1 instead of 2.08. Curious . . . our two-year-old specification for the 240 gives 1st as 2.957 to 1, 2nd as 1.858 to 1, 3rd 1.311 to 1, 4th direct, 5th 0.852 to 1 and reverse 2.992 to 1. Equivalents for the 260 given in the Press release to more approximate figures are: 2.91, 1.90, 1.31, 1.00, 0.86 and 3.38 which would suggest a major revision to the reverse gear ratio but otherwise very little difference. It might also suggest that somebody has his wires crossed . . . Whatever, I do seem to recall a fair-sized gap between 1st and 2nd, not evident on the 260. Indeed this is now one of the most delightful five-speed gearboxes on a production car and it is almost ironic that now the engine has been made so flexible as to need less gearchanging the gearbox has been made so good as to encourage cog-swapping for the fun of it. A comfortable leather knob surmounts the hefty gearlever in place of the earlier nasty plastic-wood device and this selects the lower four gears in conventional H pattern with 5th up to the right opposite reverse. There is very little spring-loading to overcome across the gate, the gearlever nonetheless being self-centring in the 3rd/4th plane,

Re-arranged light clusters and improved interior of the 260Z.

and the change is thus rapid, light and accurate although with fairly long movements. First gear synchromesh occasionally baulks when selecting this gear from rest. The 8.87 in. diameter clutch is positive and its hydraulic operation not unduly heavy.

Uprated coil springs have been incorporated in the 260Z's otherwise unchanged four-corner McPherson strut independent suspension, allegedly to compensate for the extra weight of the new engine and improved interior, but as this would appear to be fairly negligible the more logical reason seems to be that the Nips simply wished to improve the handling, which indeed the combination of these stiffer springs and wider tyres has achieved. Stability in fast bends is very impressive, there is less roll, less pitch and virtually none of the wallow which the 240Z's outside front corner would engage in when confronted by a bump in the middle of a fast corner. Near the limit on fast corners there is a predictable and gentle transition to oversteer, but the Bridgestone radials show no sign of letting go completely; even in the wet their roadholding is excellent, suggesting that at last this Japanese rubber manufacturer has discovered the purpose of tyres. Traction too is excellent, the McPherson strut rear suspension with lower wishbones using the greater acreage of rubber to advantage. In spite of the long bonnet it is a comparatively easy car to place through the lanes, though I would shudder at having to drive it flat out down a special stage. Steering is fairly heavy at low speeds but requires perfectly reasonable effort as speed increases and, after all, it would be out of character with this big brute of a car to have featherlight steering. It is controlled via a new 14 in. (at a guess) wheel with a comfortable, leather-like padded rim and heavily padded boss working a disgracefully feeble "peep-peep" horn.

Precise and responsive though that front suspension/steering is, it inherits the same annoying bump steer which we have all complained about since the 240Z's introduction. A great shame. Likewise Nissan-Datsun have failed to improve the Girling-Sumitomo servo-assisted, twin-circuit braking system (10.67 in. front discs and 9 in. finned drums at the rear). I can well believe that the majority of Z owners never find cause to criticise the brakes, for if moderate demands are made of them they are perfectly adequate. However, to drive a Z very fast is to experience almost certain brake fade, first announced by a heavy pedal and then by an embarrassing unwillingness to stop.

The single o.h.c. straight-six gains 172 c.c. and 11 b.h.p.

Adding competition friction material is not a cure, as found by Spike Anderson, who transforms the Z into that excellent Super Samuri tested in MOTOR SPORT last year: he has since had to fit ventilated discs and four-pot calipers.

Datsun claim a 127 m.p.h. maximum for the 260Z, which will reach 60 m.p.h. in less than 8 sec., average 22 m.p.g. driven extremely hard, and driven less arduously would offer over a 350-mile range from its 13.2 gallon tank. While the 240Z engine was unwilling below 4,000 r.p.m., the 260 engine offers progressive power most of the way up the range and excellent flexibility, 5th being usable down to about 20 m.p.h. The 8,000 r.p.m. rev. counter is yellow-lined at 6,500 r.p.m. and red-lined at 7,000, but very fast progress can be made without exceeding 6,000 r.p.m. Speeds available in the lower three gears are 46, 71 and 102 m.p.h., 70 m.p.h. is achieved at a quiet, effortless 3,150 r.p.m. in 5th and the 127 m.p.h maximum speed requires a mere 5,700 r.p.m., all the while the beautifully smooth, mechanically silent engine emitting an exciting, but reasonably muted, deep-throated roar.

Interior facilities are excellent, if you can stand the abundance of nasty plastic. An excellent three-speed heater and four-outlet ventilation system is controlled by a triple-lever illuminated panel, instrumentation is clear and comprehensive, two-speed plus intermittent wipers, electric screenwashers, lights and flashers are controlled by two well-contrived steering column stalks, the high-back seats unforgivably lack a reclining mechanism and the big throttle pedal, well-placed for heel-and-toeing in side-of-foot fashion is too light and sensitive for low-speed town driving.

This distinctive beast from the other side of the world is a true sports car in that it is fast, handles well, requires skill to drive it very quickly but is tremendous fun while doing so. On the other hand it is also a true GT car, for two, for it is capacious, comfortable, has a lazy, 120 m.p.h. cruising gait yet has a sensible fuel range. No wonder it sells so well.—C.R.

Front and rear spoilers enhance the hatchback lines, but wheel trims remain singularly out of character.

Road test

by John Bolster

Datsun 260Z body pressings remain unaltered though the interior is re-styled.

Smoother quicker 260Z

It is well known that, during the past four years, the Datsun 240Z has become the world's most popular sports car, largely through having won almost a monopoly of the lucrative USA market. Britain now has no car to equal it, except perhaps the TVR, which is made in rather limited quantities. The Japanese car hit the jackpot because it had a lot of performance yet a moderate fuel consumption, it was small and of very sporting appearance, but was completely practical for town use or business journeys.

In replacing the 240Z by the 260Z, the manufacturers have been careful to make as few changes as possible. It was necessary to make some basic alterations, in the interest of reducing pollution, and the compression ratio had to be lowered to suit lead-free fuel. To reduce the performance would not be acceptable so the engine size was increased by fitting a longer-throw crank, the stroke going up by 5.3 mm. The new engine meets all the requirements and there is a small increase both in maximum power and torque, which has permitted a change in final drive ratio from 3.9 to 3.7 to 1. The two lowest gears of the five-speed box have also been closed up a little and a tyre size that puts more rubber on the road has been adopted.

The same body pressings have been retained, though the interior has been re-styled in accordance with the latest trends. As always, the suspension is independent all round on the MacPherson system and the rack and pinion steering needs less than three turns from lock to lock. There is an anti-roll bar in front and the springs have been slightly stiffened, partly because of a small increase in weight. The straight-six engine cannot be mounted too far forward or the weight distribution would be impaired, so the fairly long bonnet must be accepted, but this is a traditional sports car feature which many people still admire. The scuttle is fairly high and a short driver might want to raise the seat.

The 260Z corners well with less understeer than its predecessor.

The body is strictly a two-seater, with enough room for the biggest occupants. The opening rear window is controlled by telescopic struts and there are straps to secure the luggage on a spacious platform which is, however, in view of miscreants outside. The spare wheel is enclosed in a case beneath this platform, alongside the petrol tank. Everything is well arranged for the driver's convenience and a comfortable position can be found by people of varying sizes.

The choke must be used for a while until the engine is warm, but the unit then shows true six-cylinder flexibility. For city driving, a change of leverage might be beneficial in the throttle linkage, the butterflies tending to open rather sharply from the closed position unless a little care is exercised. The five-speed gearbox is superb, with a light change and close ratios. Fourth and fifth gears can be used at quite low speeds, which is perhaps why the bigger engine actually seems to be more economical than its predecessor.

One might expect the already good acceleration to be improved and certainly the car pulls its high gearing well. Yet, the combination of this ratio with the wider tyres makes a racing start difficult, unless one is willing to punish the clutch. This I refuse to do, and so there was a slight tendency to fluff just after the getaway; below 60 mph I was therefore not quite able to equal my figures for the 240Z. However, life isn't all racing starts and a 40 mph bottom gear is ideal for sharp bends.

The engine peaks at 5600 rpm and there seems little point in going over 6000 rpm, even when obtaining the best possible acceleration figures. Curiously enough, the rev-counter is marked yellow from 6500 to 7000, where the red starts, but this seems somewhat unwise with the longer stroke now adopted. I went up to 7000 rpm once, but never again, for the crank goes through a torsional period at around that speed. It is possible that the rev-counter of the test car was reading slow at the top end, and that I over-revved in consequence, but I would prefer the red section to start 500 rpm earlier. The gear speeds in my data panel are given for 6500 rpm in the lower gears but the car will not exceed 5700 rpm in fifth, so the new gear ratio is just about spot on. The highly satisfactory 127 mph maximum of the 260Z is just 2 mph up on the 240Z.

The Datsun is perhaps a bit noisy when accelerating, though the exhaust note is a joy to the enthusiast and it does not seem to attract unwelcome attention. Cruising on a high gear, the car is delightfully effortless, and at 90 mph on a whiff of throttle it is outstandingly quiet for a sports car. On bumpy roads some thumping is heard and sandpaper surfaces create a roaring noise, but wind noise is only audible above about 100 mph. The machine is very steady at speed but side winds tend to deflect it when travelling at over 110 mph. Such speeds are somewhat academic at the moment, unfortunately.

The 260Z corners very well, perhaps with a shade less understeer than its predecessor. The steering is quite light, except when taking very sharp corners; sensitive and quick, it is responsible for much of the car's character. A tail-out attitude can be achieved on really fast bends, but the rear-end sticks down well with no tendency to break away, though a succession of bumps may call for a little correction. The ride is fairly firm at low speeds but smooths out at higher cruising rates, though the 260Z always feels like a sports car.

The brakes are entirely adequate for normal road use and are always smooth and silent in action. Racing is another matter and a determined driver might well make them fade under such conditions. This is, after all, a pretty fast car and no light weight, so the brakes have a job of work to do. For driving at ten-tenths on a circuit, a very expensive installation with ventilated discs would be justified. This is a road test, however, and I don't think that the average owner will get anywhere near the fading point — there's plenty of warning if it does begin to happen, anyway.

Similarly, the lights are reasonable for fairly fast motoring but better ones are available for the enthusiast who wants to gild the lily. In standard form, this Datsun is a fast car that will delight the man who enjoys a really potent sports model for his everyday driving. It would be much heavier if it were deprived of its roof, so a fixed-head coupe seems to be the only solution if maximum performance is required.

It must be admitted that I needed two Datsuns for this road test and the one in the photographs is not the one that gave the performance figures. The first car just didn't like me — it made me walk home in the dark when its lights failed and it sulked when I pressed the stopwatches for speed tests. During all our own troubles, it's nice to know that the Japanese can make Friday cars, too, but the second one was as fast and reliable as we have come to expect of Datsuns.

SPECIFICATION AND PERFORMANCE DATA

Car tested: Datsun 260Z two-seater coupe, price £2,895 including car tax and VAT.

Engine: Six cylinders, 83 mm x 79 mm (2565 cc); compression ratio, 8.3 to 1; 162 bhp (gross) at 5600 rpm; single chain-driven overhead camshaft; two Hitachi horizontal SU-type carburetters.

Transmission: Single dry plate clutch; five-speed all-synchromesh gearbox with central change, ratios 0.86, 1.0, 1.31, 1.90, 2.91, and 3.38 to 1; hypoid final drive, ratio 3.70 to 1.

Chassis: Combined steel body and chassis; independent suspension of all wheels by MacPherson struts incorporating telescopic dampers and coil springs, with lower wishbones; anti-roll bar in front; rack and pinion steering; servo-assisted disc front and drum rear brakes; bolt-on steel disc wheels, fitted 195/70 VR 14 tyres.

Equipment: Speedometer; rev-counter, water temperature, oil pressure, and fuel gauges; ammeter; clock; heating, demisting, and ventilation system with heated rear window; intermittent and two-speed windscreen wipers and washers; flashing direction indicators; reversing lights.

Dimensions: Wheelbase, 7 ft 6.7 in; track (front) 4 ft 5.3 in, (rear) 4 ft 5 in; overall length, 13 ft 6.8 in; width, 5 ft 4.2 in; weight, 2,425 lb.

Performance: Maximum speed, 127 mph. Speeds in gears: Fourth, 125 mph; third, 96 mph; second, 65 mph; first, 43 mph. Standing quarter-mile, 15.7 s. Acceleration: 0-30 mph 3.8 s; 0-50 mph, 6.2 s; 0-60 mph, 8.2 s; 0-80 mph, 14.4 s; 0-100 mph, 23.8 s.

Fuel consumption: 20 to 28 mpg.

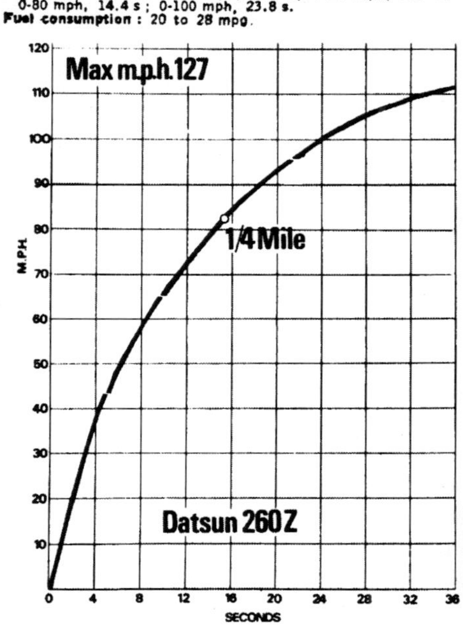

Above: High scuttle for short drivers. Below: Traditional long bonnet appearance.

2565 cc straight six engine produces 162 bhp at 5600 rpm.

DATSUN 260Z

Is taking a winner and improving on it a sure sign of greed?

PHOTOGRAPHY: GENE BUTERA

• Apparently nothing is sacred at Datsun, not even playing to a capacity crowd for four years with the same successful sports/GT car. Who knows, maybe those long lines of buyers really wouldn't have lasted forever. Rumor has it you can actually get the color of your choice now. And in some cities, the price has reportedly plummeted to what the sticker says. Not what you'd call a crash in the market, but Datsun is taking those signs seriously. As a result the 1974 Z-car has a new first name: 260. That bigger number means the factory is trying to put more into the car than the U.S. safety and emissions standards are draining out. Be forewarned: It's an obvious ploy to lengthen the waiting lines again.

The new nameplate stands for a bigger engine: the same basic 240Z single overhead cam Six with piston displacement upped by 171cc (10.4 cubic inches) as a result of an 0.2-inch increase in stroke. Also the exhaust valves are larger for better breathing and a magnetic pulse generator has replaced breaker points in the distributor. Datsun engineers claim the new electronic ignition improves starting and forestalls misfiring with the 260Z's emissions package (lean mixtures, an air pump and heavy doses of recirculated exhaust gas). And since underhood temperatures have surged in the fight against air pollution, fuel lines are now heavily insulated for protection against vapor lock. The fuel system also benefits from a rear-mounted electric pump operating in tandem with the engine-driven mechanical pump.

On the dyno, the new motor delivers 139 hp (net) at 5600 rpm, an increase of six hp over last year's 2394cc version. Torque is up by 12 lbs.-ft. to 137 (net) at 4400 rpm. Unfortunately, the dynamometer only tells part of the story; the rest is unveiled at the test track. Our test car accelerated through the quarter-mile in 17.8 seconds with a trap speed of 80.8 mph. As a result of that test, we must sadly report that the big motor Z-car is slower than last year's edition. The 1973 Z-car we tested went down the quarter-mile in 17.0 seconds at 81.3 mph. Part of that difference in acceleration can be attributed to extra weight: Our '74 test car was heavier by 80 lbs. with factory air conditioning (optional), with another 80-lb. handicap added by the 5-mph front and rear bumpers. But weight in this incidence is *not* the primary cause of the 260Z's performance fall off. Our test car also had a serious drivability problem that put a limp in its gait down the dragstrip. Halfway through the rev range in first gear, the engine simply ran out of fuel. It died like a fish out of water, with power coming back in gulps. Datsun engineers acknowledge the existence of the problem and are diligently searching for a solution. Their tests show that high underhood temperatures are boiling fuel in the carburetors, causing the temporary starvation during sustained flat-out acceleration. The old Hitachi-SU sidedraft carburetors may have come to the end of their rope. We'd suggest electronic fuel injection as a logical replacement.

That won't happen this year, but still you should not expect the 260Z to struggle through the model year slower than the 1973 car. Datsun does a sizable amount of development work in this country—often times after the cars go on sale. One whole shipload of early '73s had to have carburetors replaced on the dock due to a design defect. And later in the model year a service repair kit was issued to dealers to correct se-

vere hot start problems. The kit included the insulated fuel lines and electric fuel pump now standard equipment for 1974. Unfortunately, the basic problem is still not solved. Emissions hardware has placed such a heavy burden on the engine, that it isn't ready to make clean air and live up to its power potential at the same time. So at this point, the big motor is less an advantage and more a stop gap measure to meet the law. Any real performance gains over 1973 will depend on how successful the U.S.-based development program is.

The Datsun engineers could stand to take a look at fuel economy as well, since that has also slipped for 1974. Our tests show that mileage is down about two mpg from an average 20 mpg (for a 1973 car) to 18 mpg for the 260Z. Environmental Protection Agency tests, however, have revealed no sacrifice with the bigger engine; in its strictly city driving tests, both '73 and '74 models turned in an average 16 mpg.

Text continued on page 158

PHOTO BY MARC MADOW

Making a Good Thing Bigger

Datsun's new 260Z 2+2: The sportswagon concept becomes a reality

• Datsun's Z-car has knocked big holes in the armor-plated precept that there is no significant market in America for a 2-passenger sports car. With that dragon laid to rest, Datsun has moved on to fresh territory. Enter the 260Z 2+2, a snare for all those sports-minded buyers holding out for just a little more space.

The best part about the 2+2 is the fact that you sacrifice precious little over the standard Z-car and you gain a whole lot in return. Some of the lean rakishness is gone from the lines, but the 4-place Z will never be mistaken for an Estate Wagon. In fact you don't really see the extra foot of wheelbase at all. The only exterior clue that the 2+2 is definitely something different comes from a slightly inflated roofline.

The gentle stretching program has opened up a rear seat about halfway between a 911 Porsche and a Mustang II in volume. You slip in through slightly longer doors and plug yourself into one of the two deeply pocketed seat bottoms. There are discreet limits to the amount of romping you can do in the back, but none of the boundaries really compress you into discomfort. The backrest is nearly vertical to gain the most headroom from an extended roofline. Wheelwells determine the hip room, and shoulder width lies between two front passenger inertia reels. Leg room is available if both front and rear passengers can agree on a compromise. Every surface that you might lean against is suitably padded, and the only undue intrusion is, oddly enough, a tire-changing jack. For no obvious reason, it is clamped to the floor pan on the left side, interfering with foot room.

Even though the rear seat is definitely second-class passage, the car does not treat back passengers like second-class citizens. Big quarter windows provide a good view to the side and they swing out for ventilation. Front seats don't seal off the forward view because there is a gaping canyon between the backrests. That space is especially effective for sighting down the road because rear passengers sit quite close to the car's centerline.

Due to a little Japanese ingenuity, rear passengers aren't trapped when it's time to exit. On the right side, there is a floor-mounted release button to fold the front back-rest out of the way. And both doors have two inside handles: one in the normal location for front passengers, and one at the top rear corner of the door for those leaving from the rear.

The chassis is virtually unchanged from the standard 260Z. New sheet metal adds 12 inches between the wheels, 11.9 inches in overall length, and 0.2 inches in height. Curb weight is up in the 2+2 by 250 lbs. The only powertrain alteration consists of a larger diameter ring gear in the differential. Tire selection has not been finalized, but 185 radials are under consideration.

Even if you have no surplus of friends to haul around, the 2+2 is a good deal. Front passengers don't lose a millimeter of seat travel or legroom in the new car. And since the rear seat back folds down to make a flat load floor, the 2+2 is one step closer to a station wagon, at least on the inside. In fact, it's not too far removed from the Sportwagon concept suggested by *Car and Driver* way back in January, 1972. Not all bad, Datsun.

—Don Sherman

ACCELERATION standing ¼ mile, seconds

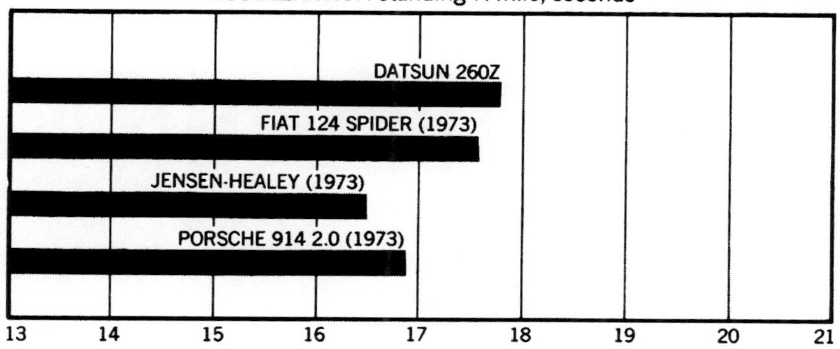

BRAKING 70-0 mph, feet

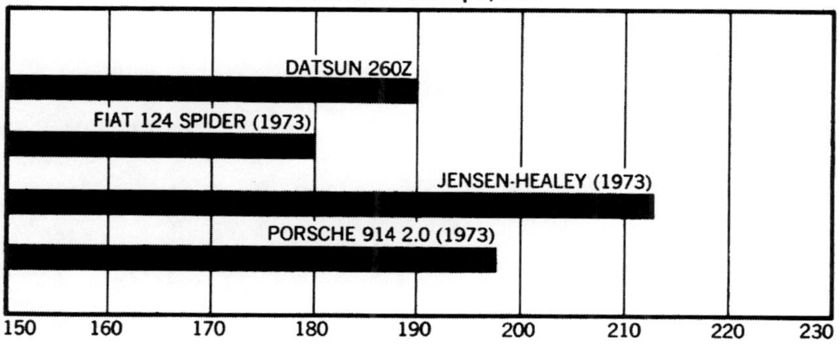

FUEL ECONOMY RANGE mpg

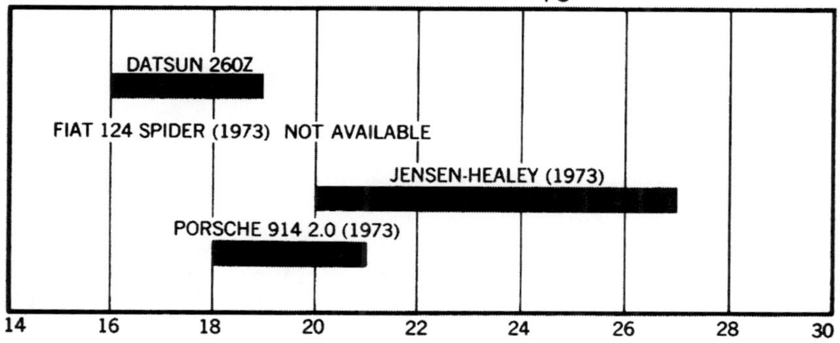

PRICE AS TESTED dollars x 1000

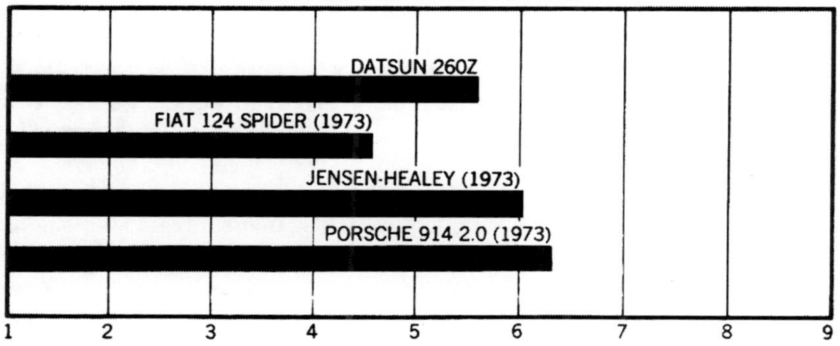

INTERIOR SOUND LEVEL dBA

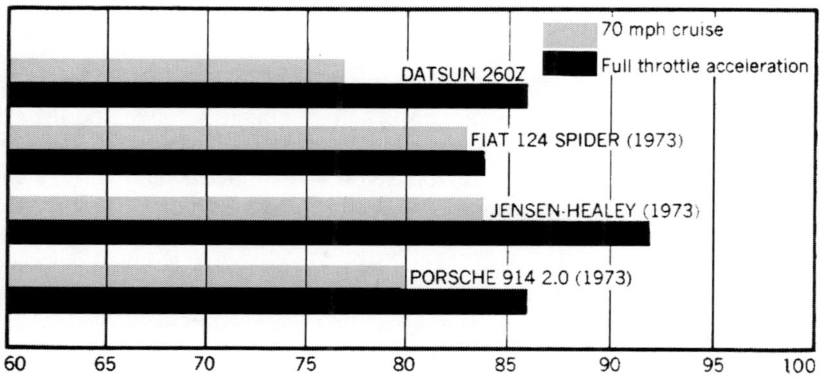

Datsun 260Z

Importer: Nissan Motor Corporation, U.S.A.
18501 S. Figueroa Street
Carson, California 90247

Vehicle type: Front engine, rear-wheel-drive, 2-passenger hatch-back coupe

Price as tested: $5610.00
(Manufacturer's suggested retail price, including all options listed below, dealer preparation and delivery charges, does not include state and local taxes, license or freight charges)

Options on test car: Base Datsun 260Z, $5125; air conditioning, $410; dealer prep, $75

ENGINE

Type: Six-in-line, water-cooled, cast iron block and aluminum head, and 7 main bearings

Bore x stroke	3.27 x 3.11 in, 83.0 x 79.0 mm
Displacement	156 cu in, 2565 cc
Compression ratio	8.8 to one
Carburetion	2 x 1-bbl Hitachi
Valve gear	chain-driven single overhead cam
Power (SAE net)	139 bhp@ 5600 rpm
Torque (SAE net)	137 lbs-ft@ 4400 rpm
Specific power output	0.89 bhp/cu in, 54.2 bhp/liter
Max. recommended engine speed	7000 rpm

DRIVE TRAIN

Transmission	4-speed, all-synchro
Final drive ratio	3.36 to one

Gear	Ratio	Mph/1000 rpm	Max. test speed
I	3.59	5.7	34 mph (6000 rpm)
II	2.25	9.0	54 mph (6000 rpm)
III	1.42	14.3	86 mph (6000 rpm)
IV	1.00	20.4	117 mph (5750 rpm)

DIMENSIONS AND CAPACITIES

Wheelbase	90.7 in
Track, F/R	53.3/53.0 in
Length	169.1 in
Width	64.1 in
Height	50.6 in
Ground clearance	5.7 in
Curb weight	2660 lbs
Weight distribution, F/R	51.5/48.5%
Battery capacity	12 volts, 60 amp-hr
Alternator capacity	700 watts
Fuel capacity	15.8 gal
Oil capacity	4.5 qts
Water capacity	8.4 qts

SUSPENSION

F:	Ind., MacPherson strut, coil springs; anti-sway bar
R:	Ind., MacPherson strut, coil springs, anti-sway bar

STEERING

Type	Rack and pinion
Turns lock-to-lock	3.1
Turning circle curb-to-curb	31.4 ft

BRAKES

F:	10.7-in solid disc, power assisted
R:	1.6 x 9.0-in fixed aluminum drum, power assisted

WHEELS AND TIRES

Wheel size	5.0 x 14-in
Wheel type	stamped steel, 4-bolt
Tire make and size	Toyo 2-1, 175 HR-14
Tire type	Rayon cord, radial ply, tubeless
Test inflation pressures, F/R	28/28 psi
Tire load rating	1230 lbs per tire @ 32 psi

PERFORMANCE

Zero to	Seconds
30 mph	3.5
40 mph	5.4
50 mph	7.6
60 mph	10.3
70 mph	13.5
80 mph	17.5
90 mph	23.7
100 mph	33.2
Standing ¼-mile	17.8 sec @ 80.8 mph
Top speed (observed)	117 mph
70-0 mph	190 ft (0.86 G)
Fuel mileage	16.0-19.0-mpg on regular fuel
Cruising range	250-300 mi

Text continued from page 155

Except for the fuel penalty and one serious flaw in drivability, the new engine is easy to get along with. With the new electronic ignition it starts eagerly when cold if you use a lot of choke and pulls like a freight train at low speeds. That makes the Z-car more flexible in traffic because you can move out smartly ahead of the flow without resorting to the top half of the rev range. It's just as well because the tachometer optimistically advertises a thousand revs that aren't useful. The 260Z is really no different from its predecessor in this respect. The Z-car's redline has stood at a lofty 7000 rpm from the beginning, and while the engine will wind that tight without bursting, only the noise level is still rising. Power noses downward after 5600 rpm and the useful rev range ends at 6000.

Although the big motor is a mixed blessing, other changes for this year are strict improvements. Datsun has chosen 1974 to unload a fix for virtually every complaint owners have lodged over the years. That's not to say the 240Z has been riddled with shortcomings. The fact is it has been one of the most popular cars in existence—at any price. *Car and Driver* readers selected it as the Overall Best Car for 1973, and Datsun is intent on preserving that stellar image.

Most of the shortcomings of the car's interior have been acknowledged and fixed . . . even the old bamboo-colored steering wheel is gone

Handling is at the top of the 1974's improvement list. In the past, directional stability at highway speeds had been the Datsun's weak suit: Pre-'74 Z-cars wandered down a windy freeway as if they were piloted by inebriates. The problem centered around a complicated interaction of aerodynamics, steering geometry and rubber bushings locating the steering rack. For the solution, Datsun has taken no small pains. First of all, the body's angle of attack into the wind is altered by raising the rear of the car slightly. That diminishes front-end lift at speed and at the same time reduces weight loss from the front tires. With a tighter grip on the road, the front of the car is not so easily swayed from its path by sidewinds. The steering gear mounting system has also been revised with special attention to eliminate lateral compliance. Side loads that might come from cornering or cross winds can no longer deflect the steering rack or turn the front wheels. So now only the steering wheel guides the car, as it should. The road feel to the driver is much too damped for our liking, but the 260Z does track down the road with solid respect for the straight and narrow.

Spring rates are higher at both ends of the car largely to accommodate the extra weight of fortified bumpers and factory air conditioning. Since that weight has favored the front end, there is a built-in tendency toward understeer. But Datsun engineers have wisely side-stepped that bed of quicksand by adding a rear anti-sway bar as standard equipment. It shifts roll stiffness to the rear of the car to counteract the negative handling influence of a heavier front end. On the whole, the new suspension calibration works in a very commendable manner. The 260Z sweeps through turns with a new level of determination: Body roll is at a tight minimum and you can feel both ends of the car working right up to the limit. In the front, there is a gradual loss of response to the steering wheel, but the tires never yield to severe understeer. It's the rear tires that actually signal the limit as they lose their side grip and begin to audibly scratch at the pavement. You feel the tail slowly creeping out, but the drift angle stabilizes at a perfectly manageable limit because the front end also begins to slide. And it all happens with no feeling of impending doom. In fact the Datsun is so stable that normal interruptions—more throttle, less throttle, braking and even wet surfaces—don't shake its composure. It's enough to make you bypass the freeway every time in search of a twisty back passage.

No matter what route you take, the Datsun's interior will deliver you in fine style. None of the strong attributes have been tampered with—excellent instrumentation, wrap-around seat backs and a station wagon's cargo hold under the hatchback. But most of the shortcomings have been fixed. The hair trigger gas pedal is gone. And all the rubbery vagueness is out of the shift lever with a new linkage this year. Even the old bamboo-colored steering wheel has been upgraded with padding and a leather cover. Not real hand-sewn cow skin, but a man-made facsimile accurate right down to the wrinkles, stitches and pores, realistic enough to fool a glove manufacturer. Thankfully, the cheap looking heat-stamped plastic coverings for the transmission and rear suspension towers is gone, replaced by vinyl with a richer texture and a finer pattern.

Factory air conditioning is also a major upgrade this year. The hardware is a marvel of technology—lightweight aluminum materials for the evaporator and condenser, and a compact swashplate compressor similar to the GM/Frigidaire design. The compressor is vibration free in operation and there is no underhood clutter with the new system. Inside the car, the hardware is shrewdly interfaced with the instrument panel. The heater/AC control module is one of the simplest and most informative layouts we've seen. Three carefully marked levers regulate the interior climate: one 4-speed blower switch, one temperature selector and one function knob. Since the latter is graphically coded with red and blue arrows, you know if the air has been heated or cooled and exactly where it's going. At last cryptic labels like "Bi-Level" take on a solid meaning.

The air conditioning system is the only convenience Datsun doesn't include with the base price. For $5125, you get tinted glass, intermittent wipers (new this year), a dead pedal for your left foot and even an AM/FM radio . . . complete with an electric antenna.

True, it's not the bargain it was in 1970 at $3526, but a serious competitor to the Z-car still hasn't materialized. The opposition is slimmer by two cars this year with the demise of the Opel GT and Triumph's GT6. The remaining field, the Alfa GTV, the Jensen-Healey and the Porsche 914, may delight purists, but the technical fascination doesn't seem to sway the masses shopping for a sports car at Datsun. Face value is the key: The 260Z offers a bigger engine at a lower price. Not to mention the comfort of joining a crowd—a mass stronger by 54,000 happy customers in 1973.

We don't expect a downturn in popularity even with the drivability problems wrought by emission controls. The upgrade program has been too thorough for that to happen. And if the carburetor engineers can get their act together, they'll wipe out the 260Z's most menacing competitor—last year's 240Z. •

The 2+2 version shown here is the latest model in the Z range of sports cars; the two-seater is also available

260Z

Datsun's famous best-selling sports car with ohc engine and all-independent suspension, now available also as a 2+2

DATSUN CREATED a sensation with the 240Z when it first appeared, and went on to take a very large slice of the (formerly British-dominated) American market for sports cars. Last year the engine was enlarged to 2.6 litres, the gear ratios were changed and wider wheels and tyres adopted.

Autocar has not tested the two-seat 260Z, but the performance is unlikely to differ significantly from the 240Z we tested in 1971, which achieved a mean maximum of 125mph and reached 60mph in 8.0sec.—sufficient to put it high in the sports car performance league. For this sort of car it was also very economical, managing 21.4mpg overall. Most 260Z owners should achieve 24mpg in normal, legal driving.

The 260Z engine is essentially the same as that of the 260C, and is therefore closely related to the smaller Datsun ohc power units. Suspension design is advanced, the all-independent layout using MacPherson struts all round. We rated the steering (by rack and pinion), the handling and the ride better than average in our 240Z test; the 260Z seems to have better roadholding but a stiffer ride, probably an effect of the wider, low-profile tyres.

A very recent introduction is the 2+2 version of the 260Z, based on a floorpan stretched by 10in. and mounting a longer body giving enough room for four adults on short journeys. This version is even better equipped, with a combined radio and cassette player as standard, for instance. Since it is bigger and heavier, it cannot match the ultimate performance of the two-seater; our recent road test of the 2+2 gave it a maximum of 120mph, and a time of 9.9sec. to 60mph. It still proved very economical, however. □

BRIEF TEST

DATSUN 260Z

FOR:

Good roadholding and excellent handling; tremendous interior and luggage space for two; thoughtfully equipped interior

AGAINST:

Noisy and unrefined; engine rough at high revs; difficult gearbox

With more than 153,000 Datsun 240Zs sold throughout the world (America taking more than 130,000) there is some substance to Datsun's claim that it is the world's best-selling sports car. Two successes in the tough East African Safari have enhanced its reputation as a rugged sports car with good roadholding and handling. The layout is not advanced by modern standards, with a front-mounted straight six engine driving the rear wheels, although a single overhead camshaft, a five-speed gearbox and independent suspension all round are rare enough to be noteworthy. With the introduction of the 260Z the model has had its first major specification change since its introduction at the 1969 Tokyo Motor Show, the main revisions being to the engine with consequent modifications to the transmission and running gear. The sleek two-seater monocoque body, with a large luggage platform behind the seats, remains much as before apart from 260Z motifs on the front wings and restyling to the rear panel and tail lights.

The increase in engine capacity, from 2393 to 2565 ccs, comes from a longer stroke, up from 73.7 to 79 mm; the bore stays the same at 83 mm. The compression ratio has been dropped from 9.0 to 8.3: 1 to allow running on low lead fuel, while valve overlap has been reduced by 4 deg and ignition timing retarded by 7 deg, the last two changes being apparently all that was necessary to meet E-mark 15. The overall result is to raise the power output from 151 bhp (SAE) to 162 bhp (SAE), both at 5600 rpm. [Note incidentally that the net (DIN) figure for the 260Z, 151 bhp as quoted in our table, is now the same as the previous gross (SAE) figure for the 240Z—an interesting guide as to the sort of differences that can be expected from these two methods of testing.]

To cater for the extra power Datsun have beefed up the five-speed transmission and at the same time slightly rearranged first and second gear ratios. First is now 2.91:1 instead of 3.32:1, while second is 1.90: 1 instead of 2.08:1. The final drive ratio has changed from 3.90:1 to 3.70:1, thus raising the mph/1000 rpm figure in top to 22.3 for a slightly more relaxed cruising ability. The only other changes worthy of mention are wider tyres, up from 175 to 195/70-14s, and stiffer springs to take the extra weight of the bigger engine and extra equipment.

Blanket speed restrictions have prevented us from conducting any proper two-way maximum speed runs on fast cars for some time now, so we have accepted Datsun's figure of 127 mph. The 240Z managed 125 mph, which corresponds to 5800 rpm; with 11 more bhp but with higher gearing and more weight 127 mph is therefore reasonable as it corresponds to 5700 rpm, a little over the peak power point.

But it is unfortunate in this particular case that we were unable to check, for in all other performance respects the 260Z is actually slower than the 240Z. The 0-60 mph time is slower by half a second, the 0-100 time by 3.6 sec, the top gear 30-50 mph time by one second, and the equivalent fourth gear figure by 0.8 sec.

The lusty six-cylinder engine, with a single overhead cam, twin Hitachi (SU type) carburetters but no cross-flow head (although it is made from aluminium) was reluctant to fire, run or pull from cold without extensive use of the choke, but once warm it was smooth and tractable enough, in spite of maximum torque occurring at 4400 rpm—a high speed for this sort of engine. Although maximum power occurs at 5600 rpm the red line on the tachometer is much higher at 7000 rpm, which means effectively that anything much over 6000 rpm or so is really only for show, as power is then dropping off quite rapidly; engine noise and roughness at such revs would deter most owners from using them anyway.

With all the changes made to the engine we would have expected fuel consumption to drop, but not plummet quite so drastically. Overall consumption is down from 25.7 to 22.9 mpg, while the touring consumption (calculated from steady speed conditions) has fallen from an excellent 31.2 to a poor 24.7 mpg. Nor can excessive hard driving be to blame, since the 50 mph limit was in force while we had the car. Fortunately the engine will now run on 95 rather than 98 octane petrol—or three star rather than four—a small consolation.

With five gears and well-chosen ratios the transmission ought to be excellent, but a number of detail faults spoilt it. The clutch has a long travel, the throttle action is sudden, and an apparent backlash or looseness in the drive train made smooth changes difficult, although racing style changes, with a quick dab on the clutch, a swift pull on the lever and then full throttle were superb, a real delight. But you had to be very delicate with the clutch under

PPX
39 M

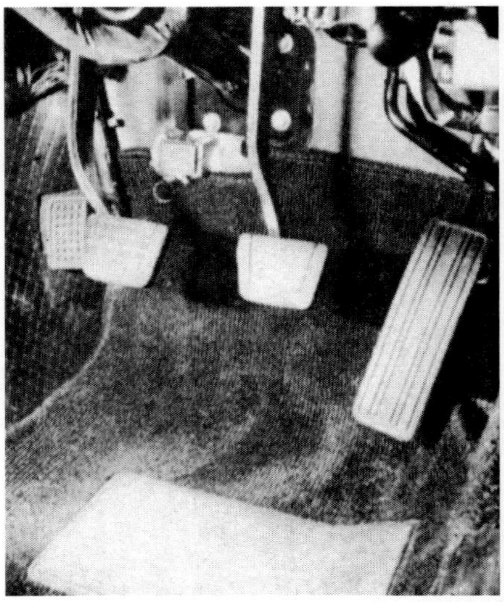

Left : no attempt to provide rear seats means 11.4 cu ft of suitcases can be carried. Above : pneumatic struts hold up the tailgate ; straps hold down the luggage. Right : well-positioned pedals and a left-foot rest

Left : good seats with excellent range of adjustment. Below left : well-filled engine bay, but all essential components are accessible. Above : well-designed instrument layout

normal conditions to avoid annoying jerks and loud clonks. On top of this fifth was almost impossible to engage when the gearbox oil was cold, and little better when hot ; reverse was almost as bad.

The handling, always good, has been improved in at least one respect to our way of thinking, and that is wet road grip. An increase in tyre width, all else remaining constant, generally results in poorer wet grip, so we can only conclude that the tread pattern or the rubber mix of the Japanese-made tyres has been brought more into line with British thinking. Our experience of Bridgestone tyres up to now has not been all that happy, but the RD 102 Wide 70s now fitted compare very favourably in all respects with the other, better known, makes.

The steering is direct, responsive and with good feel, but is heavy ; too heavy for some. There is also a fair bit of kickback. The cornering power on smooth roads is very high, although perhaps not outstanding for a sports car, so corners and bends can be taken very quickly, with understeer giving way to eventual oversteer. This sequence happens undramatically and controllably, however, so that sideways motoring is quite easy—and entertaining—but not very tidy since bumps and, even with the improved grip, injudicious use of the throttle in the wet can scuttle the tail out quite sharply.

The brakes (10.67 in diameter discs at the front, 9.0 in diameter drum at the back) are vacuum servo assisted, with a front/rear split and a pressure limiting valve in the rear line. With such a set-up there should be no problems, but in fact several of our testers experienced severe fade on the road—an unforgivable fault for a high performance car. Two severe stops from high speed are enough. We have experienced this trouble before with 240Zs, although it must be admitted that during our fade test we experienced only relatively moderate fade (an increase in pedal pressure from 35 to 48 lb) but it was accompanied by harsh juddering and a smell of cooking linings. Perhaps as well as harder linings, ventilated discs are required, since the interval between stops in the fade test is one minute, just enough maybe for the brakes to cool and recover. Any harder treatment (say from a higher speed, with less time between stops, or with a deceleration of more than 0.5 g) shows that the brakes are right on the limit.

We regard the 260Z as one of the most sensibly planned two seaters built today. There is plenty of room in all respects, with no cramping at all. Leg-room is particularly good, while the volume of luggage that can be swallowed (11.4 cu ft) is exceeded only possibly by the Reliant Scimitar GTE, for which we have no comparable figures.

As might be expected the ride is firm, emphasised by harshness and crashing noises on indifferent surfaces, but is just right at higher speeds so that you can take full advantage of the roadholding.

Most people found the driving position very comfortable, partly because of the good available space—tall drivers can stretch their legs due to the large range of seat adjustment. The seats are quite comfortable (if a bit hard) and give adequate support. The pedals are ideally placed for heel-and-toeing, and—a typical touch—there is a brace for the left foot, while the gearlever position, close to the steering wheel, could hardly be bettered. Two stalks on the steering column look after lights and wipers, the slender right hand one just operating the indicators and dip/flash facility. The more substantial left hand one works the light by flipping a fingertip switch, the wipers by turning the knob on the end, and the washers by pressing the same knob. This may sound a little complicated but the system is quickly learned and after that is a pleasure to use. The upper mountings for the non-inertia reel seat belts fitted to the test car meant that the upper strap sat poorly across the shoulders, chafing and cutting into the neck and the door handle, down at the bottom of the door, is awkwardly placed.

With a relatively high scuttle and waistline short drivers may have to crane their necks to see out (although the seat can be raised using washers on the mounting bolts), and drivers found the nearside front quarter difficult to judge. The large rear window fortunately covers most of the blind spot created by the heavy rear three-quarter pillars.

The facia, in black moulded imitation leather plastic, is very transatlantic in style, with the two major dials (speedometer and tachometer) buried in wells in front of the driver. In spite of this they are of the no-nonsense sort, being large and clear, with no reflections, and are well lit at night. The ancillary instruments, comprising clock, combined ammeter and fuel gauge, and combined water temperature and oil pressure gauges, are ranged across the centre of the facia, and for that reason are a little out of the sight line.

The latest, more sophisticated, heating and ventilation system worked quite well, and we all liked the "Bi-level" setting of the air direction control, which allowed cold air to the face and warm air to the feet—the right combination. Unfortunately the air vents at each end of the facia had a poor throughput.

Noise suppression is one of the less refined aspects of the 260Z. Apart from the fussiness of the engine at high revs the sealing around the door and other areas is poor—a trip through a car wash left one driver with wet feet—which accounts for loud wind roar at higher speeds. On top of the crashes from the suspension on rough roads there were loud clonks, and whines from the transmission and a lot of bump-thump as well. In all, one of the less pleasant aspects of the car.

The finish, both aethetically and as regards fits of panels and components, is about average. The poor sealing around the door has already been mentioned, and another little fault that showed up while we had the car was that the fuel filler lock fell out. When it comes to fittings, though, the 260Z is full of thoughtful details. There is a left foot rest; straps to hold the luggage down; there are two interior lights, including a powerful one in the middle of the facia; an inspection lamp in the engine bay; a "defogger" (heated rear window); small flaps either side of the bonnet to get at the battery and windscreen washer bottle; a toolkit hidden in a small compartment at the front of the rear floor and other such details too numerous to mention.

The 260Z carries on the tradition of the 240Z. being a rugged handsome car with good handling and plenty of performance from the big six cylinder engine. Any loss in performance and economy compared to the 240Z must be blamed firmly on emission control requirements.

MOTOR ROAD TEST No. 22/74 • Datsun 260Z

PERFORMANCE

CONDITIONS

Weather	Cloudy; Wind 8-15 mph
Temperature	50° F
Barometer	29.95 in. Hg
Surface	Dry

MAXIMUM SPEEDS

	mph	kph
Banked circuit	see text	
Terminal speeds:		
at ¼ mile	85	137
at kilometer	103	166
Speed in gears (at 7000 rpm):		
1st	47	76
2nd	72	116
3rd	104	167

ACCELERATION FROM REST

mph	sec	kph	sec
0-30	3.0	0-40	2.0
0-40	4.5	0-60	4.0
0-50	6.6	0-80	6.5
0-60	8.8	0-100	9.5
0-70	12.0	0-120	13.3
0-80	15.1	0140	18.0
0-90	19.6	0-160	27.3
0-100	27.5		
Stand'g ¼	16.8	Stand'g km	31.2

ACCELERATION IN TOP

mph	sec	kph	sec
20-40	10.4	40-60	6.3
30-50	10.0	60-80	6.3
40-60	10.1	80-100	6.3
50-70	10.6	100-120	6.9
60-80	11.1	120-140	7.7
70-90	12.6		

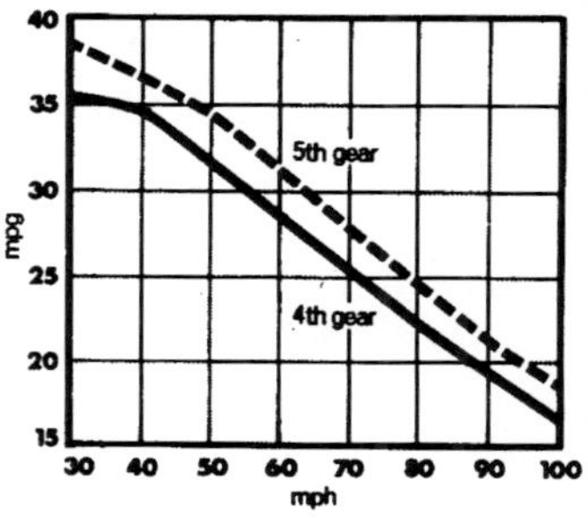

ACCELERATION IN 4TH

mph	sec	kph	sec
20-40	7.9	40-60	5.2
30-50	7.7	60-80	4.6
40-60	7.6	80-100	4.5
50-70	7.9	100-120	5.1
60-80	8.3	120-140	5.9
70-90	9.3	140-160	7.5
80-100	11.6		

FUEL CONSUMPTION

Touring*	24.7 mpg 11.4 litres/100 km
Overall	22.9 mpg 12.3 litres/100 km
Fuel grade	95 octane (RM) 3 star rating
Tank capacity	13.3 galls 60.5 litres
Max range	316 miles 508 km
Test distance	849 miles 1366 km

* Consumption midway between 30 mph and maximum less 5 per cent for acceleration.

SPEEDOMETER (mph)

Speedo	30	40	50	60	70	80	90	100
True mph	29	38.5	48	57.5	67	77	86	96

Distance recorder: 2.5 per cent fast

WEIGHT

	cwt	kg
Unladen weight*	21.7	1102
Weight as tested	25.4	1290
Distribution front/rear	52/48	

* With fuel for approx 50 miles

Performance tests carried out by Motor's staff at the Motor Industry Research Association proving ground, Lindley.

GENERAL SPECIFICATION

ENGINE

Cylinders	6 in line
Capacity	2565 cc (156.5 cu in)
Bore/stroke	830/79.0 mm (3.27/3.11 in.)
Cooling	Water
Block	Cast iron
Head	Aluminium alloy
Valves	Sohc
Valve timing	
inlet opens	16° btdc
inlet closes	52° abdc
ex. opens	54° bbdc
ex. closes	14° atdc
Compression	8.3 : 1
Carburetter	2 Hitachi HJG46W
Bearings	7 main
Fuel pump	Mechanical
Max power	151 bhp (DIN) at 6000 rpm
Max torque	147 lb ft (DIN) at 4400 rpm

TRANSMISSION

Type	Manual
Clutch	Hydraulically operated sdp diaphragm spring

Internal ratios and mph/1000 rpm

Top	0.86 : 1/22.6
4th	1.00 : 1/19.5
3rd	1.31 : 1/14.9
2nd	1.90 : 1/10.2
1st	2.91 : 1/ 6.7
Rev	3.38 : 1
Final drive	3.70 : 1

BODY/CHASSIS

Construction	Unitary steel
Protection	Phosphate treatment prior to painting

SUSPENSION

Front	Independent by MacPherson struts, lower links, coils, telescopic dampers, anti-roll bar
Rear	Independent by MacPherson struts, lower wishbones, coils, telescopic dampers

STEERING

Type	Rack and pinion
Assistance	None
Toe-in	0.08-0.20 in.
Camber	0° 50′
Castor	2° 55′
King pin	12° 10′
Rear toe-in	Parallel

BRAKES

Type	Discs front, drums rear
Servo	Yes
Circuit	Dual, front/rear
Rear valve	Yes
Adjustment	Self-adjusting

WHEELS

Type	Steel 14 x 5½J
Tyres	Bridgestone 195/70VR14

ELECTRICAL

Battery	12V 60 Ah
Polarity	Negative
Generator	Alternator
Fuses	10
Headlights	2 x 75/50W

COMPARISONS

	Capacity cc	Price £	Max mph	0-60 sec	30-50* sec	Overall mpg	Touring mpg	Length ft in	Width ft in	Weight cwt	Boot cu ft
Datsun 260Z	2565	2896	127.0†	8.8	10.0	22.9	23.8	14 2.25	5 5	21.7	11.4
Jaguar E-type V12	5343	3812	146.0	6.4	6.0	14.5	16.1	15 4	5 6	28.8	3.8
Jensen Healey	1973	2420	120.0	7.5	7.7	21.0	24.0	13 6	5 3.25	18.7	7.6
Lotus +2S 130§	1558	3306	121.0	7.7	8.5	21.0	26.1	14 0.5	5 3.5	16.8	4.2‡
MGB GT V8	3528	2408	125.3	7.7	6.2	19.8	25.7	12 9	5 0	21.2	6.6
Reliant Scimitar GTE	2994	2939	—	8.7	7.6	21.7	28.2	14 2.25	5 5	22.8	—
Triumph TR6	2498	1949	117.0	8.5	7.8	20.8	28.0	12 11	4 10.25	21.7	3.6‡

*in top †see text ‡measured with boxes not cases §4-speed version

Make: Datsun
Model: 260Z
Makers: Nissan-Datsun, Tokyo, Japan
Concessionaires: Datsun UK Ltd, Datsun House, Brighton Road, Worthing Sussex.
Price: £2430 plus £202.49 car tax plus £263.25 VAT equals £2895.74.

ROAD TEST
DATSUN 260Z 2+2

PRICE
List price, all POE .... est $5750
Price as tested .... est $6510
Price as tested includes standard equipment (AM/FM radio with electric antenna), air conditioning ($410), automatic trans ($275), dealer prep ($75)

IMPORTER
Nissan Motor Corp in USA
18501 S. Figueroa Ave
Carson, Calif. 90247

GENERAL
Curb weight, lb 2855
Test weight 3155
Weight distribution (with driver), front/rear, % 51/49
Wheelbase, in. 102.6
Track, front/rear 53.3/53.0
Length 180.9
Width 64.9
Height 50.8
Ground clearance 5.5
Overhang, front/rear 37.6/40.7
Usable trunk space, cu ft 5.9
Fuel capacity, U.S. gal. 15.8

ENGINE
Type .... sohc inline 6
Bore x stroke, mm ...... 83.0 x 79.0
Equivalent in. .... 3.27 x 3.11
Displacement, cc/cu in..... 2565/157
Compression ratio 8.8:1
Bhp @ rpm, net .... 139 @ 5200
Equivalent mph 108
Torque @ rpm, lb-ft .. 137 @ 4400
Equivalent mph 91
Carburetion .... two Hitachi-SU (1V)
Fuel requirement ...... regular, 91-oct
Emissions, gram/mile:
Hydrocarbons 3.0
Carbon Monoxide 22.0
Nitrogen Oxides 1.6

DRIVETRAIN
Transmission ...... automatic; torque converter with 3-speed planetary gearbox
Gear ratios: 3rd (1.00) 3.54:1
2nd (1.46) 5.17:1
1st (2.46) 8.71:1
1st (2.46 x 2.0) 17.42:1
Final drive ratio 3.54:1

CHASSIS & BODY
Layout .... front engine/rear drive
Body/frame .... unit steel
Brake system 10.7-in. disc front, 9.0 x 1.6-in. drum rear; vac assist
Swept area, sq in. 310
Wheels .... steel disc, 14 x 5
Tires .... Toyo, 175HR-14
Steering type .... rack & pinion
Overall ratio 18.0:1
Turning circle, ft 36.1
Front suspension: MacPherson struts, lower lateral arms, compliance struts, coil springs, tube shocks, anti-roll bar
Rear suspension: Chapman struts, lower A-arms, coil springs, tube shocks, anti-roll bar

INSTRUMENTATION
Instruments: 160-mph speedo, 8000-rpm tach, 99,999 odo, 999.9 trip odo, oil press., coolant temp, ammeter, fuel level, clock
Warning lights: brake system, choke on, rear-window heat, seatbelts, hazard, high beam directionals

ACCOMMODATION
Seating capacity, persons ...... 2+2
Seat width, f/r.... 2 x 21.0/2 x 15.0
Head room, f/r 37.0/34.0
Seat back adjustment, deg 40

MAINTENANCE
Service intervals, mi:
Oil change 3000
Filter change 6000
Chassis lube 30,000
Major tuneup 12,000
Warranty, mo/mi 12/12,000

CALCULATED DATA
Lb/bhp (test weight) 22.7
Mph/1000 rpm (3rd gear) 20.5
Engine revs/mi (60 mph) 2920
Piston travel, ft/mi 1515
R&T steering index 0.97
Brake swept area, sq in./ton 197

RELIABILITY
From R&T Owner Surveys the average number of trouble areas for all models surveyed is 12. As owners of earlier-model Datsuns reported 13 trouble areas, we expect the reliability of the Datsun 260Z 2+2 to be average.

ROAD TEST RESULTS

ACCELERATION
Time to distance, sec:
0-100 ft 4.4
0-500 ft 11.0
0-1320 ft (¼ mi) 19.2
Speed at end of ¼ mi, mph .. 76.0
Time to speed, sec:
0-30 mph 5.0
0-50 mph 9.3
0-60 mph 12.2
0-70 mph 16.3
0-80 mph 21.4
0-90 mph 29.3

SPEEDS IN GEARS
3rd gear (5400) 112
2nd (6000) 84
1st (6000) 52

FUEL ECONOMY
Normal driving, mpg 20.5
Cruising range, mi (1-gal. res.) ... 311

HANDLING
Speed on 100-ft radius, mph .. 32.6
Lateral acceleration, g 0.709
Speed through 700-ft slalom, mph 52.4

BRAKES
Minimum stopping distances, ft:
From 60 mph 173
From 80 mph 288
Control in panic stop .... good
Pedal effort for 0.5g stop, lb 35
Fade: percent increase in pedal effort to maintain 0.5g deceleration in 6 stops from 60 mph 29
Parking: hold 30% grade? .... yes
Overall brake rating .... very good

INTERIOR NOISE
All noise readings in dBA:
Idle in neutral 57
Maximum, 1st gear 84
Constant 30 mph 68
50 mph 71
70 mph 76
90 mph 82

SPEEDOMETER ERROR
30 mph indicated is actually 29.0
50 mph 50.0
60 mph 61.0
70 mph 71.0
80 mph 81.0
Odometer, 10.0 mi 10.5

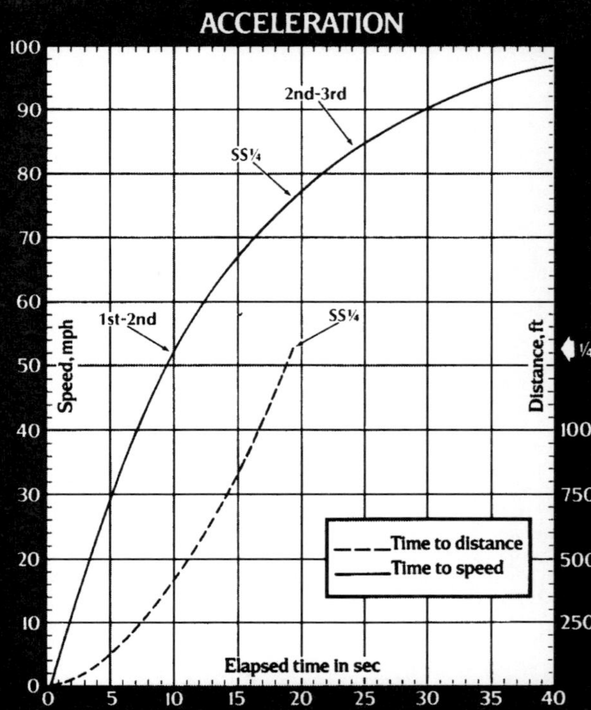

DATSUN 260Z 2+2

Smooth transition to an occasional 4-seater

PHOTOS BY JOE RUSZ

THOUGH PURISTS MIGHT cringe at the thought of a 4-seater 260Z, it certainly makes sense from a marketing standpoint. There just had to be a market for a 2+2 with the Z-car character and value for money. And because the distinctive shape of the Z seemed to lend itself to a 2+2 treatment, Datsun designers decided merely to stretch the wheelbase a foot (11.9 in. actually) without making any other major changes—an approach similar to what Jaguar took when the E-Type 2+2 was brought out many years ago. This should be no surprise, as the E-Type influenced Nissan strongly when the 240Z was still in the concept stage. The only dimensional changes of note in the new 2+2 are the increase of wheelbase (from 90.7 to 102.6 in.) and overall length (the same amount, to 180.9 in.); all sheet metal forward of the windshield posts is identical with that of the 2-seat car. Overhangs are the same, the windshields appear to be the same and the tailgates seem to be the same too. The difference in height between the two cars is also so slight as to go unnoticed; here the Z stretch is different from that of the E-Type, where the windshield height was increased by 1.5 in. in the 2+2.

Perhaps it's unfair to say that the overall appearance of the 2+2 isn't as pleasing as the original, but that was the staff's consensus. If the longer version had appeared first maybe we'd feel differently, but to our eyes the 2+2 seems too long and heavy through the middle for best harmony with the two ends. The long-nose version shown on our March 1974 cover appears better proportioned, but with the Z's already very long front end we wouldn't ask for a still longer one! Don't misunderstand us, though; the 2+2 is still an attractive car, and the transformation from a 2- to a 4-seater is in most respects so subtle that many will never notice it from the outside.

What will be noticed is the extra seating. As in most 2+2s (after all, the name implies "occasional" seating in the rear) the two front passengers fare much better than the two in the rear. Sitting squarely between the rear wheelwells and flanking the driveshaft tunnel, the rear seats are of necessity narrow, low-slung and deeply recessed to provide even minimum head room. They're most appropriate for two children, although two adults of moderate size (say up to 5 ft 8 in. tall and 150 lb) can get fairly comfortable back there if the pair up front are willing to move their seats well forward.

The rear seats have a common backrest that can be folded down to provide extra luggage space, and with it folded the driver could look forward and backward and not immediately realize he was in the 2+2. Controls, front seats and instruments are identical; the only inward differences other than the rear seating area are carpeting on the transmission tunnel (finally!) in place of the horrible quilted vinyl of the 2-seater, an extra door-opening lever accessible to rear passengers, and the neat packaging of the shoulder belts' inertia reels in panels under the push-out rear quarter windows. Two less positive notes:

there's an unsightly jumble of wires and relays under the passenger's side of the dash, and the terrible-looking vinyl upholstery on the seats (we call it "unborn alligator hide") mars an otherwise well appointed interior. Luggage space is a trade-off in the 2+2, compared to the 2-seater: 5.9 cu ft vs the smaller car's 8.5 behind the seats, but with the backrest folded an extra 9.2 cu ft below the window line.

Living with the handicap of 200 lb added weight, an optional automatic transmission and no power advantage over the regular Z, our test car couldn't begin to keep up with the manual-shift 260Z we tested earlier this year. Zero to 60 mph took 2.2 sec longer in this car, of which probably 1.2 is attributable to the automatic, and the quarter-mile took an additional 1.3 sec of which probably half is the automatic's loss. That we weren't able to get a stickshift 2+2 reflects some drivability trouble Datsun was having with it at introduction time; unable to sort out the manually shifted car, the Nissan people turned the automatic over to us instead, rationalizing that a larger proportion of 2+2 sales will likely be automatics anyway.

The automatic is a conventional 3-speed converter type, basically a Ford design and used by both Ford and Toyo Kogyo (Mazda) as well as Nissan. It's smooth and quiet in normal operation, though a bit too eager to downshift to 2nd gear at city speeds. For a sporting car it also upshifts a bit too soon: at 5000-5200 rpm on wide-open throttle, well below the engine's peak power. So we shifted it manually at 6000 rpm when doing the acceleration tests to get maximum performance. Our test car suffered from two problems that seem to plague most Z-cars: differential whine and an annoying clunk in the drivetrain every time the throttle opening is changed. They're surely nothing serious and presumably won't cause an owner mechanical problems, but they should have been eliminated long ago.

The biggest transformation in the Z character when it becomes a 2+2 is the way it drives, and there are both pluses and minuses in comparison with the 2-seater. The steering is a bit quicker on all Zs this year, so with the extra weight of the 2+2 it becomes quite heavy for parking; at speed the steering is light and precise as always. Spring rates have been increased to compensate for the weight and carrying capacity, but the 2+2's handling is normal Z-car: well balanced and neutral, with understeer at the limit and gentle oversteer obtainable by backing off the throttle in a turn. The 2+2 was slightly faster through our slalom course, indicating a bit more understeer, and slightly slower on the skidpad where its extra weight and identical tires mean less ultimate cornering power. Braking distances are about 10 ft longer from 60 and 80 mph, and all-out stops are accompanied by more front-wheel lockup than we got with the 260Z 2-seater.

The longer wheelbase has a marked effect on the ride. Freeway hop has all but disappeared, and there's even less jerking of the car over large bumps than with the short car. The wheelbase also gets some credit for the 2+2's stability at speed in a straight line: the 260Z was much improved over the 240Z but the 2+2 is better yet. A negative aspect of the longer wheelbase surfaces when the 2+2 traverses lane dividers and other sharp, small bumps, though. There's little compliance in the Z's front suspension and these cause a drumming in the body cavity. The larger cavity also lets an engine resonance at 2300-2400 rpm turn into a real racket.

Overall, the 260Z 2+2 is as practical for the family man (or woman) as the 260Z is for those who never have to think about carrying more than one passenger. It has lost little in the transformation except straight-line performance, and not much of that. The extra luggage space available could be handy for a long trip by two people, too, and at an estimated price of $5750 it represents the by-now traditional Z-car value for money in a new category of car.

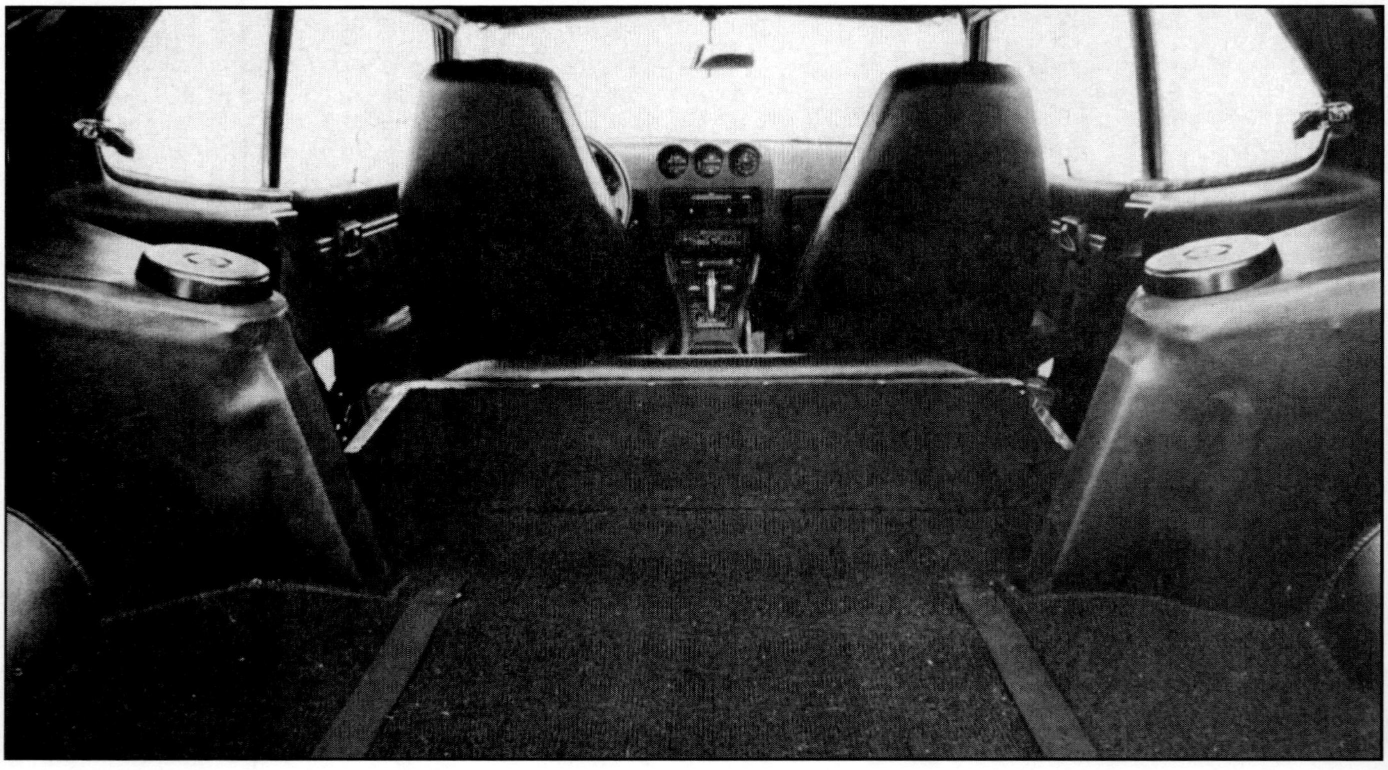

DATSUN'S LATEST Z-CARS

The 260-Z, successor to the famed 240-Z, contains numerous improvements, including a longer 2+2 four-seater version, but certain areas of driveability need further attention.

Datsun set new standards for sports-GT cars when it introduced the 240-Z four years ago. The styling was "right on" for everyone's taste, and the specifications made it an exotic car by any standard. But the really stunning thing about this four-wheel independently sprung GT was it's unheard of low price of about $3500. At the time of the Z-car's announcement, the Opel GT was the rage among sports-GT buyers, with waiting lists, dealers asking and getting hundreds more than the suggested list price etc. But once the more powerful 240-Z showed its pretty face, Opel GTs became easy to get, and they even lowered the suggested list price.

For the record it must be mentioned that few 240-Zs, if any, sold for that low figure. Datsun dealers loaded them with accessories, including "mag" wheels, that brought the selling price to over $4000, but even at that price it was still considered a bargain. Devaluation and inflation have swelled the price of the successor 260-Z to over $5000, making it not the giveaway value it once was. However, one only has to look around at what else is available and at what price to see that the latest Z-car is still very much of a bargain.

The original Z was by no means a perfect car (its crosswind stability was wanting for one thing), but it had so many virtues that owners were willing to overlook its shortcomings. With the advent of even more stringent emissions controls in the ensuing years since its introduction, however, driveability (and performance) deteriorated to the point that, by the 1973 model, people were having second thoughts about the desirability of owning one. Hence the introduction of the 260-Z.

We're happy to report that gone is the crosswind wander at high speeds that led 240-Z owners to fit nose spoilers, different shocks, etc. Also, with certain reservations that we will get to later, much of the driveability and performance of the early Z has been restored. The crosswind problem was eliminated by using stiffer front and rear spring rates (coincidental with fitting heavier 5-mph bumpers) and the addition of a rear anti-sway bar. The trim of the car was also altered by increasing the rear riding height to give the car a nose-down attitude so as to increase aerodynamic loading at speed. Undoubtedly the increased polar moment of inertia resulting from the placement of the massive bumpers at the extreme ends contributes to yaw stability, too. Our test car had air conditioning which imposes even more weight on the front end.

The restoration in performance came from stroking the sohc L-6 engine 5.7 mm, resulting in a displacement increase of 172cc or 11 cu in. The low and mid-range torque was correspondingly improved, but at the cost of smoothness at the upper end of the rpm band. In a long engine like an L-6 these few silly millimeters increase in stroke have a marked effect on dynamic balance and, consequently, the isolation of the engine mounts. The last 1000-1300 rpm before the 6800 rpm redline come very laboriously and accompanied by noise and vibration. To avoid the unpleasantness, one must refrain from going much beyond 5000 rpm in the gears.

Being in the grip of the fuel shortage and reduced speed limit of 55 mph on the highway, we confined ourself to conservative driving until it came to performance testing on the test track. Consequently, we had no idea what lay in store until we tried some standing start acceleration runs. The first three or four attempts resulted in the engine's quitting completely each time. Then, rather than dumping the clutch, we tried slipping it. This got us underway but with the engine giving a surge of power then quitting, a surge of power then quitting, causing the car to proceed slowly down the drag strip in a cantering gait. This behavior would persist as long as the foot remained on the throttle, and the car would only regain its composure when backing off then getting on it again.

Apparently, the Hitachi carburetors are sensitive to forward acceleration and stop carbureting as the fuel surges and sloshes in their bowls. Whether this phenomenon has anything to do with emissions calibrations, we have no way of knowing, but we suspect it may be. We were forced, therefore, to compromise our off-the-line starting technique by slipping the clutch to the point of getting a smooth but lackluster departure. Without fail when we got off to a rousing good start, surge set in and we had to abandon the attempt.

As we said, we encountered none of this on the street due to our conservative driving, but woe unto us if we had decided to try to get the jump on someone at a stoplight. We would have ended up in the middle of the intersection grinding away on the starter while our victorious adversary motored away and left us. Each reader will have to decide for himself just how much of a handicap this really is in view of the energy shortage. It seems to us that Datsun will certainly come up with a fix for this if they haven't already. Whether Bosch fuel injection like the 2+2 prototype (actually 2 by 2) had on it at the Tokyo auto show will be the ultimate remedy is not known. But it would certainly work and would also eliminate much of the plumber's nightmare that accompanies the present emissions controls/carburetion setup. Without this handicap, the engine feels like it's perfectly capable of propelling the car into quarter-miles in the upper 16-second bracket.

Besides salvaging most of the lost performance with the 260 engine, Datsun managed to pretty much hold the line on fuel economy, which is no mean feat. About the only penalty is the ever present tendency for the engine to "run on" or "diesel" after turning off the ignition whenever it is warm. A manual choke which is controlled from a lever on the center tunnel console was an absolute must, we found, any time the engine was cold or even cool. A big yellow-orange annunciator warning lamp won't let you forget and leave the choke on any longer than necessary. Hot starts never presented any problem so long

as we remembered to depress the throttle pedal slowly to about the half-way point while engaging the starter.

The general feel, the seating position and placement of the controls when behind the wheel of the 260-Z can hardly be improved upon. There are European style inside door pull/arm rests which in combination with the rather high center console provide armchair-like comfort. The wipers, washers, headlamps, beam control and turn signals have fingertip controls on a pair of stalks on the steering column. The gear selector mechanism has a marvelously precise, natural feel for quick crunchless shifts, ranking with the best we've encountered. The clutch pedal pressure is light, and its action is smooth and progressive, making it a perfect companion for the gear selector.

The general handling demeanor of this latest Z-car is such that, of all the sports-GT cars available today, it is among the least likely to get you into trouble. It is a very "natural" car to drive and is totally without quirks and surprises. Basic cornering behavior is on the understeering side of neutral which the driver can, at will, convert into slight oversteer at lower speeds in the lower gears with the throttle. The transition comes very gradually, allowing all the time in the world for corrective action and recovery.

Our test car had Toyo radial tires which have rather firm riding qualities below 40 mph or so. (Those experienced and well-versed in Z-car lore tell us that the Bridgestone radials that are also supplied as original equipment are somewhat better in this regard.) But at higher speeds the ride was always comfortable, even on not-so-good surfaces. Dry pavement traction, as evidenced by our braking and skid pad tests, was quite good. The limit on the skid pad, by the way, came as a result of the inside rear wheel spinning which is in turn a result of increased rear roll stiffness.

The brakes also have a good progressive feel to them that is in keeping with the rest of the controls. Stops were straight and without any tendency toward premature wheel locking.

Passenger and luggage accommodation are unchanged from earlier models, both of which are more than adequate for a sports-GT car. There is a lip at the front edge of the luggage area to prevent items from sliding forward when braking, but, like just about every other hatchback available today, it sorely needs some additional straps and tiedowns to prevent cargo from constantly shifting about. The rear hatch now has a pair of pneumatic spring supports instead of one for better support in the open position.

The Z has a pretty fair flow-through ventilation system, which we never used because of the air conditioning. There is a new multi-cylinder, wobble plate a/c compressor similar to the type made by Frigidaire that is smooth and vibrationless and of which Datsun is justifiably proud. There are a total of four vents on the dash with directable outlets, and the heater-a/c controls are easier to decipher than before. When it comes to climate control, the Z ranks with the best available on any car.

Until relatively recently, noise, both interior and exterior, seemed part and parcel of a sports-GT car, but that's outmoded. Except for the previously mentioned ruckus the engine raises at top rpm, the 260-Z is a fairly quiet car, having a noise level profile at various speeds about like that of the Corvette. Our test car had a distinctly audible final drive whine that seemed to peak at about 55 mph, the present speed limit on California highways. We also drove two other 260s, a 260-Z and a 260 2+2, on which final drive noise was barely discernable, so we assume this was a non-typically noisy gearset.

The fit, finish and interior furnishings of the new Z are in keeping with the sports-GT concept. There is, however, a group of electrical components that protrude into the interior space in the vicinity of the passenger's right leg that looks extremely out of place and is obviously added on as an afterthought. Neither Datsun engineers nor anyone else could have foreseen the mushrooming requirements for switches, relays, buzzers etc. brought on by the legally mandated interlock and warning systems at the time when

Top two photos of regular Z versus 2 + 2 show stretch between door and wheel well, also less slope in 2 + 2's rear window for more rear passenger headroom. Bottom photos show 2 + 2's concave cushions, backs that fold flat, adding about 2 more feet in length and several more cubic feet to the already generous cargo area.

the Z-car was first laid out, but it does seem that they could have come up with something more cosmetically acceptable than this.

The instrument panel has undergone some recontouring to accommodate twin vents in the middle, and the instrument array remains impressively complete and legible. A trip odometer is a useful addition in this age of mileage consciousness.

On the whole, the 260-Z's virtues far outweigh its weak points, in our opinion, and the car is a definite improvement over its immediate predecessor. If the compromises at first seem too much, pondering alternatives quickly puts things in perspective. If not the Z-car, then one must accept one or more of the following: Less space and comfort, poorer fuel economy with reduced cruising range, vastly increased purchase price.

And as if the Z weren't enough by itself, there's the 260 2+2 with four useable seats, obtained by stretching the car between the aft edge of the door and the fore edge of the rear wheel well. The rear seat backs have socket-like cavities to make the most leg room for the rear passengers. They're fine for children on longer hauls or for adults in a bind. This makes GT ownership practical for certain one-car families where it never was before.

The feel of the 2+2 is practically identical to that of the Z-car in ordinary driving, and the ride seems even better. The Z with its shorter wheelbase will out-maneuver it in tight places, but the 2+2, not being overly long compared to most cars, still rates as an agile car. With no rear passengers, the seat back folds flat forward to make an absolutely cavernous cargo space.

With this pair of new cars, the Datsun dealership remains the premier place to shop for those looking for the best in sports-GT car values. •

DATSUN 260Z

PERFORMANCE DATA

Acceleration, sec:	
0-30 mph	4.3
0-40 mph	6.0
0-50 mph	8.1
0-60 mph	10.9
0-70 mph	14.2
0-80 mph	17.2
Standing start, ¼ mile	17.34
Speed at end ¼ mile, mph	80.50
Avg accel over ¼ mile, g	0.213

Speeds in gears, mph:	
1st (6500 rpm)	38
2nd (6500 rpm)	63
3rd (6500 rpm)	102
4th (4200 rpm)	93
Engine revs at 70 mph	3200

Speedometer error:

Electric Speedometer	Car Speedometer
40 mph	42 mph
50 mph	51.5 mph
60 mph	61 mph
70 mph	71.5 mph
80 mph	81.5 mph

Brakes:	
Min stopping distance from 60 mph, ft	155
Avg deceleration rate, g	0.774

Fuel economy (on closed test course):	
Overall avg	19.8 mpg
Range on 16.0 gal tank	316 miles
Fuel required	Regular

Skid pad:	
Max speed on 100-ft rad, mph	33.0
Lateral acceleration, g	0.726

Interior noise, decibels (dBA):	
Idle	61
Max 1st gear	90
Steady 40 mph	67
50 mph	69
60 mph	74
70 mph	77

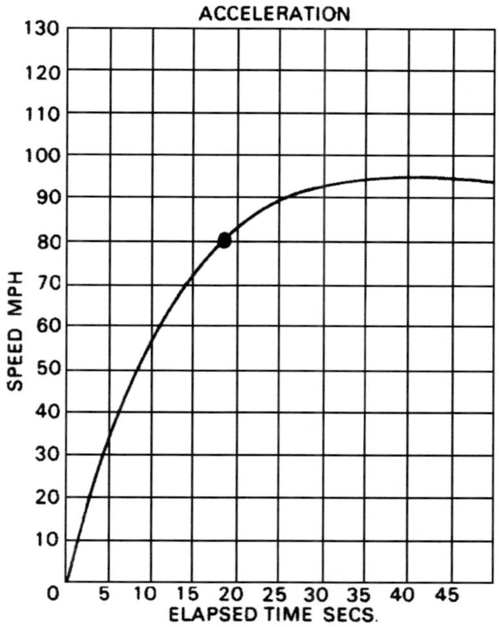

Graph Of Recorded Data Expressed In Percentage of 100 (100 = best possible rating)*

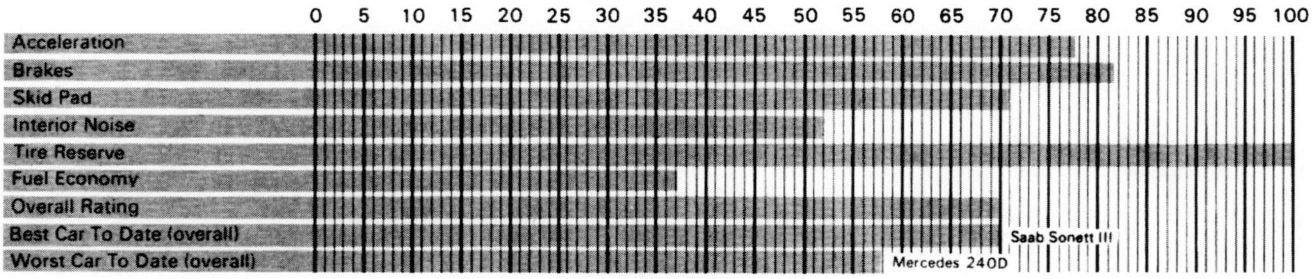

SPECIFICATIONS

Engine:	
Type	SOHC L-6
Displacement, cu in.	156.8
Displacement, cc.	2565
Bore x stroke, in.	3.27 x 3.11
Bore x stroke, mm.	83.0 x 79.0
Compression ratio	8.8:1
Hp at rpm, net.	139 at 5200
Torque at rpm, lb-ft, net	137 at 4200
Carburetion	2 1-V
Emissions, gm/mile:	
Hydrocarbons	2.7
Carbon monoxide	22.0
Nitrogen oxides	1.3

Manufacturer's guarantee and service:	
Warranty (mos/miles)	12/12,000
Oil change (mos/miles)	–/3,000
Lubrication (mos/miles)	–/30,000
Tune up (miles)	
Minor	6,000
Major	12,000

General:	
Wheelbase, ins.	90.7
Overall length, ins.	169.1
Width, ins.	64.1
Height, ins.	50.6
Front track, ins.	53.3
Rear track, ins.	53.0
Trunk capacity, cu ft	10.0
Curb weight, lbs	2645
Distribution, % front/rear	52/48
Power-to-weight ratio, lbs/hp	19.0

Prices:	
Factory list, as tested	
West Coast	$5774.00
East Coast	$5774.00

Accessories included in price:
$410.00—Air conditioning

Drive line:	
Transmission	4-spd manual
Gear ratios:	
1st	3.59:1
2nd	2.25:1
3rd	1.42:1
4th	1.00:1
Final drive ratio	3.36:1
Driving wheels	rear

Wheels	5J-14
Tires	175HR 14
Reserve load, front/rear, lb	807/807

Body and chassis:	
Body/frame construction	Unit
Brakes, front/rear	Disc/drum
Swept area, sq in.	308.00
Swept area, sq in./1000 lb	116.50
Steering	Rack-and-Pinion
Ratio	18.0:1
Turns, lock-to-lock	3.0
Turning circle, ft	31.4
Front suspension:	MacPherson struts, lateral arms, compression links, coil springs, tubular shocks, anti-sway bar
Rear suspension:	strut type, lower A-arms, coil springs, tubular shocks, anti-sway bar

Test Equipment Used: Testron Fifth Wheel, Esterline-Angus recorder, Ammco decelerometer, General Radio Sound Level Meter

* Acceleration (0-60 mph): 0% = 34.0 secs., 100% = 4.0 secs.; Brakes (60-0 mph): 0% = 220.0 ft., 100% = 140.0 ft.; Skid pad lateral accel.: 0% = 0.3 g, 100% = 0.9 g; Interior noise (70 mph): 0% = 90.0 dBA, 100% = 65.0 dBA; Tire reserve (with passengers): 0% = 0.0 lbs., 100% = 1500 lbs. or more; Fuel economy: 0% = 5 mpg, 100% = 45 mpg or more.

NEW MODEL

Datsun Fairlady Z 2 by 2

The rear seats are too small for adults on long trips.

Datsun 240 Zs and 260 Zs are primarily produced for the US and other export markets, but domestically, a 2,000cc version is sold.

Vehicles with engines displacing less than 2,000cc are considered "light cars" in Japan and are given special tax breaks.

In Japan, the Z series is sold under the name of Fairlady Z, and even this "underpowered" 2,000cc Z is capable of attaining more than ample performance on Japan's 100 kph (63 mph) limited highways.

Although the 2,400cc and 2,600cc engines still have some marketability in Japan, Nissan is hesitating to sell big-engined sports models locally because of the critical fuel shortage. So Nissan has compromised and is selling the 2+2 export model fitted with a 2,000cc engine.

This smaller engine is identical with the powerplant equipped in the two-seater Zs, a Nissan L-type 6-cylinder OHC engine, displacing 1,998cc, with two SU-type carburetors producing 125 bhp.

In order to meet Japan's emission control standards for 1974, various countermeasures have been adopted. These include the addition of a charcoal canister-type mechanism to prevent gasoline evaporation, changing the ignition timing to reduce NOx, joint idle adjustment of two carburetors at one point, along with inner venting of the carburetors. Consequently, this detoxified engine has lost a great deal of the sharp performance found in the two-seater Zs.

This L-type engine is Nissan's most mass-produced engine. From the same assembly lines and milling machines comes the 1,400cc, 1,600-cc and 1,800cc 4-cylinder engines, plus the 2,000cc, 2,400cc and 2,600cc 6-cylinder versions. With alterations in parts such as the carburetor and camshaft, Nissan produces various engines with a variety of characteristics ranging from sports to luxury cars.

Though the L-type engine might not be the best engine produced in Japan, it is a very dependable powerplant which is both economical and durable.

The L-type engine in the Z cranks out 125 bhp with its twin SU carburetors and sports-type camshaft. This sports engine is mounted only on the Z and the Skyline GTX.

The overall length of the car has been extended by 310 mm (12.2 in.) and the doors have been widened to create the 2+2 configuration. The wheelbase is now 2,605 mm (103 in.), up from 2,305 mm (91 in.) to make space for the rear seats. The roof has also been slightly altered, taking on a shape resembling other hardtops in Nissan's stable.

Although these alterations have increased the weight by 100 kg (220 lbs.), maximum top speed has remained the same at 180 kph (113 mph) and 190 kph (119 mph) for the 5-speed version.

In Japan, this 2-liter Z is sold in three versions, the Fairlady Z, the ZL and the ZL-AT. The Z is equipped only with a 4-speed manual gearbox, while the ZL uses a 5-speed manual, the top gear being an overdrive, while the ZL-AT is the automatic version of the ZL.

It was rumored that the 2+2 would probably uses semi-trailing arms on the rear suspension, but Nissan elected to keep the four-wheel MacPherson strut setup as on the two-seater Zs.

Tire size has remained the same at 6.45H-14-4PR. On the inside, minor alterations have been made, including the addition of thick protective padding to the dashboard. At the same time, all the gauges now are angled toward the driver. The radio, stereo, air vents and various switches have been placed on the center console box, which is now integrated with the instrument panel.

The steering wheel is a three-spoked wood-grained plastic type, one of several economy measures aimed at keeping the Z's price down. Like the front seat, the rear seat is a one-piece folding bucket-type seat. When the back of the rear seat is folded forward, a reasonably-sized trunk space is created. Along the inside of the door, thick pads have been heavily lined. Also, for ventilation, the 2+2 Z has a new fan and recirculation system which blows hot air towards the feet and cold air towards the face of the driver and passengers.

Beside these improvements, for safety measures Nissan has added such items as a tandem master cylinder brake system with lock-up prevention by means of a pressure control valve at the rear and hydraulically-boosted discs up front, collapsible steering column and steering lock, flexible fender mirrors and a non-glare collapsible interior mirror.

Being the largest-produced sports car in the world today, the Datsun Z series would seem to be aiming to increase its popularity with the new 2+2 model. But in Japan, even the 2,000cc version is considered large and combined with the current oil crisis, public enthusiasm will not likely rise too high.

Domestic model of the Fairlady 2 by 2 uses a 2,000cc engine.

2+2 adds up

DATSUN'S new 260Z and 260Z 2 Plus 2 were introduced to the Japanese public at the Tokyo Motor Show only six months ago and already Nissan Australia has the 260Z on the market.

The 2 Plus 2 is not yet available but don't be surprised if Nissan doesn't go overboard with the usual fanfare and hoo-hah associated with new car releases.

After all, its predecessor, the 240Z enjoyed so much success on the Australian sports car market that a hard-sell program was just not necessary.

The 240Z's good looks, crisp performance and plain charm made it what could only be described as a winner in terms of sales for the Japanese giant.

The 260Z follows on with this tradition. The new two-seater is not a new motor car, but the 2 Plus 2 260Z is.

A quick drive in one of the "old" 240Zs was almost enough to convince you that its designers had only recently gone out of the business of designing 14 ft. racing skiffs — those nippy power boats that have their driver's seats at the very rear of the boat.

The 260Z 2 Plus 2, on the other hand, with its extra 12 inches of wheelbase and additional 12 inches of overall length (tacked on between the door and rear wheel arch) is a different kettle of fish altogether.

While the 240Z managed to retain its marketing appeal throughout the whole of its almost four-year-long stay in Australia, the long wheelbase 260Z takes this appeal even further.

The car we drove this month was the first 2 Plus 2 260Z in Australia. In fact, after we were to finish the test, the car was destined to be pulled down by Nissan Australia engineers for evaluation.

It was terribly young with only a shade over 500 kilometres on the clock and we really felt that it needed a few thousand miles more before it was ready to give its best.

But, after running figures out at Calder Raceway, we were in for a surprise.

It returned a 17 seconds dead time for the standing quarter mile which is spot on what a 5000-mile old 240Z did late last year.

The 260Z, as its name implies, is a more powerful version of the 240 model. The engine has been stroked from 73.7 mm to 79 mm while the bore has remained at 83 mm. Brake horsepower is up from 151 at 5600 rpm to 162 at the same rpm and torque has been increased from 145 at 4400 rpm to 151 at the same rpm.

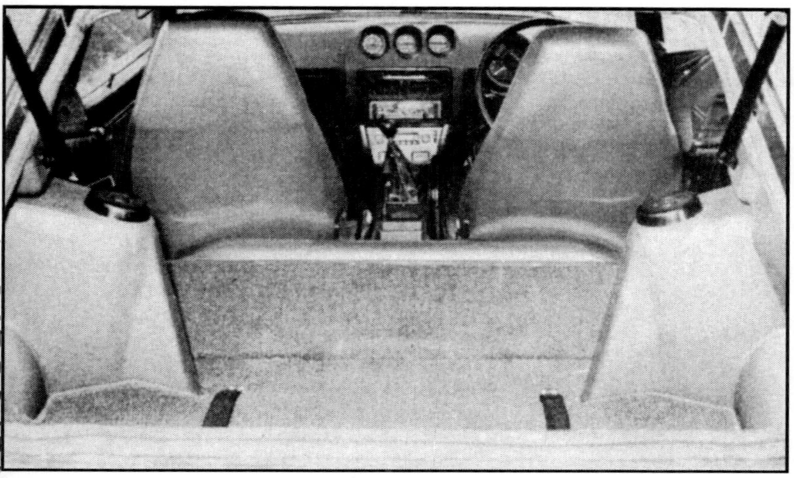

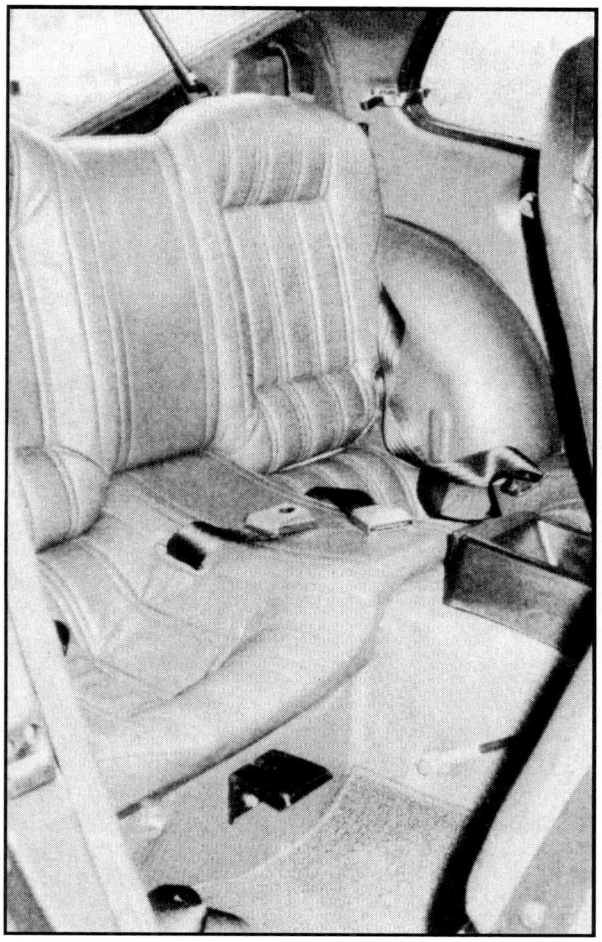

So, one would expect better times. But, combined with a taller final drive of 3.7:1 (240Z had 3.9:1) one would also expect acceleration times to suffer.

As we have said, this does not appear to be the case.

The main question to be answered with the new long wheelbase version however, is whether it is a proper four-seater. Well, all we can say about that is that it all depends on who's driving the thing. The fore and aft adjustment on the driver and front passenger seats is remarkable. It's one of the few cars we've tested in which the furthest aft adjustment is even a shade too much for even the tallest bloke in the office (6 ft. 3 in.).

Top left: 2 Plus 2 retains the Z's generous luggage space with back seat folding down.

Above left: Another 200cc takes Z engine to 2.6 litres.

Above right: The 2 Plus 2 borders on genuine four seater.

With the seat set in the proper position for a five foot six driver, the room in the rear seat was enough to take that same person. So, as a 2 Plus 2, the 260Z measures up to scratch.

The second most important improvement accompanying the 240Z-260Z transition is the extra stiffening to the suspension. Spring and shock absorber rates have been increased by about 250 per cent to change the marshmallow wallow ride and handling to a tight, firm proposition.

The improvement was even more marked when we put the 260Z through its paces. The 260Z, in 2 Plus 2 form anyway, is beautifully predictable. It's quick to respond (despite lower gearing in the steering) and it gives plenty of warning when you push it too hard through a corner.

The rest of the changes to the new model are all in the convenience-safety mould.

The doors have been modified slightly — the arm rest, door pull and panic handle have been incorporated into one unit and there is even an extra inside door handle for the rear seat passenger's convenience.

The tail door is now supported by two hydraulic stays instead of one and trim has been changed to improve the car's appearance. There's even a little touch of polished woodgrain here and there.

But gone is the wood-grained steering wheel. It has been replaced with a urethane-filled, leather covered rim which makes for better grip and control.

The heater-demister system has also been changed to the extent of better, easier to operate controls. The 240Z had controls all over the place — two on the centre console and a few others on the dash. Now everything is controlled by two sliding switches on the dash.

To sum it up succinctly, the new 260Z is a well-thought stretched version of the 240 sports; it's been refined and up-dated sensibily.

Price of the 260Z 2-plus-2 will be $5790 (manual) and $6065 (automatic). The 260Z two-seater will sell for $5250 (manual) and $5525 (auto). That's only a shade dearer than the pre-tariff prices last year.

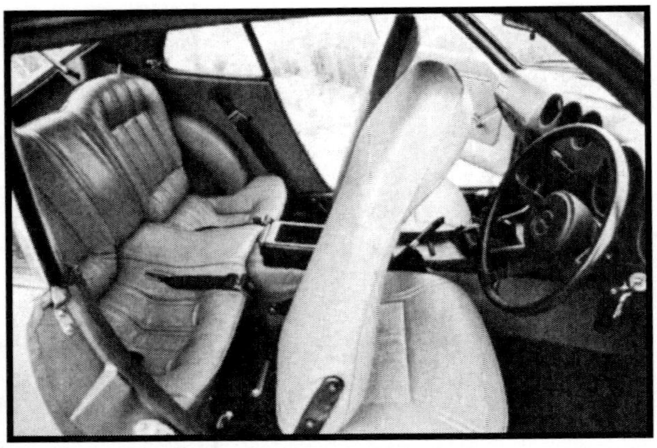

Rear seats fold down neatly to form a flat space which is almost big enough to sleep in!

For $5800 Datsun gives you...

An Even Better Z-Car!

With sports car looks, handling and performance, accommodation for four, a hatchback and folding rear seat Datsun's 260Z has provided the best of a number of worlds. It's value on wheels . . .

IT ALWAYS SEEMED a pity that the old Datsun 240Z, with its generous body proportions, was so thoroughly a two seater.

The bonnet was long, the space for the two passengers was wide and generous, but behind the seats there was no room for anything except the hatchback and "display case" boot.

But now, with a minimum of alteration to the highly successful two-seater formula, Datsun has produced a far more practical sporty car, lost nothing in performance, gained a good deal on the handling side and given the car appeal to a far wider range of buyers than it had before. And the price is still very reasonable.

Datsun's done it by adding 200 cc to the engine size, taking the two-seater's body and adding in about 200 mm of wheelbase (that's about eight inches), fitting two usable rear seats and squaring off the roofline just enough to give real people enough headroom.

On the styling side, we all agree here that the two plus two is, if anything, better looking than the two-seat car and certainly prettier than, say, a four place E-type Jag. That's not bad when you consider that the Datsun costs only $5790. There's still a two-seater version of the 260Z and that sells for $5250.

We were able to pick up a 260Z two plus two from Sydney's Capitol Motors for an impressions drive. The car had only something like 400 km on the odometer, so it couldn't be used hard, but we nevertheless learned very smartly that Datsun had increased the appeal of an already good car with the latest developments.

The engine is now bored to 2565 cc but it's the

An Even Better Z-Car!

same L-type SOHC six that Datsun has been using for years — the one that surprises you with its size when you open the bonnet. It seems just about as long as the big old 4-odd litre thing they put in the 4-wd Datsun Patrol!

The donk is superbly accessible and everything is conventionally and neatly laid out under the bonnet.

The engine feels little different from the old 2.4-litre mill. It's still smooth, fuss-free and pulls quietly and quickly from very low revs. The extra 10 bhp is enough to offset the extra weight of the two plus two body, so performance is little changed. Probably the two-seat 260Z is a little quicker than the 240, but we doubt if there's going to be a REAL difference. That means a top speed of 195 km/h (121 mph) and standing quarter-mile times in the mid-16s.

The 260 engine, because it feels so like the 240, will doubtless run out of puff after about five and a half thousand revs, which is not a very sporty way for it to behave.

It's a damn shame that the cam isn't a bit more sporting because the red sector doesn't start till seven grand and these engines really *can* take those revs.

Incidentally, did you see the Tokyo Show story in WHEELS in which Japanese correspondent Jack Yamaguchi was speculating that there might be an experimental turbocharged 260Z around? The car shown at Tokyo had a mysterious fourth pedal (to bring a turbocharger into action?) and the Datsun people stubbornly refused to open the bonnet.

The production 260Z gearbox is the dependable five-speeder with the same ratios as the 240Z. Final drive is unchanged at 3.9. As a result, the 260Z feels very high-geared and would be better off in most circumstances with a shorter diff ratio.

There's been a real improvement in the handling of the 260Z. The longer wheelbase does nothing but benefit the car, making it close to equally balanced front and rear.

Handling initially is very mild understeer, but when you really start to pile on the pace, the 260Z has a mild, predictable brand of oversteer.

You can come howling into a medium fast corner, lift off the power for just a moment, then clamp it on again just before the apex and suddenly the car's drifting at a slight but noticeable angle to the road. Backing off will tighten the nose into the curve and this is a far better course than fiddling with the steering wheel rim. It's a very neat cornering attitude and makes your exit from bends very fast indeed.

Extreme provocation can get the tail out eventually, but we feel that ordinary, mistake-free fast driving will never hang it sufficiently out of line to require conscious correction on bitumen. Truly, the handling is quite beautiful.

It's a pity we can't say the same thing for the steering. It has all the 240Z's vagueness at the straight-ahead, and that's a problem in a car capable of running above the ton for long periods and which also has a tendency to lighten at the front end as the speeds rise.

You find yourself spearing along straight roads without the comfort and confidence that the power and comfort will allow, because you're worried that a cross-wind gust will blow you into the other man's lane.

We drove a spoilered 240Z not long ago and found

Cockpit and controls are pretty well unchanged except for details like steering wheel boss and gear lever knob.

Even with rear seat in use, luggage space is quite good. Retaining straps are a very handy feature.

that the front end lightness was greatly reduced by the "chin" spoiler. We'd recommend that to any 240Z/260Z buyer.

It's a good thing that the Z can be steered so easily on the throttle because it's not much fun making fine alterations to the steering in 100 mph sweepers when you have to move from one side to the other of the two or three inches of free-play to do it.

On the other hand we do like the high gearing of the steering for round-town work. It's fairly light and the directness is damn handy. It's also quite an awe-inspiring sight in your first few miles of driving to see that long bulbous nose respond markedly to quite small hand movements of the steering wheel.

The long wheelbase does a whole lot for the 260Z two plus two's ride, too. Maybe it's because the last 240Z we drove had rather tired shock absorbers, but this new car rode very much better than we remember. There's still the fore/aft movement on

acceleration and braking that's always been a legacy of the car's strut-type independent rear end, but in the 260Z it's barely noticeable. Bumps and ruts were dealt with more quietly than the two-seater could do it and bump absorption seemed more . . . er, complete.

And another thing. The 260Z is quieter than its predecessors. Our test car had an air leak at the top of the passenger's wind-up window, but other than that there was little wind noise at any speed (provided the windows were wound up). The engine was very quiet — even at fairly high revs.

The 260Z has a cruising ability that can't be matched except by cars with considerably bigger engines. You have to keep reminding yourself that this well-equipped torquey road runner with its very high gearing really does only have about 2½ litres up front.

The inclusion of the rear seat — which really can be occupied by reasonably sized adults for round-town work — has not encroached on the generous driver accommodation. You seem to be sitting in a 240Z (apart from detail cockpit changes) if you keep your eyes front.

The bootspace is either bigger or smaller than it used to be, depending on whether or not you have the rear seat up or down. In the down position, there's nearly enough space to sleep in the car, while with it up there's still enough room for a fair amount of soft baggage. It can't go very high, though, because it's likely to blot out your rearview.

The best way to describe the Datsun 260Z's equipment is that it's ALL THERE. The only things we can think of (short of bobble fringe or whoopee locking pins in the bonnet) are air-conditioning and a tape deck — and they're optional anyway.

This Datsun's imported and we liked its finish very much. Cockpit furniture was well assembled and looked durable. Paintwork was good and tough. We did notice that there was a bit of a squeak as though something was flexing when we drove over diagonal gutters once or twice.

So that's the 260Z two-plus-two. We're betting that this car will outsell the two-seater because of its practicality. The $540 extra you pay for the rear seats is peanuts when you consider the advantages.

But the Datsun's not radically altered — there's no reason why it should be because the formula has been so successful. It's just a shame that the few faults in the 240Z are still there.

Faults or not, if you're thinking of a Datsun two-seater you'd better get in line right now. They're going to sell like mad. *

Even though you can now get four people in the cockpit, the car's lines aren't impaired. Some say the car has become more attractive.

DRIVING ROAD TEST

Datsun 260Z

Photos by John Plow

The Datsun 240Z caused a sensation in the market place when it was introduced in 1970. And why shouldn't it have. There wasn't a better buy anywhere. For just a shade over $4000 you could get great looks, a potent six cylinder engine, independent suspension all around, radial tires, the practicality of a hatchback with large carpeted storage space and good gas mileage to boot. It was in effect the poor man's Corvette or E-type. It had sex appeal.

Since then, things haven't changed much. Well, except for one important item — the price. In 1972 it was listed as $4580, in '73 it sold for $4770 and this year it's jumped to a staggering $6195. Now that amounts to a 30 percent price increase in one year and though the car retains all the features that made it a sensation in 1970, their impact is diluted considerably by the price tag. What was once a bargain is now a rather expensive proposition. Granted everyone's prices have been climbing at an alarming rate, but we question whether the person who could afford a 240Z in 1970 can afford the 260Z in '75.

Obviously the biggest change in the car from last year to this, is the name

Comfortable buckets and excellent design of major controls and instruments underline the 'grand touring' concept

change indicating an increase in engine size. Last year's 2393 cc engine with a bore and stroke of 83mm and 73.7 mm respectively, has been enlarged by increasing the stroke to 79mm. Displacement is now 2565 cc's or 157 cu. in. Power is 139 horesepower at 5200 rpm — which at first appears to be almost the same as last year's 130 hp. However the '74 figure is expressed in terms of net horsepower. The gross rating for the '74 model, which would be comparable to the '73 is 162 hp. So you can see, there has been an increase in power.

Exterior sheetmetal has been left more or less the same, with the exception of the 260Z emblems and the larger, mandatory bumpers. Inside a few, and welcome, modifications have been carried out. Gone are the tacky-looking steering wheel and shift knob made of cheap plastic. Now instead of imitation wood, the customer gets a leather wrapped wheel and shift knob - eminantly more practical and certainly more attractive.

In the suspension department a rear anti-sway bar has been added as part of the standard equipment and this has helped the handling somewhat.

There's no denying that one of the 240Z's strong features has been the inordinate amount of legroom afforded the driver and his passenger. Traditionally, two-seat sports cars have been a trifle uncomfortable as hip and legroom have been a bit on the stingy side. With the Datsun 260Z however, there's legroom for those over six foot. Large comfortable bucket seats, adjustable for rake as well as front to rear positioning help make the Datsun sports car a truly comfortable Grand Touring automobile. And in keeping with the GT definition, the 260Z comes with a huge cargo area for all manner of suitcases and luggage. Access to this area is via the large hatchback at the rear or through the twin bucket seats. Straps are also provided along the flat, carpeted area for tying down objects that might roll around while the car is on the go.

The dash is certainly attractive and in step with the car's performance in that there's no scarcity of instruments. Twin dials directly in front of the driver give the speed and engine revolutions, the tach being redlined at 6500 rpm, though the peak power is obtained at 5200 rpm. Towards the center of the dash are three smaller dials housing the water temperature and oil pressure qauges, the ammeter and fuel gauge and finally the clock. Flowing from the center of the dash is a broad console area in which are located the air vents, heater and air controls as well as the standard AM/FM radio. The last item also employs an automatic antenna that extends the moment the radio is switched on. As the console levels out to the horizontal, one finds the manual choke lever, the four speed shift lever and the hand brake. At the far end of the console, between the seatbacks is a box-like depression for placing loose articles such as cigarettes so they won't roll around when driving. The seat belts are easy enough to use being located by the outside shoulder and requiring little more than a constant pull across the chest and buckling into the clasp located between the seat base and console. The door handle on the other hand is a bit awkward as it's located far down at the base of the door. The space below the dash on the passenger side is marred by an ugly arrangement of wires and heater boxes. At first we thought that a covering panel had been left off, but closer inspection revealed that this was the normal set up.

The first thing we noticed when starting the car was a loud ticking noise eminating from the right side of the car just behind the passenger's ear. Though the 260Z comes standard with a mechanical fuel pump, this extremely loud ticking sounded for all the world like an electrical pump; however it didn't make a noise until the engine was firing, underlining the fact that it was indeed a mechanical pump. We've never heard of anyone complaining of this before so it may well be a fault common to the test car.

As the car moves through the gears, it becomes obvious that the 260Z is a quick automobile. The power is definitely there and starts to come on

Horsepower has been increased to 162 gross

strong after 4000 rpm. Beyond 4000 rpm the engine gets loud and sounds almost strained though we're certain that it isn't. At 75 mph the engine is turning over at a liesurely 3500 rpm.

Above all, the Datsun 260Z is still a fun car and an exhilarating performer. It's a little slower than it once was, qetting to 60 mph now in 9.9 seconds rather than the 8.7 of previous years and top speed is 'now set at 115 mph versue 120+ mph. But the combination of strong six cylinder engine, good disc brakes up front and a positive four speed transmission, allows the car to be driven smartly in most situations. When pressed hard, there's enough power to get the rear end out in an envigorating slide while the steering is quick enough to catch it and retain driver control. Gasoline mileage is eighteen to twenty mpg depending upon driving habits which isn't bad these days considering the performance the car provides. Like everything else, it eventually boils down to price. The car has a lot to offer, and will no doubt continue to attract that special market which it serves, better than any other model on the market.

Practical hatchback opens onto useful luggage area

The 260Z still provides the enthusiastic driver with plenty of excitement

DRIVING ROAD TEST

technical data

DATSUN 260Z

SPECIFICATIONS

ENGINE	
Location	front
No. of cylinders	six, in-line
Valve operation	single overhead camshaft
Compression ratio	8.8:1
Carburetion	two, two-barrels
Bore	3.27 ins. (83 mm)
Stroke	3.11 ins. (79 mm)
Displacement	156.5 cu. ins. (2565 cc)
Power	139 hp @ 5200 rpm
Torque	137 lb. ft. @ 4400 rpm

TRANSMISSION	
No. of forward speeds	four
Gear ratios	1st – 3.592; 2nd – 2.246; 3rd – 1.415; 4th – 1.00
Final drive	3.36

BRAKES	
Front	10.7 in. dia. discs)
Rear	9.0 in. dia. drum) power assisted

DIMENSIONS	
Wheelbase	90.7 ins.
Track	53.3 ins. front; 53.0 ins. rear
Width	64.1 ins.
Height	50.6 ins.
Weight as tested	2710 lbs. (50.8% front; 49.2% rear)
Fuel capacity	13.2 gals.
Tires	175HR x 14, radials

STEERING	
Type	rack and pinion
Turning circle	31.4 ft.
Turns lock to lock	3.1

SUSPENSION	
Front	MacPherson strut, coil springs, anti-sway bar tubular shock absorbers
Rear	independent, lower A arms, coil springs, tubular shock absorbers, anti-sway bar

CALCULATED DATA

Braking distances in feet: average of 3 stops

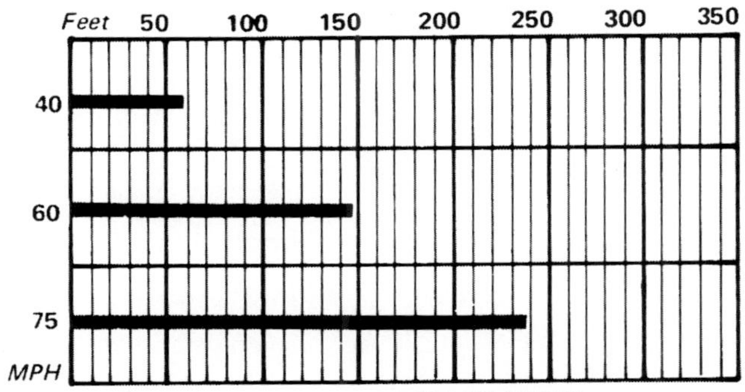

Acceleration in seconds

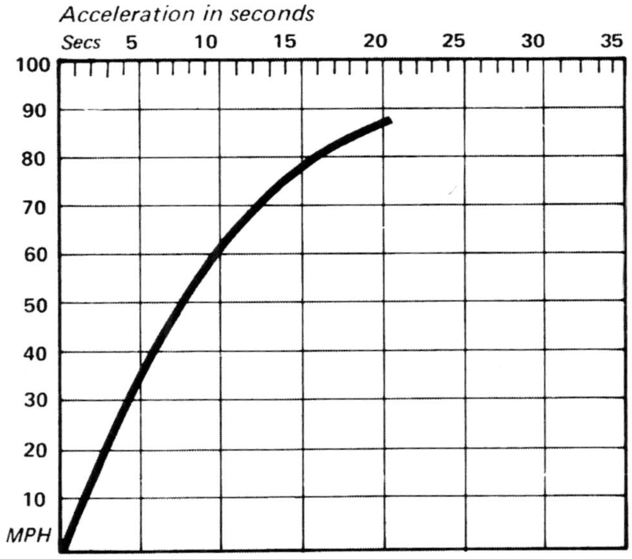

BRAKING		ACCELERATION	
75-0	238 ft.	0-40	6.0 sec.
60-0	149 ft.	0-60	9.9 sec.
40-0	59 ft.	0-80	16.1 sec.

Quarter mile 17.3 sec./83 mph

Shell

Skid pad	.69g
Fuel consumption	18-20 mpg (Shell regular)

SUGGESTED RETAIL PRICE $6195.00

AUTO TEST

Datsun 260Z 2+2

2,565 c.c.

Stretched version of 260Z two-seater provides reasonable accommodation for two in rear without loss of car's attractive lines. Engine noisy and harsh at high revs, yet lacking in punch at bottom end. Axle noisy at medium speeds. Well equipped, but expensive by comparison with European rivals

From the front, the 2+2 configuration is not evident, but from the side, the larger rear quarterlight and square trailing edge of the roof are identification points

FOLLOWING its début at the 1969 Tokyo Motor Show, Datsun's 240Z won instant acclaim as the best-looking car to come from Japan. Adding to the model's appeal was the fact that its performance and handling were just as good as its looks. Nor did it end there; as the months went by, it became increasingly clear that ruggedness was another of the car's many attributes. So much so, that in the spring of 1971, 240Zs won premier and team awards in the tough East African Safari rally. Proving that this was no fluke, a second outright win was achieved in 1973 – this in addition to numerous successes in European events.

When road-tested by *Autocar* at the time of its introduction to the UK (May 1971), the 240Z fully lived up to its reputation. Maximum speed was an impressive 125 mph, whilst acceleration times to 60 and 100 mph were 8·0 and 25·6sec respectively.

So much for the 240Z. In the autumn of 1973 (January 1974 in the UK), it was superseded by the 260Z. Virtually unchanged in appearance, the later model is powered by a long-stroke version of what basically is a 240Z engine. Also changed are the gearbox and final-drive ratios, whilst slightly wider rims now carry fat, low-profile tyres.

Inevitably, the lack of rear passenger accommodation had limited the appeal of the 240Z and 260Z. In November 1973 (April 1974 in the UK), Datsun put this to rights by introducing a supplementary model known as the 260Z 2+2. Essentially a 260Z stretched by some 13in., this new model has the same mechanical specification as its two-seater counterpart. The ability to carry two more passengers incurs a cost penalty of almost £600, tax-paid prices currently being £2,843 and £3,435.

Performance

Before taking a look at the model's performance, it may be as well to note the major differences between 240Z and 260Z engines. The most significant change has been the lengthening of the stroke from 73·7 to 77 mm, resulting in a displacement increase of 172 c.c. (from 2,393 c.c. to 2,565 c.c.). Compression ratio of the larger engine is 8·3-to-1, enabling it to operate on 94 octane (RM) fuel; with its 9·0-to-1 compression ratio, the 240Z called for fuel having a minimum octane rating of 98 (RM).

Although intended as anti-pollution measures, these changes have resulted in useful improvements in both power and torque. Peak power now is 150 (DIN) at 5,400 rpm, compared with the former figure of 130 (DIN) at 5,600 rpm. No directly comparable torque figures are available, but some indication is given by the fact that the current engine's peak output according to the DIN (nett) standard is higher than the smaller unit's SAE (gross) figure.

To compensate for the fact that the larger engine develops its peak power at low revs, overall gearing has been raised. To this end, the axle ratio has been changed from 3·9 to 3·7. Offsetting this to some extent is the fact that the ratio of the indirect top has been changed from 0·85 to 0·864. Change of tyre equipment has had negligible effect. In simple terms, the overall result has been to change the gearing from 21·6 to 22·6 mph/1,000 rpm.

Frontal area of the 2+2 is much the same as that of the two-seater. Even so, notwith-

standing the claimed power increase and the modified gearing, the top speed of 120 mph is 5 mph down on that of the 240Z. At this pace, engine speed is 5,300 rpm – just 100 rpm below the peak of the curve.

In fourth (direct), top speed is 115 mph, equivalent to 5,900 rpm. Again, this is down in comparison with the 240Z, which achieved a best of 118 mph and 6,440 rpm. This adds strength to our view that the later unit's power curve falls pretty steeply beyond the peak.

As in the 240Z, the unusually accurate tachometer is yellow-lined at 6,500 rpm and red-lined at 7,000 rpm. However, the current unit is decidedly unwilling to rev beyond 6,800 rpm at which speed it gives every indication of running into valve bounce problems. Not that this need be regarded as a shortcoming, for there seldom is anything to be gained by exceeding 5,500 rpm.

In terms of high-speed cruising ability, the model has nothing to fear. On German *autobahnen*, an indicated 110 mph (a true 106 mph) was held with the utmost ease whenever traffic conditions allowed. At such speeds, the level of noise inside the car is by no means objectionable. Indeed, the model's long-legged feel constitutes a major attraction. Incidentally, speedometer error is negligible below 90 mph.

In addition to the changes to the axle and fifth-gear ratios, first has been slightly raised (2·906 instead of 2·96) and second slightly lowered (1·902 instead of 1·86). This, together with a kerb-weight penalty of 3·1cwt (in comparison with the 240Z results in a fairly leisurely step-off. From rest, 30 mph comes up in 3·5sec, 60 mph in 9·9sec and 100 mph in 31·1sec. Equivalent times for the 240Z are 3·0, 8·0 and 25·6sec.

As always, what really matters is how the model compares with equivalent cars of rival makes. As a look at the comparison table will confirm, there is little to choose in terms of maximum speed. Nevertheless, it should not be overlooked that the Capri 3000 GT (a car costing £1,365 less) does have a 2 mph advantage. By the same token, we cannot help feeling that the test model was somewhat down on power.

Moving on to the 0–60 mph and standing quarter-mile comparisons, the Datsun is at the bottom of the league. However, it compensates by taking second place to the BMW 2002 Tii in the economy table.

The Datsun engine's comparatively poor showing at high speeds might tempt one to think that it is endowed with extraordinary flexibility at low speeds. Unfortunately, such is not the case Whilst the unit is utterly smooth and tractable, it is noticeably lacking in punch. This is well illustrated by comparing 50–70 mph times in top. The 260Z takes 11·9sec – a full 4·4sec longer than the Capri 3000 GT. True, the latter is a little lighter (22·5cwt, compared with 23·5cwt) and a mite lower geared (21·7 mph, compared with 22·6 mph per 1,000 rpm). Nevertheless, it is clear that the engine is somewhat lacking in this respect.

As already mentioned, economy is good. Over the total test distance of 2,800 miles, the model averaged 23·9 mpg. At one stage, it achieved no less than 26·5 mpg over a distance of 370 miles, but this was at somewhat lower speeds than a typical owner could be expected to drive. At the other end of the scale, the 200-mile period embracing testing at MIRA yielded 10·9 mpg – a creditable enough figure under the circumstances. All-in-all, we have no hesitation in quoting 25 mpg as a typical figure.

Unlike rival models from European factories, the Datsun calls for only economy-grade (three-star rating) fuel. Tank capacity is around average at 13·2gal giving a safe range in excess of 250 miles. So far as could be ascertained, the fuel gauge under-read to the tune of 3gal at the lower end of the scale.

The fuel filler cap lives under a locked flap on the right-hand rear quarter. It accepts full pump delivery right to the top. Thoughtful points are the provision of a security chain for the cap and a plastic "apron" to protect the paintwork.

No measurable quantity of oil was used during the test. Small wonder, therefore, that the engine remained spotlessly clean. Typically Datsun, access to the dipstick and filler cap could hardly be bettered.

Engine and driveline

With the console-mounted choke lever fully "out", the engine starts promptly from cold. Returning the choke to a fast-idle setting allows the car to be driven away without any sign of temperament. Even at this stage, the unit emits little mechanical noise. In contrast, the large, light-bladed fan makes quite a roar – this in spite of its viscous drive. To be fair, the fan noise is evident more to bystanders than to the occupants of the car itself. In any case, the criticism does not apply at normal idling speeds (possible within half-a-mile of starting from cold). Neither is there objectionable fan noise when the car is driven hard.

Hot starting is less certain, the engine sometimes requiring considerable turning before it will fire. On two occasions (both in warm weather) we also experienced slight surging when driving away after a period of idling. Both symptoms point to mild percolation or vapour-locking problems.

Almost the first thing one notices about the Datsun is the jerkiness of the throttle linkage at small openings. This lack of progression makes the car somewhat difficult to drive smoothly in traffic, although it is something one becomes acclimatized to after a period.

Clutch action is light (28lb) and smooth, although the pedal fulcrum developed a creak during the course of the test. This manifested itself only when the car's interior was cold.

The combined effects of high gearing, good traction and appreciable all-up weight gave the clutch a hard time during performance testing. Any attempt to break traction on get-away resulted in appreciable power fade. Even so, the unit proved equal to the task of restarting the car on the 1-in-3 test hill. The parking brake, too, just managed this check.

Five-speed manual transmission is standard on all cars still in the UK. The lower four ratios are arranged in conventional H-pattern, with the fifth and reverse placed on the right. There is the merest trace of spring loading away from the first-second plane, but there is very much stronger loading away from fifth and reverse. By-and-large, the mechanism works very well, although one or two of our testers found fifth a little awkward at times.

One of the difficulties associated with having a spring final-drive unit (a feature of all independent and de Dion layouts) is that of insulating gear noise from the car's interior. Here, Datsun have achieved only partial success. Above 50 mph, there is considerable whine under drive conditions. It peaks at 60–65 mph, then diminishes to be lost in the generally higher noise levels which prevail farther up the range.

Ride, handling and brakes

Although fairly firm at low speeds, the suspension (MacPherson type at all four corners) provides a good ride over most surfaces. Very occasionally, long undulations can generate a degree of float at the rear end, but this is never troublesome.

Potholes and the like cause a fair amount of bump-thumping. Likewise, cobbled or rippled surfaces can result in considerable roar. Nevertheless, the noise level in general is well within acceptable limits for this type of car.

With just 2·9 turns of the wheel between locks, the rack-and-pinion steering mechanism feels high-geared. This gives a feeling of precision and tautness, but results in considerable heaviness at parking speeds and when cornering hard. Indeed, the sheer physical effort

Right: The handsome underbonnet appearance is unchanged. Access to items requiring routine maintenance is good. Two flaps provide access to the battery and windscreen washer bottle whose flap can be seen in the open position

AUTO TEST

Datsun 260Z 2+2

involved can be the limiting factor when hurling the car along a winding road. On the credit side, only at low speeds on very rough roads is there any appreciable kick-back.

A feature of the 260Z is its beard-type spoiler, made of a resilient plastics material. Another, more rigid spoiler is mounted across the back of the bootlid. It may well be that these measures contribute to the model's reassuring stability at very high speeds.

In all normal cornering situations, the car feels reassuringly stable. The harder it is pushed, the more it understeers. Eventually, however, its balance changes to an oversteering condition – a change which is accentuated should the throttle be suddenly closed. Although

Comparisons

MAXIMUM SPEED MPH

Ford Capri 3000 GT	(£2,064)	122
Reliant Scimitar GTE	(£3,036)	121
Alfa Romeo 2000 GTV	(£2,939)	120
Datsun 260Z 2+2	**(£3,429)**	**120**
BMW 2002 Tii	(£3,135)	116

0–60 MPH, SEC

BMW 2002 Tii	8·3
Ford Capri 3000 GT	8·3
Reliant Scimitar GTE	8·9
Alfa Romeo 2000 GTV	9·2
Datsun 260Z 2+2	**9·9**

STANDING ¼-MILE, SEC

BMW 2002 Tii	16·4
Alfa Romeo 2000 GTV	16·4
Ford Capri 3000 GT	16·6
Reliant Scimitar GTE	16·9
Datsun 260Z 2+2	**17·3**

OVERALL MPG

BMW 2002 Tii	25·4
Datsun 260Z 2+2	**23·9**
Alfa Romeo 2000 GTV	21·1
Reliant Scimitar GTE	20·8
Ford Capri 3000 GT	20·7

Performance

ACCELERATION

True speed mph	Time in Secs	Car Speedo mph
30	3·5	31
40	5·2	41
50	7·3	50
60	9·9	60
70	13·5	70
80	17·6	81
90	23·4	93
100	31·1	104
110	46·1	114
120	—	124

Standing ¼-mile
17·3 sec 79 mph

Standing kilometre
32·0 sec 101 mph

Mileage recorder:
(0·4 per cent under-reading)

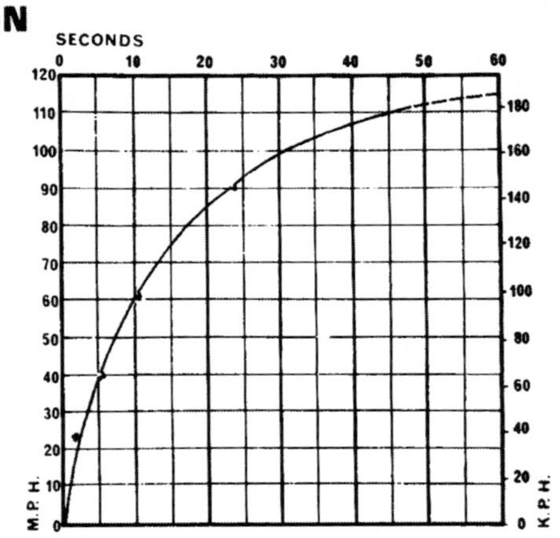

GEAR RATIOS AND TIME IN SEC

mph	Top (3·20)	4th (3·70)	3rd (4·84)	2nd (7·04)
10–30	—	—	6·6	4·6
20–40	10·9	8·8	6·3	4·3
30–50	10·7	8·7	6·2	4·2
40–60	11·4	7·9	6·4	4·8
50–70	11·9	9·1	6·7	7·3
60–80	12·4	9·8	7·3	—
70–90	14·1	11·3	9·8	—
80–100	18·6	13·8	19·1	—
90–110	—	22·7	—	—

GEARING
(with 195/70–14in. tyres)

Top	22·6 mph per 1,000 rpm
4th	19·5 mph per 1,000 rpm
3rd	14·9 mph per 1,000 rpm
2nd	10·2 mph per 1,000 rpm
1st	6·7 mph per 1,000 rpm

MAXIMUM SPEEDS

Gear	mph	kph	rpm
Top (mean)	120	193	5,300
(best)	121	195	5,350
4th	115	185	5,900
3rd	101	163	6,800
2nd	69	111	6,800
1st	46	74	6,800

BRAKES

FADE (from 70 mph in neutral)
Pedal load for 0·5g stops in lb

1	30–25	6	30–25
2	30–25	7	30–25
3	30–25	8	30–25
4	30–25	9	35–30
5	30–25	10	30

RESPONSE (from 30 mph in neutral)

Load	g	Distance
20lb	0·33	91ft
40lb	0·64	47ft
60lb	0·92–0·97	32ft
80lb	1·00–1·10	29ft
120lb	1·15	26ft
Handbrake	0·39	77ft

Max. gradient 1 in 3

CLUTCH
Pedal 28lb and 5·9in.

Consumption

FUEL
(At constant speed-mpg)

30 mph	43·5
40 mph	38·5
50 mph	34·5
60 mph	31·2
70 mph	27·8
80 mph	24·1
90 mph	19·5
100 mph	14·5

Typical mpg 25 (11·3 litres/100km)
Calculated (DIN) mpg 25·3 (11·2 litres/100km)
Overall mpg 23·9 (11·8 litres/100km)
Grade of fuel Economy, 3-star (min. 94RM)

OIL
Consumption (SAE 10W/40) Negligible

TEST CONDITIONS:
Weather: cloudy
Wind: 11–16 mph
Temperature: 7 deg C (45 deg F)
Barometer: 29·78in. Hg
Humidity: 80 per cent
Surface: Dry concrete and asphalt
Test distance: 2,800 miles

Figures taken by our own staff at the Motor Industry Research Association proving ground at Nuneaton and on the Continent

Dimensions

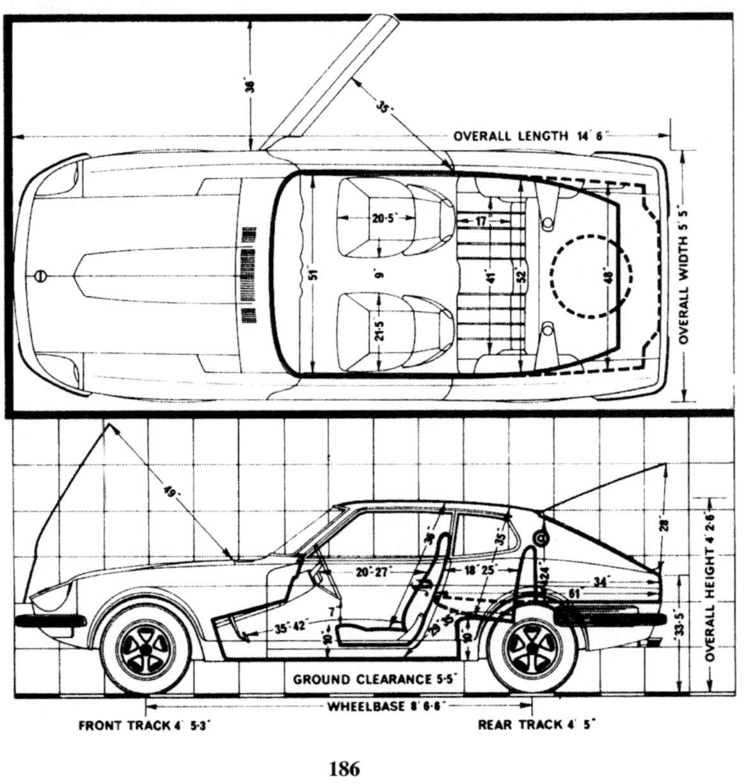

STANDARD GARAGE
16ft×8ft 6in.

TURNING CIRCLES
Between kerbs
L, 36ft 5in.; R, 34ft 8in.
Between walls
L, 38ft 0in.; R, 36ft 3in.
Steering wheel turns, lock to lock 2·9.

WEIGHT:
Kerb weight 23·5cwt (2,632lb–1,195kg) (with oil, water and half full fuel tank).
Distribution, per cent F, 51·1; R, 48·9.
Laden as tested: 27·3cwt (3,056lb–1,387kg)

these characteristics are correct in essence, the transition takes place rather more abruptly than it should.

Braking behaviour is excellent, the test car achieving one of the highest deceleration rates we have ever observed on a road-going car (1·15g). The fact that this calls for a pedal effort of 120lb is no ground for criticism; indeed, this may well be regarded as a safety feature in that it minimises the risk of inadvertent wheel-locking. Such would not be the case were a high effort be required for normal check purposes. It so happens that 60lb suffices for a mean deceleration of 0·95g.

Some of the credit for this excellent balance must go to the inertia-type pressure-regulating valve which is incorporated in the hydraulic line to the rear (there being separate hydraulic systems for front and rear). No low-fluid warning device is fitted, but there is a system to warn of a pressure differential between front and rear systems. The warning lamp itself serves also as a parking brake reminder.

From the fade viewpoint, the brakes perform equally well. In fact, the Datsun has the rare distinction of requiring precisely the same pedal effort at the commencement of the first stop and the termination of the last. The only criticism which can be levelled concerns the considerable roughness evident from the seventh stop onwards. A similar trait was noted when braking hard at the end of the through-the-gears acceleration runs.

Specification

Datsun 260Z 2+2

FRONT ENGINE, REAR-WHEEL DRIVE

ENGINE

Cylinders	6, in line
Main bearings	7
Cooling system	Water, pump, viscous-coupled fan and thermostat
Bore	83·0mm (3·27in.)
Stroke	79·0mm (3·11in.)
Displacement	2,565 c.c. (156·6 cu. in.)
Valve gear	Single overhead camshaft, chain-driven
Compression ratio	8·3 to 1. Min. octane rating: 94 RM
Carburettors	2 Hitachi HMB 46WI
Fuel pump	Nikki mechanical
Oil filter	Full-flow, replaceable cartridge type
Max. power	150 bhp (DIN) at 5,400 rpm
Max. torque	158 lb. ft. (DIN) at 4,400 rpm

TRANSMISSION

Clutch	Diaphragm-spring, mechanical operation, 8·87in. dia.
Gearbox	Five-speed, all-synchromesh
Gear ratios	Top 0·864
	Fourth 1·0
	Third 1·308
	Second 1·902
	First 2·906
	Reverse 3·382
Final drive	Hypoid bevel, 3·70-to-1
Mph at 1,000 rpm in top gear	22·6

CHASSIS AND BODY

Construction	Integral, with steel body

SUSPENSION

Front	Independent; MacPherson struts, lower transverse and drag links, coil springs, telescopic dampers, anti-roll bar
Rear	Independent; MacPherson struts, lower wishbones, coil springs, telescopic dampers

STEERING

Type	Rack and pinion
Wheel dia.	14·8in.

BRAKES

Type	Disc front, drum rear, dual-circuit, pressure-regulating valve in rear line
Servo	Vacuum type
Dimensions	F 10·67in. dia.
	R 9·0in. dia. 1·57in. wide shoes
Swept area	F 305 sq. in., R 88·7 sq. in.
	Total 393·7 sq. in. (288 sq. in./ton laden)

WHEELS

Type	Pressed steel disc, four-stud fixing, 5in. wide rim
Tyres—make	Bridgestone RD102
type	Radial ply tubed
size	195/70 VR 14

EQUIPMENT

Battery	12 volt 60 Ah
Alternator	Hitachi 50 amp
Headlamps	Lucas sealed beam, 100/150 watt (total)
Reversing lamp	Standard
Electric fuses	10+2 fusible links
Screen wipers	2 speed+intermittent
Screen washer	Standard, electric
Interior heater	Standard, water-valve type
Heated backlight	Standard
Safety belts	Extra
Interior trim	Vinyl seats, pvc headlining
Floor covering	Carpet
Jack	Screw pantograph type
Jacking points	2 each side under sills
Windscreen	Laminated
Underbody protection	Phosphor treatment prior to painting

MAINTENANCE

Fuel tank	13·2 Imp. gallons (60 litres)
Cooling system	16½ pints (inc. heater)
Engine sump	9 pints (5·1 litres). SAE 10W–40. Change oil every 3,000 miles. Change filter every 6,000 miles
Gearbox	3 pints. SAE 80EP. Check every 6,000 miles
Final drive	2 pints. SAE 90EP. Check every 6,000 miles.
Grease	No points
Valve clearance	Inlet 0·010in. (hot)
	Exhaust 0·012in. (hot)
Contact breaker	0·018in. gap; 35–41 deg. dwell
Ignition timing	10 deg. BTDC (stroboscopic at 650 rpm)
Spark plug	Type: NGK BP6ES. Gap 0·033in.
Compression pressure	170 psi at 350 rpm
Tyre pressures	F 28; R 28 psi (normal driving)
	F 32; R 32 psi (high speed)
Max. payload	882lb (400kg)

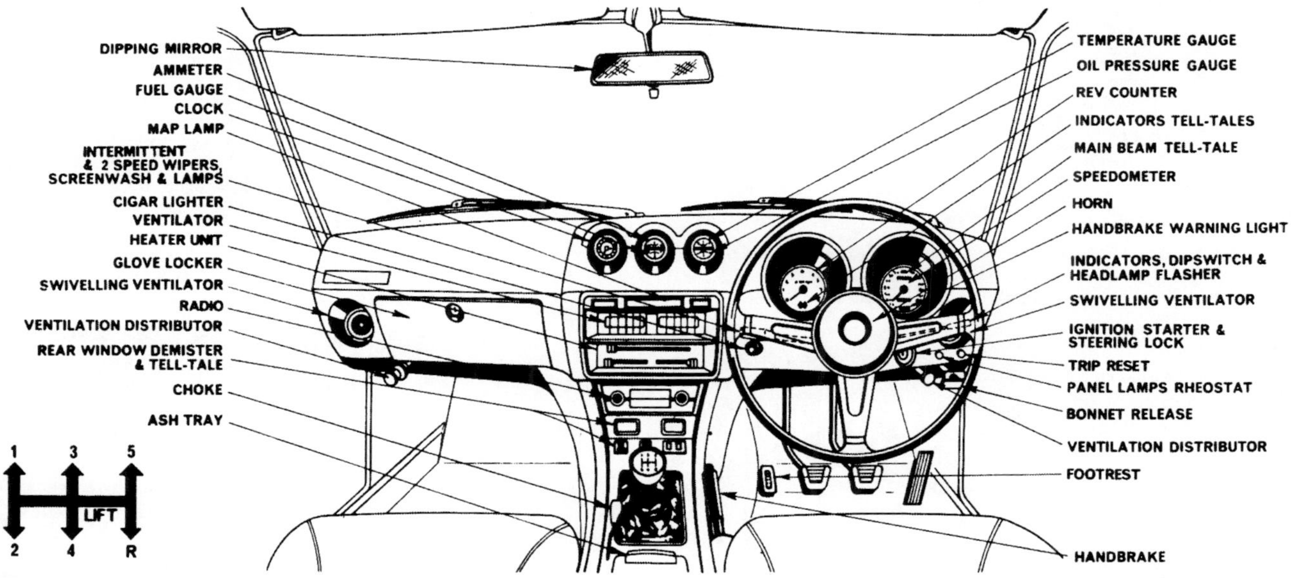

Servicing

	3,000 miles	6,000 miles	12,000 miles
Time allowed (hours)	1·0	3·0	5·0
Cost at £3.30 per hour	£3.30	£9.90	£16.50
Engine oil (cost of oil)	£2.61	£2.61	£2.61
Gearbox oil (cost)	—	—	—
Oil filter (cost)	—	£1.99	£1.99
Air filter (cost)	—	—	—
Contact breaker points (cost)	—	—	—
Sparking plugs (cost)	—	—	£2.60
Fuel filter (cost)	—	—	£1.11
Total cost:	£5.91	£14.50	£24.81

Routine Replacements:	Time hours	Labour	Spares	TOTAL
Brake pads/front (2 wheels)	0·6	£1.98	£3.93	£5·91
Brake/shoes – rear (2 wheels)	1·0	£3.30	£5.36	£8.66
Exhaust system complete	0·7	£2.31	£48.68	£50.99
Clutch (centre+driven plate)	2·9	£9.57	£10.01	£19.58
Dampers – front (pair)	3·2	£10·56	£27·95	£38·51
Dampers – rear (pair)	5·0	£16·50	£29·68	£46.18
Overhaul drive shaft	1·2	£3.96	£14.15	£18.11*
Overhaul alternator	1·2	£3.96	£39.29	£43.25*
Overhaul starter	1·4	£4.62	£27.92	£32.54*

* *Maximum charges.* ALL PRICES INCLUDE VAT

Above: Facia and control layout are shared with the 2-seater 260Z. The instruments are clearly marked and easily read, sloping lenses effectively eliminating any reflections. Wiper pattern and bonnet release are sensibly for a right-hand drive car

Below: With the rear seat back folded down, considerable load space is available. There are straps firmly attached to the boot floor to secure luggage

Below: A pair of substantial gas struts support the big rear window through which surprisingly large objects can be loaded. The suspension strut housings intrude less than they appear to

Above: Rearward adjustment of the front seats is more than adequate. Although the seat cushions are flat, they give comfortable location aided by the wrap-round edges to the seat backs

Below: Provided that front and rear seat passengers are prepared to compromise over the space available, there is adequate room for four adults, but the rear seats are most comfortable for children

Below: The spare wheel and abbreviated tool kit live beneath the boot floor. A pair of wheel chocks are provided. The jack is stowed against the heelboard of the rear seats

AUTO TEST

Datsun 260Z 2+2

Fittings and furniture

Apart from the loop-pile carpet which covers the floor and luggage platform, the whole of the inside is trimmed in black vynil – albeit, attractively grained and "pleated" where appropriate. The only other relief is provided by the narrow band of mock-wood decor which traverses each door.

The front seats have adjustable backrests which incorporate head restraints. Fore-and-aft adjustment – rather coarse – is provided by the usual slides.

Both backrests may be tipped forwards to provide access to the rear. Oddly however, only the passenger's one has provision for doing so without losing the original rake setting.

Contrasting with this is the sensible provision of a pair of release catches for each door, one each for front and rear passengers.

The full-width rear backrest is held in the raised position by a catch at each end. Releasing this allows the rest to be lowered so as to extend the luggage platform.

Although not unduly obstructive from the visibility viewpoint, the head restraints do hamper loading and unloading of luggage via the doors. Easier by far is to use the tailgate. Hinged at the top, this is counterbalanced by means of a pair of compression struts. It provides a good-sized opening with a sill of not unreasonable height. The "boot" itself is more spacious than it looks, the suspension strut housings making less of an intrusion than would at first appear. A thoughtful detail is the pair of straps to tie down luggage. Also appreciated is the automatic switch which controls a roof-mounted lamp.

An electrically heated back window is standard. Surprisingly, the leads which supply it are left to dangle untidily when the tailgate is closed.

The spare wheel lives in a well in the load platform, with a moulded hardboard cover to provide a flat floor. You have to release the luggage straps to raise the carpet in order to get at the cover and wheel.

Strapped to the left of the platform is the toolkit, contained in a plastic bag. There is a compact but effective jack handle, a wheel nut wrench with trim-disc remover, and a pair of collapsible wheel-chocks. The jack itself, a screw pantograph affair, lives in the right hand rear footwell out of the way against the heelboard.

Facia and control layout are exactly the same as in the 240Z and the 260Z two-seaters. Deeply recessed ahead of the driver are the revcounter and speedometer. Both have sloping lenses which eliminate all reflection problems. Inset into the face of the revcounter are the tell-tales for the indicators. In the speedometer face is the warning lamp for the braking system (already mentioned) and the tell-tale for main beam. The only other warning lamp is that for the rear window, sited ahead of the switch on the centre console.

In the middle of the dashboard is a group of three supplementary instruments. From left to right these are the clock, ammeter cum fuel gauge, and temperature cum oil pressure gauge. Our only complaint here concerns the slow response of the oil pressure gauge; some damping is desirable, but the amount displayed by this particular item could be downright alarming.

To the right of the steering column is a stalk which takes care of indicating, flashing (by means of a button at its end) and dipping (a double-acting pull arrangement). All of this works very well and has a light and precise feel.

On the left is a much stouter stalk which carries a pair of rotary switches. The outer one controls the wipers, providing pause (7 to 8sec delay), slow and fast facilities. The inner one controls the lamps. Finally, a push-button at the end gives a wash-wipe facility (wipers continue for four cycles after release of button). Home (Japanese) market models being right-hand drive also, it is no surprise to find that the wiper pattern is good. Likewise the bonnet release pull is on the right.

Beneath the supplementary instruments are a pair of adjustable face-level vents. These are supplanted by an eyeball vent at each end of the dash. Yet another pair of vents live on the cowl sides, each with its own pull-push control and solely dependent on ram-flow effect.

Immediately below the central pair of vents are the heater controls. These comprise three slides – one for control of stratified distribution, the second being connected to a simple water-valve, and the third taking care of a quiet and effective three-speed blower. A good point is that the last is arranged to boost the flow through all four facia vents.

Some measure of stale-air extraction is provided by small vents in the rear quarters, beneath the circular "Z" motifs. Additionally, the rear quarter windows are hinged at their leading edges. We found the system quite effective – surprisingly so after the 240Z's mediocre showing.

Also mounted on the centre console is the Hitachi radio/cassette player which is standard on these models. Also standard is an electrically raised telescopic aerial, with its own switch built into the radio facia. Loudspeakers are sited at the extreme rear, one on each side of the luggage platform. The radio, which has a self-seeking setting, performs extremely well, and the same goes for the tape player.

There is very little that the Datsun lacks. Rheostat control is provided for the instrument and dashboard lighting, which includes the heater slides and radio. Tinted glass is standard, as is a laminated screen. There is a dipping rear-view mirror with an unusual rotary actuating knob. A thoughtful detail is the nicely sited rest for the driver's left foot. Oddly, the passenger has no vanity mirror; in contrast, the driver's sun vizor incorporates a document pocket.

Living with the 260Z 2+2

In view of its comprehensive specifications, it may not be surprising that there are no extras listed for this car. Even so, there must be a lot of potential customers who would prefer seats trimmed in some cloth material. Halogen headlamps are another item which spring to mind (those fitted are 75/50-watt Lucas "Brighteyes" tungsten units). Judging by the Datsuns we see on the road, wider wheels (possible light-alloy ones) are another extra which might appeal. This raises an interesting point, for the 240Z's standard 5in. wide rims are somewhat borderline for the tyres used (195/70–14). On the credit side, there would appear to be ample room within the wheel-arches for larger non-standard tyres and wheels.

Now for some more practical observations. The driving position and control layout are good, and the seats are reasonably comfortable. As a further aid to comfort, the four ventilation eyelets at the base of each backrest (front seats only) seem to do some good.

As long as the driver is willing to compromise, four medium-size adults may be accommodated without too much discomfort. This involves the rear passengers splaying their knees to clear the front seats. Other than this and the fact that the backrest is a trifle too upright, rear seat comfort is not at all bad. Nevertheless, this 2+2 is better suited to the role of a spacious two-seater, or as a car for parents and two small-ish children.

Seat belts, which are a compulsory "extra", are Britax static type. They are easy enough to fasten and release, but need to be adjusted fairly tightly if the diagonal strap is not to slip down one's shoulder.

In addition to the generous "boot", there is a fair amount of space for odds and ends. This comprises a lockable glovebox on the left of the dashboard, plus two sizeable wells atop the centre console.

One area where the Datsun scores handsomely over its competitors is that of easy access to mechanical parts. Lifting the front-hinged and effectively counterbalanced bonnet reveals a layout which should be an object lesson to many design teams. Neat, workmanlike and beautifully finished, it is arranged so that there is nothing which cannot be inspected or got at with more than the minimum of effort.

Conclusion

As an adaptation of the 260Z two-seater, the 2+2 is a complete success. It provides enough extra room without losing the visual appeal of the shorter model. We are less happy with the mechanical changes which have taken place since the 240Z days. The longer-stroke engine is harsh and noisy at high revs, yet lacks punch at lower speeds. In comparison with Ford's Capri 3000 GT, it is grossly over-priced; alongside most of its other rivals, it makes a fair amount of sense. □

MANUFACTURER:
Nissan Motor Co. Ltd., 2 Otemachi Building, Otemachi, Chiyodaku, Tokyo, Japan
UK CONCESSIONAIRES:
Datsun UK Ltd., Datsun House, Brighton Road, Worthing, Sussex

PRICES	
Basic	£2,936.00
Special Car Tax	£224.69
VAT	£254.46
Total (in GB)	**£3,435.15**
Seat belts	£12.00
Licence	£25.00
Delivery charge (London)	£24.00
Number plates	£6.60
Total on the road (exc. insurance)	**£3,502.75**

Insurance	Group 7
Extras (inc. VAT)	None listed
TOTAL AS TESTED ON THE ROAD	**£3,502.75**

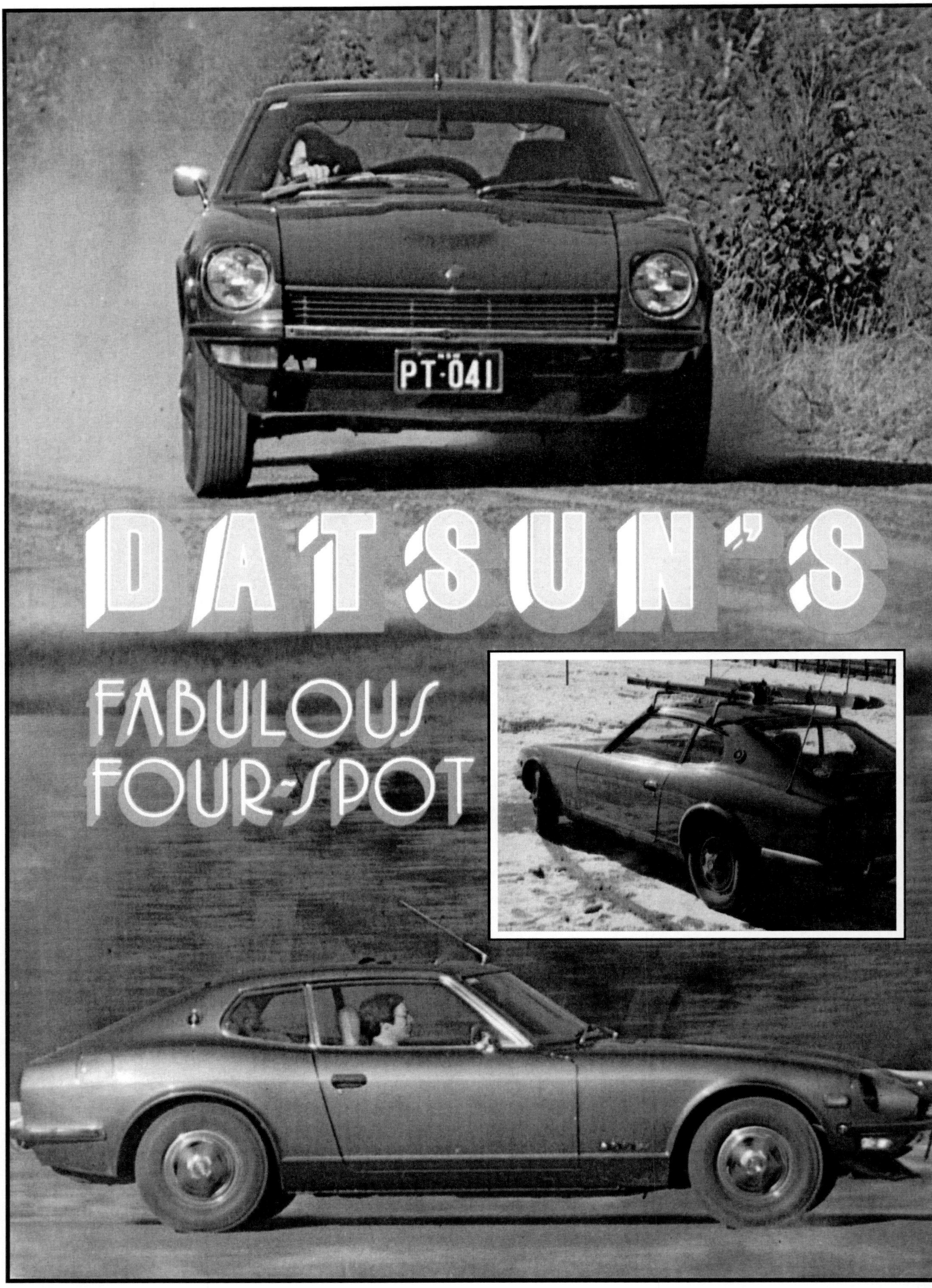
PT·041
DATSUN'S
FABULOUS
FOUR-SPOT

JAPAN'S top sporty car has been stretched to squeeze in two more people but the successful coupe concept remains virtually unchanged. Our 3000km road test confirms the car's practicality and appeal. Datsun's 2+2 is a debonair and dynamic delight . . .

WHEN DATSUN opted for code-numbering for the title of their new sportscar, it didn't take the wits long to deliberately misread the lettering and produce the humorous title of Twenty-four Ounce Datsun. Well, it seems that an endless string of successes from international rallies to international showroom floors convinced Datsun they got the last laugh on their "ocker" mockers.

Accordingly, the new "stretched" version of the super-successful sportscar was dubbed the 260Z. If the Twenty-four Ounce was the small pack, then I guess you could call the Twenty-six Ounce the economy pack. After more than 3000kilometres of testing, I can only ask where's the giant pack?

The Datsun 260Z is, on the surface, a car suffering from E-typeitis. This is a common problem that seems to afflict many successful sports cars and can be attributed to something approaching "corporate greed." Interpreted, that means the car company involved gazed fondly at the glowing sales graphs, and decided to maximise the success story by establishing a series of derivatives.

It didn't work for the E-Type — the car fell in a mine shaft deeper than the one some testers use to record top speeds — and it remains to be seen whether it will work for the Datsun 260Z. Its potential for success unfortunately cannot be gauged on the car's product quality alone — in any case, no-one would willingly be dragged into an argument on the

ABOVE: Hole-in-the-head was a super-effective extra cost option. Wind deflector worked very efficiently and operation is all electric.
LEFT: Hatchback concept enhances the 2+2's appeal. Overall styling is little different from the 240Z.

TOP: Desperate Datsun manoeuvre — steering "feel" is just OK, gravel road handling is vague. Top dead centre 'dead spot' is very apparent.
INSET: Good touring suspension at the expense of precise handling makes the 2+2 a comfortable long distance machine.
BOTTOM: Only real clue to Datsun's four seater sports is the extended cabin roof line and larger three-quarter window. Tape measure test reveals a welcome wheelbase increase.

relative merits of this vehicle compared with the E-type 2 plus 2. But it could well be that the Datsun's introduction to the marketplace is better timed.

Certainly, the sportscar ranks have been seriously depleted by the steady attrition of legislation, rising costs and falling demand. For those who survive, the available market seems richer and less populated than before. And with the increase in consumer demand for motoring sophistication, the luxury-packed economy-priced package will always have a better chance. Unlike the situation in days of yore, sportscar performance and handling are minority issues.

Enter the Datsun 260Z. An economical luxury-packed sporty car it certainly is. A sportscar it is not. And if you need any further proof, check the registration figures that show a sales break-up of 50/50 manuals/automatics. Now really, what square-rigger would be seen tugging at a T-bar?

Let's get the record straight — I'm not knocking the 260Z. For fast families of two adults and up to two small children, the 260Z is a very viable formula. It cruises fast and smoothly, it handles reasonably, with better-than-sportscar ride, it takes the littlies in the back in good comfort and a reasonable bunch of holiday luggage can be jammed into the exposed tailgate area.

The equipment is superb — with everything from good basic gear for fatigue-free driving to all the little luxuries such as heated rear glass, radio or tape deck, good instrumentation and so on.

Economy is good too — at all levels. The car is relatively cheap to purchase — at $6545 (manual $6260) — find me something cheaper with the same specifications. Registration and insurance aren't too prohibitive, and reliability is high with maintenance and tuning requirements low. Fuel economy is more generous than you find in most sports or sporty cars — the worst I recorded wearing my lead boots on a windy mountain road was 21mpg (13.5l/100kw) and the best was in excess of 30mpg (9.4l/100km) averaging 80km/h (50mph) on open road cruising.

The gentle gentlemen will put more than 26 miles into any city gallon but Fred Fleetfoot is likely to consume a

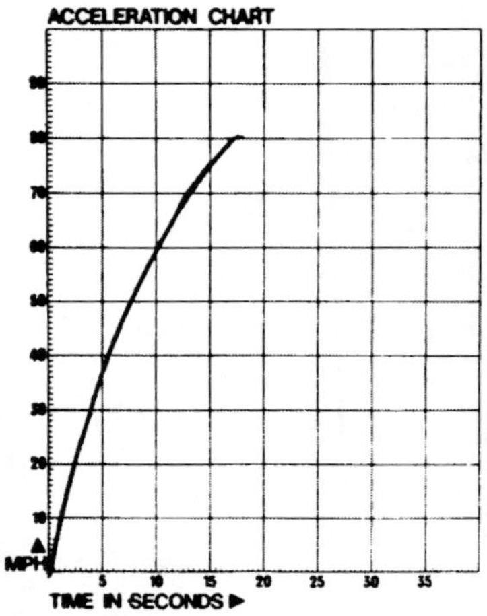

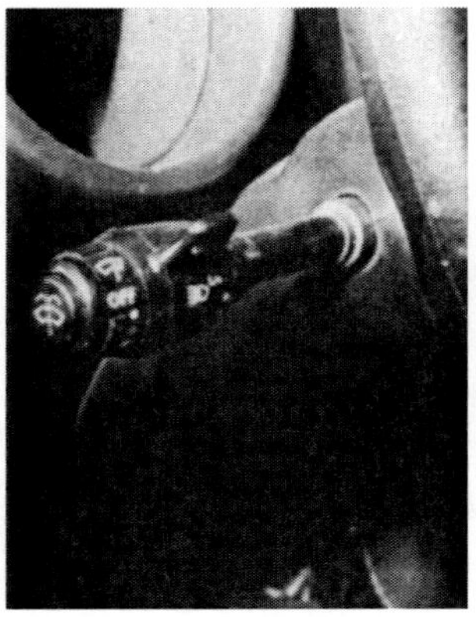

LEFT: Multi-function steering column stalk operates wipers, washers and lights — it's fuss and fumble-free. RIGHT: Dashboard layout is typically thoughtful Japanese. Ventilation is average, but Datsun designers get top marks in the ergonomics department.

ROAD TEST DATA & SPECIFICATIONS

Manufacturer: Nissan Motor Co (Japan)
Make/Model: Datsun 260Z 2+2
Body Type: 2-D Sports
Pricing: as tested $6545
basic Manual $6260
options/prices: Electric, s/roof $499 Spoiler $75 Auto $285
Test car supplied by: Capitol Motors Pty Ltd Parramatta Road, Auburn
Mileage start/finish: 3422 km (2126 ml) 6410 km (3982 ml)

ENGINE

Cylinders: Six in-line
Bore x stroke 83 x 79mm (3.26 x 3.11 in)
Capacity: 2565cc (156CID)
Compression: 8.3 to 1
Aspiration: Two Hitachi side-draught SU-type
Fuel pump: Mechanical Type Diaphragm
Fuel recommended: Maximum Octane (90 Plus)
Valve gear: SOHC
Max. power (gross): 120 kw @ 5600 rpm (162bhp SAE)
Max. torque: 206.1 nm @ 4400 rpm (SAE 151.8 lbs ft)

TRANSMISSION

Type/locations: T-bar Automatic/three speeds

Gear	Direct Ratio
1st	2.458:1
2nd	1.458:1
3rd	1.000:1
Final drive	3.364:1

CHASSIS AND BODY

Type: Integral
Weight as tested: 1350 kg (2977 lbs)
Kerb weight: 1217 kg (2677 lbs)

SUSPENSION

Front: Indep. McPherson coil springs with telescopic damper struts and lower trailing links, with compression rod, and anti roll bar.
Rear: Coil springs, telescopic damper struts, lower trailing links.
Shock absorbers: Double-acting telescopic
Wheels: 5J steel disc wheels
Tyres: 195/70 VR 14 Low Profile Radials
Pressures: 32psi/32psi (220.5kp)

STEERING

Type: Rack and Pinion
Ratio: 18.0 to 1
Turns lock to lock: 3.25
Wheel diameter: 15in.
Turning circle, between kerbs: 11.0 m (36.0ft)
between walls: 11.7m (38.4ft)

BRAKES

Type: Disc front/drum rear with servo assistance
Dimensions: 271mm (10.7in) Front/228.6mm (9in) rear

DIMENSIONS

Wheelbase: 2605mm (102.6in)
Track, front: 1356mm (53.3in)
rear: 1347mm (53in)
Overall length: 4445mm (175.0in)
width: 1650mm (65.0in)
height: 1290mm (50.8in)
Ground clearance: 155mm (6.10in)

EQUIPMENT

Battery: 12V/50 amp hour
Alternator: 50amp
Headlamps: Twin 50/40W Circular 7in
Jacking points: In rocker panels front and rear of doors — both sides

CAPACITIES

Fuel tank: 60 litres (13.2 gals)
Engine sump: 4.6 litres (10 pints)
Final drive: 1 litre (1.8 pints)
Gearbox: 2 litres (2.4 pints)
Water system: 10 litres (2.2 gals)

PERFORMANCE

Test conditions for performance figures:
Weather:
Wind: 5 knots
Humidity: 65percent
Max Temp: 21c
Surfaces: Hotmix bitumen

gallon in as little as 18miles with a bit of dicing and a lot of Greenlight Gee-Pees. That's all with the automatic — the only car we were able to test. With the manual, you could expect a little better economy in all areas except outright attempts on the land speed record.

While we're in the "highly inflammable" department, it's worth noting a few other points about the Datsun's design specifications. This is a compact sporty car, yet the fuel tank bulges with 60 litres (13.2 gals) which gives it a range of up to 466 kilometres (290 miles) for the frugal motorist.

Furthermore, the fuel tank is filled by opening a lockable, hinged flap, folding out a piece of protective plastic onto the sideflank, unscrewing a huge, easily-removed cap and lowering it on a chain from which it can't be detached. The tank can then be filled at the fastest pump speed available almost to the top of the filler neck — without air bubbles, spitback, fuel loss or other problems.

Compare this systematic, unfussy, fault-free design with the quite unforgiveable installations in every Australian product, and you rapidly realise why 25 percent of the Australian market swung to Japanese cars last month. And remember — the Japanese have achieved all these attributes including the rapid-fill system in a car of considerably more compact dimensions, sitting as much as 109 mm (4.2in.) lower! In other words fellas — you have no excuse.

But then, neither does Datsun have any excuse for some of their little boo-boos. Faults that relate to the safe or efficient use of a performance vehicle's performance become quite intolerable — and the Datsun 260Z has a handful of these. The lights are inadequate for anything much over 95km/h (60mph), and the driver's side wiper lifts off at anything over 80km/h in most conditions — less in some crosswind conditions.

The seatbelts are sub-standard — hard to adjust, poorly located, badly designed and out-of-step with the sophisticated, well-equipped interior. This is a Datsun sorepoint — this company markets vehicles with some of the worst seatbelts locally available.

The car's good highway performance is not underwritten by some of the support engineering that normally contributes to a complete and

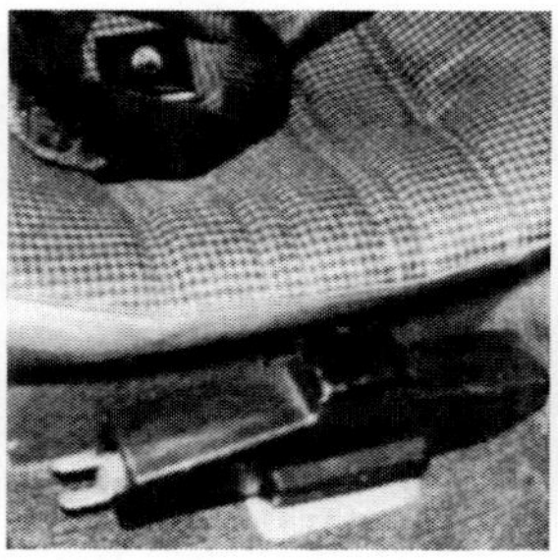

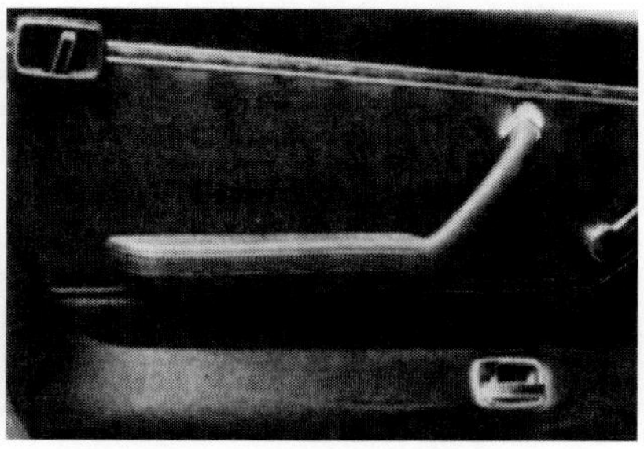

REAR seat (left) looks well-shaped and comfortable, but it's just bearable for big people. Plus point is the fold-down back which gives a welcome increase in luggage area. Making use of all available space the jack has been located in the rear passenger floor area (centre), where it fouls feet. Consideration for back seat passengers led to double door locks (right) — it's a great idea.

Top Speed:
Average: .... 185 km/h (115 mph)
Best run: .... 189.9 km/h (118 mph)

Standing Quarter Mile:
Average: 18.3secs
Best run: 18.1secs
Speed at end of Standing Quarter: .... 130.6 km/h (81.2 mph)

Acceleration:
0-30mph: 4.4secs
0-40mph: 6.3secs
0-50mph: 8.2secs
0-60mph: 10.8secs
0-70mph: 13.7secs
0-80mph: 17.5secs

Speeds in gear:

Gear	Max. km/h Drive	Max. km/h Held	mph Drive	mph Held	rpm Drive	rpm Held
1st	62.7	96.5	39	60	4800	7000
2nd	109.4	160.9	68	100	4800	6800

Acceleration in drive:
20-40 .... 3.7secs
30-50 .... 3.8secs
40-60 .... 4.5secs
50-70 .... 5.7secs
60-80 .... 6.7secs

Fuel consumption:
Average for test: .... 11.1 litres per 100 kilo (25.6mpg)
Best recorded: .... 9.4 litres per 100 kilo (30mpg)
City average: .... 13.5 litres per 100 kilo (21 mpg)
Country cruising: .... 10.9 litres per 100 kilo (26 mpg)

Braking: Five maximum stops from 60 mph

Stop	G	Pedal	Time
1	0.86	42psi	3.3secs
2	0.82	44psi	3.4secs
3	0.78	41psi	3.4secs
4	0.76	46psi	3.1secs
5	0.74	49psi	3,2secs

30-0mph: 11.7m (38.5ft) in 1.8secs with an average G-force of 0.8g
60-0mph: 1 137.6m (150.5ft) in 3.4secs with an avge. G-force of 0.76g

Calculated Data:
Bhp/ton: 135.5bhp/ton
Piston speed at max rpm: 884.5m/min (2902ft/min)

Speedo Corrections:

Km/h	40	60	80	100	120	140	160	180
Mph	24.8	37.2	49.7	62	74.5	86.9	99.4	111.8

INSURANCE, WARRANTY, MAINTENANCE AND RUNNING COSTS

Registration: $80

Insurance:
Quoted rates are for drivers over 25 with 60percent no-claim bonus and where the car is under hire purchase. This is the minimum premium level — decreasing rates of experience and lower age groups may have varying excesses and possible premium loadings.
Non-tariff: $211
Tariff: $207
N.R.M.A.: $221

Warranty:
20,000 km or 12 months.

Service:
Initial service at 1000 km

Other service:
Lubrication and maintenance services every 5000 km. Listed below are manufactures recommended charges.
5000 km $5.00
10,000 km $54.00
15,000 km $13.50
20,000 .... $65.00

Spare parts — recommended cost breakdown:
Disc pads (set of four) $12.75
Muffler front $51.55
Muffler rear $57.66
Windscreen laminated only $152.20
Shock absorbers — front $119.35
— rear $112.50
Headlamp assembly — right hand side $17.40
— left hand side $18.30
Tail-lamp assembly $40.95
Bumpers front $75.57
rear $70.92
Front guard — left $139.71
— right $92.01

Color range:
Red, White, (non-metallic)
Metallic: Brown — Bronze — Green — Gold — Blue — Silver — Royal Blue.

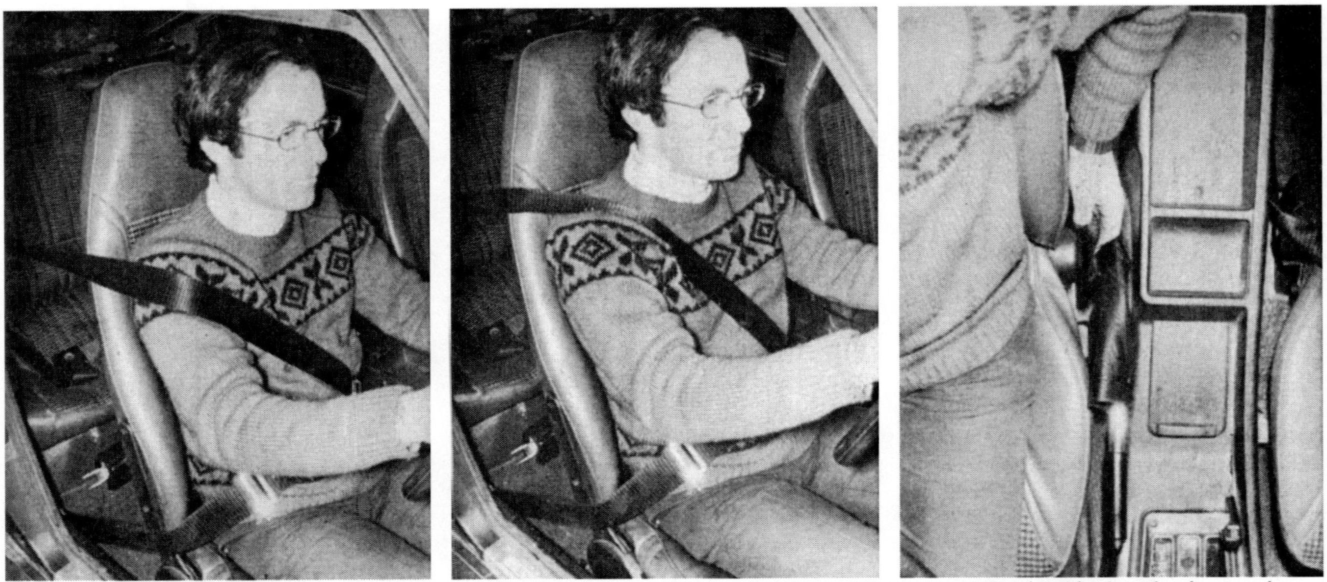

SEATBELTS are a complete disaster — they are difficult to adjust, placement is inconvenient and over-the-shoulder location is poor. In addition the retaining buckle drops down between the seat and the console which results in a fingernail splitting recovery exercise.

DATSUN 2+2

harmonious package. The transmission is particularly suspect — it is noisy and clunky at times, and the differential is particularly rough.

In situations requiring rapid changes of application in throttle and brakes, the diff seems to protest with a series of clicks. In both test cars this developed as the test wore on, and on one, the diff clunk became quite noisy. Both rear ends whined at high speed.

Pinning down the faults in the transmission is not so easy. It is smooth and relatively fast on the upshifts, but extremely reluctant on the downshifts. Surprisingly for a sporty car, the kickdown is adjusted at a much lower speed than the maximum for the relevant gears. So, for a cornering situation that demands a lower gear, the car must frequently be "forced" down into the lower ratio by manually selecting the lower gear.

Perhaps this has been adjusted for economy. In any event, the sporting driver will find that the autoshift requires constant manual attention, although his wife will no doubt be content with its boulevarde performance.

The ratios are poorly chosen. First gear only revs willingly to 60km/h (about 4800rpm) although it can be persuaded up to the yellowline and 90km/h (56mph) with a lot more effort and accompanying noise. Absolute maximum is a screaming 100km/h (60mph).

By contrast, second gear runs out all the way to 161km/h (100mph) at the redline (only 20km/h short of the top speed) with lusty acceleration available all the way up to 150km/h (94mph).

These ratios may have been chosen for a combination of economy and expressway performance — particularly for the US market. They work well for Australian open-road situations where faster-moving traffic is encountered, but they are a little less satisfactory for jabbing out into the oncoming traffic lane to scrabble past slow-moving cars on the tighter, more crammed roadways.

Steering has never been a Datsun (or Japanese) strongpoint for directional control at the straight-ahead position — and the 260Z represents the state-of-the-art. About a quarter turn of freeplay each side of top dead centre is the Datsun answer to lightening that first turn of the lock when you move out from the curve.

And it sure needs lightening! The 260Z is noticeably heavier in the steering than its baby brother at idling and parking speeds, and is quite annoying for women driving in the city. Conversely, at speed, the vagueness annoys the sporty driver, and unfortunately the typical front-end float was all too evident, despite the addition of a neat fibreglass spoiler.

I've heard all the arguments about steering rack adjustments for Datsuns, and we've noted them in most road tests in the past — but after-sales attention is still no substitute for engineering attention in the first place.

Despite its faults in these areas, the 260Z is still an immensely comfortable and enjoyable touring machine. Our long-distance miles were achieved with speed, comfort and pleasure. After a 600km section of straight driving over some of Australia's nastiest roads (including the Hume and Federal highways) driver and passenger emerged untired and relaxed.

Cornering standard is acceptable, and the ride control is more than adequate for a sportscar driven fast on our woeful roads.

Rear seat passengers other than small children could certainly last only short distances. Leg and headroom is poor (the rear seat passenger's legroom on the driver's side is even reduced by placing the jack there!) and the seats are only contoured to fit small mortals.

Luggage area is acceptable for such a car — one of our test crews crammed-in two medium suitcases, lots of small-sized, odd-bags and a couple of suitbags without difficulty, and the whole lot can be safely secured under the retaining straps supplied.

In other respects, the 260Z is not much different from its successful baby brother. It has virtually identical control and instrumentation layout, and the radio is equally bad (it is sorely stretched to hold a 65 kilometre range). Visibility is much the same despite the extra 30 cm (11.8in.) spliced into the wheelbase, and that's a fair standard for a sportscar.

Fitments and luxury appointments are similar, and it's safe to say the car is virtually complete for a lifetime of driving as it stands on the showroom floor (front-end spoiler and better lights would be the two major exceptions).

The option list is small — a good electric steel sunroof that's quiet and buffet-free up to 165km/h and radio/tapedeck (at least the tapedeck is reasonable).

In most departments, it's simply a case of "the package as before". The extra wheelbase has provided good accommodation for flying families incorporating various-size small children, or passable accommodation for larger children and/or adults for short city hops. The very same factor has brought a natural increase in price and an unsurprising loss in refinement of steering, suspension, roadholding and performance.

It's still a reasonable car for reasonable people with these requirements in mind — at a not unreasonable price. But it's also important for any prospective purchaser to establish whether this car's specifications suits *his* specifications.

As they say in all the good commercials, try before you buy.

DATSUN

Datsun 260Z

considering the smog equipment the car carried and the weight. Next year's enlarged and fuel-injected engine should do better by at least a second, not to mention adding punch all throughout the rev range.

Bumpers and other body bits will remain as they are for '74 on both the Z-models, the 'standard' and 2 + 2, which means that the 2 + 2 will still have enough space for two occasional passengers while meeting the tough '75 crash requirements.

Not too many Datsun owners should be involved in crashes; if the 280 Z is as good as the 260, they will be able to drive around most emergencies. Which is what a sportscar is all about, right?

Datsun 260Z 2+2

It's axiomatic that when you've got a good thing going, you don't mess with it. Datsun, with its Z-car series has a *very* good thing . . . and since the corporate awareness of Datsun is high, the engineers and marketeers won't mess with the super-successful formula for the Z-cars at all in 1975.

Well, maybe just a little bit. The engine will be jumped up .2 liters to 2800 cc, and fuel injection will be added instead of the carburetion currently available. You could hardly call those earth-shaking new developments.

Not that Datsun *needs* revolutionary gimmicks to sell Z-cars. The 240 and 260-Z series have so far outstripped even the expectation of the manufacturer that what started life as a limited-production sportscar has turned into a *cult* car. You can't go *anywhere* without seeing a Z-car, it seems. There is, of course, a reason for that.

The Z-car is the sportscar built to end all the traditional complaints about sportscars. Lack of heating, wind noise, graunchy gearboxes, temperamental engines, hard-to-find bits . . . all those hassles so well known to the sportscar freak are absolutely absent in the Z-car series. Which means that the car has such a wide appeal that you can see as many being driven by harrassed secretaries as by hairy-chested *macho* types. If that speaks well for the car as a car, it should; possibly no other sportscar has ever been the result of so much market research.

Street drivers aside, the 240, 260 (and probably the 280) Z-cars have all been instant successes on the racetrack. The inline six-cylinder engine coupled to an excellent gearbox (four-speed: no overdrive) and all-independent suspension make the car agile, responsive and quick. Our latest test of a Z-car (December '74 *RT*) gave us a 0–60 time for the 2 + 2 of 11.6 seconds . . . not AA/Fuel dragster time maybe, but respectable

DATSUN 260Z
Data in Brief

GENERAL	
Wheelbase, ins	90.7
Overall length, ins	169.1
Width, ins	64.1
Height, ins	50.6
Curb weight, lbs	2645
ENGINE	
Type	6-cyl. inline SOHC
Displacement, cc	2565
DRIVELINE	
Transmission	4-spd manual
Driving wheels	rear
BODY AND CHASSIS	
Brakes, front/rear	disc/drum
Steering type	rack and pinion
SUSPENSION	
Front: MacPherson struts, lateral arms, compression links, coil springs, tubular shocks	
Rear: strut type, lower A-arms, coil springs, tubular shocks, anti-sway bar	

GIANT TEST Triumph Stag Scimitar GTE Datsun 260Z

FOR

Triumph Stag

Triumph Stag has clear instructions for raising the roof, big red lights warn when doors are open at night and the steering wheel is adjustable

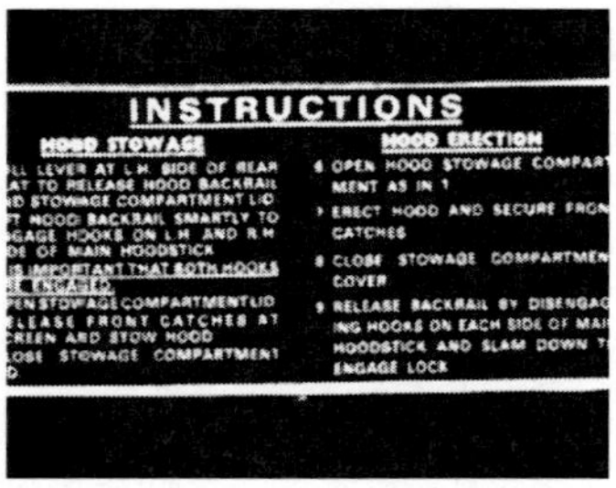

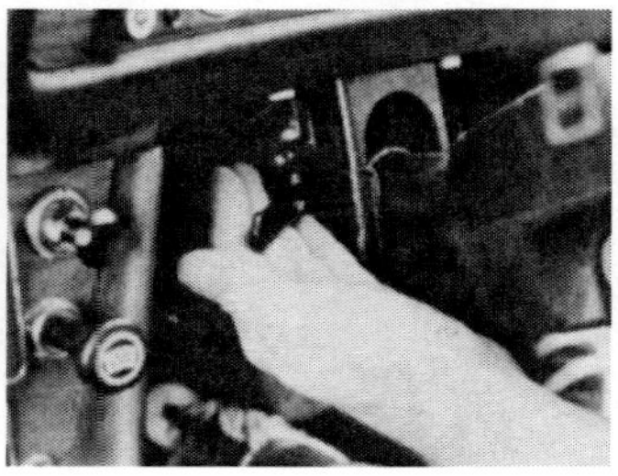

AGAINST

Triumph Stag

Triumph Stag's spare wheel is hard to extract, checking battery levels is difficult and the steering wheel rim obstructs the view of the instruments

Scimitar GTE

Scimitar GTE gets a fold-out cover to hide valuable luggage, switching in overdrive is fingertip work and a powerful wash-wipe system keeps the rear window clean

Scimitar GTE

Scimitar GTE has four halogen headlights but on our car, at least, poor adjustment made them ineffective; wheel is cheap-looking and bends, fuel filler doesn't lock

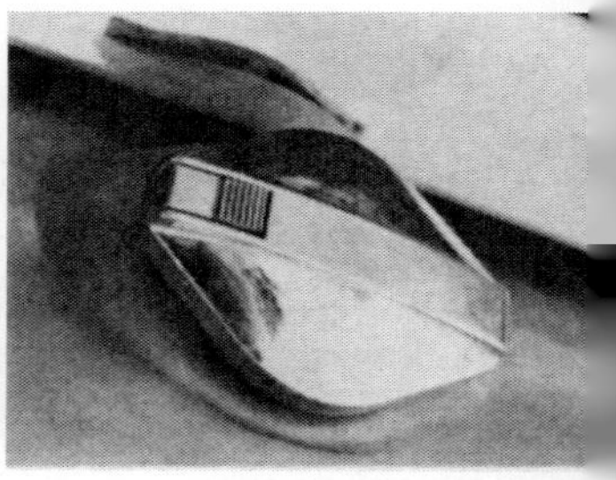

Datsun 260Z

Datsun 260Z lists among its excellent detailing an under-bonnet trouble light, a fuel cap that can't be lost or damage the paintwork and straps that hold luggage in place

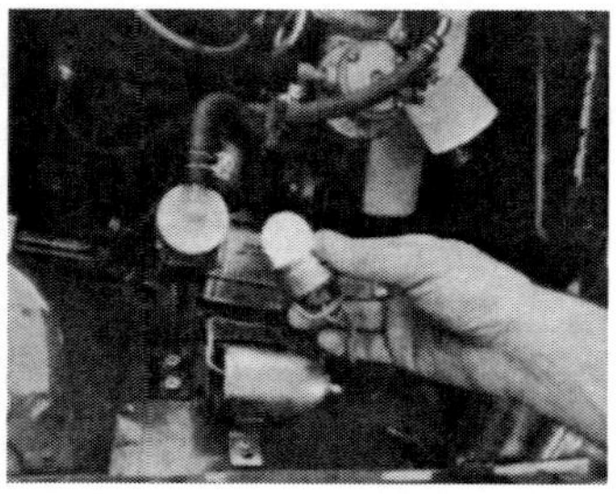

Datsun 260Z

Datsun 260Z's luggage must be disturbed to change a wheel, the tinny hubcaps carve up fingers trying to remove them and the seats are too thin for day-long comfort

GIANT TEST

Photographer: Mervyn Franklyn

SHOPPING FOR A SPORTING CAR COSTING between £3000 and £3500? Individuality ranks high among your priorities, and so does strong, torquey performance. You want a fifth gear for effortless and economical long-range cruising, and a measure of practicality as well—enough to allow a couple of kids or the occasional in-law to ride in the back. You have a good choice: there are three popular cars that fulfil all these needs, scoring especially highly on individuality. They have so much individuality, in fact, that each has its own special something to stand apart from its opponents. For instance, the recently-arrived Datsun 260Z 2+2 is a low and smooth 2+2 with a convenient hatchback, the Reliant Scimitar GTE is a sort of sporting estate car (*very* sporting), and the Triumph Stag is a 2+2 with a detachable roof. These special features—each a rarity—give these cars unique appeal. There is just enough overlap in their purpose and the way they carry it out to make them true competitors.

After the latest price rises, the Reliant Scimitar GTE Overdrive is the cheapest of the trio at £3337. The Stag (with hardtop) is just a few pounds more at £3342, while the 260Z 2+2 is up another £100 at £3435. When the 260Z was released about six months ago, it was very much more expensive than the other two. Now the dreaded inflation has levelled things up.

STYLING, ENGINEERING

The Datsun is a development of the original 240Z which Nissan introduced five years ago, the 2+2 configuration coming at the same time as the first major mechanical change: upgrading of the in-line, six-cylinder engine from 2.4 to 2.6litres. Styling was altered greatly for the 2+2—rather, a fistful of inches were slotted into the wheelbase and the roofline was altered to suit. The result is a longer car that is visually better balanced than the 260Z two-seater, although the ruggedly handsome look is still there.

As before, the tailgate lifts up to reveal a large luggage platform behind the seats: the rear ones fold down to give even more carrying capacity. Although the Datsun looks a big car, it is, in fact, fractionally shorter than the Stag, the largest of our group.

Stag styling is completely different from the Datsun: because it has a removable roof, it is built on more conventional lines

GIANT TEST

Triumph Stag

Despite Motocar's *insistence that it's a latterday Lotus Elan, the Stag is in fact not a very sporting vehicle. It behaves tolerably well in corners but its limits are low. If they are transgressed, surprises follow—fast*

Scimitar GTE

In these photographs the GTE is going 10mph faster than the Stag (above), yet it is rolling less and still has a bit in hand. Its handling is very progressive, and for such a commodious vehicle it is surprisingly 'chuckable' when driven hard

Datsun 260Z

The beefy Datsun reminds us of certain British sports cars of the '50s and early '60s. It feels strong, even crude, but in fact behaves remarkably well and, thanks to radically improved Japanese-built tyres, now offers outstanding adhesion wet or dry

with a normal boot following on after the cockpit—in brief, a Triumph 2000 coupe with a lift-off roof. An unusual feature is the integral roll-over bar.

The Scimitar is different again. Thoroughly unique in the motoring world now that Volvo's imitator 1800ES has died a welcome death, it is essentially a two-door estate car that has been neatly styled to make it both very appealing to the eye and highly practical. It is, no doubt, the car that inspired the increased practicality of the Capri II. A further point where the Scimitar differs from the Datsun and Stag is in body construction: while they have unitary chassis/body construction, it uses a steel chassis with separate fibreglass body. That the GTE's styling is effective becomes apparent when you stand it alongside the Stag: although introduced two years later, the Stag looks a good deal older with its ornate front and rear treatment and coke bottle flanks.

There are as many variations in the mechanics of the three cars as there are in their styling. The Stag is powered by a V8, the GTE by a V6 and the 260Z by an in-line six. The Stag and GTE both have four-speed gearboxes with electric overdrive; the Datsun has a five-speed gearbox. The GTE has a live axle; the Stag and Datsun have independent rear ends. The Datsun isn't a highly-advanced car mechanically, but it does have enough interesting features to rate it as above average. The in-line six has an overhead cam and twin carburettors, the gearbox has five speeds and the rear suspension is independent. All three have disc brakes at the front with drums at the rear, and they all have servo assistance. The Datsun alone has a rear pressure-limiting valve.

The Stag's 2997cc V8 is the largest engine —by a mere 3cc from the GTE's Ford V6. More than 400cc behind comes the Datsun's 2565cc in-line six which, like the other two, has oversquare cylinder dimensions. While the GTE V6 has a super-staid cast-iron block and cylinder heads, the Stag and Datsun engines have alloy heads on iron blocks. Their valves are operated by overhead cams as well, compared with stodgy pushrods in the V6 (which uses a solitary twin choke carburettor against the twin setups of the other two). Power outputs? The Datsun engine might be the smallest, but it gives the most power: 151DINbhp at 6000rpm, with 147lb/ft at 4400rpm. While the Stag V8 doesn't have quite as much power (146DIN at 5700rpm) it has, not surprisingly, a good deal more torque—167lb/ft at 3500rpm. The GTE's V6 has an even greater discrepancy between bhp and torque, giving 135DINbhp at a tame 5000rpm and 172lb/ft at 3000rpm. Final product of the gearing is a very high 25.9mph/1000rpm for the Reliant, 24.1 for the Triumph and 22.6 for the 260Z.

PERFORMANCE

If you're expecting the mythical might of the V8 to let the Stag kick up its heels at the other two cars, you will be disappointed. It's the slowest of the three by quite some margin. Not only is it the slowest against the watch, but it feels that way too, since the burbly V8 spreads its torque right over its rev range and makes the acceleration process seem unfussed. Mated to such high final gearing, it is an engine well-suited to effortless cruising at ton-up speeds—a point the Triumph engineers no doubt favoured over outright acceleration, although by most standards the Stag is, of course, a quick car.

But if the Stag power plant is thoroughly unfussed at speeds above 100mph, then it is matched rev-for-rev by the V6 in the GTE. On the one hand, the overdrive gearing in the Reliant lets it cruise with even fewer revs for a given road speed; on the other, the intermediate gearing and the hefty torque mean that the GTE can blow the pants off the Stag while it's getting there. It manages just to shade the Datsun too, although the difference between their times is hardly worth worrying about. Years of refinement have turned the Ford V6 into a smooth, pleasant engine with excellent flexibility, although it still isn't really happy to be cranked right out: it gets noisy and a little harsh beyond 5000rpm. You drive the GTE on torque and the wide range of gearing available, and never need to worry about lack of revs.

The Datsun's straight six is a lusty old thing that can never be accused of having too little torque for the job in hand. Datsun even want us to think the engine is capable of as many as 7000rpm too, but the redline on the tacho dial is in reality only for show; although the engine will, in fact, pull that far, it becomes far too harsh and noisy to tempt you more than once or twice. Power drops off sharply after 6000rpm anyway, so there's just no point in trying for the extra 1000rpm. For fast touring, the 260Z engine has to turn over quicker than the V8 and V6; up to 4000rpm (90mph in fifth) it is fine, but beyond that it begins to rumble and intrude.

However, the six is almost as flexible as the other engines and has a notable advantage in fuel consumption to back up its solid acceleration. Driven as hard as it will possibly go in all conditions, we could not get its fuel consumption to drop below 23mpg—an impressive figure. Cruising at 85 to 90mph for hours on end it returns a steady 27.9mpg. The Reliant is only slightly less impressive, dropping to 21.6mpg when thrashed and giving around 28mpg during fast cruising in overdrive top. The Stag logs 21mpg as its worst, but is very hard pushed to give better than 25mpg at cruising speeds—a pity, since the Stag V8 is easily the most pleasant of the three engines.

RUNNING COSTS

Tot up the total fuel consumption for 12,000 miles running and the difference between the three cars is not great. Just on 23mpg is the figure most Stag owners will return most often, so that means a year's fuel bill will be around £283. GTE buyers

GIANT TEST

should average 24mpg, which means an annual cost of around £270. At an average 25mpg, the Datsun's yearly tally will be £259 (all three run on four-star fuel, although you can get away with 3-star in the 260Z).

Maintenance is a straight-forward matter for each of the test trio, with the Triumph having the edge because of a 6000-mile interval between servicing compared with 3000 miles for the others.

HANDLING & ROADHOLDING

For some time we have been scratching our heads in amazement over a *Motocar* statement that the Stag has a handling/ride compromise almost as good as that of the Lotus Elan (which is extinct, anyway). Granted, it rides quite nicely; but if you're thinking of the Stag as a really sporting car with deft handling, you're way off beam. The power steering is still far too light and has practically no feel; corners taken at any real pace leave the driver with a lot of uncertainty as to what is going to happen. In fact, because the roadholding is so modest the Stag begins to understeer strongly. With enough speed up, it is then prone to total contradiction, with a lightning switch to oversteer of often-alarming proportions. Once again, the non-communicative steering is of no help in dealing with this, and the driver feels remarkably insecure and lacking in control over the car. We must point out, should you think that we are talking of wildly excessive speeds, that in the corners we were using for our action photography, the Stag was at its limit at just on 60mph whereas the Datsun and GTE were going through at 70mph with perfect manners. So the Stag is *not* a driver's car; it needs to be taken into bends relatively slowly then guided quietly through. It is far more a boulevard vehicle than a sports car.

For a car with a live rear axle, the Reliant Scimitar has outstanding road-holding and handling. The only fault that can be found in its behaviour is some bumpsteer and the back will also joggle a little off line over bumps in the middle of bends taken near the limit. Apart from that, the car is totally trustworthy, signalling its intentions clearly and having such finely balanced handling that at the very limit it switches from the merest understeer to the mildest oversteer. The sorting could hardly be better.

The Datsun displays the same sort of handling excellence, with a similar (if not greater) level of roadholding. Because the steering is heavy and reaction-prone, the car feels as if it is a strong understeerer. It isn't, and it puts up very fast times through bends. However, it too is prone to bumpsteer and the wheel kicks strongly in your hands. One of the things that most impressed us about the Datsun was its tenacious grip on wet roads. Even using all the power in first and second, we rarely managed to break the tail away. A combination of the efficiency of the rear end and the new compounds used for the Japanese Bridgestone radials is the reason.

DRIVFR APPEAL

The Stag's V8 engine is easily its most outstanding and appealing component. The ride is good, but apart from that and the fact that the car can be a hardtop, a soft-top or roofless, it isn't rewarding or especially enjoyable to drive. You soon become disenchanted with the pleasures of the engine when the thing won't go round corners with any sense of security. Around town, the Stag is quite happy and pleasant because the steering is so effortless, the vision is so good and flexibility of the V8 is made to order for slow-moving traffic.

At first the Datsun seems a crude and harsh vehicle. Care must be taken with the clutch or else the drive train will answer with clunks and jerks. The engine, as it revs, feels more robust than anything else, and the steering is hefty. Yet, when you've lived with the Z for a while you begin to like it because of its rather crude, hefty character. It feels like a modern-day adaptation of the old Austin-Healey 3000. There is also the fact that it really does handle well, and that the roadholding can be trusted implicitly. The five-speed gearbox has well-chosen ratios and the change is good. When really flying in a series of bends, the balance becomes apparent, and the car can then be driven enjoyably on the throttle in a way that the Stag can't hope to match.

The Reliant offers similar enjoyment during spirited driving: perhaps even more so because it does not require such a firm hand on the wheel. At low speeds, the steering is fairly heavy, but it lightens quickly with speed and has excellent feel. Despite the bumpsteer on poor surfaces, and the occasional tail hop, it feels a more refined car than the Datsun. Of course, the four-speed gearbox, with its two overdrive ratios (third and top), means that there is a gear for every possible situation. Or you can simply play about with them all if you're feeling so inclined.

All three cars have good instrument and control layout. The Stag is perhaps the least impressive, since its steering wheel (which does adjust, alone in this trio) obscures the instruments in certain positions. The instrument glasses also reflect. Both the Datsun and GTE have excellent instrument displays, although they are laid out in different styles. Very American, the Datsun's dash has deep nacelles which house the instruments. Even if it looks gimmicky, it does work well and the dials are clear. Minor instruments include water thermometer, oil pressure and temperature (in one nacelle), ammeter and fuel (combined in another) and a clock. In the Stag, the minor instruments include a battery condition gauge, but surprisingly no oil pressure dial. Contrasting with the Datsun, the Stag's instruments are set into a wooden panel, and the GTE's fascia looks almost as traditionally British, even if it doesn't have wood facing. Thoughtfully, the GTE instruments are laid out from left to right in order

Triumph Stag

Single-ohc-per-bank V8 is a tightish fit but delivers ample torque as smoothly as one might wish. Cockpit is in keeping, not well integrated but almost luxuriously equipped, and with an adjustable steering wheel. Padded bench in back is for occasional use

Scimitar GTE

Accessibility suffers because the Scimitar's Ford V6 engine is squeezed right back under the bulkhead in the interests of good weight distribution. Interior is a masterpiece of uncluttered planning, flexibly arranged to take two, three or four adults plus their baggage

Datsun 260Z

Plenty of space around the 260Z's simple, inline engine for routine access. Interior is uncompromisingly sporting, yet really does have space behind the front seats for two small adults or large children. Luggage room is quite generous, too

GIANT TEST

GIANT TEST

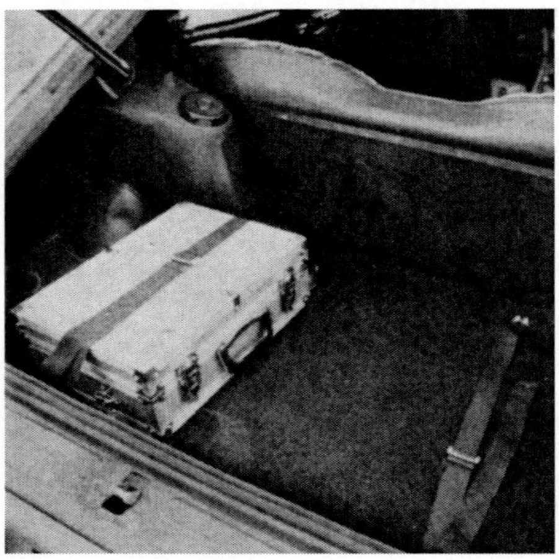

Triumph Stag (top) has the smallest boot, but is by no means inadequate and has the advantage of being covered and lockable so that valuables are out of sight. Scimitar (centre) features a novel rear seat which folds half at a time. Datsun rear seat folds more conventionally

of importance, and they're all easy to read. Pedals are fine (as in the Stag and Datsun, there is a footrest), the gearlever is easy to reach and works easily and the overdrive switch juts out from the dash so that the right index finger can flick it without the hand having to move from the wheel. The overdrive comes in and out very quickly and is unusually smooth. Minor switchgear is well located on the edge of the dash, to the left of the wheel, but because there are wipers front and rear, washers and lights, it can be confusing. The only thing that really does detract from the GTE driver's pleasure is the nasty steering wheel: it flexes under pressure in the middle of bends and looks cheap.

Pedal layout is equally good in the Datsun and Stag, and so are the gearlever locations. Both have twin stalks for the minor controls, but the Datsun's are more pleasant to use because they work more smoothly.

COMFORT

The Stag wins hands-down for ride, especially around town. Its suspension is soft and soaks up bumps with a relaxed, easy style that it retains on motorways and most backroads as well. The seats have excellent squabs but the cushions are fractionally too flat. The driving position itself is good, thanks only to the adjustable wheel. But no matter how comfortable the Stag may be as a long-range motorway car, it is let down by frightful wind noise. The rush around the window frames starts to drown the radio at 45mph, and from then on just gets steadily worse until at 80mph you give up and turn the radio off. At higher speeds, conversation is difficult and at 100mph becomes tiring. So this point, together with the tricky handling and inadequate roadholding, means the Stag is more suited to boulevard purposes than anything else. Although it is the largest of the three cars, the Stag uses its space poorly by comparison with the GTE and 260Z, although two, even three kids can squat on the padded back shelf. Equipment and finish is good (overdrive and power steering are standard) and the car has an air of some luxury. The integrated roll-over bar offers permanent protection as well as providing vital body stiffness. The car comes with either soft-top or hardtop or both if you pay extra money. While the tops both fit well and keep out water and draughts with equal efficiency, the soft-top is hard to erect and the hardtop needs two men to lift it on and off. A good point of the ragtop's function is that it folds down into a well behind the cockpit and is concealed by a metal cover. Boot space is poor and getting the spare wheel out from under the boot floor is difficult.

The Datsun 260Z's interior is among the best-planned of any car. As a 2+2 it is a resounding success, with the available space being utilised so well that two small adults (say two women of around 5ft 3in) can travel there for hundreds of miles in some comfort. In that respect alone, the Datsun is rare among its 2+2 contemporaries. But one of the sacrifices made to achieve this carrying capacity is the thinning of the front seats so that their squabs are hard and lack the necessary lumbar support for long trips. Although it has an independent rear end, ride isn't one of the Datsun's finer points. There seems to be enough spring travel, but the damping is inadequate and at low speeds the ride is harsh and juddery over bumps. Going quickly on open roads, the ride becomes quite comfortable. In all, the Datsun shows enough crudeness in its ride to point to it being thoroughly underdeveloped: the Japanese just don't yet understand about a good ride.

The Stag—and the GTE as well—are well-equipped, but they can't compete with the Datsun. Bringing the others up to an equivalent level means that the price moves in the Datsun's favour. The car is full of impressive detail points, too. Points like a ventilation system that directs cold air onto the face while sending hot air to the feet; trouble light on an extension lead mounted under the bonnet; straps to hold luggage in place, rubber under the fuel filler cap so the paint won't be damaged and so on. With the rear seat folded, the luggage area in the 260Z is vast, although there is nowhere to hide valuables. Under-bonnet accessibility is excellent, with all the ancilliaries laid out for easy reach—things are a lot more cluttered under the Stag bonnet, and with the V6 so far back in the Reliant's bay it can be difficult to work on during tune-ups.

The Scimitar is another firm rider at low speeds, covering uneven surfaces with a deal of knobbiness but not thumping so loudly as the Datsun when it strikes hefty bumps. With speed it, too, becomes thoroughly comfortable although the limits of the rather basic suspension are shown up by bumps in fast corners. Seats are comfortable, but they need higher backrests. As in the Datsun, foot space in the front is formidable and all the creature comforts are present. Space in the rear is better than in the Datsun and adults can travel there in comfort so long as their knees are tucked either side of the front squabs. Of course, the Scimitar's rear seats can be folded flat, one seat at a time, to provide the optimum seating/load space combinations. With both seats down, there is enough platform space to cart as much as in a small conventional estate car. Like the Datsun, the rear window lifts up on self-supporting struts and incorporates electric demisting, as with the Stag. Alone, the GTE has a rear-window washer and wiper—a necessary touch. Reliant's approach to the interior appointments has been so thorough that you now get a fold-out cover that clips into place to hide luggage.

SAFETY

Roadholding and handling of the GTE, and especially the Datsun, are strong safety factors unto themselves, whereas the Stag can't be called a truly stable car if driven briskly. It just doesn't have enough road-holding and handling to come up to the standards of the others. But that hefty rollbar is a first-class safety feature and so are the strong headlamps and good wipers. Vision in all directions is excellent and the seatbelts are well-mounted and comfortable. Heating is good, but ventilation on really hot days isn't potent enough (presumably, you have to take the roof off). A dual-line braking system is standard.

Dual-circuit brakes come in the Datsun too, and so does that pressure-limiting device. But the 260Z's brakes can be made to fade all too easily in high speed stops, so one good point is balanced out by a bad point. Seat-belt mountings are not perfect in the Datsun and some people find the belts uncomfortable. Headrests are standard though, and there is good padding on the steering wheel boss. A laminated windscreen is standard.

The Scimitar has no sharp cowls inside the cabin to cause injury, and has good seat-belts. Its windscreen is laminated and it too has four halogen headlights (although the Datsun only has two, they are big ones). Glass is Sundym all round, and a full rollbar (concealed under the trim) is part of the basic construction.

CONCLUSIONS

After a great deal of soul-searching, we've decided that we would settle for the Scimitar. It is an extremely versatile car with a great deal of appeal stemming from its originality. The only real faults are occasional bumpsteer and its slightly harsh ride at town speeds. You can easily live with that in the knowledge that the car behaves so nicely at high speed and is so pleasant to drive quickly.

On the other hand, we could be as happy with the 260Z—a car with superior roadholding overall (and a good deal of potential for developing the suspension) and faultless handling. The Datsun does indeed have a very robust, strong sort of character that can be off-putting at first. But you learn to like it the more you drive the car: it has the same sort of hairy-chested, vintage appeal of the old Austin Healey sixes. Suspension noise, engine harshness above 4500rpm and seats that aren't quite comfortable enough are the only significant faults, although the steering is really too heavy for women to manage around town. The amazing equipment level is a strong selling point.

A poor third, the Stag is outclassed by the GTE and 260Z for open road performance. It does have a fine engine, a good transmission, comfort, svelte looks and a lot of dash when the roof is removed. These are points that will make it a very good car indeed for the Highgate ladies to use on shopping trips, or for your commuting office manager to impress his friends. Meanwhile, it's left to Scimitar and 260Z to look after the real drivers. ●

Scimitar GTE

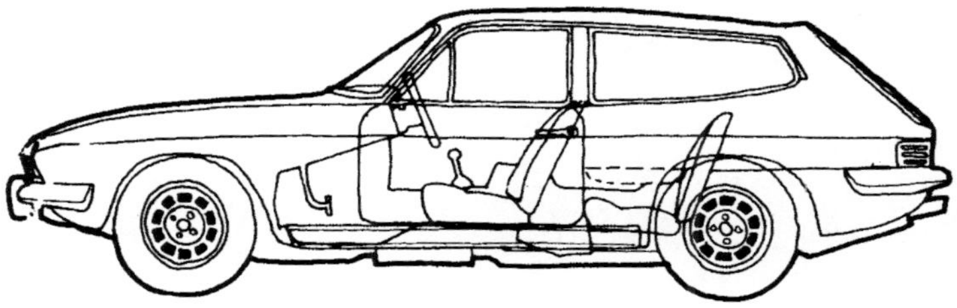

Datsun 260Z

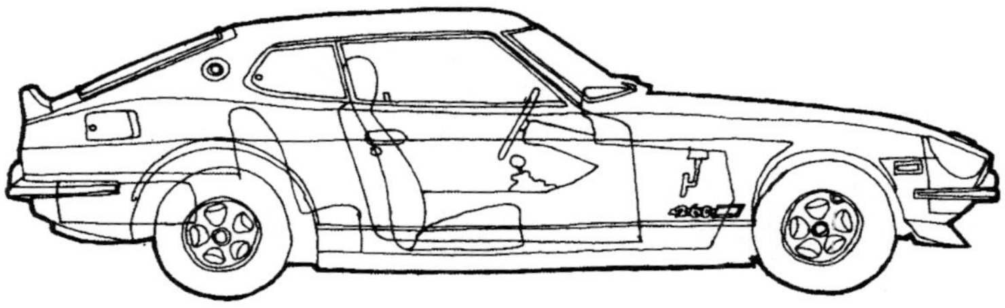

Triumph Stag

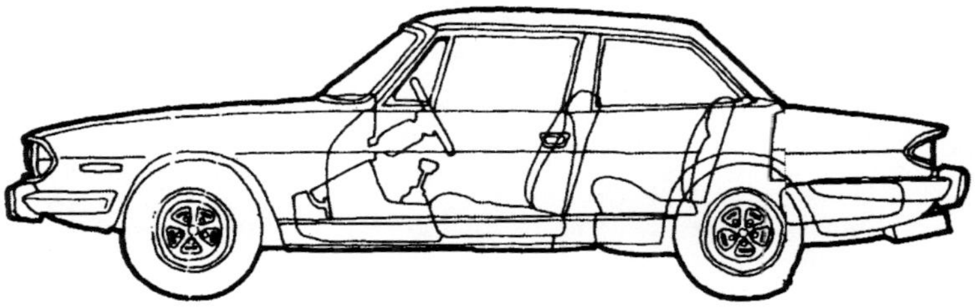

SPEEDS IN GEARS

	FIRST	SECOND	THIRD	FOURTH	FIFTH
Scimitar	0-40	0-65	15-90	20-106	25-122
Datsun	0-47	0-72	18-104	21-117	27-125
Stag	0-42	0-60	10-91	15-118	20-120

PERFORMANCE

	0-30	0-40	0-50	0-60	0-70	0-80	0-90
Scimitar	3.1	4.5	6.6	8.8	11.7	15.6	20.2
Datsun	3.1	4.6	6.7	8.9	12.2	15.3	19.8
Stag	3.5	5.4	7.5	9.8	13.2	17.1	22.3

FUEL CONSUMPTION

Scimitar 22-28mpg, Datsun 23-28mpg, Stag 21-25mpg

Datsun's Tough Turnpike Thumper

So it's got a lorry chassis, but it looks plenty sharp and wow !—you can get four people in it !

Back in the good old days, in this case before 1969, it was a general rule that when a manufacturer slightly increased the size of an engine, that engine gave better performance for a minimal increase in fuel consumption. But this is 1974, and a small increase in engine size, while boosting the power rating, actually reduces performance, has a drastic effect on fuel consumption, and all for what purpose? Why, so that (in theory at least) the amount of toxic substances released into the air for you and I to breathe is cut down by an amount that probably has absolutely no effect on you or me.

Well, that's show business. If the Japs hadn't bombed Pearl Harbour, thus enabling them to lose the war and build their economy up from scratch on American lines, it's unlikely that the Nissan Motor Co would have mushroomed into the mammoth setup it is today. One thing is certain—it was the American pollution regulations which persuaded our old mates Katsuji Kawamata (chairman) and Tadahiro Iwakoshi (president) to squeeze an extra 5.2mm into the stroke of the Datsun 240Z's straight six, thus creating the 2565cc 260Z.

Silly old Kat and Tad. The engine now produces 151bhp, 15 per cent more, but the longer stroke, allied to emission equipment, higher final drive and first and second gear ratios, have made the engine a lot lazier and less responsive than its smaller predecessor. Performance has suffered, and fuel consumption has risen alarmingly, so that you're now lucky to get 23mpg out of the car.

However, as Kat would say, 'acceleration may not be excerrent, but the Fair Rady (as it's known in Yokohama) is still a fast rady'. The car we tested was the 2+2 version, which is a foot longer (all the extra length is within the wheelbase), one inch wider and just over 1cwt heavier. Apart from a lengthened propshaft, the only other differences are stiffer rear springs, and uprated brakes, with cooling

fins on the rear drums. Not that you'd notice the extra braking power—but more of that anon.

The 240/260Z series still fulfils the role of the Austin-Healey 3000—a gap that British Leyland have never succeeded in plugging. For all its comparatively sophisticated suspension setup, independent all round, and its comfortable modern interior, the Datsun is what used to be known as a 'man's car', with quite heavy steering, clutch, brakes and gearchange, a car that gets thrown off line by bumpy roads and which is most rewarding when pushed hard. The kind of woman with muscles to match the 260Z is not the fair lady I wish to meet.

The 2+2 offers more rear head and leg room than most of its competitors, and the range of equipment you get as standard for your three-and-a-half grand is just what one would expect, plus a little bit more. The reclining front seats have integral head restraints, the windscreen is tinted, and other goodies include a rear 'defogger', cigar lighter, clock, alternator, fitted carpets, tachometer, radio and eight-track cartridge system.

The interior looks like it was designed by a European with the American market in mind, as it has an unusual combination of good taste and function. The driving position could not be bettered (although the seat belts are, as on all Japanese cars, so ill-fitting as to be dangerous), the instruments are clearly visible and well calibrated, the pedals are perfect (including a rest for the left foot), and in general the trim is clean and simple, though there are a couple of areas where it's been finished off on the cheap. Datsun ventilation is the best you can get, short of air conditioning.

The 2+2 is capable of carrying four adults in reasonable comfort, and with the rear seat down the load capacity is amazing. Filling it is easy via the flip-up rear window. Plenty of scope for gymnasts in the back, as you could easily fit a mattress in there, you dirty little people.

Lifting the bonnet reveals a massive truck-style engine. Although the compartment is crammed with this mechanism, it all looks very accessible. The head is made of alloy, there's a single overhead cam, and there are twin Hitachi carburettors.

To extract any satisfaction from this lazy lump, it's necessary to ram your right foot through the boards, and to use the five-speed box frequently. The gearchange is also a bit truck-like, rather oversprung, but very precise. No doubt there was a reason for raising the gearing on cogs one and two, but whatever it was, the car is now quite slow off the line and doesn't really start to shift until it's doing 30 or 40mph. Even then the acceleration is disappointing. Top speed is claimed to be 127mph, but I found it impossible to pull maximum revs in fourth gear, let alone top. It was difficult to tell whether this was due to wind resistance or simply the engine going rough and running out of steam, though I suspect the latter. I can remember being driven in a 240Z at peak revs in fifth over the Hammersmith flyover—and that was on the uphill part—a genuine 125mph. The highest figure I saw on the speedo of the 260 was 119mph.

The suspension, by MacPherson struts all round with an anti-roll bar up front, is very stiff, and the ride consequently firm though by no means harsh. The Bridgestone tyres—195/70 VR 14—mounted on steel rims are surprisingly good in most respects, contributing to the absolutely predictable handling, but their major defect is that they follow the contours of the road surface too closely, and can be pushed off line by the slightest ridge.

Roll is virtually absent, and a slight initial understeer soon converts smoothly into easily controllable oversteer, bringing your biceps into play. The rack and pinion steering contributes to the superb feel of the car at the limit.

If the brakes are used fairly hard they respond quite well, with very little fade, but if they are used very hard indeed the results are little short of disastrous. Until they cool down again, the fade is excessive and is accompanied by a severe shudder. It is interesting to note that nearly all the 240s and 260s you see on the road are fitted with alternative wheels—usually Wolfrace. Possibly these allow better cooling to the front discs, where all the trouble lies.

As expected, the six is a noisy brute, but doesn't intrude too much until pushed over 5500rpm, when it lets out a great throaty roar—fine old Healey stuff. Wind noise is not absent, but there is much less of it than in the smaller Datsuns, such as the appalling 160J, and the most constant internal noise comes from the fat tyres thumping along the tarmac.

The 260Z is a very well built car, feeling very solid and reassuring on the road, with no rattles or squeaks, though there is a fair amount of transmission whine, and driving over loose stones produces an unpleasant tinkling sound, which must indicate that the panels are not all that solid.

This is the best Japanese car, and one of the world's best sports coupes, as well as the most popular, and both the Sports and 2+2 are assured of a healthy future so long as it's possible to buy motor cars of this type, which may not be very long. However, one has to say that the 240Z was smoother, faster and more economical. Well, that's progress, kids. **PD**

DATSUN 260Z 2+2

ENGINE
6 cylinders in line, ohc, 2565cc. Compression ratio 8.3:1. Power output 151bhp (DIN) at 6000rpm. Torque 147lb/ft (DIN) at 4400rpm.

CARBURATION
Twin Hitachi HJG46W fed by mechanical pump from 13 gallon tank.

TRANSMISSION
8.87in hydraulically operated diaphragm spring clutch. Five-speed synchromesh gearbox.

SUSPENSION
Front: independent, MacPherson struts, lower links, anti-roll bar.
Rear: independent, MacPherson struts, lower wishbones.

STEERING
Rack and pinion. Collapsible safety column.

BRAKES
Front: 10.67in diameter discs.
Rear: 9.0in diameter drums, self-adjusting. Servo-assisted, with pressure regulating valve. Dual circuits.

WHEELS AND TYRES
Bridgestone 195/70 VR14 radials on 5½J steel rims.

PRICE
£3435.15 (as tested).

STRETCHING A BARGAIN

The Datsun 260-Z 2+2 offers greater utility with negligible sacrifice of the qualities that have made the original 2-seater Z-cars so popular

In the beginning it was decreed that a sports car should have two seats and no more lest its sporting qualities somehow be compromised. Later the GT car came into being to refute the notion that one had to endure wind and rain in one's face for the privilege of fast, enjoyable driving. Then Ferrari, banking upon its considerable reputation as builders of fast, exciting cars, gave the world the 2+2 body style. The idea was to stretch the wheelbase of what was basically a two-seater body style just enough to accommodate an additional 2 rear seats for *occasional* passengers without giving up the "ideal" styling of the shorter car. The sport sedans of recent years give little or nothing away in road holding or handling to two-seater sports cars, but most people will agree their boxy shapes do nothing to impart a sporty image.

(For historical completeness it should be mentioned that in 1955 Mercedes-Benz very nearly hit upon the idea of a 2+2 themselves when they offered optional athwartships seating of a third passenger behind the front seats on their 190-SL sporty car in a 2+1 arrangement of sorts, but the idea never caught on, even in subsequent Mercedes sporty cars.)

Thus Datsun, along with several others, borrowed the Italian idea to broaden the appeal of their Z-car line without major alteration of its styling theme. And although there are some in the Z-car ranks who will voice exceptions to the 2+2's looks, it's probably safe to say that, to a greater degree than anyone else since Ferrari, Datsun stylists have made the most of the 2+2 concept.

Occasional is the key word in describing the passenger carrying ability of the additional two seats. A pair of adults of medium or smaller build can endure the seats if the front passengers put their seats forward, but only children will be happy there for longer jaunts. Be this as it may, it's precisely what a lot of present or potential Z-car owners have been looking for: the ability to haul four in a bind. With the back seats up, luggage space is somewhat less than that of the regular Z-car, but they fold forward, exceeding both the volume of the two-seater and the lengths of articles it will carry.

The more cavernous interior seems to amplify road noise a bit more than the shorter car, but otherwise there are no disadvantages. Speaking of noise, the rear axle whine that we detected in the regular 260-Z we previously tested (May 1974) was absent in this particular car.

The good ride of normal 260-Z has been preserved and even improved in the respect that there's less pitching on undulating surfaces. Although the steering feels slightly heavier, it retains that good, natural, point-it-where-you-want-it-to-go feel. The good riding qualities of the all-independent suspension makes this car particularly well suited to long distance, high speed travel which, after all, is what any car with these pretensions is supposed to do, but unfortunately some won't.

Although the engine and running gear of the 260-Z and 260-Z 2+2 are of identical specifications, we noted several differences between our test 2+2 and the short wheelbase 260-Z we tested previously. Gone, we're thankful to report, is the irksome engine surge we noted before when attempting maximum performance standing starts. No matter how roughly we treated it the engine never missed a beat, always accelerating away strongly and smoothly. Gone too was most of the roughness and a decibel or two of the noise that we encountered near the upper rpm limit. We trust that these are some refinements that have been added since the early production run.

Performance was on a par with the previous Z we tested despite the 2+2's significantly greater weight, which we attribute to the sweeter running engine. The braking distance was somewhat shorter, too, which comes from a more favorable weight distribution. Empty, the non-air conditioned 2+2 has a 50/50 weight distribution whereas the air conditioned normal Z has a 52/48 distribution. With passengers, the normal Z balances out 50/50 while the 2+2 will actually be slightly tail heavy, and even more so with rear passengers, which enhances stopping ability.

One thing we hoped might be changed in the interim between our tests, but wasn't, was the veritable sub-station of wiring and electrical components mounted fully exposed beneath the dash by the passenger's right leg. Not that any harm results from this installation, but it sure looks add-on and awful. One onlooker thought it was part of our temporarily installed test instrumentation.

While there seems to be plenty gasoline available (as this is written), the cost is high, and there are rumblings that it may go higher yet. Consequently, fuel economy continues to be an increasingly important consideration, no matter what you drive. Datsun Z-car brochures make no attempt to portray these models as economy cars, but 55-mph normal driving nets mileages that come close to the economy car bracket. Our manual transmission test car averaged 21 mpg, driven conservatively but not resorting to "economy run" techniques. Using more of the car's performance potential will plunge the economy down into the teens, and equipping the car with optional air conditioning and automatic transmission will cost on the average an additional 2-3 mpg, judging from previous experience with such cars.

There's another aspect to Z-car ownership that will appeal to many: that of belonging and fellowship. There are nu-

merous Z-car clubs of one sort or another about the country, many of whom are affiliated with the Datsun Owners Clubs Association, a national organization. Besides the usual socializing, rallying and concours d'elegances, there is an invaluable interchange of information among members about the cars themselves. While there are no official endorsements as such, you only have to ask to find out what fixes are available for service problems that crop up and where to get them at fair prices. Just as important you can also find out where *not* to take your car for service. Of the so-called "marque" clubs the Z-car (and Datsun) organizations probably rank second only to Corvette owners when it comes to club affiliation versus total numbers sold.

For anyone moving into GT car ownership for the first time the Z-car makes selection simple. There is no such thing as a bare-bones spartan version. The standard model contains a host of items that are always extra-cost on domestic cars and some that you have to pay extra for on other imports. As an example, the standard equipment list includes tinted glass, AM-FM radio with power antenna, radial tires, wheel covers, rear window defroster and full carpeting. What options there are, are truly that: air conditioning, automatic transmission, chromed front bumper guard, stripes, rear deck rack and rear window louver.

Longtime Z-car people should be apprised that the crosswind instability that necessitated fitting of spoilers, or "spooks" as they were sometimes called, was eliminated with the introduction of the 2+2. Different spring rates, brought about by the vastly heavier mandatory bumpers, is credited with doing the trick. The 2+2's extra 11.9 inches of wheelbase and roughly 200 pounds extra weight (compared to a like equipped normal 260-Z) have further augmented the stability.

The 260-Z 2+2 is a worthwhile addition to the Sports-GT ranks. Its utility approximates that of the late, lamented Volvo 1800-ES Sports Wagon with what many will agree is better overall styling. There's nothing like the 260-Z at anywhere near the price, and there's nothing like the 2+2 version at *any* price. ●

DATSUN 260Z 2+2 PERFORMANCE DATA

Acceleration, sec:

0–30 mph	4.2
0–40 mph	6.2
0–50 mph	8.4
0–60 mph	11.6
0–70 mph	15.4
0–80 mph	19.8
Standing start, ¼ mile	17.326
Speed at end ¼ mile, mph	78.12
Avg accel over ¼ mile, g	0.205

Speeds in gears, mph:

1st (6500 rpm)	40
2nd (6500 rpm)	64
3rd (6500 rpm)	81
4th (5100 rpm)	115
Engine revs at 70 mph	3100

Speedometer error:

Electric speedometer	Car speedometer
40 mph	42 mph
50 mph	52 mph
60 mph	62.5 mph
70 mph	73 mph
80 mph	83 mph

Brakes:

Min stopping distance from 60 mph, ft	147
Avg deceleration rate, g	0.818

Fuel economy:

Overall avg	21.0 mpg
Range on 16.0 gal tank	336 miles
Fuel required	regular

Skid pad:

Max speed on 100-ft rad, mph	32.6
Lateral acceleration, g	0.710

Interior noise, decibels (dBA):

Idle	61
Max 1st gear	86
Steady 40 mph	74
50 mph	75
60 mph	78
70 mph	79

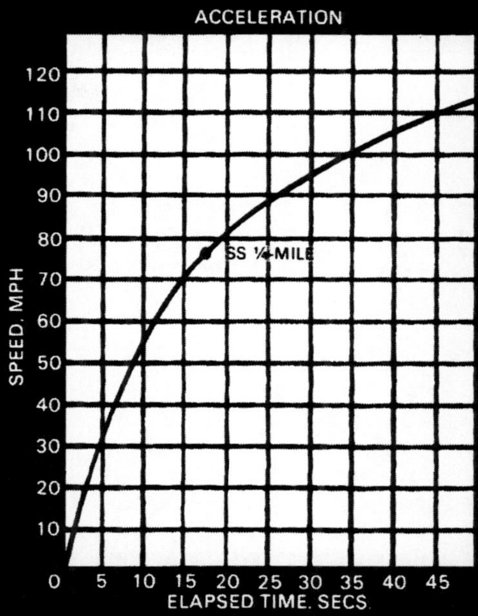

Graph Of Recorded Data Expressed In Percentage of 100 (100 = best possible rating) *

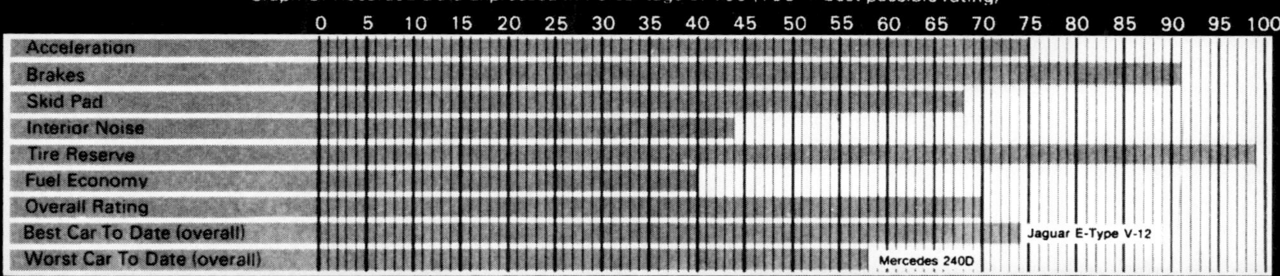

SPECIFICATIONS

Engine:

Type	SOHC L-6
Displacement, cu in	156.8
Displacement, cc	2565
Bore x stroke, in	3.27 x 3.11
Bore x stroke, mm	83.0 x 79.0
Compression ratio	8.8:1
Hp at rpm, net	139 at 5200
Torque at rpm, lb/ft, net	137 at 4200
Carburetion	2 1-V

Emissions, gm/mile:

Hydrocarbons	2.7
Carbon monoxide	22.0
Nitrogen oxides	1.3

Prices:

Factory list, as tested	
West Coast	$6089 + Transportation
East Coast	$6089 + Transportation
Accessories included in price: None	

Manufacturer's guarantee and service:

Warranty (mos/miles)	12/12,000
Oil change (mos/miles)	-/3000
Lubrication (mos/miles)	-/30,000
Tune-up (miles)	
Minor	6000
Major	12,000

Driveline:

Transmission	4-spd manual
Gear ratios:	
1st	3.59:1
2nd	2.25:1
3rd	1.42:1
4th	1.00:1
Final drive ratio	3.36:1
Driving wheels	rear

Wheels and tires:

Wheels	5J-14
Tires	175HR14
Reserve load, front/rear, lb	875/615

General:

Wheelbase, ins	102.6
Overall length, ins	180.9
Width, ins	64.9
Height, ins	50.8
Front track, ins	53.3
Rear track, ins	53.0
Trunk capacity, cu ft	5.9/15.1
Curb weight, lbs	2750
Distribution, % front/rear	50/50
Power-to-weight ratio, lbs/hp	19.78

Body and chassis:

Body/frame construction	unit
brakes, front/rear	disc/drum
Swept area, sq in	308.0
Swept area, sq in/1000 lb	112.0
Steering	rack-and-pinion
Ratio	18.0:1
Turns, lock-to-lock	3.0
Turning circle, ft	36.1

Front suspension: MacPherson struts, lateral arms, compression links, coil springs, tubular shocks, anti-sway bar

Rear suspension: Strut type, lower A-arms, coil springs, tubular shocks, anti-sway bar

Test Equipment Used: Testron Fifth Wheel, Esterline-Angus recorder, Ammco decelerometer, General Radio Sound Level Meter

* Acceleration (0-60 mph): 0% = 34.0 secs., 100% = 4.0 secs.; Brakes (60-0 mph): 0% = 220.0 ft., 100% = 140.0 ft.; Skid pad lateral accel.: 0% = 0.3 g, 100% = 0.9 g; Interior noise (70 mph): 0% = 90.0 dBA, 100% = 65.0 dBA; Tire reserve (with passengers): 0% = 0.0 lbs., 100% = 1500 lbs. or more; Fuel economy: 0% = 5 mpg, 100% = 45 mpg or more.

CAR OF THE MONTH

In order to save money it is necessary to spend it / By Karl Ludvigsen

THE 10 GRAND DATSUN

The success of the Datsun Z-car is well known. It is, in it's own right, a kind of duplicate in microcosm of the all-time specialty-car champ—the original Mustang. Even after four years of ever-escalating sales and corresponding price escalations from $3600 to over $6000 base, the demand is still strong. We are rife with stories of two-year-old Z's commanding higher prices now than when they were new. But, for all it's market vigor, the Datsun Z has not risen above itself. Unlike the Mustang or Camaro or Corvette, or almost any other popular automobile in today's market, there is no super-luxury model or macho-street racer model. Hold that thought. Oh yes, you can buy 260 Zs loaded with every aftermarket known to man, in fact, for the most part you cannot buy them any other way, but there is no regular factory model that points either in the luxury or racy direction. And, in a time when speciality-personal cars are some of the liveliest sellers, that may not be the wisest position for Datsun to be holding. But, there is hope. At the announcement of the new Datsun 260 Z 2+2, the editors of *Motor Trend* got together with Bob Sharp to design a real luxury touring car that would aim precisely at the executive market. A spot where, we all felt, inflation, revaluated currency and other such hangups, are creating a giant gap.

If you've heard the Bob Sharp name it's probably been in connection with his fantastic racing record with Datsuns. I well remember hearing, in the early Sixties, about this guy up in Connecticut who was meticulous in both his preparation and his driving and who was racing, of all things, one of those Datsuns that looked like an MG reflected in a fun house mirror. Since then Bob and his Datsuns have won more than one hundred first-place awards in SCCA racing plus five national championships, including the hard-fought Class C Production crown he won last year with his 240 Z with the big 33 on the side.

But this car that you see before you, this ten grand Datsun, is not a racer and does not, except for certain details, resemble one. It doesn't have the flashy stripes, brutal wheels and huge spoilers usually associated with the four-wheeled equivalent of a café racer motorcycle. Instead it's subtly lettered on the sides and front: "GT-33 Executive," which is Sharp's designation for his plush, dress-up and fix-up package for Datsun's new 2+2 260 Z. Since it lists so close to the magic figure, Ten Grand might suit it as well, recalling the famous Rollston-bodied Duesenberg that was simply called the Twenty Grand, because that's how much it cost—in 1933.

The basic intent of the Executive is to convey something of elegance and refinement that Z cars have lacked. The jump-seated 260 Z is not for racing and never will be, it was reasoned, so why not find a way to emphasize its excellence as a luxury tourer? The fender flares and ducktail spoilers were kept on the shelf, exchanged instead for some wonderful touches that recall the classics of the Thirties. It can truly be said of the Executive that its trim, paint and design details are so complementarily planned and carried out that—unlike previous bejeweled Zs—there are no jarring reminders that somebody meddled with the factory's original notions. It all works in harmony. Sharp and his crew of artisans deserve credit for that. *Motor Trend's* role was that of a market consultant group, suggesting new directions and trends we saw taking shape across the nation.

Nor is this car merely a cosmetic treatment. Drawing on racing experience, Sharp fitted special front and rear anti-rollbars, which kept the handling about the same—nearly neutral with slight understeer—reduced the amount of roll, and kept the car steadier up to the limit of grip in a corner. Of course the Michelin X tires helped, too. Koni adjustable shocks were added, which are perfectly tuned to the 260 Z's suspension. They cure the main fault of the standard car's ride, a loose, bounding motion after large bumps. In fact, with the Sharp treatment, the ride of the 2+2, already very good, is perfect for my taste. It's steady, firm without being harsh, and able to soak up whatever the road throws at it. The costliest part of the Executive, the Dunlop wire wheels, also add the right touch—that Ferrari Lusso look—to its appearance.

The normally blah engine room of the 260 Z gets sparkle and contrast from the crackle-black valve cover and bright yellow high-performance ignition wire. A tuned exhaust system adds a deep, mellow vroom to the sweet six-cylinder sound, the only drawback being a particularly noisy resonance around 2500 rpm, which just happens to be the engine speed in top gear at our wonderful national speed limit of 55 mph. At other speeds the Audiovox stereo system is worth its hefty contribution to the cost of the Executive.

Subtle though the changes are, the looks of the Executive never fail to turn heads. The vinyl demi-roof works perfectly with the two-tone paint scheme, elaborated from the all-bronze stock color. Neat striping keeps the close-up look classic too, especially around the shallow front spoiler and the transparent headlight covers. Inside the car the lighter look of deep pile carpeting and two-tone seat trim are very welcome, a refreshing change from the usual black-on-black gloom of the production 260. In fact, I'd have preferred matte silver spokes to the black spokes of the small-diameter steering wheel, which I liked otherwise, even though it made the already heavy 260 Z steering even moreso.

Right now a few of you out there may be wondering if it wouldn't be smarter just to buy a new 260 and make your own Executive. Well, you can't any more than you could have made a real Shelby 350 GT by yourself. You see, the GT-33 Executive is for all intents and purposes a completely new car that bears passing resemblance to a Datsun 260 Z 2+2. In fact, the car is so good that Datsun maybe ought to just have Sharp build these things for them. the way Shelby did for Ford. All things considered, it has all the makings of a classic—and for ten grand yet. ■

GT-33 EXECUTIVE DATSUN 260 Z 2+2

Base Price	$6,319.00
Air Conditioning	410.00
APPEARANCE ITEMS	
Custom Paint	450.00
Vinyl Top	84.00
Custom Interior	475.00
Headlight Covers	98.75
Black Crackle Finish Valve Cover	30.00
Cocoa Mats	18.00
Rear Compartment Luggage Straps	60.00
BSR Front Spoiler	65.35
HANDLING ITEMS	
Dunlop Wire Wheels	500.00
Michelin X 175X14 Tires	204.00
BSR Front Anti-Rollbar	62.30
BSR Rear Anti-Rollbar	81.05
Koni Shock Absorbers (4)	282.85
BSR Tuned Exhaust System	99.75
OTHER ITEMS	
Accel Ignition Wires	49.95
Racemark Steering Wheel	66.70
Carello Headlights	58.90
Audiovox AM/FM Stereo Sound System	345.00
TOTAL	$9,760.60

BEAUTY. Samuri's very special paint scheme enhances the Plus 2's natural lines. Few sports cars are better proportioned or create more interest. Included in the Samuri package is the deep front spoiler and seven inch Wolfrace alloy wheels; the choice of tyres is yours

BEAST. Three twin-choke Webers, Mangoletsi inlet and exhaust manifolds and (of course) a Spike Anderson head. To keep the beast under control, Samuri fit Cam-Am type ventilated discs, uprate the suspension with stiffer springs and Koni dampers

BEAUTIFUL BEAST

Samuri's startling Datsun 260Z Plus Two has performance in keeping with its appearance. reports Rex Greenslade

The trouble with this world is that the older you get the less you are allowed to make your own decisions. You gain plenty of experience along the way, but you invariably collect lots of commitments as well.

Take buying a sports car, for instance. You want one that'll do 140 mph, go round corners on rails and stop on a sixpence. Unfortunately, the wife says it has to be quiet, the children need a couple of extra seats and the mother-in-law has to be made comfortable. The friendly bank manager in the cupboard is adamant that it mustn't cost more than £5000, and Mr Denis Healey is making damn sure that you know that anything under about 17 mpg is distinctly anti-social. See what I mean?

But don't despair, you've got some friends. Spike Anderson and Bob Gathercole, lively directors of the Samuri Motor Co, recognised the need for just such a machine (yes, Bob is married with a few children, but what his mother-in-law and bank manager are like I haven't the faintest idea) and saw in the Datsun 260 Plus Two the potential to do it. The results speak for themselves; the performance, handling and (almost) economy of a Porsche 911, yet for around £3000 less.

Samuri, if anyone should need reminding, are a small tuning company that specialises in Japanese cars. Originally founded by Spike, who's an absolute demon at gas-flowing cylinder heads, Samuri have produced a series of excellent converted cars like Shoo Sam (Datsun 120A Coupe) and Super Sam (Datsun 240Z). With Win Percy at the wheel of Big Sam (a very highly modified 240Z) they took the 3-litre class of the Blue Circle Mod Sports Championship away from the semi-works Porsches last year, while this season they're showing the saloon boys how it should be done with the Toyota (GB) Celica. The abbreviation Sam always creeps into the name of any car they prepare; so far they've resisted Toy Sam for this year's racer. There's even Tiny Sam, a tiny Messerschmitt bubble-car, complete with Samuri red/brown paint scheme, tinted windows and front spoiler!

Spike and Bob design each of their conversions as a total concept. Not satisfied with a highly modified engine grafted into an unmodified chassis—in many cars, a potentially dangerous combination — Samuri modify the suspension, brakes, aerodynamics and always finish off with an immaculate, distinctive paint finish. The Plus Two follows this trend, though with the accent on torque rather than power, and handling not at the expense of ride.

Interior looks standard, but under the bonnet and under the carpets extra sound-deadening material is fitted, making the car much more refined

The standard car has a reputation for good handling, with the wider wheels and suspension mods carried out to this car the extra power is no problem

The engine modifications are less extensive than those they carry out on the 240Z. Both inlet and exhaust valves remain at standard size, for instance, though the compression ratio is raised to 9.5 : 1, and the head completely reprofiled and gas-flowed. Triple Weber 40 DCOE carburetters are fitted using a Mangoletsi inlet manifold and throttle system. Samuri owe a lot to Mangoletsi, incidentally, for they not only supply the six-branch exhaust manifold but also carried out a large amount of development work on jet and choke sizes, with the aim of producing maximum torque — rather than top end power—throughout the rev range. The result is around 30 more bhp (added to 150 bhp) but a much larger increase in mid-range torque.

Carl Shenton of Spec Fab Ltd, helped develop the suspension. The MacPherson struts are uprated on all four corners, Koni dampers added at the rear and the whole car lowered not only to bring the centre of gravity down, but also to induce some negative camber. Lockheed ventilated discs and four-pot calipers are added at the front to cure the dreaded fade that plagues the standard car, together with special Mintex linings front and rear. Apparently these brakes demand the use of massive 7 in wide Wolfrace wheels (others don't have the right offset) but as they look so good who's worried? Samuri profess a preference for Dunlop Series 70 195 VR 14 tyres, though, of course, the choice of tyres is up to the customer.

To round it all off, they add Lucas QH lamps, soundproofing under the bonnet and carpets, a deep front spoiler and a special paint finish by Kilbush Ltd, of Bedford. For the Plus Two this consists of a deep metallic bronze on the bonnet and door sills, picked out with white coach lining, on top of the car's standard colour.

A very comprehensive conversion, I'm sure you'll agree, and one that's very reasonably priced at £1310. Add that to the price of a new Plus Two (£3670) — though Samuri will convert secondhand examples — and you get a total cost of £4980. To put that in perspective, the Porsche 911 costs nearly £3000 more at £7898.

On performance there's precious little to choose between the Plus Two and the Porsche. The Samuri's probably a few mph quicker on top speed, and almost as quick on acceleration. It's fair to point out incidentally that the Samuri's figures were obtained with a badly slipping clutch — in proper trim the car should be even quicker. All Samuri Plus Two's will have specially uprated clutches which provide more than adequate strength.

We've never tested a Plus Two 260Z, so that we don't have any reference from which to make a straight assessment of the improvements given by the engine mods. The 260 two-seater (some 2 cwt lighter) figures indicate that the gains are indeed substantial; some rival magazines have recorded 0-100 mph times of around 31 s for the standard Plus Two.

The Samuri conversion makes the engine rev very freely to its 7000 rpm limit. As standard, the engine runs out of breath and becomes pretty rough much above 5500 rpm, that's just the engine speed at which the Samuri is in its element. Happily they haven't achieved all this at the expense of low speed tractability. The Plus Two will pull with full throttle from about 2000 rpm without fluffing. The only area where we'd like some improvements is on the amount of hiss that comes from those massive Webers on part throttle (though the roar on full throttle is well muted and rather pleasant); Samuri could make an air box that should do the trick.

Another area in which Samuri have done well is economy. You might be forgiven for expecting a rather dismal overall mpg figure but we achieved a creditable 17.4 mpg. Perhaps the most interesting figure is that at 100 mph the Plus Two does more than 20 mpg. Given less heavy-footed road testers, we might have approached the Porsche's 19.8 mpg.

We were also impressed with the suspension work. The handling is superb; precise, predictable, forgiving. Yet it hasn't been achieved by sacrificing the ride. Perhaps a little harsh at low speeds, the ride smooths out well when the car is travelling at motorway velocities.

The relaxed, comfortable, effortless behaviour of the car at about 110 mph is one of its greatest attributes. It's admirable that a firm that already has a reputation for producing powerful, quick rev-happy cars can also turn its hand to producing more refined Grand Tourers of outstanding quality.

Kingley Garage Bedford Road, Kempston Bedford, Tel: 854090.

MAXIMUM SPEED

	Samuri Plus Two	260Z	Porsche 911
	140+ mph (see text)	127 mph	140 mph

ACCELERATION

mph	Samuri Plus Two	260Z	Porsche 911
0-30	3.1 s	3.0 s	2.4 s
0-40	4.2	4.5	3.6
0-50	6.0	6.6	5.2
0-60	7.6	8.8	6.5
0-70	9.8	12.0	8.9
0-80	12.8	15.1	11.0
0-90	15.9	19.6	14.9
0-100	20.2	27.5	18.3
0-110	26.0	—	24.2
In Top mph			
40-60	8.8 s	10.1 s	9.1 s
50-70	9.8	10.6	9.6
60-80	10.4	11.1	10.4
70-90	10.4	12.6	10.4
80-100	10.8	—	10.5
90-110	11.6	—	12.1
In Fourth mph			
30-50	8.6 s	7.7 s	6.2 s
40-60	6.8	7.6	6.3
50-70	6.1	7.9	6.3
60-80	7.0	8.3	6.0
70-90	7.1	9.3	6.1
80-100	7.9	11.6	6.8
90-110	9.3	—	—

FUEL CONSUMPTION

Steady mph	Samuri Plus Two	260Z
30	36.7 mpg	38.0 mpg
40	30.1	37.0
50	28.7	34.5
60	26.7	31.5
70	25.5	28.0
80	23.6	24.6
90	21.8	21.1
100	20.6	18.5

* Not measured

A costly body builder

The Datsun 240Z and its more powerful successor, the 260Z, have become the world's top selling sports car. It has made its biggest impact in the USA and afficianados here in Britain emphasise this Trans-Atlantic success by calling it, American style, the 260 Zee.

But being the world's best selling sports car gives the Datsun quite a reputation to live up to and creates quite a few myths and fantasies around a car whose apparent technical specification, performance, handling and price are matched if not bettered by others on the market.

Chief of the legends surrounding the Zee is that it is a reincarnation of that fabled breed of car from yesteryear, the hairy chested muscle car that took a real man to master and scared girlfriends to death. A latter day Austin-Healey 3000, enthuse Datsun fans.

But a lot of those Austin-Healey drivers from ten years ago are now respectable married men, given to throwing odd glances at the children who now stop them trading in the Cortina for a Datsun. To let them in on the act Datsun earlier this year brought to Britain a slightly stretched version of the 260Z with seats in the back for the kids and it was this 2-plus-2 version of the legend that we lived with.

Style and Finish

The 260Z is a distinctive looking machine; very definitely a sports car with its long aggressive bonnet line and large power bulge. The bonnet slopes smoothly down to a narrow grille under which is mounted the front spoiler.

The 2-plus-2 version has 12 inches extra in wheelbase over the sports model, the side-threequarters being noticeably longer and more slab-like. But it has been skilfully done and the car retains the smoothness of line which characterises its two-seater sister.

At the rear a tailgate lifts on two gas-filled struts to reveal the luggage compartment. Once again fitted to the base of the tailgate is another spoiler, in grey plastic and it is interesting to consider whether it is symbolism or aerodynamics that determine their fitting.

The rear end treatment is rather typically Japanese, but thankfully, not as bad as on many Japanese cars, and the 260Z as a whole manages to look clean and uncluttered by the chromium nausea that is so prevalent.

Accommodation

As a 2-plus-2 the Datsun must get many more marks than most of its rivals, for far from providing 'potty-sized' rear seats into which any child of more than five must be protestingly shoehorned, those in the rear of the 260Z are surprisingly roomy.

The rear cushion is shaped into two deep wells for extra headroom and location, and although with the driver's seat back in the position for most normal-sized drivers there is little leg room, on the passenger side it is a different story.

Legroom in the front here is so enormous that the front seat can be racked well forward, leaving the front passenger still with comfortable legroom and enough space behind for an adult to sit in quite reasonable ease (provided they are not too tall).

The front seats are extremely comfortable over the longest journeys, once used to the initial hardness of the backrest. The seat cushions are much softer and well shaped, being padded for lateral support and extending well forward to give good support for the thighs. The backrests, with integral head restraints, are adjustable for recline and have a good range of fore and aft adjustment, making it quite easy to find a comfortable driving position. But after being tipped to let rear passengers in, the seats have to be reset to the correct angle of recline for one's driving position.

The seats, like most of the interior, are trimmed in black plastic; that of the seats having a simulated grain finish. A highly useful feature is that the rear seat back-rest can be folded flat to virtually double luggage space, making the car as versatile as the big Ford Capri and Reliant Scimitar which are two of its obvious rivals. But, as is so often the case, whether the seat is up or down, luggage sits plainly in view through the rear window on the open shelf.

Oddment accommodation is reasonable, but not generous: a large, lighted, but not lockable glove-box, and two trays on the centre console, one map size, the other cigarette packet size.

Equipment

Japanese cars are renowned for the fullness of their equipment, so perhaps it should come as no great surprise to find an eight-track stereo cassette player cum-self-seeking radio with electric aerial as one of the standard fittings.

Background music aside, the 260Z is quite acceptably equipped with the items one needs to actually drive the car. A heavy, moulded black facia contains speedometer and rev counter in front of the driver, set down into deep cowls, their clear white numbers being easy to read. The supplementary instruments are in the centre of the facia in shallower cowls.

Major controls are on two column stalks, the clever left hand one having one sleeve control for

The massive straight six cylinder engine fills the engine compartment of the Datsun

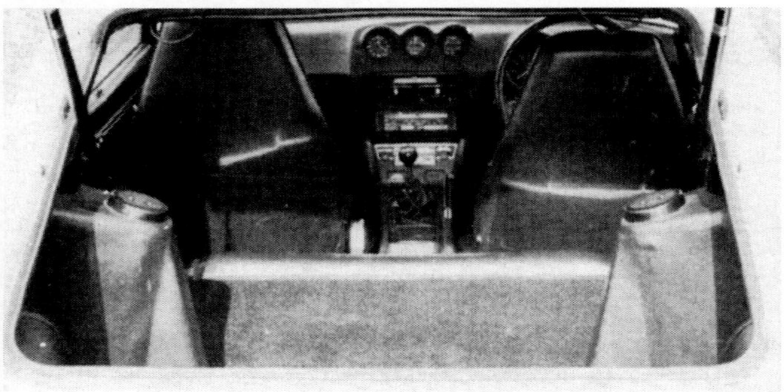

The folding rear seat gives versatile load room. Seat up (above) folded (below)

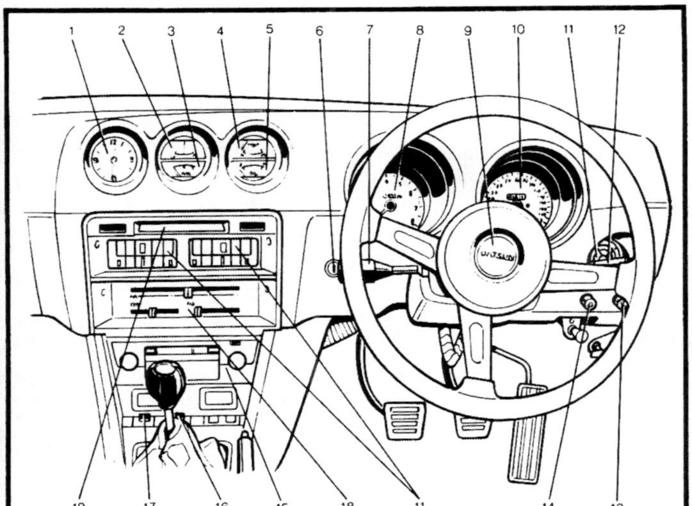

1 Clock. 2 Ammeter. 3 Fuel. 4 Temperature. 5 Oil. 6 Cigar lighter. 7 Wash/wipers/lights. 8 Tachometer. 9 Horn. 10 Speedometer. 11 Vent. 12 Indicators/flasher/dip-switch. 13 Trip reset. 14 Panel lights rheostat. 15 Radio. 16 Hazard lights. 17 Heated rear window. 18 Heater controls. 19 Interior light.

lights, a second for the wipers (two speed plus an intermittent action), and a push button end for washers (and wipers if not already on). The right hand stalk controls indicators and beam and flash of the headlights.

The heater controls are at the centre of the facia, with a light above them for map reading etc. We found the heater rather disappointing. True, it chucks out plenty of hot air thanks to a three-speed fan, but the ventilation system is linked to the heater fan so one cannot separately balance the volumes of fresh and warm air coming into the car. Again when de-misting the windscreen, the fresh air vents (at the centre and edges of the facia) are shut off automatically and the car can quickly become rather stuffy.

A heated rear window is fitted, Americanisation demanding that its control be named a 'Rear Defogger' and there are ashtrays on the centre and rear of the huge console, plus grab handles for rear passengers. Door pulls cum arm rests are fitted to both doors and the interior handles are recessed well down at the front of the doors. But, curiously, there is a second catch at the rear of each door to let rear passengers escape quickly. The car interior is carpeted throughout with a small rubber mat built into the driver's side.

The steering wheel is well padded for good grip and the pedals are large and well placed for heeling and toeing. There is also a very sensible rest provided for the clutch foot.

Performance

In use the 260Z engine sounds and feels much like the unit one sees under the car's bonnet — a huge and heavy lump.

It is this rumbling, rough engine sound that makes the 260Z's performance so deceptive. One is surprised to find the car going so quickly while sounding so slow and to this extent it is indeed just like those cars of yesteryear, rough and lumbering until they get into their not inconsiderable stride.

With 2565 cc of six cylinder, single overhead camshaft engine there is naturally plenty of low speed torque to let the Datsun lumber around all day at low revs. But its actual power band is quite narrow, maximum torque coming at the high figure of 4400 revs and maximum bhp at 5400 revs. Below 4000 rpm the car is noticeably more sluggish and the power dies away quite quickly at 6000 rpm so there is little point in rupturing the engine by continuously taking it to the 6500 warning line or the 7000 red sector even though it will go there.

Its zero to 60 mph time of 9.5 secs is respectably quick, allowing for the car's considerable size and weight and a maximum speed of 125 mph is good in any company. The car will, in fact, pull to virtually this speed in the fourth of its five gears but is over peak power by then and gaining speed only fractionally. Fifth gear being very high means also that those last few mph need a long clear road.

The gearbox has a conventionally gated first four speeds, with fifth up and to the right. It proved a little notchy in use, the fourth-fifth gate being quite slow and the third-second change occasionally baulking.

Noticeable virtually all the time was a heavy clunk from the rear axle, both on gear changing and when putting the power back on after running on a trailing throttle. Only extremely gentle letting out of the clutch could avoid it and every 240/260CZ owner we know has complained of the same phenomenon.

Road holding

Any would-be Datsun 260Z owner should take a course of press-ups before driving his new toy. The steering is extremely heavy — you won't be a seven stone weakling for long. It also has very strong self centring, manifesting itself as an unusual, and at first disconcerting, springiness back through the padded steering wheel when cornering. The car's handling is good by coupé standards but not up to the best in sports car standards. Suspension settings

Rear seat can hold an adult — just about

Front seats are very well shaped but firm

have been kept soft which gives excellent ride comfort on all surfaces but adversely affect the handling.

The soft independent rear suspension can be caught out by bumps and camber changes when cornering, making the rear rather twitchy when the car is being driven hard. Roll angles through bends are also quite noticeable.

Its great length, the extra 12 inches of wheelbase having made it a very long car, means that it resents being hustled through tight bends. But its suspension is quite safely set up with predominant understeer so that the front tends to slip towards the outside of bends and extra steering lock will bring it round. Only under extreme provocation can the tail be broken away, although enthusiasts would probably prefer this to happen more easily. It is a car that much prefers long, fast curves when it will cling to the road very well indeed.

The brakes, despite a slight spongy feel at the pedal, proved well up to stopping the big car, fading a little only after repeated heavy use. But they did develop a tendency to snatch and lock up prematurely on one side, again after heavy use.

The costs

Upped in price not so long ago to £3670, the 260Z 2-plus-2 must now be regarded as an expensive car for its specification and performance, although it does have some impressive standard equipment. With Datsun having built up a good spares stockpile here, servicing and spares should be no more than average cost for this class of machine, but likewise insurance companies will look at it with disfavour. Datsun's own insurance arrangement, at preferential rates, does not give a grouping for the 260Z — preferring to treat cases individually, but everyone else lists it as Group Seven.

On that crucial question of petrol the Datsun is quite a fair performer, the high fifth gear allowed us to return an excellent 25.6 mpg touring which dropped to a still fair 21.2 mpg during the harder test runs.

The Alternatives

Here the 260Z has many rivals: for a completely different approach to high speed motoring there is the Lotus Plus 2S 130/5, with more performance but less room for passengers and luggage. The Opel Commodore Coupé, at £3378, is a shade slower than the Datsun, but more sophisticated if not so obviously sporty. The Triumph Stag (£3342) has the performance but evil power steering and tricky handling. Possibly the two closest rivals are the fine Reliant Scimitar GTE, £3194, similar performance and space, and for far less money the 3-litre Capri in GT or Ghia form, again with similar performance and the same passenger/load carrying capability.

Verdict

As in so many road tests, the section above tells the story. The 260Z 2-Plus-2 is an excellent machine but at the price it has more equally excellent, some would say better, rivals: the Commodore is far more sophisticated — the cheaper Capri offers much that the Datsun does.

While its handling is not up to the best in sports cars, the Datsun has classically elegant lines and a tough brutality about it that make it a worthy successor to the 'muscle cars' and give it an individuality which some of its rivals lack and which will obviously persuade many buyers

Rear styling features typically Japanese lamp clusters. Note the plastic air dam

Datsun 260Z 2+2

PRICE: £3670

Importer: Datsun UK Ltd., Brighton Road, Worthing, Sussex

PERFORMANCE
Maximum speed: 125 mph
Maximum in 4th: 122 mph
Maximum in 3rd: 100 mph
Maximum in 2nd: 67 mph
Maximum in 1st: 43 mph
Speedometer error: Accurate at 60 mph

Acceleration
0-30 mph: 3.3 secs
0-40 mph: 5.0 secs
0-50 mph: 7.1 secs
0-60 mph: 9.5 secs
0-70 mph: 12.6 secs
0-80 mph: 16.1 secs
0-90 mph: 20.7 secs
0-100 mph 26.7 secs

Fuel consumption
Full test: 21.2 mpg
Touring: 25.6 mpg
Tank holds: 13.2 galls
Range: 330 miles
Fuel grade: 3 star
Fuel for 15,000 miles: £390

SPECIFICATION
Engine: Cast iron block, alloy head
No. of cylinders: 6-in-line
Bore and stroke: 83.0 mm x 79.0 mm
Capacity: 2565 cc
Valve gear: Single overhead camshaft
Compression ratio: 8.3 to 1
Carburation: 2 Hitachi HMB 46WI
Maximum power: 150 bhp DIN at 5400 rpm
Maximum torque: 158 lbs/ft DIN at 4400 rpm
Cooling: Water
Main bearings: 7

Transmission
Clutch: 8.87 ins diaphragm spring
Gearbox: 5-speed manual all synchromesh
Ratios: 2.91, 1.90, 1.31, 1.00, 0.86 to 1
Final drive: 3.70 to 1
Mph per 1000 rpm in top gear: 22.6

Steering: Rack and pinion
Power: No
Turns, lock to lock: 2.9
Turning circle: 36 ft

Suspension
Front: Independent, Macpherson struts, lower links, coil springs, anti-roll bar
Rear: Independent, Macpherson struts, lower wishbones, coil springs

Brakes: Servo-assisted dual circuit
Front: 10.7 ins discs
Rear: 9.0 ins drums
Wheels: 5J x 14 ins steel
Tyres: 195/70 VR14

Body construction: Steel unitary

Weight: 23.5 cwt
Distribution (front/rear): 51/49 percent
NCC recommended towing weight: 18 cwt
Payload: 882 lbs

SERVICING
Recommended service interval: 3000 miles
Standard time, labour only; 1 hour (3000), 3 hours (6000), 5 hours (12,000)

Parts costs
Front wing: £55.80
Front brakes pads: £3.64
Exhaust system: £38.43
Clutch unit: £23.48
Replacement engine: £265.53
Replacement gearbox: £195.69

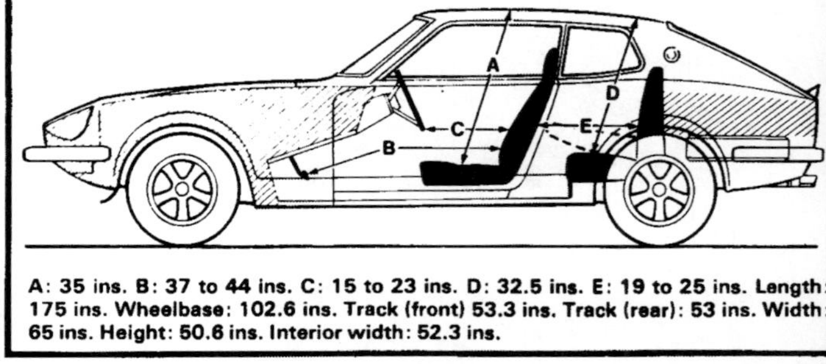

A: 35 ins. B: 37 to 44 ins. C: 15 to 23 ins. D: 32.5 ins. E: 19 to 25 ins. Length: 175 ins. Wheelbase: 102.6 ins. Track (front) 53.3 ins. Track (rear): 53 ins. Width: 65 ins. Height: 50.6 ins. Interior width: 52.3 ins.

HOW IT COMPARES

Price	Car	cc	Speed (mph)	touring (mpg)	0-60 secs	30-50 in top (secs)	Interior width (ins)	Boot (cu ft)	Length (ins)
£2831	Ford Capri 3000 Ghia	2994	120	23	8.5	8.0	51.0	81/22.6	168.8
£3194	Reliant Scimitar GTE	2994	121	25	8.9	8.0	51.0	19/36	171.0
£3342	Triumph Stag FH	2998	118	24.5	10.1	7.5	52.0	9.0	173.7
£3378	Opel Commodore GS Coupé	2784	113	19.0	10.3	6.0	59.0	11.8	181.3
£3422	Lotus Plus 2S 130/5	1558	122	27.0	7.6	11.7	51.5	8	168.5
£3670	**Datsun 260Z 2+2**	**2565**	**125**	**25.6**	**9.5**	**10.5**	**52.3**	**11.4/20**	**175.0**

What Car? tests/Datsun 260Z 2+2

Retaining the well-known shape, the 260Z now displays aerodynamic aids front and rear.

Looking the part road test

The Datsun 240Z was a much-loved sports coupé with a six-cylinder engine that gave it a reserve of smooth power but was small enough to be reasonably economical. For anti-pollution reasons, and to accommodate low-octane fuels, a longer-stroke version of the overhead-camshaft unit was developed, with a lower compression ratio. I tested both types and found that the later 260Z car was less inclined to rev, because of its longer stroke, but with its higher gearing it was still a fast and effortless sports car.

For the last couple of years, only the longer, 2+2 version has been available in the UK, but now the sports 2-seater is back. I therefore lost no time in obtaining a road-test car, for real sports cars are getting somewhat thin on the ground.

The Datsun retains the well-known shape, though it now displays aerodynamic aids front and rear. Judging by its stability in gusty winds, these appendages are rather more than merely cosmetic. The big rear door, balanced on struts, gives excellent access to the large luggage deck, but it would be well to improvise some sort of cover, for the suitcases are all too visible through the window. This is one of the few cars that provides ample leg room for today's tall young men and, though the seating is fairly low, the view in all directions is satisfactory.

Having a long bonnet, the 260Z easily assimilates an in-line six-cylinder engine, with plenty of metal in the right places. The valves are operated by a chain-driven overhead-camshaft and two constant-vacuum carburettors are mounted on well-proportioned manifolds. However, the design of the exhaust manifold cannot be applauded and a useful power increase is here available for the asking—accessory shops please note! The under-bonnet arrangements offer good accessibility.

Mounted in unit with the engine, the gearbox gives five speeds with a direct fourth, the overdrive fifth gear position being out to the right and forward, which is now the most popular arrangement. A chassis-mounted hypoid unit drives the rear wheels which, like the front, are suspended on struts and lower wishbones. Anti-roll bars are found at both ends and the steering is by rack and pinion.

The attractive lines of the body are complemented by an interior which suits a genuine sports car, with plenty of legible, round dials. The seats give good lateral location, although their head-restraints are rather in the way during reversing manoeuvres. The controls are well-placed and, while the steering is heavy for parking, it becomes reasonably light at normal town speeds. The gearchange is not of the ultra-light variety, as on some Japanese cars, but it is easy to use and absolutely precise.

Above: The interior suits a genuine sports car. Below: The big rear door gives excellent access.

The car starts instantly from cold, after which the choke should not be fully released too soon, but the big engine actually warms up quite quickly. First gear is unusually high, which is ideal for hairpin bends on mountain roads. The engine is very flexible and quiter than that of the original 260Z, but there is no point in using maximum revs in the gears and I found that I obtained the best acceleration by changing up reasonably early. Theoretically, it would be possible to reach 100mph in third gear, but 90mph is a more realistic speed. There seems little difference in the *maxima* on fourth or fifth, about 115mph being an honest figure.

The latest Datsun is more refined than its predecessors and it has a marvellously long-legged stride. It makes fine averages without ever being pressed and high cruising speeds do not empty the petrol tank too rapidly. Some sports coupés suffer greatly from booming, but the 260Z is innocent of this fault. Nevertheless, there is a good deal of tyre roar on non-skid surfaces and some thumping over bad bumps. The ride is fairly firm but by no means harsh, and the comfort of the occupants is ensured by an excellent heating and ventilation system with a truly silent fan.

Normally, there is a moderate degree of under-steer, changing gradually to over-steer during hard driving or on lift-off. The car feels stable at speed but the steering seems slightly dead on occasion, though the controllability is generally good. The brakes are powerful and responsive, coping well with fast touring, though they would need some attention for competition work. As supplied, the 260Z makes a charming road car for any purpose, with plenty of performance in reserve and a sporting character that is not over-emphasised.

Though there is still a demand for a good-looking two-seater, with no space for occasional passengers, the day has gone when such cars were expected to be noisy and intractable. The Datsun looks the part, but it has six-cylinder smoothness and a clutch light enough for a feminine foot, plus fuel economy that would not disgrace a rather dull family saloon.

Specification and performance data

Car tested: Datsun 260Z 2-seater coupé, price £5728.

Engine: Six-cylinder in line 83x79mm (2565cc).Compression ratio 9.2 to 1. 150bhp DIN at 5400rpm. Chain-driven overhead camshaft. 2 Hitachi constant-vacuum carburettors.

Transmission: Single dry plate clutch. 5-speed synchromesh gearbox, ratios; 0.86, 1.0, 1.31, 2.08, and 3.32 to 1. Hypoid final drive, ratio 3.54 to 1. Driveshafts to rear hubs.

Chassis: Combined steel body and chassis. Independent suspension of all wheels by coil-spring struts and lower wishbones with anti-roll bars. Rack and pinion steering. Servo-assisted dual-circuit disc/drum brakes. Bolt-on light-alloy wheels, fitted 195/70 VR 14 tyres.

Equipment: 12-volt lighting and starting. Speedometer. Rev-counter. Oil-pressure, water-temperature and fuel gauges. Volt-meter. 2-speed and intermittent wipers and washer. Flashing direction indicators with hazard warning. Heating, demisting, and ventilation system with heated rear windows. Reversing lights.

Dimensions: Wheelbase 7ft 6.7ins, track 4ft 5.5ins/4ft 5ins, overall length 11ft 6ins, width 5ft 4.2ins, Weight 1 ton 2 cwt 3 qrs.

Fuel consumption: 21 to 27 mpg.

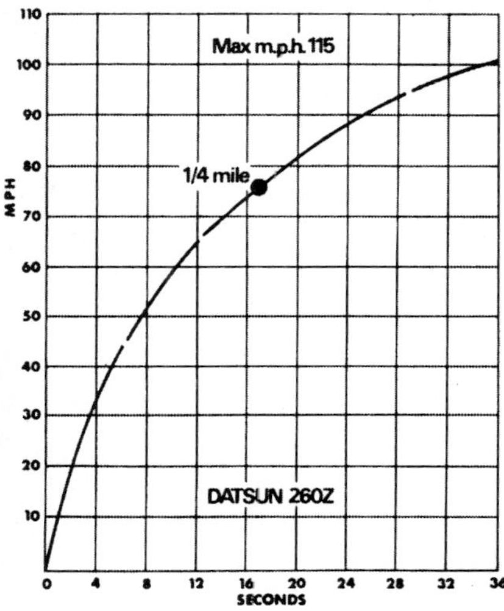

Miles Behind the Wheel

6.6 to sixty

A CAR AS rugged and understressed as the Datsun 260Z must be a godsend for the tuner who is trying to turbocharge an engine reliably with a true bolt-on kit. This conversion falls into that category and is one of the neatest I have ever seen. It is available either through Datsun (Bristol) or that prolific tuner Janos Odor of Janspeed.

To start with, the 260Z has two practical advantages for the installation: Firstly, there is plenty of space around the engine to make the work easy, and mitigate the commonly found turbocharged engine problem of under-bonnet heat build up. Secondly, the inlet and exhaust ports are on the same side of the cylinder head so there is no compressed air / mixture pipe running awkwardly across the top of the cylinder head.

The whole arrangement looks neatly inconspicuous. It employs Janspeed's well-tried formula of using the Rotomaster turbocharger to suck air through a 2in. SU carburettor, rather than blow into the carburettor as on the Broadspeed Bullit and Prophet BMW (*Miles Behind The Wheel* 18 October 1978). The compressed mixture is then delivered straight to a long fabricated buffer-ended inlet manifold which shares the same flange as six short exhaust pipes. They lead to a collector chamber on top of which the turbocharger is bolted. A standard static compression ratio of 9.2 to 1 has meant setting the wastegate (mounted on the underside of the collector chamber) to blow off at a lowly 5 psi. Other modifications are limited to the all-important oil cooler, harder-than-standard brake pads, and externally, the exceptionally attention-grabbing "Turbo" lettered sidewinders. Surprisingly, there are no transmission, suspension or further mechanical modifications to cope with the extra stresses. The standard 195/70 HR-14 Dunlop Steelmax tyres suffice.

Such a simple conversion represents considerable development time at Janspeed, but according to Jim McCubbin at Datsun (Bristol) further time spent by them on the ignition curve has made the engine even more flexible than when first supplied.

There was an element of truth in two quite independent comments from passengers in the Turbo 260Z. "Just like a latterday Austin Healey 3000," they said. "Healey 3000, or poor man's supercar?" I asked. We shall see.

Like all the other turbocharged cars that we have tested recently, that firm push in the back came with extraordinary flexibility. All right, the normally aspirated, nearly-square 2.6-litre slogging straight six could hardly be more flexible, but the blown 260Z bettered the standard car in this respect (*Autotest* 5 October 1977) by pulling quite willingly from 10 mph in fourth gear. Without a drop in static compression ratio (found on most turbocharged cars) to markedly mar unboosted or part-throttle performance, and only 5 psi boost pressure, the "step" in power as the engine climbed on to the turbocharger was wonderfully subdued — a feeling confirmed by looking at the similarity low down between the blown and unblown cars through-the-gears acceleration times. But look at the top end! There is all the relaxed torquey poke you could ever want for.

Sliding my foot off a pleasantly light clutch, it was a super machine to take off the line. When the rear wheels started to spin there was none of the Broadspeed Bullit's initial gasping gap in the power as the revs and turbocharger speed dropped momentarily. On a damp track, and with no limited slip diff, the traction was quite remarkable. It took us pouring away from rest to 30 mph in 2.5 sec, 60 mph in 6.6 sec, past the quarter-mile post in 15.3 sec (quickest Turbo so far and equal to an Aston Martin V8 Automatic), on to 100 mph in 17.7 sec and 120 mph in 30.6 sec — all well within the mile. Admittedly the

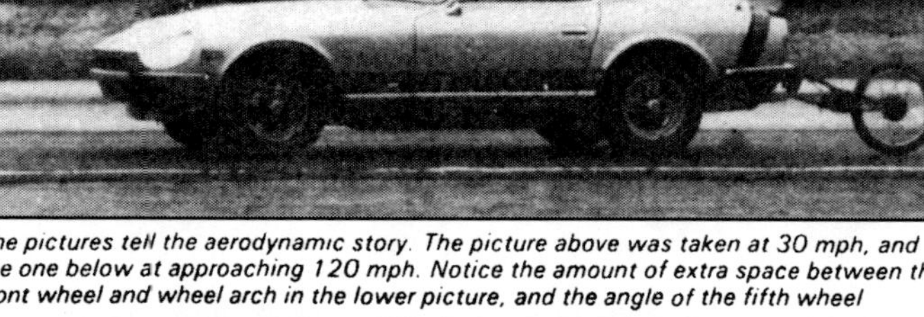

The pictures tell the aerodynamic story. The picture above was taken at 30 mph, and the one below at approaching 120 mph. Notice the amount of extra space between the front wheel and wheel arch in the lower picture, and the angle of the fifth wheel

Bullit is slightly quicker right at the top end, but the Datsun felt less frenetic — less stressed.

Starting was never a problem hot or cold, but a slight mid-range hesitation on part throttle and as the blower came in suggested the need for some fine mixture tuning. Also, on full boost, the engine surged as if intermittently held back, and this tied up with a sympathetic boost gauge needle movement varying 1 psi. Rotomaster and Janspeed say that this is caused by a "panting" wastegate and is easily cured by restricting the exhaust flow to the valve. Apparently the latest conversions have been suitably modified.

On the road neither criticism really detracted much from the sheer pleasure this long-legged, rather ponderous handling beast gave. However, in spite of the harder pads nothing could stop total brake fade on the seventh of 10 consecutive 0.5g stops from 95 mph at MIRA (the standard *Autocar* fade test). It's a hard test, but the weakness was hardly surprising because the standard car barely passed our earlier, far easier test. Ventilated discs are obviously worth considering.

For the well-heeled enthusiast without a family the Turbo 260Z has a lot going for it. Handily it's 3in. narrower than the reasonably proportioned 3-litre Capri. Sensible gearing in fifth of 23.6 mph per 1,000 rpm positively encourages all-day cruising at 90-100 mph; something the Turbo 260Z will do without boost and on a touch of throttle — were it possible. The endemic choppy and sometimes thumpy ride didn't upset me, and although cornering balance varies from slight slow speed understeer to being just about neutral at high speed, the high geared steering and a 50/50 weight distribution probably do most to help the Datsun handle predictably.

The deeply hooded instruments and pleasant to use steering wheel remain unaltered — and typically Japanese. The boost gauge was poorly sited underneath the facia. Nothing needs re-routing under the bonnet because of the conversion: There is plenty of space for and around the pipework. Accessibility is excellent.

Acceleration

FROM REST

True mph	Turbo 260Z	R/T 260Z
30	2.5	3.2
40	3.6	4.9
50	5.1	7.4
60	6.6	10.1
70	9.1	14.5
80	11.6	19.0
90	14.5	24.5
100	17.7	34.7
110	23.3	—
120	30.6	—

	Turbo 260Z	R/T 260Z
Standing ¼ mile:	15.3 sec 95 mph	17.9 sec 79 mph
Standing kilometre:	27.8 sec 117 mph	32.7 sec 98 mph

THROUGH THE GEARS

	TURBO 260Z				R/T 260Z			
mph	Top	4th	3rd	2nd	Top	4th	3rd	2nd
10-30	—	10.6	7.3	4.2	—	—	7.3	4.3
20-40	11.8	9.3	6.5	3.4	11.9	9.4	6.9	4.2
30-50	10.6	7.7	5.2	2.7	11.5	8.7	6.5	4.1
40-60	9.3	6.9	4.6	2.9	11.9	8.9	6.7	4.7
50-70	8.5	6.5	4.3	—	13.2	9.8	7.1	7.3
60-80	8.4	6.4	4.6	—	14.7	11.0	7.7	—
70-90	8.7	6.9	6.0	—	17.1	12.2	9.7	—
80-100	9.6	7.5	6.2	—	23.2	15.2	15.9	—
90-110	11.9	8.8	—	—	—	—	—	
100-120	—	12.1	—	—	—	—	—	

On the debit side, a surprising amount of wind noise spoiled motorway cruising refinement, and the wipers left the windscreen at anything over 85 mph — a failsafe system? But more importantly I felt that in blustery conditions straight line stability could have been better, where steering vagueness much over 100 mph could be photographically nailed to a lifting front end. Perhaps comments like these are slightly irrelevant these days, and overall the standard chassis, suspension, and transmission seem to accept the massive power hike without any protest or quirk, as do the engine internals.

Whether quietly trickling through the dulling commuter crush, restraining myself on the motorways, or even extending the 260Z Turbo at MIRA, I could not better 15 mpg on any of three tankfuls of fuel, yet the overall consumption worked out at 14.6 mpg. Whatever the driving style, the fuel consumption remained strangly constant.

Despite the niggles it didn't take long to become rather attached to such an unfussy, solid feeling, very high performance car. The stylised interior might put you off or the heavy steering around town, or perhaps the seats, but you tend to forget these things when a downchange and floored throttle wafts you quietly with the turbocharger whistling inconspicuously straight towards real supercar performance.

The complete package costs £1,400 from Datsun (Bristol) and raises the price of a new 260Z to a little under £7,000 (a comparable price to the Bullit).

In answer to the earlier question; perhaps it's a poor man's supercar, with very strong Healey 3000 connections.

Janspeed Engineering Ltd
Southampton Road
Salisbury
Wiltshire SP1 2LN
Datsun (Bristol) Ltd,
Berkeley Place,
Clifton
Bristol BS8 1EH

ZED CAR INSTITUTION

With the 280ZX soon to take over from the Datsun 260Z, we recall our impressions of the long lived "Japanese E Type"

THE DATSUN 260Z is like an institution. How many people do you know that have (and still are) longed to own one? Since their introduction – as the 240Z then – late in 1970, they've been the poor man's Ferrari.

Eight years on and very little has changed. Except the price. The original two seat 240Z cost $4,567 at its introduction. Today, the 260Z two seater costs a massive $13,645. Sure inflation caused some of that rise, but the rest . . . probably something to do with the economics law of supply and demand.

The 240Z became the 260Z in June 1974. The engine was stretched from 2400 to 2600 ccs — hence the model designation change — and power went up from 151 to 162 bhp. The ride was also stiffened to obviate what Motor Manual testers described at the time as the "marshmellow" ride of the 240Z.

With the regular 260Z came the most important change, the 260Z 2+2. Datsun had lengthened the wheelbase and whole car by exactly 12 inches, giving them room to install a rear seat. Or something that resembled a rear seat anyway.

Suddenly the Z car had more practicality, more acceptability(it wasn't so much of a sports car anymore) and more buyers. Datsun were on another winner.

Sales were good for the original Z car, and with its introduction, the 260Z — still fully imported — was selling even better. Datsun was selling every car it could get.

1976 saw a sales peak of 1648 units, this dropping to 1069 in 1977. Continuing sales trend (which reflects a slight waning of popularity), we see that to the end of May last year, 388 units have been sold.

In 1979 the Z car isn't cheap – as we said. For $12,570 you get the two seat 260 and for a grand more, the four seater. That puts them over two grand *more* expensive than the recently introduced (to Australia) sports car opposition, Fiat's X1/9 and Triumph's TR7.

Certainly the 2+2 Z gives you extra passenger room and the practicality of a hatchback, and that's important to lots of people. But as cars, the TR7 and X1/9 are vastly superior.

Mechanically the 260Z is dated. The engine is rough, noisy and doesn't possess much go. Over the quarter, cars with two less cylinders are quicker — it's only when the road is open and long that you get performance motoring.

Mate that with a notchy, difficult to use gearbox and a heavy throttle spring, and you've got the recipe for utterly frustrating driving. Smooth gear changes are the exception, not the norm.

Completing the drive train is a diff that literally "clunks" into each gear — no matter how smoothly the car is driven. Still at the rear, we should mention the unforgiving rear suspension. Impact harshness is very severe, road shocks vibrating through the cabin, leaving just a plain, uncomfortable ride.

Down at the front, there's a bad case of terminal understeer, which gets to almost uncontrollable proportions in the wet. The Z won't oversteer no matter what you do — except on gravel of course.

Linked with the understeer is HEAVY steering. You begin to use muscles you've never used before. How women drive it (most I know refuse to) I don't know.

In total the Z is a total disappointment to drive. But while it's mechanically dated, then it remains almost as desirable as ever. The styling, while also dated now, is still a head turner and it will probably, one day, become a classic.

Inside, the driving environment looks the part, and is quite comfortable. That's all most drivers want.

Time has caught up with the 260Z. It's still the bird puller it always was but as a sports car, it's bettered by a number of sedans.

Roll on the new Z, Datsun.

PERFORMANCE:

Speedometer error (km/h)			
Indicated	60	80	100
Actual	62	80	91

Acceleration from standstill to:

60 km/h	6.2
80 km/h	8.4
100 km/h	11.1
120 km/h	16.0
140 km/h	20.1

Acceleration from 60 km/h to 100 km/h

Standing start 400 metres:

Elapsed time	18.2
Terminal speed	130

Maximum speeds in gears:

1st	70 km/h @ 6500 rpm
2nd	110 km/h @ 6500 rpm
3rd	160 km/h @ 6500 rpm
4th	205 km/h @ 6500 rpm
5th	225 km/h approx.

Braking — 110 km/h to zero:

Average distance taken in metres	52.5

Datsun 240Z

Driving the icons

The driving experience never quite lived up to its stunning lines, says Colin Goodwin

TOM SALT

Non-standard Wolfrace alloys look just right. Understeer, heavy steering dull driving experience

I've done more than drive this icon – I owned one for nine years. I bought it in the mid-'80s for a song, sold it in the '90s as a restoration project, as it finally spluttered to a halt.

When I bought my 240Z, I couldn't believe that I'd snatched up such a gorgeous car for only £950. If it had had a different name it would surely have been worth much more. If it had worn an Austin-Healey badge, for example. Actually, classic car pundits often describe the 240Z, launched in 1970, as a modern Healey. Sacrilege, some would say; especially those who sneer at the 240Z's badge and Far East birthplace.

The Z might have been made in Japan, but it was designed by Austrian Count Albrecht Goertz, who worked for the American design company responsible for the Coke bottle. He was also responsible for the BMW 507, itself a far from ugly motor car. Not that this would have cut much ice with those who turned their noses up at anything built in Japan – the same people who accused the Japanese of being capable only of copying others.

In fairness, there's a lot in the 240Z that supports that view. Peer under the tail and you'll see independent rear suspension that's pure Colin Chapman in layout, with struts and wide-based lower wishbones. Still, it may have been copied, but it makes the MGB's ancient live axle look very agricultural.

The Z's engine increased in size a few times during its lifetime, but the 2.4-litre ohc six is reckoned to be the nicest. By today's standards, 150bhp from a unit of this size is nothing special, but it's enough to take the 240 to 125mph. Steve Bicknell, who owns this perfectly restored Z, has fitted it with an exhaust that's slightly more rorty than the standard item – and it sounds fantastic; much better than mine ever did. Bicknell's car is like new. Brand new, because 240Zs didn't stay like this for very long. There were tales of cars with serious rust while still in the showroom.

Bicknell's Z is free from several irritating faults that made driving the 240 a less enjoyable experience than it should have been. The throttle linkage, for example, is made up of several rods and rose joints. Fine when new, but when worn it makes it impossible to drive the car smoothly. You put your right foot down and the pedal suddenly sticks; push harder and you get much more throttle than you really wanted. The drivetrain includes six universal joints, and when these get a bit dog-eared, smooth progress is even more unlikely.

Z's 150bhp 2.4-litre six good for 125mph. Sticky throttle a common problem

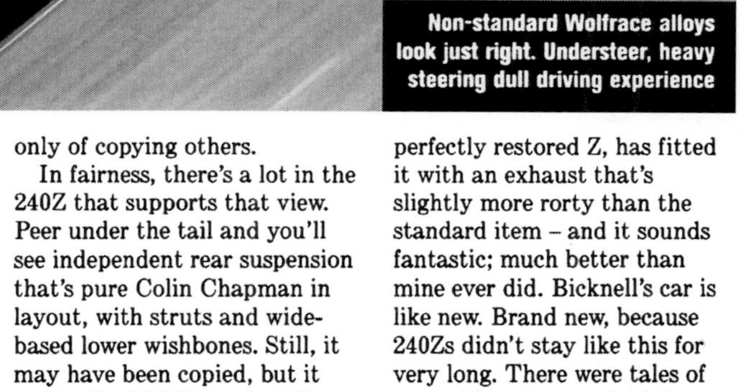

Driving a Z would be a lot more fun if it didn't understeer so much. Forget any thoughts of power sliding the rear-drive Datsun out of slow corners. It just won't play. Trying will just wear your arms out as you wrestle with the heavy steering. The brakes are another Z weakness. Drive hard and they'll start to fade. The hot tip was to fit Range Rover calipers.

A lot of non-standard kit found its way onto 240Zs in the '70s. The Wolfrace alloys on Bicknell's car are period pieces that were often fitted to Z cars; the standard steel wheels had hub caps that looked boring and refused to stay on the rims during even mildly hard cornering. Wolfies look fine, but the add-on wheel arches, huge spoilers, rear window louvres and most of the other crud that custom car nuts once fitted to their Zs certainly did not.

Non-standard exhaust sounds great

Nissan itself did its utmost to ruin the Z – and succeeded. The 260Z wasn't so bad, but the 280 and 300 models were dreadful. Only the recent (and now dead) twin-turbo 300ZX restored some dignity to the Z name. Nissan in the US has recently started buying up 240Zs, restoring them, and flogging them through selected dealers. Guilty conscience, I reckon.

DATSUN

ROAD & TRACK 1947 50 1997 ANNIVERSARY SALON

DATSUN 240Z

Japan reinvents the sports car

BY DOUGLAS KOTT
PHOTOS BY GUY SPANGENBERG

THE SLIDE'S COLORS are hazy, its cardboard frame yellowed and slightly warped, but the memories remain vivid. I was a gangly 13-year-old at the time, squeezed beneath the hatch of a dark blue 240Z that belonged to my mom's boyfriend, Jerry, holding my brand-new puppy. We were on our way back from Chino, California, to my hometown of Yorba Linda, having picked up a 7-week-old Pembroke Welsh Corgi from a breeder in the area. Maybe the thrill of sudden puppy ownership made the car seem even more distinctive, but the impressions are indelible. Seeing a nice 240Z on the street brings it all back in a flood—the resonance of its exhaust, the tacky diamond-quilt vinyl covering the rear strut towers, the faint aroma of unburned hydrocarbons mingled with puppy breath, and the way the Z's taut suspension was making my Corgi's tiny head dip rhythmically with every bump, like the counterweighted skull of a souvenir turtle.

The impact on American car enthusiasts was huge too. Here, in 1970, was a $3526 sports car with a level of styling sophistication unheard of for a mass-produced Japanese car, with a rakish fastback roofline, impossibly long hood, headlights recessed in those famous "sugar scoops" and proportions that, although undoubtedly influenced by the Jaguar E-Type and Ferrari Daytona, finally broke through the "copycat" styling for which Japanese carmakers had long been accused. And the 240Z offered something else for the American enthusiast weaned on 327 Chevys and 289 Fords: power. Of course, it wasn't in the sort of tread-peeling, smoke-producing amounts that made for great theater at the Dairy Queen, but 150 bhp at 6000 rpm and 148 lb.-ft. of torque distanced it (quite literally) from the Alfa Romeo 1750, Opel GT, MGB GT, Fiat 124 Coupe and other European competitors in the same price range.

Datsun already had a sturdy engine in the 510 sedan's L-series 1.6-liter inline-4, so it was fairly straightforward to create a cast-iron inline-6 sharing the same bore-center spacing, bore and stroke dimensions of 83.0 x 73.3 mm, pistons, connecting rods and rod bearings. In fact, as Colin Shipway notes in his book, *Essential Datsun Z, 240Z to 280ZX,* the extra two cylinders brought the design nearly full circle, as the architecture of the 510's inline-4 was most likely influenced by a Mercedes-Benz straight-6 that Prince (which was owned by Nissan) had built under license.

As with the 510's powerplant, this new engine—logically dubbed L24, for its 2393 cc—used a single chain-driven overhead camshaft to operate two valves per cylinder via rocker arms with mechanical adjusters. The aluminum head was of the side-flow design, fed by two sidedraft Hitachi-SU HJG 46W carburetors, SU clones built under license. Redline was at a lofty 7000 rpm, but road testers of the day said going past 5500 rpm or so resulted in more noise than power. When our fifth wheel was fitted, the Z delivered, with a 0–60-mph dash of 8.7 seconds and a quarter-mile posting of 17.1 sec. at 84.5 mph. Today, any hot econobox worth its 16 valves could show its high-mounted brake light to the Z at the drag strip, but consider that in its day the Z could give the Porsche 911T a good run for its money, which, at $6060, was nearly twice as expensive.

Some other pieces came from existing parts bins, albeit with minor modifications: the 4-speed manual transmission from the 2000 Roadster; the MacPherson-strut front suspension from the Japan-market 1800 Laurel. But the rear suspension deviated from the 510's semi-trailing arms and took a page from Colin Chapman's design book, essentially using MacPherson struts at the rear as Chapman did for his Elite and Elan. This simple, lightweight setup, using extremely wide-based lower A-arms for fore/aft location, certainly was partly responsible for the Z's agility advantage over the live-axle/trailing-arm arrangement favored by most like-priced competitors—and forever stamped the term "Chapman strut" into the *Road & Track* lexicon.

The combination worked. As we said in our April 1970 Road Test, "The Datsun can really be driven hard; flung enthusiastically into corners, its near-neutral handling (helped by the near 50/50 weight distribution) makes it very stable, with just a hint of oversteer, allowing the tail to hang out but not come around... On the skidpad, we recorded 33.0 mph, equal to 0.728g. This is just a hair better than the speed achieved by the Porsche 914!" Our kind of car, in other words.

At about this point, you may be thinking that the Z's design approach closely mirrors that of the Toyota 2000GT, a rather pricey ($6800), limited-production 2-seat GT with a 2.0-liter twincam inline-6 and seductive fastback bodywork that went on sale more than two years before the Z. Vehicular plagiarism? Not really, and the reasons why lead this story in an interesting direction.

Enter Albrecht Goertz, a German designer/stylist perhaps best known for the BMW 507, who was commissioned by Nissan in the early Sixties to build a sleek 2-seat coupe prototype body on the 2000 Roadster (SR311) chassis. The prototype, dubbed the Silvia, was built by Yamaha (which, like Porsche, offers its engineering services to other manufacturers) and was to be powered by a Yamaha-designed 2.0-liter straight-6 (sound familiar?). A pretty little car with retractable headlights and the Goertz trademarks of a reverse-angle nose and lower bodywork that tucked inward to expose the tires' tread, it was finished in 1964, but Nissan opted to put the project on the back burner. It's rumored that Yamaha took Goertz's ideas to Toyota, the result being the 2000GT. As Shipway observes, "the 2000GT was later cited as one of the [Z's] design influences, but it was more akin to a half-brother because it arose from the same original design concepts."

In 1966, Nissan resurrected the project, by which time the Silvia's features had evolved into other prototypes, which eventually became the basis for the 240Z. Sleeping dogs were allowed to lie until the introduction of the 280ZX, when Goertz criticized the new car heavily. Nissan responded with a statement denying that Goertz ever had anything to do with the original 240Z; the designer countered with a lawsuit. The matter was amicably

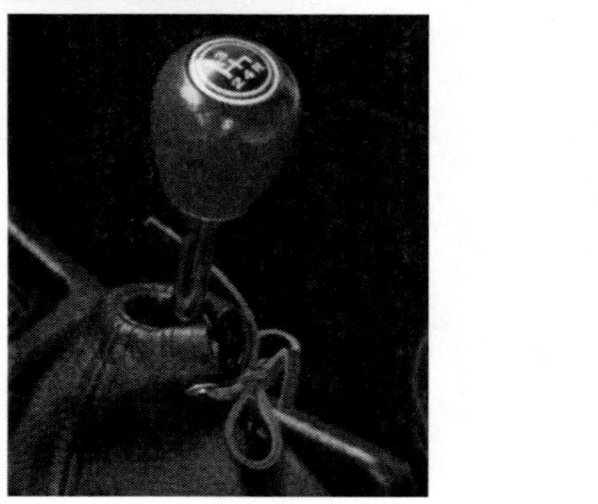

settled with a candid letter from Nissan to Goertz, which stated that although "...the design of the 240Z was the product of Nissan's design staff, Nissan agrees that the personnel who designed that automobile were influenced by your fine work for Nissan and had the benefit of your designs."

It's interesting to note that, even with the Silvia prototype, Goertz stressed that there should be adequate room for full-size Americans. The

■ The feel of our January 1970 cover photo is nicely recreated with our action shot of Todd Frazier's restored Z on the Commodore Schuyler F. Heim drawbridge in the Long Beach harbor area.

■ **Top, the Z's generous cargo area, complete with diamond-quilt vinyl; above, the famous "sugar scoop" headlight buckets.**

message wasn't lost on the 240Z, whose low-mounted thin-shell seats and roofline accommodate 6-footers with ease. Also significant was the thought given to ergonomics, an infant science even in the late Sixties. In laying out the interior, electrodes implanted in the arms of a human "test dummy" measured muscle fatigue to help optimize placement of the controls.

For our Salon, it was quite a challenge to track down an original 240Z. Though it was the best-selling sports car of its time (demand outstripped supply in the U.S., a probable first for Datsun), it appears that Japanese rust-proofing techniques were also in their infancy, so the numbers were thinned by the ravages of the elements. Also, as the cars were relatively inexpensive and plentiful, few were meticulously maintained. And modifications ran rampant, the most popular being replacing the rather homely wheel covers and steel rims with the then-in-vogue slot mags, and fitting spoilers, air dams and small-diameter steering wheels.

How fortunate we were, then, to meet up with Pierre Perot. An instantly likable, French-born former race mechanic, Perot headed the Renault racing effort in the early Sixties, preparing an M63 Alpine prototype in 1963 for his close personal friend, Mark Donohue. More recently (for the past 21 years, to be exact), he has been racing, modifying, restoring and maintaining Z-cars out of his shop, Pierre' Z, in Hawthorne, California. And one of his

SPECIFICATIONS

Curb weight	2355 lb
Wheelbase	90.7 in.
Track, f/r	53.3 in./53.0 in.
Length	162.8 in.
Width	64.1 in.
Height	50.6 in.
Fuel capacity	15.9 gal.

ENGINE & DRIVETRAIN

Engine	sohc inline-6
Bore x stroke	83.0 x 73.3 mm
Displacement	2393 cc
Compression ratio	9.0:1
Horsepower (SAE)	150 bhp @ 6000 rpm
Torque	148 lb-ft @ 4400 rpm
Fuel delivery	two Hitachi-SU carburetors
Transmission	4-speed manual

CHASSIS & BODY

Layout	front engine/rear drive
Brake system, f/r	10.7-in. discs/9.0-in. drums
Wheels	pressed steel, 14 x 4½
Tires	Bridgestone, 175SR-14 radials
Steering type	rack & pinion
Suspension, f/r	MacPherson struts, lower lateral arms, compliance struts, coil springs, tube shocks, anti-roll bar/Chapman struts, lower A-arms, coil springs, tube shocks

recent restorations is the mint 1971 tennis-ball-yellow 240Z seen here, that belongs to Todd Frazier of La Habra who has owned the car since 1991. Perot went to great lengths preparing the car for our photos, detailing the engine compartment, replacing the black air filter housing with an original orange one, and even arranging for a set of the original wheels and hubcaps. Though the car is a 1971 model (manufactured in November, 1970), it's indistinguishable from a 1970 model, having the characteristic small vents just below the rear hatch's glass.

Slipping behind its skinny-rimmed, plastic-wood wheel reminded me how exotic my Z-car memory seemed 20 years ago. The footwells are surprisingly roomy, but the high sills of the door panels do start to encroach on shoulder room. Snug the 3-point belts (this was the time just before seatbelt retractors) and enjoy the surroundings. The dash's dramatic hoods enclose deeply recessed gauges in the way of a Corvette or Sixties' Ferrari, and the view to the front is excellent—the pillars of the relatively upright windshield are about half as thick as a modern car's. There's that quilted vinyl again, this time on the transmission tunnel, and a choke lever on the center console that one magazine report said "looked like it should be for lowering the landing gear or adjusting the flaps." Many earlier cars were fitted with a second lever alongside it, a hand throttle.

The inline-6 fires instantly, and no doubt has a slightly crisper bark than the original, since Frazier has replaced the original exhaust manifold with a header. We're off, with that huge expanse of hood giving the impression we're sitting well back in the car, perhaps on top of the rear axle. We're not, of course, but the long-limbed can reach rearward through the high-back seats and touch the rear strut towers.

Efforts are high—the leverage from the big-diameter steering wheel is appreciated during parking maneuvers and the brakes require a really firm push before anything happens—but there's a wonderful mechanical honesty and a directness of feedback in the Z's every move. The 4-speed manual, shifted with a genuine wooden knob that caps a spindly chrome lever, is a perfect example. Negotiating its H-pattern requires firm, deliberate moves; none of the sloppy, ham-fisted shifting that more modern cars let you get away with. Gearing is tall, with 2nd gear being good for 70 mph, but the engine's midrange torque allows you to move along briskly even "short-shifting" at 4000 rpm. That would be a shame to do all the time, as the six really starts to sing in a turbinelike whoosh as revs continue to climb.

We pull back into the driveway of Pierre's shop and I hand him back the keys, the drive all too brief. It had been a pleasure dealing with a man whose mission is to preserve this pivotal sports car; in fact, Nissan has appointed his firm as one of the shops to restore early Z-cars that will be sold through Nissan dealerships. It's an ambitious plan, applied to an equally ambitious car that I'm sure, decades ago, infected countless other wide-eyed 13-year-olds with the sports-car bug. And will continue to do so. ■

1971 Datsun 240Z

EDITED BY

MARK H. SCHIRMER

Hawthorne, California—

The Seventies are ba-a-a-a-ck! Oh sure, you're thinking. Madison Avenue at it again, ringing the bells of pseudo-nostalgia. Well, not this time, brothers and sisters. Go fetch those flared trousers, unearth those Superfly shades, and, er, get on down: Nissan is restoring 1970–72 Datsun 240Zs and selling them—in selected new-car showrooms called Z Stores—as very special used cars. Every one comes with peace, love, and a twelve-month/12,000-mile warranty.

This remarkable walk down memory lane may have something to do with sagging brand awareness, the public's failure to connect Nissan with its Datsun heritage (the company changed names in 1983), and the lack of showroom sizzle in the troubled Japanese titan's current model range. But don't ask why.

More important, ask, "How much?" A tick under $25,000 will buy a restored, factory-authorized example of the machine that rewrote American sports car history—about the price of a loaded Altima and far less, we'd guess, than paying to restore a Z-car to this standard yourself.

We borrowed the first 240Z off Nissan's line, actually the workshop of Pierre Perrot, a longtime Southern California Z fettler whose tidy facility and staff of nine have been commandeered for a run of 200 ground-up restorations.

Rust-free donors are bought, brought here, and stripped. Bodies are sent out for repairs and paint. Back at Pierre's, they are treated to a variety of new (roughly 800 parts and assemblies) and remanufactured mechanicals, as well as fresh interiors and rubber.

A 1971 model finished in silver, our test car is box-stock original, right down to the clunky plastic wheel covers that Nissan mysteriously selected for its otherwise stylish steed. Cars must meet regulations for their year of initial manufacture, so all emissions equipment is renewed to original specification. Asbestos-free linings, improved undercoating, and slightly wider tires are among the few concessions to modernity.

BILL CASH

Settling into a low-slung black vinyl bucket seat, one surveys the Z's long hood and casts an eye around the cabin. The time trip has begun. A large, skinny steering wheel with highly polished wooden rim, an agricultural gear lever with a froofie leather boot. A full complement of ye olde sports car gauges and vast plains of black plastic and embossed vinyl. The only thing out of character is me. I miss my Afro (Jewfro, actually).

How long ago it was. The Z-car certainly seemed modern then, when it arrived on our shores to wreak havoc on the existing order. British sports cars, which passed the Sixties frolicsomely despite habitual lack of development, became terminal patients overnight.

A dab of choke for the twin SU carburetors and a twist of the key brings the Datsun's 2.4-liter six to life. On hand are 150 horses, enough to show off any wheezy old TR6 or MGB GT, but no match for a modern Honda Prelude. The Z-car sounds brisk, but, by modern standards, it isn't. No heavy breather in standard tune (power falls off over 4500 rpm), it cries for a fifth gear. But the exhaust note is to die for and the silken ways of its torquey straight-six will delight enthusiasts for generations to come.

Steering is alive and pleasingly vintage, but slower off center than we'd remembered. Soft of spring and shock, the Z was built with American tastes of the Sixties in mind. Mag wheels and aftermarket suspension tweaks, so popular for the Z last time around, still look like a good bet today.

Like the best old cars, the Datsun 240Z is remembered fondly for a reason. It's fun to drive. It has wind-up windows and no air conditioning, but we love it. It's like the Seventies all over again, minus Richard Nixon. And how cool is that?

—Jamie Kitman

The Numbers

On sale: now (limited availability)
Price: base $24,950/as tested $25,620
Engine: OHV 6-in-line, 146 cu in (2393 cc)
Power SAE net 150 bhp @ 5600 rpm
Torque SAE net 146 lb-ft @ 4400 rpm

BILL CASH

Empire of the

son

Spike Anderson's fettling turned Datsun's Z-car into a junior supercoupé. **Dave Richards** drives a rare 260Z Super Samuri survivor PHOTOGRAPHY **CRAIG PUSEY**

The Super Samuri at speed; 260 looks little different to its older brother – on first glance only the badges on the front wings give the game away. Distinctive red and bronze livery marks out the Super Samuri; original front spoiler was too low for rutted Welsh country lanes

In the nation where ancestors are not only venerated, but deified, their motoring contemporaries are barely given a second glance. Most elderly Japanese motors wouldn't merit one, but the Nissan Fairlady Z-L S30 – better known over here as the 240Z – demonstrated a new maturity in Japanese car design when it was presented to the world's press on 18 October 1969, and it remains revered to this day.

So it should be, because the team behind it – led by Yutaka Katayama with Teiichi Hara in charge of engineering and Yoshihiko Matsuo responsible for styling – bought comparison vehicles from all over the world. The target market was the USA, but perceived competitors included E-type, MGB, TR5, Alfa Spider and, somewhat surprisingly, Facel-Véga Facellia. Examples of each were shipped to Nissan's Development Section for evaluation. The design team worked to ensure that its new car would not only outperform the competition, but also withstand the rigours of export to the USA – the resultant shipping and dockside storage conditions meant that imported British cars were often rusty before they even arrived at dealerships.

The new coupé was a surprise hit, and the success of the Z in the north American market delayed UK deliveries. The biggest problem for Datsun in the British market place was that the Z, at £2288, was too expensive to compete against the budget coupés – a Capri 3000GXL was £1777 – but without enough badge kudos to enter E-type territory. During its five years as a new car in the UK, the 240Z found a paltry 1541 buyers – making it as rare a sight on British roads as the then-new S3 Jensen Interceptor.

But with exclusivity comes desirability and one young engineer, who was already used to tuning Bluebirds, had his sights set on the Z. Spike Anderson noticed the car's efforts in international rallying and its sales success in the USA. He had been working for Broadspeed, but set up his own business, Race Head Services, near Leamington Spa. Anderson was joined by Arthur Carlisle and ex-Broadspeed engine builder Barry Hudson, and their conversions of Datsun 1200s wore the nickname 'Samuri' to symbolise the warrior nature and pluck of these little cars. The mis-spelling was deliberate because an electronics company already owned the Samurai name.

Up close, this 110 red and Tango bronze 260Z Super Samuri – based on the 240Z's two-seater successor, introduced in '73 – is eye-poppingly bold. This particular example's conversion began in 1980, when it was owned by Z specialist, racer and one-time partner in the Samuri business Kevin Irons. "I saw an advert in the paper for a TR6 and when I came back from driving it I saw the 260 in the paint shop," recalls Irons. "I took it for a test drive and there was no comparison with the TR so I bought it. A lad I worked with, Ross Ferguson, who had been working at Silverstone as an apprentice with the F1 Arrows team, told me: 'There's a guy you have to meet if you want this thing to go quicker' – then he introduced me to Spike." The work was carried out in stages, as and when funds allowed. "We did about nine or 10 260s," recalls Anderson, "They wouldn't rev like 240s – the redline was about 500rpm lower – but it was still a fine, torquey engine. We used to rev the 240s to 8000rpm, which was unheard of in those days."

Clockwise, from main: two-tone paint shows off Z's lean shape; deep cowls shield instruments; muscular straight-six wears triple Webers in Super Samuri spec – as spoiler proclaims; badge gives 260Z away; FFA 196L was first Z to get Samuri mods; ungainly 2+2 also converted

There are few external clues to the 260Z's identity – at least the 260Z 2+2 version that arrived a year later could be picked out by its rather ungainly roofline. The two-tone colour scheme emphasises the coupé's lean, muscular proportions, making the Samuri seem lower than ordinary roadgoing Zs. One 2+2 was also given the Spike treatment – bearing the legend 'Samuri Plus Two' and finished in bronze over blue. Says Anderson: "They came in all sorts of colours – it was the scheme that mattered." Irons remembers how that unusual paintwork was born: "Spike's first Z, FFA 196L, was painted Datsun 110 red. He took it to Santa Pod and put in some impressive times. One of the car mags saw him and said they wanted to do an article on the car. He had a chat with the guy in the paint shop next door about tarting it up, but the only colour he had was Rootes Tango bronze. So they came up with the scheme and Spike told me that to do the white stripes the guy with the paint brush stood still while he drove past – that's why the lines aren't quite where you expect them to be!"

Settle into the 260's thin seat and crank it over. The high-compression motor takes longer to fire up, the camshaft runs a lot of advance and, even once all cylinders are firing – triple Webers aren't known for making an engine easy to start – the motor hunts with an uneasy tickover and the body rocks on its suspension. Back home in Japan, the high-performance Z432 variant featured the S20 Skyline's twin-cam straight-six (with four valves per cylinder and triple carbs).

'Keep your foot in and each upchange releases a furious burst of acceleration: this car responds to a maximum attack driving style'

British Zs made do with a single-cam L24 motor based on the L16 510 Bluebird unit, itself a four-cylinder derivative of the single-overhead-cam Mercedes six that Prince built under licence before being taken over by Nissan. With valvegear from the 1600 SSS, an alloy head and new crank and camshaft, the L24 was a gutsy unit. "The strong engines are part of the appeal," says Irons. "You've got to be be really stupid to break one." Anderson's trick 2.6-litre engines – such as the motor that ran in 'Big Sam', his racing car – used a 240Z crank and 280 block to produce a 2.6-litre short-stroke 'bullet-proof' engine, capable of revving safely to at least 7000rpm.

The tachometer settles as the oil warms through – you can sense that this unit is race-inspired. Press the throttle and it picks up easily and revs more cleanly as the lightened flywheel spins faster. The winding road up a Welsh mountainside awaits so drop the clutch – not too heavy – snick into first and give it some welly. Change up at 3000rpm and the engine bogs down – the cam, "quite warm" according to owner Glyn Jones, is actually pretty hot and works best above 4000rpm. Keep your foot in and each upchange releases a furious burst of acceleration: this car responds to a maximum attack driving style.

Blip for a downchange, swing the steering wheel and enter a hairpin corner. Boot the throttle at the apex and, if you've been driving the Samuri right, it'll reward with a howling exhaust

DATSUN 260Z SUPER SAMURI

Sold/number built 1973-'78/622,649 (all 240/260Zs)
Construction all-steel monocoque
Engine front-mounted, iron-block, alloy-head 2565cc sohc six, three 45DCOE Weber carbs
Max power 190bhp (standard 162bhp @ 5600rpm)
Max torque n/a (std 152lb ft @ 4400rpm)
Transmission five-speed manual, driving rear wheels **Suspension** independent at **front** by MacPherson struts with anti-roll bar **rear** MacPherson struts; telescopic dampers f/r
Steering rack and pinion
Brakes discs front, drums rear, with servo
Length 13ft 6¾in (4135mm) **Width** 5ft 4in (1628mm) **Height** 4ft ¼in (1225mm)
Wheelbase 7ft 6¾in (2303mm)
Weight 2282lb (1035kg)
0-60mph 6.4 secs **Top speed** 140mph
Mpg 16
Price new £3790 **Price now** £12,000

Sam's saviour
GLYN JONES

Long-time Z fan Jones has owned his 260Z Super Samuri for six years: "I had 240Zs and 260Z 2+2s 25 years ago and always sold them on when they got too rusty – they were just old cars then, and weren't worth much." The Datsun arrived as an off-the-road project and before running it Jones first had to unseize the brakes and change the fuel. When bought, the Z wore the correct, road-hugging air-dam, but it proved impractical around Jones' mid-Wales home: "It kept grounding out and bits kept flying off. It was just too deep." The shallower replacement it now wears is less vulnerable for road use, and on occasional track days. Jones has taken the car back to former owner Kevin Irons too: "He seemed pleased to see it, and set up the triple 45s perfectly!"

and a pair of scrabbling back tyres. Get it wrong and the three carbs will bog down, acting as if you've just lost all spark as the mixture slows and then stalls in those polished inlet tracts, running to the base of the inlet tubes and fouling the plugs. The screaming nature of the conversion requires absolute commitment to release the full-on assault the Samuri is capable of.

"The appeal of the Sam is that it's not all show and no go," says Irons. "It looks great and drives brilliantly – it's what the next Big Healey should have been. One of the best days I had with the car was when I went to a Z and Corvette meet at Goodwood and, because my car had been Sammed, it set fastest time of the day. I also took it to Santa Pod several times and ran 14 secs dead [for the quarter-mile] at a terminal speed of 101mph." No wonder contemporary motoring scribes loved the Samuri – Anderson was really building road-legal racing cars. And that's what appeals today. Here is a car that was rare when new – only around 70 Samuris are believed to have been built – that has instant recognition and provides huge driver satisfaction. It's difficult, yet like a true thoroughbred it will only give its best when you are fully in charge.

The long gearlever swaps cogs easily enough, the lowered and uprated suspension allows the car to be placed accurately, whether heading nose-first into an off-power apex or wrangling, tail-out, around any curve you can set with the throttle. The brakes, often the Z's Achilles heel on-track, are fine for road use, with progressive bite and even grip. Yet your memory of the Super Samuri is always of the engine – its fierce camminess and the bellow of its exhaust.

'Standard' Super Samuri spec included a gas-flowed and port-matched cylinder head. The flows were equalised across all the ports and each

GETTING DESIGNS ON DATSUN

Born in Kobe in 1934, Yoshihiko Matsuo was educated at Nippon University. He joined Nissan in April 1960, working on the development of the 1600 SSS Bluebird – the triple S initials dreamed up by Matsuo to signify 'Super Sports Sedan'.

After the Bluebird was signed off, Matsuo was appointed chief designer for the new Sports Car Section. He worked on the car that was to become the 240Z, assisted by Itsuki Chiba and Akio Yoshida, producing a series of styling clays (above) labelled A-I to A-V. The SP-A, the final design buck, was closely related to A-V.

Matsuo identified the support of Yutaka Katayama, then president of Nissan USA: "[He was] a great help. He said Nissan could not sell cheap cars for ever, so we got the go-ahead for the Z. My only regret is that we never made the open or targa-style versions, even though we had running prototypes."

Nissan Japan's president Kawamata was so pleased with the huge Z sales that he gave the team members responsible for the design a large bonus. The modest Matsuo used his to commission silver tie pins, which he gave to his staff. He left Nissan to run his own design consultancy in August 1973.

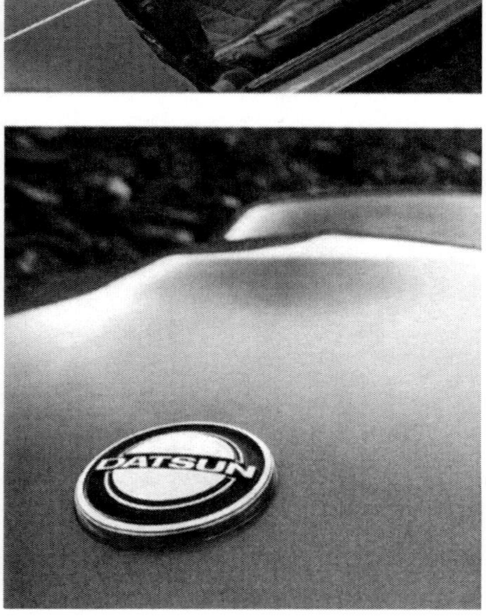

From top: de-bumpered rear with neat exhaust cut-out adds to the aggressive look, famous script lets other road users know what has just roared past; superb driving position with deeply dished three-spoke wheel; Datsun badge signifies purpose rather than kudos

was modified to exactly the same combustion volume – necessary after skimming the head to raise the compression ratio. A Mangoletsi inlet manifold was added, again port-matched to the head tracts, with gaskets shaped and modified to prevent anything impeding the inlet charge's speedy flow to the piston top. Triple 45DCOE Webers mixed the air and fuel, and a straight-through exhaust created the memorable tune. The engine work alone cost £425. Lowered springs and uprated dampers were also available, plus a 'Big Sam'-style front air dam at £130 and alloy wheels, grippier tyres and better brakes (using Range Rover Lockheed four-pot calipers from nearby Solihull). Top of the options list came the evocative paintwork.

Strengths such as unburstable mechanicals, luxurious trim levels and superb build quality meant that no sports car buyer could afford to ignore the Z in period. And yet they did, a high price and anti-Japanese sentiment preventing the UK market from experiencing the Z effect the US had seen, where 135,813 examples were sold from 1970-'73. Some sections of the classic market still snub this characterful coupé today but, faced with a British-developed, British-built Super Samuri, a few mountainous switchbacks and a throttle-full of 7000rpm, only the most diehard traditionalist wouldn't marvel at this warrior's heady, cross-cultural potency. ■

BORN FOR THE USA

Conceived for the streets of LA, the Datsun 240Z has been stunning the world since 1969 – and an adventure through rugged Yorkshire reveals why

WORDS ROSS ALKUREISHI
PHOTOGRAPHY LYNDON MCNEIL

240Z name stems from Nissan's original Design Project Z and denotes a 2.4-litre engine

'Forget binge drinking, opiates or a ready suppl

DATSUN 240Z DRIVE

HOW DO YOU MEASURE DESIRE? Trundling through the historic North Yorkshire market town of Pickering you quickly become aware that this is a car that creates waves. At 5mph its straight-six burble gently resonates off surrounding buildings, and heads start to turn. But it's when onlookers' eyes settle on that classic fastback shape that you see a distinct change in their demeanour: old men stoop their heads admiringly; a pimple of teenagers (is that the right collective noun?) points, ogles and fires off a barrage of complimentary expletives; and a young man breaks off a conversation with his girlfriend to mouth 'What's that?', earning himself a yank on the arm as if he's just had the temerity to look at another woman's cleavage.

Even behind the wheel I'm not immune. Catching the 240Z's reflection in a shop window, my eyes are captivated by that sleek, alluring outline. But it's the reaction of a young boy who stops mesmerised in mid-lick of his ice-cream that makes you realise you're sitting in something special.

It's time to be kind, to remove the spell from this picturesque town and let it return to normal, so I turn on to the Whitby Road and head out towards the North York Moors National Park. Gunning the accelerator opens up the twin Hitachi SU-type carburettors and allows the 2393cc ohc engine to reveal its gutsy, free-revving nature; there's ample torque available, but it's the smooth power delivery that brings an instant smile to your face. Thundering along the open moorland roads the exhaust note builds with the revs, eliciting a honed pneumatic-drill note at about the 6000rpm mark. Ten minutes into this drive and the throttle pedal has become an addictive vice; forget binge drinking, opiates or a ready supply of groupies – throw me the keys to a 240Z.

After an engaging drive across the moors an instruction to 'stop, engage first gear and retain to next sign' gives your arm muscles a welcome rest from wrestling the heavy Z round corners

Heavily European-influenced styling was about as far from typical Sixties Japanese design as you could get

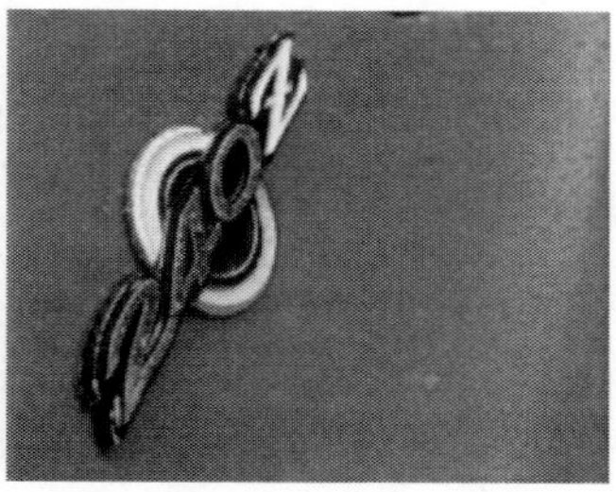

# of groupies – throw me the keys to a 240Z'

The powerplant is a masterpiece. It may not have the huge capacity of the engines coming out of Detroit at the time but, breathing through twin carburettors, it provides a rival set of throatily gruff sound effects which were perfect for luring the target audience in its chosen market.

Ah, America. Without the Land of the Free the Z probably wouldn't exist. During the Fifties Nissan sent advertising and sales promotion executive Yutaka Katayama to the USA to survey the market. The idea of a dedicated sports car for the States came to him when he saw large numbers of sporting imports on the roads around Los Angeles.

Nissan hired Albrecht Goertz as a consultant and design work on a prototype began in earnest. By 1963 a fixed-head coupé with beautiful sweeping lines, pop-up headlights and a clearly sporting nature was ready – but then a complicated relationship with development partner Yamaha, which would build the engine, saw the project shelved.

By coincidence Toyota launched its 2000GT in 1965. The car known as 'the Japanese E-type' was a two-seater fixed-head coupé with beautiful sweeping lines, pop-up headlights and sublime twin-cam engine by, you guessed it, Yamaha. This remarkably similar car was well-received but a complex manufacturing process and prohibitively high price resulted in just 337 made.

Nissan continued to research exactly what the US market wanted from its sports cars and, spurred on by Toyota's efforts, resurrected its own project. By this time Goertz was gone and responsibility had passed to an in-house team of designers and engineers. In 1969 the first 240Z was presented to rapturous response from press and public.

Rapturous is an emotive word but it fits my own sentiments as I power the Z along the gently undulating road and up into the moors, the landscape's heather cladding punctuated now and again by an oasis of lush green vegetation.

Sometimes external beauty can deceive you because that's all there is. But this car fulfils all its aesthetic promises and drives as good as it looks. The engine is mounted far enough back to prevent nose-heavy traits and the all-round independent suspension enables you to corner fast, very fast, confident in the excellent traction.

The rack-and-pinion steering – unusual for Japanese cars of the period – is direct and instantly responsive, giving you confidence to build speed quickly. It's like pulling a nubile glamour model on a drunken night out and waking up to discover she can hold a coherent and cohesive conversation; astounding.

Turning off the main road, I point the Z towards one of those green oases, Goathland, home to TV's *Heartbeat* and its fictional village of Aidensfield. As you approach, a sign tells you to engage first gear – you know you're in prime driving territory when long straights and sweeping bends are followed by instructions like this. Pootling into town I give silent thanks to the heavens for the absence of actor Nick Berry and park the car outside the Goathland Arms. I'm barely out before tourists surround the Z and begin to visually devour it.

'What is it?' asks one.

'Datsun 240Z,' I reply.

'Really, a Datsun?' he says in a voice full of amazement. 'Are you sure?'

I'm sure. Just the same as Nissan was sure it had a winner. The 240Z was no accident; the company's researchers had done their job well. Before starting to style the car they bought a Porsche 911, Jaguar E-type and a selection of other sports and GT cars. It's no coincidence that the Z is exactly the same size as a 911 and the long bonnet is almost a carbon copy of the E-type's. Overall, its looks are distinctly European with more than a hint of Ferrari Daytona.

But it was mechanically where this car stood out. The technology combined to offer a driving experience that was a quantum leap ahead of its rivals. An overhead camshaft engine, all-synchromesh gearbox, all-independent MacPherson strut suspension and front disc brakes,

Extensive market research produced a coupé the same size as a Porsche 911 with a bonnet like a Jaguar E-type and a distinct dash of Ferrari Daytona about it

combined with a user-friendly price tag – in the States at least – meant customers got Porsche performance for the price of an MGB. And how Joe Public queued up to buy them, though exorbitant import tax in the UK unfortunately placed it in an altogether more expensive class.

Nissan kept production costs low by using components from its existing models. The engine is a six-cylinder version of the 1.6-litre single overhead camshaft L16 unit fitted to the 510 Bluebird, itself a four-cylinder version of the Mercedes-Benz 'six that Prince (acquired by Nissan in 1966) had been building under licence. The five-speed gearbox came from the Fairlady 2000, independent front suspension from the Laurel and the rear brakes were also from the Fairlady 2000. Only the Chapman strut-type rear suspension was new for the Z.

It starts to rain as I fire up this collection of amalgamated parts and head back on to the moors. I flick on the wipers, the lights and the heater. This car has four-point harnesses, but I'm able to do all this without unbuckling myself because all the switches are handily placed around the steering column. The all-black interior reinforces the sporting feel with its dashboard dominated by the large cowled tachometer and speedometer. Pedals are well spaced for heel-and-toeing. The one-piece moulded fascia feels a bit plasticky but the level of equipment is beyond criticism and most of the Z's competitors. Importantly it was designed – at the insistence of Goertz – to accommodate the larger gentleman comfortably; a capacious cabin meant Nissan didn't ostracise a sizeable (no pun intended) portion of its target American market.

The sudden change in the weather reminds me how unforgiving this part of Yorkshire can be – which is apt, as the contrast of beauty and ruggedness fits both the environment and the car. The 240Z's build quality – though not rust prevention – and reliability put its rivals to shame and quickly gave it a reputation for toughness, which meant its transition to rally car was only a matter of time.

The Dalby Forest Complex, my target destination, gives a chance to explore this further. Used extensively on RAC/Lombard Rallies, its gravel roads are infamously fast and unforgiving. Thankfully – or unluckily – the rally sections are only accessible for competition. I'm of the former viewpoint, as this freshly restored car will be delivered to its new owner next week, so I'm happy to settle for the toll road running around the forest, which has more than enough to keep me entertained.

The forest itself is the antithesis to the bleak open moorlands I've just driven through. Here there's a comforting feeling of safety among the stands of Scots pines dominating the scenery. The road rises and falls and twists and turns, leading you on a mesmerising dance through this thick, ancient wood with only the bark of the exhaust audible as it rebounds in a multitude of directions from its surroundings.

It's here that the Z starts to show another side to its character. Up on the moors it was in its element, devouring mile after mile of meandering A-road, but here it's a different story; constant changes of direction make you immediately aware of just how long and heavy this car is. Shifting between the first three gears and thrusting the car into corner after corner, I start to work up quite a sweat.

The grip is phenomenal. Any attempts at wheelspin are firmly rebuffed. It simply hunkers down and powers through with barely any skittishness at all, even in the wet. That said, I've been warned that when they do lose grip all four wheels go at the same time. This is what earned the Z its reputation among rally drivers for four-wheel drifting, and it also ensures a demanding, riotous, wrestling drive. The combination of grip, length and weight means that it's hard work as your forearms work overtime while the lactic acid levels begin to soar.

Specialist Duncan Pearcey of The 'Z' Farm explains why: 'They weren't competitive on the tight, twisty rallies in the UK where they were very difficult to handle.' Couple this with poor visibility and its no surprise the 240Z couldn't compete with its lighter and nimbler Renault Alpine A110, Fiat 124 Abarth, and Ford Escort RS1600 contemporaries.

Conversely, it was the length, plus its mechanical toughness, that led to a remarkable record on the East African rally, with two wins in four attempts including an unprecedented debut win in 1971 at the hands of Edgar Hermann. 'The length of its floorpan gave the Datsun 30 per cent more stability on rough roads than most contemporary rally cars on the East African Safari Rally,' says Pearcey. 'It was able to withstand the undulating bumpy surfaces better than shorter cars, which had a tendency to porpoise.' The suspension could be working like fury but the driver still had a relatively stable platform with which to work. 'Combine that with an under-stressed powerplant – in comparison to Ford BDAs of the time – and genuine long leggedness, and you have a recipe for success.'

1970 DATSUN 240Z

Engine 2393cc, in-line six-cylinder, ohc, two Hitachi SU-type carburettors
Power and torque 150bhp @ 5600rpm; 146lb ft @ 4400rpm
Transmission Five-speed manual, rear-wheel drive
Brakes Discs front, drums rear, servo-assisted
Suspension Front: independent, MacPherson struts, lower links, coil springs, telescopic dampers, anti-roll bar. Rear: independent, MacPherson struts, lower wishbones, coil springs, telescopic dampers
Steering Rack-and-pinion
Weight 1038kg (2284lb)
Performance Top speed: 125mph; 0-60mph: 8sec
Fuel consumption 20mpg
Cost new £2288
Value now £25,000

Leaving the forest, I pull over to let my adrenalin levels subside and reflect on the day I've spent with the Z. Nissan didn't invent the overhead-camshaft engine, independent suspension or disc brakes but it did its research before combining them into this special package. From the purposeful roar of that high revving 'six to its precise transmission and rugged build, this supremely resilient sports car was everything its target market wanted. So it's no surprise that this value-for-money package was enjoyed in its hundreds of thousands in the Seventies.

What a sight it must have been to witness a Z of Datsuns – now that *is* the collective noun – being unloaded on America's West Coast on their way to conquer a land that rejected most things foreign as inferior. Flushed with success, Nissan developed the Z into the larger-engined 260Z in 1974 followed by the 280Z of '78, but the cars quickly turned to fat, losing the toned and honed form that had made the Z great.

Today there's only one model to go for and that's an original, and prices have hardened in recent years. Expect to pay £20,000 or more for a car that's just had a full restoration. 'It's underneath the skin that costs the money – anyone can make a car look pretty, but it needs to be structurally sound,' says Pearcey.

Larger panels, including inner wings and rear three-quarter panels, aren't available, so restorers may need to source a donor car from the US, where they're still quite plentiful. Ten years ago owners had problems sourcing trim items, but everything is now being reproduced in the States. In many cases it's better than original – for example, stainless steel bumpers are available for £700, front and rear, and will last a lot longer than the original rust-prone chrome items.

Check first for rust when looking at a prospective buy; the 240Z was built from thin metal, has plenty of water traps and there was a distinct lack of rustproofing at the factory. The 'Z' Farm will seam seal lap joints to stop water getting into the cavities, chassis rails and wings.

If you're on the lookout for something a bit special, £75,000 and beyond will buy you your very own full rally-spec, fire-breathing samurai. 'You're looking at around £50,000 of specialised parts and twice as much labour,' explains Pearcey.

If your pocket doesn't run to that, a really nice, previously restored car will fetch £15,000-18,000. There's a strong market for such cars now that the old snobbery against Japanese cars is subsiding as a new generation finds out for itself just how special the 240Z is. It may have been the Toyota 2000GT that was immortalised in the James Bond film *You Only Live Twice* and now commands the earth, but it was the bargain-basement Nissan 240Z that truly conquered the world. CC

Thanks to Duncan Pearcey at The 'Z' Farm.

ABOVE 2.4-litre ohc straight-six has its roots in a Mercedes-Benz design
LEFT Wearing a four-point harness doesn't restrict access to the Z's well-placed switches

240Z: a question of concept and design

ALBRECHT GOERTZ is often credited with the design of the Datsun 240Z – but that's simply untrue, says The 'Z' Farm's Duncan Pearcey.

Japanese industry celebrates the combined efforts of a team rather than one individual's input; it is also reluctant to acknowledge outsiders' involvement in a project. In this case both factors combined to create confusion over who designed the 240Z.

Nissan snapped up Goertz's services as a design consultant in the early Sixties and assigned him a team of designers to execute his ideas. The concept car was completed in 1964, but Nissan shelved the project.

Goertz was no longer involved when it was resurrected two years later, and in 1967 the 240Z shape was finalised with subtle changes to the original design. The controversy began in 1979 when Goertz criticised the design of the later 280Z and Nissan Motor Corporation executive vice-president Hiroshi Takahashi released a statement saying: 'It is absolutely unthinkable that he had a hand in designing the 240Z.'

This prompted Goertz to take legal action. The case was settled out of court in 1988, at which point Nissan sent him a letter saying: 'While it is our view that the design of the 240Z was the product of Nissan's design staff, Nissan agree that the personnel who designed the automobile were influenced by your fine work for Nissan and had the benefit of your design.'

Those personnel included chief designer Yoshihiko Matsuo and assistant designers Fumio Yoshida and Utsuki Chiba and, although Goertz was certainly influential, the true credit should go to them.

Goertz was apparently happy with this, claiming it isn't the design that's imperative but the concept: 'They designed the car, but I showed them how.' Maybe he took his true feelings to the grave, dying in 2006 aged 92.

DATSUN 240Z

While the British sports car industry limped on in the early 1970s, Nissan rewrote the rules with a newcomer that blended power, looks and balanced handling

Words: Richard Heseltine. Photography: Mark Bramley

Time was when Japanese cars were rubbish. A generalisation perhaps, but until you've experienced the full horror of an Isuzu Bellet in the wet, or a Datsun Cherry 100A in the dry for that matter, then you're frankly in no position to argue. Think of the miserable knock-offs that China produces right now that lack the stimulation, flair and excitement that European players so effortlessly embrace. For now at least, because all the signs suggest it won't take the Chinese long to catch up. Then we'll see who's laughing.

History has a tendency to repeat itself. Backtrack to the 1960s and, as the British automobile industry embarked on an orgiastic merger spree, the much-mocked Japanese were busy studying, copying and improving Blighty's motorbikes. They then sold them in vast numbers, which caused the source of inspiration to wither and die. This car – the Datsun 240Z – had pretty much the same effect on the British sports car. By looking, listening and cherry-picking, Datsun – or rather Nissan – engineers fashioned a car that sated North America's unflagging susceptibility to a good deal and rendered traditional British fare obsolete at a stroke. A cramped, leaky and not especially quick ragtop suddenly seemed less appealing. And just to rub salt into the wounds, the 240Z proved handy in competition on a global scale.

Designed specifically to earn lucrative US dollars, the 240Z broke the mould for Japanese sports cars. There had been earlier attempts – Nissan's own string of Fairlady roadsters were reasonably successful, even if they did crib Abingdon products. Honda's S800 was an intriguing curio, with its DOHC head and roller-bearing crank, as was the barking Wankel rotary-powered Mazda Cosmo. Then there was the sublime, Yamaha-devised Toyota 2000GT which

Above: On the road, the handsome Z is powerful, balanced, and accompanied by a wonderful six-cylinder howl. Just don't expect a comfortable ride

As the British embarked on an orgiastic merger spree, the Japanese improved Blighty's motorbikes and then sold them in vast numbers, which caused the source of inspiration to wither. The 240Z had the same effect on the British sports car

sold in tragically small numbers. The distantly related 240Z was, however, the first truly credible Japanese sports car.

Having hitherto toyed with producing another four-cylinder roadster, the decision to build a coupé with an extra pair of cylinders was made in 1966. And, contrary to popular belief, the 240Z wasn't penned by a German aristocrat. The late Count Albrecht Goertz, former affiliate of design god Raymond Loewy and architect behind the BMW 507, is often cited as the man responsible for the car's perfect proportions. When the Z first did its trotting on the show circuit, Goertz – then on a Nissan retainer – was a well known and erudite figure in the design community and his attachment stuck. Japanese decorum insisted that the company received credit, rather than an employee, but Yutaka Katayama is now widely considered to be the man behind the outline. Goertz, having previously styled the attractive Nissan Sylvia 1600, did indeed come up with the concept, but that's about it, according to the factory. Some years later he had his day in court and there the Count was acknowledged as having, at least, *envisaged* the 240Z.

Certainly Goertz was astute enough to realise that, with the US in mind, the new strain had to be roomy enough to house two six-footers in comfort – and all within a package that aped the layout of the Jaguar E-type within a Porsche 911's footprint. And it did both: the monocoque construction, in-line six-cylinder power and all-round independent suspension echoed Coventry's finest, while the dimensions almost mirrored those of the compact Weissach masterpiece.

The 240Z caused a furore upon its introduction at the 1969 Tokyo Motor Show – and an even bigger one in the US when it was released that September. Cheaper than mainstream British sports cars, cheaper even than a Corvette, sales went stratospheric with eager punters paying a premium over the list price to land one. The 240Z instantly left its mark on the track, too, when John Morton won the 1970 SCCA C-production title in a Brock Racing Enterprises entry: he would repeat the feat one year later while Bob Sharp lifted the 1972 and 1973 titles.

In Europe it was all a bit more subdued. The 240Z was officially launched at the 1970 Earls Court Motor Show and reaction was encouraging, although Datsun UK stopped short of bringing many over, due in part to protectionist tariffs levied against Japanese imports. And none of the 2-litre Z and ZL models, or the sexy, fat-arched Z432 and Z432R editions made it this far, more's the pity. Of the 150,076 Datsun 240Zs made to the end of 1973, a whopping 146,000 went to the US: rather fewer made it to these shores. Import taxes meant it wasn't such a bargain. At £2535 (in 1973) when a 3-litre Capri could have been yours for almost £700 less, it was always going to be on a loser. Nonetheless, the 240Z soon attracted a small if select retinue in Great Britain, with even the legendary Donald Healey reputedly being a fan.

> The new strain had to be roomy enough to house two six-footers – and all within a package that aped the layout of a Jaguar E-type within a Porsche 911's footprint. And it did. The 240Z caused a furore upon its introduction

All of which is understandable, because the 240Z always was like a Healey 3000 in spirit: tough, hirsute of chest and rather vocal (engine and transmission). As *Autocar* put it: "There is a tendency to describe the 240Z as the natural successor to the Big Healey. Perhaps it is, but it's so much more comfortable, so much roomier and so much better-handling that comparisons are difficult. There is no denying, however, that the character is there."

The simile took on extra emphasis following the model's success in rallying. For a marque that made its first, faltering steps into the rough and tumble stuff in 1958, it was with the 240Z that Datsun really took on the elite. Edgar Hermann and Hans Schuller won the 1971 East African Safari (admittedly only after Björn Waldegård's Porsche and Hannu Mikkola's Escort had retired), leading home the sister car of Shekhar Mehta and Mike Doughty. Two years later it was Mehta's turn (second place going to the Datsun 1800SSS saloon of Harry Källström), while a bit closer to home Tony Fall won the 1971 Welsh Rally. Rauno Aaltonen and Jean Todt finished third on the 1972 Monte Carlo – not an outright success, but impressive nonetheless.

So if the constituents of a true classic are good looks, a competition pedigree and historical importance, the 240Z has every base covered. The thing is, its lifespan was short. It lasted only until late 1973, when it was replaced by the larger displacement (2565cc, up from 2393cc) 260Z. With the subsequent arrival of the longer wheelbase 2+2, and the heinous but bafflingly popular 280ZX boulevardier, it was all downhill for the Z concept: an uncomplicated driver's car made way for a series of corpulent old tuggers where power-assisted steering, air-con and an auto 'box became increasingly central, at least until the gutsy and, mercifully, vastly more compelling 350Z reaffirmed our faith in the breed from midway through 2002.

Below: Rauno Aaltonen, Paul Easter and a factory 240Z head for seventh place in the 1970 RAC Rally. Below right: Shekhar Mehta and former *Motor Sport* rallies editor Gerry Phillips make waves during the 1973 Morocco Rally

LAT Photographic

Of the few 240Zs that made it here, the ones that staved off V8 engine conversions and crass faux-Ferrari 250GTO makeover kits are now highly prized, not least by the historic rallying community. This example, Nissan UK's own, looks delicious, especially on Minilites in place of the original domed wheel trims (the only exterior feature that ever really gave away the car's national origin). Up close, Jaguar E-type leaps more readily to mind than Big Healey, that long, priapic snout and tapering fastback being more Browns Lane than Miller Road. It's only when you step – sorry, stoop – inside that it all begins to unravel.

Positives first: there's plenty of room, no elbow crowding or random pedal placing. The well shaped buckets are comfortable enough and nothing is a reach away. The instruments are easy to read, despite the hooded cowlings, with the three minor dials – clock, fuel gauge/ammeter and oil pressure/water temperature – being placed in the centre of the fascia and angled towards the driver. Ventilation is acceptable, while only the blind spot in the chunky C-pillars mars all-round visibility. There's also useful carrying capacity, even if MacPherson struts eat into the luggage area. A pity, then, that the overall effect is one of abject poverty. The extensive use of coarse-grained plastics and shiny vinyl (prone to splitting, incidentally) serves only to short-change the 240Z; it's a mite unpleasant.

On the move the straight six (iron block and alloy head) sounds fab, all snarl and bluster, pulling vigorously from low revs and even more so past 4000rpm. You would never know that the unit was supposedly, erm, inspired by Mercedes-Benz: it's playful and spins eagerly up to the 6500rpm red line. The sonorous backbeat encourages you to work hard, and maybe change down when the torque spread would carry you, just to hear it change tempo. The change itself is well defined, but hardly delicate. That said, there's enough torque to pull cleanly from just 20mph in top.

Top left: straight six provides a fantastic soundtrack on the move. Top right: A name from the past. Above left: The 240Z was a bargain in America but much more expensive than a 3.0 Ford Capri in the UK. Above right: controls were all conveniently located

With near 50:50 weight distribution the Z is predictably well balanced with a touch of understeer when cornering gently. The rack-and-pinion steering loads up swiftly: attack a challenging sequence with a bit more vigour and the handling is neutral rather than tail-out heroic, at least in the dry. The ride quality, however, is unforgiving to the point where you wonder if shock absorbers were optional.

Thing is, the Z is critic-proof and has been ever since the first reviews came in. And it's not as if the initial British reports were in the least begrudging. This was obviously the future. Think about it. When the 240Z was announced, its closest British challenger, if only in ethos, was the MGC. Or, to put it another way, an MGB with a higher centre of gravity and an extra 200lb of nose baggage. And then the UK specialist press got a roasting for having the temerity to praise a Japanese car. Less how the West was won, more how the West stuck its head in the sand. And then lost.

Thanks to Terry Steeden and Wayne Bruce of Nissan UK

DATSUN 240Z/260Z

Japan's thrilling Z-car serves up a heady blend of cool styling, intoxicating power, sublime handling... and its fair share of rust

WORDS RICHARD DREDGE **PICTURES** JOHN COLLEY

BUYING GUIDE

1969–1979

Datsun's Z-series was the first Oriental car to be truly accepted by the classic fraternity. Z-cars were designed for the Japanese and American markets – but not by German genius Albrecht Goertz, as is often assumed. It was Datsun's in-house team that penned this masterpiece of sleek styling, lusty power, sublime handling and Swiss-watch reliability.

BODYWORK

You'd think these cars were Italian, they're so keen to rust. Like most of its contemporaries, the Z was poorly rustproofed so be prepared for lots of lacy bodywork; there are few original cars left and bodged restorations are common. These bodies are made up of lots of subtle curves, which you don't fully appreciate until somebody tries to recreate them and gets it wrong. A restored car may well suffer uneven panel gaps and swage lines that don't match up – which is why it's sometimes better to go for a tatty unrestored car, although these too are few and far between.

One of the killer areas is just behind the doors. Three swage lines converge here and getting them to line up can prove a real labour of love; if someone got them wrong during a resto they are very hard to sort.

The floorpans are also rot-prone, so ensure you get the car on a ramp. The main areas to check are the longitudinal crossmembers that run underneath the front seats, but all the metal needs close scrutiny. Also open the bonnet and look at the front chassis legs; they run the length of the engine bay. Next poke your head under the front wheelarches and take a look at the rot-prone inner flitches and the double-skinned base of the strut towers.

Finish off by checking the tops of the front wings (just above the wheelarches) as well as the

HOTLINKS

- www.zclub.net
- www.zcar.com
- www.zcca.org
- http://zhome.com

'Whether for occasional use or rallying, the 240Z and 260Z make sense'

SPECIFICATIONS

	240Z 1969-1973	260Z 1974-1979	260Z 2+2 1974-1979
■ ENGINE	2393cc/6-cyl	2565cc/6-cyl	2565cc/6-cyl
■ POWER	151bhp@5600rpm	162bhp@5600rpm	150bhp@5400rpm
■ TORQUE	146lb ft@4400rpm	152lb ft@4400rpm	158lb ft@4400rpm
■ TOP SPEED	125mph	127mph	118mph
■ 0-60mph	8.0sec	8.8sec	9.9sec
■ CONSUMPTION	24mpg	24mpg	25mpg
■ GEARBOX	5-speed manual	5-speed manual	5-speed manual
■ LENGTH	13ft 7in (4.14m)	13ft 7in (4.14m)	14ft 7in (4.45m)
■ WIDTH	5ft 4in (1.63m)	5ft 4in (1.63m)	5ft 5.5in (1.63m)
■ WEIGHT	2355lb (1067kg)	2425lb (1098kg)	2630lb (1191kg)

bottoms of the doors and the trailing edges of each front wing. Don't forget to check the base of the windscreen either, or the tail panel both above and below the rear lights.

ENGINES

It's possible to extract a reliable 250bhp from the overhead-cam straight-six, so with just 151bhp in standard form, the unit is unstressed. As long as the oil is changed every 6000 miles you should expect a quarter of a million miles easily; Z expert Mike Feeney recommends Millers' semi-synthetic 20W-50.

Aside from infrequent oil changes, the biggest threat to the engine's health is low coolant levels and lack of the correct anti-freeze mix; it should be maintained at 50:50. Thanks to the head being made of alloy, there's a risk of it warping if allowed to overheat, so check the head gasket and coolant level.

Get the engine up to temperature and check the oil pressure; it should register 55psi while cruising but it's quite normal for barely anything to register at idle and for everything to still be fine. This is because the oil sender for the gauge is notoriously unreliable, so check it – but this can only be done by substitution. If anything is amiss there'll be plenty of rattling from the top end and rumbling from the bottom, signalling a rebuild. If you need to revive the powerplant, expect to pay £800 just for the parts, or you could drop in a 2.8-litre unit from the 280ZX.

The limiting factor with most Z engines, in terms of their efficiency, is the carburation. The 240Z came with Hitachi SU-type carburettors which work fine; the 260Z's aren't so good. If the top of the carbs are flat (like a tin can), rather than rounded like an SU, the original units are fitted. It's worth swapping these for SU HS2 items which are the same as fitted to the Rover P6 2000TC. If you want something really fruity go for triple Webers or Dell'Ortos – but you'll need to upgrade the exhaust, valves and the camshaft too for the best results.

OWNER

The 1971 240Z pictured here is Peter MacDonald's third Z-car; he's previously owned a 260Z 2+2 and a 280ZX. 'I love the simplicity of it – both the concept as well as the construction. The car has no pretensions, it's a basic two-seater sportscar and all the better for it. I suppose the real reason I like it is because of the era it represents. I love Seventies American sportscars like the Camaro, Mustang and Firebird. The Z is the closest thing I can get to an American car without buying something American – although this example was imported from the States. It's completely usable, especially now I've made a few upgrades. The beauty of the 240Z is that aside from minor tweaking, there's nothing it really needs.'

SPECIALIST

Mike Feeney has owned, raced and worked on Z-cars for 30 years. He started running the Z Club's parts service in 1983, which he then turned into a full-time business called MJP Auto, in 1996. Still the technical adviser for the Z Club, Mike has owned at least one example of just about every Z made, perhaps the hairiest being a Chevrolet-engined drag racer, now owned by Matt Watkins but still sponsored by MJP Auto. Always a motorsport fan, you'll still find Mike in the pits at Seventies Roadsports HSCC races, tending Matt Bannister's impressive 240Z.

BUYING GUIDE – DATSUN 240Z/260Z

PRICE CHECK: MINT: £7000-£10,000 | AVERAGE: £4000-£7500 | ROUGH: £1000-£2000

WHICH IS WHICH?

1969: 240Z goes on sale in Japan.
1970: The UK and America get the 240Z; American editions have a four-speed manual gearbox while UK cars have an extra ratio.
1971: The transmission and location of the differential are improved. A Jatco three-speed auto is offered in some markets while the rear quarter panel and hatch are redesigned.
1972: The compression is lowered from 9.0 to 8.8:1, reducing emissions and power. Automatic seat belt retractors are installed.
1973: Carburettors, manifolds and cylinder head are changed to meet emission standards. Intermittent wipers, tinted glass, three-point adjustable seat belts and a collapsible steering column are fitted.
1974: Engine capacity is increased to 2.6 litres, and the car is renamed the 260Z. There's also a new 2+2 bodystyle.
1975: The US gets a 2.8-litre model, the 280Z, with Bosch L-Jetronic fuel injection.
1975/76: UK market loses the coupé; only the 2+2 is marketed for this period.
1977: The 260Z coupé is relaunched in the UK. Coupé and 2+2 continue until the introduction of the 280ZX.
1978: Second-generation Z-car debuts in America and the UK as the 280ZX. The engine, transmission and differential are carried over.

TRANSMISSION

All UK-supplied Zs featured a five-speed manual gearbox, but three-speed auto and four-speed manual transmissions were available elsewhere. You're unlikely to stumble across anything other than a five-ratio manual car though, and as it's a long-lived unit there's little to worry about. Examples in hard-driven cars might be suffering from worn bearings though, while the synchromesh on a high-mileage car will be the worse for wear.

If a gearbox rebuild is necessary you can expect to pay £500-£1000 for the parts alone, so it's an expensive business. If you find yourself in this position it's worth considering a 280ZX unit, if you can get one. These later units have improved synchro design over the 240Z and 260Z hardware, so they're even more durable. Beware the mix and match on ratios, however – only the later 280ZX manual box matches the 240Z's 3.9:1 differential ratio.

Clonking noises from the rear as you take up the drive are a sign that the outer universal joints have worn on the driveshafts. It's a standard universal joint so good replacements are nice and cheap at £35 and fitting them is easy.

STEERING & SUSPENSION

The rack-and-pinion steering makes the Z a delight to pilot, but watch out for mounting bushes that have gone soft. Once the rubber has perished the steering will become vague, so check for play by turning the steering wheel and getting somebody to see how quickly the road wheels respond. Urethane mounting bushes and a plastic steering coupler (in place of the original rubber item) improve steering precision by a huge margin and the cost is just £26 for the set.

With MacPherson struts and coil springs at each corner the Z's suspension is unusually advanced for its era. Its simplicity means the set-up is usually long-lived, but tired or leaking dampers along with sagging springs are par for the course. Drive the car along a poorly surfaced road and feel for a crashy ride. The car should soak up the bumps with ease – if it doesn't, you'll need new springs (£147 per set) and/or dampers (from £117 per pair) at each corner.

US-market cars had softer suspension than UK versions. If you're buying a US import it's worth fitting shorter, stiffer springs to sharpen things up along with beefier anti-roll bars. While you're at it, polyurethane bushes are a good idea.

'Rack-and-pinion steering makes the Z a delight to pilot'

NEED TO KNOW

PRACTICAL CLASSIC?
More than you'd think, but not ideal for everyday use thanks to that thirsty straight-six; 25mpg is attainable in a standard car.

THANKS TO
Mike Feeney of MJP Auto and Peter MacDonald, owner of the car pictured. Also Alan Thomas, Z historian extraordinaire.

WHAT ARE THEY LIKE TO DRIVE?
Massive fun, thanks to a torquey straight-six (red-lined at 7000rpm) and rear-wheel drive. Weight distribution is almost 50:50 and the ride is great.

WILL I FIT BEHIND THE STEERING WHEEL?
Yes, but it's best to view all these cars strictly as two-seaters.

WHAT ARE THE KEY PROBLEMS?
- Corrosion
- Over-sized wheels
- Damaged trim

WHAT SHOULD I PAY?
240Z restoration projects start at £1500 while the best examples can cost up to £10,000; a nice car that's not perfect fetches £7500. It's harder to value 260Zs because they're so rarely available, but the equivalent figures for a two-seater version should be £1000, £7000 and £4000; knock perhaps 20 per cent off these values for a 2+2.

INSURANCE COSTS...
Comprehensive cover for a £7000 1971 Datsun 240Z is £115, based on a 5000-mile annual limit. Driver must be over 25 years old and the 240Z a second car. Quote from RH Specialist Car Division on 01277 206911.

WHO ARE THE SPECIALISTS?
- Auto Active, Bristol. 0117 9442068, www.auto-active.co.uk
- DJ Road and Race, Glos. 01453 833451, www.djroadandrace.com
- Fourways Engineering, Kent. 01732 884288, www.fourways-engineering.co.uk

WHEELS & BRAKES
Steel wheels were fitted to all 240Zs, while the 260Zs featured alloys from 1975 onwards. Most cars now sit on alloys of some sort, either period Wolfrace rims or Minilites. Whatever wheels are fitted, ensure they're not too wide; many owners get carried away and fit wheels that destroy the ride and can put too much of a load on the suspension and steering. The original wheels were 5.5J items; you can go up to 7J and get away with it, but anything wider may cause problems with premature wear. The limited supply of performance rubber in period sizes means many owners are stepping up to a 16in alloy to improve their roadholding.

TRIM
The Z's interior is now fabulously dated and is a real piece of Seventies cheese with its quilted gearbox cover trim and resin-coated wooden steering wheel. The quilted trim often gets replaced by carpet, while all sorts of aftermarket steering wheels get fitted. Tracking down an original wheel is still possible, while repro quilted trim is available at £235 for the set. The rest of the vinyl trim will soon be available as a supplementary kit. Door trims have a habit of warping while the seat trim often splits; replacement seat re-upholstery kits are £223 for the pair.

Cars that have been left in the sun may suffer cracked dash tops; fading and discolouring are also common. In the case of fading it's possible to recolour the plastic, but cracks are harder to deal with as new replacement surrounds are almost impossible to find.

ELECTRICS
There's little to worry about here; column stalk and switch contacts sometimes give problems, but the units can be rebuilt. Alternators and starter motors are amazingly durable but can be refurbished if necessary. The front wing indicator repeaters rot badly and are hard to source, but they can be swapped for similar units if necessary.

CONCLUSION
Whether you're after a toy for occasional play, one for historic rallying or even a car for more regular use, the 240Z and 260Z make a lot of sense. They're less suited to everyday use because of their thirst, but with stylish looks, a great chassis and superb reliability, the Z makes a sound classic buy.

However, you don't have to settle for a UK-supplied car. There were all sorts of derivatives available elsewhere and remember Japanese-market cars are right-hand drive. Some home-market cars had smaller engines or four valves per cylinder. Nice 240Zs are now very rare, do your homework on a variant that didn't originally sell in the UK and you could end up with a real classic novelty.

LOOK OUT FOR...

1 Rot is the biggest likely problem with any Z; start by checking the sills.

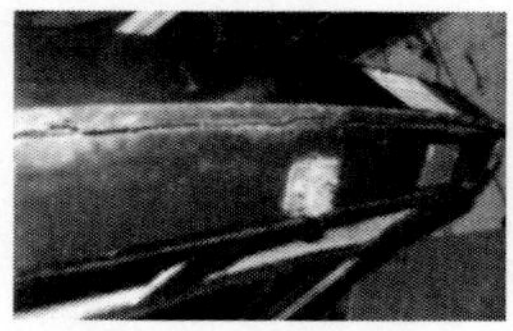

2 The underside of the tailgate corrodes badly and is hard to repair.

3 Check the condition of the inner wings, which are often full of holes.

■ MJP Eastern Auto. 01277 374201, www.mjpauto.com
■ Z Farm, Yorks. 01845 587100

WHAT ABOUT THE PRICE OF SPARES PARTS?
■ Exhaust (stainless) £400+
■ Wing £230
■ Bumper £275 (when available)
■ Dampers from £118 per pair
■ Clutch kit from £140-£175
■ Alternator £120 exch
■ Starter motor £75 exch

HARD TO FIND PARTS ARE...
■ Original panels

CAN THEY COPE WITH UNLEADED?
Post-1977 260Zs are fine, but earlier cars need hardened valve seats or an additive. The timing should also be retarded by a couple of degrees. This is not necessary if super-unleaded is used – super was not available when Nissan made their original statement about the 260Z. Millers VSP is the best additive and provides an octane boost automatically. Most 240Zs, however, will have been converted by now.

WHERE ARE THE IDENTIFYING MARKS?
The chassis number is stamped on the bulkhead and there's also a plate on the nearside inner wing behind the strut tower on the 260Z, or at the base of the offside strut housing on the 240Z strut tower. A USA car will have the chassis number stamped on the instrument panel on the lefthand-side.

OWNERS' CLUBS
■ The Z Club, www.zclub.net
■ Classic Z Register, www.s30.org
■ Datsun Owners' Club. 07941 299 854, www.datsunownersclub.co.uk

WHICH IS THE BEST BOOK?
■ *Datsun Fairlady Z to 280ZX* by Brian Long. Veloce, ISBN 978-1-904788-07-6
■ *Datsun 240Z & 260Z Gold Portfolio 1970-78*. Brooklands, ISBN 0-1-85520-395-2

Déjà Vu Meets Déjà New

Forty years may separate these two Zs, but they both celebrate the BRE Datsun 240Z's historic SCCA National Championships in 1970 and 1971

BY ANDREW BORNHOP PHOTOS BY JOHN LAMM

MOST PEOPLE FAMILIAR WITH BROCK Racing Enterprises immediately think of John Morton and the Datsun 510. With good reason. The boxy red, white and blue No. 46 BRE car won the SCCA 2.5-liter Trans-Am championship in 1971 and 1972. And the affordable 510 adapted so well to racing that scads of them, many painted like original BRE cars, popped up at racetracks around the country. Even today you'll see the occasional 510 road racing, often in BRE-inspired paint.

Before the 510, however, Peter Brock and crew—who were already campaigning Datsun S2000 Roadsters in SCCA club racing—hit the track with the sleek 240Z...and with great success. Aided by Datsun's West Coast President Yutaka Katayama, BRE obtained an early Z (chassis No. 492) in January 1970 and turned it into an SCCA C Production race car at their shop in El Segundo, California. This No. 46 Z, in fact, graced the cover of our November 1970 issue. James T. Crow reported on the build of the car and concluded that the new racing Z was well on its way to doing well. "Watch for it," he wrote. "It will be worth seeing."

Indeed it was. This was the heyday of production-based amateur road racing in America, and at the SCCA's 1970 American Road Race of Champions held at Road Atlanta (the precursor to the Runoffs), Morton's C Production BRE Z won easily, defeating the likes of Bob Tullius and Lee Mueller in Triumph TR-6s, Alan Johnson in a Ginther-prepared Porsche 914-6 and Bob Sharp, who was building

Peter Brock played a key role in making the Tribute 370Z look just like a modern BRE Z.

240Zs out of his shop in Connecticut.

Quite a debut for the BRE car and the sleek new Z in general, which swept the top three positions that fall day at Road Atlanta. And the following year, it seemed that the harder the Zs pushed, the more the Triumphs and Porsches broke. At the 1971 ARRC, two BRE 240Zs (Morton and Dan Parkinson) were on the front row, alongside Sharp. Allan Girdler, reporting in our March 1972 issue, described Morton's winning drive: "[He] put on an exhibition, leading all the way in his routine madman style and power always fully on, into each corner at seemingly impossible speed, out with wildly spinning tires, using all the road in the process."

All told, Datsun Zs went on to win 10 straight SCCA C Production titles, but that 1971 national championship marked the end of the BRE Z era. Brock—with Z sales booming and 510s languishing on dealer lots—had decided to go professional racing with the latter in the SCCA's 2.5-liter Trans-Am championship.

And sadly, the original championship-winning No. 46 BRE Z was destroyed a couple of years later. Brock had handed the car back to Datsun after the 1971 season, who in turn gave it to Parkinson, the former BRE driver who subsequently totaled the car in a rollover crash at Phoenix.

Although Parkinson, who Morton says is very fast, has never publicly admitted writing off the historically significant No. 46 car, one man who knows it's true is Ron Carter, an avid Datsun vintage racer who's built the beautiful BRE 240Z featured here, which is considered by many

Déjà Vu Meets Déjà New

to be the most faithful re-creation there is of the original No. 46 BRE 240Z.

"I loved the research; it was so much fun," explains Carter, who said he was the only guy crazy enough to undertake such an historically accurate re-creation of Morton's car. He methodically started collecting parts in 2002, beginning with a clean 1972 Z chassis that he had media-blasted down to the bare metal and stitch-welded.

An early fuel door and rear hatch gave the Z the proper 1970 look. BRE spoilers went on front and rear, as did aerodynamic headlight covers. The rollbar was copied from that of a BRE 240Z pace car used at Ontario Motor Speedway. As for the strut suspension, Carter wanted to keep it as original as possible but still be competitive in vintage racing. In went Hypercoil springs, Tokico Illumina 5-way-adjustable shock absorbers, camber plates and adjustable rear toe. And with the large anti-roll bars and sticky Hoosier DOT race tires, size 205/50ZR-15, Carter thought it prudent to reinforce the Z's suspension pickup points.

Under the hood is an original BRE-built L24 2.4-liter, a sohc inline-6 purchased from a vintage racer who was upgrading his Z to a larger engine. This Z was quite a find, as it supplied Carter not just with the powerplant but also the original triple Solex/Mikuni carburetors, the Nissan Competition intake manifold and original American Le Mans magnesium wheels. The gearbox is also from Nissan Comp, an early 5-speed overdrive unit (with "medium-close" ratios) that sends power to an R190 limited-slip differential with 4.44:1 gearing.

Differences from the original No. 46 are numerous but not that major, done mostly for added performance or safety but without changing the simple, honest character of the car. The ATL fuel cell, by vintage rules, is isolated by a bulkhead, and the original rollbar has been built into a full cage with door bars. What's more, the rear brakes are discs, whereas the original BRE Z raced with finned aluminum drums. All told, Carter's BRE Z weighs about 2100 lb., and the engine, redlined at 7000 rpm, puts out around 240 to 250 bhp. The headers, of note, are an exact copy of the original BRE exhaust on the blue No. 3 BRE 240Z, the sole remaining true BRE Z in existence.

Given that it's the 40th anniversary of both the production Z and the BRE Z's first championship, Nissan helped us take Carter's vintage BRE replica out to Spring Mountain Motorsports Ranch for some lapping fun. Making things even sweeter, we'd get to drive it back to back with Nissan's one-off 370Z BRE Tribute car, a modern Z done up in a paint scheme that pays homage to those folks who put the Z on the sports-car racing map.

The BRE Tribute car is a Nissan 370Z built by Stillen essentially to the SCCA's T2 class rules. As such, it's not overly tweaked. It has a gutted interior and a cage, plus race seats and belts. The car started out as a 2009 Touring Sport model, to which Nismo bodywork, wheels and shocks were added, the last teamed with Eibach springs that lower the car a bit. Stillen anti-roll bars are fitted to the car front and rear, and the 4-cam 3.7-liter V-6 is untouched internally. It is, however, stripped of its catalytic converter and fitted with a Stillen cat-back exhaust, a reflashed ECU, a Nissan Motorsports oil cooler, an aluminum flywheel and a heavy-duty clutch. Power is in the neighborhood of 350 bhp, and stock brakes (with braided stainless-steel lines and Hawk pads) handle stopping chores. The car also had a stock viscous limited-slip differential, although Nissan plans to fit the car with a tougher clutch-type LSD from Nissan Comp soon.

First up, the BRE 240Z. As Ron Carter is a big guy, I fit in his seat well. With this being the first time the car has run in anger on a track—and it being dearer to his heart than just about, well, anything—I tell myself: *Don't do anything stupid.* The car fires easily with the pushbutton starter and a squirt of gas from the pedal. And boy, is it loud! The clutch takeup is simple, and soon I'm out on the track being deliberate with each shift. The Z is spacious but has a narrow feel, and the pedals are placed for easy heel/toe downshifting. Nothing feels assisted. During my familiarization laps, the steering is heavy, the brakes are heavy...drivers really were men back then. I shift at about 6800 rpm, as Ron suggested, and the straight-line power is excellent. In steady-state corners, the grip is great; however, there's a miss from the engine that only clears out on the straightaway, so I head into the pits.

"Are you channeling John Morton yet?" asks Carter after I shut off the car. "Not yet," I admit. Second time out, though—after Carter's crew tweaked the float bowl levels a bit—I pick up some speed and begin probing limits more aggressively. The grip from the Hoosiers is exceptional. I'm shifting at 7000 rpm now, carrying more speed into corners and exiting them with a lot more side load because of the added pace. It felt fantastic, very mechanical, and the Z really came alive when picked up by the scruff of the neck and driven hard. Only then did I begin to imagine what it must have been like to be Morton in a BRE Z, dicing with the likes of Tullius in a TR-6 at Road Atlanta. As I pulled in, it was hard to wipe the smile off my face. Our best lap of the day: 1 minute, 56.27 seconds, a decent effort given that the engine still sputtered a bit in Turns 1 and 2.

Brock, on hand for the test, quickly pointed to a couple of potential causes for the misfire. One, the car needed a shield between the headers and the carbs to keep heat from causing issues. Two, the carbs needed to be isolated with rubber to keep fuel from frothing in the float bowls at high rpm. Carter took mental notes as Brock, a youthful 73, recalled the details from 40 years ago...

The Nissan 370Z Tribute car—with BRE livery personally created and directed by Brock in the paint booth—felt quite different from the old 240. With its full cage it's actually tighter on space than the 1970 240Z, but it's much easier to hop in and immediately drive faster. And the first time I hit the assisted brakes, I nearly put myself through the windshield. Although the grip of the Yokohama Advan

›› With its triple Solex/Mikuni carbs, high-lift cam and other parts, the BRE-built inline-6 in the vintage 240Z (below) puts out 240 loud bhp. Open fuel door (below right) provides a secret place to keep an eye on diff temps. Gutted interior (bottom right) even smells like the original's, says Peter Brock.

AD08s, the stock Nismo tire, felt remarkably good, it was still not quite up to the level of the stickier Hoosiers.

All the controls of this modern Z feel Teflon-coated for ease of use, and the adjustable rear anti-roll bar from Stillen (which was set on full stiff and may not be legal in T2) makes the car quite tail-happy, with power oversteer on tap while exiting tight corners. Road Test Editor Jonathan Elfalan (who did the timed laps) and I both agree that the Z was tuned great for the Corvette Loop we were on but would be hairy on a big fast track such as Willow Springs.

Second session in the car, with all driver aids turned off, I'm having more fun. It's hot, over 100 degrees, and I'm keeping an eye on oil temps as I continue to be impressed with how well the new Z hides its 3300-lb. curb weight and laps with no apparent vices. It's clearly better damped than a stock Z. Toward the end of the session, though, I notice more inside rear wheelspin on corner exit, an indicator that the limited-slip diff was not working well. Turns out that differential cooler hadn't been installed on the car yet, and our lapping on a hot day proved too much for the diff. Our best lap of 1 min. 55.53 sec. would have been considerably better had the car been on Hoosiers and fitted with the limited-slip diff from Nismo, with a remote cooler.

So, neither the Nissan nor the Datsun had a perfect day at Spring Mountain, but these siblings—40 years apart in age and effectively on shakedown runs—proved to be remarkably close indeed in performance. More important, they provided me with a sense of what it must have been like to be John Morton back in the day, and perhaps what a modern BRE 370Z might be like, had BRE stayed in the business of racing Datsuns or Nissans.

Will we ever see Carter's BRE 240Z on the track at vintage races? "Probably not," he admits. "I put too much energy into building the car. I built it too well. I'm afraid to crash it. And I even put a clear coat on it. Everybody knows you're not supposed to do that to a race car." That said, we can only hope to see the Stillen-prepared Tribute car in T2 action soon, keeping the BRE flame alive and putting the Z where it's repeatedly been since 1970...at the front of the field. ■

›› The BRE Tribute 370Z looks great going by, so good in fact that Brock says it reminded him of the original BRE 240Z when it blasted past on the straight. Even on street tires, this Stillen-built 370Z lapped quicker than the 240Z on sticky Hoosiers. Yes, the new 370Z is significantly heavier, but it's much easier to drive fast.

DATSUN 240/260Z

BUYER'S GUIDE

Japan's world-beating sports coupé is becoming highly sought-after, says **Malcolm McKay**

PHOTOGRAPHY **TONY BAKER**

The perfect sports car for the '70s came from the least expected source: Japan. It was targeted at the lucrative US market, then largely the preserve of British and Italian brands, and rapidly became the world's best-selling sports car because the Americans couldn't get enough. It's hardly surprising: over there, it cost just 10% more than an MGB GT and offered so much more.

The 125mph top speed and 8 secs 0-60mph time grabbed the headlines and pulled customers into showrooms, where they were then won over by the car's attractive lines, quality build and great packaging. It had plenty of interior and luggage space, a long-range fuel tank, good noise suppression and extremely comfortable, high-backed seats (pioneering integral head restraints), plus good heating and ventilation. All of which made the Z very pleasant to live with, both every-day and for long-distance touring.

We now know that the input of German stylist Albrecht Goertz into the 240Z has been over-stated in the past. It was the concept of Yutaka Katayama and designed by Yoshihiko Matsuo, assisted by Akio Yoshida, with – at most – distant memories of a stillborn c1964 design by Goertz.

The 240 had an oversquare 2.4-litre straight-six that gave its best past 4000rpm. Japan had an even more revvy 2-litre for tax reasons, initially single-cam but later with the option of twin-cam with triple Mikuni twin-choke carbs. This Z432 had 160bhp, but the ultimate Z was the 250bhp Z432-R racer, of which 362 were built.

The 260Z got a longer stroke and, though still oversquare, felt a great deal more torquey. Its introduction coincided with the launch of the 2+2, which was a much bigger car, with a foot longer wheelbase and 16in-longer body.

As rust has decimated survivors and rebuild costs have soared, the 240Z has at last begun to be appreciated. In Europe, where smaller numbers were sold, values have risen dramatically in recent years, partly thanks to top-quality specialist restorations and the cars' popularity for rallying. Many both here and in the US have been modified but, apart from historic rally cars – which command double the concours price – the big money is paid for standard-spec Zs.

Front wings, bonnets and headlamp cowls are still available from Nissan, while specialists, particularly in the USA, can supply pretty much everything else, new or second-hand.

Shekhar Mehta on his way to his first Safari win in 1973

Press shot shows higher roofline of four-seater 260Z 2+2

Rot spots

1. Front of bonnet, headlamp cowls (post-'72) and valance
2. Crossmember under rad; suspension/steering mounts
3. Front inner wings and suspension turrets
4. Footwells and chassis rails
5. Scuttle at base of windscreen; battery tray
6. Sills, esp front/rear ends (also wings in these areas)
7. Door bottoms
8. Rear wheelarches
9. Closing panel for tailgate and behind rear lights
10. Rear hatch/screen corners

Check dash top for cracking: sunshine destroys it. Also look for electrical maladies; the clock often fails and the oil-pressure sender can be misleading

Listen for worn bearings and check for worn synchro, esp on 2nd and 5th. UK cars all 5-speed, imports may be four. Early 'box has straight lever, later bent

Engines are immensely durable if well looked after, even 400,000 miles is possible. Neglect can play havoc with them, though. Inspect the cam condition through the oil filler (use a torch and turn the engine on the starter) and watch out for signs of head-gasket failure; expect 55psi oil pressure on the move

As with any alloy head, lack of rust inhibitor leads to silting, inadequate water flow, overheating and potentially a warped head and blown gasket

Pre-'77 vinyl seats prone to splitting and ultimately disintegrating, but replacement covers are available. Cloth panels last better but discolour

Simple and robust, the suspension is unlikely to give more trouble than weak dampers and worn bushes. Beware of rust or cracks around inner mountings

Standard wheels were steel; alloys (here Dan Gurneys) look better. Listen for diff whine and clonks: may be just worn UJs, but could be a slack diff

Purists prefer the classic 240 shape, which gained weight over the years

On the road

Using SU carburettors built under licence by Hitachi, the 240Z engine was simple, durable and reliable – but it will wear out eventually, so listen for untoward noises and pay close attention to engine temperature and oil pressure. Unleaded fuel is no problem (though the 240 prefers super), but infrequent oil changes lead to worn cam lobes and noticeably lacklustre performance. Zs gained weight disgracefully over the years, especially in 2+2 form, which slowed acceleration but barely affected top speed except in the USA, where emissions demands took their toll: fitting earlier carbs is worthwhile. Check to see if the car still has its original engine: the serial number is stamped both on a plate under the bonnet and on the block.

Most road testers preferred the 260 to the 240 due to its wider tyres and torque spread, though European 260s were considerably faster than emissions-hampered US models. Many enthusiasts prefer the revvy nature of the 240 engine.

Check the gearbox for signs of wear, and for number of gears: European cars were five-speed, but almost all US cars were fours. The independent rear suspension is robust, but mountings can suffer, diffs are prone to whine and universal-joint wear will cause clunks from the back end.

The Z should give a firm but comfortable ride with excellent, predictable handling – anything less means suspension wear or misalignment. Check for accident damage in the chassis rails or poor repairs to suspension mountings. The steering, which is light and direct on 175/80 tyres, is heavy at low speeds on wider rubber.

A well-sorted Z is fun to drive, with plenty of lusty power

OWNER'S VIEW
Rob Smith

Rob Smith has owned this 240Z for 10 years, but it all started with a 260. "My son bought a 260Z that needed restoring and he didn't get around to it, so I rebuilt it," he explains. "I joined the Z Club and started going to various shows. I enjoyed driving it and also had a 300ZX for a while. Then I had the chance to drive a 240Z and I loved it – you really feel a part of the car. So I started looking and found this one locally. The rear end had been custom-painted with newsprint, so I had it resprayed. I also bought an interior trim kit from the US and retrimmed it. It was remarkably solid for a UK example, but at some point it had been fitted with a Laurel engine, so I put the motor from the 260 in temporarily – and it's still there!"

The knowledge

WHAT TO PAY

Show/rebuilt 240	£20,000+
Average 240/260 2+2	£10,000/6000
Restoration	£1000

PARTS PRICES

Front wing (genuine)	£282
Stainless-steel bumper set	£881
Brake master cylinder	£148
Full sill	£61
Triple Webers, manifold, linkage	£940
Seat retrim kit 240	£265

ON THE WEB
www.zhome.com; www.240z.org; www.datsun260z.co.uk

CLUBS
Z Club 01455 213284; www.zclub.net **Classic Z Register** 07530 349639; www.s30.org

BOOKS
Fairlady Roadster to 280ZX Brian Long, Veloce **Essential Datsun 240Z to 280ZX** Colin Shipway, MBI **How to Restore your Datsun Z-Car** Wick Humble, California Bill

SPECIALISTS
MJP Eastern Auto 01277 374201; www.mjpauto.com **Fourways Engineering** 01732 884288; www.fourways-engineering.co.uk **The Z Farm** 01845 595100; www.thezfarm.co.uk **Auto Active** 0117 944 2068; www.auto-active.co.uk

TIMELINE

1966 Yoshihiko Matsuo creates clay model
1967 Glassfibre prototype with 'Z' designation
1969 Nov: Fairlady Z 2.0 and 240Z 2.4 launched
1970 240Z's rally debut on RAC, finished 7th; also wins US SCCA Production Class C
1971 Auto option announced, rear vents move from hatch to C-pillar; UK sales begin August; 240Z 1st and 2nd on East African Safari Rally
1971 Oct: centre console and seat changes
1972 Aug: larger bumpers and overriders; US cars lose power with head and carb changes
1973 Oct: 260Z replaces 240 in US and Japan, with 2+2 option, wider tyres, stiffer springs
1974 260Z replaces 240 in Europe
1975 Fuel-injected 280Z replaces 260 in USA
1976 Feb: two-seater dropped in Europe
1977 US cars get 5-speed 'box; 260Z 2-seater reintroduced in UK; seat centres now cloth
1979 260/280Z replaced by 280ZX 2+2

FACTFILE

Sold/number built 1969-'78/531,601 **Construction** steel monocoque **Engine** iron-block, alloy-head sohc/dohc 1988cc or sohc 2393/2565/2754cc 'six', with twin Hitachi-SU carburettors or Bosch K-Jetronic-pattern electronic fuel injection **Max power** 150bhp @ 6000rpm-162bhp @ 5600rpm **Max torque** 148lb ft @ 4400rpm-163lb ft @ 4400rpm **Transmission** four/five-speed manual or auto, driving rear wheels **Suspension** independent, by MacPherson struts, anti-roll bars (no rear anti-roll bar in the USA) **Steering** rack and pinion **Brakes** 10¾in (272mm) front discs, 9in (229mm) rear drums, with servo **Length** 13ft 7in-14ft 8in (4135-4715mm) **Width** 5ft 4in-5ft 5in (1630-1650mm) **Height** 4ft 3in (1285mm) **Wheelbase** 7ft 7in-8ft 6in (2305-2605mm) **Weight** 2355-2875lb (1070-1305kg) **0-60mph** 8.2-11.7secs **Top speed** 125-127mph **Mpg** 18-30 **Price new** £2690 (1973)

INSURANCE

£136.50, based on a 30-year-old London driver with full no-claims and a clean licence on a '73 Z as a garaged second car, agreed value £10k, 5000 limited miles. Lancaster: 01480 484848.

THE ALTERNATIVES

MGB GT V8

Though sold in tiny numbers and only on the home market, the BGT V8 was a serious rival to the Datsun in performance. It lacks space and only has a live rear axle, but it's desirable now, especially in chrome-bumper form.
Sold/no built 1973-'76/2591 **Mpg** 19-26 **0-60mph** 7.7 secs **Top speed** 125mph **Price new** £2294 (1973) **Price now** £7000

FORD CAPRI 3.0

The Capri rivalled the 260Z 2+2 at half the price with very similar pace: no wonder it was also a best-seller. Rot and neglect have decimated numbers and they are costly to rebuild, with poorer parts availability than you might expect.
Sold/no built 1969-'77/1,576,512 (all MkI/IIs) **Mpg** 18-25 **0-60mph** 8.5 secs **Top speed** 120mph **Price new** £1824 (GXL, '73) **Price now** £8000

One to buy **£11,995**

Year of manufacture 1971 **Recorded mileage** 49,272 **Vendor** Simon Cass, Chard, Somerset; tel: 01460 68112 **For** cared-for car in original spec; much work done **Against** no history; it's an auto

This '71 auto was one of two imported from California earlier this year. Its low mileage is believed to be genuine, but there are no documents to back it up. The car has been resprayed at some point – well – and the shell appears very sound, with solid sills and no obvious nastiness beneath. There are blemishes – notably small bubbles towards the front of each wing – but the paint retains a deep lustre, the panelfit is good and the overall impression is of a smart car.

Inside, the Z is tidy but pleasantly patinated. A neat plastic cover hides the inevitable dashboard cracks, and the ventilated seats look good. The boot area is perfect, with a new carpet, but there is some corrosion appearing under the sound-deadening in the unwelded footwells.

Under the bonnet, there's a new starter motor, plus a recent exhaust, servo and radiator. There's an air-con compressor, too, but no belt fitted. The antifreeze is fresh, the oil clean and to its lower mark. Warm when we arrived, the 'six' fired with a dab of throttle, giving a fruity bark through twin exhausts. The oil-pressure gauge is sticky, but shows 30psi at idle and 50psi under load, while the temperature needle settles in the centre of the dial. The car tracks straight, but there is some judder from the brakes, uprated with four-pot calipers. The auto 'box kicks down smartly and doesn't blunt the Z's pace too badly, but does make it feel more GT than sports car.

Minilite-style 15in Panasports wear fresh Aquaflow tyres

Original steering wheel would benefit from refurbishment

Light corrosion beneath battery, but inner wings are solid

Comfortable seats and huge boot make the Z a fine tourer

Our verdict

With customers paying £25,000-plus for rebuilt 240Zs from the top specialists, it's clear that the Z is out of the doldrums, but there are still plenty of bodged ones around from the days when proper restoration wasn't worthwhile. Take a really good look underneath and probe everywhere to be sure that you buy a good one, then enjoy it!

FOR
- Eye-catching styling
- Robust, well-engineered mechanicals
- Good parts supply
- Smooth and rapid performance

AGAINST
- Rust takes hold and is expensive to put right
- Became heavier, softer and slower (esp in USA)
- Parts often swapped for lesser models

Z car revival

Words Adam Mamo **Photos** Dan Wakelin

The evolution of Nissan's Z cars hasn't come without setbacks and growing pains. The Z badge has never enjoyed a long uninterrupted evolution like the benchmark Porsche 911. But with pain comes strength, and Nissan is back flexing its design and engineering muscle with the most recent branch on the Z family tree – the 370Z

The exterior aesthetic of the 370Z offers a buffet of styling cues and athletic lines, but it's not until you slide into the car's enveloping leather and suede bucket seats that it becomes clear this is a modern sports car without compromise. Surrounding the driver is a range of soft, tactile, leather-bound surfaces and high quality materials. It's a dark, purposeful cabin lightened by silver and brushed metal accents and the use of various circular shapes.

Modern touches collide with traditional Z elements, such as a digital clock amongst the three, dashboard-mounted auxiliary gauges. With the main instrument cluster tied to the adjustable steering column, power adjustable seats and a closely located gear-stick, finding a comfortable driving position presents no difficulty. Once that's achieved, hit the push-button start and the engine awakens with a raspy note. Bury a foot into the floor-hinged accelerator pedal, and any notion that the 370Z is a mere retro-themed toy will be left behind – rapidly.

As the sixth vehicle to wear the 'Z' badge, the 370Z has a range of ancestors from which to draw comparisons, but the yardstick for measuring any Z car remains the original Datsun 240Z.

The First Z

The significance of the 240Z is greater than just being the first Z produced, it played a starring role in changing the world's perception of Japanese performance cars. Before the 240Z, Japanese sports cars were often viewed as simply too small, too uncomfortable and worse, underpowered. This harsh global opinion lit a fire under one Nissan executive, Yutaka Katayama – who would later become known as Mr K. During the late 1960s, Mr K set about creating a Japanese sports car to silence the critics. Fuelled by a passion for the Jaguar E-Type, which he viewed as perfection, Mr K sketched out his pivotal design criteria.

The new Nissan coupé had to be designed for safety and comfort with a unique style, it would make use of part sharing for low development costs, be innovative in its design and technology, be functional and, most importantly, fast.

It was a tall order, but in 1969 Mr K's dream became reality with the launch of the 240Z. The 240Z fulfilled the challenging criteria, impressed critics and, thanks to low pricing, became a sales success. The rest, as they say, is history.

Mr K's story is an interesting one, but that was 40 years ago and we now live in more cynical times, so fresh evidence of the 240Z's merits is required.

We needed a 240Z with a story, not some garage dust magnet but a regularly raced, occasionally modified and always loved example. Surprisingly, all it took was a single phone call to locate such a car. The president of the Datsun Z Club of New Zealand, Dee Collins, brought out her own personal Datsun 240Z to show us how a real Z car rolls.

Racing Career

Dee's 1971 240Z was purchased late 1979 in circumstances probably familiar to many classic car owners. Dee's late husband, Graham, left home one day to buy a different car, but when he returned it was at the wheel of a Datsun 240Z. The car had a high odo reading and, due to a good dose of rust, had been purchased for a bargain price.

Over the next 15 years Graham and Dee's 240Z was treated to regular tweaks and modifications to better facilitate its race-track duties. Once the rust was removed, the car was lowered on sports springs and shocks, and dressed up with after-market wheels.

Under the bonnet the original six-cylinder, cast-iron block and alloy head was retained but bored out from the standard 2393cc displacement to 2690cc. The camshaft was reground, while enlarged extractors and a sports exhaust system were also fitted.

The standard twin carburettors also received attention to further increase power. Maintaining an original-looking engine bay was important to Graham, and by resisting the urge to fit triple carburettors, this goal was achieved.

In return for Graham's investment and affection the 240Z gave back 10 years of solid service on the track. From 1982 to 1992 Graham and his 240Z competed in almost every classic car race they could gain entry to, including support races for both the Benson and Hedges Series and the Australian Touring Car Championship.

While the 240Z was always competitive on the track with Porsches and Jaguars of the same era, its reliability would ultimately prove its most impressive characteristic. Graham would drive the car to each race meeting, and after every race he would drive it back home again. In all the years it raced, not once did the 240Z return to his garage on the back of a tow truck.

Today, the 240Z has retired from the rigours of circuit racing, but its throaty exhaust note can still be heard every week or two when Dee takes it out for an open road run or to attend a Z Club function. Dee still enjoys the 240Z for reasons away from all the memories it holds, she finds the styling timelessly beautiful, and she loves the sound of it and the raw driving experience it has always offered.

The 240Z understandably has a nostalgic value to Dee and the Collins family, but it is also a special vehicle amongst Z Club ranks.

The club was founded in 1981 by five initial members and their Z cars – Dee's 240Z remaining the sole founding vehicle still in the same hands. By 1983 the Z Club had a 200-strong membership base, and it has continued to grow into one of New Zealand's most active car clubs.

The 1980s was the heyday for modifying and racing 240Zs in New Zealand, and the first 15 years of the Z Club was defined by frequent race meetings. Now, fewer members are willing to put their classics on to the track, but the performance capabilities and driver enjoyment of the 240Z continues to be exercised by Dee and other club members during runs and organised events.

Back to the Beginnings

Since the final 240Z rolled off the line in 1979 Nissan had kept the Z badge alive, but slowly it drifted away from Mr K's original design criteria. Progressively bigger, heavier, more expensive and over-equipped models marked a distinct departure from the original's lightweight, agile charms.

However, in 2002 – with the release of the 350Z – Nissan took a step back towards the styling and the ethos behind the 240Z, and the new 370Z nudges even closer.

Parking our two vehicles side by side it's easy to identify aesthetic similarities. The roofline and window shape on the 370Z is a purposeful throwback to its ancestor, with

the pinched-off belt line and wide C-pillar reinforcing the resemblance. General dimensional similarities are evident in the cab-forward design and short rear overhang on the 370Z, which adds visual length to the bonnet – a signature feature of the 240Z. Other evidence of shared DNA can be found in the retro, dual-purpose Z badge and the indicators on the front guards of the 370Z.

The 370Z mimics the strong physical presence of the 240Z while adding width – and those unmissable rear haunches.

When asked her thoughts about the new model parked beside her beloved 240Z, Dee was quick to comment on the 370Z's beautiful design, and her pleasure at seeing a return to form for the Z cars after the disappointing intermediate models. But would she swap her 240Z for the new model? No way! Mind you, not surprisingly, Dee could happily live with both cars in her garage.

Dr Jekyll and Mr Hyde

The 370Z offers more than a passing nod to the 240Z in styling terms, but cut through the new model's sheet metal, and it's all modern technology underneath. Jammed into the engine bay is Nissan's latest VQ-series six-cylinder powerplant. Unlike the 240Z's straight-six, the 370Z is home to a 3.7-litre V6 unit that thumps out 245kW of grunt and 363Nm of torque.

This bent-six will rocket the 370Z from standing to ›

100kph in a mere 5.3 seconds and packs enough innovative tricks to appease Mr K himself. The pick of the new gear is Nissan's Variable Valve Event and Lift (VVEL) technology. This helps the Nissan achieve both blistering performance and almost decent economy (10.4l/100km). How? The conventional lobed camshaft in the VQ engine is replaced by a complex variable reciprocating mechanism that can adjust the intake valve lift and timing infinitely for either maximum performance or more frugal economy.

On the road the VVEL system gifts the 370Z with an almost a Dr Jekyll and Mr Hyde personality. Under light throttle the 370Z is a relaxed suburban cruiser, but put your foot down and it quickly turns leery. During spirited driving there is nothing gentle about the 370Z, the motor sings out gruffly and vibration can be felt through the wheel as the revs climb. The cabin fills with a variety of mechanical and tyre noises and the driver connects through thick, meaty controls that are heavy enough to warrant a firm hand. Power delivery arrives in a linear fashion without the surge of torque you'd get in a turbocharged vehicle. Smooth, naturally aspirated acceleration makes the 370Z easy to anticipate and adjust its attitude using only the gas pedal.

Ride quality is suitably firm but with enough compliance to disarm most bumps and dips on uneven roads, while body roll is kept to a minimum. It's also well balanced with a near-optimal 53 per cent front, 47 per cent rear weight distribution.

The 370Z changes direction with agility thanks largely to an all-alloy double wishbone front and multi-link rear suspension set-up. Generally a high level of grip is on offer, and pushing too hard will initially result only in predictable understeer. Deactivate the stability control and you'll need to be much sharper to avoid getting out of shape.

The bottom line is that the 370Z is an unapologetic sports car that makes little attempt at any real refinement or multi-purpose use. Through this uncompromising approach it pushes all the right sensory buttons for those seeking excitement.

While is shares definite styling similarities with the 240Z, what will really excite Z-car fans about the new model is how it revisits the thinking behind Mr K's original design criteria – an exact recipe on how to cook up an affordable sports car; one that could inspire genuine passion from those who owned one and those who wanted to. The 240Z is still inspiring such passion from Dee Collins and her fellow Z Club members.

The new 370Z scores points for its evolutionary, rather than revolutionary approach, but the final test is one that only time can tell. If the 370Z can one day match the reliability and timeless appeal of the 240Z, then it may prove a worthy successor to the crown. But until that day comes, there remains **only one iconic Z car.**

Facts & Figures

	Datsun 240Z (1969-1973)	**2009 Nissan 370Z**
Engine	In-line six	V6
Capacity	2393cc	3696cc
Bore/stroke	83mm x 73.7mm	95.5mm x 86mm
Fuel system	Twin Hitachi	Fuel injection
Valves	sohc	dohc per bank
Comp ratio	9.0:1	11:1
Max power	112kW at 5600rpm	245kW at 7000rpm
Max torque	198Nm at 4400rpm	363Nm at 5200rpm
Transmission	Five-speed manual	Six-speed manual
Brakes	Disc/drum	Disc/disc – ABS
Front suspension	Independent by MacPherson struts, lower links, anti-roll bar, coil springs, telescopic dampers and anti-roll bar	Independent, double wishbones, multi-link, coil springs, telescopic dampers, stabiliser bar
Rear suspension	Independent by MacPherson struts, lower wishbones, coil springs and telescopic dampers	Independent multi-link, coil springs, telescopic dampers and anti-roll bar
Steering	Rack and pinion	Variable PAS rack and pinion
Wheels	14x4.5J pressed steel	19-inch alloy
Tyres (O/E)	Dunlop SP 165 HR14	245/40R19 (F) 275/35R19(R)
Dimensions:		
O/all length	4140mm	4250mm
Width	1626mm	1845mm
Height	1590mm	1315mm
Wheelbase	2305mm	2550mm
Track F/R	1359/1346mm	1550/1595mm
Kerb weight	1041kg	1471kg
Performance:		
Max speed	202kph	250kph (limited)
0-60mph (claimed)	8.1 secs	5.3 secs
Standing quarter	15.8 secs	13.3 secs
Fuel economy (claimed)	9.7-14.1l/100km (20-29mpg)	10.4l/100km (27mpg)
NZ new price		$71,200

ROAD TEST SERIES

Abarth Road Test Portfolio 1950-1971
AC Cars 1904-2011
AC Ace Aceca Road Test Portfolio 1953-1962
AC & Cobra 1962-2011
Alfa Romeo A Brooklands Portfolio 1920-1940
Alfa Romeo Giulietta Gold Portfolio 1954-1965
Alfa Romeo Giulia Berlina Lim. Edit. Extra 1962-76
Alfa Romeo Giulia Coupes Lim. Edit. Ultra 1973-76
Alfa Romeo Alfasud 1972-1984
Alfa Romeo Alfetta Gold Portfolio 1972-1987
Alfa Romeo Alfetta GTV6 1980-1986
Alfa Romeo Spider Ultimate Portfolio 1966-1994
Alfa Romeo Spider & GTV Perf. Port. 1995-2005
Allard Limited Edition Ultra
Alpine Renault Ultimate Portfolio 1958-1995
Alvis Gold Portfolio 1919-1967
AMC Rambler Limited Edition Extra 1956-1969
AMX & Javelin Gold Portfolio 1968-1974
Armstrong Siddeley Gold Portfolio 1945-1960
Aston Martin Gold Portfolio 1921-1947
Aston Martin Ultimate Portfolio 1948-1968
Aston Martin Ultimate Portfolio 1968-1980
Aston Martin Ultimate Portfolio 1981-1993
Aston Martin Ultimate Portfolio 1994-2006
Auburn Cord Duesenberg - A Brooklands Portfolio
Audi Quattro Gold Portfolio 1980-1991
Audi TT Performance Portfolio 1998-2006
Austin Seven & Ten Road Test Portfolio
Austin-Healey 100 & 100/6 Gold Port. 1952-1959
Austin-Healey 3000 Road Test Portfolio
Austin-Healey Sprite Bug-Eye Mk 1 Road Test Portfolio
Bentley & Rolls-Royce Portfolio 1990-2002
Berkeley Sportscars Limited Edition
BMW 700 Limited Edition 1959-1965
BMW 2002 Ultimate Portfolio 1968-1976
BMW 6 Cylinder Coupes & Saloons Gold P. 1969-1976
BMW 320, 323, 325 (6 cyl.) Gold Port. 1977-1990
BMW 3 Series Gold Portfolio 1991-1997
BMW M3 Ultimate Portfolio 1986-2006
BMW M5 Gold Portfolio 1980-2003
BMW 5 Series Gold Portfolio 1988-1995
BMW 6 Series Ultimate Portfolio 1976-1989
BMW 7 Series Performance Portfolio 1977-1986
BMW 7 Series Performance Portfolio 1986-1993
BMW 8 Series Performance Portfolio
BMW X5 Limited Edition Extra 1999-2006
BMW Alpina Performance Portfolio 1967-1987
BMW Alpina Performance Portfolio 1988-1998
BMW Z3, M Coupe & M Roadster Gold Port. 1996-02
Bond Cars 1949-1974 Road Test Portfolio
Borgward Isabella Limited Edition
Bristol Cars Portfolio HARD COVER
Bugatti Type 10 to Type 40 Road Test Portfolio
Bugatti Type 41 to Type 55 Road Test Portfolio
Bugatti Type 57 to Type 251 Road Test Portfolio
Bugatti Type 10 to Type 251 Road Test Portfolio
Buick Performance Portfolio 1947-1962
Buick Muscle Portfolio 1963-1973
Buick Riviera Performance Portfolio 1963-1978
Cadillac Performance Portfolio 1948-1958
Cadillac Performance Portfolio 1959-1966
Cadillac Eldorado Performance Portfolio 1967-1978
Cadillac Allante Limited Edition Extra
Caterham Seven Road Test Portfolio 1974-1999
Caterham Seven Road Test Portfolio 2000-2010
Checker Automobiles Road Test Portfolio
Impala & SS Muscle Portfolio 1958-1972
Corvair Performance Portfolio 1959-1969
Chevy II & Nova SS Gold Portfolio 1962-1974
Chevelle & SS Gold Portfolio 1964-1972
Camaro Muscle Portfolio 1967-1973
Blazer & Jimmy Limited Edition Extra 1969-1982
Blazer & Jimmy Limited Edition Extra 1983-1994
Camaro Performance Portfolio 1993-2000
Chevrolet Caprice Road Test Portfolio 1965-1990
Chevrolet Corvette Gold Portfolio 1953-1962
Chevrolet Corvette Sting Ray Gold Port. 1963-1967
Chevrolet Corvette Gold Portfolio 1968-1977
Chrysler Imperial Gold Portfolio 1951-1975
Citroen Traction Avant Limited Edition Premier
Citroen 2CV Ultimate Portfolio 1948-1990
Citroen DS & ID 1955-1975
Citroen DS & ID Gold Portfolio 1955-1975
Citroen CX Road Test Portfolio
Shelby Cobra Gold Portfolio 1962-1969
Damlier SP250 Dart & V-8 2.5 litre 250 RTP 1959-69
Datsun Roadsters Performance Portfolio 1960-71
Datsun 240Z & 260Z Road Test Portfolio
Datsun 280Z & 280ZX Road Test Portfolio
Delahaye Road Test Portfolio
Delage Road Test Portfolio
DeLorean Gold Portfolio 1977-1995
De Soto Limited Edition 1952-1960
Dodge Limited Edition 1949-1959
Dodge Dart Limited Edition Extra 1960-1976
Dodge Muscle Portfolio 1964-1971
Charger Muscle Portfolio 1966-1974
Elfin Sports and Racing Cars
Elva Sports Racers Road Test Portfolio
ERA Gold Portfolio 1934-1994
Facel Vega Limited Edition Extra 1954-1964
Ferrari Road Cars 1946-1956 Road Test Portfolio
Ferrari Dino Limited Edition Extra 1965-1974
Ferrari 308 & Mondial Ultimate Portfolio 1975-85
Ferrari 328 348 Mondial Ultimate Portfolio 1986-94
Ferrari F355 & 360 Gold Portfolio 1995-2004
Fiat 500 1936-1972 Road Test Portfolio
Fiat Dino Road Test Portfolio
Fiat 124 Spider Performance Portfolio 1966-1985

www.brooklandsbooks.com

Fiat Abarth 1972-1987 Road Test Portfolio
Fiat X1/9 Gold Portfolio 1973-1989
Fiat Barchetta Road Test Portfolio
Ford Zephyr, Zodiac, Executive Mk. III & IV 1962-1971
High Performance Capris Gold Portfolio 1969-1987
Capri Muscle Portfolio 1974-1987
High Performance Fiestas 1979-1991
Ford Escort RS & Mexico Limited Edition 1970-1979
Ford Thunderbird Performance Portfolio 1955-1957
Ford Thunderbird Performance Portfolio 1958-1963
Ford Thunderbird Performance Portfolio 1964-1976
Ford Fairlane Performance Portfolio 1955-1970
Ford Ranchero Muscle Portfolio 1957-1979
Falcon Performance Portfolio 1960-1970
Ford Galaxie and LTD Gold Portfolio 1960-1976
Ford GT40 & GT Ultimate Portfolio 1964-2006
Ford Torino Performance Portfolio 1968-1974
Ford Bronco 4x4 Performance Portfolio 1966-1977
Shelby Mustang Ultimate Portfolio 1965-1970
Mustang Muscle Portfolio 1967-1973
High Performance Mustang IIs 1974-1978
Mustang 5.0L Muscle Portfolio 1982-1993
Ginetta Cars Limited Edition Ultra 1958-2007
Goggomobil Limited Edition
Hispano-Suiza Road Test Portfolio
Honda - Acura NSX Ultimate Portfolio 1989-2005
Honda CRX 1983-1987
Hudson Performance Portfolio 1946-1957
International Scout Gold Portfolio 1961-1980
Isetta Gold Portfolio 1953-1964
ISO & Bizzarrini Limited Edition Ultra 1962-1974
Jaguar Mk 7, 8, 10 & 420 Road Test Portfolio
Jaguar Mk 1 & Mk 2 1955-1969 Road Test Portfolio
Jaguar E-Type Ultimate Portfolio 1961-1975
Jaguar XJ6 Series I & II Gold Portfolio 1968-1979
Jaguar XJ6 Series III Perf. Portfolio 1979-1986
Jaguar XJ-S V12 Ultimate Portfolio 1988-1996
Jaguar XK8 & XKR Performance Portfolio 1996-2005
Jeep CJ-5 Limited Edition 1960-1975
Jeep CJ-5 & CJ-7 4x4 Perf. Portfolio 1976-1986
Jeep Wagoneer Performance Portfolio 1963-1991
Jeep J-Series Pickups 1970-1982
Jeepster & Commando Limited Edition 1967-1973
Jeep Cherokee & Comanche Pickups P. P. 1984-91
Jeep Wrangler 4x4 Performance Portfolio 1987-99
Jeep Cherokee & Grand Cherokee 4x4 P. P. 1992-98
Jensen Road Test Portfolio 1934-1965
Jensen Interceptor Ultimate Portfolio 1966-1992
Jensen - Healey Road Test Portfolio 1972-1976
Jowett Road Test Portfolio
Kaiser - Frazer Limited Edition 1946-1955
Lagonda Gold Portfolio 1919-1964
Lancia Aurelia & Flaminia Gold Portfolio 1950-1970
Lancia Fulvia Gold Portfolio 1963-1976
Lancia Montecarlo & Scorpion 1975-1982 RTP
Lancia Stratos Limited Edition Extra
Lancia Delta & integrale Ultimate Portfolio
Land Rover Series I, II & IIA Gold Portfolio 1948-71
Land Rover 90 110 Defender Gold Portfolio 1983-94
Lamborghini Performance Portfolio 1964-1976
Lamborghini Performance Portfolio 1977-1989
Lamborghini Gold Portfolio 1990-2004
Lincoln Gold Portfolio 1949-1960
Lincoln Continental Performance Portfolio 1961-1969
Lola Sports Racing Cars Lim. Ed. Premier 1958-1985
Lotus Sports Racers Portfolio - covering 1951-1965
Lotus Seven Gold Portfolio 1957-1973
Lotus Elite Limited Edition 1957-1964
Lotus Elan Ultimate Portfolio 1962-1974
Lotus Cortina Road Test Portfolio
Lotus Elite & Exlat Road Test Portfolio 1984-1972
Lotus Excel Road Test Portfolio
Lotus Europa Gold Portfolio 1966-1975
Lotus Elise & Exige Gold Portfolio 1995-2005
Marcos Coupés & Spyders Gold Portfolio 1960-1997
Maserati Cars Performance Portfolio 1957-1970
Maserati Cars Performance Portfolio 1971-1982
Maserati Cars Performance Portfolio 1982-1998
Maserati Cars Ultimate Portfolio 1999-2007
Matra Road Test Portfolio
Mazda Miata MX-5 Performance Portfolio 1989-1997
Mazda Miata MX-5 Performance Portfolio 1998-2005
McLaren F1 • GTR • LM Sportscar Perf. Portfolio
Mercedes-Benz 1925-1939 - A Portfolio
Mercedes 190SL 300SL 300SLR - A Portfolio
Mercedes S & 600 Limited Edition Extra 1965-1972
Mercedes S Class Limited Edition Extra 1980-1991
Mercedes 230SL 250SL 280SL Ultimate Port. 1963-71
Mercedes-Benz SLs & SLCs Ultimate Port. 1971-1989
Mercedes SLs Performance Portfolio 1989-1994
Mercedes E-Class W124 Road Test Portfolio 1986-1995
Mercedes G-Wagen Gold Portfolio 1981-2005
Mercedes AMG Gold Portfolio 1983-1999
Mercedes AMG Ultimate Portfolio 2000-2006
Mercury Gold Portfolio 1947-1966
Mercury Comet & Cyclone Lim. Edit. Extra 1960-1975
Mercury Cougar Muscle Portfolio 1967-1973
Messerschmitt Gold Portfolio 1954-1964
MG Gold Portfolio 1929-1939
MG TD & TF Gold Portfolio 1949-1955
MG Y Type & Magnette Road Test Portfolio
MGA & Twin Cam Gold Portfolio 1955-1962

MG Midget Road Test Portfolio 1961-1979
MGB Roadsters 1962-1980
MGB MGC & V8 Gold Portfolio 1962-1980
MGF & TF Performance Portfolio 1995-2005
Mini Gold Portfolio 1959-1969
Mini Gold Portfolio 1969-1980
Mini Gold Portfolio 1981-1997
High Performance Minis Gold Portfolio 1960-1973
Mini Cooper Gold Portfolio 1961-1971
Mini Moke Ultimate Portfolio 1964-1994
Starion & Conquest Performance Portfolio 1982-1990
Mitsubishi 3000GT & Dodge Stealth P.P. 1990-1999
Morgan Three-Wheelers Ultimate Portfolio 1909-52
Morgan Four-Wheelers Ultimate Portfolio 1936-67
Morgan Ultimate Portfolio 1968-1990
Morgan Ultimate Portfolio 1991-2009
Morris Minor MM & Series II Road Test Portfolio
Morris Minor 1000 Road Test Portfolio
Nash Limited Edition Extra 1949-1957
Nash-Austin Metropolitan Gold Portfolio 1954-1962
Nissan 350Z Road Test Portfolio
Nissan Skyline GT-R Ultimate Portfolio 1969-2010
Noble Sports Cars Road Test Portfolio
NSU Ro80 Limited Edition
Oldsmobile 1948-1963 Limited Edition Premier
Cutlass & 4-4-2 Muscle Portfolio 1964-1974
Opel GT Ultimate Portfolio 1968-1973
Packard Automobiles 1920-1958 - A Portfolio
Pantera Ultimate Portfolio 1970-1995
Panther Gold Portfolio 1972-1990
Plymouth Limited Edition 1950-1960
Plymouth Fury Limited Edition Extra 1956-1976
Barracuda Muscle Portfolio 1964-1974
Plymouth Muscle Portfolio 1964-1971
Pontiac 1946-1963 Limited Edition Premier
High Performance Firebirds 1982-1988
Firebird & Trans Am Performance Portfolio 1993-00
Pontiac Fiero Performance Portfolio 1984-1988
Porsche Sports Racing Cars UP 1952-1968
Porsche 917 • 935 • 956 • 962 Gold Portfolio
Porsche 365 Ultimate Portfolio 1952-1965
Porsche 911 1965-1969
Porsche 911 SC & Turbo Gold Portfolio 1978-1983
Porsche 911 Ultimate Portfolio 1990-1997
Porsche 911 Ultimate Portfolio 1998-2004
Porsche 912 Limited Edition Extra 1965-1976
Porsche 914 Ultimate Portfolio
Porsche 924 Gold Portfolio 1975-1988
Porsche 928 Gold Portfolio 1977-1995
Porsche 928 Takes On The Competition
Porsche 944 Ultimate Portfolio
Porsche 968 Limited Edition Extra
Porsche Boxster Ultimate Portfolio 1996-2004
Railton & Brough Superior Gold Portfolio 1933-1950
Range Rover Gold Portfolio 1970-1985
Range Rover Gold Portfolio 1985-1995
Range Rover Performance Portfolio 1995-2001
Riley RM Series Pathfinder 2.6 A Brooklands Port.
Rolls-Royce Silver Clould & Bentley S Ultimate Port.
Rolls-Royce Silver Shadow Ultimate Port. 1965-80
Rover P4 1949-1959
Rover P6 1963-1977
Rover 2000 & 2200 1963-1977
Studebaker Ultimate Portfolio 1946-1966
Studebaker Hawks & Larks Lim. Edit. Premier 1956-66
Avanti Limited Edition Extra 1962-1991
Subaru Impreza WRX Performance Port. 2001-2005
Sunbeam Alpine Limited Edition Extra 1959-1968
Sunbeam Tiger Limited Edition Extra 1964-1967
Suzuki SJ Gold Portfolio 1971-1997
Tatra Cars Road Test Portfolio
Toyota Land Cruiser Gold Portfolio 1956-1987
Toyota Land Cruiser 1988-1997
Toyota Supra Performance Portfolio 1982-1998
Toyota MR2 Road Test Portfolio 1984-1989
Toyota MR2 Road Test Portfolio 1990-1999
Toyota MR2 Road Test Portfolio 2000-2007
Triumph TR2 & TR3 Road Test Portfolio
Triumph TR4, TR5 & TR250 Road Test Portfolio
Triumph TR6 Road Test Portfolio
Triumph Herald 1959-1971
Triumph Vitesse 1962-1971
Triumph 2000, 2.5, 2500 1963-1977
Triumph GT6 Gold Portfolio 1966-1974
Triumph Spitfire Road Test Portfolio
Triumph Stag Road Test Portfolio
TVR Limited Edition Ultra 1958-1985
TVR Performance Portfolio 1986-1994
TVR Performance Portfolio 2000-2005
VW Beetle Gold Portfolio 1935-1967
VW Beetle Gold Portfolio 1968-1991
VW Bus Camper Van Perf. Portfolio 1954-1967
VW Bus Camper Van Perf. Portfolio 1979-1991
VW Karmann Ghia Gold Portfolio 1955-1974
VW Golf GTI Limited Edition Extra 1976-1991
VW Golf Cabriolet 1979-2002 Road Test Portfolio
VW Corrado Limited Edition Premier 1989-1995
Volvo PV444 & PV544 Perf. Portfolio 1945-1965
Volvo 120 Amazon Ultimate Portfolio
Volvo 1800 Ultimate Portfolio 1960-1973
Volvo 140 & 160 Series Gold Portfolio 1966-1975
Forty Years of Selling Volvo
Westfield Performance Portfolio 1982-2004

MILITARY VEHICLES

Complete WW2 Military Jeep Manual
Dodge WW2 Military Portfolio 1940-1945
German Military Equipment WW2
Hail To The Jeep
Combat Land Rover Portfolio No. 1
Land Rover Military Portfolio
Off Road Jeeps Civilian & Military 1944-1971
US Military Vehicles 1941-1945
Standard Military Motor Vehicles-TM9-2800 (WW2)
VW Kubelwagen Military Portfolio 1940-1990
WW2 Allied Vehicles Military Portfolio 1939-1945
WW2 Jeep Military Portfolio 1941-1945

RACING & THE LAND SPEED RECORD

The Land Speed Record 1898-1919
The Land Speed Record 1920-1929
The Land Speed Record 1930-1939
The Land Speed Record 1940-1962
The Land Speed Record 1963-1999
Can-Am Racing 1966-1969
Can-Am Racing 1970-1974
The Carrera Panamericana Mexico - 1950-1954
Le Mans - The Bentley & Alfa Years - 1923-1939
Le Mans - The Jaguar Years - 1949-1957
Le Mans - The Ferrari Years - 1958-1965
Le Mans - The Ford & Matra Years - 1966-1974
Le Mans - The Porsche Years - 1975-1982
Le Mans - The Porsche & Jaguar Years - 1983-91
Le Mans - The Porsche & Peugeot Years - 1992-99
Mille Miglia - The Alfa & Ferrari Years - 1927-1951
Mille Miglia - The Ferrari & Mercedes Years - 1952-57
Targa Florio - The Porsche & Ferrari Years - 1955-64
Targa Florio - The Porsche Years - 1965-1973
Brabham Ralt Honda The Ron Tauranac

RESTORATION & GUIDE SERIES

BMW 2002 - A Comprehensive Guide
BMW 02 Restoration Guide
BMW E30 - 3 Series Restoration Bible
BMW E36 - 3 Series Restoration Tips & Techniques
BMW - 5 & 6 Series Restoration Tips & Techniques
Classic Camaro Restoration
Engine Swapping Tips & Techniques
Ferrari Life Buyer's Portfolio
Land Rover Restoration Portfolio
PC on Land Rover Series I Restoration
Lotus Elan Restoration Guide
Lotus Twin Cam Engines
MG T Series Restoration Guide
MGA Restoration Guide
PC on MGB Restoration
Mustang Restoration Tips & Techniques
Practical Gas Flow
Range Rover - The First Fifty
Restoring Sprites & Midgets an Enthusiast's Guide
Solex Carburettors Tuning Tips and Techniques
SU Carburetters Tuning Tips & Techniques
The Great Classic Muscle Cars Compared
Weber Carburettors Tuning Tips and Techniques

ROAD & TRACK SERIES

Road & Track on Aston Martin 1962-1990
Road & Track on Austin Healey 1953-1970
R & T BMW Z3, M Coupe & M Roadster Port. 96-02
R & T Camaro & Firebird Portfolio 1993-2002
Road & Track Dodge Viper Portfolio 1992-2002
Road & Track Ferrari V-12 Portfolio 1992-2002
Road & Track Ferrari F355 360 F430 Portfolio 95-06
R & T Jaguar XJ-S - XK8 - XKR Portfolio 1975-2003
Road & Track MX-5 Miata Portfolio 1989-2002
R & T Mercedes SL - SLK - CLK Portfolio 1990-2003
Road & Track on MG Sports Cars 1949-1961
Road & Track on MG Sports Cars 1962-1980
Road & Track Mustang Portfolio 1994-2002
Road & Track Nissan 300ZX & 350Z Portfolio 1984-03
Road & Track Porsche 928 Portfolio 1977-1994
Road & Track Porsche 911 Portfolio 1990-1997
Road & Track - Peter Egan Side Glances 1983-1992
Road & Track - Peter Egan Side Glances 1992-1997
Road & Track - Peter Egan Side Glances 1998-2002
Road & Track - Peter Egan Side Glances 2002-2006

HOT ROD 'ENGINE' SERIES

Chevy 265 & 283
Chevy 302 & 327
Chevy 348 & 409
Chevy 396 & 427
Chevy 454 thru 512
Chevy Monster Big Blocks
Chrysler Hemi
Chrysler 273, 318, 340 & 360
Chrysler 361, 383, 400, 413, 426 & 440
Ford 289, 302, Boss 302 & 351W
Ford 351C & Boss 351
Ford Small Block
Ford Big Block

MOTORCYCLES

To see our range of over 70 titles visit www.brooklands-books.com

Printed and bound in Great Britain by
Marston Book Services Ltd, Oxfordshire